INTELLIGENCE AND STRATEGY

John Ferris's work in strategic and intelligence history has been widely praised for its originality and the breadth of its research. At last several of his major pioneering articles whose publications were scattered across time and venues are now available in this one single volume. In *Intelligence and Strategy* these essential articles have been fundamentally revised to incorporate new evidence and information that were withheld by governments when they were first published. This volume reshapes the study of communications intelligence by tracing Britain's development of cipher machines providing the context to Ultra and Enigma, and by explaining how British and German signals intelligence shaped the desert war. The author also explains how intelligence affected British strategy and diplomacy from 1874 to 1940 and world diplomacy during the 1930s and the Second World War. Finally he traces the roots for contemporary intelligence, and analyzes intelligence and the RMA as well as the role of intelligence in the 2003 Gulf War.

This volume brings new light to our understanding of the relations between intelligence, strategy and diplomacy between the end of the nineteenth century and the beginning of the twenty-first century.

John Ferris is a Professor of History at The University of Calgary. He has written widely on military history, strategy and intelligence studies. Among his works are *The Evolution of British Strategic Policy, 1919–1926* (1989) and *The British Army and Signals Intelligence during the First World War* (1992). He is a co-author of *A World History of Warfare* (2002).

STUDIES IN INTELLIGENCE SERIES
General Editors: Richard J. Aldrich and Christopher Andrew

BRITISH MILITARY INTELLIGENCE IN THE PALESTINE CAMPAIGN 1914–1918
Yigal Sheffy

BRITISH MILITARY INTELLIGENCE IN THE CRIMEAN WAR, 1854–1856
Stephen M. Harris

SIGNALS INTELLIGENCE IN WORLD WAR II
Edited by David Alvarez

KNOWING YOUR FRIENDS
Intelligence inside alliances and coalitions from 1914 to the Cold War
Edited by Martin S. Alexander

ETERNAL VIGILANCE
50 years of the CIA
Edited by Rhodri Jeffreys-Jones and Christopher Andrew

NOTHING SACRED
Nazi espionage against the Vatican, 1939–1945
David Alvarez and Revd. Robert A. Graham

INTELLIGENCE INVESTIGATIONS
How ultra changed history
Ralph Bennett

INTELLIGENCE ANALYSIS AND ASSESSMENT
Edited by David Charters, A. Stuart Farson and Glenn P. Hastedt

TET 1968
Understanding the surprise
Ronnie E. Ford

INTELLIGENCE AND IMPERIAL DEFENCE
British intelligence and the defence of the Indian Empire 1904–1924
Richard J. Popplewell

ESPIONAGE
Past, present, future?
Edited by Wesley K. Wark

THE AUSTRALIAN SECURITY INTELLIGENCE ORGANIZATION
An unofficial history
Frank Cain

POLICING POLITICS
Security intelligence and the liberal democratic state
Peter Gill

FROM INFORMATION TO INTRIGUE
Studies in secret service based on the Swedish experience 1939–45
C.G. McKay

DIEPPE REVISITED
A documentary investigation
John Campbell

MORE INSTRUCTIONS FROM THE CENTRE
Andrew Gordievsky

CONTROLLING INTELLIGENCE
Edited by Glenn P. Hastedt

SPY FICTION, SPY FILMS AND REAL INTELLIGENCE
Edited by Wesley K. Wark

SECURITY AND INTELLIGENCE IN A CHANGING WORLD
New perspectives for the 1990s
Edited by A. Stuart Farson, David Stafford and Wesley K. Wark

A DON AT WAR (REPRINT)
Sir David Hunt K.C.M.G., O.B.E.

INTELLIGENCE AND MILITARY OPERATIONS
Edited by Michael I. Handel

LEADERS AND INTELLIGENCE
Edited by Michael I. Handel

WAR, STRATEGY AND INTELLIGENCE
Michael I. Handel

STRATEGIC AND OPERATIONAL DECEPTION IN THE SECOND WORLD WAR
Edited by Michael I. Handel

CODEBREAKER IN THE FAR EAST
Alan Stripp

INTELLIGENCE FOR PEACE
Edited by Hesi Carmel

INTELLIGENCE SERVICES IN THE INFORMATION AGE
Michael Herman

ESPIONAGE AND THE ROOTS OF THE COLD WAR
The conspiratorial heritage
David McKnight

SWEDISH SIGNAL INTELLIGENCE 1900–1945
C.G. McKay and Bengt Beckman

THE NORWEGIAN INTELLIGENCE SERVICE 1945–1970
Olav Riste

SECRET INTELLIGENCE IN THE TWENTIETH CENTURY
Edited by Heike Bungert, Jan G. Heitmann and Michael Wala

THE CIA, THE BRITISH LEFT AND THE COLD WAR
Calling the tune?
Hugh Wilford

OUR MAN IN YUGOSLAVIA
The story of a secret service operative
Sebastian Ritchie

UNDERSTANDING INTELLIGENCE IN THE TWENTY-FIRST CENTURY
Journeys in shadows
Len Scott and Peter Jackson

MI6 AND THE MACHINERY
OF SPYING
Philip H. J. Davies

TWENTY-FIRST CENTURY
INTELLIGENCE
Edited by Wesley Wark

INTELLIGENCE AND
STRATEGY
Selected essays
John Robert Ferris

INTELLIGENCE AND STRATEGY

Selected essays

John Robert Ferris

Routledge
Taylor & Francis Group
LONDON AND NEW YORK

First published 2005 in Great Britain
by Routledge
2 Park Square, Milton Park, Abingdon, Oxon, OX14 4RN

Simultaneously published in the USA and Canada
by Routledge
711 Third Avenue, New York, NY 10017

Routledge is an imprint of the Taylor & Francis Group

© 2005 John Robert Ferris

Typeset in Sabon by
Taylor & Francis Books

All rights reserved. No part of this book may be reprinted or reproduced or utilized in any form or by any electronic, mechanical, or other means, now known or hereafter invented, including photocopying and recording, or in any information storage or retrieval system, without permission in writing from the publishers.

British Library Cataloguing in Publication Data
A catalogue record for this book is available from the British Library

Library of Congress Cataloging in Publication Data
Ferris, John Robert, 1957–
Intelligence and strategy : selected essays / John Robert Ferris.
p. cm. -- (Studies in intelligence)
Includes bibliographical references and index.
ISBN 0-415-36194-X (hardback) -- ISBN 0-415-36195-8 (pbk.) 1. Military intelligence--Case studies. 2. Strategy--Case studies. 3. Military history, Modern--19th century. 4. Military history, Modern--20th century. 5. Military history, Modern--21st century. I. Title. II. Series: Cass series--studies in intelligence.

UB250.F47 2005
355.3'432--dc22
2004024828

ISBN 0–415–36194–X (Hbk)
ISBN 0–415–36195–8 (Pbk)

CONTENTS

	Introduction	1
1	Lord Salisbury, secret intelligence and British policy toward Russia and Central Asia, 1874–1878	8
2	"Indulged in all too little"? Vansittart, intelligence and appeasement	45
3	Image and accident: intelligence and the origins of the Second World War, 1933–1941	99
4	The British "Enigma": Britain, signals security and cipher machines, 1906–1953	138
5	The British army: signals and security in the desert campaign, 1940–1942	181
6	Intelligence, uncertainty and the art of command in military operations	239
7	NCW, C^{4}ISR, IO and RMA: toward a revolution in military intelligence?	288
	Notes	328
	Bibliography	379
	Index	387

INTRODUCTION

When I became a research student in 1979, the future looked bleak. Mike Dockrill, my supervisor, who taught me how to write, accepted me only after warning there were no jobs. He was right. Fortunately, matters improved in the fields in which I work, and not just in terms of employment. After continuing to decline toward death watch, diplomatic history has recently shown signs of life. International and strategic history have grown slowly but steadily, the study of intelligence has boomed, and military history has entered a golden age. There are more military historians today than ever before, and more good ones. New areas of the field, such as airpower history, have been born and dead ones, such as naval history, reborn. All these fields, along with international relations and strategic studies, share a focus on power, strategy, armed forces and war, on ideas about these matters and the human experience with them. They are different parts of one whole—so, at least, it seems to me.

I never know for sure whether I am a strategic historian specializing in intelligence, or a scholar of intelligence who focuses on strategy. It depends on the question of the day. Though primarily an historian, I was trained in strategic studies, and the issues I address concern both disciplines. I study the history of strategy and intelligence, and use that record to assess ideas about them. Theory shapes my questions, which determine the files I open in the archives, while the evidence I find there redefines my theories. I am a realist who believes in the power of ideology, and a dialectical materialist, but no Marxist. I work on the margins of disciplines. I concentrate on the links between matters which often are placed in watertight compartments—how the financial, foreign and military policies of states are related to each other and to technology, economics, politics and ideas; how soldiers, diplomats and statesmen perceive the world, and their ideas shape their actions and thus the objects they observed in the first place; with the interactions between states; with what power and influence are and why they matter; with intelligence, perceptions and images as factors in power politics. I study diplomatic history from the perspective of an intellectual historian, and vice versa; so too, military and cultural history. My central focus of research is the British state between 1815 and 1945, but I use this material to address questions about international and military history, strategic studies, and the world tomorrow.

Accident as much as intention leads my work. My PhD thesis addressed British defence policy during the 1920s. This decade, then a scholarly backwater, proved to be a bridge for the study of power and policy throughout the world, and for the decades before 1914 and after 1929. That topic, so inchoate that it could not be understood simply by looking at documents about defence, drove me to work on foreign, financial, imperial, naval, air and military policy, to master the archives in these areas, and to redefine my topic as the formulation of strategy. As that process, and the links between these issues and departments, often was unspoken, or indirect, I had to learn how to join them, useful experience to an historian. So was another lesson. When I began my research, I accepted the standard view that my period was dominated by disarmament, Treasury control, and an articulated doctrine for defence, embodied in the "ten-year rule" and the "one power standard". One day I realized, no contemporary evidence supported any of these ideas. Reexamination of all the data I had collected showed every one was false. They had been accepted because, years after the fact, decision makers erroneously thought they were so, and scholars accepted that assumption; I discovered the truth because I was the first historian to examine the evidence thoroughly, but only after months of work, which this undiscovered error had undermined. This taught a lesson in how easily assumptions can be projected onto the evidence, but it also made my thesis original. I concluded that in my period, Britain formulated its strategy through politics rather than policy, made better decisions than usually thought, if in a complicated fashion, and led the world in rearmament. In 1929, Britain was the only world power, a secure, strong and respected state, at one of its peaks of strength. This conclusion challenged broad assumptions about Great Britain as a great power between 1815 and 1945, especially the idea that it was in steady decline from 1890, doubly so after 1918, which triggered appeasement and the outbreak of the Second World War; and claims about how and why this decline occurred. In their place, I offered more complex accounts of rise, decline and fall, which emphasized the scale of British power even in 1939, as well as its limitations, and redefined its causation, including the roles of ideology and economics.[1]

I also learned the value of serendipity. Early in my research, I opened a Foreign Office file, filled with material on British assessments of the Japanese Army and the transfer of technology on naval aviation, which sparked many publications and a research agenda I pursue today.[2] At the same time, I read a War Office file on the Greco-Turkish campaign of 1921. Halfway through, I noted that many of its telegrams were sent to and from not Britons, but Mustapha Kemal and Ismet Inonu. Having read Roberta Wohlstetter's *Pearl Harbor* and David Kahn's *The Codebreakers*—still the best historical works on intelligence—I understood what I was seeing. In the margins of my notes, I wrote, "They're reading Turkish codes!" As I continued my research, I often stumbled across reports from British intelligence agencies, especially from the cryptanalysts at the Government Code and Cypher School (GC&CS). This material was not supposed to be there, yet there it was, illuminating the formulation of policy in complex and fascinating ways. By coincidence, the "weeders" who determined whether files should be released to the Public Records Office had left much of the intelligence record in the files for the 1920s which I, but few others, used. The first draft chapter for my PhD thesis, not published until years later, tried among other things to correlate the records on intelligence and strategy, and to assess how information shaped decision making during one crisis.[3]

Since I kept finding intelligence by accident, I thought perhaps I could discover more by looking for it. So, as I wrote a dissertation about an historical case of strategy, I began to research others about intelligence. I was encouraged by a veteran from Bletchley Park, a professional researcher and tablemate at the PRO, Mary Paine, and by David French, Keith Neilson and Bradley Smith, researchers I respected who had written about intelligence and were kind to neophytes. Initially, I was moved by the challenge of the hardest problem I knew, which others thought unsolvable but significant. For some time, I aimed only to sketch British codebreaking and show where the records were, for other historians to use, but then decided to use them myself, systematically. Though my primary focus remained codebreaking, I took notes on all aspects of intelligence and related matters of policy, so I could find enough material to justify the work. I refused to assume that intelligence had affected anything unless I could prove it had done so. In hindsight, this approach was slightly conservative, but unavoidable. At that time, in this field, any step from the path of documentation led to quicksand, which swallowed many a don. Instead, I tried to double guess the "weeders", to find evidence they had forgotten to forget.

Discovery of these flakes of gold required panning through masses of files, far more than necessary for research in military or diplomatic history. I started with blind searches in issues parallel to those where I (or others) had found evidence on codebreaking. Discoveries in one series sparked tangential searches through related files. When I realized solutions in the 1930s often were related to Germano-Japanese relations, I looked through every file I could find on the Anti-Comintern Pact, with some success; the term "absolutely reliable intelligence" almost always indicated the presence of cryptanalysis, as did references to reports with the six figure identification numbers (000000) used by the GC&CS. When discovered, in turn, these dated reports (or "flimsies") showed the size of this particular hidden dimension: 75,000 published solutions of foreign diplomatic telegrams between 1919 and 1939. If ever a vein of research produced gold, I mined it to exhaustion. Thus, records on signals provided much evidence on security, snippets on intelligence, and led me to make the relationship between command, communication and strategy a research topic in its own right. In order to make sense of my material, to understand why some things appeared to be happening and why others were not, and to guide further searches, I learned the technical side of cryptology and communications. I found the obvious—changes in signals technology shaped signals intelligence, and its effect on policy. Again, I discovered that before 1924 "weeding" was spotty while intelligence often ended in private papers. In search of signals intelligence, I spent five months each working through records from the British Army in the First World War, those at the India Office Records and Library from 1825 to 1948, and private and official collections on military, naval and foreign policy between 1815 and 1914. Often, these searches were futile—I spent three days searching every file I could imagine was related to the role of cryptanalysis in the "Sabzawar incident" of 1908, without effect, but this work broadened my expertise as an intelligence historian, and a strategic one. In search of intelligence, for example, I learned the eastern question. Usually, I did not find what I was looking for, but what I found was useful.

It led me to question prevailing ideas about British signals intelligence, which I labelled the "Room 40 view", as they stemmed from the demi-official historians of naval intelligence in two world wars. According to this view, Britain had no interest in codebreaking between 1844 and 1914, largely because decision makers thought it a practice unacceptable to gentlemen; cryptanalytical agencies sprang from nothing in August 1914; Room 40 conducted all British signals intelligence during the great war; and it was the only fount for later developments. During the interwar years, decision makers were indifferent or hostile to signals intelligence, and made the GC&CS inefficient. This work contributed little to the success of signals intelligence between 1940 and 1945 when, after a second revolution in cryptanalysis, Bletchley saved Britain. I concluded that these tenets were wrong, or mostly so; that view was confirmed during the 1990s, when HMG gave the PRO most of its remaining archive on intelligence from before 1945.[4] In their place, I sketched an alternative history.

Between 1892 and 1945, signals intelligence was always a normal practice for the British state, developing through evolution rather than revolution, more useful in terms of small contributions to daily issues than decisive contributions to dramatic events. After 1890, Britain moved from the rear of the pack in that practice. By July 1914, it was already above the average among the great powers. During the First World War, Britain became perhaps the world's leader in signals intelligence, which contributed as much to its victory as ULTRA did between 1939 and 1945. Signals intelligence was significant for Britain in the war at sea, but no more so than in the blockade, in diplomacy or on land. During the interwar years, statesmen and diplomats trusted cryptanalytical intelligence and used it

INTRODUCTION

whenever they could, while British intelligence services matched those of any other country in size, and quality, and beat most. Between 1940 and 1945, Britain led the world in signals intelligence and took that discipline from the craft bench to the industrial age, but the study of that matter has suffered from a focus on British sword and German shield at the height of Bletchley's success. The cryptological war was more closely run, the German buckler stronger and Britain's weaker, than sometimes is assumed, and the question remains: how many divisions did Bletchley Park have?

Scholars of intelligence have only begun to answer this sort of question, because the area is so new, and subject to transformation. In 1980, intelligence barely ranked as a topic worth academic study; new work was written in a vacuum, almost without the benefit of a secondary literature, the relevant primary documents in the public domain were limited and often hidden, while even basic details about structure, techniques and product were unknown. Anyone working in the field was a pioneer, trying to reconstruct a whole from a fragmentary basis of evidence, like a forensic anthropologist with a shattered skull. Over the past decade, however, the British and American governments have released their hold on the evidence. Now, studies of intelligence are common—some practitioners even imagine themselves in a field entitled "intelligence studies", revisionist works are possible, while primary documents on intelligence flood the archives—to such an extent as to swamp specialists. In 1980, intelligence historians worked despite a lack of records—that was the charm of the field; in 2005 their documentary base matches that of diplomatic and military historians. More data, alas, do not necessarily yield better interpretation. The past thirty years have shown that little attention is paid to the intelligence record, while most of that attention goes to new material on old things. Progress requires not merely new evidence but new approaches, and more material causes an unexpected danger.

The official records always contained more material on intelligence than generally was realized, but finding them took time and effort. The new releases make intelligence easier to discover, but at a price. Once, when found, such records were embedded in their decision making context, easing judgement as to what they affected, and how. Now, intelligence is more accessible but stands alone; the problem is to find not evidence, but its context, and to learn what to do with it. This situation magnifies the tendency to fetishize and to sensationalize intelligence. The study has acquired an odour of mystery, which has caused some historians and strategists to view the matter with suspicion and underrate the significance of intelligence and other commentators to overstate it: the hidden dimension is filled with trainspotters. Anyone interested in the effect of cryptanalysis on diplomacy might remember that intelligence influences decisions but does not make them. Better read the FO 371s and not the HW 12s, than the latter and not the former—though most readers of FO 371s will gain something from HW

12s. Students of intelligence should aim not just to astonish their audience, but to bore them, and always to answer the key questions—why and how did intelligence really matter? If not, why bother? Rather than aim at a field which cannot stand alone, better to incorporate intelligence into military and international and diplomatic history, and strategic studies and international relations, and so widen all of them; best of all, use intelligence as a bridge between them.

Without my explicit intention, that is where my work has led me. Since 1982, I have written on strategy and intelligence, and combined them. I showed how intelligence affected decisions. I used it as a mirror for decision making and decision makers, believing that to know what statesmen or commanders knew, and thought their options were, illuminates their character and choices. I tried to make generalizations about the relationship between intelligence, state policy and the international system. I worked on the margins of signals intelligence, communication systems and military organizations, showing how this relationship shaped technological and tactical innovations, producing such things as British success with Fighter Command, and failure against Rommel. When assessing Anglo-Japanese relations, I fused cultural and strategic analyses. I treated images, perceptions, learning and decision making as topics for historical research. Inspired by the late Michael Handel, who taught me strategy, I wrote on the theory of intelligence. Later, I found myself writing on the theory of strategy, and about the history of matters central to contemporary military policy, like C4ISR and strike warfare, and this work has reshaped my study in history.

The pieces in this collection are here because they please me. They represent my work as a whole, though leaning somewhat more toward intelligence than strategy. Some are histories, of British power and strategy; of intelligence, its assessment, and impact on policy; and of signals, security, command and strategy. Others combine theory and history, using the intelligence record to reassess ideas about strategy, the theory and practice of international relations, or contemporary American doctrine and practice; and vice versa. With one exception, the pieces are mine, and different from their earlier versions, either because they were cut from larger works, or else grew in the archives after the telling. That exception, "Clausewitz, Intelligence, Uncertainty and the Art of Command in Modern War", was co-written with Michael Handel, and published here as we finished it in 1995. It addresses issues about intelligence and strategy, history and strategic studies, which are central to my work, and his. I wrote the draft of this work as a present to Michael, an attempt to link intelligence history and Clausewitz's theory of war. When he read it, he liked the work but saw its limits. As he and I argued, we found something for both of us. So the work grew in size and into a collaboration, through correspondence and a week of debate in Michael's living room at Newport, Rhode Island, with Jill Handel serving as referee and aiding in composition.

INTRODUCTION

Historical research is like freemasonry, except you are allowed to live after naming your co-conspirators. I am grateful to David Alvarez, Chris Archer, Uri bar Joseph, Andrew Barros, Chris Bell, Tami Davis Biddle, Brian Bond, John Chapman, Seb Cox, Mike Dockrill, Jill Edwards, Ralph Erskine, David French, Ian Gow, Jill Handel, Michael Handel, Michael Herman, Hamish Ion, Edward Ingram, Peter Jackson, David Kahn, Greg Kennedy, Andrew Lambert, Mary Paine, Gordon Martel, Toni McArthur, David Marshall, Brian McKercher, Keith Neilson, Ian Nish, Doug Peers, Jane Priestland, Yigal Sheffy and Brad Smith. My colleagues in The Department of History and The Centre for Military and Strategic Studies at The University of Calgary recognize the significance of studying intelligence and strategy; I thank them for support. The Anglo-Japanese History Project, The University Research Grants Committee at The University of Calgary, and The Social Sciences and Humanities Research Council of Canada, helped to pay for these pieces, by funding my research. My children, Edmund, Owen and Morgan, helped me to take time on my work. I dedicate this book to Elizabeth, who had to live with it, and did so with grace.

John Ferris
The University of Calgary

1

LORD SALISBURY, SECRET INTELLIGENCE AND BRITISH POLICY TOWARD RUSSIA AND CENTRAL ASIA, 1874–1878

Scholars have rarely examined the Victorian intelligence system and its influence on British policy. Many have assumed that the former did not exist, hence, neither could the latter. During the nineteenth century, in fact, Her Majesty's Government did collect secret intelligence, and such material did affect its diplomacy and strategy. This chapter addresses one episode in that relationship—how intelligence influenced the policy toward Russia and Central Asia of the government of Benjamin Disraeli, Lord Beaconsfield, during the great eastern crisis of 1874 and 1878. This crisis, the most significant event in European politics between 1871 and 1891, led to conflict between Russia and Turkey and almost to a world war, and reshaped territories and the balance of power in eastern Europe. It witnessed extraordinary confusion in the formulation of British strategy. Conflicts between statesmen paralyzed action over a major matter, and then suddenly threw Britain to the gates of Istanbul and war. This chapter particularly, although not exclusively, studies the relationship between intelligence and one statesman. Robert Cecil, Lord Salisbury, was a central figure in this episode. The evidence reveals in unusual detail how he, and to a lesser degree others, used and were influenced by intelligence. Nor do the insights provided by this material apply solely to one crisis of a single decade. The lessons learned during this period shaped Salisbury's actions as the leading British statesman of the later nineteenth century—experience with secret intelligence was an important part of the education of a Foreign Secretary. Examination of these issues will illuminate British diplomacy and intelligence during both the great eastern crisis and the later Victorian era.

A central problem for British foreign policy during the 1870s was the future of the Islamic states ranging from the Balkans to Sinkiang. The decay in the strength of these states and the rise of Russian power in those regions created the conditions for what might be called either an "eastern" or a "Russian" question—one that linked developments in the Balkans to those in the Middle East and Central Asia.[1] By the 1870s Russia simultaneously was threatening several strategic buffers for the British Empire. Russian control over Istanbul and the straits would imperil British strategic interests in the Mediterranean Sea and the Middle East; further Russian expansion in Central Asia might endanger Britain's hold in India. Neither of these views of peril held undisputed sway in Whitehall. Many Liberal and a few Conservative statesmen denied that British security would be threatened should Russia eliminate Turkish power in Europe; some leaders of the Liberal Party and members of one school of Indian defence held that Russia could dominate Central Asia without necessarily endangering the Raj. Differences over these matters also affected the strategic decisions of Disraeli's government between 1874 and 1878.

The debate was linked to questions of intelligence. During this period the Russian and Indian frontiers were separated by 700-odd miles of territory, controlled by independent tribes or states such as Persia, Afghanistan, the Tekke Turkomans, Merv, Khiva and Yarkand. Britain needed to acquire information not so much on an immediate Russian threat to India, which virtually no one expected, but rather on intermediate steps in Central Asia that might ultimately create such a menace. Tsarist intentions in this sphere were not easy to assess. Nor was it a new problem. In 1854, the British ambassador to St. Petersburg had written: "When every thing depends upon the will of one Individual, and that Person or Personage is under the influence of strong passions and of contending parties and interests, it is difficult to say what decision may be taken."[2]

During the 1870s, Russian policy on the "eastern question" was formulated and executed in a byzantine fashion. Three departments of state—the Ministry of Foreign Affairs, the Ministry of War, and to a lesser extent, the Ministry of Finance and many of their executive agents, could pursue different ends without reference to the rest. While all these groups aimed to strengthen Russia's position against Britain, they disagreed about the means; at any time some could favour and others oppose a direct challenge to Britain in Central Asia. Thus, in the late 1850s Nicolai Ignatiev advocated Russian expansion in Central Asia precisely to challenge Britain. By the mid-1870s he opposed such actions because these would hamper his plans for Tsarist aggrandizement in the Balkans. Only the will of the Emperor could coordinate the actions of these agencies; the Tsar in question, Alexander II, frequently failed to ensure this condition. Thus, these ministries and their servants—ambassadors, governors, and field commanders—pursued contradictory policies. The Tsar's decisions might be ignored by his subordinates and be overturned at any time without notice.[3] In order to assess Russian intentions, Britain had to identify which factions and individuals influenced Russian policy on the eastern question; determine their aims and influence; calculate the range of outcomes of the struggle between them; and then guess at the relative probabilities of the possible results, which might not occur for years ahead. The aim was accurate prediction; the means, by necessity, must be knowledge of extraordinary precision. The task was of extreme difficulty. It was also affected by history.

Between 1842 and 1869, following the first Anglo-Afghan war, Britain abandoned its earlier attempts to establish a forward defensive system for India through alliances with Persia, Afghanistan, or even the khanates of Central Asia.[4] Indeed, the "close frontier" school of Indian security held that India could best be defended on the northwest frontier itself, without any commitments to states beyond. Exponents of these views, best exemplified by John Lawrence as viceroy of India, pursued little diplomatic contact with such states or with independent tribes on India's borders. Nor did they view Russian expansion in Central Asia as a threat. By the early 1870s, these tenets of thought were facing challenge. The Liberal government of William Gladstone sought, without success, permanently to divide the Islamic states in Central Asia between Tsarist and British spheres of influence. Gladstone's Foreign Secretary, Lord Granville, held that "the best way of preserving our enormous Indian Empire is to remain where we are". Yet even he warned the Tsarist ambassador to Britain in October 1872 that any further Russian expansion in Central Asia "alarmed me for the future relations of the two countries (Britain and Russia). The British people were much alive to anything which could possibly excite alarm as to the Indian Empire". While emphasizing the "moderate" attitudes of the authorities in India, Granville pointedly stated "that peace at all price was not the special tradition of the Indian Government".[5] Meanwhile, Lawrence's successors as viceroy, Lord Mayo and Lord Northbrook, pursued greater contact with neighbouring states than had occurred for a generation. On the northwest frontier Northbrook followed a Lawrencian policy. On the northern and northeastern frontiers, conversely, he established regular political representation with local tribes and seriously considered doing so with Yarkand, the major Islamic state in Sinkiang.[6]

Simultaneously, a "forward school" emerged among many Indian officials, which opposed the close frontier. These men did not agree in all particulars—Henry Rawlinson, for example, wanted Persia and Bartle Frere, Afghanistan, to become the forward bastion of Indian defence. All these men, however, agreed that Russian expansion in central Asia could threaten the Raj, which must establish a defence zone beyond the northwest frontier.[7] Russia, meanwhile, expanded in Central Asia: by the mid-1860s, it annexed the khanates of Bokhara and Kokand, followed by that of Khiva in 1873. These actions halved the distance between the Russian and Indian frontiers. Any further steps would threaten the Raj. This view might be deemed alarmist. In 1872 Russian Turkistan contained barely 30,000 regular and irregular troops, which could not easily be reinforced;[8] 40,000 British and 120,000 Indian soldiers stood to arms in the subcontinent. Against this, the traditional idea of an internal–external threat centred on the belief that Britain's hold in India was weak; a single spark from beyond the Hindu Kush might raise a fire against the Raj. As one commander in chief of the Indian army wrote in 1871, "if ever they [Russia] possess themselves of that country [Afghanistan] they will command the services of the best fighting races with the prospect of unlimited plunder in India, against the now limited advantages of our service. There could be no doubt which side the border clans would take". In 1891, another commander, Lord Roberts, held that any Russian victory over Britain in Afghanistan would trigger an avalanche of enemies to the south, Cossacks joined by "almost every Afghan capable of bearing arms" and many tribesman on the northwest frontiers, while Indian soldiers and people would revolt against Britain.[9] The Russian threat was largely a euphemism for an Indian one. With the uprising of 1857 a mere generation away, such fears were not entirely irrational. In any case, they affected the decisions of Disraeli's Cabinet.

Foreign and imperial affairs particularly concerned that government. Disraeli intended to bolster British prestige and security by whatever means were needed: diplomacy, bluff, the use of armed force as a deterrent, perhaps even war with a major power. He was eager to disrupt the diplomatic status quo in Europe, which left Britain irrelevant, and to strive for strokes of policy. For Disraeli and his colleagues, Russia posed a central challenge.[10] Decisions on British policy in Central Asia were made by a few men. During 1875–1878 the Cabinet scarcely influenced the matter and the Foreign Secretary, Lord Derby, little more. It was determined by the government of India, senior figures within the Council of India, and above all, by Disraeli and his India Secretary, Salisbury. As Disraeli told Salisbury on 28 October 1875: "I am anxious, and a little disquieted, about Central Asian affairs. Before you bring them, even indirectly, under the consideration of the Cabinet, I think it would be better that we should confer together."[11] The personalities of these two men and their personal politics shaped the decisions at hand. Disraeli was cynical, shrewd, aggressive, a gambler willing to play for the highest of stakes and at the greatest of risks—or so he said. Salisbury was a masterful man, with a sharp mind and a sharper pen. He viewed foreign policy through the eyes of a classical realist—cold eyes, tinted with prudence, racism and high-church inclinations. Never before had he held an office responsible for foreign affairs; within two years he was impervious to the manipulations of a Bismarck. The two men differed on internal politics—Disraeli's policy on expanding the franchise during 1867 enraged Salisbury, ideologue and reactionary. However, the two men had some respect and need for each other, and were willing to put cooperation to trial. That relationship emerged in the context of their connections to another man, Derby. Disraeli relied heavily on Derby for political and personal reasons, while Salisbury stood aloof from the Foreign Secretary, second husband to his widowed stepmother—the "man who shares my mother's bed", he called his colleague. Ultimately, these relatives became rivals in more public spheres. Disraeli's choice between them reshaped British politics and policy for a generation.

Despite great differences on all other issues, Disraeli and Salisbury initially had pronounced and similar views on Central Asia. On entering office in February 1874, Salisbury held that "there is no immediate danger. But if Russia goes to Merv, I think we shall have to make definite promises to the Ameer of Cabul or see him go over to Russia". While far from alarmist—"Everything which tends toward encouraging a belief that Russia and England are on good terms, tends toward peace, both in Europe & Asia", he wrote; he did "not see at present any elements of trouble at home—though plenty on the Continent: & some-a little way off-in Asia"[12]—still Salisbury thought any further Russian expansion in Central Asia would force Britain either to ally with Afghanistan or else see Russia dominant there. Disraeli, meanwhile, had "no great faith in a real 'understanding of Russia' as to our eastern possessions, but much faith, at this moment, in a supposed understanding which will permit us to avail ourselves of the present opportunity of settling and strengthening our frontiers". Troubles with Russia during the next twelve months were "quite on the cards".[13] Both Disraeli and Salisbury sympathized with the arguments of the forward school and anticipated a more or less imminent strategic crisis with Russia in Central Asia. Over the next four years, their views changed in accordance with experience and intelligence.

The Salisbury of 1874 was not the statesman of later years who damned experts and small-scale maps alike. He requested and often accepted the advice of his experts within the India Office on the Central Asian question. He soon rejected the views of the close frontier school and of Rawlinson. Frere's arguments, however, marked Salisbury's analyses during the 1870s and for the rest of his life.[14] Salisbury agreed that Britain's hold in India could be broken by a combination of an internal and external enemy; Russia could play the latter role. Russia was intrinsically aggressive. "'Let those take who have the power, let those keep who can' is practically the only rule of (Tsarist) policy wherein, I am bound to say, she does not differ widely from many other civilised states."[15] Salisbury believed Russia was following a forward policy in Central Asia, which could seriously threaten the Raj. As he told Northbrook in February 1875:

> I agree with you in thinking that a Russian advance upon India is a chimera. But I am by no means sure that an attempt to throw the Affghans [sic] upon us is so impossible. Russia has all the Oriental capacity for intrigue, and all of the advantages which are conferred by a despotic form of Government, and a population in which plenty of adventurers and unscrupulous persons can be found.[16]

Salisbury argued later that Russia wished to gain influence in Afghanistan so, "as the Russians themselves say, 'to besiege Constantinople from the heights above Peshawur'".[17] These views were largely correct. The Russian Minster for foreign affairs, Prince Gorchakov, once informed a British diplomat that " 'one of Russia's main objects in drawing near to us in India was to make her Asiatic politics react on our European politics', so that 'for every act of nagging on our part at Constantinople there would be a corresponding act of nagging' on the Indian frontier".[18] For Gorchakov, this provided simply a diplomatic bargaining chip against Britain. Other important Tsarist decision makers, however, such as the minister for war, Dmitri Miliutin, leading generals like Mikhail Chernaiev and Mikhail Skobelov, the governor of Russian Turkistan, General von Kaufmann, and the commander of the Russian army in the Caucasus, the Grand Duke Michael, had greater ambitions. They held that Russian power in central Asia would provide the means permanently to blackmail Britain over Turkey. The ideas of an alliance with Afghanistan or an invasion of India attracted them.[19] They had the will to threaten British interests, if not necessarily the means. It was reasonable to fear that they might carry St. Petersburg in their wake and to prepare against this risk.

Salisbury's perceptions were also shaped by ideas. In 1878 he expressed views he had held in an inarticulate form throughout the mid-1870s:

> All the way from the Aegean and Mediterranean seas to the Indus there is a vast region in which the existing forces of Govt. are slowly perishing. It is not the case of bad laws or a temporary feebleness or rapacity of rule. The vital forces of the body politic are dying out. The expense of govt. is incessantly increasing, taxes are pushed to their utmost limit, trade is wasting away: depopulation is setting in: and all the distinctions which separate these peoples from mere nomad tribes threaten to disappear. They are conscious of it themselves and are on the look out for some govt. more living than their own, which shall rescue them in time. Few who are acquainted with the East think that England can safely look on till the forces of decay have eaten out all the powers of resistance. The domination of Russia in those countries might not enable or incline her to march on India: but it would not the less make our hold of India more difficult and condemn us to a more costly and repressive govt. in that country.[20]

The sources for such views were curious. Thus, in January 1877, during her stay in Istanbul, Lady Salisbury wrote of the

> melancholy (state) of the upper classes here. The condition of women must, unless it can be modified[,] injure the whole race more and more. A rich man here generally buys a few Circassian slave girls one or two of whom he makes wives of. When his sons are born they are left in the sole care of these women (who are ignorant to a degree you have no notion of and often vicious) till they are eleven or twelve. Then, they are taken into the Salamlile or men's part of the house and sometimes but not very often sent to some

> college—otherwise they are taught a little reading and writing and a smattering of French and that is all. Now when a young man brought up thus travels afterwards in France or England he generally gains nothing but good manners and a knowledge of the more dissipated side of Western life. So that, it is a common remark here that a Turk who has travelled is worse than one who has not. I have refrained from touching on the darker shades of the picture—as for instance, the way that young female slaves are bought for these boys when they are mere children—and other things worse. But you will see at once that full of good qualities as the lower classes of this people seem to be, such a governing class can lead to nothing but utter corruption and evils of all sorts in the government.[21]

Lord Minto, who soon followed Salisbury's footsteps, noted that the British Military Attaché reported Lady Salisbury had spoken of "the iniquities of the cities of the plain, alluding to the Turks—& they seem to have kept a careful look out over their son, while at Constantinople for fear of the Turks. Madame Ignatieff seems first to have put them up to it, alluding to her son as a beautiful boy—which however is not a reputation he bears".[22]

Such ideas shaped Salisbury's views of the eastern question during and after the 1870s. Thus, in 1877, he held the close frontier school to be

> condemned by the fact that for near 40 years the mountain tribes of the Punjab frontier have been living side by side with a British administration, exposed to all the influences which British Officers in contact with rude Native minds have innumerable opportunities of exerting, and that they are as untamed, and as little disposed for peaceful intercourse with us, as they were when we first set foot in Peshawur. The Khyber Pass, whose threshold is in our own territory and which is the highway to Cabul and Central Asia, is even to this day impassable to a white man; and that is a state of things not creditable to our civilizing powers.[23]

Leadership was rotten in the east. A few English gentlemen or Russian adventurers could easily dominate Turkey, Persia or Afghanistan. Unless checked by an outside force, Russian influence would advance to the Mediterranean or to Peshawur. This view was fantastical—even men like Nicolai Ignatiev and Stratford Canning never ruled in Istanbul—while the Turkish state was twenty years into a renaissance which made it matter in 1877, and 1914. Yet Salisbury acted upon this idea in 1874–1876; his long-term policy toward Turkey and Afghanistan in 1878 still rested on the naive belief that a few English officers could control these states through moral influence. His grasp of the politics and power of European states was remarkable, that of polities in Asia misconstrued.

During his first months in office, Salisbury formed a clear strategic policy regarding Central Asia. While there was "no immediate danger" of a Tsarist advance, Russia "is slowly getting hold of Persia"; nor could Britain halt that process. Sooner or later Russia would move to dominate Persia and conquer the remaining independent peoples of Central Asia. Until Russia sought to seize the city of Merv and the Akkhal (territory claimed by Persia but controlled by Tekke Turkoman tribes, south of the Attrek River and east of the Caspian Sea), it would not pose a threat to Britain; once Russia did so, Britain must act to defend its vital interests. Britain, of course, should slow any Russian advance through diplomatic means, but it must take further steps. While Persia stood beyond Britain's defensive sphere, Afghanistan did not: That state could not be allowed to fall under Russian influence.[24] Here intelligence gathering entered Salisbury's calculations, and to a significant extent.

More than any other Victorian statesman, Salisbury believed secret intelligence was essential for the formulation and execution of external policy. During the 1870s, the British Empire collected intelligence as a matter of course and through two distinct means. First, Britain had no permanent, specialist, and secret intelligence networks in Europe. Instead, whenever Britain needed to collect secret intelligence, it did so in an *ad hoc* and amateur fashion.[25] Agencies were established to gather information on specific problems and abolished once these had vanished. British officials collected the information both personally and through agents. Such work was financed by the Secret Service Fund, which during the 1870s hovered between £23,000 and £25,000 per year.[26] Although some of this money was not allocated for intelligence gathering, most of it was used to bribe a horde of statesmen and to feed a host of spies. However ramshackle, the system was similar to that of every European state. It could be effective; this system, however, was not always available when necessary.

European states collected intelligence in roughly similar ways: through subscriptions to newspapers, the observation of officials in foreign lands and, when necessary, through spies. Intelligence was usually assessed by general staff officers, diplomatic officials and statesmen, rather than by specialist personnel. Such sources provided a landslide of information, frequently unreliable, inaccurate or irrelevant. In 1878 Lord Cranbrook, the India Secretary, expressed a common view about spies:

> I am rather suspicious of the nation who offer their service, as spies upon Russia and masters of espionage. We should probably be paying the expenses of their own tools, and receiving not the information we need but that which the Russian Govt. desired us to have. These dirty weapons must be carefully handled—not contemptuously cast aside but tested before trust is placed in them.[27]

There were two more reliable and useful sources of intelligence than these. Two European states, Austria-Hungary and Russia, gained information through codebreaking. In particular, Russia intercepted and solved telegrams to and from Her Majesty's embassy in St. Petersburg, which provided ample opportunity to monitor its concerns on any given day. While Britain did not practice these black arts,[28] this self-denying ordinance was not necessarily a major handicap. Telegrams carried more about detail than policy. Another source of secret intelligence was no less valuable than codebreaking—the surreptitious acquisition of state papers from the offices of foreign governments. Victorian officials practiced this art with a combination of embarrassment and enthusiasm. At least during the mid-1830s, in 1856, in the 1860s and 1870s, and around the turn of this century, British officers regularly purloined, copied and returned without notice important Russian military and diplomatic documents.[29] Authentic documents, of course, were not easily distinguished from forgeries, nor even necessarily reliable or useful. As Salisbury remarked in August 1878,

> A real state of the Russian army is probably not in existence and certainly would not be shown to a foreigner. Like the Turkish returns, the Russian are probably falsified with corrupt objects. ... The present state of foreign affairs would diminish the value of such information, even if we got it. When we seemed possibly upon the eve of a war of course it was worth having.[30]

As Britain discovered between 1872 and 1876, however, this source could provide a unique and irreplaceable insight into the policy of another state.

The government of India controlled the second of the intelligence systems of the British Empire.[31] Contrary to Kipling, this government did not rely on trained agents continually traveling into the heart of Tsarist power in Central Asia and out again, although that practice did sometimes occur. Its intelligence system consisted primarily of indigenous newswriters in a few towns of Persia and Afghanistan, augmented by British officials in Persia and a Muslim agent in the Afghan capital of Kabul. These sources were permanent. They provided useful material on Persia, untrustworthy and untrusted news on Afghanistan, and virtually nothing about Central Asia. Members of the close frontier school realized that this was so and were not overly concerned. They did not perceive a Russian threat to India and did not seek information about one; they believed that any attempt to do so would create more problems than it would solve. Such information could only be acquired through human sources, European or indigenous. The government of India doubted that natives could provide accurate information. As a firm advocate of the value of secret intelligence, Lord Lytton wrote, "natives will always bring us whatever news they suppose to be wanted or expected by their employers".[32] Only Englishmen could provide reliable information. British representatives in Afghanistan or Central Asia, unfortunately, might become involved in political intrigues that could embarrass Indian interests; they might be murdered or held hostage. This raised not only moral problems but political ones—such actions would weaken British prestige or force the government of India to take undesirable military steps. Consequently, that government had not maintained an effective intelligence system in Afghanistan or Central Asia. The need to do precisely this was central to Salisbury's strategic policy.

Salisbury held that a Russian advance in Asia was probable but that Russia must never dominate Afghanistan. As he told Northbrook in April 1875, moreover:

> My feeling as to Afghanistan is that the idea of neutral territory is fundamentally impossible. That country must either be in our attraction or that of Russia. Persia is passing rapidly into the hands of Russia. I do not imagine that the strongest partizan [sic] of inaction would wish Afghanistan to do the same. But then we must gradually foster our influence and power within it.

If not, the danger was obvious.

> Afghanistan was the fairest field for intrigue in Asia, a nation of which the Chiefs are venal, and the people combatative [sic], both in an exceptional degree. It is Russia's interest to make herself mistress of this territory, not by force of arms, which would be costly and hazardous, but by "influence": and the advantage taken of this mode of attack is that, as we are absent from the country, and it is therefore, separated from us by an impenetrable screen, we shall not know what she is doing till it is done. Whenever she is in possession of the dominant party in Affghanistan [sic], and has seated its nominee upon the throne, she will then be able, as the Russians themselves say, "to besiege Constantinople from the heights above Peshawur".[33]

Only through the collection of effective military, political and topographical intelligence could Britain forestall this threat. In principle, Salisbury's argument was correct—indeed, after 1874, von Kaufmann's increasingly close relations with the amir of Afghanistan, Sher 'Ali, posed precisely the danger that so concerned the India Secretary. Ironically, however, this menace stemmed directly from the means by which Salisbury hoped to avoid it.

Salisbury held that the act of collecting intelligence would have desirable political consequences. Intelligence and political work should be carried out by a British official. In particular, Sher 'Ali must allow English representatives to reside at the main Afghan towns of Kabul, Kandahar and Herat.

This in itself would eliminate the Russian threat: as Salisbury wrote:"Probably you [the government of India] could checkmate her [Russia], outbid her, meet her in some form or other if you had the warning. But without a resident Englishman upon the Affghan [sic] frontier you cannot know what is going on."[34] Such Englishmen, however, would provide not merely news but "predominating influence" in Afghanistan, through a process that Salisbury outlined in 1878. He held that Britain could meet the inevitable decline of the Islamic states of the Middle East through

> an intermediate course between military occupation and simple *laissez faire*. It is a process of which there are already some examples: but for which there is at present no expression. I will call it the pacific invasion of England. ... The principle of it is that when you bring the English in contact with inferior races they will rule, whatever the ostensible ground of their presence. As merchants, as railway makers, as engineers, as travelers, later on as employees like Gordon, or McKillop, or as Ministers like Rivers Wilson, they assert the English domination not by any political privilege or military power, but by weight of the strongest mind.

If effective, the British military consuls in Asia Minor established in 1878 after the Russo-Turkish war and the Congress of Berlin would "furnish the best of bulwarks against Russian advance. Cannot something of the same kind be done in Affghanistan [sic]? Once obtain the unrestricted right of access and in a few years you will govern without ever drawing a sword".[35] This puerile assessment stemmed from the presuppositions of Orientalism and imperial anthropology; thus, Salisbury's policies in Afghanistan and Turkey could not have succeeded as he thought, if at all. Nonetheless, Sher 'Ali believed that a permanent British representative at Kabul would destroy his own independence. His fear was Salisbury's hope.

Upon entering office, Salisbury pressed continually for improvements in Northbrook's intelligence service. Northbrook must carefully monitor Russo-Afghan relations—he "ought to be in possession of any correspondence that is passing between the Ameer and the Russian agents". Britain required "agents unavowed—if avowed cannot be had" at Kabul; a European who could operate concealed in Islamic areas, such as the famous traveler Giffard Palgrave, might organize an intelligence network in Central Asia. British officers should more freely visit independent Central Asian states such as Yarkand. "I cannot see any reason for interfering with the natural right of a Briton to get his throat cut when and where he likes—except of course upon your immediate frontier."[36] Disraeli agreed that such were "the only means of which safe intelligence can be attained in Asia".[37]

Northbrook rejected most of Salisbury's arguments. By character phlegmatic, he also had more experience with policy, threat and intelligence in

Asia than his superiors at home, from which he derived wisdom. He learned the need to monitor danger, and the risk that focus on threats might destroy vision. Northbrook became Viceroy because a Wahabi Muslim had assassinated his predecessor, triggering fears of subterranean peril throughout the subcontinent, which he examined thoroughly while controlling any tendency toward panic.[38] So to handle more general problems of instability, Northbrook inaugurated a political intelligence system within India. The viceroy was no slave to the close frontier; although he opposed Salisbury's policies regarding Afghanistan, he was a greater advocate of political contacts with Yarkand. Northbrook also wished to collect intelligence from beyond India's frontiers. He simply declined to do so in the fashion and in the area demanded by Salisbury, because he believed that strategy impossible. After thoroughly considering the issue with his experts, the viceroy denied that British representatives could reside safely at Kabul and refused to try to place them there. He held that to do so would throw Afghanistan straight into the arms of the bear, which otherwise would not occur. These views proved prescient. Demands that a British ambassador be placed in Kabul drove Sher 'Ali to pursue an alliance with Russia in 1878, while during 1879 a British representative was murdered in the Afghan capital, in both cases forcing the government of India to invade Afghanistan, rather against Salisbury's inclinations. Northbrook, above all, denounced Salisbury's proposals about gathering intelligence through secret rather than open means. Native intelligence sources would "collect a mass of lies 'of sorts', and, perhaps, some truths we are better ignorant of". The viceroy refused to use any of "our Eastern adventurers", such as Palgrave or Richard Francis Burton. "I would far sooner have a plain straightforward English officer in a place of difficulty in the East. The natives would beat us at intrigue, and we should risk our character in the bargain, which is of the greatest importance to us." He vetoed all Salisbury's proposals save those that involved the use of straightforward English officers, but he used them thoroughly. Northbrook placed new political officials on the northern and northeastern frontiers of India. In 1873 a mission visited Yarkand. It provided extraordinarily detailed information that demonstrated that this state was far more ramshackle than expected. As a result, Northbrook abandoned his hopes for close ties with Yarkand. In 1874, Captain Biddulph and three other officers surveyed the paths and politics of the Pamirs and Hindu Kush, demonstrating that the area was more problematical than hitherto supposed, leading to the establishment of an advanced post, the Gilgat Agency, to monitor dangers and establish influence in the area. Meanwhile Captain Napier was sent to the city of Meshad in northwest Persia, from where he monitored military and political developments in Central Asia and established direct contact with the Tekke Turkomans. Four members of the Corps of Guides surreptitiously acquired expertise and contacts in that region.[39]

Northbrook took more effective steps to collect intelligence beyond India's frontier than virtually any other viceroy in history, but not in the areas that most concerned Salisbury: Afghanistan and Russian Turkistan. This irritated the India Secretary, who held that "Northbrook's intelligence department is very bad. He disdains the use of secret service money: and without a liberal use of that kind of investigation it is impossible to know what is going on in Affghanistan [sic]".[40] This position changed only in spring 1876, when Northbrook resigned as viceroy. Disraeli, with Salisbury's consent, handpicked a successor ignorant of India and willing—indeed, ready—to adopt a forward policy. Lytton, injured, neurotic, energetic, over-polished in style and policy, vain, vainglorious, able, pursued these aims despite opposition from his administration—"I might as well consult a Committee of Undertakers as to the best means of prolonging my life."[41] Within a year, citing "the growing importance of our frontier politics,—their gradual merging into one great Central Asian question, and so into the Imperial policy of our British Government", he pushed to reorganize all of the northwest frontier. His aim was to sustain British power and allow "a direct attack in case of need, at a given moment, by British troops on the Russian position in Central Asia"; his military staff forged plans to throw a corps to Kabul and beyond to Tashkent, so as to spark rebellion through Russian Turkistan and annihilate its empire. One of his officials deplored

> the prospect of some of the ablest officers in India being planted along the frontier to carry out this policy, and with the Viceroy's Minute in their hands as their handbook of action. This policy would result, I am convinced, in sanguinary wars, in vast expenditure, and in the annexation of worthless territories. It would extend our frontier in a direction westwards, to which I see no natural limits. Moreover, it would create amongst the venal, faithless, but freedom loving Afghans a tendency towards Russia that certainly does not exist now.

By early 1877, Lytton wished to send a British mission to Merv "with authority, after ascertaining the position of affairs there, to afford to the Turkomans all the assistance in their power, if the prospects of resistance seem favourable".[42] As part of this grand design, a central part, Lytton endeavoured to place British representatives in and to establish hegemony over Afghanistan. He believed that diplomacy required "the utmost secrecy of design and celerity in action"; moreover, that while "the Government of India is dependent on the merest guesswork for its knowledge of what is passing in the mind of Sher 'Ali, the Russian Cabinet know every rupee that we give him and almost every word that we write or talk about him"—a slight exaggeration. Lytton also emphasized the collection of intelligence through secret means. By early 1877 he had established five agents in Kabul, five at other towns in Afghanistan, and two "first rate" men at Tashkent.[43] Their role was to collect political and strategic intelligence in Afghanistan and Russian Turkistan. By the summer of 1876 the government of India began to acquire copies of von Kaufmann's letters to Sher 'Ali. Though they revealed more about how the governor of Turkistan aimed to impress the amir than the real policy of either man, senior military and political figures in Calcutta and London read them with interest.[44]

During 1874-1876, another source of intelligence developed in India, supported by Northbrook.[45] The Indian army created an Intelligence Branch, focused as much on acquiring geographical as strategic data. Its task, Roberts wrote, was

> collecting statistics, and ... arranging in time of peace, the mass of important records which doubtless exist in the several offices of the Supreme and local Governments. ... Our knowledge of the frontier is perhaps less now than at previous periods, owing, in a great measure, to the want of some department held responsible for carefully collecting every fragment of information which could possibly be of use in war.

Its duties also included "the collection, siting, and arrangement of all information required by the Government of India for the rapid commencement and vigorous prosecution of war in any direction", "the spreading of useful military information to the army of India" and the formulation of "a staff which should be able to transfer its functions to the field, when the emergency for which preparation has been made, occurs". Several officers of the Indian army traveled through Persia, as tourists and intelligence personnel. General Frederick Roberts, the Indian army officer responsible for intelligence, told one of these individuals, Colonel Charles Metcalfe MacGregor,

> What we want are routes. Any number of these will be most valuable; and you will assist the Department greatly if you will send me every route you can get hold of. I have got sanction for two additional officers to be attached to our office for six months, to collate information; and I intend to set them to work at routes beyond our border, so as to have a Central Asia Route-book. Any help towards the completion of this I shall be most grateful for.[46]

MacGregor responded with a military survey of eastern Persia, complete with a commentary on the defensive capabilities of virtually every pass in Khorassan. In late 1876, moreover, Salisbury sent MacGregor and a comrade on a similar semi-official mission to Persian Baluchistan. MacGregor quickly published this material in two books—quick publicity for secret intelligence characterized Victorian Britain.

These officers and agents were useful sources of intelligence, far better than any the government of India had possessed before. They provided accurate military, economic, and topographical intelligence regarding areas of strategic concern, such as Persia and Yarkand. This material showed that the government of India misunderstood basic matters such as the demography and economy of Merv. Such information was mundane yet vital for any military planning. Its acquisition was the greatest success achieved by the Indian intelligence system during the 1870s. These sources, moreover, provided much more reliable accounts than had previously been available of the activities of Russian frontier officials and of political developments between India's northern frontier and Turkistan. Thus, the government of India followed with general accuracy the course of Russo-Afghan relations during 1874–1878. Of course, it never understood the reasoning of Sher 'Ali and bungled its relations with him. Lytton complained, moreover, in May 1878 that "we have no trustworthy means of obtaining information as to the doings of the Russian agents at Cabul nor of the Russian designs generally"; his intelligence chief at Peshawur, Louis Cavagnari, noted that "it will be difficult for me to get prompt intelligence" of Russian troop movements. The government of India remained ignorant of important aspects of the amir's negotiations with Russia. Nonetheless, it at least knew that such negotiations were occurring. In 1878, when Sher 'Ali sought an alliance with Russia and Tsarist armed forces began to advance on Afghanistan, the government of India received sufficiently accurate and timely information to respond as Lytton deemed necessary.[47] Between 1875 and 1880 that government possessed by far the best early warning system beyond its frontiers of the entire nineteenth century, one that met many of its strategic needs. Those sources, unfortunately, did not and could not illuminate the most crucial of issues, the intentions of Russia and the state of its armed forces.

One British source could do precisely this: its military attaché in Russia. Colonel Frederick Wellesley was a shrewd observer with entrée to the highest levels of Russian military decision makers, who appreciated his connections and found his character homely. Wellesley was a man of mixed reputation. He acquired his position in St. Petersburg through marriage to the daughter of the British ambassador and remarkable patronage from the Queen's cousin and commander in chief of the British army, the Duke of Cambridge. He was notorious for extravagance; not merely in matters financial. In 1878, while serving as military attaché in Vienna, Wellesley wrecked his career through a scandal in Bohemia—he ran off with an actress who had been another gentleman's mistress, destroying his credibility with patrons like Salisbury and Cambridge. Nor was this Wellesley's only slip from the standards of the public-schoolboy. Since early 1872 he had, through the medium of agents, been stealing official papers from the Russian government. Wellesley usually could examine such documents for only a few hours—long enough to photograph or to copy them by hand. Throughout most of his tenure as spymaster, Wellesley acquired material from one source, the Russian War Office, and especially its "Asiatic Department" (which should not be confused with the bureau of the same name under the Ministry of Foreign Affairs). At least one other source provided intelligence on the Russian navy, while by 1877 Wellesley was grooming another agent with access to the archives of the Ministry of Foreign Affairs. The evidence does not indicate whether this agent was hired; probably not.[48] The names and positions of these agents are unknown.

From these sources between 1872 and 1877 Wellesley continually followed the deployments, the order of battle, and the policy of the Russian army. He traced any signs of mobilization for war and provided extraordinarily detailed information on the military matters that most concerned Britain, such as the defences of the main fleet base at Kronstadt and the condition of the Russian army adjacent to Central Asia.[49] In December 1872, moreover, Wellesley began to procure the War Office's copies of material on Persia and Central Asia: the correspondence of Russian diplomats and generals; the minutes of interdepartmental deliberations. Wellesley sometimes saw documents containing comments written only a few days before by Miliutin or the Tsar. Conversely, Wellesley rarely provided information specifically on Russian diplomacy in Europe or in Turkey. He proffered remarkable intelligence on one half of the eastern question, much less upon the other. Wellesley provided by far Britain's most valuable information on Russian policy during the 1870s—indeed, over a century later his reports still ranked among the best sources on the matter available to Western historians.[50]

Simultaneously, Wellesley stole Russian documents and Tsarist codebreakers read British telegrams, because neither source could betray the other. Granted, by 1876 Tsarist authorities sought to manipulate Wellesley by giving him misleading material which exaggerated Russian power—this merely ameliorated his sweeping contempt for the Russian army, which angered the latter when they learned of it by reading his telegrams while attached to the Russian army on campaign in 1877. In turn, through his own sources Wellesley, late in the day but still in time, demonstrated that either the British Foreign Secretary or his wife, Lord and Lady Derby, or both, were revealing rather too much of the deliberations of the British cabinet to the Russian ambassador in Britain, Count Petr Shuvalov. Wellesley believed that his work was "simply a matter of money—and that anything could be obtained by paying for it". Conversely: "The more papers I buy, the greater the expenditure, and the more irons I have in the fire, the greater the risk."[51] His superiors did not initially appreciate these problems. Shortly after Wellesley began his career as spymaster, the British War Office showed his material to an officer who was about to visit Russia. Wellesley complained that the position of a Military Attaché in a Foreign Country is one which by the very nature of the appointment requires the utmost tact and discretion.

It is sometimes possible to obtain and send home most valuable and secret information, but it is of the utmost importance that a Military Attaché should have no misgivings as to such information being considered secret at home. ... Should the Russian Government become aware that I had sent home anything secret ... the result would be either that I should be unable to obtain any information worth having in the future, or more probably still that my recall would be applied for.[52]

This particular practice stopped.

Wellesley once informed the Foreign Office that "I can obtain anything, but I would like to know what is of special interest at home, so as to be guided in my future conduct".[53] He did not usually receive such guidance but was left to determine which documents warranted the purchase and given the funds needed to acquire them. The response to his material was odd. The Foreign Office did not direct Wellesley to acquire material on Russian diplomacy in the Balkans or Europe, which would have interested it more than that which he did procure. Nor did the Admiralty press him for more material on issues such as proof that Russians were stealing plans of British warships, and using them for their own, or on the defences of Kronstadt, even though attack on them was central to planning for an Anglo-Russian war and, as he told Cambridge, such material was "without any exception ... the most secret information which could possibly be obtained in this country, and without doubt of the utmost practical value in case of a rupture between the two countries at a future period".[54] Perhaps Whitehall was put off by the price he suggested, £800, possibly the single largest expenditure from the Secret Service Fund ever suggested between 1816 and 1913. Her Majesty's Government, nonetheless, regarded these papers as important. They were read by senior figures in the Foreign Office and the War Office. They were regularly circulated to Derby, Disraeli and Salisbury, often to Queen Victoria, more sporadically to other ministers, such as the Secretary for War, Gathorne-Hardy, and rarely if ever to most members of the Cabinet. Wellesley also sent some reports directly to the Duke of Cambridge. Though this action was proper, given the contemporary role of military attachés, it reflected personal considerations and it had political consequences. Cambridge, Wellesley's mentor in a factionalized army, had pushed his appointment to St. Petersburg, even though it was several ranks above his present one as captain. This secured Wellesley a higher provisional rank and salary, a matter of great concern to him.[55] In return Wellesley sent some of his more alarming material to a senior decision maker who perceived a Russian menace in Asia. In order to spur on the cabinet, Cambridge sometimes circulated this material to the Secretary for War. This attempt failed since Gathorne-Hardy refused to challenge government policy. Meanwhile, Salisbury circulated some of this material to his viceroys, under strict instructions regarding "absolute secresy [sic]"; they were to consider such information "for your eyes only".[56]

Wellesley had strong opinions about British relations with Russia. He believed that, unless checked, Russia would develop road and water communications and an advanced base which would let the entire Caucasian Army operate in Central Asia. From that moment Russia would dominate Central Asia and threaten India. Yet

> [Russia] knows how weak she is both from a military and a financial point of view, but is too delighted if any one will think her strong—in fact she is glad to bark, because she dare not fight. ... She knows how precarious her position in [Central Asia] is, but as long as the English Press continue to write alarmist articles about the great "Colossus of the North", which is some day to sweep us out of India—so long will Russia be content to derive what empty glory she can from the prevalence of such ideas—to trade on her false reputation.[57]

Wellesley favoured firm actions against Russia—including, both before and during the crisis of 1876–1878, a preventative war and an offensive in Central Asia.[58] He held that Britain could drive Russia out of Central Asia "simply by appearing on the Oxus, which would have the immediate effect of raising the whole native population against the Russian invaders by whom they are only now kept in order by a rule of terror".[59] His reputation rose high in the eyes of the government—few captains have had greater influence on the British state. By 1876 Cambridge supported Wellesley's appointment to the influential position of Military Secretary to the Viceroy. In May 1877 Salisbury told the Cabinet that Wellesley lay "under strong suspicions of corruption"[60]—an allegation rebuked by several ministers, including Derby. Still, Wellesley's material impressed no one more than the India Secretary. As Salisbury wrote in 1875: "We receive pretty constantly copies of the most important reports and references that reach the Foreign Office and War Office at St. Petersburgh: but the supply if known would soon cease."[61] In 1878, despite his prior concerns, Salisbury gave Wellesley a plum appointment in Vienna and asked the army to give him favourable terms of pay and rank.[62] By 1876–1877, Disraeli borrowed his military strategy toward Russia from Wellesley, and used him as a secret channel direct to the Tsar, to warn Russia that it could not lightly disregard British interests and power, while Britain would intervene should the Russian attack last into a second campaigning season. (This may well have had the unintended consequence of driving Alexander to finish it in one.) In April 1878, at the height of the

Anglo-Russian crisis, Wellesley told Disraeli: "I am trying to get all the military information I can—but it is difficult. ... They fear war with us and are fully aware of the dangers attending it, but will they have courage enough to give in?"[63]

Wellesley appears to have procured material of diplomatic value about only one matter under Gladstone's government. In December 1872 he provided several documents showing that, stung by the humiliating defeat of a Russian column on the frontier of Khiva, Alexander II was on the verge of authorizing an invasion of that state. Wellesley also revealed a division in Russian counsels. The Ministry of Finance opposed this action, backed by a surprising ally. Von Kaufmann's predecessor as commander in Turkistan, Chernaiev, opposed further expansion in Turkistan. Chernaiev held that von Kaufmann's administration was unpopular with its subjects.

> In a political point of view, we have changed places with our old rival England. Instead of being a formidable neighbour of hers in Asia, we are compelled to fear her interference even in that part of the world. It would be quite sufficient for her to spend a few tens of thousands of rupees in order to place us in the most embarrassing position. England seems to look on with pleasure at the progress we are making in Central Asia. Is it not on account of the altered dispositions of the natives towards us?

Chernaiev also wrote:

> The development of our conquests in Central Asia was brought about, and will always be brought about as it were by a spontaneous action on the part of the local administration, very often in contradiction to the wish and frequently even in defiance of the orders of the Home Government. We find similar cases in the history of the English conquests in India.

Despite his own anti-Russian opinions, Wellesley noted that Chernaiev's letter showed "how much the Russian Home Government have attempted to check the increase of Russian territory in Central Asia".[64]

Since this material was reproduced in the Foreign Office Confidential Print, one can assume that it was seen by Gladstone and his senior ministers. While this intelligence arguably did influence the latter's assessments, they did not act upon it. Gladstone's government believed Anglo-Russian relations could easily become worse and wished to avoid that danger. It did not regard Russian power in Central Asia as a threat to Britain, or Khiva as essential to the security of India. It believed Khiva had been threatening Russian interests for years, that a punitive expedition was a reasonable and, in part, a defensive action. Wellesley's material would have reinforced the impression that events and frontier officials had finally driven a somewhat reluctant government toward a limited sort of forward policy. Knowledge of how and why Russia's decision was reached may well have encouraged Gladstone's government not to oppose the action. Wellesley did not provide more than a few more days' warning of the intention than would otherwise have occurred. Almost exactly when his material arrived in London, so too did another message from St. Petersburg. A personal emissary of the Tsar pledged that while Russia would attack Khiva, it would neither annex nor permanently occupy that state. He also offered to meet an important British objective, a definition of the frontier between Afghanistan and Russia's subject states in central Asia. The Cabinet had hoped for years to reach such a formal arrangement. In January 1873 it exploited the opportunity to acquire one.

The arrangement, however, did not explicitly cover the Akkhal or Merv and was sufficiently vague to allow two different interpretations. To Her Majesty's Government, Afghanistan was to remain internally independent but within a loose British sphere of influence, in which Russia would never interfere. The opposite would be true of Khiva. While the Russian decision of 1873 to make Khiva a protected state was a case of sharp practice, it also arguably stemmed from different and legitimate views of the imprecise arrangement at hand. Alexander II seems to have interpreted the latter to mean that Afghanistan would be a neutral state, equally free from Russian and British dominance although under a greater degree of British influence. Russia, meanwhile, was entitled to do anything toward Khiva except formally annex it.

Wellesley's material, finally, may have shaped British assessments of the causes for the violation of Alexander II's pledge about Khiva. Before the event, Granville denied that Russia would gain from making Khiva a protectorate, and held that if this did occur, it would be to appease Russian public opinion, which had been enraged by "the language of our press, and by our somewhat ostentatious lecturing on the subject [rather] than from nature of self interest".[65] Granville held that "the Russians are all intriguers". Since he expected bad faith from Russians on minor issues, he did not treat the announcement of a protectorate over Khiva as a new or notable indication of their long-term policy.[66] However, when analyzing the event, Granville wrote:

> I believe the Emperor was perfectly sincere at the time; but he is not a strong man, and it would require a very strong man to resist the military element by which he is surrounded, and who naturally think it necessary to have some quid for costly and troublesome expeditions, and some security against the recurrence of the grievances of which they have complained.[67]

In this instance, the analysis was not entirely accurate. In general, however, it was virtually identical to that which Wellesley's information led Derby, Disraeli, and Salisbury to adopt.

Thirteen months passed between Wellesley's acquisition of intelligence on the Khivan expedition and his next extant document on Russian policy in Central Asia. Within four months of Disraeli's government entering power, however, Wellesley began to produce a flood of such material. The causes for these events are obscure. They may stem from changes in the access of Wellesley's agents or, perhaps, in the instructions from or the apparent concerns of his government, or in his own ambitions. Wellesley presumably knew or was informed that Disraeli's government was very interested in material on such topics. Between September 1874 and October 1876, he continuously provided current effective intelligence on Russian policy in Central Asia. He acquired, for example, a memorandum by the Russian ambassador at Istanbul, Ignatiev, that opposed the Khivan operation, because "Russia does not require an extension of frontier. Such an increase of territory, especially in Central Asia would pose a source of weakness, rather than of power". Alongside these arguments, Alexander II wrote "*certes*". The Tsar accepted Ignatiev's reasoning that Russia need not destroy Khiva (as opposed to making it a subject state)—indeed, Alexander II even considered a proposal that Khiva be given to Persia, so to strengthen Russian influence at Tehran. Conversely, Wellesley revealed that von Kaufmann favoured further expansion in Central Asia. Many senior Russian commanders, however, regarded Russia's position there as weak and held that adjoining powers such as Khiva and the Tekke Turkomans could spark revolts among Russia's Islamic subjects. Wellesley concluded that: "Russia in Central Asia is at present miserably weak, but she knows it; and intends to become strong."[68] During November–December 1874, Wellesley procured several memoranda from von Kaufmann and the Russian diplomatic agent at Tashkent, and in particular a secret report intended to give the Tsar an independent view of affairs in Turkistan from General Doudeville, lately von Kaufmann's chief of staff and now his rival. These documents painted a complex picture of events. They showed that the Ministries of War, Finance, and Foreign Affairs all criticized von Kaufmann's policy. They generally described a weak, unpopular, and corrupt Russian government in Turkistan, one threatened by adjacent Islamic powers; consequently, most Russian commanders urged, the latter must be eliminated. Doudeville and von Kaufmann, moreover, independently urged that spies acquire knowledge of the terrain between Turkistan and India. The Ministry of War pledged to gain such information through other means. Miliutin noted that in order to invade India, Russia must prepare to fight both the Indian army and the intermediate peoples. This, Wellesley wrote, "offers an additional proof of that restless feeling of aggression which there can now be hardly any doubt exists".[69]

Between January and October 1875, Wellesley's material illuminated Tsarist policy toward Persia. Russian diplomats discussed—often in dispassionate terms—local politics and British activities, including Napier's work; they noted rumours that Britain had supplied 6,000 rifles to the Tekke Turkomans. Similarly, the Russian envoy to Kashgar reported that Yarkand was hostile to Russia and possessed twenty battalions equipped with English rifles. This led von Kaufmann to state that in Asia England sought "*a nous mettre des batons dans les jambes*". In fact, the governments of Britain and India had not supplied arms to Yarkand or the Tekke Turkomans. Von Kaufmann also wished to establish a permanent base on the Attrek River for eventualities "*plus ou moins probables*" against the Akkhal or Persia; as Wellesley noted, this allusion "speaks for itself".[70]

The most crucial material provided by Wellesley during 1875 was correspondence between St. Petersburg and the commander in the Caucasus. The Grand Duke Michael held that Persian policy toward Russia was "shifty and ambiguous" and marked by "much arrogance". Russia must act "in a more resolute manner and ... be guided exclusively with reference to our own interests without attributing too much importance to so called political etiquette". In "a future more or less remote", Russia must annex the Akkhal and the Persian provinces along the southern shore of the Caspian Sea, "in defiance of all hostile influences the object of which is to frustrate our plans". In order to further these aims, to suppress the Turkomans and to keep the subject state of Khiva in check, Russia must immediately establish garrisons of perhaps 7,000 men on the northern bank of the Attrek River. Once communications between the Caucasus and Central Asia were secure, Russia could "strike decisive blows in every place where the force of circumstances might lead to the necessity of aggressive action". This would provide strategic mobility to the Caucasian army, "the nucleus of our future power beyond the Caspian. ... Its real part, that of a great reserve destined for all active operations which sooner or later will take place in Central Asia will only be realized on that day. ... Such is the importance which the future has in store for the army of Caucasus"—and its commander.[71] Michael wished to annex the political heart of Persia and much of Central Asia, to establish effective physical communications within Russian Asia, and to make the army of the Caucasus the striking force of the Tsarist Empire. This policy would make Russia the military master of half the Middle East and a serious potential threat to India. This in fact occurred by 1885, when most of Michael's aims had been achieved.

In 1875, however, Alexander II rejected these proposals. Instead, in an important and unusual action, he met with Michael's adjutant, von Kaufmann, and Count Petr Shuvalov, to coordinate and to control the policies of the Ministries of War and Foreign Affairs. The Tsar noted that any Russian action in Central Asia provoked "jealous suspicion" in Britain. Derby had officially warned that should Russia advance on Merv, Britain would do so in Afghanistan. Although these British "pretensions ... have no lawful basis, and do not emanate from the preceding diplomatic arrangement" (the Afghan frontier delimitation of 1873), the "supreme will" of the Tsar for the moment was that Russia must not imperil its relations with Britain. Frontier authorities "should endeavour to avoid as much as possible any measures of aggression, and should not cross our present frontiers without absolute necessity". Reconnaissances along the northern bank of the Attrek River were acceptable, but not anything "which could be regarded as an aggressive movement towards Merve". While obviously favourable to British interests—even Wellesley noted that "the Emperor's wishes as regard to the pacific conduct of Russia in Central Asia are strongly expressed"—this dictum did contain loopholes. By June the grand duke requested authority to carry out a reconnaissance along the Attrek in "the most amiable spirit"—with 2,000 soldiers, four guns and a rocket battery! The Tsar approved this request. Wellesley carefully followed the planning for this operation, in particular informing his superiors that it did not show "as yet the slightest indication of a move on Merv", and for a similar one planned for 1877.[72]

Wellesley's reports of 1876 showed a similar pattern of events—authorities in St. Petersburg rejected continual proposals for expansion by Russian frontier officials. The latter, for example, feared that the "powerful and independent Musalman power" of Yarkand was threatening Russia's hold throughout the region. An interdepartmental conference in St. Petersburg, however, chose not to conquer Yarkand but to hope that China would do so; in the interim Russia would pursue good relations with China, perhaps even offering the latter minor territorial concessions within inner Asia, such as the region of Kuldja. Similarly, Alexander II declined to play a powerful card against Britain—to use a deadly rival, Abdur Rahman, against Sher 'Ali, "in view of certain explanations which took place between the Imperial Cabinet and that of London concerning the question of Afghanistan and its frontiers".[73] Finally, the Grand Duke Michael twice sought to overturn his brother's decision of 1875 and immediately to pursue Russian control over the Akkhal. The Tsar categorically rejected these proposals, which were "not required by actual necessity" while the time was "not ... quite convenient". He "absolutely" forbade any advance toward Merv. The Ministry for War emphasized that

> political difficulties of no small importance are involved in the proposed movement to Ashkabad.
>
> This place is at most 350 versts from Merve—that sore place in the latest Central Asian policy of Great Britain.
>
> Any trivial encounter between the Turcomans of Merve and our detachment might necessitate our following former further than it enters into the view of our Government to do. ... Lastly, in conse-

quence of all this, we should be led to the [in such circumstances] inevitable explanations with the English Government which, on account of our present relations with the London Cabinet, it is deirable to avoid.[74]

By 1876, even for the Ministry of War, Russian policy in Central Asia was subordinated to that in the Balkans. So as not to provoke a forward English policy in Europe, Russia declined one in Asia. From that time until 1878, the central issue in Anglo-Russian relations became Turkey. This affected Wellesley's value as a source of intelligence. His espionage interests increasingly centred on the Balkan crisis, while during the Russo-Turkish war of 1877–1878 his official duties took him away from St. Petersburg. He ceased to provide much material on Central Asia. During 1878, however, Wellesley did offer the first hint about Russia's abortive attempts to form an alliance with Afghanistan and to threaten India by armed force. Contrary to conventional beliefs, some British authorities had intelligence on these developments—they simply did not act on it.

In late April 1878, during a temporary sojourn in St. Petersburg, Wellesley acquired a three-week-old dispatch in which von Kaufmann stated that his forces were mobilizing to attack the subject state of Bokhara which, von Kaufmann argued, was subverting Russia's position in Central Asia, backed by that "perfidious" and "evil enemy", Britain. (The dispatch revealed only part of the story. In a simultaneous, independent and perhaps coincidental action, Alexander II accepted Miliutin's argument that Russia should match Britain's display of force off Turkey by a military demonstration against, but not an attack on, India, combined with the dispatch of an embassy to form an alliance with Sher 'Ali. Subsequently, von Kaufmann sent this mission to Kabul while all his forces moved toward the southern border of Russian Turkistan to demonstrate against India. British authorities were not aware of this context.) Wellesley noted that von Kaufmann's dispatch showed "General Kaufmann meditates an immediate and apparently uncalled for invasion" of Bokhara but referred to no other targets. The British ambassador in St. Petersburg, Augustus Loftus, warned the Foreign Office that the "contemplated movement against Bokhara appears to me a mere blind to cover the eventual designs of Russia" to place Abdur Rahman on the throne of Afghanistan. While neither assessment was entirely accurate, each was alarming. The fact that Russian forces in Turkistan were mobilizing and the possibility that they might advance on Afghanistan would have been clear to Salisbury, who was, by then, Foreign Secretary. The British government, however, took no action on this information, which apparently was not even transmitted to Lytton.

Although the matter is obscure, there are two plausible interpretations. As the classic scholar of the great Eastern crisis, B.H. Sumner, argued, British statesmen might have misunderstood the "not very circumstantial" information. This interpretation seems unlikely: Disraeli and Salisbury interpreted Wellesley's intelligence in a shrewd and suspicious manner, and that dispatch was sufficiently circumstantial to provoke alarm. Conversely, Salisbury was deep in complex negotiations with Tsarist authorities to settle the Turkish crisis which, he held, forward parties in Russia and India, or problems in the Balkans or Afghanistan, could easily wreck. As he told Disraeli in February 1878, just after becoming Foreign Secretary,

> The Russian military party, exaggerating our embarrassment in Afghanistan, are making a desperate effort to push the Emperor into war—using the atrocity argument, which has succeeded so well before. My impression is that it will fail—the internal state of Russia is too serious. But I wish our people at Constantinople did not lose their heads so very quickly. We must continue to use firm language about the Treaty—but any idea of breaking up the Rumalian negotiations must I think be discouraged.

Subsequently, he informed Loftus, "matters are looking grave, but I do not yet think we are on the brink of war and I believe we shall avoid it if the Russian statesmen do not allow the soldiers to run away with them"; and a Cabinet colleague:

> I do not think there will be war: but this result can only be obtained by maintaining an attitude in word and deed which, 1st, shall show no flinching in our resolution; 2ly, shall show no inclination to inflict any gratuitous humiliation upon Russia. Both precautions are necessary—because if, on the one hand, they are likely to be impressed in their cooler moments by our resolute attitude, they are, on the other hand, very youthful in their temperament, and might fling themselves into any mad adventure rather than submit to any fixed design of humiliating them [sic].

Precisely as Wellesley's warning appeared, Salisbury refused to offer political objectives to the British fleet off Istanbul in case of war with Russia, on the ostensible grounds that everything indicated "that an attack by the Russians is not probable". Equally, perhaps, he aimed to moderate the ardour of admirals developing war plans against Russia, and fearful of attack by torpedo.[75] It seems possible that Salisbury expected to reach a quick settlement with Russia that would automatically neutralize any potential danger from von Kaufmann, and hence chose not to act against the possible threat in Central Asia; moreover, that he did not wish to provoke Lytton into aggressive actions over Afghanistan that might wreck negotiations with Russia regarding the Balkans. Certainly, that is how Salisbury did respond when the Viceroy took such actions in the autumn of 1878. In May,

Salisbury arguably had reasons to believe that this would occur should the viceroy receive Wellesley's material. The Foreign Secretary doubted Lytton's judgment, regarded his aggressive approach toward Russia as being dangerously counterproductive, and no doubt thought the crisis would spur them forward. If this analysis is correct, Salisbury was taking a remarkably cold-blooded gamble—one that paid off regarding von Kaufmann but not Lytton.[76] Salisbury defeated the Russian gambit by ignoring it—and intelligence on it—but this sparked the unsuccessful British occupation of Afghanistan of 1878.

Analysis of Wellesley's material leads to the following conclusions. First, Russian decision making was fragmented; the departments and their agents did pursue contradictory policies. Second, Tsarist statesmen intended (exactly as Gorchakov had informed the world) ultimately to expand in Central Asia until Russia reached the frontiers of established states. Third, many Tsarist leaders purported to believe that Russia's hold in Central Asia was shaky, and they phrased aggressive strategic arguments in defensive terms, in a fashion strikingly similar to that of the English forward school. Many Russian leaders, meanwhile, wished to advance in central Asia precisely to blackmail Britain; others seemed eager to subvert or to attack India. Fourth, by 1875 Alexander II deliberately restricted Russian advances for any unspecified period of time. Seen in hindsight, Wellesley's material suggested that in the long term Russia would seek to dominate all of Central Asia and Persia but not for the moment. The Soviet academic specialist on these matters, N.A. Khalfin, argued that British policy toward Russia in Central Asia throughout the nineteenth century was cynical, hypocritical and aggressive, because British intelligence showed that Russia was too weak to threaten India.[77] Khalfin's views were mendacious and fallacious—British intelligence provided a complex picture of Russia, one combining elements of strength and weakness, for which there was no self-evident interpretation. It demonstrated that many Russian decision makers possessed the will to threaten the Raj, although not necessarily the means. British statesmen were not wrong to fear Russian intentions toward Central Asia; the question is over their assessment of the timing and the scale of the danger, and of the appropriate countermeasures.

The influence of Wellesley's material on British policy is not easy to gauge. Granted, the evidence is good for intelligence history. Wellesley's information was of high quality and was treated seriously by senior decision makers. Most—perhaps all—of his reports and many assessments of them by Salisbury and Northbrook survive. Here, however, and even more so with Derby, Cambridge, Disraeli and Lytton, conclusions about the effect of the information rest to some degree on arguments by coincidence—on the tracing of similarities between his information and the ideas of his consumers. Nor are these the only problems at hand. Decision making was no less chaotic in London that in St. Petersburg. Several different men pursued contrary policies toward Russia. Intelligence affected them all in different ways and moved British policy in contradictory directions. Wellesley's information often led statesmen not to take specific decisions that were carried into effect (thus allowing one to judge how information affected actions) but instead to favour policies that were never realized—or not to take certain actions at all. It is difficult to trace the causal significance of intelligence in such cases, which are characteristic of diplomacy—one reason, perhaps, why the effect of intelligence on foreign policy in peacetime is studied less than that on military operations during war.[78] However, the task is not impossible.

Wellesley's intelligence was perhaps most valuable in illuminating the nature of Russian decision making on Central Asia. Throughout the 1870s, Disraeli's government had a shrewd idea of the aims and influence of the factions that shaped Russian policy. They correctly appreciated the policies and the power of the forward party in St. Petersburg and on the frontier; they realized that Alexander II was deliberately not challenging British interests but under other circumstances might do so. Her Majesty's Government did not fully appreciate the nuances of Russian decision making. Derby exaggerated the differences between the long-term (as against the immediate) aims of the Tsar and his soldiers. Salisbury, Derby and Disraeli sometimes misunderstood the position of the Emperor. Thus, Disraeli wrote that if Alexander II did not enforce greater control over Russian policy, he "will be reduced to the position of an Emperor of Delhi or a Mikado before the Japanese Revolution".[79] In fact, Alexander II's stance was no less consistent and powerful than Disraeli's own; Russian generals sometimes disobeyed Alexander's formal instructions because he had given contrary but informal ones (a fact one might have expected a Beaconsfield to grasp, given his own view of the Prime Minister's prerogative of choosing who to work with, and of using private instructions to generals, diplomats and viceroys in order to pursue a policy the Cabinet would not approve). British statesmen, nonetheless, grasped with remarkable accuracy the dynamics of Russian decision making regarding Central Asia, largely due to Wellesley's information. Although many individuals who did not see this material reached similar conclusions, Disraeli and Salisbury could act not on suspicion but on certainty, and extrapolate the lessons to other issues. Each understood the roots and the branches of Russian policy.

Such knowledge could be translated into different policies. Here Wellesley's information played a complex and critical role. British decision makers generally interpreted the material in the fashion outlined above, concluding that Russia's position in Central Asia was weak and that, for the moment, further Russian expansion was unlikely. In itself, this ensured that from 1876 to 1878 British statesmen could handle the Balkan crisis without fearing Russian countermeasures in Asia. Hence, Wellesley's intelligence was most significant in the formulation of British policy regarding not Central

Asia but relations between Russia and Turkey. Historians of British policy during the Turkish crisis of 1876–1878 have not come fully to terms with the effect of Wellesley's influence and intelligence on this matter. Until this occurs, however, British strategy and diplomacy during the great eastern crisis will be inexplicable.

Wellesley's intelligence and assessments fundamentally shaped Disraeli's policy during the crisis, particularly his ideas for armed intervention against Russia. They led the Prime Minister to believe Russia was (and knew itself to be) militarily weak in Europe and Asia, and that Britain could deter or defeat Russian aggression toward Turkey.[80] A memorandum by Wellesley directly sparked Disraeli's initial (and abortive) attempt of late 1876 to dispatch a small British expeditionary force to Istanbul so as to deter Russia from using the threat or the application of force to bolster its diplomacy against Turkey. Subsequent British investigations concluded that a much stronger force would be needed than Wellesley had assumed—one larger than Britain could muster. The agitation over the Bulgarian massacres, meanwhile, rendered politically impossible this action or practically any firm policy for some time. Wellesley's assessments shaped another aspect of Disraeli's strategic thinking. Throughout the Turkish crisis, Disraeli became even less concerned with Central Asia than before—and far more confident regarding it. From the start of the Russo-Turkish war, he turned increasingly to the prospect of British intervention, through soldiers, seapower, and cooperation with Turks and rebels against Russian overlords in Asia, whenever British public opinion would again tolerate action. He told the British minister at Istanbul,

> If there is a second campaign I have the greatest hopes that the Country will interfere, and pronounce its veto against a war of extermination, and the dark designs of a secret partition, from which the spirit of the 19th century recoils. As we have the command of the sea, why should not a British Corps d'Armee (via Batoum) march into Armenia and even occupy Tiflis?
>
> We might send another to Varna and act on the Russian flank.

Disraeli's policy excluded the possibility of a Russian ripost in Asia. He believed that Russia did not endanger India—indeed that Britain could freely use the Indian army to challenge Russia in Europe or Asia. During 1878, Disraeli brought Indian troops to Cyprus to check Russia at Istanbul. He told Victoria that in the event of war with Russia, "the Empress of India should order her armies to clear Central Asia of the Muscovites, and drive them into the Caspian. We have a good instrument for this purpose in Lord Lytton, and indeed he was placed there with that view"; words sincerely spoken, if harder to execute than express.[81] Disraeli overestimated British power—Britain could not easily have sent a significant army to Gallipoli or

Varna, let alone Batum or Bokhara, though such actions probably would have deterred Russian attack or forestalled Turkish catastrope—and these intentions were never put into effect, but they are indicative. Disraeli had contempt for Russian power, confidence in British strength, and was willing to use it whenever he felt politically free to do so. Such arguments were remarkably robust even for Disraeli. They assumed that Russia could not use Central Asia to blackmail Britain—rather, the reverse. Granted, Disraeli was ever belligerent and rhetorically flamboyant while these views were affected by other factors, but they do represent his real perceptions and intentions, they do reflect both the intelligence and the assessments of Wellesley, and they were fundamental to British policy in the great eastern crisis.

Wellesley's information merely reinforced the preconceptions and policies of two viceroys, two commanders in chief and one Foreign Secretary. Thus, Northbrook held that the Grand Duke Michael's proposals "show how utterly unscrupulous even the highest Russian officers are in their plans. I do not think there is anything in them which should lead us to alter our present policy toward Persia". Though Wellesley's material corroborated suspicions that Sher 'Ali "has entered into some kind of communications with the Russians", Northbrook did not change his policy toward Afghanistan.[82] While Russia might harm the Raj, an aggressive line toward Afghanistan would do so. Conversely, the evidence of Russian weakness in Central Asia, this proof that the Tsar was reining in his generals but further advances in Central Asia were likely, simply confirmed the expectations of Lytton and Cambridge. It probably spurred their policies forward, but in complex ways. After all, in 1876, the commander in chief of the Indian army commented that a letter from von Kaufmann to Sher 'Ali "appears to me to constitute a picture of what an Asiatic Ruler who may offend Russia or stand in her way may expect to suffer. If Shere Ali reads it in this light it may have a beneficial effect on our relations with him". By July 1877, however, Haines used Miluitin's reference to the "latest sore spot" in British policy and Michael's proposal for an "amiable" reconnaissance on the Attrek, to predict an imminent Russian drive on Merv and threat to Afghanistan, and India.[83]

Derby viewed Wellesley as an "incurable spendthrift"[84] but trusted the latter's intelligence, particularly because it often assisted his diplomacy. In March 1875, for example, Derby told the Russian ambassador that Britain had no desire to expand in Central Asia, but would seize Herat if Russia took Merv, "which would lead to complications, and place the two armies very near one another". He also denied that Britain had shipped weapons to Kashgar or Baluchistan.[85] Wellesley quickly reported that von Kaufmann and Prince Michael were using reports of such shipments to support their forward policy, and then that Derby's threat had affected Russian actions. Derby regarded Wellesley's news that the Tsar had halted moves on the Attrek as "extremely satisfactory"—"I conceive it also probable that the Russian govt [sic] is well aware of the risk of a general war in 1876, and does not wish to have any part of his army engaged in Asiatic operations, at a distance from the scene of action."[86] All this confirmed Derby's quiet policy in Central Asia. He thought it pointless to warn Russia against expansion to the Attrek—"nothing can come of it unless we were prepared to back up our words by acts, which in such a matter we are not". By September 1875, indeed, reflecting on events both in Central Asia and the Balkans, Derby told Disraeli: "The Russians appear to be rather inclined to keep things quiet."[87]

During the Russo-Turkish crisis, Wellesley's information affected Derby and his characteristic combination of penetration in analysis and passivity in action—the Derby of whom Salisbury said, with sardonic despair: "British policy is to float lazily downstream, occasionally putting out a diplomatic boathook to avoid collisions."[88] Wellesley's material led Derby to believe Russia unlikely or unable to threaten British interests. It reinforced Derby's sweeping dismissal of Russian power—"Russian finance is very bad, the Russian navy hardly exists, the army is ill-officered and weak for aggressive purposes. ... The Czar dislikes war on principle; and in his present state of health—asthmatic, weak, & depressed in spirits—would probably rather abdicate than fight"[89]— and his belief the Balkan crisis could not produce danger in Central Asia. "What men or money could Russia spare for a campaign against India, if engaged in an invasion of Turkey?"[90] Indeed, if Russia did attack Turkey, "for a considerable time we have no aggression in central Asia to fear".[91] All this reinforced Derby's refusal to treat a threat to Turkey as one to Britain. Even more, at the start of the Russo-Turkish crisis, Wellesley's material apparently led Derby to overrate Alexander's passivity and to underrate the possibility of a Russian attack. In late 1875, despite his repeated statement, "who can trust a Russian?",[92] Derby agreed that Russia's actions indicated a peaceful policy, while "the Emperor's character is peaceable".[93] As one reason for the Tsar's alleged conservatism, Derby thought "the great cost and small return of the Central Asian annexations has disgusted him with the notion of further territorial extension, at least for the time".[94] Notably, over the next two years, the experience of the crisis changed Derby's opinion. By June 1876, Derby

> agreed that we ought to have no antagonism with Russia. I do not believe the Czar or his responsible advisors desire to break up the Turkish Empire at present. But the conduct of their agents in all places is absolutely at variance with the language held at Petersburg: showing either great duplicity or great administrative weakness. I believe in the existence of both, but more especially of the latter. I am as anxious as anyone to keep well with the Russians, but there is no acting with people when you cannot feel that they are telling truth.

"The Czar's personal character ... is truthful", and he "may be, and probably is, sincere in wishing to keep the peace, but if sincere, it is plain that he is not master in his own house."[95] By December 1877, Derby thought Alexander "essentially a weak man, influenced by the last speaker".[96] Wellesley's reports of a cautious Tsarist policy in Central Asia, of its unwillingness to challenge British interests, of its military weakness, and of the duplicity and unpredictability of Russian officials, confirmed Derby's disinclination to intervene in continental affairs, and his refusal to support Turkey. These attitudes were fundamental to British policy during 1876–1877. They helped to check Disraeli's aims and forced him to pursue them through subterranean means, they shaped paralysis in London and then its sudden lurch to action when Russia, just barely, defeated Turkey in one campaigning season and stood poised before Istanbul.

Wellesley's material influenced Salisbury in an odd fashion. This influence is clear, if implicit, in Salisbury's assessment of October 1874 regarding the possibility of British assistance to Persia—written at a time when the India Secretary probably, although not certainly, first began to see Wellesley's material on Central Asia. Salisbury rejected such a policy for several strategic reasons, including its probable effect on the balance of power in Tsarist decision making.

> In these questions we must bear in mind the condition of the Russian Counsels. The peace party have the Emperor; the war party have the whole military strength and some influential members of the Imperial family. It appears certain that the Emperor holds his own with difficulty. We know the effect of Russian advances on the public mind in England and India. What will be the effect of English advances on the more impulsive, and more military public mind of Russia?

Salisbury reiterated this central concern in a more acute and alarmed sense in December 1874, referring explicitly to the material provided by Wellesley. The "general purport" of this intelligence "is that proposals of a more or less warlike character are being constantly made by the authorities of Russian Turkistan, and of the army, and are being constantly rejected by the Emperor. I think that this state of things is full of danger". Much of Wellesley's information suited Salisbury's fears of an imminent Russian menace and spurred his demands for improvements in India's intelligence system. As Salisbury noted, "information of this kind is of more value for what it indicates than for what it tells". Careful reading between the lines of Russian correspondence convinced him Russia was closely monitoring internal threats to the Raj. Although Wellesley said nothing directly about von Kaufmann's relations with Sher 'Ali, through this mode of reasoning Salisbury correctly concluded that Russia was in regular contact with the amir—the India Secretary noted in particular that St. Petersburg had established tight control over the movements of Abdur Rahman. In April 1875 "some secret transcripts of importance"—presumably the proposals of Grand Duke Michael—led Salisbury to believe "that the first step of Russia, which will cause serious difficulties, will probably be taken at the cost of Persia". Alexander II's decisions about the Akkhal merely indicated that the Tsar believed "his troops will be wanted further west". The potential Russian menace to British interests had simply shifted from Asia to Europe, and might yet return to endanger India. As Salisbury held:

> Michael evidently means to force the Emperor's hand and to go on. Probably he hopes to get his troops insulted, and to be forced to avenge the insult. If he succeeds, which is possible, as the Emperor seems weak, he, Michael, will be the real author of Russian policy in those parts. It is therefore important that we should know something of his way of viewing things; and that information would be, in part, supplied by the despatch of which Wellesley speaks.[97]

Gradually, however, Wellesley's intelligence shook Salisbury's assessments. Alexander II's rejection of Michael's proposals "gives us more time than I thought we had" regarding Afghanistan. Among Salisbury's contemporary arguments for placing a British representative in Kabul was this: "It would also be a great security for peace, if we were able to keep the Czar, who wishes for peace, informed of the intrigues of his frontier officers, who do not." Salisbury, that is, intended to use Indian intelligence to manipulate the actions of a Tsar whose attitudes had been uncovered by British intelligence. The India Secretary also noted not only aggressive but defensive attitudes among Tsarist authorities. Russia seemed more concerned with defending itself against Yarkand than in conquering the Tekke Turkomans. Russian authorities "complain of an oppression" regarding Yarkand and Afghanistan. They "have a fixed idea, from which it is difficult to move them, that we are importing arms and sending military instructors (to Kashgar) in order to get up a war with the Russians"; they "indulge in similar myths" regarding Merv. In May 1876 Salisbury told Lytton:

> I do not guarantee the genuineness of these secret papers. You know the elements of the calculation with respect to them. On the one hand what has afterwards come out publicly has never contradicted them. On the other they always present precisely the view which the Russian Government would naturally desire that we should entertain.[98]

By late 1876, Salisbury recognized that his presuppositions might be wrong—that any Russian menace to India was latent rather than imminent; however temporarily, Russia was rejecting a forward policy in Asia. Of course, Russia might return to such a policy. As British concern switched to the Balkans, Salisbury noted that things looked "ugly. There can be little doubt that if Russia does resolve to cross the Danube, some kind of diversion on the Asiatic side will be attempted".[99] This statement possessed a hidden corollary—so ugly a diversion need occur only if Britain blocked Russia on the Danube. Any assessment of how this intelligence influenced Salisbury's policy toward Turkey must be, to some extent, speculative. During 1876–1877, however, Salisbury did not oppose the elimination of Turkish power in Europe. While anger at the Bulgarian massacres and distaste for Turkish rule over Christians created these views, at all other times in Salisbury's life as an imperial statesman, strategic arguments inevitably neutralized such moral ones. It is curious that this did not occur in 1876–1877; this ceases to be so when one accounts for Wellesley. Salisbury had entered office expecting Russia sooner or later to threaten British security, regarding the Central Asian and Turkish questions as two halves of one problem. By 1876 Wellesley's material indicated that Russia was consciously not threatening India. Notably, when Salisbury formulated his policy toward Russia and Turkey, he did not simultaneously fear a Russian threat to India, save in the sense that British support for Turkey might spark one. During the summer of 1877, as he broke with Disraeli over Turkey, still he supported Lytton's reorganization of the northwest frontier, to bolster British power in Asia, and the despatch of British forces to Malta, in order to bolster its diplomacy in the Balkans.[100] The development of power and deterrent capability were one thing, their application another. Salisbury was fundamental first in preventing Britain from blocking Russian moves against Turkey until December 1877, and then in unleashing Lord Beaconsfield. It seems hard to believe that the India Secretary would have adopted this approach had he regarded Russia as an imminent threat to India. If the foregoing analysis is correct, these views were significantly affected by Salisbury's reading of the information provided by Wellesley.

Similarly, in late 1876 Salisbury changed his policy toward Central Asia. He still favoured British hegemony over Afghanistan. However, this was no longer an immediate necessity; it should be furthered by gradual and cautious steps. Salisbury also began to oppose the more adventurous elements of Lytton's policy. Not only did the viceroy's decision to invade Afghanistan in 1878 irritate Salisbury, but so too did Lytton's desire in 1877 to provide covert support to Afghans or Tekke Turkomans to fight Russia in Central Asia. Salisbury held these ideas "foolish", which "would tax our resources to the utmost":

> I do not see what we can get by giving this permission. The wound to Russia, even if all the operations are successful will not alter the events of the present war. She will pull back for a time; & the Affghans are quite incapable of conducting protracted operations away from their base.

But if the Affghans are beaten—which is quite probable—the fire will be on our own frontier. We may be in a position in Europe in which it may be impossible—or most inconvenient—for us to take any active steps—and we shall have to remain quiet possibly to the detriment of our credit.

War with Russia along the whole line is an intelligible policy, though I do not think circumstances justify it now. But peace negotiations in Europe, simultaneous with "unofficial" war on the Attrek or the Oxus, can produce nothing but embarrassment and discredit.[101]

The idea of stirring up the Turkomans is what Bismarck calls "unofficial war". Its disadvantage—to a country which cares about its honour—is that you have all the evils of war, and none of its advantages. If the people you stir up succeed, you gain nothing by it; and if they fail, you have to come and help them, and helping the Turkomans at Merve would not be an easy task.

The best way I think would be to repeat at St. Petersburg the warning about Merve Derby gave two years ago.

Until they make up their minds to go to war with us they will not touch it: and then—they will go further.[102]

These statements clearly reflect Wellesley's material. Salisbury recognized that Russia was "much too weak"[103] to challenge Britain. Russia would not advance in Central Asia unless it chose to threaten Britain throughout the world, which would occur only if the British endangered Tsarist interests in Turkey or Central Asia. By late 1876, indeed, Salisbury entirely reversed his Central Asian policy. He favoured an approach that 18 months earlier he had regarded as "fundamentally impossible"; he reverted to the policy followed by Gladstone's government between 1867 and 1873. Salisbury hoped to exploit all the factors outlined by Wellesley in order permanently to limit Russian expansion in Asia—and to end the Russian danger to India by acquiring a formal commitment from the Tsar, which even his most unruly subordinates would dare not violate. Salisbury later regretted the Balkan crisis

> from an Indian point of view, for I had some communications with the Russians on the Central Asia question, which I thought promised well. I was proceeding on these bases—abandonment of all claim to political influence in Kashgar—promise of both sides not to communicate without leave with Bockara [sic] on one hand

or Cabul on the other neutralization of Merve with regulated system of chastisement of Turkomans when necessary, and lowering or abolition of tariffs along the Asiatic–Russian frontier. If a peace could have been made (between Russia and Turkey), I think the Emperor would have been very anxious to make everything secure by settling all difficulties on our Indian frontier. But these inconvenient Turks have made any hope of this kind chimerical.[104]

Contrary to the conventional view, Salisbury was no innocent abroad during 1876–1877, or at home.[105] In return for letting Russia eliminate (without replacing) Turkish power in Europe—which Salisbury regarded as a good thing in itself—he intended to extract a high price in Central Asia. Ignatiev, presumably, was the Russian authority with whom Salisbury had these discussions. Salisbury was not Ignatiev's puppet; he was as much manipulator as manipulated. Each had read the other's mail. Wellesley's intelligence had indicated that Ignatiev opposed further Russian expansion in Central Asia and influenced a Tsar who was unusually sensitive to British susceptibilities there. On the foundation of material provided by Wellesley, Salisbury made a subtle and precise attempt to pull the strings of Russian decision making to further British interests. This material also illuminates another issue. From mid-1877 to early 1878, Derby and Salisbury viewed policy toward Russia and interpreted information on it in identical terms. This reinforces the notion that Salisbury broke with Derby and moved toward Disraeli, with all its fundamental consequences for British politics and foreign policy, largely for cynical reasons of personal advancement. Yet strategic considerations still mattered. Salisbury regarded the need to keep Russia from control of Istanbul as a vital interest and was willing to run the risk of hostilities in order to preempt that eventuality; Derby was not; and that was the question of January–February 1878. Again, Disraeli and Salisbury could agree on India and Istanbul, but not on Turkey in Europe. Only when that issue ended could they find common ground and a common policy, and the Conservative Party find a new master, in waiting.

British intelligence on the Central Asian question during the 1870s was unusually successful in technical terms. It achieved its finest performance before 1918. Nothing suggests that any contemporary European state possessed a better intelligence system. By 1870 Britain had no means to acquire information on the matter. By 1875 it had penetrated Russian intentions and immeasurably improved its monitoring of events in the intermediate states. It demonstrated that Britain could act as it wished in Europe without fears for Asia, thus stripping a trump card from the Tsarist hand. This intelligence reinforced a plethora of different British policies toward Russia in Europe—that of Derby, which failed under test, and those of Salisbury and Disraeli, both able but neither successful, in part because each checked the other, mostly because the British elite and public could not agree on what interests were at stake and what policy could best achieve them. British policy may be criticized, but it was based on extraordinarily good intelligence. This allowed British authorities to sidestep a dilemma that hampered their policy toward Russia between 1881 and 1904. During these years British authorities could never acquire certain intelligence about Russian intentions and capabilities regarding India. This left Britain vulnerable to blackmail and forced Indian strategic planning to rest on worst-case assumptions—which strengthened Russia's position *vis-à-vis* Britain. During the 1870s, conversely, British intelligence provided an extraordinarily precise and reliable account of Tsarist capabilities and intentions, which strengthened Britain's bargaining position. Britain's informed policy achieved some notable if temporary successes. By 1878, with Salisbury and Disraeli together defining policy, Britain seemed on the verge of a triumph over its rival, as it bluffed Russia from the table of victory in Turkey and prepared to feast on Afghanistan. Internal British politics, however, negated what might have been. The fall of Disraeli's government carried many of these diplomatic gains in its wake—along with much of Britain's intelligence system. Russia quickly strengthened its position in Central Asia by conquering the Akkhal and Merv. This created the preconditions for the strategic nightmare that haunted imperial decision makers between 1885 and 1904.

The intelligence, nonetheless, had shaped British decisions on Central Asia and Turkey. Northbrook, for example, abandoned the idea of using Yarkand as a strategic buffer once his intelligence services demonstrated the weaknesses of that state. Indian strategic planning rested on the enhanced military, political and topographical intelligence available on Central Asia. This intelligence affected British policy at high levels in a complex fashion. It led principal decision makers (1) to believe that, contrary to their preconceptions, Russia was weak in Central Asia and its policy cautious, that Britain could decouple its actions in Turkey and Central Asia; but (2) to act in contradictory ways. Disraeli favoured an aggressive line and Salisbury (joined by Derby) a pacific one. Wellesley's product canceled some of its own effect because it led its consumers to favour contrary policies, or reinforced their predisposition to do so.

Wellesley's material echoed in British policy over the next 20 years. This is most obvious regarding Britain's reading of the dynamics of Russian decision making. The idea that St. Petersburg had limited control over Russian frontier officials began almost precisely when Wellesley's material became available; it affected imperial decision making for a generation. Salisbury, moreover, dominated British policy toward Russia and India between 1885 and 1902. He formed mature views on this issue between 1874 and 1877; he acted on these ideas for the rest of his life. During this formative intellectual period, the information provided by Wellesley allowed Salisbury to see how Russia reached its decisions, to compare his perceptions with the reality of the matter. This is the context in which Salisbury uttered the celebrated statement that announced his liberation from the alarmist views of the English forward school. As he told Lytton,[106]

> you listen too much to the soldiers. No lesson seems to be so deeply inculcated by the experience of life as that you should never trust the experts. If you believe the doctors, nothing is wholesome: if you believe the theologians, nothing is innocent: if you believe the soldiers, nothing is safe.

Salisbury had learned to know his enemy—and his experts. That knowledge shaped British decisions until the close of the nineteenth century.

2

"INDULGED IN ALL TOO LITTLE"?

Vansittart, intelligence and appeasement

> Sentiments have nothing to do with facts, or with policy which has to follow facts. The only trouble—in theory—should be to ascertain them.
>
> Robert Vansittart, 1936[1]

> The principal trouble, of course, remains that we cannot possibly tell, however much we might guess, what is going on inside the brains on the one man who matters.
>
> Lord Halifax, 1938[2]

Over the past generation, scholars have increasingly come to recognize that intelligence shaped British diplomacy during the 1930s, the period of Robert Vansittart's tenure as Permanent Under Secretary (PUS) to the Foreign Office and Chief Diplomatic Advisor to His Majesty's Government. Most recent works on appeasement and virtually all on Vansittart refer to his use of intelligence. Often they assert its significance. Thus David Dilks, the leading student of intelligence and appeasement, has emphasized that "Vansittart had his own sources of intelligence, outside the official machine, together with special skill in reading the signs". Dilks held that this intelligence and its interpretation caused Vansittart's differences with the Cabinet, his "incessant admonitions" to ministers and his ultimate decline in influence. These are major claims. Christopher Andrew, Donald Graeme Boadle, Norman Rose, Wesley Wark and D.C. Watt have also treated Vansittart and intelligence as being a significant part of appeasement and its study.[3] This article will address that issue from a different perspective, a biographical one. It will treat Vansittart, intelligence and appeasement as a single and coherent topic. This paper will define his experiences with intelligence before he became PUS, and examine how this shaped his actions of the 1930s. It will consider how Vansittart used intelligence, how well he did so, and how his usage mattered. It will argue that this did matter—that one can reconstruct the logic behind decisions only by examining the data considered by decision makers, that one man's experience with intelligence can illuminate his times. The intelligence record—what Vansittart's successor as PUS,

Alexander Cadogan, called the "missing dimension" of diplomatic history—can illuminate the minds of the appeasers and of their opponents, the nature of their policies and the rationale for them.[4]

During the course of Vansittart's career, Britain ceased to collect intelligence through *ad hoc* means and turned to permanent agencies for the purpose. Between 1844 and 1914 normal British officials, especially consuls and military attachés, collected secret intelligence as part of their normal work. Sometimes they acted on their own initiative, sometimes on superior orders.[5] Thus, in 1890 Lord Salisbury and his Permanent Under Secretary, Philip Currie, ordered all the consuls in Black Sea ports to monitor signs of a Russian strike at Istanbul, through their own observations or any means they might wish to employ.[6] Nothing better characterized the Victorian system of intelligence than the fact a Prime Minister and a PUS should personally direct an espionage network consisting primarily of British officials. When collected, secret intelligence was assessed not by offices but by individuals—by the statesmen who acted on it. The main exception to these rules was the Intelligence Branch of the War Office, a combination of general staff and intelligence-assessing bureau which often worked directly for Prime Ministers and Foreign Secretaries between 1876 and 1900.[7]

Throughout the Victorian period, many diplomats kept their distance from this haphazard system of espionage. That tendency increased during the Edwardian era, when the Foreign Office became reluctant to let even consuls serve as spies. As PUS, Charles Hardinge wrote, "the paid agents of the Admiralty should do such work". Still, as ambassador in St. Petersburg a few years before, he had spies of his own in the Russian Ministry of Foreign Affairs.[8] Diplomats and consuls continued intelligence work until 1914 and the Victorian approach toward espionage survived to serve during the great war. In 1914–1915 diplomatic officials throughout the world were ordered to collect intelligence. In some cases this became their main task; in some places they were British intelligence.[9] During this same period, however, Britain increasingly came to rely less on *ad hoc* networks established for special purposes and more on specialist and general service bureaus. After 1919, a permanent and bureaucratic system supplanted the older one. Most notable among these bureaus were the Secret Intelligence Service (SIS; frequently called the Secret Service, or SS) for agents and the Government Code and Cypher School (the GC&CS) for codebreaking.[10] Nor was the process of bureaucratization limited to collection. Intelligence was no longer analyzed primarily by statesman but by offices, by the intelligence branches of the fighting services and by the regional sections of the Foreign Office.

Vansittart witnessed this evolution of intelligence, and participated in it. As a junior diplomat, he saw the informal system at work. How far he was personally involved with it is not entirely clear, but three points are worthy of note. In 1907 he served with the British Legation in Persia, one of the most active centres under the old system of espionage and among the first to adopt a permanent bureaucratic structure. The Legation was also receiving Tsarist consular telegrams solved by the codebreakers of the Indian Army, during the first incident since 1844 in which cryptanalytical intelligence assisted the Foreign Office.[11] Whether Vansittart knew of that material or not is beyond proof, but he was on that spot, and he would have had to be blind not to see some of the Legation's work in espionage. In 1915, he stood at another centre of spying. While based with the British Legation in Stockholm he witnessed German attempts to recruit seamen as agents against Britain. British security, he recorded, found "these Scandinavian greenhorns were easy meat. I have always wondered at the low price for which men and women can be inveigled into the most dangerous and thankless job in the world".[12] Even more: he shared a formative experience for the Foreign Office, its involvement with blockade and intelligence. Between 1914 and 1918, for the first time in decades, the Foreign Office constantly handled intelligence reports and assessments of high quality and learned what they could do; in particular, through the experience of blockade, its regional sections became intelligence assessing bodies, and its personnel experienced analysts. Managing the blockade was the greatest thing the Foreign Office did during the great war. A striking proportion of its best members served in that effort, and then rose to leading positions over the next generation. As a middle-level member of the Ministry of Blockade, Vansittart had access to a wide range of human and communications intelligence, perhaps as much as any other member of Whitehall, and served in effect as an intelligence analyst.[13]

Again, as a middle-level official during the 1920s, especially as chief of the American Department of the Foreign Office, Vansittart himself assessed information and intelligence and applied it to policy. As Private Secretary to one Foreign Secretary, Lord Curzon, and to two Prime Ministers, Stanley Baldwin and Ramsay MacDonald, he not only observed the machinery of intelligence—he served in it. As the official cog through which intelligence reached Curzon, Vansittart saw virtually every report which crossed the Foreign Secretary's desk during an unusually well-documented period.[14] Vansittart witnessed failures and successes of intelligence. He saw the GC&CS uncover Soviet intentions to subvert British interests. He learned how often intelligence could not be turned to advantage but he also watched Curzon use it to seize triumph at the Lausanne conference of 1922–1923 when, as one British witness put it, "the information we obtained at the psychological moment from secret sources was invaluable to us, and put us in the position of a man who is playing Bridge and knows the cards in his adversary's hand". Indeed, during Lausanne, one of Vansittart's roles was to determine precisely which intelligence reports were of sufficient import to be forwarded to Curzon from London. The Private Secretary also learned how intelligence was related to internal politics, as he endeavoured, on his master's behalf, to have Scotland Yard intercept mail within Britain which was related to a political intrigue between the press magnate, Lord Rothermere, and the French government.[15] Under Baldwin, Vansittart continued to watch the relationship between intelligence and external policy and received advanced tuition in the areas of espionage and internal politics. In particular, if after the fact, Vansittart acquired some inside knowledge about the affair of the Zinoviev Letter. He also knew about the political espionage conducted by Joseph Ball for Conservative Central Office against the Labour Party. His memoirs of this period refer with affection to "Joe Ball [and] his Intelligence Corps, of whom more was heard in the days of Chamberlain". Vansittart and Ball even considered the possibility of launching a burglary against the office of Maundy Gregory, the unauthorized salesman of political honours![16]

On his appointment to office in 1930, Vansittart had greater experience with intelligence than any other PUS between the wars—indeed, as much as many members of the intelligence services or any of the Foreign Office's liaison officers with them, such as Neville Bland. Vansittart quickly acquired greater expertise than anyone outside the SIS and the GC&CS. He oversaw all of Britain's official sources of overseas intelligence and directed all of its secret ones. More precisely, he directed Admiral Hugh Sinclair, the Chief of the Secret Service (CSS), who controlled the SIS and the GC&CS—the most important intelligence chief Britain had known in peacetime for centuries, just as the SIS and GC&CS had more influence on policy in peacetime than any earlier service except the Intelligence Branch between 1876 and 1900. Vansittart's interest in intelligence, however, differed in degree but not in nature from that of his colleagues. Sometimes it is alleged that the Foreign Office was indifferent or hostile to intelligence. On the contrary. Just months after the war, Curzon praised the "very wonderful achievement" of Room 40 and MI1b, which had "the result today there is hardly a single Foreign Government whose messages we are unable to read provided that we can obtain the figures of their telegrams"; he emphasized the need to maintain this power in peace.[17] Similarly, Hardinge insisted that the Foreign Office required "control of secret service operations in foreign countries".[18] Though diplomats tried to avoid personal participation in the collection of intelligence, this attitude declined in force compared to those before 1914. In a radical break from Edwardian attitudes, after 1919 the Foreign Office incorporated intelligence personnel within its organization—the GC&CS in London, and in a more grudging and confused fashion, many SIS officers as Passport Control Officers (PCOs) in consulates abroad—and defended their institutional and personal interests within Whitehall. Throughout the interwar years, the assessment of information and action on it were the Foreign Office's main functions. Intelligence provided as much of the significant evidence on diplomacy as any other source, including the reports of ministers. As with every element of information, it was rarely read in isolation, but mostly in an alloy with material from all sources, the whole being greater than the sum of its parts. Secret intelligence became integral to the Foreign Office's view of most matters, and experience with it standard to the professional education of diplomats.

Typically, Foreign Secretaries after the days of Curzon left the management of intelligence to their PUSs, being concerned only with the product. Thus, in 1937 Anthony Eden wrote that "control of the secret service" was "under the exclusive direction of the Permanent Under Secretary. The Secretary of State has nothing to do with it, and I at least have always avoided asking anything about it in detail".[19] While the intelligence departments of the fighting services constrained Vansittart's power, he exercised an unmatched authority over the SIS and the GC&CS and the assessment of their material. His authority combined a personal connection between PUS and CSS, with a formal relationship between the Foreign Office and the intelligence services. That relationship is easily defined. The Foreign Office was the director and protector of the intelligence services and the prime consumer of their information. Sometimes politicians and the fighting services challenged this status, but without much success. The Foreign Office trusted the GC&CS, which justified that attitude. It was as effective as any other codebreaking bureau on earth and better than most. Each week, on average, it gave Whitehall seventy-four solutions of the encoded telegrams of foreign governments, and usually was breaking the important systems of at least two great powers and many smaller ones.[20] However, the power of the GC&CS waned during Vansittart's tenure at the top of the Foreign Office. In 1929–1930, it had near mastery of the code systems of Japan, the United States, France and Italy, and some power against those of the USSR. By the mid-1930s, it had lost access to Russian diplomatic systems, balanced by excellence against Comintern traffic, had decreasing success against French and American traffic, gained much less than before from access to Italian diplomatic traffic (though still feasting on its military and colonial systems), and had little luck against Germany. In 1939, its access to Japanese diplomatic systems collapsed. While the Foreign Office doubted the value of spies, it did respect the quality of the SIS. In the 1930s, that quality was higher than is commonly accepted, but it was uneven—abysmal in Asia while good in Germany.

The nature of the personal connection—the mixture of authority and independence, of cooperation and trust, between PUS and CSS—remains veiled and must be inferred from random snippets of fact. One thing is clear: it varied with personality and with circumstances. In 1919, when the SIS was a fledgling bureau, its first chief, Mansfield Cumming, offered humble gratitude to Hardinge for rewarding his chequered wartime service with an honour. Eyre Crowe questioned Cumming's judgment and found he needed a firm leash, not surprising with a man whose intelligence assessments suggested he had read *The Protocols of the Elders of Zion* once too often. Crowe, conversely, trusted Sinclair, as did Cadogan, after some doubt.

Sinclair enjoyed a bluff and cooperative relationship with William Tyrrell,[21] but he was uniquely close to Vansittart. *The Mist Procession* refers to Sinclair in complimentary terms—"a man equal to Blinker Hall in natural genius for the game".[22] These feelings were reciprocated. According to Ian Colvin, a well-informed source, when Sinclair learned of Vansittart's supercession as PUS in December 1937, he immediately went to his master's flat and paced the floor, repeating "Van, this is disastrous!"[23] The two men cooperated and shared views throughout Vansittart's tenure as PUS, and afterward. "Both the Admiral and Van's sources", as Cadogan once put it, presented the same general picture about Germany and the two offered similar prescriptions to the problem, but some significant differences did emerge between their views during 1938–1939.[24]

Vansittart was more interested in intelligence than any but a few ministers or any other PUS of the interwar years, but the nature and significance of that interest are encrusted in myth. That myth, in turn, stems from self-mythologization. After his retirement as Chief Diplomatic Advisor in 1941, Vansittart increasingly turned his energy to his history. This was a fundamental motivation behind his memoirs and his Germanophobe war propaganda. It also explains his pressure of the 1940s to ensure that the Foreign Office's publications of documents from the 1930s did not misrepresent his position, on pain of a threat to publish copies of his own papers. This defence, he knew, must rest on the record of the "memoranda and minutes of warning which I continually showered upon successive Governments".[25] In order to cast himself as the Cassandra of appeasement, Vansittart needed to claim a consistent record of unheralded but accurate warning. This led him to distort the record on many points—to oversimplify his position toward Germany during the 1930s, to overstate his Germanophobia and to underrate his own influence on events. These distortions have had a significant impact. By accepting Vansittart's claims to irrelevance, the literature on appeasement misconstrues important elements in British decision making during 1938, while that on the German resistance is distorted because it accepts Vansittart's claims for irrelevance and Germanophobia.[26]

The same reflex shaped Vansittart's references to intelligence, and their effect on the literature about it. His memoirs paint himself as the only champion of British intelligence, embattled, under-funded and unappreciated. This claim is caricature. While it often was stingy, Whitehall maintained intelligence services at roughly the size normal among great powers of the era. Nor did the SIS and the GC&CS face continual and devastating pressure for economies. The best, if imperfect, numerical indicators on this matter, the size of the Secret Service Vote and of cryptanalytical staff, scarcely budged between 1923 and 1934.[27] All governments and departments agreed that intelligence had to be collected and they used whatever material they received. This was true even of the Labour governments of 1924 and 1929–1931, despite fables to the contrary. Vansittart claimed to have been hard pressed to defend the Secret Service Vote against the

Foreign Secretary of the second Labour government. Arthur Henderson, a teetotaller, "rated Secret Service like hard liquor, because he knew, and wanted to know, nothing of it. I, on the contrary, felt that we indulged in it all too little".[28] There may be some truth to this claim, but it is not the whole truth. Perhaps Henderson did grumble when Vansittart presented the Secret Service Vote for his signature, but sign it he did and his colleagues made use of the product. Henderson's Parliamentary Secretary, Hugh Dalton, used material provided by the GC&CS in warfare against the Admiralty so as to further Labour's aims on arms limitation, while Ramsay MacDonald used it to further his policy during the London Naval Conference.[29]

While PUS, Vansittart was generally satisfied with the size, funding, structures and priorities of the intelligence services. He did not energetically reform these areas, not even when the Chiefs of Staff and the Cabinet Secretary, Maurice Hankey, continually and accurately complained of problems with intelligence in Asia.[30] Nothing suggests that Vansittart tried to strengthen or to reform the intelligence services before the Abyssinian crisis. Perhaps, it might be argued, he wished to take such actions but doubted the government would accept them. Against this, it must be said, from 1935, whenever increases to the GC&CS were requested, the Treasury immediately rubber-stamped the requests.[31] Had Vansittart wished to fight for increased spending on intelligence after 1933, he would have found allies—certainly the service chiefs and Hankey, possibly the Permanent Secretary at the Treasury, Nicholas Warren Fisher. It is indicative that until late 1935, the Foreign Office did not take such steps and that it continually ignored the services' attempts to strengthen intelligence in Asia.

Vansittart used intelligence for two purposes. It gave him knowledge and it gave him power. It was his strong suit in Whitehall's debates over policy—no one could match a PUS in those cards. Vansittart assiduously added power to that suit by placing secret, unofficial and official reports on "my file of evidences of eventual German aggression".[32] He used this material in a classic way. He circulated some reports as ammunition against opponents; he withheld others which might be used against himself; he used references to secret sources and to high security classifications to draw readers and to back appeals to his own unique authority. Thus, his memorandum of 31 December 1936, "The World Situation and British Rearmament" was prefaced by this phrase—

> *MOST SECRET. Much of the material used in the following memorandum is of so secret a nature, and any leakage might be so detrimental to some of the many sources from which it has been drawn, that I would ask for most particular care in the keeping of this paper.*[33]

True enough but, equally, most of the memorandum came from ordinary sources while it thoroughly mixed together material of varying reliability taken from official, unofficial and secret reports. No casual reader could determine the authority for any statement, let alone for the synthesis.

In selecting and circulating intelligence to suit himself, Vansittart followed a practice conventional in Whitehall. Another of his techniques, however, was rare among civil servants of his day. In order to affect public opinion and the politics of policy, he frequently leaked intelligence to Parliamentary figures who opposed the government. Sometimes with his consent, sometimes perhaps not, members of his private intelligence network also leaked material to the press and politicians.[34] Vansittart had learned much from Joseph Ball. During the 1930s he ranked among Ball's greatest rivals in the use of leaks as a tool of politics.

Such practices became central to Vansittart's arguments and to his reputation in a peculiar and gradual fashion. Until 1936, intelligence had no more influence on his views than was usual with PUSs. His "Old Adam" papers of 1930–1933 combined statements of principle with analyses of public facts. His initial memoranda on the Nazi danger stemmed from the "Old Adam" series and, with the single exception of German rearmament, they too rested on evidence drawn from official, essentially from public, sources. Only during Eden's tenure as Foreign Secretary in 1936–1937 did Vansittart's arguments begin to rely notably on secret sources and to include much material from his "private detective agency". This increased use of secret intelligence stemmed from many causes but from one in particular. Vansittart referred more openly to hidden intelligence the more limited his influence became in Whitehall and the more controversial his policy. The more Whitehall rejected a policy derived from information available to all, the more he turned to information available only through himself.

This process turned to cascade after December 1937, when Vansittart lost his official hold over the Foreign Office and the intelligence services. During the negotiations about his supercession as PUS and appointment as Chief Diplomatic Advisor, one of Vansittart's fundamental demands was to retain control over the SIS and the GC&CS. In fact, he tried to make it a *sine qua non*. He lost that struggle. Eden and Neville Chamberlain did not fear Vansittart's request, but they did decline to deprive Cadogan "of direct control over a service which has always been the prerogative of the post".[35] As Chief Diplomatic Advisor, Vansittart directed neither the collection nor the interpretation of intelligence. He continued to see much material of this sort but he could not be certain that he would see all of it, nor could he prevent anyone in particular from seeing any part of it. His assessments could be challenged not only by politicians, civil servants and the military intelligence departments, but now by the very experts who once had made his cases—the Foreign Office and the SIS. He had lost control over the suit of intelligence; but Vansittart's private sources and their reputation remained a card in his hand, perhaps the strongest one he had left to play. He prayed it would prove the ace of trumps instead of the deuce of spades.

As Chief Diplomatic Advisor, Vansittart could best catch the attention and shape the views of Whitehall by providing new and otherwise unavailable information which accurately predicted events to come and plausibly explained those which had passed. The more Whitehall heard of his secret sources, the greater his influence. Hence, Vansittart cited his private intelligence openly, copiously and specifically. On 9 August 1938, for example, he told Warren Fisher that the views of his "first hand and first rate" sources tallied with those of the SIS while both contradicted the reports of the British ambassador to Berlin, Nevile Henderson—proving the latter's inaccuracy.[36] During every crisis of 1938–1939, Vansittart came forward wielding secret intelligence as the razor edge for his policy.

Vansittart's increasing use of intelligence to persuade had complex consequences, and contradictory ones. It led many observers to mistrust his views, to dismiss his policy, and to question the value of intelligence itself. Military intelligence thought his arguments "based on the fixed idea that Germany is determined to go to war, and in the near future, and that it is useless to attempt further negotiations in order to avoid such a disaster: from this he argues that the only course to pursue is one involving a race in armaments", which "will rule out any possibility of moderation or stability". Hankey judged "The World Situation", the first of Vansittart's papers to rely on intelligence as a guide for policy, "one of his most depressing Memoranda". Hankey justified Vansittart's supercession as PUS on the grounds that he paid "too much attention to the press of all countries, and to S.S. information—useful pointers in both cases, but bad guides".[37] Again, in late 1938 Cadogan and the Foreign Secretary, Lord Halifax, drifted toward Vansittart's views of Germany and his use of intelligence to bolster arguments, but in a revealing fashion. Their memoranda placed material from open and secret sources in different sections; that from Vansittart was labelled as such and published separately.[38] Clearly, by 1938, his intelligence had acquired a mixed reputation. On the other hand, it was considered even by men who despised his policy. Neville Chamberlain at least thought about Vansittart's intelligence reports—he ostentatiously returned unread some of the Chief Diplomatic Advisor's memoranda on policy—and Vansittart's material did affect the views of Cadogan and Halifax.

Intelligence involves the collection of information and its interpretation through the light of individual preconceptions, modes of thought and attitudes. Vansittart's light was the "realist" tradition of British diplomacy.[39] According to this school of thought, international politics were governed primarily by the power and the interests of states—primarily, but not exclusively, for values, sentiments, ideas and public opinion all defined the interests pursued by statesmen and shaped their use of power. Similarly, private beliefs affected Vansittart's public policy. From the 1920s, he evinced strong views on internal and external affairs, and old-fashioned ones. After the Coalition Liberals were annihilated during the 1922 election, Vansittart commended the views of his father's old retainer: "I always said the country would rather be governed by gentry than a Jumped-up-Saturday-Night like Mr. Lloyd George."[40] Threats to British interests and prestige drew the same response from Vansittart in the 1920s as in the 1930s. For France to beat Britain during the Chanak crisis of 1922, "would be a prospect fit to make one die of shame, and we might as well put up our shutters in the East for years. It would in Eastern eyes be one of the greatest humiliations a British Govt & its representatives had ever had to face".[41]

None the less, when considering the aims and means of states, Vansittart was a consistent realist and an intelligent one. He loathed communism, for example, but understood the value of the Soviet card in the game of power. He analyzed strategic issues with a strategic logic, one which combined assessments of the capabilities of states, societies and economies, the intentions of statesmen and the attitudes of masses and of elites. He applied the same logic to Hitler's Germany as to the United States of Calvin Coolidge. In 1927, Vansittart analyzed long-term American power and its short-term actions in terms of economic and demographic factors, pressure groups, public opinion and state interest. Like most educated men of his time, his analysis also applied the language of "national characteristics" and the logic of schools of thought like social Darwinism and classical racism:

> the most efficient element—at least ultimately—in the United States is the German–American: the others have drive but are often off the fairway, and at greater expenditure of self accomplish no more than their corresponding numbers here. The race is of course a biological gamble, a people in werden not in Sein: but the Anglo-Saxon element is already down to 25% and the German is increasing in the land.[42]

Vansittart's personal characteristics also shaped his reading of intelligence. In the 1950s, these characteristics were praised. Thus John Connell's statement that Vansittart was "probably the ablest, the most original in mind, the most far-sighted, the most daring" of interwar British diplomats. "His judgment in analysis, both of men's characters and of the pattern of events, was swift, penetrative and accurate."[43] The more conventional view today is less complimentary—Vansittart's prescience is praised, but little else. Gladwyn Jebb, once Vansittart's Private Secretary, described him as being "in a curious way rather simple. It was not, I think, very difficult to take him in".[44] In fact, Vansittart did misjudge figures such as the Sudeten German leader, Konrad Henlein, and his own appointee as ambassador to Berlin, Nevile Henderson. Not surprisingly, many found Vansittart's writings marked more by cleverness than clarity. The Head of the Foreign Office's News Department, Arthur Willert, once asked an old friend how he had spent the weekend: "Translating one of Van's papers into English for my master", he replied."[45] Again, Vansittart later noted that by 1936 he was regarded as "wild and hysterical" and he was right.[46] Eden feared that his PUS "is not balanced & is in such a continual state of nerves that he will end up making would-be aggressors think the more of us as a potential victim".[47] Neville Chamberlain held similar views, while in 1985 John Colville, once Private Secretary to both Chamberlain and Churchill, denounced Vansittart's judgment as poor and frivolous.[48] These views are damning, and they are fundamental to Vansittart's use of intelligence. A study of intelligence must account for them. It can also test their accuracy.

It was within this framework of attitudes, ideas and politics that intelligence took its place. It did so most significantly regarding Vansittart's policy toward Germany, but that issue is illuminated by two well-documented but little-known instances from Vansittart's career as PUS. The first comes from late 1936. After the Montreaux Conference, the GC&CS read many Turkish diplomatic telegrams. This material illuminated patterns of decision making in Ankara, the nature of Turkish strategy and its diplomatic relations with other countries, especially the USSR and Britain. It confirmed British fears that the Turkish Foreign Minister, Tewfik Rustu Aras, was dangerously attentive toward the Soviets; it also proved Turkish diplomats refused to show "any apologetic tone about having consulted us" when criticized for that fact by the Soviets. Above all, this intelligence showed that the USSR was pressing Turkey to accept a defensive alliance. Under that arrangement, Soviet naval and air forces would assist Turkey against aggression in the Mediterranean while Ankara would close the Dardanelles to any power at war with the Soviet Union. This proposal arguably contradicted the Montreaux Convention; it certainly threatened British interests. It would bring Turkey within the Soviet orbit and irritate Italy and Germany. It might let the USSR project its power into the Mediterranean Sea. All this would complicate Britain's position in the Mediterranean and weaken its hand against the Soviet Union.[49]

For several days this situation greatly concerned senior echelons in the Foreign Office. Ultimately, through the foreknowledge provided by code-breaking and their own appreciation of Aras's personality and his position in Ankara, they blocked this development. In particular, whenever any Turkish diplomat raised anything related to the idea, their British counterparts immediately warned them away from it. Vansittart's involvement in this issue is noteworthy. He kept his distance from this significant matter which was illuminated by absolutely reliable intelligence. He let the Southern Department handle the issue. He generally accepted its assessments and its proposed actions, although he did carefully watch its work. His only substantive comments concerned a tangential issue, Turkish relations with Italy and Britain: "The Turks have no interest in seeing us on bad terms with Italy. On the contrary—& they are well aware of the fact."[50]

The second of these examples stems from the greatest known triumph of

British intelligence during the appeasement era. Between April 1934 and February 1939, the GC&CS regularly read the diplomatic telegrams of Japan. These illuminated the relationship between Japan, Germany and Italy, which orbited a loose instrument, the Anti-Comintern Pact. That treaty was signed in November 1936 after months of negotiation between German and Japanese representatives.[51] "The World Situation and British Rearmament" of December 1936 discussed this development in a long paragraph, which was drafted when British authorities knew there were secret protocols to the Pact but not their content. According to "The World Situation",

> it is significant that [the Anti-Comintern Pact] has been negotiated not by the two Foreign Offices, but by Herr von Ribbontropp's [sic] rival office of amateurs and the equally short-sighted Japanese military. Between the two general staffs there have been some previous symptoms of an intimacy which necessarily rouses suspicion as to the true substance of the agreement. We do not yet know the full contents, but we do know that there is without question a secret agreement which may result in something like staff conversations. At present the appearance is that of co-operation against communism; but the appearance convinces no one, and the Russian Ambassador in Tokyo has not ineptly retorted, that the German and Japanese police cannot possibly need each other's assistance! What the agreement clearly does do, however ... is to introduce Japan into the orbit of European affairs at a particularly delicate and dangerous phase, and to increase the probability that, in given circumstances, Germany and Japan would now act together.

In support of this last sentence, the memorandum cited the opinion of the Japanese ambassador to Britain. It also stated that Herman Goering regarded "ideological window-dressing" as irrelevant—what mattered was "that an agreement between the world's best soldiers had now been reached. It was particularly desirable that England's smug complacency should be shaken". Similarly, "a high official in the confidence of Dr. Goebbels" allegedly held that the pact was intended to weaken British influence in Tokyo and to ensure that Japan and Russia remained on bad terms.[52]

This section of "The World Situation" was drafted by the Far Eastern Department of the Foreign Office, but the memorandum appeared under Vansittart's name and he was free to rewrite it. With one single exception—the addition of the material on Goering and Goebbel's assistant—he did not.[53] As ever, he followed the Far Eastern Department's analyses of Japan. That assessment, in turn, rested on secret intelligence. While official sources provided all the comments from ambassadors, they offered only background information about relations between the Japanese and German military and the negotiation of the Pact. Here, the GC&CS and the SIS were the main source.[54] The SIS or Vansittart's private contacts also provided the alleged views of Goering and the "high official"—at least, neither Foreign Office files nor the FO 371 Index refer to them.

The assessment was accurate. Much remained unknown, but the GC&CS and the SIS had uncovered the main lines of the secret relations between Japan and Germany. They had demonstrated with clarity, if not absolute precision, the origins of and the intentions behind the Anti-Comintern Pact and its consequences. Vansittart and the Foreign Office used that intelligence to make powerful calculations about the intentions of potentially hostile powers—indeed, of factions within those states. This was no mean feat, given the confused nature of these relations and the vague phrasing of the Anti-Comintern Pact itself. The Japanese and German factions which pushed the Pact had done so to confuse and alarm other powers. Ironically, the Pact had the opposite effect on Britain. By monitoring its development, Britain could determine the real nature of relations between Japan, Germany and, later, Italy.

"The World Situation", however, misinterpreted one part of the issue and in a revealing fashion. In November–December 1936 the Foreign Office knew it did not know the full story behind the Anti-Comintern Pact and it did fill in the gaps by assuming the worst case.[55] This produced the most alarming element of its paragraph on the Pact—the suggestion that the secret (and, as yet, unknown) section might indicate "something like staff conversations". In fact, that section indicated nothing of the sort and no staff conversations ever occurred under the aegis of that Pact. Notably, after "The World Situation" was drafted but before it was printed, the GC&CS finally solved the secret section. The Foreign Office concluded this material neither supported nor disproved its conjecture about staff conversations. That view was reasonable, but the Foreign Office's actions were political. It did not update "The World Situation" to state that the secret protocols were known and did not support the conjecture in question—one may wonder what it would have done had this information supported its position.[56] In any case, the same information led the Military Intelligence Division (MID) toward a more accurate and less alarmist interpretation. "We know that the German–Japanese Secret Supplementary Agreement is a colourless document." The secret protocols had only one notable feature—Germany and Japan would consult should either fall victim to an unprovoked Soviet attack. The "worst thing about it" was that Germany and Japan had denied that the Pact did contain secret protocols; but leaving aside this proof of concerted lying, the MID concluded that the pact seemed "innocuous, judged by its face value".[57]

These two examples illuminate Vansittart's use of intelligence as PUS. In most ways, it was identical to that of them all. Sometimes he ignored intelligence or else used it purely as a political tool. Sometimes he handled it with skill, sometimes not. Vansittart was usually not the basic analyst of the intelligence he received and used. Instead, he relied on his subordinates' assessments and their proposed lines of action. Intelligence never determined his policy, but simply shaped its execution in specific areas. Its primary purpose was to indicate the direction of the policies of foreign governments and, above all, the specific positions on particular issues of individual statesmen. For that matter, Vansittart's vaunted "private detective agency" was scarcely novel. It was similar in structure to the Victorian system of intelligence, to the networks of informal relationships maintained by other diplomats. In the early 1920s, William Tyrell ran the News Department, to conduct propaganda and gather information. Its representatives explored the political catacombs of Rome, while he used Charles Mendl as his guide through the sewers of Paris.[58] Vansittart was no innovator, but rather the last master of a century-old system of personalized intelligence analysis, with decision makers at the top directing sources and their readings; right after his retirement, Britain was pioneering a new bureaucratized system. Vansittart did not use intelligence in a way unusual among PUSs until he ceased to be one.

In particular, secret sources neither dominated nor created his views of the German danger. Before 1933, Vansittart was not the Germanophobe he later claimed to have been, but he was suspicious of all powers and certainly of Germany. In 1930 1931 he warned the Cabinet of that "ridiculously dangerous demagogue", Adolf Hitler, of the desires of Germans and their leaders' designs.[59] In 1933 he quickly accepted the warnings proffered by the British embassy in Berlin and the Central Department.[60] Between 1933 and 1935, he sought to persuade the government of his case primarily through the collation of public statements of Nazi policy. Vansittart's policy was less straightforward than he later claimed, and it did incorporate some aspects of appeasement, but his analysis was prescient and consistent, and it did have effect. In February 1936, for example, he warned the Cabinet that external German objectives were unlimited and intrinsically linked to its internal policies. Germany would seek, first, to remilitarize the Rhineland; and then more or less simultaneously, to annexe Austria, Memel, Danzig and the Sudetenland. All the while, it would pursue economic hegemony over the Danube basin and territorial aggrandizement in Poland and Ukraine, militarize its own economy, create a war industry of "unprecedented magnitude" and pursue "the militarisation of an efficient race from one end of the social scale to the other". Only "a complete reform of the German spirit" could produce peace. Only massive and immediate rearmament could restrain Germany until then.[61]

This analysis centred on psychology. Vansittart held that German decision makers interpreted the "chorus of peace-bleating" in Britain as proof of "a decline in virility, capacity and will to resist". "The only way", he emphasized, "to find any lasting cooperation with the Third Reich is to command its respect."[62] That was the aim of rearmament. It would symbolize resolution. It would strengthen Britain's psychological and material hand. Perhaps, ultimately, it would free Britain to find a negotiated settlement and "lasting cooperation" with Germany. Precisely this focus on intangibles crippled the success of Vansittart's case. Most British decision makers were materialists who emphasized capabilities. If Britain was weak and endangered, they argued, it must be cautious: nothing more than caution, Vansittart retorted, would signal weakness and attract danger. His superiors regarded this as a high-risk policy of bluff, and rejected his logic—indeed, many of them literally could not understand it. Cadogan, for example, once wrote, "Van, as far as I can make out, wants to talk big, but then—? He's an idiot with an *idee fixe*—a very simple one. He's all facade and nothing else. Nothing constructive: with all his big talk he's got no idea at all. And that is what we are suffering from!"[63] What Cadogan suffered from was a simple mind.

Precisely because Vansittart focused on will rather than material, he understood Hitler's thought and German policy better than his contemporaries, or for that matter, most students of appeasement. There were, of course, weaknesses in his approach. As intelligence analyst, he was less scientist than seer—forcing his audience to take his word on trust. This weakened his credibility by 1937, and forced him to rebuild it during 1938—the most important year in these events, and also the one in which he handled intelligence best. He was trying to deter a man and to manipulate a decision-making system which he did not fully understand. Whether he was using material from secret, official or public sources, Vansittart's assessments of Germany had certain characteristic flaws. His analysis of economic–strategic matters was inconsistent. In the space of six months, he could swing from describing Germany's economy as being weak to strong, from arguing that weakness would provoke adventurism, to holding that it would force restraint.[64] Until 1938, his warnings of the tempo and location of danger were imprecise. At worst, he indicated that every enemy would strike everywhere and at once. When analyzing any debate between German decision makers, Vansittart identified "radical" and "moderate" factions and presumed a struggle between them to influence a malleable but unpredictable *Fuhrer*. Such views were expressed by many authorities, but always in error.[65] This mode of analysis distorted the nature of authority within the Nazi state and the politics at Hitler's court, and sapped the accuracy of Vansittart's assessments. In 1936 he advocated a policy which combined concession, firmness and restraint: "By this threefold recipe alone can moderates and moderation have any chance in Germany. If we firmly follow this threefold course, they may have a chance." Again, in 1937 Vansittart advised Eden that: "By making any bad, because over-hasty, agreement with Germany we shall be destroying the reasonable people who, if given a chance, might be able to bring about a good one."[66] But this policy was impolitic. No one whom Vansittart might have defined as reasonable could come to power unless and until the Nazi regime was destroyed.

Vansittart took a long time to appreciate this point. Until the autumn of 1937, he sought to use multilateral diplomacy as the key to turn the clockwork of German politics. He wished to create international constraints to German expansion and then to play for a stalemate, thus strengthening the "reasonable" Germans who would, in turn, restrain Hitler. Then, a moderate Germany would be rewarded with moderate concessions, while the Versailles order would be amended in detail and bolstered as a whole—a somewhat more schematic and rushed version of British policy since 1919. This policy could not have worked as Vansittart intended, because of its scale and complexity and because he misconstrued German politics. Vansittart wished to create a series of diplomatic alignments and a balance of power which did not exist, and then to change attitudes virtually everywhere on earth: quite literally, his German policy was his world policy. This policy could succeed only if everything worked out right all at once and remained so for years. Most great powers would have to oppose armed revisionism to the status quo by any of them. Each would have to restrain its narrow ambitions and treat Hitler as the overriding problem for all. If not, the multilateral solution would collapse and Germany divide and conquer. The powers would have to remain united during the period required not only to change attitudes in Berlin, but also to appease the newly moderate Germany. Once that Germany was bought, it would have to stay bought.

None of these conditions existed. Had they done so, there would have been no problem in the first place. Vansittart's first policy failed; it probably could never have succeeded; this demonstrates some of his limits as a policy advisor. By late 1937, he coined a new one. He realized Hitler was master of German policy while the "moderates" would do nothing until the *Fuhrer* had first been weakened. Vansittart also believed that Germany was ready to strike, instead of gathering its strength and biding its time. He aimed to defeat any such act of aggression, for its own sake, and as a means to create circumstances which would produce a lasting international coalition against Germany, weaken Hitler, raise the "moderates", and force a political struggle in Berlin which would at least cripple the *Fuhrer* and perhaps destroy him.

During the 1930s, Vansittart followed two German policies. The first was ambitious, the second risky, neither could be achieved easily, nor did he make either of them fully clear to Whitehall. This was a fatal problem for the first of his policies, which required unusual patience and resolve from Britain—the skill to produce a diplomatic draw through multilateral means and the wisdom to realize stalemate was victory. Instead, British decision makers misunderstood his policies. Many came to think that he did not have one. So have some historians, misled by their failure to realize he had two. In fact, whatever the faults in Vansittart's analysis and prescription, he put forward the only practicable alternatives to the diplomacy of drift of the governments of MacDonald and Baldwin between 1933 and 1937 and the pursuit of high appeasement by Neville Chamberlain, Halifax and Cadogan in 1938. His policy could not have achieved its precise intentions. On the other hand, it might still have checked Hitler in unintended ways, and no other means could have done so better than his.

The question is how far this policy rested on intelligence. Public and official sources provided good material on Germany and in large quantities, but much remained hidden about modes of decision making in Berlin, about German capabilities and intentions. British intelligence would be of value precisely to the degree that it filled these lacuna. It did so with effect—this is not a story of failure, but of unusual success, with limits. Intelligence provided some material on German military and industrial capacity, more about the nature of decision making in Berlin and the direction of its policy over the long term, and a great deal about the positions on specific issues of individual German leaders. This material was often striking in accuracy and detail; but, equally, it was often misleading or misguided. Nor could contemporaries easily determine its accuracy and reliability. The best sources of British intelligence offered little on Nazi Germany, and thus could not even be used to indicate the accuracy of those sources which did. The GC&CS had no luck against important German ciphers, although traffic analysis and the solution of low-grade codes provided excellent quantitative data on German armed forces, especially the *Luftwaffe*. In 1987, again, a well-informed source, Peter Wright, claimed MI5 had tapped Joachim Ribbontrop's telephones while he was ambassador to Britain. This claim is plausible, and such means may have produced the "incontrovertible evidence" Vansittart once gave Eden to prove Ribbontrop "is a violent Anglophobe".[67] Incontrovertible evidence on Germany was rare. Such material generally came from human sources and through the SIS or Vansittart's "private detective agency"—more precisely, the firm of Vansittart & Christie Ltd.

Vansittart first heard of Malcolm Graham Christie during 1924–1926, when he oversaw the American Department and Christie was Air Attaché in Washington. Christie made the acquisition of technical air intelligence his main task. Vansittart watched him milk the American press and aviation industry, and exploit differences within the Army and Navy about the exchange of technical information with Britain. He also used means which bordered on espionage.[68] Thus, Christie hoped "to secure through a reliable source a classification of all the Army Air Service Engineering Division's secret and confidential reports, memoranda, etc, in order to enable me to accurately estimate the value and extent" of material offered for exchange. Soon, he came to favour the official exchange of information: "it is becoming more and more difficult to secure the technical data of real value, i.e. it takes practically the whole of my time planning and effecting indirect means of getting the information without risk of detection outside the plain 'quid pro quo' basis". He pursued these objectives through clever negotiation. On his own initiative, Christie persuaded both American air services to exchange research with the RAF—indeed, to give him such material before Britain had accepted this proposal, no mean feat, given their suspicions of manipulation. Only then did Christie inform his superiors of his actions. Alas, Whitehall rejected this proposal. American authorities held no animus against him, but they did feel a need to retaliate: the United States Naval Attaché in London stated publicly that "Christie endeavours to obtain information in an unauthorised manner and is regarded in Washington as very little short of a spy." This alarmed the Chief of the Air Staff. Hugh Trenchard ordered that Christie be told "in the plainest language ... that he is to engage in no activities outside the normal duties of a British Attache". Over the next two years, Christie managed the exchange of technical information in a different but hard-headed way.[69]

Between 1927 and 1930, he harnessed his talents to similar ends as Air Attaché in Berlin. Christie, a wealthy businessman, had lived for nine years in Germany before 1914, obtaining the degree of *Doktor Ingenieur* at Aachen University.[70] This background, and his status as a veteran pilot from the Western Front, helped Christie make contacts in German political, military, aviation and industrial circles. Edward Milch and Hugo Junkers, one the head of the German Air Ministry, the other a leading German aircraft manufacturer, sent letters of regret when he retired from the RAF in January 1930.[71] As in Washington, Christie acquired intelligence by playing official and business sources against the other, but with one difference. In Germany Britain expected such activities of an Air Attaché. Both his predecessors acquired information through means verging on espionage, and sources amounting to agents in the German Air Ministry.[72] So did Christie, as he and his staff "wander aimlessly around amongst the Boche herds with our ears laid back, eyes front, but our mental antennae extended in the endeavour to select and sift from the bewildering multiplicity of wavelengths a few significant signals".[73] In the process he established a reputation in the British embassy and the Foreign Office's Central Department, which managed relations with the states of Central Europe.

Christie paid close attention to the foreign subsidiaries of German aircraft manufacturers, the combines which linked industry and military, the means by which Germany contravened treaty restrictions on the development of air forces, and the firms and foreign states which helped it to do so. Through "a prominent person employed by the Junkers firm", he monitored that concern's finances, its links with the German Air Ministry and the production by its Swedish subsidiary of civil aircraft which could easily be converted to military models. "A source which is usually *entirely reliable*" detailed Germano-Soviet cooperation in military aviation.[74] "Based upon personal observations and upon information that has been collected from many sources and very carefully sifted", Christie brushed up his opinions on the German people, their politics, ambitions and power. His message was mixed. "The old prusso-german war machine" was largely dismantled. Americanization and republicanization were changing German society. Ultimately "the old militant die-hards" might be defeated by

> the democratic sentiments of the younger generation brought up to play games and to take part in athletics and sports; the onflow of youth averse to military discipline should produce a people less aggressive and more amenable to principles of fair play ... the Teuton has a prosperous and powerful future if only he is well lead [*sic*] and acquires a sense of sportsmanship.

This future, however, was decades away. For years to come, the "virile, martial-minded, German people", lacking "a befitting measure of political sense", would wish to restore German status and its military power, especially in the air. In 1929, Germany could not take on France in the air—not even Poland. Still, it maintained military expertise, sophisticated technology, large reserves of trained pilots and ground crew and a great industrial capacity. Germany could immediately increase its air production sixfold; and, within nine months, raise its maximum construction capacity from 230 to 2,500 machines, its monthly peak of production in 1918. Given four months of freedom, Germany could develop air power which could throw "such a weight of force on the one side or the other as to decide almost any European conflict in her own favour". These calculations of extant German airpower were distorted, but they gave Christie experience in tracking issues which soon became crucial. Rather more prophetically, Christie warned that the Allied evacuation of Germany would "prove a turning point in the aero-political policy of the Reich, perhaps not wholly noticeable at first but gradually becoming more obvious. The hostage will have been released, the military grip relaxed and replaced by the trustful embrace of the League". German power would rise sharp and fast. Germany would expand its air strength to pursue frontier revision against Poland, possibly more.[75]

Following his retirement, Christie became an international businessman, well connected in Germany and Britain. Until then, he had followed a conventional pattern in life, but within eight months, that changed. Apparently on his own initiative, Christie sought out contacts among all right-wing German parties, including the National Socialist German Workers Party, and reported on them to the Foreign Office. Initially, his assessments were inaccurate—between 1928 and 1936 his political predictions usually proved wrong—but even so Christie was well connected and his accounts did improve. His analyses always rested on crude ideas of German characteristics combined with a militaristic Germanophilia, but precisely these flaws gave him insight into a militaristic and racist state. Indeed, when added to his formidable and attractive personality, they gave him influence and information. As an analyst of German airpower and industrial mobilization for strategic purposes, he was first rate—among the best available in Britain. Ultimately, Christie developed genuine expertise as a collector and analyst of intelligence.

Between 1930 and 1933, Christie developed extraordinary access to material on German politics and air strength and to those who made decisions on these matters. He also presented his findings to the Foreign Office, with notable effect. At first he was a freelance amateur, acting out of curiosity rather than at the behest of the Foreign Office. After 1933, however, Vansittart came to regard Christie as Britain's best source on the inner workings of the Nazi state. Christie did influence Vansittart's ideas and the two gradually formed one view of Germany. Meanwhile Christie's connections, augmented by those of the PUS, became the basis for Vansittart's private intelligence system.[76] The evidence on this network is fragmentary. Much remains uncertain or unknown, but some important points can be established directly or by inference.[77] Christie's success stemmed from his long years in Germany, and his membership in the curious fraternity of airmen during this period—men of reactionary politics, who worked with representatives of other countries even at the risk of betraying their own. This situation is epitomized by Gustav Lachmann, a German-born aerodynamic engineer who worked twenty years for a British aircraft manufacturer, and two for a Japanese one, all the while maintaining close touch with German firms and officials. Interned in 1940 because MI5 thought him a security threat, "one of the Freemasons of aeronautical research and, therefore, almost international in his outlook", he spent the war in Lingfield prison conducting aeronautical research for Handley Page![78]

More broadly, the Christie–Vansittart network tapped several distinct circles of dissidents within Germany alongside dedicated Nazis. It was loosely organized and its focus changed frequently. Between 1933 and 1936, the network essentially combined Christie's open contacts with senior Nazis and other Germans, and his secret sources in the German Air Ministry. Between May 1937 and July 1938, the importance of these sources was matched by Carl Goerdeler's contacts among conservative dissidents. During and after the Munich crisis, Vansittart discarded Goerdeler, while Christie abandoned his official Nazi contacts and acquired new sources through the dissident Nazi leader Otto Strasser and anti-Hitler elements in the German diplomatic service and the *Abwehr*, the internal and external security service of the German Army. From then until it faded in 1940, the network centred on soundings from resistance circles taken by Christie and others. It may also have been augmented by family connections—Vansittart's brother, Guy, was a senior executive for the European division of General Motors, with responsibility for plants used in Germany's military preparation.[79]

The Vansittart–Christie network consisted of two rough groups: sources—people whose views carried authority in themselves or who possessed direct access to important information—and their contacts with London. While not all of the dissident sources are known, those who are stemmed exclusively from the strands of conservative to reactionary opposition. They included several junior members of the German diplomatic corps and its press service (Erich and Theodor Kordt, Wolfgang zu Pulitz and Klop Ustinov) and two businessmen in firms central to German armament, Robert Bosch, a south German industrial magnate, and Hans Ritter, an employee of Junkers who assisted the German Air and Military Attachés in Paris between 1934 and 1938. Bosch and Ritter always ranked among Christie's main sources, while the others were of peripheral significance before July 1938. Bosch had been a friend of Christie's since 1910. Ritter may have been the "prominent person employed by the Junkers firm" who aided Christie as Air Attaché in Germany. Each provided information and introductions. Bosch, himself significant in the German opposition, may well have introduced Christie to Goerdeler (whom the businessman employed from April 1937 for purposes of cover, with the aim of unifying the opposition and negotiating for it abroad). This issue, however, is controversial: Vansittart claimed to have met Goerdeler first in 1935, while A.P. Young recorded that he introduced them in July 1937.[80] Meanwhile, after the Munich crisis and his own resignation from German service, Ritter became an aggressive and accomplished talent scout for Christie; the two shared a taste for humourous pseudonyms (Colonel Blimp, Naphtali Mentelbaum) and contempt for fools.

Still unidentified are several of the sources whom Christie praised most highly. Two of them, "Don" and "X", reported frequently from within the German Air Ministry during the 1930s. One or both may have been Ritter, but definite identification is uncertain: between 1922 and 1939 British intelligence constantly recruited people from that bureau. Meanwhile, many unnamed informants serviced Christie. He occasionally referred, for example, to "Q", whom in early 1939 he described as "a very trustworthy old friend occupying privileged position in the German press, with access to the *Auswartigesamt*. He lives outside the *Reich*". This description fits Rudolf Pechel, editor of the tolerated but non-Nazi *Deutsche Rundshau*, who often visited Britain during this period, did associate with Christie, and did mention Ritter after the war.[81] Other unknown sources appeared during the Munich crisis. While Ritter remained Christie's leading correspondent, and Bosch an important one, by 14 August Christie reported that "a very old friend of mine ... an absolutely cautious reliable fellow" (Ritter) had found two new sources. One was in the German diplomatic service, most likely Theo Kordt, although from these days forward, many members of the German embassy in London reported to Christie. One of them, Edward von Selzam, later rated Christie among his "oldest and most reliable British friends".[82] The identity of the other new figure, described as "an entirely different source (Vatican)", is uncertain, but Ritter did later handle Christie's contacts in that direction. Thereafter, Christie frequently referred to German Catholic sources, of uncertain identity.

Between October 1938 and September 1939, Christie's known sources included Ritter, Bosch, Strasser, the Kordt brothers, zu Pulitz and Ustinov; but equally important are several unknown ones. One of them emerged by October 1938. Christie described him as:

> A certain highly educated and extraordinarily well-informed German, named Y, who is supported by the great Catholic interests in Germany, whose bureau contains archives dealing with subjects of the most valuable political and cultural nature, has recently been able to establish contact with me. This person is no emigre, but one whose intimate contacts reach as far as the immediate entourage of the Fuehrer, the highest offices of the Wilhelmstrasse, of the Party and of the German Secret Service. I would guarantee, as in the past, the accuracy of his information.[83]

"Y" may be the "Vatican" source, but again, identification is impossible. The description does not fit any well-known German Catholic opponent of Hitler, such as Joseph Muller, the link between the *Abwehr* and the Vatican in 1939–1940. By the turn of 1939 Christie found another source, "Fish", who provided material from "only the highest proven sources"; perhaps he also was the person Christie described as being in "a responsible strategic position".[84] This man/these men probably was/were linked to the entourage of Hans Oster, leader of the resistance in the *Abwehr*—with whom Ritter was soon on close terms, as he already was with General Beck. There is, however, no direct evidence on this point. Finally, by March 1939, two of Christie's old friends (most likely Bosch and Ritter) correctly learned of Hitler's intentions to devour the rump of Czechoslovakia from a person (or persons) described variously as "an Assistant Under Secretary [*Ministerial direktor*] in the War Ministry at Berlin", an "informant in German Ministry of War, in close touch with German Foreign Office", and

> a high official in the German Ministry of War, from whom we have received much valuable information in the past. He works in the section of the War Ministry which deals with foreign affairs and therefore receives up-to-date information from the Foreign Office, the Ribbentrop Bureau and the Propaganda Ministry. It must be emphasised that he is in possession of such knowledge of foreign affairs and plans as Ribbentrop considers it necessary for the German military authorities to be given, but in addition he receives supplementary information from the War Ministry's own sources …

He is in a position therefore to check up on Ribbentrop's statements in most cases.

These descriptions fit both Dr. Otto Kieper and Gottfried von Nostitz, each conservative opponents of Hitler and Foreign Office officials attached to the General Staff.[85]

In late 1938, the politics of resistance and espionage led Christie to find new sources and change his network. Characteristically, he no longer met his contacts in Germany but in Switzerland, from where Ritter built links to all elements of the opposition, the *widerstand*. Goerdeler claimed to speak for the opposition. Ritter was a contact with it, though he knew many of the same people as Goerdeler, and others. In taking these steps, Vansittart and Christie sidestepped Goerdeler and Christie's Nazi contacts, pursued direct links with the opposition, and encouraged them to express their recommendations on the best British tactics to counter Hitler. Meanwhile, the opposition in the *Abwehr* and the *Wilhelmstrasse* were searching for direct contact with Britain. Thus, both ends of the chain discarded Goerdeler as middleman. Consideration of Christie's known sources and a reading of the material given him, suggests that the Wilhelmine resisters within the *Wilhelmstrasse* were the network's main source from October 1938 to January 1939, especially since it already knew better than the *Abwehr* conspirators how to make contact. Then, Oster's entourage probably provided some of Christie's new sources, increasingly so from March 1939. During the early stages of this development, reports declined in accuracy and rose in alarmism. While some of this matter may reflect deliberate disinformation from Nazis or resisters, aimed to make Britain offer more to Hitler or his enemies, equally it stemmed from the confusion within German decision making, to a sincere reportage of rumour, or an overestimate of transient attitudes. Equally, the opposition was only just becoming self-conscious as a resistance. In attempting to learn what it was and to assess its product, Vansittart and Christie were doing something new and hard.[86]

Christie's various contacts could and did report on views and information stemming from further individuals. He was also close to men like Goering and Henlein, and his reports of their views were happily cited by Vansittart.[87] Some of these sources spoke in the sure knowledge their words would be carried to the ears of foreign governments; others did not necessarily know this would happen. Nor can one determine whether the contacts carried these words accurately. Christie was the central cut-out in the network. In 1937–1938, however, his significance as a contact was matched, perhaps exceeded, by Goerdeler, previously Mayor of Leipzig and Reich Price Commissioner. This minor politician held conservative but anti-Nazi views. He provided a link to circles with similar inclinations, particularly to two chiefs of the German General Staff, Ludwig Beck and Werner von Fritsch, and one of the *Reichsbank*, Hjalmer Schacht. Between July and December

1938, Vansittart came to doubt Goerdeler, and the network shifted focus. In July Vansittart recruited A.P. Young, a businessman connected to Goerdeler and Bosch, with good reasons to visit Germany but ignorant of Vansittart's other men, to liaise with Goerdeler. Meanwhile, Ritter established a new base in Switzerland, from which he assumed Goerdeler's function of linking with the *widerstand*. During the Munich crisis Philip Conwell-Evans, the Secretary of the Anglo-German Fellowship, joined the ranks of Vansittart's contacts, providing useful connections to German business and government agencies, to Ribbontrop and to the opposition.

Vansittart's private detective agency was managed by leading English Germanophiles and Germans. Though usually described as an intelligence system, it combined open but non-official contacts with German government figures, and secret means to contact the opposition. The network reported intelligence less than opinion—it stood halfway between diplomacy and espionage. Until July 1938, Christie maintained security by hiding in plain sight—so well known was his role and so good his rationale for visiting Germany, he could safely meet sources there; nor were the opposition's contacts with authorities abroad always hidden. From August 1938, the network moved toward secrecy and with skill. Just before war broke out, Vansittart and Conwell-Evans showed their command of tradecraft when giving Theo Kordt a means to meet them in Switzerland. He would send an unsigned postcard carrying a specific citation from Horace; fourteen days later Conwell-Evans would arrive in the district noted on the postmark.[88]

The great strength of the Vansittart–Christie network was its breadth and depth of access, ranging from senior Nazis to junior officials and some dissidents. This was balanced by great weaknesses. All of its members were biased. While these biases often worked in different and perhaps self-negating ways, sometimes they reinforced each other. Neville Chamberlain dismissed von Kleist-Schmenzin, as a "Jacobite".[89] However inadequate and self-serving the metaphor, the criticism had force. Goerdeler, his sources and many of Christie's diplomatic contacts, had Wilhelmine views on foreign policy: only compared to Hitler were they moderates, and even that was not obvious until 1939. By 1938, Goerdeler demanded that Britain prove its good faith by pledging officially to his shadowy constituency that if they acted against Hitler, Britain would restore the Polish corridor and a sizable colonial empire, offer a huge interest-free loan to Germany and create a permanent Anglo-German strategic axis which would check Italy in the Mediterranean, Japan in China and perhaps overthrow the Soviet regime. This offer was not far different from those Goering or Hitler proposed, or Kaiser William II. Vansittart's memoirs state that he always recognized and thus avoided this problem. Some historians have accepted this claim, but contemporary evidence points in another direction. During 1937–1938, Vansittart continually cited the views of Goerdeler and his circle as authoritative. He described (often without naming) Goerdeler as "an impressive person, wise and weighty, a man of great intelligence and courage, and a sincere patriot", "a German of high standing and well known to me", who knew Nazi policies would destroy Germany and Europe, a man well connected to the Army's leaders, a source whose reports had always been absolutely accurate.[90] Vansittart never mentioned Goerdeler's biases—admittedly, he may have seen no need to do so in these cases or may have feared such a discussion would cast doubt on the German's value. By December 1938, however, Goerdeler approached Cadogan, and for the first time directly told the Foreign Office what his contacts wanted. Then, for the first time, Vansittart discussed Goerdeler's true desires. He told Halifax Goerdeler was "merely a stalking horse" for military expansionists, as against Nazi expansionists, and should be trusted only "as an occasional informant". Vansittart added this twist of bitters: "He is quite untrustworthy and he is in with the wrong kind of person because his own mind is wrong."[91] After 1945 he repented of his verdict, slightly. It stemmed from Vansittart's disappointment with Britons and Germans during and after Munich, the date when his Germanophobia began.

Nor was bias the only problem with these sources. Christie boasted that they were well connected and he did take care not to conflate or distort their views, but his reports were often simply his or their opinions, one multiplying the other, about German public opinion or of events which had not yet happened. Such views carried no authority in themselves—Goerdeler's assessment of Hitler's intentions had no more significance than those of a well-informed mayor of Luton on Neville Chamberlain—and were merely guesses, no matter how prescient. Above all, the system often relied on testimony far from the original source, sometimes fifth-hand: Vansittart's gloss of Christie's account of Goerdeler's reports of Beck's assessment of Hitler's intentions. Vansittart denied that any of his

> sources has any connection with the Secret Service. They are all quite independent and individually reliable. It is therefore the more significant that they are nearly always in accord with the reports of the Secret Service; and it should now further be noted that they are borne out by the information that has come into Colonel Christie's possession.[92]

This statement was right and wrong at the same time. Without coordination, several British contacts were tapping several sources in Germany, some of whom were approaching many British officials. The SIS and the Vansittart–Christie network did have separate sources: between 1933 and 1938, for example, the SIS had no direct access to Goering, but could reach circles around Alfred Rosenberg and the *Aussen Politisches Amt* of the Nazi Party and the German military, which were beyond Christie's reach; it also received and respected much useful material on German military capabilities and intentions from the Czech intelligence service.[93] None the less, the two systems did tap some of the same people and rumours, as, for that matter, did the British embassy in Berlin. Again, the various British sources within the German embassy in London, Theo Kordt, Klop Ustinov and zu Pulitz, provided information to Vansittart and to MI5.[94] Under these circumstances, British intelligence and His Majesty's Government alike made the most basic of mistakes. One report repeated through two contacts reinforced itself. It was easy for rumour to be multiplied and the network to be manipulated. This certainly happened in the winter of 1938/1939, when the Cabinet's Foreign Policy Committee received material from the ostensibly different sources of the Foreign Office, the SIS and Vansittart. Yet all of them were relying to varying degrees on Goerdeler—in effect, Cadogan and Vansittart simultaneously repudiated Goerdeler's authority while citing him as authoritative! Meanwhile, some of the ostensibly independent warnings of Vansittart and MI5 stemmed from their shared agents in the German embassy; Christie's new sources essentially consisted of people Vansittart was indirectly repudiating, by rejecting Goerdeler; while the resistance within the *Abwehr* gave similar reports to Christie and Mason-MacFarlane.

The "opposition", meanwhile, was loose and fissiparous, always mutating, its leadership and membership often vague and hard to distinguish from servants of the Nazi state, especially before 1938. Its contacts with outside parties confused both sides. Resisters pursued different aims and sent conflicting messages, because of confusion, security and the stresses of personality and conspiracy. Thus, in August 1938 the opposition in the General Staff sent von Kleist-Schmenzin, to convince Whitehall toward tough steps. "Bring me certain proof that Britain will fight if Czechoslovakia is attacked and I will make an end of this regime", allegedly said the head of the German General Staff, General Beck—who promptly resigned just as his emissary reached London! Several weeks later, Oster sent an emissary to London, Lieutenant-Colonel Bohm-Tettlebach, who found it hard to deliver his message because he lacked the right contacts. On 6 September Theo Kordt spoke to Lord Halifax on behalf of the opposition in the Foreign Ministry and the *Abwehr*; but he presented the views of the latter rather than the former, without informing his masters in the *Willhelmstrasse*.[95]

The opposition was a difficult creature to comprehend. Vansittart did not entirely succeed in this. Indeed, had he or any other Briton understood the opposition better, they would have trusted it even less than they did. Goerdeler, after all, sent reports on his first mission abroad not just to members of the opposition but also to Goering. The opposition within the *Wilhelmstrasse* pursued aims like those of the Wilhelmine government in 1913. Again, Whitehall treated Prince Hohenlohe as a major politician, and did not understand German intelligence. It did not know Admiral Canaris headed the *Abwehr*, let alone that he aided the opposition at home and espionage abroad. One *Abwehr* officer captured in 1942 claimed "CANARIS's main aim has always been to secure big stuff through big people. Princely hosts such as HOHENLOHE and neutral diplomats such as ROCCAMORA are his meat". Hohenlohe was "one of CANARIS's very special and very trusted 'gentleman agents'. The Prince is only used for matters necessitating penetration into high diplomatic or social circles abroad". In 1945, a *Gestapo* officer claimed that Canaris's successor and SS officer, Walter Schellenberg, personally ran Hohenlohe who, with another figure, was called "the chief's personal checking system" in Spain. In 1938, notably, Hohenlohe was one of Vansittart's sources and a significant advocate of Sudeten independence.[96] The opposition was ambiguous in nature and uncertain in effect: a wild card. Some of its members were people of honour; more were opportunists. Could they really launch an organized strike against Hitler? Would they? Perhaps with British encouragement, the opposition would have destroyed Hitler's regime; perhaps not. This question is important to consider but impossible to answer. Vansittart ensured that Whitehall considered the question when it most mattered.

Nazis obviously were not monitoring all the Vansittart–Christie network—had they been doing so, Goerdeler or Beck would have been arrested long before they were. Several of the contacts, however, were widely known to be unofficial conduits of information. In his visits to Britain during 1937, Goerdeler freely offered his views to British officials and journalists. By September 1938, just three months after his recruitment, A.P. Young informed British politicians and journalists about Goerdeler's views. By the early spring of 1939, Young briefed American journalists about attitudes within Germany and was quoted as an authority on the topic.[97] In August 1938, the French ambassador knew the rough details of von Kleist-Schmenzin's visit to London; members of the military opposition leaked similar material to Christie and Ian Colvin, the *News Chronicle* correspondent in Berlin.[98] Christie did not even try to disguise much of his role. In 1936 he met the Conservative politician Leo Amery at two social functions. Amery and others knew Christie did "all sorts of miscellaneous intelligence work on the Continent" and was connected to important Germans. Christie passed intelligence alongside the port—had France marched during the Rhineland crisis, the army would have overthrown Hitler, the German elite was divided between the army and "Goering with the Air Force, the SS and the Gestapo", *Anschluss* was inevitable, Czechoslovakia doomed and German rearmament terrifying.[99] Many of his Nazi contacts, like Henlein and Goering, knew Christie was an unofficial conduit to Whitehall and so used him. Goering used Birgir Dahlerus and contacts with French air and military officers in the same way, while Christie was Henlein's sponsor through British society. French authorities kept a dossier on Christie, whom they regarded as an anti-Nazi Germanophile with a dangerous influence on Vansittart. As the French ambassador in London put it, Christie was:

a convinced Germanophile who, while seeming hostile to the Hitlerian regime, seeks by every means to support a rapprochement or at least to prevent a conflict between England and Germany. He is close to Sir Robert Vansittart, and to that friendship one must attribute the latter's endless insistence on basic reforms to the Czechoslovak state.

French authorities knew Christie had organized Henlein's visit to London in May 1938 and they monitored the Sudeten German leader's discussions with Ribbontrop and British authorities.[100] Ribbontrop, in turn, used Henlein to spread lies which fooled Vansittart and Winston Churchill and shaped British views toward Czechoslovakia. Opportunists in the resistance used Goerdeler and other contacts to destroy Hitler while swelling Germany, by passing material indicating British authorities should make an offer the generals could not refuse.

Some Nazis and their conservative opponents knew parts of the Christie-Vansittart network and tolerated them because these could be used to spread disinformation whenever they wanted, which was often.[101] They each controlled parts of Vansittart's private detective agency. To make matters even more complex, Christie and Vansittart recognized that fact to some degree, discounted some of the disinformation and tolerated it in order to acquire information, and did squeeze some truth from lies. This network provided superb information about such things as memoranda on the war economy written by the German General Staff and the *Langnamverein*, the Rhineland Association of Heavy Industry in 1937, Hitler's intentions toward Czechoslovakia and preparations for its invasion in 1938, and German negotiations with Italy and attitudes toward the USSR in 1939.[102] Thus, Vansittart's sources at any moment tapped a host of different sources—truth, lies, rumours and whispering campaigns inspired by Hitler, Goering or Ribbontrop and several groups of their foes on the conservative part of the German political spectrum.

The main aspect of intelligence during appeasement was its assessment of the intentions of Germany, its decision makers and especially of Hitler, but it was also significant in its picture of present and intended German capabilities. Secret sources were always fundamental to Vansittart's warnings about Nazi armament, especially in the air. This, the best-known instance of his use of intelligence, focused less on the question of what German strength was at the moment than on what it would be at some future point. Calculations on that matter were uncertain, involving a series of guesses about a host of technical and interrelated issues. Vansittart himself recognized that the issue was not fact about capabilities but prophecy regarding intentions. The problem was doubly great because Hitler's rearmament programmes called for Germany to produce more than it proved able to do. Thus, information on the strength which one German agency expected to have at some future point might be genuine but misleading. Vansittart's campaign in this area had several characteristics. Christie, who had gained experience with such calculations as Air Attaché, provided much valuable and genuine intelligence, some of which was misleading. Vansittart interpreted all of this in an alarmist way and then used it in bureaucratic warfare with the Air Ministry, with the aim of speeding air rearmament. He and his associates leaked much of this intelligence, especially to Churchill, so to affect public attitudes and government policy. Vansittart also refused to share all of his information with the Air Ministry or let other official bodies provide an authoritative interpretation based on the collation of all relevant material. He used intelligence as a weapon and virtually expected Whitehall to take his own conclusions on trust. All this had several consequences. Initially, Vansittart did understand the rate of German air expansion better than the Air Ministry. By 1936 he ended Whitehall's underestimate of the German danger.[103] Then, however, his evidence, his alarmism and his leaks contributed to an exaggeration of German strength, which hampered strategic assessments and policy. Finally, his use of intelligence contributed to confusion in Whitehall and made enemies.

Between 1933 and 1935, however, secret intelligence had little effect on any other aspect of Vansittart's views about Germany. He sometimes used intelligence from the SIS or Christie to illuminate Nazi decision making, but generally he relied on public and official sources, which provided a mass of accurate, consistent and trusted material. Christie's material from that period generally focused on broad matters—German public opinion, the power of components within the Nazi state, Germany's ultimate hopes for expansion along the Baltic coast and central Europe—but said relatively little about immediate issues of foreign policy. From early 1936, however, the point increasingly ceased to be the general direction of Nazi policy but rather its specific intentions on immediate issues. Vansittart followed the conventional practice in Whitehall when confronting such circumstances and relied more and more on secret intelligence.[104] Precisely as this happened, however, his reputation collapsed. The Cabinet blamed him for the debacle of the Hoare–Laval Pact; Eden, the new Foreign Secretary, questioned his judgment, his analyses and syntheses as, increasingly, did junior officials within the Foreign Office; past allies like the service chiefs, Hankey and Warren Fisher, fell away. By mid-1937 Neville Chamberlain, the new Prime Minister, complained continually that the Foreign Office was blocking his attempted rapprochement with Italy. Once, when he wished to contact Eden when the latter was abroad, Chamberlain complained "I never know how Van interprets my messages or what comments he adds".[105] Vansittart's views were respected within the Foreign Office, but many junior colleagues disagreed with him on fundamental issues. No longer did he routinely represent its views in Cabinet Papers—their shape was usually determined by Eden and featured the opinions of junior officials rather than their chief.

Thus, in the spring of 1936 Eden let the Central Department and Vansittart present their views about Germany, based essentially on public sources, direct to the Cabinet; in December 1936, he let Vansittart do so with secret sources in "The World Situation". Conversely, in July 1937 Eden refused to give the Cabinet a lengthy memorandum on "material and psychological conditions in Germany", drafted by Vansittart largely from secret sources, perhaps two-thirds of which derived from Goerdeler. Vansittart wanted this paper, which was already set up in the form of a Cabinet Paper, to have "a rather broader circulation" than "The World Situation". Eden refused and the memorandum was merely entered in Foreign Office files.[106] On his own copy, Vansittart inscribed the phrase, "suppressed by Eden". The PUS was increasingly less authoritative within the Foreign Office; and without.

It was in this context that Vansittart used intelligence during his last two years as PUS—to shape his own analyses of German intentions and actions, but even more to convince Eden and the Foreign Office of his views. Thus, he sought to use secret sources so to persuade Eden that Ribbontrop was anti-British and Nevile Henderson misinformed, and to affect the Foreign Secretary's views about German ambitions for expansion in central Europe in the spring of 1936 and the fall of 1937, and about British strategy in the Mediterranean and diplomacy throughout Europe in July 1937.[107] Meanwhile, this material shaped Vansittart's own views. By mid-1937 Goerdeler's sources agreed that both the Party and the army wished to create a "*Totaler Wehrstaat*", a nation with its military and social policies harmonized and harnessed to the chariot of total war. This view was correct, though Goerdeler overestimated the Army's opposition to Hitler and to that policy—the generals had always hoped precisely that the *Fuhrer* would create a total war state. In any case, toward the end of 1937, Vansittart and Christie overcame the problems in Goerdeler's analysis, and their own earlier views. Both concluded that the radicals within the Nazi Party were increasingly dominant, that the army would cooperate largely with the regime, while the moderate generals were liable to be replaced. From this time, they usually assumed that a power struggle within the German elite could not hamper Hitler's hold on the state until the latter had first been shaken from outside. Faith in the "reasonable people" no longer crippled their analysis.

Simultaneously, Christie and Vansittart concluded, other factors in German society could restrain the intentions and capabilities of the Nazi state. Many leading civilian and military figures feared the consequences of a radical policy, and preferred safer courses. There existed a "widespread fear among the masses that their Nazi government's foreign policy is steering them into another catastrophic war". Hard work for few material rewards had sapped the morale of the working classes, as the struggle between the Party and the generals had done to the army. According to Goerdeler, Fritsch and Beck believed these psychological factors "would considerably weaken the fighting spirit of the nation in a major war and impose great hesitation and caution upon the Fuhrer". Hitler's actions, Christie argued, were crippling the social basis for the *Totaler Wehrstaat*, and the economic foundation for total war—and German decision makers knew it. Only when Britain showed resolve could the potential opposition to Hitler's policy be mobilized. It might dissipate, Vansittart warned, if Britain did not do so.

> Everything points to circumstances as well as spirits being in considerable confusion in Germany. Economic conditions are making themselves felt on the government and within the Party; and although the latter still preaches in undiluted purity, Germany's divine right to expansion as laid down in Mein Kampf, there are those in authority, both in the Party and outside it, who, realizing the approaching strains and stress, are grasping for some immediate policy and some expedient for tiding over the impending crisis. But ... [there is no sure way to read the mind of] ... the incalculable and emotional figure of Hitler, on whom no one can count from one day to the next.

Referring to the views of Fritsch and Beck, as reported by Goerdeler, Christie emphasized a danger and a promise. One "shrewd and experienced German officer" held:

> A major war is clearly out of the question for the Reich. Both social and economic difficulties forbid it. Germany could only risk war if a certain and quick victory could be achieved ... this remains impossible as long as our potential enemies grow stronger and stronger. The Reich, however, in combination with Italy, will bluff to the eleventh hour.

Another stated, "Germany cannot face a war of major duration" but would "force the pace and bluff".

> If you British continue to dictate that you will avoid war at almost any cost, you will be presenting a temptation that may well prevent settlement by peaceful means ... Peaceful advances on your part will only be interpreted as a further sign of fear, and will increase the Nazi appetite for domination.

The more Britain advertised its desire to "avoid war at almost any cost", the more Germany would bluff.

From material of this sort, primarily third- and fourth-hand, interspersed with some original documents, and through an analysis which no doubt seemed contradictory to many readers, Vansittart drew consistent conclusions. These were widely known in Whitehall, but little believed. He held that German decision makers, especially within the military, were divided about aims and means. Therefore, German decisions could be determined by British actions and by German perceptions of Britain's attitude. Germany was striving to get everything it could but would not dare pursue its aims through war. It was trapped between "unsatiated ambitions on the one side and inadequate material resources on the other". Bluff and greed were the hallmarks of its policy; resolution and rearmament must be Britain's response. Anything less would advertise weakness. The weaker British will appeared, the greater the radicals' influence over Hitler. The more resolute London, the less adventurous Berlin.[108]

After his supercession as PUS, Vansittart retained these views and redoubled his reliance on intelligence. He had been forced from influence because Whitehall rejected his aims and means. He had to justify both of them from the start in order to get back in, and he had only one tool left to do so. Meanwhile, his supercession wrecked Whitehall's system for intelligence on Germany. Since 1930, Sinclair, Christie and Vansittart had managed the collection of such material while the PUS and the Central Department had dominated its interpretation. However imperfect, this system was better than its successor. Throughout 1938–1939, the collection and analysis of British intelligence on Germany became increasingly disjointed, in part because Vansittart deliberately heightened the politicization and confusion surrounding it, in order to strengthen his claims to expertise. Decision makers were unsure of the value of intelligence, inexperienced in its interpretation, yet driven to read it. When the Foreign Office tried to assess intelligence without Vansittart, its efforts even on key issues were amateurish and inconclusive, whether comparing reports by the SIS and the British ambassador in Rome about Italo-German relations, or assessing telephone intercepts of Czech diplomats provided by Germany at the height of the Munich crisis.[109] Several different people received raw intelligence and interpreted it without coordination or assessment by specialists. Intelligence had little immediate effect on British actions but it did become central to the education of statesmen. During 1938 they considered different interpretations of German aims. Intelligence guided the selection between them, the mistakes which statesmen concluded they had made and the lessons which they learned. Here, Vansittart had advantages—more flair and experience with intelligence and an environment which justified his past warnings in unprecedented ways. Events followed the pattern of his predictions, which became increasingly plausible. In this, his hour, he shaped Britain's meanderings down the road to Munich and then off it and toward war.[110]

After his supercession as PUS and Eden's resignation as Foreign Secretary, Vansittart's minutes became more imperative and numerous. With nothing to lose and more time on his hands, he began to shower secret reports on Halifax, the new Foreign Secretary.[111] Once Vansittart's warnings had been vague as to time, place and sequence; now they were precise and falsifiable. Once they had been overwritten; now their style was stark. Initially, Halifax was unimpressed: in March 1938 he gave Chamberlain one of Vansittart's reports from "the usual highly-placed and patriotic German" only because "Van begged me to do so" and only after telling the Prime Minister so.[112] In early 1938, Vansittart argued that Nazi leaders expected Britain to accept German hegemony in Europe, but they also believed their nation faced increasing economic and social strains. Thus, they would act immediately to split Britain from France and dominate Europe and they would do so in central Europe. Shortly thereafter occurred the *Anschluss*. Then, Vansittart concentrated his attention on German intentions toward Czechoslovakia. On 21 March 1938, he reported, several authentic, well-placed and independent sources claimed that, in order to alleviate internal tension and further external ambitions, Hitler would soon attack Czechoslovakia. These were not facts—Hitler had not yet issued orders on that topic—merely predictions: but accurate ones. The German army, Vansittart continued, was in poor shape, and it was, according to "a German of high standing and well known to me", still a moderating influence on German decisions. "As I have often pointed out—and as Goering, the industrialists and the army well know and admit to each other—Germany is in no condition to sustain a protracted war." No one in Berlin knew how Britain would answer German aggression toward Czechoslovakia. Hence, Britain should publicly state that this would not be tolerated. That might shake Hitler or strengthen the army's resistance to his policy. In any case, it would buy time which Britain could use to settle the crisis and prevent Hitler from exploiting it for greater aims.[113]

On these issues, Vansittart stood alone in Whitehall during the spring of 1938. The SIS's reports were less alarming, if less consistent. They indicated that German leaders were not looking for war with Britain or Czechoslovakia, nor using the Sudeten issue for ulterior ends, but were determined to settle that matter on their terms, not necessarily unreasonable ones. Some of them might demand that Germany annexe the Sudetenland, others accept its autonomy within Czechoslovakia; but if negotiations failed, all of them would try to solve the issue by forcing a general crisis which might produce a general war.[114] Whitehall held that Germany wished to settle the Sudetenland rather than use it as a cynical excuse to provoke a crisis, but would adopt force if talk failed and so produce a catastrophe. All decision makers, including Vansittart, believed the Czechoslovak state had oppressed the Sudeten Germans. Chamberlain, the Chiefs of Staff and the Cabinet Committee on Foreign Policy concluded Czechoslovakia was strategically untenable. If war broke out, it would be overrun. It could be restored only through another world war, one Britain might not win; in Chamberlain's view, "we could not help Czechoslovakia—she would simply be a pretext for going to war with Germany. That we could not think of—unless we had a reasonable prospect of being able to beat her to her knees in a reasonable time, and of that I see no sign". Nor did statesmen see catastrophe as foredoomed. "It might be rash to forecast what Germany would do", Chamberlain thought before the *Anschluss*, but seizing all Czechoslovakia would contradict Hitler's racial policies. Hitler, instead, wanted "to dominate Eastern Europe ... [and] ... much the same things for the Sudetendeutsche as we did for the Uitlanders in the Transvaal"—perhaps an unfortunate comparison for a son of Joseph Chamberlain to make. Germans, he thought, "who were bullies by nature are too conscious of their strength and our weakness", but still they could be reasoned with, by British standards of reason, over the Sudetenland and the world. Similarly, Halifax denied that Hitler had "a lust for conquest on a Napoleonic scale", or "when Germany had done this and that and the other in Central Europe, she will in overwhelming might proceed to destroy France and ourselves". Halifax, Chamberlain and Cadogan hoped to pursue a policy of systematic appeasement, settling the Sudetenland crisis alongside other international disputes, and so laying the foundation for peace, stability and a new concert of the powers.[115]

These hopes immediately miscarried—by 21 May 1938 the Cabinet believed Germany was preparing to attack Czechoslovakia and publicly warned it away from such an action. This belief was mistaken and that action counterproductive: it led Hitler to order preparations to attack Czechoslovakia on 1 October 1938, and Whitehall to believe that Hitler would explode if confronted by a second British ultimatum. Ironically, Britain was soft during the real crisis of September precisely because it had been hard during the nonexistent one of May. Vansittart played a minor part in Whitehall's belief and action, but they fit with the intelligence he had provided and his views on policy. So did Whitehall's next move, the attempt to defuse the crisis by convincing Czechoslovak and Sudeten German leaders to establish Home Rule for the Sudetenland. During May–July 1938, Vansittart was central to these negotiations. This was his first step back to significance.

His reports on these negotiations were taken seriously by the Foreign Office and served as a peg on which to hang his general views. He did so in a sustained and virtuoso performance from July to September 1938, throwing forward one statement after another, especially from Henlein, Hohenlohe and Conwell-Evans, men recognized to have access to Nazi leaders. These sources, he emphasized, presented a "rather striking unity" of views, one shared by the SIS. "I have shown this memorandum to our own Intelligence authorities, who agree with me that the odds are still on and not against German military action, in spite of any assurances hitherto received." The little surviving evidence on the SIS's views generally confirms that argument. He and Sinclair provided parallel information on Nazi control of the

Sudeten German movement.[116] Right after Munich, Sinclair analyzed German aims in terms virtually identical to those of Vansittart (Germany sought hegemony over Europe and ultimately the world, while its policy rested on "first and foremost, *force*, or the capacity to use it ... Force always behind German diplomacy") and offered similar solutions.[117] Above all, Vansittart warned, "the Germans are making all necessary preparations for a military coup against Czechoslovakia at any time from the latter part of August onward". Other sources predicted that danger would not arise until September or October, but all concurred that rise it must. Hitler, Vansittart warned, intended to fool Britain, smash Czechoslovakia and then divide and conquer Europe. "Hitler definitely does not intend to allow the duration of any settlement which would preserve the integrity and sovereignty of Czechoslovakia." Henlein and Conwell-Evans agreed that "the aim of the Nazi bosses is to destroy Czechoslovakia and absorb Bohemia and Moravia into the Reich and to bribe Hungary and Poland with the remains".[118]

In July, Halifax, Chamberlain and the Foreign Office considered Vansittart's first reports on these lines alongside others, especially those from the Berlin embassy. The latter agreed that unless the Sudeten problem was settled quickly, a general crisis would arise, but it rejected Vansittart's evidence, analysis and prediction. The Military Attaché, Neil Mason-MacFarlane was "quite unconvinced that the military evidence now at our disposal definitely indicates a clear intention to march this autumn". Nor did the Central Department share Vansittart's interpretation. It concluded that German leaders had decided not to gamble on war in 1938 nor to provoke an immediate crisis. It saw no more proof for the worst view of Hitler's intentions than the best. As William Strang wrote: "We are at the mercy of the Fuhrer's incalculability." George Mounsey saw "plenty of interesting evidence", but thought it "very difficult to draw conclusions in existing circumstances".[119]

This difficulty was soon resolved. On 9 August, Vansittart warned:

> the Germans are going to force the pace, and that very soon; and we are going to be faced immediately with the question whether we are going to prevent them from subjugating all Europe—and we can still do so without a war—or whether we are going to become a second or third-class power.[120]

Almost immediately the crisis erupted, as Vansittart and no one else had predicted. During the Munich crisis his influence slowly began to rise, even though he and his sources advocated a risky policy. In several interviews with Christie and A.P. Young around 8–10 August 1938, Goerdeler reported that Germans and their generals opposed war. Hitler, however, was mad, bad, and bound for war. He was manipulated by the extremists and "believes that France and Britain are bluffing". The generals and industrialists, conversely, might still revolt against the Party: therefore, Britain must issue a statement of resolve to defend Czechoslovakia—in the hope not of deterring Hitler but of sparking civil war. Young concluded that Goerdeler anticipated a revolution by "the reasonable and liberal forces opposed to Hitler", victory and his own elevation to Chancellor. Such arguments from such a source would have carried no weight in Whitehall. Since the Blomberg affair, the Foreign Office and Vansittart had dismissed similar assessments by Goerdeler of the willingness of the generals to resist Hitler. Ultimately, Christie held that Goerdeler's nerve was cracking and discounted his analysis.[121]

The rest of Vansittart's sources offered different analyses alongside similar prescriptions. Christie emphasized that "everything we've foretold step for step is proving absol. true". Several different sources reported "a great and increasing feeling against war amongst the German people". They felt "a catastrophe is pending". The Party leaders, however, believed Britain and France would not fight if Germany invaded Czechosolovakia. Hitler had told his generals—"I know that England will never fight". So, Christie declared, "A declaration to the contrary would rock Berlin to its foundations". The Western Powers must demonstrate their resolve to defend Czechoslovakia through a prolonged war and they must mobilize if German forces did.[122] Failure to do so would produce catastrophe. Bosch reported, "one thing is certain": if Hitler scored yet another triumph

> with bluff and lies over the Western Powers ... the whole opposition that exists today in Germany will collapse. The army will then see in Hitler a supernatural genius who can never fail, and it will follow him blindly anywhere. The conviction, that the weak and senile Western Democracies are ripe for retirement [*reif zum Abtreten*], will impel both the German Government and people to further conquests which will force you [Great Britain and France] to fight or resign yourself to be stripped, for Hitler would then have an entirely different people behind him in the German people than he has today when it would not outlast more than a few weeks of war. He would then have quite different sources of war material, etc. at his disposal. The postponed war would be a long and bloody one, whereas today you could finish Hitler quickly if you would only force yourelves to energetic action and say "Thus far and no further". Surrender on this issue means war without end. Resistance will yet save the Peace.[123]

On 18 August von Kleist-Schmenzin, emissary of the generals, made similar points. So Vansittart told Halifax, he

> said (and this coincides with a great deal of information which I have given you from entirely different sources) that war was now a certainty unless we stopped it. I said "do you mean an extreme

danger?". He answered: "No, I do not mean an extreme danger, I mean a complete certainty". I said "do you mean that the extremists are now carrying Hitler with them?". He said: "No, I do not mean that. There is only one real extremist and that is Hitler himself. He is the great danger and he is doing this entirely on his own. He receives a great deal of encouragement from Herr von Ribbontrop who keeps telling him that when it comes to the showdown neither France nor England will do anything." (You will remember that I gave you the same information from an entirely different source this morning as to Ribbontrop's present attitude and influence.)

Von Kleist-Schmenzin categorically denied that "extremists" or "moderates" mattered. Hitler alone would decide for war or peace. He had set a date for war—28 September. The generals, even Goering, opposed war, but they could not restrain Hitler unless outside powers acted. Only a clear and public warning might convince Hitler that Britain and France would act and make him back down.[124]

Throughout the crisis, Vansittart's arguments within Whitehall followed the general line of his sources, above all of Christie. He scored a triumph of intelligence: he ensured that Whitehall knew the assessments and attitudes of German generals, the positions of senior Nazi leaders and Hitler, and the possibilities of opposition. "Germany intends to realize her ambitions by force if she cannot get the whole of what she wants—which is everything—by other means." The opposition to Hitler was irrelevant to the immediate issue, though it might be a factor if war broke out or if Hitler was defeated in the crisis. "There is practically nothing now to hope from the Army as a brake. That common and relatively comfortable illusion must henceforth be dispelled, at least as regards a short war." "There really is a division in Germany as to the immediate future", but only resolution could force it into the open, bring German public opinion into play against Hitler, strengthen the moderate's nerves and discredit the extremists who demanded an immediate drive on Czechoslovakia. Otherwise, the consequences would be dire. "The present controlling gang", with Hitler "the chief warmonger", cared nothing about the Sudetenland, but victory here would produce "adventure after adventure on the part of the gangsters" who sought "unlimited expansion which will leave Germany as the only first-class power in Europe and perhaps in the world". Vansittart also abandoned the argument that had underlain his views of the past two years, that Hitler was bluffing. He described Hitler's views as incalculable—*unberechenbar* (quoting Beck, without naming him). He told Warren Fisher and Halifax in almost identical language that the *Fuhrer* intended to invade Czechoslovakia: "Only the strongest and clearest action on our part can prevent the catastrophe. Hitler ... has come down on the side of the extremists but he is not too balmy to be scared back over the fence if we have the nerve to do it." Only a public and unambiguous statement of intent could avoid that danger. "If we leave Berlin under any illusion as to where we should stand in the event of a European war, there shall be a European war." He informed Hugh Dalton that the "war party" in Germany, "of which, in fact, Hitler is the head", did not believe Britain would act over Czechoslovakia. If Hitler was not stopped, the "moderate party" in Germany, already weakened, "would simply disappear". Again, Vansittart told Halifax, "Hitler has made up his mind as to 75 per cent. on violent action, and ... nothing but plain speaking on our part will prevent the other 25 per cent. from filling itself in automatically." Vansittart's "plain speaking" involved a public declaration that Britain would resist German aggression against Czechoslovakia but would pursue a "Home Rule" policy for the Sudeten Germans. Publicity for these policies would show that Britain was just and dangerous and thus mobilize against Hitler his own public opinion. It would maintain Britain's status as a great power. It might also cause a world war.[125]

Prognosis was the strength of the anti-appeasers, not prescription. They knew Hitler's aims, the appeasers did not; they were superior in clarity and resolution, less so in policy. By this time, no policy Whitehall could have accepted would have appeased Hitler. Even those who sought to do so enraged him—Chamberlain's piece of paper wrecked his policy. The appeasers' means could not achieve their ends, and must produce deadly unintended consequences—they knew that would happen if their assessments were inaccurate. Arguably, the same was true of the anti-appeasers. Had the line of Churchill or Vansittart prevailed in September 1938, Hitler might well have called Britain's bluff, and forced it into war or humiliation, as he did in August 1939. This outcome was likely. During most of the Munich crisis Hitler willed victory or war. He did not think he was bluffing. Ultimately, he did not act on these intentions. He did back down when confronted with a choice between war, or a victory of substance without a triumph of prestige. This last minute loss of nerve stemmed from the actions of Mussolini, but even more those of Chamberlain, who did save peace that time. Yet had the line of the anti-appeasers been followed, had Hitler been confronted from the start with a choice between war or diplomatic defeat, he might have chosen war; probably he would have done so. Then, Britain would have waited for war and the turn of the wild card of the *widerstand*. Had Britain and Hitler triggered a coup in Berlin, events might have gone rather better than they did; but the odds of that outcome seem small.[126] Britain would not clearly have done better by going to war in September 1938 rather than a year later, the only major advantage being the remote possibility of a *coup*. One can scarcely blame Whitehall for doubting the weight of that factor, especially since men could not believe their only choices were war now or later, rather than war or not.

The anti-appeasers understood the risks of their policy and were ready to meet it; their willingness to risk war, to provoke it, was an admirable thing, and a terrible one. By aesthetic and strategic judgments delivered in hindsight, they stand justified—better to see than be gulled; if war must come, face it like a man; stand rather than submit. Vansittart advocated a policy which he knew could produce only victory or war; so too Churchill advised the Czech ambassador in London, Jan Masyrk. These men were war mongers; they were right. Yet denied hindsight, contemporaries might well ask, why fight great wars for small issues? Or take major risks over minor differences in policy? Everyone wanted Czechoslovakia to offer massive internal concessions to the Sudeten Germans, no one to bow to German bullying, none believed specifically British interests were at stake. Geoffrey Dawson, editor of *The Times*, thus justified a fabled moment of Munich, his newspaper's advocacy on 7 September that Germany receive the Sudetenland through plebiscite: "I feel more and more that it is important to cut the ground out from under Hitler's feet by reiterating that the whole situation is fluid and that any permanent solution will be considered—except indeed force or the threat of force."[127] To multiply these problems, Britons argued less about issues of interest than of morality. Warren Fisher and Halifax began to break from appeasement in September 1938, when they concluded that Hitler was lying to Britain and making it responsible for bad treatment to Czechoslovakia. Decision makers saw the crisis through a kaleidoscope, in which issues turned suddenly and without warning from nightmare to farce, when world war might be provoked by the wording of a remonstrance to Germany which Hitler might never even read.

The Munich crisis marked the peak of Vansittart's success as intelligence analyst. His facts were accurate, his reading excellent and his policy Britain's only option other than surrender. All this is a useful mirror for British decisions, so long as one remembers the flaws in the glass. Vansittart believed Germany intended to destroy Czechoslovakia and use the crisis to achieve mastery in Europe; he wished to block these aims through a public commitment which might be taken for bluff or force Britain into war. His assessment was correct; his policy is a might-have-been. It might have deterred war and won the crisis and even solved the problem of Hitler. It might also not have done so and, had this policy failed, it would have forced Britain into war or humiliation—the trap of August 1939. Hitler was a problem without simple solution, except the one Vansittart had urged so long, the creation of more British power. Chamberlain's advisor, Horace Wilson, claimed Hitler "was *not* in ignorance of the risk that invasion of Czechoslovakia might well involve a war of nations; that, on the contrary, he had weighed the risk and was, if necessary, prepared to face it".[128] Chamberlain was not entirely wrong to tell the Cabinet

> No State, certainly no democratic State, ought to make a threat of war unless it was both ready to carry it out and prepared to do so ... Herr Hitler was withdrawn from his Ministers and lived in a

state of exaltation. He might well take the view that the statement was bluff. If he did we should then have to choose between being shown up as bluffers and going to war.[129]

Vansittart's policy rested on calculations about Hitler's psychology and German opinion which were uncertain then and now. He ignored those material factors which would rule if a gamble failed; and these were not favourable. They pointed toward a prolonged and costly war with no certainty of success. The MID held that "Germany has created a situation enabling her to undertake at will a sudden and overwhelming concentration against Czechoslovakia, and to view with growing equanimity the outcome of an attack delivered against her from the West".[130] Few decision makers anywhere would like such a policy and such odds, certainly not the cautious liberal materialists of Whitehall. They held that a general war would have deadly consequences and yet might be unnecessary. They feared that any action which might stop Hitler from flirting with war easily might goad an undecided *Fuhrer* toward it. They were uncertain about the extent of Hitler's ambitions, despite Vansittart's categorical reports. Their real concern was not capabilities, but intentions. Nor did decision makers see Czechoslovakia as a vital interest, except insofar as the crisis had linked it to British prestige. Many of them did wish to signal that Britain would not be ignored in this issue; all agreed that this would be difficult. Such a signal could not easily be sent through normal channels, because Henderson might not deliver it, nor Ribbontrop pass it on, nor Hitler understand it—or be able to do so. Halifax and Chamberlain both thought that the *Fuhrer* might be mad. By 12 September the Foreign Secretary told the Cabinet that any public warning might drive Hitler "over the edge".[131] If so, Britain would have no choice except surrender or a high risk of war.

Under these circumstances, manufactured by Hitler and itself, the central issue for Whitehall became the *Fuhrer*'s immediate and ultimate intentions. Would he go to war unless he received his demands about the Sudetenland? Would those be his last demands? Did he want a general war or general hegemony? Did he know what he wanted? These questions were not posed by cowards. Precisely the men of Munich took a firm line with Hitler in 1939. Between 1935 and 1939 they played a weak hand against Japan with resolution, because it threatened concrete British interests. During the Munich crisis, however, these men were cautious and uncertain. So many issues were involved that they did not realize what the issue was until after the fact. They thought their hand was weak. They feared another world war would wreck British power and Western civilization. They refused to risk a general war for a secondary interest and they were not sure Hitler would threaten vital ones unless they forced him to do so by blocking his aims over a minor issue. As Chamberlain told Joseph Kennedy, "we ought not to accept the view that war is inevitable, at any rate until we have exhausted every effort to prevent it by the exercise of influence, moderation, etc".[132] To these decision makers, the least risky bet seemed the assumption that Hitler was not and did not want to be a threat to Britain. Hitler had thrust the burden of uncertainty onto them and stolen their courage in exchange—over Czechoslovakia.

For diplomacy as for war, Carl von Clausewitz's words ring true: "Timidity is the root of prudence in most men"; "Given the same amount of intelligence, timidity will do a thousand times more damage in war than audacity." This was true of Whitehall during the Munich crisis. Strang emphasized the need "not to play the game of bluff too high", Chamberlain, that the whole essence of British strategic policy was "you should never menace unless you are in a position to carry out your threats". After the crisis, Cadogan wrote, "Herr Hitler is said to have succeeded in bringing off a bluff. This is not entirely true. It is not, in poker parlance, a bluff to bid high on four aces, which he held in his hand", while Wilson rejected a policy which must "mean either that if the bluff was called we should at once be involved in war, or else that we should have to confess that it was bluff and withdraw our bold words with the maximum of ignominy".[133] These men let Hitler bully and bluff without responding in kind. So strong were their hopes and fears that no warning could convince them of Hitler's intentions, only his actions; intelligence could not help them until experience had done so; and then the issue of what lessons they would learn remained unclear.

Vansittart's position was extreme but he knew his mind. Hence he, with Henderson, became one of Whitehall's poles of reference on the central issues at hand: Hitler's intentions, how British actions could affect them, whether Britain dared bluff or run the risk of war or warn Hitler from aggression. Given the ambiguities of appeasement, Vansittart and Henderson did better in wrecking each other's cases than in proving their own. Instead, each made predictions, to be taken on faith at the time, and proven after the fact; and their cases were considered. Leading figures read Vansittart's reports alongside those from MI5, the Berlin embassy and the SIS.[134] All of this material had some similarities because all of these bodies tapped the same veins of rumour and some of their sources overlapped. Thus, during the crisis Mason-MacFarlane became Vansittartian. Neither "Germany as a whole" nor "the Army High Command" wanted war. Elements in the party, however, including Hitler, were willing to run that risk and the army, unready for war or revolution, would obey Hitler's orders. Still, Mason-McFarlane held, a resolute stand by Britain and France might force Hitler to back down, perhaps wrecking his regime. Even Henderson agreed that a "forward party numerically weak but influentially strong" wanted war, while that idea "frightened" the people and their army. Henderson, however, differed from Vansittart over Hitler's intentions and the consequences of a warning to him. Until early September, Henderson held that Hitler did not want to fight Britain and would back down before an ultimatum—but at a price. This would make a later war between Britain and Germany inevitable; but if Britain met Hitler's Sudeten aims, a lasting rapprochement was on the cards. As the crisis rose, Henderson changed his views, and unintentionally addressed another of Vansittart's arguments, that Hitler was not "too balmy" to be deterred. Instead, Henderson argued, Hitler "driven by megalomania inspired by military force which he has built up, etc. ... may have crossed the border-line of sanity" and would fight unless he received his demands. A madman could not be deterred; Czechoslovakia was not a British interest; thus Henderson denounced any attempt to warn Hitler or to take any risk for Czechoslovakia.[135]

Although many of Vansittart's minutes were simply "entered for record", and conceivably never seen by Cadogan or Halifax, others were considered in detail and frequently discussed. Halifax met Christie on 10 August, when the latter's sources first reported crisis as imminent. On 6 and 7 September Theodor Kordt, who was attached to the German embassy in London, briefed Halifax, Cadogan and Wilson. Initially, the Foreign Secretary and his PUS viewed this material with some suspicion. On 5 August 1938 Halifax wrote:

> I sometimes wonder whether it can be true that the Germans are the only people in Europe today who are not afraid, and whether they on their side may not be getting reports from their secret sources (just as we are from ours on the other side!) suggesting that the democracies are going to have a preventative war, etc., etc., and that they must prepare for it. I am constantly struck by the recurrence of reports of troop movements in this or that place, which when investigated turn out baseless. But it suggests that there is much mischief making about, and that nerves are strained.[136]

Cadogan later recorded: "There's certainly enough in the Secret Reports to make one's hair stand on end. But I never quite swallow all these things, and I am presented with a selection". "I don't think I'm very impressed by it on the whole."[137] Yet Vansittart's labour was not in vain; he lit the slow fuse for an explosion. During the crisis—because of it—the Central Department came to share his views on issues such as mistrust of Nevile Henderson, the idea that Germany controlled the Sudeten movement and was using it to exacerbate the crisis, and the need to warn Hitler from aggression.[138] Vansittart influenced bureaucrats; and he stretched the rubber soul of the Foreign Secretary toward resolution.

Vansittart used intelligence not as a light but as a sabre. He aimed to turn men's minds, especially that of one man. Detailed examination is needed to comprehend this process. The evidence about Halifax's position between 10 August and 25 September is problematical. He expressed different views to the Cabinet and a well-informed figure, the American ambassador, possibly because he used Joseph Kennedy as a sounding board for his own fears, presumably because he wished to manipulate American attitudes, certainly because his attitudes changed daily. Halifax did not express his thoughts fully to anyone. He aimed to leave his colleagues guessing until he had made up his own mind, and he rejected few ideas. On 7 September, after a lunch with Halifax, Geoffrey Dawson reported the Foreign Secretary as saying his office disliked a leading article which hinted at a dismemberment of Czechoslovakia but "he did not seem to dissent from it himself"; in fact, all other evidence indicates that Halifax would have deplored this proposal.[139] When the full evidence on his views is assessed in a chronological fashion, Halifax clearly had no settled mind, and occasionally veered from one extreme to another from one day to the next. None the less, the general trend is clear: he moved increasingly toward a firm and untrusting line. The latter became the key which turned Whitehall from Munich to war.

By 5 August Halifax agreed "there is a good deal of evidence to show that a party at least" was "planning the worst" but still he doubted Germany would risk "a general war". There was "a strong element of bluff" in German policy—"therefore we on our side should hesitate to bluff, and still less to take military action against them". On 10 August Halifax wavered between Vansittart and Wilson about whether Britain should respond to Germany's mobilization with a clear warning, before settling on safety's side.[140] By 21 August Halifax told Chamberlain "this German stuff may not be true but …there is enough in it to warrant our doing what we can … to keep Hitler guessing: & strengthen the hands of the generals", so long as Britain avoided "a false position", either of drifting to an undesired commitment or of having "too big a bluff called".[141] By 30 August, Halifax had moved some distance back toward Vansittart's views, though not all of the way. He told Kennedy that Hitler's approach was not "all bluff. [Halifax] thinks that Hitler hopes to get everything he wants without fighting and that by taking advantage of the situation as he thinks he sees it, it might be as good a time as any to march". In Halifax's view, Hitler intended to settle the issue "by force if necessary" and he must be warned off before he committed himself publicly to an extremist position.[142] These were precisely the points which Vansittart and no one else had made to the Foreign Secretary. Almost immediately, Halifax moved away from this idea, only to fall back on it, as his policy wavered between appeasement and resistance from day to day.[143]

On 30 August, again, Halifax gave the Cabinet an analysis he retained for several weeks. Two views could be taken of "the position as a whole". "One view—and there was a great deal of evidence in support of it—much of it from good sources—was that Herr Hitler, against the advice of the Army and of the moderate party, was determined to intervene by force", because he thought only this means could achieve his ends and "he wanted a spectacular success for internal reasons". The other view was that Hitler intended to answer the Sudetenland question in 1938, was preparing all means to do so, "in a mixture of bluff and reliance on force", but "he had not yet made up his mind to use force for this purpose". The latter view, Halifax noted, was Henderson's; the former, and the great and good evidence for it, though the Foreign Secretary did not say so explicitly, came from Vansittart. Halifax thought "the conflict of evidence was such that it was impossible to say which view was correct", nor could the problem easily be solved. The "only deterrent which was likely to be effective would be an announcement that if Germany invaded Czechoslovakia we should declare war upon her. He thought that this might well prove an effective deterrent". Unfortunately, it would split British and Dominion opinion and perhaps drive the *Fuhrer* into a general war he might not otherwise start. Hence, Britain should simply try to bridge the gap between Sudeten and Czechoslovak leaders, and "to keep Germany guessing as to our intention".[144]

Halifax, it seems, regarded Vansittart's evidence and policy as plausible and listened to his views, but would not act on them. Again, by 10 September, Kennedy reported, Halifax and Cadogan stated that their

> secret information is that Hitler is prepared to march ... They are advised by their confidential sources that Hitler cannot stand out very long; that the generals are a little bit disturbed at the regime. Their secret advises are that Hitler has reached his decision and that he has made up his mind this is as good a time as any to strike. Halifax and Cadogan think their advices are more than likely correct.[145]

These comments echo Vansittart's analysis and show its double-edge. Cadogan and Halifax moved toward his views of Hitler's intentions but not his policy, because they were convinced of the dangers of war and of British weakness. Whatever influence Vansittart had over their thinking pressed them as much away from his proposals as toward them—in the short term. None the less, so Halifax claimed later, on 11 September he took the action which on 30 August he had told the Cabinet involved high risk and high returns. He had the Foreign Office press spokesman state that if Germany attacked Czechoslovakia, France and Britain would enter the war. Then, on 12 September, Halifax told the Cabinet that

> Hitler was possibly or even probably mad. He might have taken a definite decision to attack Czechoslovakia *coute que coute*. This view of the position ... was supported by a good deal of information from responsible quarters, conveyed to us at some risk ... If Herr Hitler had made up his mind to attack, it was possible that nothing which we could do would stop him.

Halifax now regarded the claim that "Hitler could be stopped by a direct ultimatum" as "at the best a very doubtful view". As proof of Hitler's irrationality and extremism, and of the ease by which they might be detonated, Halifax cited a "responsible person who had just returned from Germany", Conwell-Evans—he might equally have quoted Christie. "Any serious prospect of getting Herr Hitler back to a sane outlook would probably be irretrievably destroyed by any action on our part which would involve him in a public humiliation. This view of the situation was supported by all those who were in a position to judge the facts." If Hitler "has not definitely made up his mind" to attack Czechoslovakia, an ultimatum would make him do so. Bluff was dangerous while "to say without qualification that we were prepared to go to war to defend Czechoslovakia would, in fact, put the decision of peace or war in the hands of other than ourselves".[146]

In any case, Vansittart had no influence on the greatest decision maker of them all, the Prime Minister. As the French ambassador noted, Chamberlain was "accustomed, particularly because of his time at the Exchequer, to think about exact problems, he is tempted to reduce international matters to the simplest possible formulas and he thinks that, in this area, there is no problem which cannot find a solution".[147] Chamberlain, Henderson and Horace Wilson formed a school apart from other decision makers, opposing the idea of any warning to Hitler, almost treating the issue as though it would not affect Britain's prestige and power, convinced Hitler had reasonable and limited aims and one great act of trust and reasonability by Britain could transform European politics entirely. To Vansittart's use of the 1914 analogy, Wilson retorted,

> surely the difference is that we were in a position to enforce our threat, if one had been made. And it is arguable that it was reprehensible not to have taken advantage of our state of preparedness.
>
> Today we know (with Chiefs of Staff reported advice) that neither we nor the French are in a position to enforce the threat.[148]

After the crisis, Wilson argued, if a

> transfer of territory is justified and required ... you cannot refuse the adjustment because of the threatening or brutal attitude of one side. As between individuals a man may well say to another that, though he agrees he ought to give something or to hand something over, he won't do so if the other man blusters or snatches. But can you say that as between nations where the lives and fortunes of millions of people are at stake?[149]

Chamberlain and his entourage paid attention to intelligence, but not to Vansittart's interpretation. Again, by 30 August, Chamberlain believed that

Hitler, isolated and in exaltation at Berchtesgarden, received only that news which suited "the group that want to go to war". He told Kennedy "Hitler has made up his mind to take Czechoslovakia peacefully if possible but with arms if necessary" and accepted Henderson's view that "no more speeches should be made because instead of giving courage to the moderates to fight against a war in Germany, it was having the opposite effect and was urging them to get into it". Britain was in no "position to stop Hitler (there is, for example, the question of the position in the air, the weakness of France, etc.) and, in the circumstances it would be unwise to utter threats".[150] Chamberlain never wavered from his course during the crisis, nor from his guides, Henderson and Wilson, and he made British policy. Munich was Chamberlain's hour. Ministers and officials resented Hitler's efforts to wreck British prestige. His Cabinet, hand picked for servility, wavered for war. Had Chamberlain not preempted events by finding a simple solution to many problems, they would have drifted to war. He saved the peace.

These events affected Vansittart's position in complex ways. During the crisis he was in contact with elements in Parliament which sought to destroy the Prime Minister and his policy, which were working closely with the Czech government. Soon he was suspected of being central to these intrigues. After seeing an account of Vansittart's exploits and a photograph of his "grinning mug" in the *Daily Mail*, Cadogan wrote: "How does he manage to advertise himself so blatantly?" The Chief Diplomatic Advisor's political activities concerned Cadogan, Hankey and Eric Phipps, ambassador to France, Vansittart's brother-in-law and his enemy. On 28 September, Phipps warned Chamberlain that the Czech ambassadors in London and Paris were "carrying on a regular campaign against yourself and the French Government and working in with all the forces in favour of a 'preventative war'. Later, Phipps told Hankey that Vansittart "is almost certainly in touch with Churchill, Eden, the Labour leaders" and Alexis Leger in the Quai d'Orsai. After the crisis Hankey and Phipps both warned Horace Wilson of Vansittart's political threat. Hankey noted, "V dangerous because controls all the instruments of propaganda". Chamberlain appears to have monitored Vansittart's links with Dalton and Churchill during the crisis, and perhaps read intercepts of telephone calls by Czech diplomats, provided by Germany. Some of these fears, perhaps, stemmed from one odd event in which Vansittart may not even have been involved. On 11 September, one of his protégés, Rex Leeper, head of the Foreign Office's News Department, informed the press that if Czechoslovakia were attacked, France would aid it and would then be joined by Britain and the USSR. Vansittart wanted Britain to issue such a declaration, but after the war Halifax stated that he had prompted it in order to warn Hitler that British patience had limits.[151] Though firm and final evidence is lacking, some of the suspicions of Vansittart were merited. He freed Young to distribute his own account of Goerdeler's views to anyone he pleased: "You are one of the few people who know the truth, you are a British subject. It is your stuff. You can do what you like with it." Young immediately sent his report to Eden, Wilson, two left-leaning newspapers, the *Daily Herald* and the *News Chronicle* (which repeated the fact to the Foreign Office), and to several leading American officials. Vansittart told Young that he favoured the dissemination of Goerdeler's views in the United States. Young wondered whether Vansittart had inspired one leading article in the *News Chronicle*.[152]

Vansittart was more suspect than ever in the eyes of Chamberlain, Wilson and Cadogan but he had also moved closer to the centre of decision making than he had been since 1935. His arguments were known to the main decision makers and remembered by them, above all, by Halifax. He is a man easy to mock, but no Western statesman since 1945 has ever had to face problems so dire as he did in 1938–1940. His record is honourable and his learning curve steep—alas, it started low. In the spring of 1938 the Foreign Secretary had not known quite what to do with diplomacy or his Chief Diplomatic Advisor. Then and later, his chief advisor really was Cadogan. Halifax rejected Vansittart's views but read the latter's papers. By the summer Halifax paid increasing attention to them and slowly became his own man—a wobbly man. This shaped the Chief Diplomatic Advisor's calculations. Throughout the Munich crisis he aimed his arguments not at Whitehall or even the Foreign Office, but at Halifax. His influence on his master was more straightforward than with many others, tired of his views or unwilling to concede that he had won an argument with them. Thus, striving to follow Lord Grey's example from the 1905 crisis, the Foreign Secretary was the great exponent of "keeping the Germans guessing". Vansittart retorted: it "is the policy that obtained in 1914. We did keep the Germans guessing, and they ended by guessing wrong, and war followed". Again, Halifax sought to keep the French guessing, When the French ambassador held that Germany's aim in the crisis was not justice for the Sudetenland but hegemony in Europe, and France's "turn would come next. I said that this really was an argument in favour of a certain war now, against the possibility of war, perhaps in more unfavourable conditions, later. With that argument I had never been able to feel any sympathy; nor did I think the conclusion of it could be justified". Vansittart warned this attitude would push the French to defeatism, for which they would blame Britain. That outcome happened almost immediately.[153] He bombarded the Foreign Secretary daily in an attritional struggle for influence, and with effect. Much to Cadogan's irritation, Halifax insisted that Vansittart attend the ministerial conferences on the crisis.[154] The Foreign Secretary circulated several of Vansittart and Christie's reports to Chamberlain and had the Chief Diplomatic Advisor comment on letters from Henderson which were given to the Prime Minister.[155] Halifax wanted the inner Cabinet to test its views and Henderson's against Vansittart's criticism; and it shaped his choice between the two views "of the position as a whole".

By 25 September, after Chamberlain's second meeting with Hitler, and the first crystal-clear proof that Hitler did not mean what he said, Halifax began his break with Chamberlain. He told the Cabinet he "had found his opinion changing somewhat in last day or two, and even now he was not too certain of his view". The issue "turned on Herr Hitler's future intentions" and on Chamberlain's hopes for rapprochement, but "he could not rid his mind of the fact that Herr Hitler had given us nothing and that he was dictating terms, just as though he had won a war without having had to fight". While Halifax "did not altogether share" the view of his colleague, Duff Cooper, "as to the "March to the East", he none the less felt some uncertainty about the ultimate aim which he [Lord Halifax] wished to see accomplished, namely, the destruction of Nazi-ism. So long as Nazi-ism lasted, peace would be uncertain. For this reason he did not feel that it would be right to put pressure on Czechoslovakia to accept. "We should lay the case before them. If they rejected it he imagined that France would join in, and if France went in we should join with them." And, Halifax wondered, if Hitler "was driven to war the result might be to help bring down the Nazi regime?"[156] These views were not simply the product of Vansittart's influence. Churchill and Duff Cooper expressed similar ideas, while much of what Halifax said after his conversion on the road to Munich referred to morality—"We could not press the Czechoslovakian Government to do what we believed to be wrong."[157] When Chamberlain complained of this "horrible blow to me" and threatened resignation should Britain be dragged into war, the Foreign Secretary replied, "I feel a brute—but I lay awake most of the night tormenting myself & did not feel I could reach any other conclusion on this point of coercing Czechoslovakia".[158] Nor did the conversion have great effect during the crisis. Before and after his break with Chamberlain, Halifax let the Prime Minister do his running. This influence would soon, however, bear fruit—poisoned or otherwise.

A private rebuke from Cadogan was the spark for Halifax's greatest wobble toward resolution, on 24/25 September, but Vansittart caused others. At the time Chamberlain and the Minister for the Coordination of Defence, Thomas Inskip, credited some of Halifax's actions to "R.V.'s influence", while Joseph Kennedy told the State Department, "I judge that Vansittart is back more or less in favor here and is being consulted a great deal on moves that are being made". In 1941 Horace Wilson condemned Vansittart for "his usual overbearing vehemence", for being an "obstructive critic" and for influence on Halifax. Without his own intervention, Wilson thought, the Chief Diplomatic Advisor would have "negatived" Chamberlain's policy during the Munich crisis, "though not by anything that Germany or Italy might do". In mid-September, "when it seemed war would be upon us", Wilson recalled, "I thought it would be hard not to place upon him a good deal of the responsibility for it."[159] Vansittart's wife later informed Dalton that while Cadogan was jealous of the Chief Diplomatic Advisor, Halifax "is friendly to him and can be influenced a great deal, but he is subject to the Inner Cabinet, which contains some bad men". "All very womanly!", Dalton commented, but even distaff influence was more than Vansittart had known for years.[160]

Nor was this alone turning in his favour. Immediately and increasingly after Munich, British statesmen and officials became ashamed of their actions, themselves. Now the issues were settled, they knew what these were. They had known Germany could threaten Britain; now they believed Hitler would do so. Munich had bought not peace, just time. Hitler was a bad man. He had made them do bad things, and from fear. After hearing Chamberlain's account of his first meeting with Hitler, even Inskip noted: "It was plain that H. had made all the running: he had in fact blackmailed the P.M."[161] Meanwhile, Hitler's wrongs seemed to prove Vansittart right. During the summer and autumn of 1938, he made specific predictions: Germany would provoke a crisis in August, would prepare to pursue it through force if necessary, would annexe all of Czechoslovakia, and its relations with Britain would worsen after the Sudeten issue was settled. Soon, these predictions all came true. The reputation of his past prophecies strengthened the credibility of his present ones, and of his incessant refrain that rearmament and resolution alone could prevent Germany from mastering Europe. As Cadogan wrote on 15 March 1939, following the annexation of Bohemia and Moravia: "I must say it is turning out—at present—as Van predicted and as I never believed it would. If we want to stem the German expansion, I believe we must try to build a dam *now*."[162]

Between October 1938 and March 1939, Vansittart found new credibility within the Foreign Office, precisely as the accuracy of his reports fell off, as various Germans pumped much disinformation into his system, which Vansittart did not realize was such. Probably this stemmed from the disruptions caused by Christie's reconstruction of his network. Christie felt the need to caution his consumers that he was treating his new sources with caution. He told Vansittart he "will always discriminate between absolutely reliable facts obtained first hand, and other reports which come second hand, though of course from usually quite trustworthy sources". Again, when his sources indicated Germany would settle its score with Britain and France before turning east, he noted:

> I would like Hali [*sic*] to know that a good part of this & the previous memorandum came from me & my friends, otherwise he will gather from past reports of mine which spoke of "main concentration Eastward" that I have been fooled. We always knew Hitler to be incalculable, but we have given some good reasons in previous reports why he has for the time being changed his mind.[163]

Slowly, haltingly, Cadogan and Halifax began to view Germany in Vansittart's terms. As he had done years before, they used intelligence to read the augurs; less well. They came to play in his strong suit, to see the game in his terms and to adopt a version of his policy. In the process, they turned Britain off the path to Munich and down the road to war. Judgments on the causation of this process must be cautious. In describing only one cause in a over-determined process, one must overstate its significance. Many things pushed in the same direction and toward the same target—the views of the Foreign Office and its uncertain master. Vansittart was not the only cause at hand. A closely related one, the effect of SIS reports, is uncertain. Events might have moved the same way had Vansittart died in January 1938. He was, however, necessary to the specific form which this process took in the world as it was.

A surfeit of causes can be found, nor is it easy to determine the main point, their effect on Halifax. Even in the days of high appeasement, he believed Britain must never lose its own status as a great power, never let Germany defeat France and master Europe, never tolerate Nazi misbehaviour or behave badly itself: "The Anschluss", for example, "or rather the methods by which it was brought about, shocked this country profoundly ... Such methods will always have such an effect here and will always be likely to block attempts to bring the two countries together."[164] During the Munich crisis, Cadogan, Halifax and their subordinates lost much of their optimism about Germany, and acquired some of the pessimism associated with Vansittart. They believed they had behaved badly.[165] They accepted concepts and favoured policies similar to those of Vansittart, but not consistently, because they did not share his certainty that Hitler intended to master Europe. They still hoped, in Halifax's words, that "when Germany had done this and that and the other in Central Europe", it would not "proceed to destroy France and ourselves".

Until November 1938 most of the Foreign Office remained willing to work on this assumption and the Munich accords. Cadogan held that one further and final act of appeasement would solve the problem. These men were willing to give Hitler a chance to prove he had achieved all of his territorial aims, though they also believed one more aggressive act would demonstrate German bad faith, the failure of high appeasement, and they all insisted on rapid rearmament. Chamberlain, in a state almost of megalomania, believed appeasement was approaching its apotheosis: however, Wilson and Henderson warned, additional rearmament or public expression of mistrust of Hitler would produce an "inevitable result ... to force the Germans to do what they have not hitherto done—prepare plans for war with this country".[166] They were correct on these points, but few shared these views. Vansittart, MI5, and to varying degrees SIS and a few Foreign Office officials, retorted that Munich had been a disaster and Hitler would strike again.[167] Halifax shared the opinion of the majority of his officials, but less optimistically than Cadogan, and with his views permanently advanced from those of August. He accepted the fact of German "predominance" in central Europe. He expected Germany to consolidate its strength there, perhaps even to drive on Ukraine. He was willing to give peace a chance but demanded that Britain and France ensure "their predominant position" in western and southern Europe and hasten their rearmament. This was the "great lesson" of Munich—"It would be fatal to us to be caught again with insufficient strength."[168] Although he did not realize it, this policy would steer Britain straight to war. One of the forces pressing toward conflict after Munich was the contradictions in the lessons each side thought it had learned: both concluded that they should not bow to threats, while the other would bend under pressure. Halifax's policy would anger Hitler, who would reciprocate with threats to Britain—at a time many sources would carry such information to Britain and Whitehall was finally ready to see threats as threats.

This was especially true of Halifax. Even in late October, a third-hand and uncertain report that Hitler was considering the abrogation of the Anglo-German Naval Agreement concerned him. Such an action, Halifax held, would prove a German menace to Britain—and precisely that agreement did collapse between November 1938 and January 1939.[169] Meanwhile an avalanche of reports from a host of sources signalled danger, including the possibility of direct German attacks on Britain or on western Europe, an area inextricably linked to British security. What Sinclair termed "alarmist rumours put forward by Jews and Bolshevists" in France for their own ends indicated Italian mobilization against the Western powers.[170] Most significantly, solutions of Japanese diplomatic traffic showed that Ribbontrop, for the first time, was trying to make the Anti-Comintern Pact a military alliance and to direct it against Britain; he also told the Japanese ambassador to Germany that that was Hitler's wish.[171] This, the great case in which code-breaking shaped policy toward appeasement during late 1938, reinforced the credibility of Christie's sources, which twice had reported that German and Japanese strategic relations were becoming dangerously close.[172] Public statements by Hitler and other Nazis indicated hostility to Britain. When Henderson returned to Britain for medical reasons, the Berlin embassy reported alarming news.[173] Soon Henderson's reputation collapsed, shaping the lessons statesmen derived from Munich and eliminating the main source of information which could sustain high appeasement. Other sources, including Goerdeler, warned diplomats, the SIS and the Vansittart–Christie network of German hostility and of possible attacks on London.[174] Though these reports often did reflect statements made by Hitler and Ribbentrop to their subordinates, many of them were inaccurate; some were disinformation spread by German reactionaries and Nazi officials and possibly Czechoslovak intelligence; all shook the Foreign Office to the core.[175]

By the last weeks of 1938 even Cadogan came to fear German threats and "stoked [Halifax] up about secret reports we have had all tending to show Hitler, Rib and Co., are *'exaltes'* ".[176] Uncertainty and rivalry with

95

Vansittart shaped Cadogan's attitude, but these reports did progressively change his views of Hitler's intentions and British policy. It is difficult to compute precisely how any one of these reports affected the Foreign Secretary, assessing intelligence on his knees, with God his co-pilot, and such computation is beside the point. The whole was greater than its parts. What most affected Halifax were four general facts: that some of the intelligence obviously was true; that so many sources agreed so closely about German threats to vital British interests; that reports of menace constantly came in; and that all this fit the most dire warnings from the Munich crisis and afterward—Vansittart's predictions. As Halifax told the Cabinet Committee on Foreign Policy in January 1939,

> Readers of the Papers which he had circulated might perhaps feel that he had served up to them a collection of rumours without first passing them through a sieve ... While it was impossible for him to vouch for the truth and accuracy of every fact and statement contained in these documents, it should be noted that the information in them came from a number of different sources which were the same sources from which we had received information in the summer and early autumn of last year which had so unhappily proved, on the whole, accurate and correct. In these circumstances he did not think that it would be right to neglect this information and the warnings embodied in it ... while it was derived from many different well tested sources it showed on the whole considerable unanimity.

These reports "might represent an element of bluff and have been deliberately put about by the German authorities with a view to creating alarm in the minds of foreign nations". Still, however "fantastic" they might seem, several sources shared the "consensus of opinion".[177]

Between November 1938 and April 1939, this material affected British policy in a complex way. Much of it was never entirely trusted—much of it should not have been. As Cadogan noted in February 1939: "Our sources of infn. have lately become so prolific (and blood-curdling) that I am beginning to regard them with a degree of suspicion". Yet, it was widely used. When in January 1939 Halifax asked how far "the various prophecies made in our secret sources" tallied with Hitler's speech at the Reichstag on 30 January, it proved that "nearly all our recent red papers are in action and cannot be recovered".[178] This intelligence did not establish certainty in British minds. It did budge the balance of uncertainty. It did lead Whitehall to conclude the surest bet was to assume Hitler might be a threat, rather than not. In late January 1939, for example, and for the first time in months, Vansittart attended the Cabinet Committee on Foreign Policy. In the high water mark of his tenure as Chief Diplomatic Advisor he dominated the meeting and two strong supporters of

Chamberlain, as Horace Wilson helplessly stood by. The Home Secretary, Samuel Hoare, held that for purposes of discussion the committee should accept as true Vansittart's information that Germany was contemplating an invasion of the Netherlands. Privately, Inskip noted Vansittart's information "cannot be other than reports of 3rd hand conversations between Hitler & Ribbontrop". Still, he took it seriously.[179] Thus, the Cabinet made its first break with high appeasement—it decided a German attack on the Netherlands was possible and would be a *casus belli*. The reports on this topic were erroneous, as were others. Right or wrong, over coming months all this intelligence drove the Foreign Office, Halifax and some other ministers away from Chamberlain's policy and toward a tougher line. Ultimately, this produced confusion in policy, it led Britain to act on the basis of inaccurate intelligence and disinformation; it led Britain down the road to war.

This was Vansittart's triumph. He was central to this process, though his significance varied from week to week. In October his views were noted but not believed. By December Cadogan and Halifax valued his opinion. In January Whitehall acted on the assumption his most alarmist material might be true; in February the Foreign Office ignored him. Jebb, the Foreign Office official in charge of handling intelligence, thought "the recent absence of alarmist reports from all our secret sources" indicated that Germany might become quiescent. In early March Halifax refused to see Vansittart regarding his warning that Germany soon would annex Czechoslovakia.[180] The situation was confused by the fact that many of his reports were false (at various times he warned that Germany planned to launch a surprise attack against half of Europe) but at their heart was truth. Economic crisis was driving Hitler to conclude "in substance, 'Very well, all this means that the vital decision must come at once and it is coming at once'": and from 20 February he predicted the target with accuracy.[181] By March he warned precisely when Germany would annexe the remnants of Czechoslovakia so to prove German mastery and British impotence, and so won his greatest triumph—his last.

Over previous weeks Halifax and the Foreign Office had lost faith in high appeasement but had not formed an alternative. It held that "Hitler has for the time being abandoned the idea of precipitating an immediate crisis".[182] It heard Vansittart's warnings about Bohemia and Moravia, where Hitler aimed "to demonstrate the complete impotence, gullibility and lack of honour of the West" and that "Germans are tough, irresistible and determined" but, struck by the inaccuracy of his other warnings, it concluded:

> Hitler is clearly preparing for every possible eventuality. Rumours of one or other of these plans are continually reaching us, and cannot be lightly discounted. On the other hand, there is no evidence at present that any one of them has been irrevocably adopted by Hitler and the date fixed for it being put in force.

Once again, Vansittart had predicted Hitler better than they. The Foreign Office accepted his view of Hitler's intentions and adopted his line of policy—to play a psychological game against Hitler and German public opinion, to build a diplomatic dam in eastern Europe while still offering concessions to German opinion, to play for a stalemate, to bluff, to dare Hitler to start a war.

Precisely then Vansittart's influence plunged, and for good. He had helped to change minds about Hitler, but he differed fundamentally from his colleagues on other issues. In particular, Soviet support would bolster Britain's commitment to Poland, but Whitehall was suspicious of Russia. Meanwhile the GC&CS and the British embassy in Tokyo indicated that a close arrangement with the USSR might drive Japan into Germany's arms. Britain wished to create a diplomatic counterbalance which would check Germany and force its leaders and people to reconsider their aims. This process would take years to work. It would fail if it provoked Japan into an alliance with Germany against Britain. Consequently, Whitehall pursued the smallest possible link with Russia. Vansittart, virtually alone, held the opposite view.[183] His views on this matter were ignored. Moreover, now that the Foreign Office accepted his views of Hitler's general aims, he had nothing new to say about policy and less novel and plausible intelligence to offer. His well-known material on Russo-German negotiations appears to have been inaccurate in detail it certainly was disregarded.[184] In the last weeks before the outbreak of war he again provided good intelligence, but without great effect on events. Throughout 1939–1940, his contacts with the German opposition deepened, but this track ran slowly into the sands.

The time between July 1938 and March 1939 was his heyday as Chief Diplomatic Advisor—arguably, the high point of his career. Historians conventionally assume that when Vansittart ceased to be PUS he became Cassandra. This view is wrong. Vansittart's real triumph came after he was driven out as PUS, when those who had been appointed to find another policy found that they could not do so and under his guidance had to return to his. Vansittart was more influential under Halifax than Eden, and largely because of his use of intelligence. The key word is "influence". Vansittart did not control the thinking of Halifax and Cadogan, but at one key point and on one key issue he did change it. Nor did intelligence shape his views on fundamental issues. It is in the political dimension that one finds the historical significance of intelligence and Vansittart. Intelligence never changed his mind—he did use it to change other minds. Thus, he made intelligence central to Britain's debate over appeasement between 1937 and 1939. The intelligence record must be central to students of that policy.

3

IMAGE AND ACCIDENT

Intelligence and the origins of the Second World War, 1933–1941

Intelligence is more than espionage. It is the collection and analysis of information in order to let one use one's resources in the most effective way possible, against rivals doing the same. Information is collected and knowledge acquired so as to support action, rather than for their own sake. Intelligence is not a form of power but a means to guide its use, whether as a force multiplier, or by helping one to understand one's environment and options, and thus how to apply force or leverage, and against whom. Intelligence is a rational activity but its significance, like that of rationality itself, is limited. Intelligence shows what can be understood in the context of what cannot be known. It addresses several related questions, which can be answered only in probabilistic terms, with the uncertainty to any one answer multiplied by that of the rest. Subjects under observation resist the observer through denial and deception, and change their behaviour in response to one's own. They use intelligence to guide their actions—and so affect yours. The truth is not just out there; one can create the truth one deserves.

Intelligence is collected through open sources, such as diplomats, and secret ones, including agents and codebreaking. Each source has strengths and limits. Agents produce vast amounts of unreliable and inaccurate intelligence, as well as the rarest of gems—high-level documents from other states and inside commentary on their meaning. Sources are valuable not because of their secrecy or technical complexity but through the provision of accurate, relevant and timely information for action. A primitive source may equal a sophisticated one in value, an open source a secret one. Even the best sources rarely tell the whole truth and nothing but the truth. The best intelligence is useless without an efficient link between the organs which collect, evaluate and act upon it. Flaws are possible anywhere along the chain; when one link breaks so will the whole. Accurate intelligence may not be collected or assessed properly. It may not reach a statesman in time for him/her to act; s/he may be unable to use knowledge or may mishandle the attempt to do so. A good army with bad information may beat a bad army with good intelligence. Two first-rate espionage services may neutralize each other while, when fighting an incompetent adversary, mediocre intelligence may give its master a razor. Intelligence does not necessarily let one achieve the effect one intends—it may be counterproductive. Nor does intelligence affect diplomacy exactly as it does war. It is merely one factor in a game with many actors, where intentions and effects become tangled. In a game with five players, the best stroke possible against one rival may alarm a third and lead them to bump a fourth into deflecting one's shot—perhaps toward one's own net. Diplomatic intelligence often leads statesmen not to take specific actions that were carried into effect—thus allowing one to judge how information affected actions—but also to favour policies that were never realized, or not to take certain actions at all. In diplomacy, to wait is to act, with consequences perhaps greater than from any stroke of policy. The causal weight of intelligence in diplomacy is difficult to gauge—this does not make it less significant than it is in the case of military operations.

The specialist literature on intelligence and the origins of the Second World War is small and of mixed quality, good in some places, poor in most. The works of the first generation of intelligence historians were often commendable—pathbreaking, retaining worth in major areas; but they were written before the archives were available, and they suffer the fate of every pioneer.[1] Authors struggled to find where they were going and how to get there—to discover evidence, to make sense of fragments, to create a context and a chronology; not surprisingly, their work has flaws. One can criticize scholarship without condemning scholars. The literature focuses too much on estimates of the military capabilities of other states, against the intentions of their leaders; on the views of middle-level bureaucrats, against those of statesmen; their assessment of these assessments is coloured by the liberal materialism of our time; these works fail to address the intellectual foundation for perceptions or to link intelligence systematically to policy; sometimes they treat diplomacy purely as a function of cryptology—it should be so simple. By necessity, these writers aimed at the reconstruction of specific matters rather than general explanation, and sometimes distorted the influence of intelligence on particular events while missing its systematic import. Meanwhile, the general literature on the origins of the Second World War incorporates intelligence in different ways. Most works, including virtually everything written before 1974, ignore the matter, sometimes at a crippling price. Many subsequent ones, and all the most significant of them, incorporated the matter as well as was possible at the time, based on partial access to evidence on a big topic, or to a large body of evidence on a small issue.[2] A tiny literature makes full use of the record at present available. That record is large. Over the past decade, an increasing amount of primary documentation on intelligence has become available: British material released by Her Majesty's Government; American and international documentation unleashed by United States' authorities; and French records captured by the Red Army in 1945 and freed by the Russian Federation fifty years later. In 1980, intelligence barely ranked as a topic worth academic study; new work was written in a vacuum, almost without the benefit of scholarship, while the relevant primary documents in the public domain were limited and often hidden. Now, studies of intelligence are common, revisionist works are possible, and specialists are swamped in primary documents. The intelligence record is good for the United States, Britain, France, Sweden and Italy, tolerable about Germany, and illuminating if incomplete on the USSR, Japan, Poland, and some other significant secondary powers. Intelligence can be incorporated into history.

When doing so, certain fallacies of evidence and argument should be avoided. The most common is the Bloomsbury syndrome, the focus on anecdote instead of analysis. The most dangerous is the assumption (as against the proof) of influence, the ideas that because secret intelligence was available to a decision maker, it must have affected his decisions, and in a significant and simple way; or that intelligence was the key to policy and hence its records must transform our understanding of events. Such arguments are not necessarily wrong but simply unproven, and therefore of limited use even if accurate. What really matters about intelligence is not what it is but what it does; what it did not do is as important as what it did. Discussions about how intelligence affected decisions must rest on the strongest and most precise argument the evidence will allow. Even in well-documented instances, doubly so with the usual suspects, this may be no more than a case by coincidence resting on circumstantial evidence, on the tracing of similarities between a source's information and the ideas of its consumer, but that fact must at least be recognized and tested in the most rigorous fashion possible. Ideally, in order to determine the function of intelligence within the evolution of any event, one should define its status relative to all other relevant factors in the framework of cause and effect. This ideal is difficult to achieve. Specialists have acquired a method for this purpose, which rests on two sources. The first is a didactic literature about how intelligence should be assessed and used, best exemplified by Sherman Kent's classic study, *Strategic Intelligence for American World Policy*,[3] which framed the method of professional intelligence analysts throughout the Western world during the cold war. The second source, often called the "no-fault" school, arose in reaction to the theory and practice of the first. This academic literature—part empirical, part theoretical—about how intelligence is actually assessed and used, includes Robert Jervis's assessments of the links among information, perception and action, and the studies of surprise, deception, interpretation and intelligence failure of Richard Betts and Michael Handel. Its classic is Roberta Wohlstetter's study of the intelligence failure at Pearl Harbor.[4] The didactic literature assumed that so long as a specific approach was followed, one that married rigorous social science method to proper institutional structures, such as the creation of Chinese walls between analysts and actors, intelligence could be assessed with a high level of accuracy and produce material of great significance. Any failure to achieve these standards was a failure of intelligence. The "no-fault" school, conversely, assumes that some kind of error, whether of omission or commission, is unavoidable in intelligence, that no method can always lead to truth, and that the truth is often useless. Failures of intelligence are common—unavoidable. The question is their nature and significance.

Most academic students of intelligence probably would accept a view like the following. The effect of intelligence depends upon its interpretation in the context of a set of conditions that govern expectation and usability. Decision makers can understand the world, and they do affect it. They are not mere prisoners of perception, unable to learn from error or to change their minds. But decision makers are reluctant to change their minds, and they do tend to interpret bits of information on the basis of preconception. Nor is it ever easy to assess intelligence. A given event may well have an unambiguous meaning. Information about it rarely has an unambiguous interpretation. Intelligence generally provides pieces of background information which are read in the light of complex patterns of preconception, often unconscious or unexamined. The meaning of some pieces of intelligence, such as when a statesman outlines his imminent intentions, are intuitively self-evident against the framework of common sense. This sort of material is easy to understand, trust and use, but hard to find. The typical piece of intelligence is not absolutely certain proof acquired two days after the fact that Adolf Hitler said on 5 November 1937, "This is my reading of the balance of power, my aims are X, Y, Z, and I will start World War II on 3 September 1939". Even the Hossbach memorandum did not reach that standard of precision and accuracy, because that was not Hitler's intention even on 1 September 1939. Had Western intelligence services received an accurate account of Hitler's statements at that meeting, they would have known his attitudes but been misled about specific issues, such as the mode by which he planned to launch diplomatic aggression. More typically, intelligence consists of news provided five months after the event to His Majesty's Government by British codebreakers of a report from the French ambassador in Bucharest, which he received though the intermediary of a Greek journalist, of the views of Hitler's aims offered by a drunken Japanese *charge d'affaires* in Sofia. Intelligence services usually provide masses of material, often utterly irrelevant, of unknown accuracy or on a tangent of relevance, drawn from the hearsay of third-hand sources.

A preexisting body of ideas shapes the assessment of such material. These range from broad matters such as social, political or religious schools of thought, to official doctrines about specific topics or the eccentricities of individuals. This whole process is dogged by problems, such as ethnocentrism and the tendency to project one's own way of thinking onto others, that produce well-known errors like mirror-imaging and best-case or worst-case logic. These problems are difficult to avoid because intelligence is hard to handle. It embraces both description and prediction. Description is difficult enough. Intelligence services, however, are often asked to explain not only how other states will behave at a given moment but also to guess how they will do so years in the future—to predict decisions that have not yet been made. Above all, they have to determine not what another state should do but what it will do. If you know better than the party you are analyzing what line of policy it should follow, then if it makes a mistake so will you. British policy toward Italy between 1936 and 1939 went wrong in part because the Foreign Office understood Italy's position better than Benito Mussolini did, holding that Italy would cease to be a great power if Germany incorporated Austria and stood on the Brenner Pass.[5] Bad intelligence can lead to good decisions. Good intelligence may not affect policy. It may be unusable or it may be used counterproductively or it may invalidate itself. If one accurately determines another side's intentions and forestalls them, one may force it toward a new and unexpected policy. Intelligence can fail by succeeding, or vice versa.

In theory, states need information in order to formulate and follow a grand strategy and a foreign policy: to determine which aims they can or must achieve, the means by which they best can do so, the options that are open to them, and the optimum way to allocate their resources and to elucidate the power and the policies, the intentions and the capabilities, of every player in the game. In practice, intelligence rarely affects the determination of policy—although this does happen. Frequently, however, it shapes the background to decisions, how statesmen understand and learn about their environment, and very often intelligence determines the execution of policy. Intelligence affects tactics more than strategy; operations or bargaining more than the formulation of policy. Intelligence on another's bargaining position can guide one's own, it can be applied immediately, and its effect on action can be gauged with precision. Greater problems occur with the broader aspects of intelligence: when it provides knowledge—lets one understand another's attitudes or long-term policy, reveals the existence of something one did not know or confirms that of something in which one believed, proves statesmen are honouring their promises—or not; and when it provides leverage—indicates an opportunity and means to take the initiative or disrupt another's efforts to do so, or shows what messages one should deliver to whom so to check their manoeuvres, or those of another; and when it contributes to learning, to making people change their minds. It is difficult enough to understand the capabilities of other powers. The answer to the question "what can X do?", varies with the questions "why?", "against whom?" and "where?" and with calculations about the outcome of the interaction between luck, types of tactics, styles of diplomacy, and untested pieces of technology. To uncover intentions is an even more ambitious undertaking. Governments often reach their decisions in literally unpredictable fashions—or in ways that can be predicted only if one knows the aims and means of each element in their bureaucratic political processes.

Statesmen frequently do not know what they will wish to do in the future; even should they think they do, they may change their minds or have them changed. Nor are all of their actions taken in order to achieve these intentions. Necessity may force leaders to march one step forward, two steps back; opportunity may alter one's calculus of aims and means. Policy—especially for the long term—often is formulated and executed in a byzantine fashion, with different departments of state (and many of their agents) able to pursue different (sometimes contradictory) ends without reference to the rest. Even when all of these groups pursue the same ends, they can easily differ over the means. All too often central authorities fail to coordinate these bodies; even the most central policies may be ignored or overturned at any time without notice. In order to assess another state's policies, one has to identify which factions or individuals influence its policies on any given issue; calculate the range of outcomes of the struggle between them; and guess at the probabilities of the possible results—which might not occur for years ahead.

The aim is accuracy of prediction; the means must be knowledge of precision. Intelligence officers, however, are neither mind readers nor seers. It is rare for any state continually and certainly to know the central elements of another's policy, those that shape each of its specific actions. States usually understand the intentions and capabilities of their peers only in particular instances, and in a fragmentary way. This information can illuminate some aspects of a problem but cannot reconstruct the whole. These partial successes are sometimes counterproductive. Correct knowledge of capabilities but not intentions can easily lead to best- or worst-case assumptions; knowledge of the intentions but not the capabilities of a hostile but impotent power may produce hysteria; lessons learned from the behaviour of a party in one crisis may fail when applied to the next, because it too learns from the past and changes for the future. Yet, sometimes one really needs only partial successes: one need not know why an action is being taken so long as one knows that it is, or understand capabilities that are never used. The problems about determining intentions are redoubled by those with the evidence on it. Usually, intelligence provides first-rate material on second-rate issues, and second-rate information on first-rate matters. It rarely provides unambiguous statements by the chief authorities as to what they will do on a specific topic at a given date, but rather indicators of that matter, drawn from the views of middle-level officials whom one uses as a proxy for their masters—even though what they are really trying to do is to influence the latter. Again, intelligence moves people, not calculators. Emotion is intrinsic to decisions, so too personality and politics. With data incomplete or uncertain and analysis conjectural, one can always find some doubtful detail to derail any assessment one dislikes. Policy decisions are rarely final; most are preliminary compromises which many participants are willing to drop. Intelligence is always interpreted according to preconception; it can simultaneously justify every position in any debate; its primary effect may be to reinforce factionalization and a dynamic tension underneath policy which at any moment may wreck the surface without warning. Intelligence can have chaotic consequences, varying with personality or faction; its effect has to be gauged by looking at each participant; it may not help effective action—but often it does. Rarely, it strikes events like lightning; and one cannot know the consequences until they have happened.

Between 1933 and 1941, intelligence was fundamental to the formulation of policy by the great powers. It provided as much good information as did any conventional source, which decision makers used in a fashion complex even by the standards for the genre. Explicitly or intuitively, they saw every detail in the context of the whole. They analyzed issues from a strategic perspective, combining assessments of the capabilities of states, armies, societies and economies, the intentions of statesmen, and the attitudes of masses and of elites. Decision makers did so not in a value-free and bureaucratized fashion, but in one dominated by personality and ideology and factionalization. No state had a simple policy—their agencies pursued several at once, often contradictory, sometimes kept secret by one bureau from its rivals. Everywhere, bureaucrats used intelligence to achieve their normal policies, which comprised most decisions, but the man at the top had remarkable autonomy on the greatest of issues in "totalitarian" states and liberal democracies alike. In 1938–1939 Edouard Daladier dominated foreign and defence policy in France, as Neville Chamberlain aimed to do in Britain; during 1940–1941, Winston Churchill controlled British policy toward the United States and Japan while Franklin Roosevelt conducted an end run around the constitution. Their power over policy matched that of Hitler, Mussolini and Joseph Stalin. Nor did any state handle intelligence by committee. Everywhere, assessment was confused and politicized, these problems redoubled by specific ones; in Britain and France, bureaucrats and politicians wielded intelligence in wars over policy; so too in Italy, the United States and Germany, where men also used intelligence to curry favour at the top; all this, in the USSR, was multiplied by the influence of the purges. In theory, Britain had a centralized system of intelligence, the Foreign Office controlling the collection agencies and dominating assessment of their material, which was primarily diplomatic in nature. By 1937, this system had collapsed. The key issues became strategic and interdepartmental. Modes of assessment splintered, some authorities deliberately spreading alarm, others ignoring material they disliked. In France, the army dominated collection; its product was good but its assessments distorted German strength, often intentionally so, and were mistrusted by the Quai d'Orsai. In the USSR, politics killed intelligence, while fear and favour ruled assessment. In Germany, collection and assessment were divided between institutions that did not cooperate, distorted by the competition between Herman Goering and Joachim Ribbentrop for influence over Hitler, and dominated by the *Fuhrer*'s trust in himself. Yet not just in Germany did one leader's intuition rule intelligence. Everywhere, the personal quirks of top leaders determined interpretation—Stalin's paranoia and logic, the megalomania of Chamberlain and Hitler and Churchill; the self-satisfaction of Mussolini and Roosevelt; the self-delusion and willingness to gamble for the highest of stakes of Hitler and key decision makers in Japan. General Tojo Hideki likened Japan's decision to fight the United States to leaping from Kiyomizu Temple, the tallest structure in Kyoto, a proverb indicating one's determination to risk all for the greatest of gains. Intelligence is interpreted from an unusual perspective when standing on Kiyomizu's brink. These statesmen used intelligence to understand their environment and to alter it, relying on their own intuition as against the elaborate, and seemingly arbitrary, estimates of professional analysts. They all thought they knew their counterparts abroad better than did their advisors below. One French ambassador held that the British Foreign Secretary, Lord Halifax, thought "he had special insight into the psychology of Nazi leaders"; this was true of him, and others.[6] Chamberlain projected his thinking on people who thought differently, and sabotaged official policy by pursuing a private one. Experience at Munich led him to think Hitler a man he could work with; meetings with "umbrella men" led Hitler to believe he could make worms turn at will. Both were wrong.

Statesmen were also affected by ideology, whether the liberal democratic forms of Britain, France and the United States; or the variants of social Darwinism, militarism and racism in Italy, Germany and Japan; or Marxist–Leninist and militarist ideas back in the USSR. It has become fashionable to denigrate the importance of ideology on actions. The most recent (and excellent) study of Soviet policy in 1940–1941 even denies that Marxism–Leninism affected Soviet assessments or actions![7] This fashion has many founts. The triumph of liberalism has made that way of thought seem natural—meta-ideological—and all competitors idiotic. Modern liberal materialists export their ideas to the minds of decision makers past, making it easier to understand appeasers than anti-appeasers or revisionists, or to assume they were all the same; not so. We are all liberal materialists now; they were not all then. "Realists", meanwhile, think interests self-evident, and "realism" the natural means to understand power: thus, statesmen must be pure realists, viewing power, interests and systems in the same way; and anyone who applies sentiment to diplomacy must be a fool, and a rarity. Laymen express such views in loose forms, theorists of international relations explicitly and systematically. In the most recent and excellent work of this sort, John Mearsheimer treats each state as a person, with only one policy at a time, and interests, power and systems as things, "like black boxes or billiard balls". All states belong to one system, which by nature or reason, statesmen comprehend accurately, and attempt to shape in identical ways. That system defines a game, an unbreakable set of rules, and the perceptions and actions of all its players. They must play that game—all they can gain from trying not to play it is to do so badly. States *should* behave like realists, and almost always do. If they do not, "such foolish behaviour invariably has negative consequences". Mearsheimer excludes ideology, or any motivation within states, or beyond the use of instruments in pursuit of interests, as influences on the perceptions and actions of any statesman. "It does not matter for the theory whether Germany in 1905 was led by Bismarck, Kaiser Wilhelm, or Adolf Hitler, or whether Germany was democratic or autocratic. What matters for the theory is how much relative power Germany possessed at the time."[8]

These views are wrong. Liberalism is an ideology. Realism is a form of idealism. A state is not a person but many of them, factionalized, pursuing contradictory ends and speaking in tongues. Interests are not just objects, but a fusion of things and of ideas about them. Statesmen further them by exerting power (through things) and influence (through ideas). Power is real, systems are a combination of reality and social construct. Realism is essential to the understanding and playing of power politics, but it and they are more complex than is often supposed. Realism describes instruments and environments, and the ways the former shape the latter, but does not prescribe what they should be used for. It tells you how to play games, not which ones, or why. Realism describes power and means, but it cannot define values, or the ends they indicate. A pure realist, aiming at power and victory for their sake alone, is a psychopath. Few statesmen are so, if any—none in this period. Almost all statesmen merge realism with some idea of values, which join means to ends. The word "realism" is a noun in search of an adjective, like "Marxist–Leninist", "national-socialist" or "liberal". For power politics, ideology shapes epistemology. It defines our means to know the world, and hence our attempts to shape it, our views of power, interest, force, of the game and rules. The realism of real statesmen combines ideologies and an understanding of instrumentality. By factoring out ideology from this alloy, analysts do not derive a purer form of realism, they destroy it. They reduce statesmanship to gamesmanship, just as removing copper from the smelt leaves not better bronze, but tin. This impoverished definition of realism also cripples understanding of the evidence on power politics. Analysts read events from hindsight, and intentions from effect, making statesmen seem more realist than they are, and realism easier to do—like magic: this is what they did, there must be a realist explanation, so find it; he succeeded, therefore he must have been a realist, she failed, thus she was not. If realism means a sagacious and dispassionate reading of power, interests and system, and their calculated manipulation, producing effects as intended, then good realists are hard to find. Perhaps their rarity explains their success. Realists tend to cancel each other out; the key is relative superiority. In order to know your interests and how to further them against rivals and the world, you must first of all be strong and smart, and then more so than your competitors. If systems really were filled only with able realists, realism would lose its premium—it would matter no more to statecraft than a statesman's taste in clothes. With realism, everything seems easy, but easy things are hard to execute.

Realists assume that the members of a system understand, but cannot alter, it; in fact, systems are easier to change than to comprehend, and they mutate when they are misconceived. Rules can be broken. Often they are not understood in the same way by all their members, and sometimes not at all by most of them. Players think they are playing different games, and so do not follow the same rules, which may change without notice. Players can remake rules and systems, even without knowing that they are doing or have done so. Power politics is like whist, except that without notice it may become poker, while any player may pull their gun and accuse any other of cheating. Power, interests and systems are hard to understand; this produces confusion for all and is a bonus to anyone who sees them for what they are, especially the first player to do so, or one whose competitors are slow to learn. Such a player may win a trick and rewrite the game. Differences of opinion about power and rules are natural to systems. So is misunderstanding of the system by some members, sudden revolutions in rules and power, and constant non-optimum behaviour, as seen from gamesmanship in hindsight. The default mechanism for these systems is the natural way humans play zero-sum games, in a competitive and reciprocal fashion, with war the bottom line. Realism is the best means to analyze and win such games, but it cannot always produce victory. Uncertainty and chance so affect some games that outcomes cannot be predicted by reason or by intuition, nor intentions be effected, as in multilateral systems where most states play erratically and constantly interfere with each other. Against irrational opponents, a realist usually does rather well, but sometimes the drowning men drag her down. All realism can do is shave the odds—it cannot escape them. Even more; players can reset the rules for the system, if they represent enough of its power. Systems are largely what their members think they are, or make of them—the sum total of their behaviour; but unless enough of them play the same way, the zero-sum game reemerges. One aggressive or realist player may be enough to wreck the revised settings; and if ever the system crashes, the default rules. Statesmen may try to make the world into any one they want, but reality and other wills resist them. The point is power; if sufficiently strong, liberals can force their will on realists, as can the adherents of any ideology which places values above *realpolitik* but allows the use of force, such as conservatives, Catholics or Chomskyites, as opposed to Gandhians. This view is unpalatable to liberals, who want everyone to behave like them through reason rather than force, and to realists, who do not want to admit that any ideologue might trump their views. If power underpins liberal rules, those who follow them may not suffer, while realists may not gain from breaking them. The problem is not with liberalism *per se*—strong and smart liberals can make bad states behave nicely—but with weak liberals or foolish ones, who do not understand the limits to their power and their ideology, nor what they mean. Many liberals are weak and foolish, and a system based on their principles would be hard to establish, but it is not impossible. In fact, it has existed between liberal states for a century. They abandoned armed force against each other, and turned to a more pitiless rivalry in economics.

The policy of any state stems from a synthesis of its inner views and those inspired by the system. The system makes statesmen behave as realists, their humanity and ideology prevent them from behaving only so. People are not just players; they do not simply follow the rules. The system explains part of what any statesman does and why, but the rest comes from the black boxes. Until these are opened, one cannot understand the reasons of states. Study of inner politics is not enough to understand foreign policy, but it is necessary for the latter. Ideology is not just a quirk of statesmen—it shapes the system. Between 1815 and 1939, the system was most stable either when power was balanced in a classic sense (rarer circumstances than usually supposed, found mostly between 1892 and 1914) or in periods of multilateral hegemony, when the states which dominated a system generally used their power to support the status quo (1815–1851, 1871–1892, 1919–1931). These cases of hegemony are often seen as times of balance, because states were divided over some issues; but the dominant ones stood united on the most central of them. They identified the stability of the system among their vital interests and were reluctant to risk a great war. In these cases of balance and hegemony, stability was bolstered by a thick net of alignments between states and their ideologies. The dominant powers had similar ideologies (conservative in the 1820s, liberal in the 1920s) or else, despite differences in ideas, they shared a common understanding of rules, interests and limits, and opposition to apocalypse now. The system was least stable, and the chances of great war and revolution in power greatest, in periods when alignments were weak, few states supported the status quo, all played a lone hand, and their ideologies conflicted, with some favouring great wars (1851–1870, 1933–1941). For the stability of systems, ideology is acid, or glue.

Ideologies accommodate and affect realism in different ways. Liberals in the twentieth century disliked being the first to use force. Characteristically, they started to do so only after losing a trick, or two; militarists like the first use of force too much. Each approach better suits some rivalries than others. Britons gained more from applying liberal realism to the United States than Germans did through militarized realism, while a clash between liberalism and forms of anti-liberalism dogged Anglo-German power politics. Realism is harder to do across ideological (and cultural) borders, which confuse understanding of power, games, interests and limits, though often the latter brook no misunderstanding. Thus, nuclear weapons dampened the effect of ideological conflict between 1945 and 1989. Between 1933 and 1941, conversely, every statesmen thought he was a realist and every one was wrong. Their collective lack of reality made a system in which realism was hard to apply.

Ideologies, the world views they reflect and produce, and the clash between them, have affected the diplomacy of few periods so much as this one. In the mid-nineteenth century, ideology shaped international relations—conservatism, nationalism and liberalism made gunpowder, and diplomacy sparks. During the decades before 1914, the explosiveness of this mixture fell, except in the Balkans. Nationalism became just another interest of states, liberalism a mere impediment to Anglo-Russian relations. Ideology shaped the politics of European states but not their diplomacy. All statesmen played the same game while liberal realists and reactionary ones shared similar ideas about its rules. The great war killed conservatism, revived nationalism, and birthed fascism and Marxism–Leninism. Ideological differences between states emerged in 1919, but armed liberalism kept its rivals in check until 1931. Then a change in power unleashed the force of ideas and a struggle between them, creating problems without precedent in recent memory. Ideology made pitches to groups beyond one's borders, and universal issues of class and race, into state interests. It affected one's views of ends, means, the rules of the game, and of how others perceived such issues. It raised questions that were hard to answer. Even today, aided by archives and hindsight, historians differ about how ideology affected any statesman, or act of diplomacy. To the Reichstag on 30 January 1937, Hitler stated his desire for "sincere and cordial cooperation" with Britain and his belief Bolshevism that was "a world peril for which there must be no toleration".[9] This statement reflected his real views, but it was contrary to his actions in August 1939. Commentators generally, and correctly, denied that ideology either ruled policy or was irrelevant to it; they assumed that ideology interacted with *realpolitik*, at which point imprecision emerged. In 1936 a French diplomat held that Soviet policy, increasingly "Russian nationalist" and driven by "the balance of power" and "realpolitik", still could not forget the revolution. "Ideology alone cannot determine the basic lines of Soviet policy" but "a foreign policy resting simply on *raison d'État* cannot produce the results desired by the Soviets".[10] Everyone knew they had to account for ideology. The question was, how? Their answers to that question were no better than ours.

Ideology was not the only factor in perception and policy; its effect varied with person and time. Yet it did shape everyone's policy, and the greatest of decisions, such as Operation Barbarossa, or the refusal of Britain and the USSR to align with each other against Germany. British and Soviet decision makers mistrusted each other as much as they did Germany. Before the Munich crisis, Chamberlain saw "the Russians stealthily and cunningly pulling at the strings behind the scenes to get us involved in war with Germany (our Secret Service doesn't spend all its time looking out of windows)". During it, one British intelligence officer noted a report that there are both German and Soviet agents at work in Prague and elsewhere, endeavouring to stir up trouble among Czechs, Slovaks, Poles, etc—the Germans for the purpose of providing pretexts for Germany to take action, and the Soviets with the object of precipitating a general conflagration with as many nations as possible dragged in, as Moscow considers—probably with all too good reason—that such a war would result in ultimate chaos and revolution in all the countries concerned.

Soviet leaders interpreted British policy with equal cynicism.[11] People meant what they said and said what they meant and believed their own propaganda and understood international politics through the prism of their internal ones. Liberals, Marxist–Leninists and Nazis had different forms of realism. When analyzing the power of peoples, liberals used concepts of economic determinism and national and institutional character; racists, of demographic determinism, crude social Darwinism and generalizations about "races"; Marxist–Leninists, of economic determinism and crude forms of class analysis. Ideology defined interests. The nature of power and interest was in dispute and so were the rules of the game of states, between liberals of an older vintage, liberal internationalists, and militarists of Marxist or racist inclination. Liberals conceptualized international relations as law, others as force. Liberals thought war bad and unnatural, others did not. Though Soviets were more cautious in international relations than Germans or Japanese, they shared many attitudes—opposition to the status quo and belief that war was natural and cooperation merely a tactic. Volunteerism, the belief that will created reality, shaped the interpretation of evidence and selection of actions in all the revisionist states. A perceptual gap prevented statesmen from understanding each other's policy, especially since foreigners found it quite hard to take Hitler's ideology seriously; he did. Even Italians shuddered when they realized Germans meant what they said. On 7 July 1939 Italy's ambassador in Berlin was stunned by "la fantazia di Ribbentrop"—that if others opposed German demands, "Parigi, Parige ne rimarrebbe polverizzata", Britain would face "alla distruzione del proprio impero", the USSR "non vuole far niente", the United States for less.[12]

Granted, the fundamental issue was the clash between the aims of statesmen, which would have occurred even with mutual understanding; but in the world as it was, misunderstandings about basic policy triggered mutual miscomprehension over diplomacy from day to day. These circumstances were deadly for people pursuing policies of bluff and deterrence and delicate forms of manipulation and influence, which hinged on the precise delivery and comprehension of signals, doubly so because leaders in these factionalized states delivered mixed messages, some of which were missed in the shuffle. Deterrence, for example, works only if one understands how other polities act, and how their leaders view the balance between themselves and you; these fallacies clouded that understanding; deterrence failed. It took an imaginative willingness to step out of one's own ideological framework to understand what was happening. Not many tried to take that step, few succeeded at all, fewer for long.

Soviets, for example, thought that behind the facade of bourgeois parliaments lay the master, the moneybags, and beneath it the dynamite, the people. Diplomacy was public relations, aimed to expose and explode capitalism, best conducted like Bolsheviks. "Remember we are waging a struggle (negotiation with enemies is also struggle)"; said Stalin. "Let them know what Bolsheviks are like!" Spit "in the pot of the swaggering 'great powers'—very good. Let them eat it." Soviet leaders, sensitive to manipulation, believing compromise to be a mere camouflage for who did what to whom, felt the need to win every bargain and be seen to do so. They read the world from "the logic of things", such as Stalin's political algebra that criticism equalled opposition, which meant conspiracy, which entailed treachery. In 1930, Stalin wrote: "The Poles are certain to be putting together (if they have not already done so) a bloc of Baltic states (Estonia, Latvia, Finland) in anticipation of a war against the USSR. I think they won't go to war with the USSR until they have created this bloc. This means that they will go to war *as soon as they have created the bloc* (they'll find an excuse)".[13] The logic of things explained everything. Nothing could shake it. These views, so realist as to be unrealistic, ruled the interpretation of all intelligence. Soviet views of external relations were linked to perceptions of internal threat, as leaders increasingly came to believe they were surrounded by traitors. In 1936, they unmasked "the Trotskyite–Zinovievite Terrorist Centre" as "foreign agents, spies, subversives, and wreckers representing the fascist bourgeoisie of Europe", slaves to Hitler, aiming to smash the USSR. In 1938, they claimed the "anti-Soviet bloc of Rights and Trotskyites" had allied with Poles and Germans for the same end and hoped to do so with Britons and Japanese. In both cases, intelligence services abroad allegedly ran traitors at home, as Bolsheviks extrapolated to the international arena their experience as conspirators and of manipulation by the Okhrana. The prosecutor Andrei Vyshinsky demanded that Nicolai Bukharin "admit before the Soviet Court by what intelligence service you were enlisted—the British, German or Japanese?"[14]

How far Soviet leaders believed these claims of external connections is unclear, but some did so, like Stalin and the chief of the NKVD between 1936 and 1939, Nikolai Yezhov, and most probably thought these contained much truth. The highest Soviet decision makers certainly feared internal treachery, and slaughtered their subordinates on the grounds that they were tools of foreign intelligence agencies. One can doubt that they believed these claims only if one holds that they did not believe what they said between themselves in private. Soviet leaders formally accepted these claims of external conspiracies and publicized them, because they thought they would convince the world that the USSR had foes but was vigilant. Enemies were everywhere, and a death struggle combining class and world war loomed. In 1925 Stalin said: "If war breaks out, we must not twiddle our thumbs. We must intervene, but be the last to do so." In the early 1930s, he held that the crisis of capitalism has "put war on the order of the day as a means for a new redivision of the world and of spheres of influence in favour of the stronger states". Bourgeois states were "compelled to resort to a policy of war", preferably against the USSR. Initially, Soviet leaders saw every capitalist state as out for itself, but later divided them into two loose groups. Germans, Poles and Japanese were first seen as greater threats, matched after Munich by Britain and France. By March 1939, Stalin held that "a new imperialist war is already in its second year, a war waged over a huge territory from Shanghai to Gibraltar, and involving over 500 million people. The map of Europe, Africa and Asia is being forcibly redrawn". Britain and France wished to lure Germany and Japan against the USSR, "to allow all the belligerents to sink deeply into the mire of war, to encourage them surreptitiously in this; to allow them to weaken and exhaust one another; and then, when they have become weak enough, to appear on the scene with fresh strength, to appear, of course, 'in the interests of peace', and to dictate conditions to the enfeebled belligerents".[15] Here lay roots of the Germano-Soviet treaty of August 1939. The Soviet Foreign Minister, Vyascheslav Molotov, justified it on the grounds that France and Britain wanted to force the USSR into "a policy of enmity and war against Germany" while Bolsheviks, of course, pursued the interests of peace.[16]

British statesmen, conversely, drawn from a class which believed it set standards for all, leaders of the power which had set the rules of diplomatic behaviour for generations, thought no one would want to wreck the world they had made; it was so convenient. They treated their tenets of thought and behaviour as universal norms; these were not. They came from a political culture characterized by a willingness to limit gains, to avoid recklessness, to assess others by the standard of a gentleman, by faith in progress, fair play, free trade, and limits and reason; liberals, some liberal internationalists and Cobdenite or Christian idealists, regarding war as a misfortune or a disaster. French diplomats thought British statesmen "loyal to their tradition of facing reality and of meeting misfortune with a good heart". Englishmen assumed that "time works for them and, ultimately, they will have the last word", while "international life will be impossible if one must constantly question the sincerity or honesty" of promises made by gentlemen. "These ideas ... belong to the British code of 'fair play', for all that it is imaginary."[17] Such characteristics were handicaps when assessing statesmen like Adolf Hitler, whose ideas stemmed from militarism, social Darwinism and classical racism, shrouded by play at madness and liberalism, who loved war and playing double or nothing for all at once; and states where politics was murder. So too, Hitler's attitudes blinded him to his enemies. In 1939, he thought British concessions and their willingness to make them had sapped their position and showed the weakness of their will and of their hand, so just one more blow would surely bring them to heel. Instead, since they believed they had done the right thing, finally they felt free to do the wrong one—precisely the way they were weakened made them more willing to fight, not less so, as Hitler (or, indeed, most realists) would assume, a commentary on the oddness of liberal interpretations of power. The mutual incomprehension between Britain and Germany, exacerbated because neither had a sure and strong source on the other, shaped international relations. Britons sometimes focused more on determining whether a statesman was a gentleman than on indicators of his policy. When Lord Halifax described his first meetings with Goering and Hitler, he spent much time describing their dress to his colleagues, making style the man; he broke with these Germans when their behaviour convinced him they were bad. British statesmen, like French ones, were not cowards or fools, but they had lost some of their elders' hard-edged realism and hard-won expertise. They did not fail because intelligence was bad; they used intelligence badly because they failed as statesmen. In intelligence, wisdom is to information as three is to one. At the same time, these decision makers were influenced by realism. Among them were hard realists, like Robert Vansittart, and some militarists, such as Churchill. Precisely because such men focused on will rather than material, they understood Hitler's policy better than his contemporaries, or many students of appeasement. Most British decision makers were materialists who emphasized capabilities and rejected any risk of bluff. If Britain was weak and endangered, they argued, it must be cautious: nothing more than caution, Vansittart retorted, would signal weakness and create danger. He was right.[18]

If failures of policy prove the idiocy of ideas, Britons have company. Soviets, Japanese and Italians made greater errors of assessment between 1936 and 1941, the United States and France equal ones. The greatest intelligence errors of 7 December 1941 were made not in London or Washington, but in Tokyo. The master of mistakes was Hitler, intellectually a mixture of social Darwinist, classical racist, Wagnerian and vulgarized Neitzschean; he who assessed power in terms not of blood and iron, nor of gold and steel, but of race and soil; the man who described the struggle he caused as "an ideological war for existence or nonexistence", and made it so;[19] he who asked "what comes next?" when Chamberlain declared war, who said in September 1941, "I will not live to see it, but I am happy for the German Volk that it will one day witness how Germany and England united will line up against America";[20] who a few months later declared war on the United States, perhaps the only thing that could have brought it into the European war; he who in 1940 refused to concentrate on smashing Britain when it stood alone but instead chose to start a second front against the USSR, because of beliefs—derived from racist theory and personal memories—that

Britons were most deadly when at bay, while Russians were cattle herded by Jews into a rotten barn which would collapse with one blow. In these errors, Hitler was not eccentric, but average. All Germans grossly misunderstood decision making in Britain, overestimating the power of aristocrats and royals. Hitler's foreign minister, Ribbentrop, thought a cabal of Americans, Freemasons and Jews ran Britain.[21] Ribbontrop turned against England in part because he interpreted the abdication crisis as an anti-German coup; Rudolf Hess flew to Britain in May 1941 in the belief that discussions man-to-peer could turn Whitehall. The memory of British resistance during 1914–1918 shaped German views in 1940; Douglas Haig's last victory was the battle of Britain. The memory of Russia's poor performance of 1914–1918, multiplied by ethnocentrism and racism, prevented German decision makers from understanding the danger of an attack on the USSR. Germans assumed the United States would join Britain during any great crisis, continually referred to an "Anglo-American power-sphere" or "a corporation USA/England" as though the two were one, and held that they would lose nothing from forcing Washington to side with London.[22] Racists, social Darwinists and Marxist–Leninists misconstrued liberals as much as the opposite. Hitler could talk like a liberal, but not think like one, or understand them.

Preconceptions and images—ideas of how the world worked and states behaved—also shaped assessment. These phenomena were complex. Consider just one of their elements, ideas of "national characteristics". Where liberal materialists gauge the strength of a people and its army by looking at GNP, then institutions, tactics and weapons, observers of the 1930s looked first to gross national willpower.[23] Ideas of national character were fundamental to estimates of the power of any people. A standard category in United States analysis was 'psychologic". In their combat estimates, General Staff officers were trained to include such matters as, "*Racial Characteristics*. A calm, temperamental, stoical or excitable people; war-like or peacefully inclined; strong or weak; bold or timid; intrepid or easily discouraged".[24] Similarly, the Deuxieme Bureau thought "a people's "mentalite" fundamental to military estimates, especially national tendencies toward individualism or collectivism which created "a predisposition to military discipline. Here, Germany offers a striking example".[25] Ideas about national character shaped French assessment of Germany, and military estimates everywhere, with Nazis in racial terms, in the USSR as the characteristics of classes and the morale of foreigners when fighting a proletarian army, or the degree of rapaciousness and the level of social development of their ruling class.[26] Nor was this just a military phenomenon—when gauging the effect of their policies on a people and its leaders, statesmen too relied on ideas of national characteristics, what in August 1939 Ribbentrop described to the Italian Foreign Minister, Count Ciano, as "his knowledge of the English psychology". Ciano thought

Ribbentrop misinformed.[27] So too, after Munich, a French diplomat in Berlin thought Hitler wished to work with Britain but "completely misunderstands English psychology", something his colleagues in London thought central to British policy. The latter was dominated by public opinion, and "it always is hard to understand the heart of the English people".[28]

The language of national character was loose, shared by observers ranging from environmentalists to racists, who without notice or noticing used the same words in different ways. These ideas were only one factor in estimates, alongside demographic and economic strength, doctrine and institutional qualities, but their influence was pervasive. They most frequently surface when estimates describe the nature of peoples, conscripts or officers, or assess national or institutional morale, but they also shaped views about combat and organizational efficiency. Even more, many quantitative estimates were not descriptive but predictive, reached by multiplying factors such as levels of production with concepts of "national character" (that Germans, for example, were efficient). Since most observers thought institutions shaped character, these images could change. Foreign analysts, for example, overrated Italian power because they thought fascism had altered Italians. In 1927, American estimates deemed Italian soldiers mediocre and their officers worse. "The Italians have unbounded self-confidence, are often willing to endure great privations, and at times fight with great bravery. Their moral stamina, however, has hardly improved sufficiently to permit their ensuring severe reverses without collapsing, or to enable them to carry on a prolonged war without powerful allies." Over the next decade, the assessment grew more positive. American officers thought fascism had produced "a distinct change" in an "inherently undisciplined" people. By 1939, Italian regular forces were judged "very good" despite limitations in equipment, "The organization of the nation for war is so radically improved over what it was in 1915–18 that the effectiveness of the Army cannot be judged at all by World War Performance". Eighteen months and many battles later, estimates reverted to old stereotypes. Italian aircrew were regarded as wildly uneven in courage and skill, "The temperament and mentality of the Italian is such that morale, so far as the individual is concerned, is very unstable and solely activated by condition of the moment. The Italian has a spontaneous personality, reacting with immediate fervor and harmony to conditions as they develop".[29]

Ideas about "national character" stemmed from observation of behaviour, during sports or work or war (especially the last major one a nation had fought), from the stereotypes of history and literature, and from bodies of thought such as racism. They were surprisingly international— French, German and British ideas about Russian "national character" were similar, though not identical. Such stereotypes about nations (or "class", "gender" and "generation") have some power—they may explain how a few people always behave, some people usually do and many often do; yet this power is married to weaknesses. These ideas produce overgeneralizations, predictions about group behaviour which are sometimes wrong about many of the members, often inaccurate about some of them, and always erroneous about a few. Predictions derived from national characteristics are crude; at any time they may be mostly right or wrong, but never entirely so. They are descriptive, perhaps fitting behaviour which has been observed, but useless in predicting new forms (despite the treacherous temptation they offer in that direction). These ideas of national characteristics are infected with ethnocentrism, the tendency to treat one's behaviour as the solution to universal problems, and they open the door to racism, through which the crudest of concepts became fundamental to analysis. They did not prevent people from changing their minds or learning. Individuals could alter their opinions immediately in response to experience or observation, and discard one image and replace it with a polar opposite. These ideas, however, did cause people to make specific (often misleading) predictions in the absence of evidence, and to act on these errors.

If the reality of power governs the course of war, the image of powers determines that of peace. A weak state which others regard as strong will be such; a strong nation which others regard as weak may thus become so. In international politics, the perception of power is a source of weakness, or strength, to any state. Erroneous assessment of another's military may hamper one's diplomacy and preparation for war. Perceptions are often complex and inchoate; rarely is there just one image of any nation's characteristics or army's quality. Images tend to swing between two poles, one embodying ideas of weakness and malevolence, the other of power and arrogance. Images usually are unstable, built from many ideas about specific issues which are joined in greater wholes; and ideas about others are linked to those about oneself. Estimates always compare others to oneself, and mistakes about either party may wreck the whole; even if one understands the tactical characteristics of another army, one may underrate its power because one exaggerates one's own. The effect of images on thought and action is always complex, especially as one moves from simple matters such as the power of a navy to that of a polity; and every individual can have different ideas of any state's strength. An examination of two cases will illuminate these issues: the image of Britain as a power, and that of the quality of Japanese armed forces.

Foreign perceptions of British power and policy stemmed from history, selective memories of its performance between 1580 and 1918. When condemning British leaders in 1939, Mussolini said: "These men are not made of the same stuff as the Francis Drakes and the other magnificent adventurers who created the empire. These, after all, are the tired sons of a long line of rich men, and they will lose their empire"; in 1940, Ciano thought the annihilation of the French fleet at Oran "proves that the fighting spirit of His Britannic Majesty's fleet is quite alive, and still has the aggressive ruthlessness of the captains and pirates of the seventeenth century".[30] American assessments noted

> British characteristics of courage, tenacity and self-confidence afford a firm foundation for the high morale of the British soldier. He has behind him many generations of splendid war service ... The British system of training is typical of the nation. The development of character and moral qualities is strongly emphasized ... Broadly speaking the British people may be said to be ambitious, industrious, egotistical ... No other country has such a never-ending round of sports. The British consider sport as not a dissipation for idlers but a philosophy of life, a bulwark against effeminacy and decay. This fact has much to do with their best characteristics, good humour, give and take, fair play, intuitive and universal willingness to give every man a fair chance and just rights. They are not quarrelsome, not over-sensitive, not unduly pugnacious, but they have unbounded tenacity and persistency, linked to the general stability that goes with cold common sense. They know how to take care of themselves as do no other people and maintain a deep rooted belief in their own superiority. British superiority rests upon a preference for doing rather than thinking. The British live always in the real world, not in the world of dreams ... The British lack dash and impetuosity but their bulldog tenacity that never knows when it is beaten and consistently refuses to admit defeat has made them victors on many a hard fought battlefield. The British soldier never shows to better advantage than when in desperate straits and fighting with his back to the wall. These racial characteristics must always be taken into account when making estimates or plans in regard to the British Army.[31]

In *Mein Kampf*, Hitler offered a similar (if more militarized) view:

> Is it not positively the distinguishing feature of British statesmanship to draw economic acquisitions from political strength, and at once to recast every gain in economic strength into political power. And what an error to believe that England is personally too much of a *coward* to stake her own blood for her economic policy. The fact that the English people possessed no "people's army" in no way proved the contrary; for what matters is not the momentary military form of the fighting forces, but rather the will and determination to risk those which do exist. England has always possessed whatever armament she happened to need. She always fought with the weapons which success demanded. She fought with mercenaries as long as mercenaries sufficed; but she reached down into the

precious blood of the whole nation when only such a sacrifice could bring victory; but the determination for victory, the tenacity and ruthless pursuit of this struggle, remained unchanged ... I remember well my comrades' looks of astonishment when we faced the Tommies in person in Flanders. After the very first days of battle the conviction dawned on each and every one of them that these Scotsmen did not exactly jibe with the pictures they had seen fit to give us in the comic pages and press despatches.

In reference to the future, Hitler commented, "How hard it is to beat England, we Germans have sufficiently learned"—not well enough.[32]

Foreigners believed that Britain was always selfish and treacherous; but either strong or decadent, nothing in between—two sides of one coin, minted in Carthage. When British statesmen of the interwar years compared themselves to their predecessors, they thought of Castlereagh; foreigners of Palmerston. These views were international and long standing: in 1883–1884 the Tsarist Minister for Foreign Affairs, M. de Giers, mentioned "la patience and la perseverance qui caracterisent la politique egoiste de cette Puisaance insulaire".[33] In 1895 an advisor to Kaiser Wilhelm II noted, "English policy, in holding to its old traditions, had recognized in Italy a pawn to pull its chestnuts out of the fire", while Wilhelm thought, "England will at best only seek to exploit us and then leave us in the lurch at the opportune moment". In 1935 a German ambassador noted that France feared "the dreaded realism of the British".[34] However unflattering, these views respected British power and realpolitik. Another set of images about England focused on its wealth—and therefore, its weakness. In 1895, one German diplomat thought

Nothing better could really happen to England than to be awakened from the lethargy in which she had been stagnating for the past eighty years by a few kicks delivered by the Russians and the French. If the bull were simply allowed to gather fat without any healthy exercise, its agility and powers of resistance would of course decline; but once properly shaken up, it might again become its former fighting self.[35]

Similarly, in 1934, the Italian ambassador to Britain, Count Grandi, described that country as no longer a bulldog but "a hippopotamus ... slow, fat, heavy, somnolent, weak in eyesight and even weaker in nerve".[36] A popular theme in Nazi propaganda was Britain as governess, class-ridden, arrogant and hypocritical. Many contemporaries analyzed British power exactly contrary to the fashion of liberal materialists: one sees wealth as power, the other saw it as weakness. Images of Britain tended toward two poles—"perfidious Albion" and the "nation of shopkeepers". Observers jumped from one pole to the other with the ease of exotic dancers. Mussolini thus explained the change in British policy following Hitler's annexation of Bohemia and Moravia: "We must not forget that the British are readers of the Bible and that they combine mercantilism with mysticism. Now the latter prevails, and they are capable of going into action."[37] These images produced a critical and paradoxical, and overlooked, problem for British statesmen between 1815 and 1945. They were expected to act as the best students of Machiavelli or else as the most decadent of rentiers, yet they were neither. British decision makers had never been so cynical as was thought, and could not meet their imagined reputation, yet their actions were interpreted to fit one stereotype, or the other. Behaviour in any way ruthless or calculated provoked cries of "perfide Albion". Failure to meet the expectations of that image, or even actions which merely seemed inexplicable against it, were deemed perfidy in disguise, or rot. This problem was magnified because foreigners found British policy harder to fathom than that of any other power, in part because for generations Whitehall had aimed to keep foreigners guessing, while so much of its policy hinged on deterrence; unfortunately, the interworking of its actions and archetype sapped the credibility and obscured the signals on which deterrence rested, while its failure to behave according to archetype produced cognitive dissonance. No foreigner could believe that British policy during the appeasement era was so incoherent as it actually was—they searched instead for some hidden and Machiavellian key. Hitler and Stalin entirely misunderstood British policy between 1935 and 1938, fuelling rage and mistaken policy between 1938 and 1941. The intelligence failures that most shaped the outbreak of the Second World War in Europe were those made about Britain.

Modern critics sometimes view British decision makers of the interwar years as barely able to bumble their way through decline; contemporaries regarded them as ruthless, cunning, cruel, acting always in pursuit of aims held for centuries, able to make others serve the interests of England as it left them in the lurch; dangerous. During the 1920s, British prestige was higher than had been normal since 1815, but this began to change from the mid-1930s, when Great Britain clashed directly with the central aims of Germany, Italy and Japan, while failing to live up to its name. Then, the tenor of its policy and the reaction between images and racist and social Darwinist lines of thought led revisionists to scorn, in a fashion counterintuitive to liberal materialists. Hitler thought the British empire in decline because its population and its ruthlessness were small—45 million Caucasians ruling ten times their number of non-Aryans but unwilling to do so through fire and will: "The emphasis on the British Crown as the symbol of the unity of the Empire was already an admission that, in the long run, the Empire could not maintain its position by power politics."[38] Mussolini dismissed Britain because of its age and wealth—"plutocratic and therefore selfishly conservative"; "No one over 40 years liked to go to war. The decisive factor, finally, had been that England, as a result of the revival of her trade in the last few years, had become extraordinarily satiated, and satiated people did not like to risk anything." A German diplomat recorded Mussolini as saying, "in England 24 men would play soccer while 100,000 watched, whereas in our countries we preferred the 100,000 to engage in sports themselves, he remarked that the British had their brains in their feet".[39] Foreigners measured British strength by the self-confidence of its rulers; they moved against it because they believed that action to be safe. "The British empire already is an old man", said one officer of the Imperial Japanese Navy (IJN) in 1934; after Munich, Daladier called Britain a "frail reed" and Roosevelt complained it "cringed like a coward".[40] In August 1939, no foreigner expected Britain to do what it did—fight unless its aims were met; thus it had to. British leaders seemed uncertain, therefore others thought Britain weak, and dared to strike, taking actions that wrecked them all, every one. Given the effect of its image, only a policy of resolution—of bluff and recklessness—could have served Britain effectively in the 1930s. The sooner and bolder, the better: even when they disparaged Britain, Mussolini and Hitler regarded it with respect and some fear, and seized on any sign that the lion was stirring. Nothing would have suited British policy better than to "Oran" the Italians in 1936. Britain had nothing more to fear than fear itself.

It is commonly thought that during the interwar years, Western assessments of Japanese military forces were inaccurate, and because of racism. Such views are wrong. Some foreigners did agree that for "racial" reasons, Japanese suffered from poor eyesight or balance, which must affect their military capacity; junior personnel frequently expressed such vulgar racism, and some senior ones. However, vulgar or scientific racism did not dominate the views of decision makers. Professional observers, commanders and statesmen observed Japanese military forces through the lenses of preconceptions about war, Japan and its military institutions. The problem with their views was not racism, but ethnocentrism; Western observers treated their approach to war as the universal means to measure military value. They measured Japanese quality by its ability to fight Western forces in the conditions for which they prepared, rather than their ability to engage the IJN or the Imperial Japanese Army (IJA) in eastern Asia. These forms of military ethnocentrism, not broader bodies of thought like racism, were the single greatest cause for mistaken expert estimates of the IJA, closely followed by the way foreigners linked assessments of Japanese performance in combat to its "national character". As Captain Bonner Fellers, later a senior intelligence officer under Douglas MacArthur, stated in 1935: "The psychology of the Japanese soldier is the psychology of his people."[41] For a combination of genetic and environmental factors, Japanese were regarded as lacking individualism, aptitude for machines and the capacity for innovation; and yet as having great endurance, obedience to hierarchy and organizational ability. Air and naval officers prized the first set of qualities far above the second; these ideas led them to underrate Japanese pilots and sailors. Army officers respected the qualities in both categories; these concepts led them to praise and to bury the IJA—to respect its infantry but to criticize its artillery and armour.[42] To Western observers, Japanese infantry and fighter pilots formed the opposite extremes of the spectrum; one admirable, the other incompetent, for the same reasons. Observers drew less consistently from other sets of qualities: most saw Japanese as well organized but prisoners to their preparations, unable to learn quickly or improvise, lacking individual initiative, courageous but prone to hysteria under stress. A substantial body of Japanophiles downplayed such views and emphasized positive ones, seeing Japanese as uniquely quick to learn and to overcome errors.

Opinions differed about each Japanese service, and every estimate was mixed, including negative and positive comments. In 1933, the French Military Attaché in Japan thought

> The Japanese army is a redoubtable adversary; no other army emits a comparable force of morale, nor shows a better or more vibrant collective spirit. After having been with it for two years, I think it possesses the potential, the knowledge and aptitudes needed to adapt rapidly from the start of a campaign to the true conditions of modern war. The races' faculty of adaptation will correct the errors of peace, and these magnificent soldiers will retain the advantages of instruction and training in manoeuvre and vigour in attack.[43]

In 1935, his American counterpart said of the same soldiers,

> They lack initiative. They plan things meticulously, very much like the Germans, and if they are given time to carry these plans out, they will probably be successful, just like the Russians were kind enough to stay out in South Manchuria so that the Japanese had time to plan all their turning movements and their coordinations, etc. I doubt very much their ability to change quickly to meet changing conditions. That, to my mind, is a vital defect in them, perhaps the most important one.[44]

Foreigners regarded the IJA with respect, though its reputation sagged from 1932–1936 and its mixed performance in China. In 1931, French observers thought that army an *outil parfaitement dresse*, one rather less sharp by 1937.[45] Foreigners regarded the IJN as large but not quite first rate (or second), believing it might well be inferior but not daring to rely on that assumption. Assessments of Japanese air forces were negative, though they rose before the Pacific War, when experts (but not commanders) began to rate their equipment as decent by Western standards. By 1939 the American

General Staff rated Japan's air force, equipment and industrial base as good: "While Japanese airplanes are slightly inferior in performance to German and British current production, Japan's current production in general is equal to that now in service in any other nation." By 1941, *Luftwaffe* technical experts offered similar if slightly more negative views, while British assessments were moving haltingly in that direction.[46] Assessment varied by nation and institution. French and British observers were unusually positive about the IJA, Britons about Japanese naval air forces and French about Japanese army air forces (which they had trained); American and German officers in China, who identified with that country, were more negative about the IJA than were their national counterparts in Japan. Generally, institution shaped assessment more than nation; American, French, British and German army officers had more in common with each other in their views of the IJA, than any of them did with those of their naval or air counterparts regarding the services they surveyed. Meanwhile, fundamental differences existed between the views of experts and the general officers—the problem being less the view of the experts, than their ability to sell it.

Western observers overstated the fragility of Japanese national morale and underrated their ability to improvise and adapt; they failed to sell their assessments to the units which were preparing to fight Japan. Statesmen and commanders thought Japan weaker and more cautious than was the case, and underestimated the offensive power it could wield out of its area, though everyone recognized its defensive capacity at home. Yet Western observers and staff officers assessed Japanese military forces no less accurately than they did European ones—if anything, more so; they made equal errors about Italy and greater ones about the USSR. They assessed it exactly as they did every state—not through the uniform frame of racism, but rather a malleable mixture of observation and ideas of national characteristics. Some estimates were surprisingly accurate. The errors stemmed no more from preconception than Japanese success in hiding its most modern equipment, especially aircraft. In fact, Japanese leaders estimated their power relative to Western states less accurately than Western ones did. Nor did these estimates have a simple effect. German soldiers rated the IJA less than British or French ones did, and Hitler applied racist thinking to military analysis more than other statesman, but for strategic reasons he still allied with Japan. The British army had good intelligence on Japan which was assessed well, accepted at high levels—and ignored in Malaya; so too with the American army and the Philippines, though intelligence and assessment were less good. The Royal Navy's mediocre assessment of its Japanese counterpart was saved by system and circumstances; its strategy, resting on bean counting of warships and a rejection of best case planning, was not distorted by its underestimate of Japanese quality; nor did the latter affect the destruction of Force Z.[47] So too the US navy, with one exception—the failure to realize Japan might dare to strike the American main fleet at home by surprise. The United States and even more, Britain, assessed Japanese airpower poorly, which shaped disaster. Decision makers thought they held an edge in airpower over Japan, whose morale was uniquely vulnerable to attack by air; their policies of deterrence and defence relied on these assumptions, and were betrayed by them.[48] Otherwise, the errors about Japanese military power were irrelevant at the highest levels in London and Washington, where the great mistake was deeming Japanese statesmen too cautious to risk a war simultaneously against Britain and the United States, because it must lose such a conflict. They were right, so they were wrong.

Image and estimate shaped the policy of every state in complex ways. Between 1933 and 1941, far more than in 1905–1914, decision makers misunderstood the fundamentals of power and policy everywhere. As a gross generalization, German (and to a lesser degree, Italian) strength was exaggerated, that of everyone else underrated, especially Japanese and Soviet and American, and for many reasons. Some stemmed from technical matters, shaped by fallacies such as mirror imaging. Intelligence of a statistical sort on GDP or numbers of battalions was fairly easy to collect, not so on qualitative or technological issues, even more so on how far and fast a state could rearm. The French overestimated the size of the German army because they misconstrued the calibre of its paramilitary formations, as the British did the rate of *Luftwaffe* expansion and its style of war because they assumed it must act like the RAF. British and French misread the evidence on the German army's ideas about operations because they could not believe Germans would wish to fight that way, or that such an approach could defeat them; so too, Germans with Fighter Command. Again, the politicization of intelligence had an ironic systematic effect. Hitler, Stalin and Mussolini mistook military power more than any other statesmen. They got their own forces wrong because their subordinates deceived them, and also foreigners; the Italian military misled Mussolini even though it privately exaggerated French and British power relative to its own! British and French commanders deceived their masters, overestimating their weaknesses and German power, which reinforced the misleading and miscalculation by the Axis.[49] Before Munich the German army provided worst-case estimates as much as did those of France and Britain, and for even more political reasons—the difference being that Hitler ignored them even more than did Chamberlain, though the latter, admittedly, did pursue a policy congruent with professional advice, while the former did not. Ironically, the greatest victim of the overstatement of German power was the Axis. Mussolini and Japanese decision makers took the decisions which ruined their countries because they believed Germany to be too powerful to lose. So too did Hitler. The effect of such failures in assessment is measured best not by seeing each in isolation, but by adding together all those relevant to any relationship. In the extreme case, this produced an error of about 10 million men. During 1940–1941, Soviet decision makers thought Germany had twice the number of soldiers it really did, while Germans underrated Soviet strength by half (and viewed even this capacity with contempt).[50] Some of these errors stemmed from the interplay of images. British and French estimates rested on the stereotype Germans were efficient; not quite so. When assessing combat power, Germans, Italians and Japanese fetishized willpower and spirit, assuming their races had both, but generally not their opponents; they underrated the significance of economics and organization; they misunderstood American and Soviet strength. Germans conventionally saw the USSR as plague bacillus, or colossus with feet of clay, and Americans as rich and gutless.[51] These failures in the estimation of power contributed to uncertainty in Paris and London and to aggression and bluff in Rome and Berlin between 1935 and 1938; to the way, in 1939, Germany and Britain and France, and in 1941 Germany and the USSR, and Japan and the United States and Britain, misconstrued each other's intentions and power and so entered wars of a kind none expected; to the way every state assessed intelligence and used it to pursue policy.

Between 1933 and 1941, diplomatic intelligence was higher in quality than ever before, more widely distributed and more competitive. The balance between sources and nations was complex. Generally, codebreaking is regarded as the best source of diplomatic intelligence and agents are reputed as unreliable. The medium is a greater problem with agents than codebreakers. Spies pursue secrets, matters beyond the reach of open sources, through twisted means and men, by placing trust in traitors. Yet, during the 1930s, spies were as good a source of diplomatic intelligence as any other. The mutual incomprehension on big issues could best be penetrated by acquiring documents from other states, through agents in place or by rifling the bags of foreign governments in transit. Despatches say more than telegrams. Codebreaking illuminated details more than the whole; few leaders bared their heart over the telegraph or international telephone lines. Compared to 1914 or even 1929, courier systems had improved and major outposts received more material than before, reducing the significance of the material codebreakers could strike while increasing that available to agents or burglars. The best documented codebreaking bureaus, the British Government Code and Cypher School (GC&CS), the *Forshungsamt* and *Pers Z* of Germany, and the American army's Signals Intelligence Service, provided no more material fundamental to diplomacy than spies and document stealing gave Italy and the USSR. Human intelligence services varied in quality, with the United States weakest, the USSR strongest, and the rest fairly equal. The average service was good, the best great.[52] Despite its failures in 1940–1945, during the 1930s the British Secret Intelligence Service (SIS) was able in western Europe, China and the Middle East, maintaining the quality of its networks by emphasizing their ability to procure documents, as was the German *Abwehr* in western and central Europe, using Ukranian nationalists, for example, against Poland.[53] Through consuls, traitors and work with anti-colonial forces, Japanese intelligence learned what it wanted to know before 1942; it collected good tactical and operational material which was incorporated effectively into the attacks which opened the Pacific War. Through masterly methods, the *Deuxieme Bureau* illuminated its main target, Germany, as did Polish and Czecholsovak agencies; Italian intelligence did well against Britain and France. The greatest hoard of gems was piled in Moscow by ideologues and mercenaries. During the 1930s, Soviet intelligence acquired copies—sometimes in multiple form—of British telegrams and despatches from four sources in the Foreign Office (Donald MacLean, John Cairncross, Ernest Oldham and John King), and also the agent penetrating British establishments for Italian intelligence.[54] During 1939, Soviet intelligence had great access to the secrets of all the great powers. It penetrated the German embassies in Warsaw and Tokyo (and thus also Japanese decision making), the British embassies in Rome and Paris and the Foreign Office's Communications Department; and probably acquired key correspondence from most embassies in Moscow, through black-bag jobs and chancery servants-turned-spies. Anglo-French negotiators in Moscow during 1939 stayed in local hotels where their private discussions no doubt were bugged. Intelligence has shaped few matters as much as Soviet decisions about the Germano-Soviet Pact.[55] The Soviets showed how easily good human intelligence could be collected from a parade of pathetic failures unable to get satisfaction, sexually, philosophically, or otherwise.

Less is known about diplomatic codebreaking. The cryptanalytical and intelligence personnel at the GC&CS rose from eighty to 200 members between 1934 and 1939, as was roughly the case with those in similar positions at the *Forshungsamt* and *Pers Z*. In 1938–1939, the OGPU's codebreaking section had about 100 members and that of the US army twenty-two to twenty-five. In 1940, the Italian army's "Cryptographic Section" had forty-five, of whom sixteen to twenty were cryptanalysts, the remainder being clerks and translators.[56] Each week, on average, the GC&CS gave Whitehall seventy-four solutions of the encoded telegrams of foreign governments, and read important diplomatic systems of perhaps twenty smaller powers, the United States, France and Japan. It had no access to any German systems or to Soviet diplomatic ones, but did succeed against Red Army and Comintern traffic (which met many of its key concerns regarding the USSR), Italian diplomatic, military and colonial codes, and the military messages of Japan and many smaller states. The documentation on German codebreaking is less thorough—a sample of some 0.0066% of the *Forshungsamt*'s product between 2 September 1938 and 2 September 1939, plus some impressionistic comments. It provided more reports than the GC&CS, perhaps 604 per week in 1938–1939, but most were intercepted telephone calls, something Britain did, but not through the GC&CS.[57] Together, the *Forshungsamt* and *Pers Z* seem to have been less good at diplomatic codebreaking than the GC&CS, providing fewer solutions and cracking less high-grade traffic of Latin American states and middle-level codes of three major powers, Japan, Italy and the United States, though their success against most states in the Balkans, Poland and Turkey was fundamental to the diplomatic battleground on which Germany chose to fight. In technical terms, the great German successes were in cryptography, signals intelligence in the field, and against telephone traffic. American codebreakers beat just one major state, Japan, which in turn had little success against any great power, while Britain, the United States, the USSR and Germany read its systems. The story with codebreaking by other states is less certain. Italy read much military and some diplomatic traffic of most states in the Balkans and many in Latin America, Spain, the United States, France and Britain—more or less at the GC&CS's standard. Unlike the GC&CS, the Italians relied not on cryptanalysis but on copying codebooks through black-bag jobs at embassies in Rome. When it entered the war its power quickly eroded; while not entirely a blessing, the GC&CS's focus on the techniques of cryptanalysis aided the rise of Bletchley Park. France probably did slightly better than Germany or the United States, though worse than Britain or Italy—it read some Italian diplomatic traffic, some minor British traffic, and the codes of Spain, Eire and Austria. The success of the USSR is uncertain—it rated above France and conceivably led the world in diplomatic codebreaking. Polish codebreakers were excellent, reading major systems of all their neighbours, the conquerors of Enigma; other small states also had successes. Poland and Sweden stood alongside Britain and the United States and ahead of all other countries in the most difficult and innovative of cryptanalytical achievements.[58] Other practices matched in significance the interception and solution of telegrams. Though every state rifled the bags of foreign powers and tapped the telephones of foreign embassies, Italy had a spectacular ability to seize documents, and Germany to exploit international telephone lines crossing its territory. In 1938–1939, Hitler made Germany the centre for crisis and diplomacy. The *Forshungsamt*'s ability to monitor telephone conversations to and from diplomats in Berlin, and on the European trunk lines which ran through its territory, produced a triumph of communications intelligence between 1933 and 1939. These technical successes, however, were not always useful to policy. Hitler did not like to read telephone intercepts (as against solutions of telegrams), though it is hard to accept that he did so only on one occasion, while Goering, the *Forshungsamt*'s master, did not freely share its product with his rival, Ribbentrop, nor let his service cooperate with that of the Foreign Minister. More generally, success in communications intelligence varies with one's ability both to solve traffic and to intercept it. The USSR could intercept only traffic sent to and from embassies in Moscow or on cables crossing its territory from Europe to Asia, weakening the value of its codebreaking capabilities, as occurred for similar reasons to the United

States and to Italy. Britain controlled the bulk of intercontinental cables, giving the GC&CS the same position in the world as the *Forshungsamt* had in Europe. These two states appear to have gained the most communications intelligence in the 1930s.

Security against espionage also varied. Far and away the strongest was the USSR, protected by ferocious counter-intelligence and purges at home and by great cryptography abroad; then Japan, with powerful counter-espionage but poor cryptography, and Germany, where that situation was reversed; then perhaps Italy; with Britain, France and the United States at the bottom of the list. The significance of insecurity is hard to determine. In broad terms, it is not always a problem, as when one means one's bargaining position and wants others to know what it is; in order to play chicken, one must signal the fact and have it believed. Sometimes poor cryptography can aid diplomacy—though this is scarcely advisable! Insecurity is a problem only when one is bluffing or mistaken or uncertain or fearful or pursuing a policy others can disrupt, as was true for the status quo powers of the 1930s. During 1939, Soviet penetration of British establishments shaped its reaction to a poor offer from Whitehall and an attractive one from Hitler—indeed, it helped the USSR to procure that proposal. Anyone able to read British telegrams and documents about Italy would see Whitehall took it seriously as a power and wanted desperately to get on better terms—too seriously, too desperately—but was unwilling to offer it much. Official channels would have revealed most of these views, but access to secret material sharpened them. This shaped a fundamental problem for British diplomacy (and Italian strategy)—Mussolini's contempt for England. Yet security can be too much of a good thing. The USSR hid the virtual doubling of its military in size after September 1939, one cause for the gross errors about its military power in 1941, when Nazi Germany and Britain underestimated its strength in divisions by 50 per cent. This failure usually is credited to the incompetence of foreign intelligence—it actually stemmed from changes in the competence of Soviet security. From 1932 to 1939, signals intelligence was Britain's main source on the Soviet order of battle, and an excellent one—it gave Whitehall more material on the Red Army than perhaps any other military force on earth. In this key area, Soviet security was mediocre. However, in December 1940, the MID noted, "practically no information concerning (Red Army) formations in the interior has been received since the outbreak of War". That is, Britain no longer got signals intelligence on that subject, presumably because the Red Army minimized the use of radio. Thus, Britain missed the Red Army's massive expansion in size between September 1939 and June 1941.[59] Its experience illuminates the German one. Soviet radio silence explains why these powers underestimated the size of the Red Army in 1941, as it destroyed their only good source on the topic. Yet this Soviet triumph was double-edged. Security sapped the deterrent posture Stalin thought he had established; he knew his state was strong and assumed others did so too. They did not, though Hitler might well have attacked even had he known the real strength of the Red Army.

In the balance of intelligence and insecurity, each power had an edge over some rival, led the world somewhere, and was beaten by someone. Generally, each was stronger in intelligence than security, in attack over defense, though the Soviet shield was formidable and the *katana* dull. The United States and Japan stood at the bottom of the league table, and the USSR ruled the roost, but otherwise the intelligence services of the great powers, and of Czechoslovakia and Poland, were of tolerably equal quality. Parity occurred in part because the central issue of 1937–1939 was central Europe, where a regional intelligence service could outclass a major one based outside that region, and the traffic of small states betray the position of a great power with impenetrable cryptography. In 1939, through these means, Germany followed the details of the British strategy of guarantees in eastern Europe.[60] In central Europe British intelligence was weaker than anywhere else, German stronger, Polish even more so, though this did not prevent its leaders from making a tragic overestimate of their power. More generally, secondary states with poor cryptography but well-placed ministers inadvertently provided excellent commentary on every great power to every other one; Turkey, for example. Again, the power of intelligence is tricky to define. If the USSR led the world in collection, this stream died in dust. By January 1937 Soviet leaders condemned their intelligence for treachery and incompetence in recruiting agents! In 1940, just before being shot as a spy of Poland, Yezhov claimed that in 1934: "Polish spies ... had infiltrated all departments of the organs of the Cheka. Soviet intelligence was in their hands." In order to destroy traitors and foreign spies, he "purged 14,000 Chekists. But my great guilt lies in the fact that I purged so few of them". When forced to retire from the NKVD in 1938, he warned that many of its leading members were "secret agents and conspirators", while "intelligence operations abroad will essentially have to be rebuilt from scratch since the Department of Foreign Operations ... was contaminated with spies, many of whom had been in charge of networks of agents abroad who had been put in place by foreign intelligence agencies". Thus, he died victim to agents in his agency. In 1941, Stalin believed many of his intelligence officers were traitors, or conduits for British deception—so too in 1943. Thus, Soviet intelligence was wrecked, and spies abroad lost contact with their masters. In 1941 excellent intelligence did not save Stalin from error; only in 1939 did the USSR use intelligence well, to serve a poor policy.[61] When combined with politicization and paranoia at home and the effect of images, the stream of intelligence on British policy blinded the Soviet leadership to a greater danger. British intelligence, less good against the USSR than vice versa, aided policy more. Ciano, perhaps the best informed statesman of 1937–1940, was no Cavour. Japan was easily outweighed in the balance, but still in 1941 its foes failed and fell, because it needed simple knowledge to launch brilliant attacks, while that required for defence against it was hard to collect and even harder to interpret correctly. Altogether, diplomatic intelligence was of a high quality, and balanced fairly equally between the great powers; as a whole it did not work systematically in anyone's favour against everyone else; but it did have that effect in many specific instances.

This balance of intelligence can be seen as a series of individual duels, in which most countries defeated Japan and the United States, the USSR whipped all comers except perhaps Poland, Italy beat the status quo powers and smaller states but not its fellow revisionists, generally major countries defeated several minor ones and small states were beaten by two or more great powers—Turks, Yugoslavs, Spanish Nationalists and Republicans by most. Despite its value, that approach is too linear to express the phenomenon at hand: how knowledge affected a dialectical, reciprocal and multilateral process. These duels must also be seen in systematic terms. The result—or just the process—of each affected all the rest. In 1939 Soviet and Italian success in acquiring British documents affected a third duel, as each gave Germany copies of such material, better than anything the *Forshungsamt* generated, selected to suit their interests; since each acted unknown to the other, the aggregate effect was not necessarily what either intended.[62]

The significance of intelligence and its balance varies with international systems and each state's place in them. In the 1920s, liberal states forced their will through power. Revisionist powers were weak and isolated, most states supported the status quo, the liberal order was armed. France or Britain held the strategic initiative in diplomacy, being the stronger player which set the pace in most interactions—determining their nature and consequences, thrusting the burden of uncertainty and the need to make the first move in bargaining onto others, who had to guess their intentions and how to influence them. In such circumstances, revisionists might gain little from superior intelligence and lose with parity; even with bad intelligence, status quo states could still pick the ground and the time to fight, at worst needlessly losing the occasional trick. With good intelligence they could see the cards in their opponents hands, after already having the advantage of picking the game—and the deck. In the 1920s, British and French intelligence was good and they were powerful. This combination helped them maintain the status quo, and modify it, while hampering the ability of revisionists to overthrow that order and revealing the attitudes of men such as Mussolini and Vladimir Lenin, though not Gustav Streseman. From 1933, conversely, the liberal order became less cohesive and militarily weaker, the beneficiaries of the status quo declined to support it or cooperate with each other. The balance of power ceased to work because no one tried to make it do so. Only the revisionists played power politics and they aimed to wreck the balance. They grew in strength and in number— Germany, Italy, the USSR, Japan. Though the revisionists did not work closely together, when one shook the status quo, all gained. It was easier for them to shake the system than for other states to cooperate in its support. To a rare degree, last seen in Europe between 1856 and 1871, all states played a lone hand; even mere alignments were rare and weak. The system ceased to shelter its members, offering little support to any defender nor impediment to any attacker nor counterweight to any strength or aggression. The power of the stronger party in any bilateral relationship or the multilateral whole was multiplied, because weaker parties stood alone. The revisionists' policies could be simple—they might use the most opportunistic of tactics and pursue any bilateral relationships they wished and blow them or the whole up, because they wished to destroy the system, the status quo powers did not; thus their tactics were constrained and their policies were tangled. They searched for a diplomatic solution to the revisionists when there was none, only a strategic one, the creation of power and its use. Each status quo power also faced a particular dilemma. The United States had little ability to affect events. French leaders feared they held a losing hand, doubting their ability without aid to hold off Germany in war, unsure how to meet its pressure, forced on the defensive in an area hard to defend, central Europe, trying to square the strategic circle through multilateral diplomacy. Britain pursued an active and ambitious policy, aiming to solve every problem in the world at once through multilateral and liberal internationalist means. Until 1937, it could neither achieve this policy, nor abandon it. As these states sought to pursue their policies or prevent them from collapse, they jumped to the initiative of revisionist powers, defending their interests against two or three states while jettisoning those of the international system, feeling themselves a vulnerable party in interactions, guessing at their adversaries' aims and the means to influence them.

Revolutions in Tokyo, Berlin and Moscow prevented foreigners from knowing who did what to whom; official contacts led only to bureaucrats who executed policy, which was formulated by a few men (or one man) who were hard to contact, influence or understand, who viewed power and policy in a more cynical and less-reasoned fashion than the professionals they despised. While stationed in Berlin, the French ambassador Francois-Poncet noted that "the plans of Herr Hitler and his colleagues remain an enigma" while "the Duce's projects continue to be enveloped in mystery"; even to his servants. When viewing how each other formulated policy, British, American and French observers assumed that power was divided among many men (often with one paramount), officials were powerful, while public opinion was autonomous and influential. When viewing the revisionist states, they located power in one man, surrounded by a small group of loyalists, informed but factionalized; a layer of officials, of limited influence; and public opinion, meaningless or malleable. In 1937 Francois-Poncet held that:

Contradictions and incoherence disconcert our spirit, imbued with logic. That is not true of the complex mentality of the leaders of the Reich and of their people. Impulsive, fanatical, unbalanced, their chiefs follow here their instincts for violence and appetites for domination, and there the call of reason. They place arrogance and ambition over doubt and fear of consequences, menace above worry about retaining a way out, if the menace fails. They are divided between juxtaposed currents which merge or separate, retreat or prevail, in turn.

As for the people, they form an amorphous mass, always ready, at the bottom, to follow the tendencies which are known to be the most powerful. Certainly, most of them desire peace and tranquility. They do not want war.

But they could easily be made to do so.[63] Foreign observers were left to scan for signs in the guts of the press, or in public statements—interpreting Hitler in the light of *Mein Kampf*, Mussolini in *Machiavelli*.[64] Meanwhile, elements within the Axis spread disinformation—the *Gestapo* may have leaked false documents to Moscow which triggered the army purge; Germans routinely overstated their capabilities, especially in airpower, to British and French officials, with effect; Italian intelligence fed false information about the *Regia Aeronautica* through controlled French agents. These campaigns of deception were linked to rumours from many quarters, uncoordinated and contradictory, and one of the most successful was an accident. The attempts by the Italian ambassador in London, Count Grandi, to convince Chamberlain that Mussolini longed for a deal with Britain, was his own creation, unauthorized and unappreciated by his superiors. For careerist purposes, Grandi aimed to manipulate Mussolini and Chamberlain. This campaign became deceptive only because Mussolini declined to exploit this chance, Grandi pursued such a deal almost as a freelance, and gulled Chamberlain into misconstruing a key matter.[65] British and French statesmen were thrown into uncertainty, sometimes believing that every action had such unpalatable consequences that the easiest solution was to take none, on other occasions willing to prime the pump of better relations with Germany and Italy by paying them for the privilege of starting a bargaining process.

These problems were structural and psychological: they centred on intelligence, or its absence. A reactive power needs better intelligence than a strong and active one—to understand what is happening, what to do and how, it must be right on more things. It must know the active power's intentions, the latter merely its own mind. This situation breeds tendencies like uncertainty, guessing as to the active party's aims and one's means to influence them, and worst-case planning. Between 1933 and 1939 the status quo powers needed outstanding intelligence. They did not have it. They had to look for clues to the intentions of revisionist powers through guesses based on newspaper editorials, courtier gossip, and crude means of measurement, like ranking decision makers in two groups, such as "moderates" or "extremists". The GC&CS offered Britain little on the policy of Italy, Germany and the USSR, and the SIS little on the USSR and Japan. French military intelligence was good, but much of this advantage was lost to politicization, while its diplomatic intelligence was weak until 1939. The United States had expertise against only Japan, and imperfectly. Intelligence was slow to help status quo statesmen understand the intentions of Hitler and Mussolini and their willingness to act on them. They had to guess at these matters and did so badly; the fears they might guess wrong or bluff too far helped to queer their pitch. The inability to be sure of Hitler's intentions until 1939 or of Mussolini's until 1940 crippled decision making and let Germans and Italians manipulate Frenchmen and Britons. Britain assessed far more accurately the aims of the one revisionist state whose diplomatic traffic the GC&CS still mastered and Britain intercepted, Japan; had Britain read Italian correspondence in 1937–1938 as in 1923–1926, Grandi could not so easily have manipulated Chamberlain.[66] Though the GC&CS still mastered Italian diplomatic traffic, couriers carried material which once had gone by wire. France got Italy right only at the turn of 1938/1939, when codebreaking demonstrated Italian hostility.[67] Intuition and translations of foreign newspapers gave Hitler and Mussolini a better picture of policy than their opponents received through secret sources—with Stalin in 1941 as much as Daladier in 1938. The limits to intelligence were part of the problem of the status quo powers—and an improvement would have mattered; it might have been the only means to tear blinkers from eyes when vision still mattered, and to let statesmen understand how far deterrence and concession were working, or could work. Instead, they stood divided and on the defensive, weaker than the revisionist powers in intelligence and security, unable to choose the ground of battle, made to play to their weaknesses. The key battleground became central Europe—where the position of the status quo powers was weakened and that of the revisionists strengthened, as the imbalance of power multiplied that of intelligence. The revisionist powers often forced the status quo powers to play on their ground, against their strong suit, sometimes in a contest where a trick took the game—most notably, Germany in 1938–1939, and the USSR in 1939. They could win simply by disrupting the status quo, somehow, somewhere. France and Britain had to defend specific interests without upsetting the whole.

Between 1933 and 1941, diplomatic intelligence shone most on secondary issues but it still illuminated the heights.[68] It guided Italy to triumph over Britain during the Abysinnian crisis, by showing Whitehall's reluctance to intervene.[69] In 1936–1939, Germans and Italians easily monitored French and British relations with central and southeast European powers, casting light on the diplomatic battlefield from all sides. During the Munich crisis, the *Forshungsamt* listened as the highest Czech leaders broke their hearts and the secrets of Prague, Paris and London over the telephone; it learned how foreign counsels were divided, that Britain and France aimed to avoid war and were pushing Czechoslovakia to concession. This material was irreplaceable and fundamental. It compromised Britain's policy of keeping everyone guessing, and the credibility of France. It did not change German policy, but did reinforce the thrust: it let Hitler and Ribbentrop realize they were winning and might gain more by pushing the screw.[70] During 1939, the traffic of Balkan states and the telephone calls of ambassadors in one's capital guided diplomacy for Germany and Italy (the latter aided by British and French documents), though it also led their policies to clash and Germans to split. This material led Hitler and Ribbentrop to believe Britain's bluffing, that determined action could break the logjam in central Europe and the status quo in the Continent without risk of war in the west; it led Goering (and perhaps some of Ribbentrop's subordinates) to different actions and a cacophony of mixed messages which reinforced Whitehall's belief the Germans were bluffing. Throughout, German success against low security telegrams or telephone calls showed the mood of diplomats and indicated that in their capitals. A few hours forewarning of foreign overtures let Hitler or Ribbentrop prepare an effective rhetorical response, something to which Whitehall attached real (or unreal) significance. Monitoring Neville Henderson's telephone calls to London may have led German authorities to mistake his views for those of his superiors, overestimating their panic and underrating their resolution.[71] Intelligence was fundamental to the diplomatic tactics of Germany and Italy; less so to their strategy.

Between 1933 and 1938, conversely, the GC&CS's solutions of Japanese traffic steered Britain through dangerous water. Aided by the SIS, it revealed the basis of Axis diplomacy—there was no Axis. These services uncovered the secret relations between Japan, Germany and Italy, showing with clarity, if not completion, the aims behind the Anti-Comintern Pact.[72] Whitehall used that intelligence to deduce the intentions of hostile powers and their factions, no mean feat, given the confusion in these relations and the Pact. The Japanese and German factions which pushed the Pact did so to confuse other powers. Its effect was the opposite. By monitoring discussions about it, Britain could determine the relations between Japan, Germany and Italy. In late 1938, solutions of Japanese traffic showed Germany was pressing Japan to turn the Pact from a defensive alignment against the USSR into an offensive alliance against Britain. This news sparked an anguished analysis of GC&CS solutions by the Foreign Office, and helped it understand Hitler's aims.[73] Though Britain lost access to major Japanese diplomatic systems in February 1939, it had a powerful means to analyze Japanese intentions, through reports from other sources of the debate in Tokyo about Hitler's offer; this shaped its policy toward Japan, Germany and the USSR. The United States, the USSR and Germany shared such power. Though the evidence is lacking, knowledge of this Japanese debate may well have showed Hitler that Tokyo could not meet his needs and Stalin that danger and opportunity were near, shaping the road to the Nazi–Soviet pact—though it was only one strand of the intelligence available to Germany, and even more, the USSR.

These successes were significant, and there were others (British and Italian codebreaking records may revise understanding of the diplomacy of the Spanish Civil War, for example), yet at the highest of levels, intelligence mattered less than incomprehension. Diplomatic intelligence aids bargaining and knowledge. One can more easily use it than learn from it. In the circumstances, the effect was systematic. Intelligence favoured those who needed it for tactical as against strategic purposes; those who wanted to destroy the status quo, as against those who wanted to preserve it. Fighting on their chosen ground and knowing their own minds, the revisionist powers had better intelligence and could act on it opportunistically. The status quo powers, ruled by uncertainty, were inferior in information and could use it less freely. Before they could use intelligence for tactics, they had to use it for strategy. Britain and France, playing a guessing game, needed better intelligence than they had, so to learn how to guess right. They needed to experience Munich before they could avoid it. Learning was possible, and significant. In 1939, lessons derived from Munich combined with good and bad intelligence led British and French decision makers to take a firm line, the only one justifiable in strategic terms, however poor the execution. But learning was not easy, nor was it linear. Much data and experience were needed to change any mind on any issue. These lessons sometimes were poor, while rivals at home and abroad also learned from experience, and changed their behaviour too, and so all lessons learned were invalidated before they were applied. At the turn of 1938/1939, a flood of reports, ranging from excellent solutions to deliberate disinformation, led Paris and London to understand Hitler's aims; and Germans to think Britain hostile after Munich (when it was not) and to act to make it so. Britons and Germans learned the same lesson—that if pushed to the limit, the other would back down. Within that framework they interpreted intelligence and sent mixed messages and missed them and deployed leverage, and wrecked the other's application of these insights in the weeks before 3 September 1939. For equally dialectical reasons, in August 1939 Soviet policy stunned Britain and that of Italy did the same to Hitler; as, in 1941, German policy had stunned Stalin and Japan Roosevelt and Churchill.

Intelligence points to the interaction between information and attitudes. Study of the matter shows its significance and even more that of ideology, and its relationship to perception, the real hidden dimension of diplomacy. One can reconstruct the logic behind decisions only by examining the data available to decision makers; the intelligence record mirrors their times. In the period 1933–1941, this mirror illuminates the policy of statesmen with unique clarity, but the greatest reflection is of the state system. Intelligence was better than between 1904 and 1914 and more widely distributed and used; and yet more than in 1914, great events were unintended. In the decisions for war, only Italy in 1940 and Germany and Japan in 1941 acted as they intended (though, as with most states in 1914, the results were not as expected). In 1941 Americans, British and Soviets were more surprised than any leaders had been in 1914, while on 1 September 1939 neither Hitler nor the British government expected war with each other. The correlation between two powers seeking to use deterrence to bolster a fragile status quo and avoid war, another using power politics to wreck that order and create its hegemony and war, a third grotesquely overrating its own military capacity, and another believing that war was inevitable, the only choice being when and how to enter it, produced results catastrophic for all. Reason and *raison d'État* and intelligence were bad guides for these statesman, because they viewed events and played the game so differently, in a dialectical, reciprocal, multilateral system, a remarkably atomized one, with so many actors affecting each other in such unpredictable ways, where ideas, knowledge, policy and cause and effect were linked in an ironic fashion. Intentions were not effected, nor effects intended. Statesmen thought the state system a machine where all one needed to create an effect was to pull a lever. In fact, the machine was baroque and broken. There were more levers to be pulled than in 1914, but with a less certain outcome and more people pulling away to opposite effect. People thought they knew how to get what they wanted but failed to do so, because they did not understand the system, and the way in which it worked. These statesmen thought they were all playing a game with one set of rules; instead, each was playing a different game with the same pieces. All thought they understood the world; none did. From the collective combination of their intuition and intelligence and ambition, they created the truth they deserved, which was illusion. In this context, the expectation of certainty was a source of incomprehension. The more surely one thought one understood events, the more mistaken one was; the more one trusted one's intuition or intelligence, the more misguided one was. There is a striking correlation between good intelligence and failed policy between 1939 and 1941—Germany and Britain in 1939, the USSR, Britain and the United States in 1941. Intelligence was not a tool for these statesmen as they worked in the machine of states—it was a broken saw whiplashing across the system. Nor was this characteristic without consequence. The outbreak of the different phases of the Second World War was dominated by accident. Yet had this not occurred, had statesmen seen the world as it was, differences over the interests of states still would have caused a great war though, perhaps, governments might have made fewer fundamental errors. The Second World War broke out because of a systems failure; much the same would also have happened had the system worked as intended. Interests and power were factors of the first order, with images and incomprehension and intelligence in the second rank—and yet still the latter shaped the world during 1939–1941. Ideology and image created incomprehension; intelligence could not overcome them; its success in acquiring data mattered less than its failure to penetrate preconception, or to help intention overcome accident. It is here that intelligence most shaped the origins of the Second World War. A war which should have occurred by intention did so by accident.

4
THE BRITISH "ENIGMA"
Britain, signals security and cipher machines, 1906–1953[1]

Historians have been more interested in the breaking than the making of codes. There is but one exception to that rule: the fascination with machines which encipher messages at one end of a communication circuit and decipher them at the other. Although this idea is centuries old and many such machines were patented between 1850 and 1920, many assume that the history of cipher machines began in 1920, with the development of the "Enigma" system. Amidst the emphasis on German experiences with "Enigma", that of other states with such systems has been overlooked. Britain, for example, commonly is thought to have ignored cipher machines until 1926 and not to have begun to develop them until 1935.[2] The British "Enigma" has a more peculiar history than this. It illustrates the problems which cryptography posed to every state during the first half of the twentieth century, and illuminates the forgotten half of the wireless war between 1939 and 1945. ULTRA was not enough for victory; Britain won not just by breaking German codes but by defending its own. Nor was that victory foredoomed. In 1939 Britain had neither the communication nor the cryptographic facilities which it needed to survive. Until 1942 its cryptography was no better than that of Germany, perhaps worse. Britain paid for these mistakes in blood. It had to rebuild its signals and its security as they faced deadly attack. Its successes in these endeavours, no less than the offensive victories of Bletchley Park, made 1942–1943 the turning point in the wireless war.

Governments have as much to gain from defending their own secret messages as attacking those of foreign states—if not more. The requirements for cryptography are determined by the characteristics of the media which carry traffic. Until the 1840s any government's messages could be intercepted only if they could be filched from diplomatic bags or the public post. The secrecy of messages was defended more by the security of bags than of ciphers, which made attack easy. During the telegraph age, again, some of any and every government's traffic could be intercepted, by anyone with access to cables or their offices. A new form of communication which arose after 1896, radio, was even faster and more flexible to use than cable.

Unfortunately, all of this traffic could be intercepted by anyone within range of the transmission and able to receive the frequency. Between 1900 and 1945, states responded to this danger slowly and in two overlapping ways: by refining traditional cipher systems, and by developing new ones such as cipher machines and "one-time pads" (OTP), in which cipher groups are superenciphered on a system which is never used again.

These means should have kept cryptography abreast of cryptanalysis, but codemakers have one handicap in their struggle against codebreakers. The ease of communication is as important a requirement for government messages as security. Signals authorities conventionally argue that the need to receive "our own messages quickly and correctly is more important than that of their concealment from the enemy", and rightly so.[3] A complex cipher may be very secure but will delay the transmission of messages, which can cost the Napoleonic minute. Security can defeat itself, since the use of complex systems leads to transmitting errors which compromise ciphers or policies. When dealing with easily intercepted forms of communication, states must carefully balance the needs for security and usability. Even the best of general principles sometimes will be inappropriate and many practices can degrade both secrecy and the ease of communication. Cipher machines offered a means to sidestep this danger, to enhance both these needs at the same time. Although such machines were valuable for cable traffic, essentially they were the product of the requirements for cipher security in the radio age. Britain's approach toward these machines always hinged on its attitudes toward these greater issues. Unfortunately, until 1939 it always underestimated the scale to which it would use radio and its need for signals security.

Britain was among the first powers in the twentieth century to recognize the potential value of cipher machines. Its fighting services first became interested in these devices around 1906, almost exactly when they began to consider the use of radio on a large scale. Since they believed radio was uniquely open to interception while "an expert who had sufficient material and sufficient time" could break any cipher,[4] they recognized that the use of radio posed unprecedented cryptographic dangers. They hoped to minimize these risks by using radio only when absolutely necessary and by frequently changing their cipher systems. They also pursued technical chimeras such as radio frequencies which could never be intercepted by an enemy. The services, however, misjudged the role of radio in wartime and the security of existing ciphers. The Royal Navy (RN) did not even have a superencipherment system for its codebooks, relying instead on an elementary transposition cipher which David Beatty, the commander of the British battlecruiser force, noted "can be discovered by any student of cryptography in about one hour".[5] The RN and the British and Indian armies planned to use the Playfair system, a decent substitution cipher but far from unbreakable and scarcely easy to use, to cover inter-service traffic in the field. In

August 1914 the services' apparatus of codes and ciphers did not allow radio to be used securely and flexibly.

In all fairness, before 1914 no power found it easy to balance the needs for security and the usability of radio. Only extraordinary means could safeguard radio traffic, even ordinary ciphers were cumbersome. Naturally, the services were attracted by inventors who claimed their cipher machines could make messages absolutely unbreakable yet easy to transmit. Some of these machines were complex—one studied during the July crisis, the "Cryptotyper", consisted of two typewriters. Plaintext was entered on one, and transmitted on wire to the other via a sort of plugboard which enciphered messages through the use of paper strips with punched holes, like "the roll of music in a piano player". Most did so through wheels on which the cipher key could be set in various ways. The services' approach toward these devices was marked by an ignorance of the technology and of cipher security. In 1906 the Admiralty examined one machine without realizing that it was a pirate of another patented in 1890. In 1912 it regarded one system as being entirely secure, only to discover just before the war that the messages could be solved within a few hours.[6] Yet given the novel technology, such errors were hard to avoid, and the services merit credit for making so thorough an examination at so early a stage. Between 1906 and 1914 the army and the navy considered or tested under service conditions at least thirteen such machines. They flirted with the idea of commissioning a firm to construct another according to their specifications. They thoroughly examined the question, which interested senior personnel. In 1913 the General Staff's Director of Staff Duties, George Cockerill, and one of its authorities regarding intelligence and the construction of ciphers, Francis Davies, argued that if cipher machines could be perfected, the very problem of the security and the usability of radio "will be solved". The First Lord of the Admiralty, Winston Churchill, believed such systems offered "a simple, swift and sure" method of ciphering. By 1914, however, the services decided that no "mechanical cyphering system" could meet their needs. By 1915 many cipher authorities regarded it as "nothing more than a waste of time" to view yet another prototype.[7]

Before 1914 cipher machines were a tangential but notable consideration in British signals security. The services and the Foreign and Colonial Offices showed foresight in recognizing the value of cipher machines but were naive in their attitudes. They rejected those available because these were too mechanically unreliable and insecure to serve for radio traffic in the field. This was to demand a level of performance beyond the state of the art, which none the less was at a respectable level. Several designers had devised complex if conceivably practicable means to change the cipher key frequently, which was essential for security. As Britain's leading codebreaker, Major G.R.M. Church, noted, "no mechanical contrivance which relies on a repetition of the key is absolutely safe, no matter how complicated it may be". However, the Admiralty rejected any machine which required frequent key changes, fearing this would cause "confusion" and "fatal delay". The "idea of changing the key from day to day" filled the Colonial Office "with horror".[8] This attitude was natural, given the lack of trained personnel and Britain's low standard of cipher security. Still, to demand that such machines be secure without changing the key was to ask the impossible. Conversely, the enthusiasts overestimated the speed with which cipher machines could be introduced and the degree to which these could solve the problem of security. This attitude fell into a pattern which would recur again and again.

The great war revealed major flaws in Britain's approach to cipher security and the use of radio. Its army traffic in the field was no less vulnerable than that of the enemy. Nor was diplomatic traffic better served: if, fortunately, most of it went over cables the enemy could not tap, neutral and Allied powers received tempting opportunities. Meanwhile, the Admiralty entered the war with a cryptographic system inferior to that of the *Kriegsmarine*. Fortunately, Room 40's successes in breaking German traffic revealed the vulnerabilities in these systems, and the Admiralty redressed these problems with skill. Britain handily won the defensive part of its cryptological war against Germany, largely through accident and geography.

In 1918–1919 British authorities moved to overcome these problems, by establishing a W/T Board to coordinate the service's research into radio, an Imperial Communications Committee (ICC) to oversee the empire's signals systems and the Government Code and Cypher School (GC&CS), among other things, to improve cipher security. As a result, by 1921 the departments had adopted more secure and cumbersome codebooks, which took 50–100 per cent longer to use than their previous ones, while by 1919 the services and the Foreign Office used superenciphered codebooks to cover all their important messages.[9] However, these systems were designed for cable traffic. The use of more vulnerable forms of communications soon dictated the needs for cipher security. Britain held that a "properly trained cryptographic bureau can in course of time break down the security of practically any code or cypher provided sufficient data—in the form of messages—are available to work on". Radio, being "particularly susceptible to interception was a most unreliable vehicle for secret messages".[10] Britain's instinct was to minimize the use of radio, so as not to endanger its ciphers. Yet radio was an admirable vehicle for urgent messages and was continually rising in value. Britain's attitude towards this dilemma fluctuated just as continually during 1919–1939.

Between 1919 and 1921 the ICC decided to complete the imperial wireless chain to make radio available for government messages. However, British cipher authorities wanted to limit its peacetime use to cases of "extreme emergency", since only cumbersome and never entirely secure systems could defend this traffic.[11] The War Office did not want any government message at all to be sent by wireless. By 1923 this attitude had changed fundamentally, because radio was simply too useful a medium to be ignored, given the revolutionary move from the spark system toward continuous wave and short wave and the mass production of sets. Cipher authorities accepted that radio would frequently carry important messages. In order to overcome the heightened problem of cipher security, they established the principle that all government messages sent by radio should be superenciphered on frequently changed tables.[12] While these systems could defend radio traffic, they were slow and hard to use. Simultaneously, the idea of cipher machines reemerged as a means to circumvent the dichotomy "between urgency and security".[13]

In the early 1920s several new machines, including the first versions of Enigma, were patented. Some of them, including Enigma, rested on a new basic concept, the use of a series of rotors to encipher messages, with adjustments to the settings in order to change the key. Such systems could be made electro-mechanical by adding wiring systems within the rotors. Through rotors, which British authorities called "drums" or "wheels" until 1945, designers had finally squared the technical circle and developed the means for a secure and yet mechanically reliable cipher machine. Whatever their immediate limitations, these machines could be modified to provide greater usability or security as desired, for example by adding a further electrical superencipherment system, like the plugboard of the German military version of Enigma. Codebreakers and engineers discussed the potential value of cipher machines in the international technical literature. A host of inventors and companies brought their wares to public and official attention, usually exaggerating their quality, the likelihood another government would seize sole rights and the price being offered for them. The American army adopted primitive systems of this sort by 1921, the German navy adopted such machines in 1921 and 1926, by the 1930s Japanese authorities examined some prototypes and the USN dozens, from German, Dutch, Swedish and Swiss inventors. Japanese, American and, most effectively, German, military services developed cipher machines, with the aim of making them standard equipment. There was a surprising amount of international cooperation in this regard. In 1931, the German army showed its Enigma system, including the plugboard, to an American army officer. In 1932, the German manufacturers of Enigma let a USN officer see an experimental model, an office system with a printer replacing the lampboard, being developed for the German military. German cryptographic authorities considered letting the officer examine this system more closely. American and French signals authorities later exchanged views on other systems.[14] Nor was Britain slow to note the value of such devices. During the 1920s cryptographic experts from the GC&CS and the War Office examined standard machines, such as the Hebern, Kryha and Enigma systems. By 1923 senior service figures believed these devices could solve the dilemma of radio traffic while the W/T Board held "that the advent of a secret mechanical system of cyphering is near at hand". The GC&CS "hoped that in a few years' time automatic machines would have reached sufficient perfection" to eliminate any need to superencipher radio traffic. The departments and the GC&CS agreed to work on this question. In 1926 an interdepartmental committee was formed to deal with cipher machines.[15]

Yet between 1923 and 1927 Britain did no more than examine prototypes while Germany began significantly to improve its cipher security by adopting and developing Enigma. Like other contemporary failures in British signals security, this one stemmed from a lack of interdepartmental coordination and interest. More than this, until June 1927 the RN insisted that cipher machines be mechanical, which blocked refinement of the best systems of this era, the Enigma, Hagelin and Hebern devices, all electro-mechanical. Still, the War Office commissioned the Accounting and Tabulation Co. to build a pneumatic rotor system designed by Sidney Hole, while one signals authority, Lieutenant Colonel Peel, pursued other designs.[16] Britain was concerned with the vulnerability of radio traffic. It also recognized that radio was rising in value and would sometimes carry the most crucial of messages. In 1928 it resolved a debate over using the radio in wartime by prohibiting any civilian department from doing so, an embargo which was removed only in 1939.[17] This self-denying ordinance did not solve the problem of security, since every department could use radio freely in peacetime (though the Dominion Office and Dominions sent cipher telegrams only by "a *British cable route throughout*", and never by "*wireless*"), as could the services in war.[18] It also hampered the use of a valuable form of communication.

At the same time, the government concluded that cipher machines could overcome these problems. In 1928 Britain established a Wireless Messages Committee to examine the "reliability" of radio communication. The GC&CS and the War Office's experts told it cipher machines could "render messages beyond the power of human ingenuity to decypher". While machines "of an inferior type are already on the market", a small initial outlay for research would allow the rapid, cheap and large-scale production of "much superior" ones. Possibly this statement refers to the O'Brien system, which received its first patent at this time and soon attracted much official attention. The committee favoured this proposal, believing these devices would make radio easy to use and "absolutely reliable from the point of view of security". It also noted "minor difficulties and breakdowns" would occur in the initial stages of the use of these machines.[19] This proved to be an understatement. This recommendation was timely, although Britain would have had to spend some years in order to procure the best possible model. The problem lay in the way that it did so. Since British hopes for the ease of manufacture of such machines were pitched too high, the disappointments inherent in the process of research, development and production might combine to crush its interest further than was justified. For almost a decade, Britain did something unique regarding cipher machines or, rather, two things. When other states adopted cipher machines, they generally worked with established inventors and patents, often giving them access to secret military patents, and developed the best available commercial models at the state of the art, as did the United States with Hebern's systems, Germany with Enigma and France with Hagelin devices; nor did they care about the nationality of the inventor. Britain chose to force the pace by commissioning a new system on the leading edge of technology, and to rely on indigenous inventors. It regarded proven commercial models, including the refined version of Enigma, as too "inferior" to serve even as a basis for development. It believed indigenous inventors and firms could build better and all-British ones. This belief was the greatest error in Britain's experiences with cipher machines before 1940, closely followed by the price of pinning all its trust on untested prototypes. British inventors of the era were no worse than those of other nationalities, but few people anywhere were able to build good cipher machines, nor did this happen on command; Britain was pursuing the most difficult way forward.

War Office experts appear to have taken the lead in this matter, and with some foresight. About this time, Peel advocated a "universal" rotor cipher machine, to handle all secret British traffic. This was an idea rather than an artifact: a model rotor, and drawings for a machine "designed on definite principles to meet the needs of a vast organization in the most simple manner". These principles rested on careful assessment of the best systems of the 1920s. They were a generation beyond the state of the art, applicable even to systems used in the 1980s. The aims were convenience, economy of men and money, but mostly security. In order to address "the possibility of mechanical attack in the future", Peel and his collaborator, Mr. G. Critchley, proposed a level of security exceeding that of any contemporary system and matching Typex in 1941: ten rotors ("five split drums making in effect ten drums with five setting points, giving a key length of security of 26^{10}"), their power multiplied by careful arrangement of the wiring within each rotor and differentiation of traffic through different wheel settings. This technical approach to security matched that of the German military experts of the period who were adapting Enigma, and the Americans who refined Hebern's systems. Like the Germans, Peel and Critchley sought means to avoid the flaws in Enigma wiring which left it vulnerable to isomorphic attack, and considered but rejected as infeasible the idea of a plugboard between two typewriters, as in the Cryptotyper of 1914 and one in Hebern's patent of 1915. Peel and Critchley also proposed two ideas later adopted in Typex: that the machine print on paper tape (used in teletype systems) and be able to work directly to teleprinters ("the mechanism can be adapted to punch a tape ready for automatic transmission, instead of typing, if such a design is required"). Their system may also have used the stator drums and the reversible inserts ("split" rotors) featured in Typex, though the description is not clear on that point. In fact, Peel proposed the idea of an on-line cipher teleprinter, though with reservations: one could "equip each W/T station with a tape punching cipher machine", but would "any Department or Service ... be prepared to pass secret messages in an unsafe form to a W/T operator"? The GC&CS thought this system would provide "absolute" security, while an engineer, Keith Elphinstone of Messrs. Elliott Bros., believed it could be made "practical".[20] This design, however, led nowhere; the ideas were innovative, the mechanics unsuccessful. This was an ideal machine, not a practicable one, but it may have influenced the development of Typex, and beneficially so.

In 1929, the Cipher Machine Committee pursued a different system, recommending that three "O'Brien–Gardner" devices be constructed and tested. The Treasury also stopped "all research" into cipher machines, probably referring to other systems, although this may have delayed the O'Brien ones. No evidence explains why officials liked this system, but O'Brien's patents prove the point. To the normal modes of rotor and wire security, it added a "scattering mechanism". A "worm drive" within the system caused eccentric movements in the rotors as they turned, in a mechanically complex and precise fashion. O'Brien pioneered the next major advance in security for cipher machines—a means for irregular rotor motions, first embodied during 1940 in the American Sigaba system. His system also printed the plain and enciphered text of messages, an improvement on the Enigma lampboard later used by Typex. That is, in 1929 British authorities turned down all existing systems because they saw their security flaws, and hoped to leap to the next generation.[21]

American naval authorities also admired O'Brien's system and its prototypes. Its expert in cipher machines, Lieutenant Wenger, praised the system for allowing mechanical "*effect* ... to react upon original *cause*", so producing "a tremendously long and complex cipher", which he calculated at more than "$73^5 \times 26^{25}$ starting points" (the equivalent of rotor settings—trillions of times more than the commercial variant of Enigma, or the German military versions of 1939). Wenger's assessment came shortly after he viewed the most recent versions of Enigma, including one using a system for irregular rotor systems which, significantly, he compared to "the 'scatter gears' of the O'Brien Machine". By implication, he too thought the O'Brien system more promising than Enigma. According to USN files, O'Brien and his firm Auto Cyphers Ltd, owned the patent for the system. Presumably because of limited finances, during 1930–1932 he worked for and assigned manufacturing rights to the Ougree Steel Trading Co., which hoped to sell thousands of machines to Britain, and even more to foreign governments. Ougree claimed to have spent £14,000 in preparing prototypes for testing, though this claim was perhaps exaggerated. W. Watson and Sons, Ltd, a leading firm of instrument makers, built the prototypes. American authorities thought O'Brien "a rather egotistical person who ventures to make rather broad statements which are so far-reaching that one is immediately inclined to question them as to facts". His sales pitch exaggerated British interest in the system, and his knowledge of British cryptanalysis, betraying some secrets, inventing others. He led Americans to think that the RN ran British codebreaking, "undoubtedly the best organization of its kind in the world and he glibly and directly infers that the British organization has little difficulty in reading the secret messages of practically all foreign governments", or "knows everything that goes on in the world". Though this statement had some truth, O'Brien largely made it up, perhaps based on inferences from gossip by GC&CS personnel. More seriously, he told Wenger that British cryptanalysis was led by Edward Travis, in fact, head of the GC&CS's security section, no doubt the most senior of its figures he knew. According to O'Brien, "he had received little encouragement at the beginning, ... the Cipher Bureau had told him that it was an axiom among cryptographers that a mechanical device cannot be made secure". Travis, however, was a strong advocate of his system, the first one he had supported, and complained of the Treasury's refusal to fund its development, which it had earlier done for systems the GC&CS disliked (and by extension others that, most likely, the War Office favoured); that Whitehall had ordered three prototypes, at £500 each, one for the Army, the RN and the RAF, "after seeing only the plans and the original model", and wanted to purchase complete patent rights, which O'Brien refused; and that the system had been tested by four "mathematicians" from the "Cipher Bureau" (possibly Travis, Dilwyn Knox, W.F. Clarke and L.H. Lambert). O'Brien even offered to sell the USN the same extra security procedures which, he claimed, the Admiralty wanted on its version! His behaviour was unusually mercenary for an inventor of cipher machines. Wenger noted that O'Brien "is a New Zealander by birth and an Irishman by extraction, which may account for his lack of what might be called loyalty, or at least discretion". O'Brien also feared Whitehall might leave him financially "high and dry"—his worst breaches of discretion occurred when his prototypes were undergoing British tests, and failing them. During this period, Ougree offered to loan (or sell) the USN two copies of the system for a test, along with O'Brien's services; but otherwise would entertain only large orders or nothing—the sale of American manufacturing rights for US$200,000, or of 200 machines for the same price.

Wenger noted that "satisfactory performance of the machine depends upon absolute accuracy of the timing, meshing, or registering of certain parts", while representatives of Ougree and Watson admitted that the prototypes needed much more development.[22] This was the problem. O'Brien's system was ingenious but impossible—too complex and fragile. These three machines, "first models hand-made and of rough workmanship", were not completed until autumn 1931 and frequently broke down in testing. Though the nature of the problems is unclear, a later O'Brien patent probably refers to them. It noted that all automatic (including scattering) functions of the new machine "are inter-related so that they cannot fail to take place in the proper order, and so that the possibility of disturbance of the cipher sequence owing to inadvertence on the part of the operator is eliminated. A further object is to provide a higher standard of mechanical perfection of the kind of machine described". In any case, by autumn 1932 an interservice committee recommended that the O'Brien system be abandoned. However, impressed with the potential of such devices, it wanted other prototypes to be tested.[23] Britain was no further advanced with cipher machines than in 1928, or in 1908. Nor would it progress much further during the next two years.

The causes for this inaction are obscure. Perhaps, as in 1915, cipher authorities had seen one too many unsuccessful prototypes to keep the faith. Experiences with the O'Brien machines marked many attitudes, as did the crisis of 1931. The influence of financial stinginess and limits on all the actors was remarkable. Ougree claimed that cryptographic authorities were attracted by the security of the O'Brien system, but wanted a private concern to subsidize the development of a workable machine. One signals authority later claimed the Cypher Machine Committee rejected any further work in the area between 1932 and 1934 "because it entailed spending further money without any certainty of success and owing to the difficulty of finding a person competent to develop an idea and produce the suggested model".[24] During this period, moreover, British attitudes toward cryptography changed again. Travis believed its new superencipherment system was extremely secure and reasonably flexible,[25] and the GC&CS seemed to have lost interest in cipher machines. It was not reactionary; its members enthusiastically supported machine cryptology from 1939, and paid professional attention to cipher machines during the interwar years. In 1930, however, they were less experienced with the matter than American or German military cryptanalysts; notably, W.F. Clarke and L.H. Lambert, the GC&CS's naval and radio experts, outside the mainstream of an organization focusing on diplomatic codebooks, dominated its investigation of cipher machines, where they were less significant than the service's signals and cryptographic branches.[26]

Meanwhile, in 1932–1933 a Strategic Cables Committee (SCC) reexamined the value of radio and telephones. It was spurred by their steadily rising use for government messages and stung by security problems such as the interception by an amateur operator of a radio telephone conversation between the Prime Minister and Britain's delegation at the Imperial Economic Conference in Ottawa. No one on this committee even mentioned cipher machines when discussing the question of security. Instead, the services hoped a system parallel to telephone "scrambling" devices could make radio messages "unbreakable" or even prevent them from being intercepted at all.

The GC&CS correctly denied this was possible. On the other hand, it claimed codebooks could defend whatever radio traffic the services would need to use in wartime, so long as they changed their supereciphering tables every fortnight. This prediction, coming from a bureau which demonstrated daily that foreign codebooks were vulnerable, indicates that the standard level of cryptography in international diplomacy during the 1920s was low; it was erroneous because the GC&CS assumed no one could change their ways, even though the Soviets had already done so and many other powers were soon to follow their example. Until 1940, British codemakers and codebreakers alike grossly overestimated the effect of any one change in superencipherment tables, and that problem was multiplied by the underestimation of how much radio traffic would be used.

The SCC reported that while large volumes of radio traffic could never be entirely secure, superencipherment would make a "good deal" of it sufficiently so. By "the time the enemy had succeeded in unravelling the cypher, not only might the information be out of date, but in any case the cypher would have been changed, and therefore he would have to start again *do novo*".[27] In cryptographic terms, these views were frighteningly naive. Superencipherment systems could offer great security, but only if properly constructed and used; only if, despite wide circulation, they were not physically compromised; only if the quantity of traffic carried on any one table (the "depth on the table") did not exceed a certain level. Britain's superencipherment systems of the 1930s and 1940s often fell short of these standards, as did those of every state. By 1943, Britain concluded that only when tables were changed up to 13 times per month, instead of once, could superencipherment systems defend large quantities of radio traffic. Earlier British practices did not meet these standards. In 1940 the RAF's basic book was five years old. It had only two tables—a "special" one for higher formations and a "general" one for all other traffic. These tables were universal—used by every RAF unit or formation on earth—and changed only once every three months. Few tables were held in reserve. So flawed a system was scarcely secure. Enemy cryptanalysts could pool all RAF traffic intercepted from the world in order to attack one table which, if broken, would expose all RAF traffic in Britain, in Egypt, everywhere. One physical compromise could strip naked all RAF traffic on earth. Precisely these problems did emerge during 1940–1942, not only for the RAF.[28]

In any case, between 1933 and 1935 several developments eroded the assumption codebooks would safeguard British radio traffic. Contrary to expectation, radio became "an everyday means of communication for all types of traffic".[29] While still not deemed a primary means of communication, it was used far more frequently than had been expected even in 1928. This increased quantity of messages would be correspondingly difficult to defend, while the steadily worsening international environment increased the need for cipher security. Codebooks could allow this only if they were further refined. By 1937, so the Air Ministry noted, "cypher book methods have become increasingly complicated owing to the necessity of obtaining an higher and higher degree of security as the art of the cryptographer progresses".[30] Superencipherment systems alone could not defend large quantities of radio traffic. Radio operators already found these systems hard to use; if their complexity was increased, the speed and flexibility of radio use, the characteristics which made it valuable for communication, must decline. Meanwhile, rapid means of ciphering were needed to service the high speed teleprinters which were just becoming an adjunct to military signals. Superencipherment systems could not easily defend large volumes of radio traffic: probably they would prevent such volumes from being transmitted at all. Had they been Britain's only high-grade systems in 1940, its strategic communications and cryptography alike might have foundered. Cipher machines again seemed a quick fix to immediate problems.

Here His Majesty's Government received a break like that which broke Enigma. A few dedicated men, working on their own initiative, gave Britain the means for speedy and secure communications. Central among them was the Chief Signals Officer of Coastal Command. O.G. Lywood is best remembered through an unsympathetic account by R.V. Jones, as the technician who almost stopped the genius from destroying the radio beacon system which guided the *Luftwaffe* against Britain in 1940, among other mistakes.[31] Lywood deserves a better memorial. His contribution to British victory matches that of Jones. During the mid-1930s, Lywood guided the British government's development of teleprinter systems, which multiplied the speed and hence the volume of signals, something desperately needed in 1940 and afterward. He was among the world's leaders in military communication and architect of the "Defence Teleprinter Network" (DTN), the backbone of British strategic communication during the Second World War.[32] Meanwhile, he and a small team ensured such traffic could survive the enemy, by developing the "Type X" (Typex) cipher machine. That is, first Lywood developed a communication system and then he built the cryptography for it. Signals personnel adapted a cipher machine to serve their needs, and only then consulted cryptographic experts.

After the O'Brien–Gardner debacle, Lywood concluded that the only way forward was back: to abandon research into prototypes and devise a variant of a proven system, "Enigma".[33] When the Cypher Machine Committee declined to finance this proposal, Lywood and an unofficial community acted on their own, relying on, "as far as possible, such readily obtainable commercial apparatus of which details were in possession of the Government and which appeared to offer reasonable possibilities of success". He did benefit, however, from previous research and development and some support from the Air Ministry, though this appears initially to have been semi-official in nature, until a viable prototype was developed. Lywood's "vision and energy" (as an official commendation later stated) were aided by Mr. Ross, a Deputy Secretary at the Air Ministry, Flight Lieutenant Coulson, the RAF's cryptographic expert and liaison officer with the GC&CS, several other ranks, and E.W. Smith, foreman at the RAF's wireless and electrical workshops at Kidbrooke and a man of "inventive genius and practical electrical and mechanical ability". Lywood claimed that he had "the main idea" and some thoughts about details, which Smith turned into "working facts". Lywood praised Smith and pushed his career but their superiors had different views, assessing their "comparative contributions ... as a minimum—Lywood 4 to Smith 1". In fact, Lywood made the design and Smith the machine. In this task, mechanical expertise mattered as much as conceptual capacity. It was easier to conceive a machine than to make one work, and on matters of cryptography, Lywood had no expertise; he simply borrowed good ideas from other systems, but this showed. Together, they had all the attributes of a classic inventor. They acted on their own time and at their own expense—Smith frequently worked with Lywood "until late at night, catching the 5 a.m. train back to London" and his day job, paying for his tickets and much of the kit.

Those attitudes were not accidental, but cultural. The RAF was the world's most progressive military service in the application of science and technology to warfare, particularly with regard to electronics and radio and their ancillaries. It pioneered the integration into operational systems of radio-telephones, radar, teleprinters and on-line cipher machines. Its wireless operators and officers, caught up in the contemporary enthusiasm which surrounded the technology and medium, made their work their hobby; on their own time, during the 1920s, they developed the RAF's worldwide wireless service.[34] Added to these general circumstances were particular ones. Cipher machines rose from an intersection between two rare faculties, the ability to invent machines and to break codes—few men fused these characteristics, most notably William F. Friedman, and even he failed to turn ideas into devices—all in a broader context. The development of a cipher machine was not an end but a beginning; its point was to serve signals. Most officials who worked with cipher machines were cryptologists, focused on security. Most signals officers who did so concentrated on communications, but had no expertise in security. Among them, Lywood was unusual, already used to work with innovative technology and to converting civilian kit to military functions. Smith too was experienced in developing civilian electro-mechanical equipment to military use. These two were experienced with signals and machinery, albeit with teleprinter and radio equipment. Their knowledge about cipher machines came from theory, Lywood's reading and observations, his thinking influenced by Enigma but also perhaps by the basic structure of Hebern's 1915 patent and the ideas of Peel and Critchley, and perhaps O'Brien (with the exception of his best but hardest-to-embody idea, the "scattering" mechanism).

Even more: Lywood worked with teletype traffic. When he thought of cipher machines, he wished them to service teleprinter systems; he wanted not just a cipher machine, but one working on-line. As he wrote, experience with the O'Brien–Gardner machine indicated "that the only scrambling principle that appeared to show any promise was the one incorporated in the 'Enigma'. The problem was how to make it into a mechanised printer instead of merely a visual indicator" (as on the Enigma lampboard). Lywood designed Typex Mark I around not just one but two sets of equipment, "Enigma" rotors and DTN teleprinters. He had all the right contacts within Whitehall and without to make this idea reality. In particular, his team was helped by the firm of Messrs. Creed and Co. of Croydon, which American signals officers rated among "the foremost makers of automatic telegraph equipment", manufacturer of the teleprinter equipment Lywood was adapting for the DTN and Typex.[35] At its own risk, though with visions of sugarplums in its head, Creed started production models even before it knew if it would be paid for them. This access came at a price. After Typex entered production, problems of delays and quality control occurred because Creed was poorly equipped to build cipher machines as opposed to on-line cipher teleprinters, while ultimately 90 per cent of Typex machines were manufactured without telegraphic attachments. In hindsight, the best firm to develop a cipher machine was the British Tabulating Machine Corporation (BTM), which held the rights to IBM patents within the British empire and to adapt its data-processing machines. BTM, the only firm outside the United States able and allowed to redesign the IBM variants of Hollerith machines, had an indigenous design capacity. It built versions of the best data-processing systems of the era with a large staff (603 in Britain during 1933, rising to 1,061 in 1939), matching any other such firm outside the United States where, however, IBM's staff were ten times larger. BTM's capabilities enabled it to build the "bombes" used by Bletchley Park. Lywood did not approach BTM because of his contacts with Creed, but perhaps because BTM, a well-connected firm, backed a rival in contention for selection as a British cipher machine, O'Brien's revised system.[36]

In two years, Lywood's team advanced further than Britain had done in twenty. "Investigation and development" for what became Typex Mark I began in August 1934. Five months later, in January 1935, the Cipher Machine Committee ordered the RAF to build three variants "of an improved 'Enigma' type through the agency of the so-called 'Type X' attachments".[37] Development involved two stages: first, the construction of five prototype cipher machines, derived from the commercial versions of Enigma, and from this the creation of a suitable device; and second, their marriage to Creed teleprinters. This system had three main parts: (a) the cipher machine proper, wired to (b) a base containing an electro-magnetic encipherment system (the functional equivalent of an Enigma plugboard), which was linked to (c) a " 'Type X' attachment", a " 'cypher' teleprinter" (or a morse reperforator to send teletype traffic by radio) modified to work with the cipher machine. This system could be linked by telegraph or wireless to another set. "The 'cypher' teleprinters of transmitting and receiving stations are connected to the ends of the line, and as the message is typed out on the transmitting scrambler keyboard, so the encyphered version is simultaneously printed on the tape of the teleprinter at the receiving station". The idea of linking two typewriters by an enciphering system was well known, as was the Enigma system. All Lywood really did was add the two ideas together, and to existing equipment which made one typewriter a cipher machine and the other a teleprinter. By May 1936 the Air Ministry had received its first experimental models, and it received the first working version of Typex Mark 1 by February 1937. Only then was the GC&CS asked to assess the cryptographic qualities of the device. It pronounced the machine "absolutely secure" when, despite having both the original and enciphered versions of several messages, it failed to penetrate the enciphering process. Here, however, the GC&CS's authority was limited—until 1939, leaving aside the electro-magnetic superencipherment system, Typex was technically less secure than the German military versions of Enigma, which had problems of their own, because of the way rotors were used.

Then, Lywood's team turned to develop a new machine, Typex Mark II, one of its two standard models of the Second World War. Contrary to expectation, the more Typex was developed, the more it became like Enigma, not less. Indeed, Lywood's first step was to detach the attachments which gave Typex its name! Typex Mark I was "somewhat bulky and immobile" and complex, prone to breakdowns, because its designers were inexperienced and trying to synchronize the operation of two automatic systems, cipher machine and teleprinter. Typex Mark II was intentionally simpler than its father because it was designed to work apart from the "Type X" attachments. It was a tolerably portable and robust electro-mechanical off-line cipher machine for use down to station headquarters, though it could also be carried on trucks. Again, communications governed cryptography. Fourteen Mark Is (with twelve more in reserve) covered both ends of the Air Ministry's seven teletype links overseas, but hundreds of cipher machines were needed to cover lower-level networks using manual means. Ultimately, Typex Mark II received plugboards allowing them to work with the "cypher teleprinter", and so on-line, whenever desired. Lywood's team developed Typex Mark II with greater speed than before—the preliminary design stage began in February 1937, while an experimental model was demonstrated on 14 June 1938. This immediately led to orders for 350 Mark IIs. From 1940, finally, most orders went to Typex Mark III, its best-known version, a manual off-line machine, rather like Enigma.

Britain finally had a means to cut the Gordian knot of cryptography and communication. In terms of basic security, of the rotor system, Typex was a variant of "Enigma", so much so that Britain had to look hard for ways not to admit it was using the patent, although enough mechanical and especially electrical changes occurred to make a lawyer's brief.[38] Even so, Lywood and Smith, developing older commercial versions of Enigma, improved rotor security for Typex less than the Germany military had done for its variants with more cryptographic expertise during a longer period of work. Their Enigma, with its plugboard, should have been more secure than the early Typex Mark IIs. Amazing technical errors negated this edge, however, while from 1940, continual refinements raised Typex's security far above that of Enigma. On balance, Typex Mark II matched Enigma in quality from the start and outstripped it from 1940, providing better communication and security. Typex Mark I, with electromagnetic superencipherment and on-line capacity, had the greatest security and signals capacity of any machine cipher of 1939, or 1942. However, because it incorporated irregular rotor motion, Sigaba was more secure than any Typex machine used manually, and better than Typex once it was available and mechanically reliable. This balance was restored only in 1950, when Typex Mark X (Mercury) adopted Sigaba-like means of irregular rotor rotation. Friedman and USN cryptographic authorities regarded Typex with disdain, as inferior to Sigaba, though their comments pertain only to Mark IIIs.[39] Between 1939 and 1946, cipher machines were engaged in an extraordinary and complicated race in quality, Enigma leading in 1939, Typex in 1940, Sigaba in 1941, all overshadowed after 1942 by the rise of on-line cipher teleprinters.

All versions of Typex had advantages in usability over the German military versions of Enigma. Whenever a character on an Enigma keyboard was pressed, its enciphered or deciphered equivalent was lit by an electric bulb behind a screen, which a second operator had to copy. Typex required just one operator, freeing up 12,000 cipher operators in 1945, compared to Enigma, and avoided errors, because the enciphered or deciphered text was automatically printed on paper tape. Unlike Enigma, all Typex I models were organically linked to teleprinters, while all Typex II models could be so. They were the world's first on-line cipher teleprinter, creating a combined ciphering, transmitting and printing system working at high speed. Normal signals, even from Enigma and Sigaba, were written, enciphered, transmitted, received, deciphered and printed in plain language, all in separate steps. Typex teleprinter messages were typed and automatically enciphered and transmitted in one step, and received and automatically deciphered and printed in another. Though this idea had been known since 1918, and commercial systems had been patented, Lywood was the first to make a cipher teleprinter suitable for state service. Despite its clumsiness and immobility, Typex Mark I was the leading edge of the first fundamental advance in cipher machines since 1920. As an adjunct to a communication system, it beat Enigma from the start, designed both for manual service in the field, like Enigma, and for teleprinter traffic at major commands, like the Lorenz online system which Germany deployed for its most significant traffic in 1942–1943. Though nothing indicates how many Typex Mark IIs were joined to Typex Mark I "cypher teleprinters", presumably this was done on most or all RAF and perhaps some army intercommand teleprinter links, given the ratio between the size of their staffs and the daily volumes of Typex traffic they sent. Thus, Typex enabled a uniquely large amount of traffic to be transmitted with a uniquely high level of security. However, no evidence suggests that any other departments, including the Admiralty, used Typex in an on-line mode.[40] Most Typex machines were used off-line and most users were unaware of its potential. After the war, Hugh Denham, a naval codebreaker in the Indian Ocean, involved in transmitting solutions of Japanese naval traffic with London, thought Typex was an "off-line" system; "as far as I am aware, at that time we did not possess the means of transmitting teleprinter traffic securely by high frequency".[41] When used as a cipher teleprinter, Typex was the world's most accurate, speedy and easy-to-use cipher machine, and ultimately the most secure of them; when used manually, the machine retained its edges of security and ease of use and accuracy, but lost most of its advantage of speed (though it remained somewhat faster than codebooks and, it appears, Enigma). Typex outclassed all older British systems even more than it did Enigma. It was more secure than codebooks and quicker to use—enciphering, transmitting and deciphering an RAF message of 110 groups took eighteen and a half minutes with Typex Mark I, compared to two hours with codebooks. The advantage declined when Typex was used manually, but still it was about twice as fast as book systems.

Yet Typex was forged dangerously late in the day. Britain could have built its own Enigma at any time since 1928. It did not have a single cipher machine suitable for field service and ready for production until 1938. This late start multiplied the significance of another problem. Creed's, a manufacturer of telegraph equipment, had not merely to conduct crash production in that field but also suddenly to establish a new branch, to construct cipher machines. This required different forms of technical expertise, producing problems of managerial and labour expertise and lack of machine tools. They slowed production until 1945 and perhaps degraded the quality of the manual versions of Typex, which suffered from rotor problems that damaged communications and threatened security. This delay in development, conversely, had advantages; without it, Typex might not have been able to work on-line nor multiply its security in 1940. Again, among the great powers only Germany outclassed Britain in the consistency and quality of the development of cipher machines. The French, Italians and Soviets placed little emphasis on cipher machines, and then used Hagelin systems, which proved vulnerable. The United States Navy and Army, more constantly interested in cipher machines than Britain and assigning their development to experienced cryptanalysts, handled the matter no better. Had the United States entered the war in 1939, its position would have been worse than Britain. Bureaucratic divisions and overconfidence in the power of technology and American ability to manage it crippled the United

States's remarkably innovative approach to machine cryptology.[42] Although in 1933 and 1936 Friedman sketched an innovative approach toward the next generation of cipher machines, and Frank Rowlett later made a workable system for irregular rotor motions, the development of Sigaba did not begin until 1938, prototypes were not ready until early 1940, nor did production start until 1941.[43] At this point, however, the United States had a better off-line cipher machine than Britain and better means to manufacture it.

For Britain and cipher machines, however, Germany was the standard for comparison. Britain did not meet it before September 1939 because it mishandled the process of research and development, and misunderstood the requirements for high-grade cipher facilities. Whitehall underestimated the degree to which radio would be used and hence the amount of its traffic the enemy would intercept. Thus, it misconstrued the balance between security and usability. It approached cryptography in a technically poor and uncoordinated fashion, failed to develop cipher machines effectively, and was unwilling to adopt OTP, the most secure if cumbersome system available. All this left Britain relying far more than was wise on one type of high-grade system—superenciphered codes—which Axis experts were able to break. Italian naval codebooks were better than British; the GC&CS thought them unbreakable, and easier to use than OTP. "They showed such an uncanny knack of closing a gap soon after we found it, that we are forced to believe that they (or the Germans) were watching the traffic as closely as we were." The Italian navy's only cryptographic weakness was the vulnerability of its Hagelin systems. As with the Japanese army, codebooks well used were as secure as (if less convenient than) cipher machines.[44] In 1939, again, the German navy had far better cryptography than Britain, with Enigma and high-grade books for central traffic, and dozens of separate codebooks for ships liable to capture. In 1939–1941 Britain's communications and cryptographic apparatus was weak, and Britain lost as much as it gained through cryptanalysis. This position was redeemed only by the presiding graces of modern British cryptology: luck, skill and a willingness to accept the possibility its ciphers might have been compromised. Britain's experience with Typex contributed to these weaknesses, and to its recovery from them.

The Official History of British Intelligence in the Second World War implies that events progressed smoothly after 1935: the RAF and the army adopted Typex "with enthusiasm"; by September 1939 they were fully "ready" with it down to a divisional or equivalent level; and thereafter Typex adequately met Britain's needs for high-grade traffic, with the special exception of the navy. In fact, between 1935 and 1939 Britain remained confused about the technical situation which governed its approach to cipher machines. The services and the GC&CS grossly underestimated the degree to which they would use radio—in 1939 the Navy and Bomber Command regarded "complete unbroken wireless silence" as a viable policy—and overestimated the security of the codebooks used for radio traffic. In 1936 the War Office believed that if properly used these ciphers "are not capable of being broken down", while any reciphering table would "remain secure for a period of at least a month under the worst conditions".[45] Such attitudes did not provide an incentive to hasten the completion of Typex.

In any case, years were bound to pass before prototypes could be tested and mass production started. Britain had problems in the initial stages of the development of Typex. The RAF's command in India had "a good deal of trouble with their own machine which died on them" during the Munich crisis. That Typex was ready by the outbreak of war in September 1939 was coincidental. Britain constructed just twenty-nine Mark Is and ordered its first Mark IIs only in June 1938. At that time authorities expected to have 350 of these machines ready within fourteen months, or by September 1939. This forecast was optimistic. Only 350 Mark IIs were available on 25 January 1940. By September 1939 Britain probably had no more than 250 Mark Is and IIs in service, though, by that time, so wrote the ACAS, Nutting, "practically all communications between Air Ministry and H.Q.s of Commands both Home & Overseas are now dealt with by means of the mechanized systems".[46] This RAF lead explains why its radio system became the backbone of British strategic communications between 1940 and 1945. Even so, at the outbreak of war just six of the 190 personnel of the Air Ministry Communication Centre worked with Typex.[47] Meanwhile, the War Office was only beginning to issue Typex to its overseas commands. The need soon exploded. By July 1940, 1,432 Mark IIs had been ordered, including a manual version, 518 for the RAF, 284 for the Army, 630 for the RN, eleven for India, 78 for the Dominions, two for the Dominions Office, and none for the Foreign Office (which had tested a Mark I but decided against machine systems until mid-1942). By August 1941, 1,885 Mark IIs had been ordered, and another 1,350 were being requisitioned; by May 1944 Britain had manufactured 5,016 Typexes but was some 4,000 short of the desired establishment.[48] By August 1945 probably 12,000 high-grade machines were in service, both Typex and the "Combined Cypher Machine" (CCM) which, after 1943, the services used as much as Typex. Comparatively, Germany had some 30,000 Enigmas in service at its peak period of use during the war. Britain also developed at least another three models of Typex, which became increasing simple and manual, and radically altered the workings of every version.

Typex was a good cipher machine in both 1939 and 1945. It was rapid, easy to use and robust. Along with the CCM and the American Sigaba system, it was never broken by the enemy.[49] Britain did well in the development and production of Typex between 1939 and 1945 and always had enough such machines to cover the most fundamental needs. Thus, when Italy cut British cables in the Mediterranean in 1940 and radio carried "the whole weight" of RAF inter-command communications, the two Typex machines in the Air Ministry's Whitehall radio station were able to support this burden. Still, the late start with Typex bequeathed major problems in the supply of these machines and of trained personnel, and dangers both on the front and in Whitehall. The orders of 1938–1941 were too late and slow to meet Britain's needs for speedy and secure communication. In July 1940, perhaps only 625 Mark IIs had been produced, including 300 for the RAF, 146 for the army, thirty-eight for the RN, eleven for India and thirty for the Dominions and the Dominions Office. Orders for Typex twice exploded suddenly in scale, 600 in October 1939, and 1,350 in August 1941, causing shortfalls in production for long periods. Creeds', the only British firm able to manufacture Typex, could not meet the demand for them nor, it appears, for technical innovations. By 1945 the Ministry of Supply doubted Creeds' was competent to produce the next generation of cipher machines for His Majesty's Government, and other government authorities agreed. Without American assistance in manufacture, Britain's requirements for cipher machines during the Second World War could not have been met.

Throughout 1940–1941 British forces often lacked the machines and personnel needed to transmit much high-level traffic. Even in 1944 the RAF suffered from "grave" shortages of Typex. Consequently, many important messages of the army and the RAF were carried on slower and less secure systems, or not sent at all. In January 1941, Whitehall gave its commanders in Egypt only four days, warning that they might have to further denude their already weak RAF strength by dispatching several squadrons to Turkey. The Air Ministry understood the "astonishment" of its commander over this short notice, but stated that it had been unable to notify him earlier because the "limit of cypher signals makes it impossible to keep you fully informed of situation outside your theatre".[50] This limit also helps to explain the communications failure between Singapore and London during 1940–1941 which shaped disaster in Malaya. Nor was Typex ever used for tactical traffic within divisions at the front. The army wanted cipher machines for this purpose, but those available, the "Syko" and "Morsex" devices, were slow and insecure. This crucial category of traffic was carried by vulnerable and cumbersome methods like the Slidex R/T Code. These problems surrounding Typex and strategic communications gave the enemy major cryptanalytical opportunities in 1939–1942 and notable ones even in 1944.

Every British cryptographic calculation between the wars assumed its strategic communications would be carried on all British telegraph lines, secure from interception and unavailable to foreign cryptanalysis. Italy's entry into the war crippled that cable system and British communications security. The carrying capacity of British cables to Asia declined markedly when Italy cut those in the Mediterranean; in December 1941, as Japan wrecked those in the Pacific, one cable around South Africa, "rather wonky ... and not to be relied on", became Britain's sole telegraphic link with its eastern empire.[51] By 1942 just the transatlantic components of Britain's cable network remained intact. Britain could meet its rapidly growing needs for strategic communication only by expanding, and hastily, its radio services. Their carrying capacity quickly multiplied. In May 1941 the army's high-speed radio section in Cairo sent 20,000–25,000 groups per day, four times the level of nine months before. In November 1942 the army's new wireless link between London and Cairo carried 62,000 groups daily, sustaining an adequate level of communication even when it had to carry "practically all" traffic after the loss of the Pacific cable. By March 1942, virtually all military traffic went by radio, but 25 per cent of that of civilian departments went by cable. Censorship authorities, warning that "cable congestion has become so serious that it is seriously interfering with the War Effort", asked all departments to "take *immediate* steps to ensure that their cyphers are sufficiently secure to enable their traffic to be normally routed by W/T", which would carry all save perhaps their most secret traffic.[52] This decision marked a complete reversal in policy.

British signals confronted revolutions not just in forms of media but quantity of messages. In 1927 the services assumed that during wartime, they would send 110,000 cipher groups by all means to and from Britain each day. Between 1943 and 1945, the wireless stations in the Air Ministry and the War Office alone handled ten times this load, approximately 1,110,000 groups per day. In 1939 the War Office dealt with 20,000 groups per month; by 1945 it handled 20,000,000 groups in high-grade cipher alone. In 1944 the Foreign Office Communications Department sent four times as many cipher groups per day (41,000) as in 1939 because, as the main conduit for the civil departments' traffic, it lost a battle against verbosity in messages. Just one of Isaiah Berlin's reports on American politics in 1943 occupied thirteen "cypherer hours" on the "few" Typex machines (obviously used manually) on the Washington–London circuit. No doubt the Foreign Office had Churchill in mind when it complained the War Cabinet's telegrams abounded in "luxuriant phraseology". By 1941 the Communications Department could transmit only the most crucial of messages without "considerable delay". It neared that point at later moments.[53]

Whitehall lacked the high-grade facilities to carry all important messages quickly and adequately even on the crucial link between London and the British embassy in Washington. This enhanced volume of traffic solved problems of communication but it exacerbated the fragility of Britain's cryptographic shield. By late 1940 and early 1941, Whitehall recognized this danger and sought to buttress that shield. It multiplied its orders for Typex machines and bolstered the internal security of the device, and with effect. Whatever categories of traffic that machine covered were secure, while those it could not protect were vulnerable. Typex covered strategic traffic far better than operational traffic, leaving serious problems in that area as it turned first to solve others. Until mid-1942, Typex could defend Britain's most crucial categories of communication, such as the transmission of signals intelligence material, but not all of its important ones. Given the ratio between the increase in radio traffic and in cipher machines, Typex probably covered only the same proportion of traffic as in 1940—that is, the absolute quantity of important messages it could not defend rose, most notably in Britain's most active theatres, in, to and from the Atlantic, Mediterranean and Middle East. Through the initiative of the Foreign Office, by 1941 Britain brought OTP into service, which provided absolute security for a small quantity of messages, but could not fill the gap. The GC&CS devised a superior superencipherment system, the "stencil subtractor frame". Problems of testing, of production, of distribution across seas haunted by U-boats, all delayed the introduction of these new systems. The "S.S. Frame", while ready for trial by April 1941, was not adopted officially until March 1942, nor brought into effective service until June 1943. By spring 1941, Britain understood how to repair the cryptographic errors of a generation. Time was needed to do so. Until then, communications to and between British commands in the Middle East and South Asia were the most exposed to interception and codebreaking of any strategic traffic on earth. In order to cover high-grade traffic, Britain had to use systems ranging from on-line cipher teleprinters to the superencipherment of groups from a codebook known to be in the enemy's hands.

In the interim, older versions of British superenciphered codebooks again carried far more intercommand traffic than in 1940. This included all operational RN traffic and signals to and from army headquarters without Typex, in Abysinnia, Crete and Greece; non-operational traffic between all commands in the Middle East (and sometimes between Cairo and London); and all communications between higher formations before and during operations. These superencipherment systems were improved technically. By May 1941, for example, the RAF had special superencipherment tables for the Middle East. It sought to maintain many tables in reserve and to change those in service several times a month. Their security, however, hung upon a knife edge. Thus, in May on Crete the enemy captured a "complete set of S. [signal] and C. [cipher] Publications"—including copies of all save a few RAF superenciphering tables.[54] In 1941, Britain confronted this dilemma—it could defend the security of its current level of radio communications only through the use of superencipherment systems which were cryptanalytically vulnerable and often known to be in the enemy's hands. Britain had to take this risk and the integrity of these systems cracked under the strain. At the turn of 1940–1941, the RAF codebook was compromised because "of the existing depth [about 150] on the table"—RAF signals security aimed to cut that vulnerability by 98 per cent, to an "average depth of 3", which meant the superencipherment table must be changed thirteen times each month, instead of the then-current rate of once every three months."[55] Soon, Britain increased the security of its superenciphered traffic by another 50 per cent, defining the acceptable "depth on the table" as no more than two.

From early 1941 until November 1942, albeit with growing difficulty, German codebreakers read superenciphered RAF traffic in the Mediterranean area, with an average time lag of two to four weeks. In 1941, through cryptanalytical means they reconstructed the army's standard high-grade codebook, War Office Cypher "W", and captured a copy of it in early 1942. The War Office was not able to replace this system with "W 2" until July 1942—fourteen months after the enemy was known to be reading it currently![56] German cryptanalysts broke at least one variant of the superenciphered traffic in "W" between Whitehall and Egypt from "at least" August 1941 and January 1942, with infrequent success thereafter, sometimes solving messages with a time lag of one week. Material of this sort was augmented by German success in breaking the British Interdepartmental code system used in the Near East. Even worse, *B-Dienst* triumphed over mid-level superenciphered book systems of the RN and merchant navy. Given the scale of physical compromises and German use of mechanized procedures for cryptanalysis (particularly Hollerith machines for data processing), older British superenciphered codebooks, the systems most frequently used for the middle range of important traffic, were frighteningly vulnerable.

As so often in the history of cryptology, god chose to be an Englishman. Precisely as Germany shattered this old cryptographic shield, it confronted a new one. After June 1941 the superencipherment systems of the army and the RAF increasingly were relegated to non-operational traffic (mostly of an administrative nature) and to subordinate headquarters and higher formations. This process was complete by the start of 1942, containing German cryptanalysts at parts of the middle levels of the cryptographic pyramid and then steadily pressing them down to the bottom. Even in 1941 Typex and OTP, systems the enemy never penetrated, carried all important traffic on intercommand links: by mid-1942 they covered all of that within the Mediterranean and Middle Eastern theatres. From summer 1941, meanwhile, British forces in the Middle East improved all forms of their cipher security, in particular that of their superencipherment systems. They established a centre to produce books and tables for local formations. By June 1942 the RAF always had two high-grade books in use at any time with four separate "series of tables". Each individual table in the Middle East series was changed several times each month. Such steps restored integrity even to Britain's superencipherment systems—the Germans lost access to the codebooks from the Near and Middle East which they had exploited in 1941, and to middle level naval traffic in 1943. Thereafter, they broke only one other such system, the local variant of War Office Cipher "W" used by the Home Forces in the United Kingdom. German generals later boasted that by late 1944, they could intercept the plain language radio traffic of American infantry battalions!

Perhaps cryptographic struggles are best envisaged not as sprint but sumo. Certainly, after 1942, British cryptography was obese. A belt of redundancy crippled German cryptanalysts everywhere they turned: OTP, several distinct kinds of Typex machines, their internal working routinely upgraded, with those on different circuits using different settings which were frequently changed, and dozens of superenciphered codebooks with tables changed at blinding speed. This British system required more resources than the German one, but was also more secure. In order to crack any level of British communications, the Germans had to engage and defeat one or more distinct cryptographic systems—and success against any one rarely eased attack against any other. All Enigma traffic was vulnerable, conversely, once Britain learned how to crack one basic system, which let success against traffic of minor value compromise that of great significance. Ultimately, Britain found a better way to harness cipher machines to signals security than Germany did, but through accident and with cost.

The provision of Typex was the key variable in the improvement of British signals security. Between 1940 and 1942, the security of British traffic varied dramatically, often irrationally, with how departments had moved to procure these devices before the fall of France. By April 1940 the Admiralty had made 44 per cent of the total orders for Typex machines (575 of 1,307)—90 per cent of them requested in October 1939—but by July 1940 it had received only 38. It aimed at an establishment of 692 Typex machines, more than any other service proposed, so to service all categories of RN traffic, including operational messages for warships at sea. Ultimately, however, the RN used Typex purely for strategic traffic. Thus, it gained absolute security for its most fundamental messages while it switched from reliance on cable to radio, without bolstering its greatest cryptographic weakness, the book systems used for operational traffic. Why the RN should have abandoned its efforts to use Typex for operational messages is unclear; perhaps delays in production (exacerbated by the destruction of forty-seven machines in an air raid on Deptford in March 1941) reinforced naval officers' doubts about cipher machines. In any case, the Admiralty was far less reactionary in this field than has often been suggested.[57] Again, by January 1942, 300 Typex machines (15–20 per cent of Britain's total number in service) and two high-grade books covered RAF operational traffic at "Home Stations" in the United Kingdom—a bastion even Bletchley could not have scratched, one so well staffed as to became a target for economies.[58] Yet this category of traffic scarcely warranted such defence, doubly so since these forces could use landlines. Meanwhile, the RAF in the Middle East, seriously short of Typex, reported: "Every endeavour is being made to speed up the manufacture of Type X and the Air Ministry agreed to give Middle East first priority of a further 33 machines for the Middle East."[59] This problem, and the army's delay in ordering Typex in large numbers, created the weakness in traffic between London and its commands in Asia and Africa.

From mid-1941, Typex was the main means for intercommand traffic on intelligence, operational and strategic matters between Britain and its overseas headquarters, but unlike Enigma for Germany, it covered neither all major administrative messages, nor operational traffic within commands. Many Typex machines in Africa and Asia "showed distinct signs of wear". "Type 'X' paper rolls arriving in Middle East are very often stuck solidly in one mass, having passed through tropical climates on the way out. They should be packed as the Far East rolls are packed, in tins with driers."[60] But the tide turned fast, carrying with it the fruit of earlier orders for Typex. From the summer of 1942, Typex became standard on links down to Army Corps/RAF Group level in the Middle East.[61] From August 1942, it carried all but the most secret of Foreign Office messages between London and its outposts in the United States.[62] This traffic had never been broken, but Typex protected its growing volume. The RAF was the first service to order large numbers of Typex machines, including 350 in January 1939, and to manage the switch to teleprinter radio circuits (standard for home stations by 1939, and rising from one of eleven intercommand links in March 1940 to eight of twenty-two in June 1944). It had more and better communications and cryptographic facilities than it needed; hence, it came to carry most messages for the War Cabinet and the Chiefs of Staff (COS). By 1943, RAF Typex machines carried most (1,600,000 groups) of the major traffic between Britain and North America each month; meanwhile, it sent signals intelligence traffic between theatres, rising from 80,000 groups per day in March 1943 to a peak of 400,000 daily in August 1944.[63] By mid-1943, the War Office's radio section in London carried 555,000 groups per day over 100 Typex machines.[64] In early 1942, all COS traffic went by the time-consuming form of OTP, but soon it covered merely all War Cabinet messages "whose very long term Top Secrecy is of paramount importance", while the RAF's Typex and teleprinter network carried all other War Cabinet and COS messages—perhaps 90 per cent of key British traffic.[65] In April 1945, Typex carried 49,000,000 groups, or 413,000 messages across the world.[66]

Meanwhile, from December 1942 Typex finally matched the value of Enigma for operational traffic, and whipped in it security. Typex became fundamental at this level during TORCH, when communication systems throughout Anglo-American forces and the Sigaba system at Allied headquarters both collapsed; General Eisenhower complained of "overloaded signals communications" and "extraordinary difficulties with static, codes and ciphers to Washington and to London". His headquarters, finding the "lack of [a] universal cipher machine extremely costly in time and labour", used Typex for all inter-formation traffic, with success.[67] Typex first covered the operational traffic of British divisions during the Tunisian campaign, though the Eighth Army did not so use it until HUSKY. Initially, attitudes toward the value of Typex for operations were tepid, but slowly they warmed while problems declined. From HUSKY Typex served this sphere well, providing complete security while letting each operator send twice the number of groups possible with a codebook.[68]

By 1940 British cryptography and communications confronted deadly dangers; by 1942 they smashed them, a triumph parallel and complementary to that of Bletchley Park. These successes stemmed in part from the source of earlier failures—the delay in Typex's development. During 1940–1941, few Typex machines were distributed, precisely as the GC&CS began routinely to break Enigma keys, and to learn the weaknesses in Germany's use of the system. Radical modifications could easily be incorporated in the machines and rotors already out, and new procedures stamped on operators; when the German Army discovered the vulnerability of Enigma in 1942–1943, conversely, so many sets were in service and bad habits in practice that the problems could not be solved. In 1941, Germany used perhaps fifteen times as many Enigma machines (about 30,000) as Britain did Typex ones, which eased the British process of monitoring operators. That British process also began with more impetus because the GC&CS was moved by fears about cryptography. After the fall of France, it thought all Army and RAF code systems, including Typex, compromised by capture and other means; "the enemy has obtained possession of all information on military cyphers and cypher methods. Further reports have come to hand suggesting misuse of cyphers by the R.A.F., which if true have the result that information vital to our work as well as to the Army and R.A.F. may be becoming available to the enemy."[69] This fear was correct, with key exceptions— neither Typex nor the GC&CS were compromised, while British cryptography was most weak at the middle levels of RN traffic. Despite the GC&CS's efforts, Whitehall did not address these dangers adequately; hence, until 1942 British cryptography remained weaker than that of Germany.[70] In the case of Typex, however, these fears occurred precisely at the right time to kill error.

In November 1939, when considering whether to use Typex within divisions, the War Office asked what "effect the capture of the machine, complete with cipher drums, would have on future security". The GC&CS replied that Typex was safe even if captured, but "to provide against some method of solution at present unknown to us, it would be advisable to provide spare drums which can be substituted for any that may be captured or mixed with them for subsequent machine settings. I suggest the provision of ten drums per machine, any five of which can be used, those not in use being held in a place of comparative safety".[71] By February 1940, as the army and the RN began to use Typex Mark IIs, the GC&CS and the services agreed greater security was needed: each service should develop its own sets of drums, and another for inter-service traffic; every machine should have at least seven drums, (soon raised to ten), using five of them to determine any setting; no external indications should reveal which "particular set of drums" covered any message; a secure and standardized system should be used to signal which settings were in use on any circuit; and "each service should segregate its traffic as much as possible, using different drums or special message settings as appropriate". These decisions reflected the state of Bletchley's art.[72] Without informing the GC&CS, however, the army gave the BEF Typex machines equipped with only five drums, "which means a difference in security of 120 only as compared with 30,240 possible wheel orders" produced by ten drums (i.e. 5×4×3×2×1=120, as against 10×9×8×7×6=30,240). In June–July 1940, the GC&CS believed (correctly) that an army Typex machine had been captured and concluded its traffic might be compromised, with further dangers possible. Even so, the GC&CS thought the attackers would confront "a very difficult problem"; and probably could be beaten so long as message settings were selected with care (as "now done by the Air Ministry") and were "changed twice daily at irregular intervals, best chosen for splitting the traffic", while "the various lines of traffic [were] segregated so as to render as little as possible available to the enemy on any one machine setting".[73]

Soon, all Typex settings were made from five drums out of ten, tougher to crack than the *Luftwaffe* or *Kriegsmarine* versions of Enigma (which selected, respectively, three drums out of five or eight, allowing sixty, or 336, rotor settings), or even those of the U-boats, which from 1942 chose four drums (three out of eight and one out of three, allowing 1,008 rotor settings, 8×7×6×3=1,008) and from late 1943 had 1,344 settings (8×7×6×2×2). In its ultimate form with fourteen split rotors, Typex was able to select 7,687,680 rotor settings(28×26×24×22×20). That power was magnified because Britain avoided the elementary errors in usage and plugboard wiring which wrecked the security value of the German system. Typex traffic was also subdivided far more than that of Enigma, bearing in mind that Britain used fewer machines. By January 1941, the RAF first began to divide its Typex traffic between two different drum settings. By January 1942, its operational traffic in Britain went in three "main" settings. Soon, its worldwide messages were divided into four (general, Middle East, empire, home); joined, later, by a second setting for the Middle East, and another two each for India and Australia, and one each for Canada and expeditionary air forces. By November 1944, every day the RAF used thirty Typex settings, with another each for COSC and signals intelligence traffic, and many others for the army and the RN.[74] Meanwhile defences were instituted against physical compromises. From 1942, each Typex machine was equipped with tools to destroy it if under risk of capture—"considerable strength is required for this purpose"; American authorities used thermite devices to protect Sigaba and CCM machines. Emergency replacement systems were readied for use if any machine was captured, as occasionally happened, as in the Arakan in 1944, when immediate damage assessment was conducted.[75] That Britain applied its lessons from the attack to the defence is yet another unsung story from the wireless war.

In cryptology as in war, that side wins which makes fewest mistakes. Between 1939 and 1941, Germany, Italy and Britain were neck and neck in a race to make the most. German and Italian codebreakers won this race—they failed to exploit their opportunities against high-grade British systems. Indeed, they gained surprisingly little from their efforts, because of the limits to their skill, and imagination. Italians did not even try to break British cipher machines.[76] Germans attacked Hagelin machines with frequency and success, including the American M-209 and the French C-36, but refused to contest Typex. *B-Dienst* knew Enigma was vulnerable in theory, but was reassured when material seized in 1940 showed the French Admiralty could not break it. *B-Dienst* thought the RN used a machine cipher, and tried to attack it, but stopped because the task was hard and personnel were few. "Later on it was impossible to resume work on this code, because increasing difficulties in deciphering the military systems engaged all the personnel." In early 1940 German army cryptanalysts did basic research on Typex, which led nowhere. The capture of an army Typex machine, without rotors, at Dunkirk, discouraged German army codebreakers from attempting more than continued monitoring for research purposes, although they appreciated that attack was possible if they could determine the wiring within rotors (which was unknown). A senior cryptanalyst at OKW/Chi, Dr. Erich Huettenhain, wrote, "as we believe that the enigma can not be solved no great effort was made to solve Typex. Typex has seven wheels and we therefore believe it to be more secure than our enigma". When properly used, Enigma "is unbreakable. It might be broken if a vast Hollerith complex is used but this is only slightly possible". What most interested the Germans with Typex was its system of printing plaintext and cipher messages. The faint German interest in attacking Typex was swamped because the task was hard and resources scarce. Only massive and centralized cryptanalysis could break a good Enigma system, and this the divided German system could not provide. A leading member of *B-Dienst* called such a unified system "a monster organization".[77]

Even more, Axis signals intelligence services were limited in ambition because they thought their achievements good, which was true—by 1918 standards. They followed the best models of the great war, with innovations like the use of Hollerith machines; their success against Britain during 1939–1942 was above the average for 1914–1918, and close to Britain's standard of that period; they were impressed by their own success and skill. In 1944, the chief of Italian air signals intelligence warned the Allies that the main signals intelligence unit of the *Luftwaffe* and its many Hollerith machines could reconstruct Syko tables within five hours, thus determining "complete Allied Air Force and Naval orders of battle in certain areas". He was impressed by this feat and thought Allied codebreakers would be too. Given their knowledge of Bletchley and Syko, they are more likely to have seen this as a case of sledgehammer against nut, or to have concluded that Syko was safer than expected. Again, in 1944, a captured German intercept officer:

rated the achievements of the German Army intercept orgn very high, and believed that the complete OB of US and British forces in the USA and GREAT BRITAIN as well as on the Italian front, had been obtained ... German intercept was of great tactical value also, since intercepted messages of tactical importance could ... be passed back to the comds in the fd within minutes of their being deciphered and collated at Intercept HQs [sic].[78]

The continued success of signals intelligence in the east masked failures in the west. Axis signals intelligence did well at everything they could conceive; but they thought on a smaller scale than the British and Americans. Between 1939 and 1943, Italian signals intelligence services stagnated in quantity and quality, while German ones rose marginally in quality and perhaps tripled in size. British and American services expanded by thirty times, and pursued unprecedented forms of organization and technique. Divided Axis cryptanalysts assaulted different bricks of British cryptography—a massive and united Anglo-American attack wrecked the whole Axis building.

Italian and German diplomatic codebreakers continued to work as in 1939, their quality and success slowly eroding, and always below the GC&CS's standard, though the tapping of transatlantic telephone traffic produced substantial success until autumn 1943. *B-Dienst*, Britain's toughest foe, resembled Room 40 in structure, work and quality, and had greater effect on operations, though of course, Room 40's real successes had been at the strategic level. Its numbers rose from ninety in September 1939 to 1,800 between 1941 and 1943, including perhaps 300 cryptanalytical and intelligence personnel, but then rapidly slid in strength. Before the war, *B-Dienst* devastated RN traffic. Its focus on the "mental skill" of cryptanalysts, combined with "the English being very conservative in the employment and development of their radio ciphers", let it track changes to RN cryptography until 1944. This material was most successful in betraying British intentions to attack Norway in 1940, and its operations in the Mediterranean during 1941–1942 and on the Murmansk run, leading to defeat in the first case and the wreck of major warships and convoys in the other. Indeed, signals intelligence was involved in the destruction of more large British than German warships. Access to mid-level RN systems gave Germany useful and otherwise unavailable insights into British views on the battle of the Atlantic, and bolstered the U-boat campaign during 1940, and for almost a year during 1942–1943. In these cases, *B-Dienst* matched Bletchley in effect, and intelligence was a force multiplier. Often it let an inferior force choose its time and place of attack and have more success than otherwise would have been possible; the German navy won only when *B-Dienst* did. Yet at a strategic level, these successes were minor and their pursuit broke the German navy, in a tolerably even exchange with the RN; their main effect was to weaken British seapower against Japan.[79] Italian naval codebreakers relied on stolen copies of foreign systems; their cryptanalytical abilities were limited. In 1939–1940, they barely penetrated the weak Franco-British interallied cipher, with superencipherment tables changed just once every three months, though they were not driven out. Similarly, even with a copy in hand of the "W" codebook in 1942, Italian military cryptanalysts could not crack its superencipherment tables. Still, traffic analysis and solutions of low-grade RN systems provided much useful intelligence. The head of the Italian navy's Signals Intelligence Service, Admiral Maugeri, held that

> The departure of an enemy naval force or a convoy from East to West never escaped the SIS, and it was almost always possible to establish within a few hours its composition and even its objectives; which permitted immediate measures on the part of our naval command, and the most important naval encounters [battle of Punta Stile, of Cape Tulada, of Cape Matapan, the two actions off Sirte, and that of Pantellaria] originated through information from the SIS.

Notably, half these battles were British victories, in one of them, Cape Matapan, largely because Ultra beat Italians. So too, the RN.[80] Between 1939–1942, the Y services of the German and Italian armies and air forces provided excellent operational intelligence, but their codebreaking outfits were smaller and less able than SIS or *B-Dienst*. The "Cryptographic Section" of SIS had forty-five men, including sixteen to twenty cryptanalysts. German army codebreaking was split between Intercept Commands EAST and WEST, which shared seven Intercept Headquarters. Between 1942 and 1944, the main office of Intercept Command WEST had seventy-five to 160 people, with perhaps fifty or sixty in the "Deciphering Department". Intercept Headquarters Seven had 170 men, including 100 in a "Deciphering Department". These outfits had many Hollerith machines, but their targets were tactical, with one main exception. An Italian officer witnessed over thirty German technicians using several Hollerith machines to attack "W". Germany, however, failed to penetrate "W2". Similar Hollerith attacks sometimes broke into the M-209, used for field traffic. Otherwise, German successes were against field ciphers and tactical codes intended to provide just 24 hours security, like the British Syko, Slidex and Codex and the American Divisional Field Code. These attacks used Hollerith punch cards to weed out impossible solutions. "These were held up to the light and the only possible charts were those corresponding to the holes through which light showed."[81] This system was like that at Bletchley, with one exception—Germans attacked the simplest systems, Britons the hardest. In some ways, these simple systems were a sacrifice, which distracted Axis attention from better things. Meanwhile, the central office of

Luftwaffe signals intelligence had about 350 people, with a sixteen-man Hollerith section, and its main outstations had between 100 and 280 people, with Hollerith sections. It had some success against a mid-level RAF superenciphered book in 1941–1942, and also against many similar Soviet systems, but from 1942 in the west it focused all these resources on simple systems—plain-language traffic, low-level air, convoy and meteorological codes, and Syko, Slidex and Codex (against which success rarely reached more than 30 per cent). More than its Axis counterparts, that of the *Luftwaffe* tried to overcome the change in Allied cryptography. One well-informed deserter reported that in March 1943, *Luftwaffe* signals intelligence people were withdrawn from the field "for unified work in Berlin on high grade ciphers", where in 1939–1941 we had "great successes".

> However, through complications it has been rendered impossible to break the principal W/T traffic sufficiently fast for strategic and tactical purposes. Today, on Goering's orders, efforts are being doubled in Berlin and elsewhere to make a breach in the English–American cipher system. For this purpose small parties of parachute sabotage personnel were put into action in Africa to bring in important material or keys.

But this was without apparent success—except to preempt OKH IN/7's effort to find British cryptographic material lost at Tobruk in 1942.[82]

In 1941–1942 these successes, while not violating operational or strategic planning, gave the enemy excellent intelligence on the RAF and army's order of battle in the Middle East and the Mediterranean basin. Meanwhile, Axis signals intelligence provided valuable operational intelligence against the RN in the Mediterranean and the British army in Egypt. All told, Britain arguably lost the signals intelligence war in that theatre between January 1941 and May 1942, and certainly did worse and suffered more damage there than it ever did in the Atlantic. Even in 1943–1944, Axis signals intelligence often provided good information on the deployment of reinforcements to North Africa and shipping movements across the Mediterranean, while poor signals security and material derived from tactical systems like Syko and Slidex remained the German army's best source of operational intelligence, and a fairly good one. None the less, this information was not valuable enough. The astonishing thing to note is how poorly Axis cryptanalysts exploited their opportunities. The British cryptographical record defines the level of incompetence of Axis cryptanalysis.

No sooner had British cryptography whipped its foe than another problem emerged—a friend. By 1943 diplomatic differences between Britain and the United States were on the rise. Simultaneously, Britain instituted a series of messages—first called "NONSUCH", later "GUARD"—for the small category of traffic which American authorities were intended *"never"* to know had even been sent. Cryptology was the root of this revealing development. By December 1943 the Cypher Security Committee saw "an urgent requirement to decide and define British cypher policy *vis-à-vis* the United States". Whereas Britain had given American authorities copies of Typex and unparaphrased messages from the system, the latter had never "officially" given Britain access to Sigaba, and rarely passed unparaphrased texts. British practices had assumed that

(i) U.S. were not attempting to break British cyphers.
(ii) they hadn't the necessary trained staff or equipment to do this even if they so wanted.

> Both these assumptions are ... *now* out of date; the U.S. have the necessary men and equipment ... [and] ... valuable material ... for an attempt to break British cyphers, and the inclination must obviously be assumed.[83]

Years later, the Joint Intelligence Committee held that Britain had simply feared that the United States was "in a position, albeit most unlikely, to carry out a crypt-analytic attack on our high grade cyphers".[84] In fact, during early 1944 the British believed the United States would attack Typex traffic and that it would succeed, partly because they thought the Germans were doing so. In August 1943, captured German intelligence officers claimed that during the Tunisian campaign, codebreakers in Tunis and Berlin had broken much Typex traffic, sometimes within twelve hours of receipt. Allegedly, the Germans had captured a Typex machine at Tobruk in 1942, and attacked it via mechanical means, and apparently a sophisticated and substantial effort. Though these reports were sketchy, British cryptographers smelled a Bletchley. They concluded that Typex had been read, and its security must be reconsidered. By December, "comprehensive investigation" by the GC&CS, using "certain new possible methods of attack which had been discovered", showed Typex was vulnerable when any key carried too much material, or messages to be published, or those in stereotyped forms.[85] This led to increased finesse in security. That is, the GC&CS applied the latest techniques of mechanical cryptanalysis—known to the Americans—to the security of their own systems, which were found wanting. E.E. Bridges, the Cabinet Secretary, told the Prime Minister that the "greatly increased efficiency" of American cryptanalysts, "which has been built up with the help of our own cryptographers, who have passed on all our methods and skill", combined with the passing of unparaphrased traffic and "numberless Plain Language 'cribs' to our cypher traffic", had compromised Typex. "I think we must assume that the high grade cypher in which the majority of our messages to the J.S.M. [Joint Staff Mission] Washington and to

Commanders-in-Chief are sent can now be read by the Americans." "GUARD" would separate sheep from goats: for purposes of convenience, older British practices would continue with most traffic, even though the Americans might well read almost all important messages they could intercept throughout the world, including matters of great material significance. Conversely, signals about issues where major British and American interests clashed, such as those between the Foreign Office and its outposts in Washington, and Churchill's with the JSM and British Commanders-in-Chief in the Middle East and South East Asia, would receive "absolute security". Churchill accepted the proposal with revealing reservations.

> I wonder however whether it would not be as well for me to suggest to the President a self-denying ordinance by which on a gentlemen's agreement both the British and American Government would refrain from trying to penetrate each other's cyphers. This would enable the existing easy circulation of messages to proceed without prejudice to the "GUARD" arrangements.
>
> I have not authorised the decoding of an American message since they came into the war with us, and I told the President so. I have little doubt they would say the same.

High authorities rejected these sentiments: Bridges doubted any such arrangement would have "a very lasting validity in technical circles". After discussion with Travis, by now operational head of the GC&CS, "C", the Chief of the Secret Service, General Stewart-Menzies, held "there could never be a satisfactory gentlemen's agreement, as even if orders were issued on the highest level, the temptation to have a peep would be more than some experts could resist". These cynics were right: USN cryptanalysts were examining Typex traffic with attack in mind, though they abandoned these efforts.[86] Whitehall convinced Churchill to abandon the idea, by referring to his communication with pet commanders, and the argument that "one of the advantages we hope to gain from the 'GUARD' procedure is that penetration by the Americans of our ordinary cyphers will not matter, while penetration of our 'GUARD' cyphers will not be possible".[87] Against enemies, the compromise of any important traffic was a problem; against a friend, only the most important messages needed protection.

Initially, "NONSUCH" and "GUARD" traffic was carried by OTP and by special Typex settings. However, by definition Typex was insecure for the purpose; that was why the problem existed. America knew the basic structure of Typex and had expertise in attacking electro-mechanical systems, transmitting errors had betrayed the existence of NONSUCH and GUARD traffic and compromised these settings, while Typex and the CCM were falling behind the state of the art. A third advance in the electromechanical age of cipher machines was at hand: the development of on-line cipher teleprinters which used OTP. Only such a system could guard this traffic against America. As soon as it formulated the problem Britain found a solution—indeed, arguably it was the arrival of the solution which caused a recognition of the problem. The solution was a creature of the mid-Atlantic caught through serendipity; inspired by American technology, invented by a Canadian professor of communication engineering, developed by leading British engineers, scientists and mathematicians; and sired by the Secret Intelligence Service (SIS).

In 1938, so to strengthen its radio facilities, the SIS headhunted Richard Gambier-Perry, previously an infantry and air officer, from Pye Ltd. of Cambridge, a major and innovative manufacturer of electronic equipment. Gambier-Perry, a bureaucratic buccaneer who lost few battles in the emerging world of transatlantic intelligence, applied radio to black propaganda, contact with agents and security against foreign spies. He gave SIS a great signals system. By late 1941, he sought to coordinate all intelligence communications worldwide, including the distribution of ULTRA to American authorities. He placed the North American end of this system under the control of British Security Coordination (BSC), which oversaw imperial intelligence in that hemisphere. The system is often named HYDRA, after its central node, a radio station at BSC's school in Ontario, "Camp X". HYDRA was run by Benjamin de Forest Bayly, "Pat", a communications engineer at The University of Toronto, knowledgeable, energetic, with an international reputation and excellent contacts among American scientists. Bayly was respected by all who met him; one of Britain's leading experts in machine cryptanalysis, W.G. Welchman, called him "an exuberant person with infectious enthusiasm".[88] Bayly's job was to ensure that HYDRA could contact BSC in New York over telegraph lines and Britain over radio, via teletype and with security, including defence against anyone able to tap landlines in the United States.[89] By definition, however inadvertently, United States authorities were among the possible threats. Bayly used American technology against its intelligence.

He adopted an unusual and commercially unsuccessful device built by Western Union. "Telekrypton" created teletype messages on the Verham principle, generating signals through five-hole paper tape, which formed characters by a binary system. A message was printed on one strip of five-hole tape. As its electrical impulses were transmitted, they joined those produced by a second five-hole strip, so changing the original message, which the receiving machine read by filtering the companion signal with a reverse image of the second strip. This system provided encipherment, and could meet the standard of OTP. "Telekrypton" itself did not do so: its second strip was merely a repeating loop. It was mechanically unreliable, and could be used only for telegraph traffic. Where Enigma and Typex used electrical impulses to encipher figures generated by keystrokes, Telekrypton enciphered not letters but electricity. It was keyed to the thirty-two-figure

Baudot–Murray system, which represented letters and also instructions to the receiving machine for matters such as spacing ("stunt" characters). Hence, Telekrypton messages were received in a jumbled form by radio, which used twenty-six-character morse. Nor did this end the complications. In 1941, to avoid political problems with the FBI, the BSC routed all its cables to London, both ways, via Toronto; and when war broke out, it found it hard to lease space on transatlantic cables. For much of the war all its traffic was routed via Toronto, and much of it always was. Thus, BSC traffic with New York and London went in incompatible systems—from New York to Toronto over cable, and from Toronto to London by radio. Every message sent from one end of the circuit to the other had to be retyped in the middle, in Toronto, at twenty-five words per minute, slowing transmission from machine to human speed. By late 1942 this problem was crippling HYDRA. In adapting Telekrypton, Bayly found an elegant solution to all of these problems of compatibility, communication, reliability and security. He created "one-time tape" for the second strip, used to cover only one message, its holes randomly generated by an IBM tape puncher—thus creating perhaps the world's first practicable one-time tape mixer; and a means automatically to translate Baudot traffic to morse (by suppressing the seven "stunt" characters, at the price of reducing teleprinter speed by 50 per cent) and so to send such messages by radio, first at 100 words per minute, ultimately at 300.[90] Prototypes for this new machine were soon ready. One was sent to London by January 1943. As Travis examined this device in Bayly's workshop in the BSC's office at the Rockefeller Center, so legend has it, he looked out a window onto the roof adjoining Radio City Music Hall. He saw Rockette dancers sunbathing, and thought them good; so he named the device, "Rockex".[91] British cryptography honoured its American legs.

In attacking these problems Bayly aided the solution of bigger ones, with help from his friends. He worked with the GC&CS's chief mathematician, Alan Turing, when the latter visited the United States in 1943, developing close relations with leading American students of signals. American intelligence eased Turing's entry; USN codebreakers were aligned to leading commercial researchers in communications and data processing. He also approved Bell Lab's "X-system", an early and excellent speech encipherment system. Turing, however, merely supplemented Bayly's access. In fact, influence flowed in the opposite direction; Bayly's work in translating the Baudot–Murray system to morse and in developing five-hole tape later helped Turing's move from data-processing machines to the computer. British cryptology shaped the birth of the computer through Rockex as well as COLOSSUS.[92] Again, Welchman, later stationed in Washington, noted that he and Bayly had a "curious position". Able to contact all American authorities, many of whom could not talk to each other because of interservice friction, imperial officials became "go-betweens" between Americans.[93]

From January 1942, BSC developed one-to-one "Telekrypton" and "Rockex I" links with the GC&CS and American signals intelligence services, so to transmit ULTRA. By May 1943 "Rockex I" carried transatlantic teletype cable traffic between the JSM and select offices in London (initially the Admiralty and Air Ministry, later the Cabinet Office joined while the Air Ministry dropped out), transmitting SIS and ULTRA material, sometimes for the Combined Chiefs of Staff.[94] On this system, two skilled teletypists could conduct an instantaneous conversation, though only one point-to-point link could be serviced at any one time. For people without such skills, "Rockex I" offered the strategic equivalent of "key conversations" on the battlefield, where two operators on one frequency but in different locales sent plain-language morse messages dictated by officers standing beside them; from mid-1944 this approach became standard drill. Meanwhile, the United States created several "X-system" (or "Sigsaly") circuits, including one between Washington and London, under American control but, with its permission, available for twenty-four named British officials to contact forty Americans.[95] In 1943, "Rockex I" and the "X-system" sapped the value of German tapping of Allied transatlantic telephones, by providing secure means to carry the most important components of that traffic. Meanwhile, British attention increasingly turned to an American threat; Turing noted that if the X-system were "operated solely by US personnel, this personnel will be in a position to decypher it", while the JSM favoured Rockex I because it allowed "key conversations" to occur "with complete security *including* security from interception from Americans".[96] Rockex I, under British control, matched "X-ray" in security, almost did so in speed and exceeded it in flexibility. Indeed, the JSM thought Rockex I would be "infinitely more useful", since X-ray had the

> very great disadvantage that the human voice is distorted so that no form of expression is possible and it sounds as if the two talkers were very old men, with very quavery and uncertain voice ... It would, I think, be quite impossible to emphasise a point by tone of voice. It is therefore unsatisfactory as a channel for debate though entirely adequate as a method of stating facts in complete security.

With Rockex I, whenever any British authority in London or Washington needed to contact another, "one should be able to go straight down to the machine and be in touch within a few moments without any fear of Allied or enemy interception".[97] X-ray eased communication with Americans, Rockex I amplified it between Britons, eliminating American security threats while helping Britain influence its allies. The JSM later noted that British views could most easily become Allied ones at "the lower levels of first and second grade staff officers" where detailed American planning was done, and

Once a plan passed out of this working level it was extremely difficult to get the Americans to change their minds, and then the higher the plan went the more set it became on the U.S. side. Much, therefore, depended on having first class British representatives on the lower levels, and on their maintaining good personal relations with the American opposite numbers, many of whom were regular officers with West Point training.

All this required "very rapid" communication with London, so that British technical specalists or senior authorities could determine how they wished to shape draft American policy; fortunately, through Rockex I, "The J.S.M. had its own direct line through Navy to the War Cabinet offices in London, and it was often possible to get a reply within three or four hours, including enciphering and deciphering at both ends"—close to the fastest times possible even in 2005.[98]

After Bayly developed "Rockex I" and began to ponder its refinement, he visited Bletchley Park, and observed the use of machines in cryptanalysis. He and Welchman pooled their knowledge of the principles of communications, cryptology and mathematics, and the practices of teletype, radio, punch-card and punch-tape technology. Once Bayly had formulated the design for an advanced Rockex, prototypes and parts were built at Hanslope Park, headquarters of the SIS's "Special Communications Unit No. 3", where British intelligence used the technical expertise of the General Post Office to aid research and development in advanced electronic equipment. R.J. Griffith, engineer for COLOSSUS, the world's leading electro-mechanical data-processing device, directed Rockex's development. The same people built Britain's new codemaking and codebreaking machines. The development of "Rockex II" took great effort. According to the BSC, "something like four hundred blueprints had to be drawn before the parts could be machined, and even when the unit was at last assembled exhaustive tests were necessary to ensure that it had no hidden weaknesses".[99] By July 1944 prototype Rockex II machines were ready, "designed to combine one time pad security with convenience of operation at all stages of cyphering", via radio and telegraph. It was on the leading edge of a new age in cryptography. The Cypher Policy Board (CPB) held Rockex II essential for all key traffic of the Foreign Office, GC&CS and the COS, and had all other departments inspect the device. According to a "weeder" more kindly than usual, Britain used this machine even in 1973; so too did Canada, until 1975.[100]

The development and production of these ciphering and transmission systems was not easy. Drawing on the lessons of the previous decade, the Ministry of Supply calculated that this process would require several years. Britain was not dealing merely with radical technological advances but also with the new age of cryptanalysis created by Bletchley Park. Since 1900 Britain had badly mishandled simpler problems. It could easily have done the same with this one. As ever, the departments underestimated the difficulties involved in the development and production of cipher machines. In December 1944, when the War Office was pursuing different on-line cipher teleprinters to Rockex II for use in the field, "Secratype", it expected "prototypes or pre-production models" to be ready within a year, although Britain had not yet defined the "principles" which would govern their design. Equally, the Foreign Office was over-optimistic about the production of Rockex II. In October 1944, the CPB aimed to produce sixty units, twenty in twenty weeks and the rest by July 1945. By February 1945 it wanted 360 machines (including 150 for GC&CS traffic); a "target production figure of 20 machines a month was satisfactory but ... a slower rate of production would not be acceptable as to be of use these machines were required as quickly as possible". These ambitions were not realized. By September 1945, thirty-three Rockex IIs were in service, just 33 per cent of the target (twenty-one from the production order and twelve of Hanslope's prototypes), with only three being delivered each month. Just as lack of machine tools had hampered Creed's production of Typex, they threatened the development of Rockex II: certainly by July 1945, the CPB complained that four tools were unavailable and "urgently required". Production was slowed by the need to develop British supplies of "one-time tape" and hole punches, no longer available through lend lease, though Menzies bought six IBM tape punches with scarce dollars from the Secret Service Fund.

None the less, this production met Britain's minimum needs, barely. Two Rockex IIs stood on the London–Washington circuit by February 1945, just in time. As one member of the Communication Department wrote regarding the production of Rockex II: "Keep them up to it! These machines may just save our bacon if peace were to break out suddenly."[101] Rockex II carried "the bulk of the traffic" for the major conferences of 1945 at San Francisco, Berlin and Moscow. Meanwhile, with the end of the war, the GC&CS's needs for these devices fell, while those for other units rose. By 1946 the CPB believed Britain needed 500 Rockex II machines, including "substantial" reserves; all of them and the requisite tape-making equipment should be produced immediately.[102] This request was not fully met. Until March 1947, the JSM still relied heavily on "Rockex I" while soon afterward Gambier-Perry thought "our major posts abroad" could not be fully equipped with Rockex II until 1950—that is, throughout the early cold war era, Britain transmitted much of its diplomatic traffic over a system it believed the United States could break and might be breaking.[103] Rockex, meanwhile, replaced Typex and OTP for strategic and diplomatic traffic, but nothing further, not surprisingly. Rockex II's main edge over Typex lay in its ease of use for teletype traffic; in terms of security, refined versions of the latter remained formidable for decades, into the era even of computer cryptanalysis. The fighting services used Typex for operational traffic even during the invasion of Egypt in 1956. Similarly, the USN relied on Sigaba until 1959. In

1949 British cipher authorities attempted to have NATO adopt Typex Mark II for interallied traffic. Ultimately, however, this niche was filled by a new American system, the KL-7, its traffic later superenciphered by the on-line electronic cipher device, the KW-26. In design terms, KL-7 was a distant cousin of Typex Mark II, and no more user-friendly: as one operator noted, "one never actually typed on a KL-7. Its keys were beat into submission!" Typex remained standard for the Australian Department of External Affairs until 1953, probably far longer, while in New Zealand, "the last Ministry of Foreign Affairs machines [were] dumped at sea about 1973".[104]

These delays in production occurred for many reasons. Creed's, earlier a world leader in teletype and reperforator equipment, could not or would not manage the transition to manufacture the tape punches and one-time tape developed by IBM and Western Union for the next generation of equipment. Granted, this material was hard to build and the market small. Creed's may have been too occupied with larger and more profitable projects to focus on so small and specialized an area, while, as a matter of policy, it was blocked from matters central to the cryptographic functions of Typex, such as the wiring of rotors; its role always had lain more with teleprinters than cipher machines. Creed's, however, was consulted in the development of Rockex II, and British authorities obviously did not think it able to handle its production. Creed's had failed to produce the desired number of Typex devices between 1939 and 1945, partly because of shortages with machine tools, had never used the reperforator technology required for Rockex II, and provided "inferior" equipment for the system.[105] British cryptographers were not willing to take any further chances of compromises stemming from poor manufacture. Later, the manufacture of Rockex tape was subject to thorough quality control.[106] BTM, the obvious commercial alternative, had expertise with IBM equipment but no experience in building cipher machines. Nor was Hanslope a production unit. The many bodies involved in the production and use of cipher machines had conflicting interests. The military authorities who ran strategic correspondence between London and Washington tried to stop the Foreign Office from taking over that function for international conferences in early 1945 because "communications are *not* the Foreign Office's strong point".[107] That office, thinking otherwise, forced its way back to run overseas communications and cryptography, aided by the Air Ministry's wish to escape its unwanted duties for that function; but this created bureaucratic upheavals.

Despite these problems, Britain approached the second generation of cipher machines far better than it had the first; probably no other country matched its work in this sphere. At least three subcommittees of the CPB coordinated the technical experts and the departments. They were led by the "acknowledged cipher cracking experts", including Travis, a specialist in cryptography, but particularly Welchman, that master of attack on machine systems, by then moving toward his second career as the designer of military communication systems. The team developing COLOSSUS provided help, as did Turing, though he focused on unbreakable speech encipherment.[108] Meanwhile, Gambier-Perry took charge of the Foreign Office's Communications Department; thus, the creator of the signals system whose needs led to Rockex II, remade British external communications, placing Rockex and radio at its heart. Again, in October 1944, the CPB agreed that Britain must form an inter-service Cypher Machine Development Committee (CMDC), to coordinate the research, development, production, use and security of machine systems. A year later, it decided to pursue two lines of work. While the CMDC would handle the "development" of conventional devices, Bayly would receive a five-year contract for £30,000, a large sum for British government scientific work, to have five staff "research into the mechanical and electrical practicability" of "the G.C.& C.S. Theory on Cypher Machines referred to as the RM (26) theory" and develop a prototype. The RM (26), perhaps meaning "Rotor Machine 26 letter", conceived by Welchman with help from Turing, was intended for field service. British cryptological authorities hoped to replicate the approach which had led to Rockex, with Bayly and a workshop creating prototypes for British authorities to develop. Their willingness to place so large a programme in his hands shows their desire to replace Typex in the field, faith in his ability and, as ever, the limits to their resources in the field. Few Britons could turn a cryptographic concept into a workable cipher machine. Though the data is inconclusive, when discussing a new *"Scrambler only"* machine for field service, Welchman told the War Office he

> had in mind a scheme whereby the security of machine cyphers would not be governed by the moving parts. Permanent rotating drums might produce the scramble within any message but ... the inherent security of the machine would be dependent on a form of plugboard which would be modified and considerably simplified relative to those at present employed with Type X. These plugboards would be incorporated into the machine between the drums.

He seems to have been conceptualizing a machine system on the model of a superenciphered codebook, using a semi-permanent arrangement of rotors as the base, with an improved (and frequently changed) plugboard providing most of the security. Such a machine had obvious advantages for use, and problems with security. For the latter reason, and because Bayly lost interest, the programme was abortive, and cancelled after two years.[109]

In 1946, the CPB decided a "Cypher Machine Development Unit" (CMDU) should oversee research and development in the area. It should have seventy-three members, led by the ablest engineer available and including all present personnel working on cipher machines. These men were able and experienced, including Wing Commander Smith; among the men considered to run the CMDU were engineers who had developed COLOSSUS. Its members were to have expertise in engineering and production, mechanical, electro-mechanical and electronic problems, speech and facsimile media, and to be able to sustain "a full development programme on three major projects concurrently". One may wonder if this body was intended to develop cryptanalytical as well as cryptographical machines. Whitehall was divided over where to house the CMDU; the Ministry of Supply (because of manufacturing experience), the Foreign Office (because of its greater concern in the matter) or the GPO (because of its technical expertise). The GPO was favoured, but to ensure that it did not "supply only their second best people" and insist on "a tight technical control of the Unit", the CMDU remained under the CMDC's "day by day" and "*detailed operational control*".[110] At this stage, records fade, and history ends. None the less, by 1944 the standard of Britain's approach to cipher machines and signals security had risen far above that between 1900 and 1939.

This development had benefits but also costs; to improve communications and cryptography has paradoxical consequences. During the great crises of the 1930s, the Foreign Office barely managed the surge of traffic. It constantly left secondary posts in the dark. It did not fully inform the Chancery in Cairo (the heart of British authority in Egypt) about Anglo-Italian relations during 1935. During the Munich crisis the British Legation in Budapest received its news from the BBC! Yet diplomats thought the only solution to this problem, to send small outposts the "information telegrams" given to the Dominions, impossible; "posts with a small staff could [not] cope with the additional decyphering involved", as such telegrams often involved "at least three to four hours work for two people where these are not skilled cypher experts". "After drafting & recyphering here and decyphering in posts abroad the telegrams would, in a swiftly moving crisis, always be out of date. It is in fact impossible to keep all Missions informed of the latest developments."[111] The rise of Rockex ended this problem but created another. Reflecting on the Trieste crisis of 1953, Hugh Grey, head of the Foreign Office's Communications Department, thought "the machine has stood up to this sudden change in conditions". No one had complained of poor communications; on the contrary, the Foreign Secretary complained of being swamped in them. Grey wondered "whether our methods of conducting correspondence in what may be regarded as normal conditions, are appropriate in crisis conditions". A closed communications circuit of teletype and "machine cyphering", moving traffic with speed and security, linked the Foreign Office and its outposts, every member able to reply to telegrams, almost through the diplomatic equivalent of "key conversations".

> If these facilities did not exist in their present state of perfection, it would not be possible for our posts abroad and others concerned to

attempt to keep pace with the hour-to-hour developments, reporting and advising in rapid fire, in the way that they have been doing lately ... "Crisis telegrams" pour in too rapidly; they nearly all carry high priority markings and nearly all are sent, whether for observations or merely for information, to five or six other posts.

Each of these posts sent its comments on all of these reports back to every other authority. "We then approach the state of several dogs chasing their own tails ... At best, even if the rapid spate does not lead to confusion of thought, it certainly must create a grave strain on those in high places responsible for the decisions." Other Foreign Office authorities found it "painfully evident" that "in times of emergency ... the apparatus of administration has evolved more rapidly than the human beings supposed to control it". They pursued means to avoid information overload; one may wonder if they succeeded.[112]

Failures in cipher security are often treated primarily as a *deus ex machina* to explain the success of the codebreakers. To view cryptography simply from the perspective of cryptanalysis, is to misunderstand the nature of cryptology. The maintenance of signals security is a never-ending and heartbreaking struggle, requiring the continual development of complicated systems and the proper training of personnel in sophisticated procedures. Since it can be wrecked by just one error, failures in cipher security are the rule rather than the exception. States can simultaneously possess a high standard of cryptanalysis and a low one of cryptography. Britain's experience with cipher machines helps to explain why it did so between 1914 and 1939. Such devices could make radio a reasonably secure medium for the transmission of government messages. Britain was among the first powers to appreciate this possibility and among the last to bring such machines into service. Its misjudgments in this regard stemmed from its attitudes toward two more fundamental issues. Decision makers misunderstood the needs for cipher security and were unwilling to take the difficult steps which alone could protect their mail from the eyes of foreign gentlemen. This problem was exacerbated by their attitude toward technological change. Rather than being reactionary, decision makers were often fascinated by the initial promise of mechanical contrivances. Their problem lay in bridging the gap between that promise and its realization, in a failure to appreciate just how slow and complex a process research, development and production would be. The white heat of technology was more attractive in anticipation than duration.

These attitudes fostered a spasmodic policy toward cipher machines. Britain saw them as a quick and complete solution to immediate problems, overestimating the speed with which such devices could be introduced and the degree to which they could provide security. When this promise was not rapidly achieved, Whitehall too easily lost interest in the idea. This weakened Britain's ability to defend the secrecy of its traffic; so also may the hopes which it invested in the idea. As with all states, Britain's interest in cipher machines was motivated by the great illusion in cryptography, the belief that a cipher system in itself can render messages absolutely secure. Of course, in the two world wars Britain refused to trust simply in systems in order to maintain its signals security. Still, at many important moments before these wars British cipher authorities did believe that systems, particularly cipher machines, could make traffic entirely unbreakable. They failed to realize that signals security hinges no more on systems than on the provision of means to change them regularly and of enough trained personnel to use them effectively. Whitehall's faith in the potential value of cipher machines may have encouraged it to believe at certain points that it could ignore these critical but difficult matters. Cipher machines helped to overcome Britain's problems with signals security, but its approach to the former may have contributed to the latter. Ultimately, Britain managed to overcome these systematic weaknesses, and to leapfrog its rivals into the age of on-line cipher teleprinters. It did so by pioneering a new approach to signals security. The lead was no longer taken by cryptologists or inventors, but by communications experts of imagination, aided by integrated teams of technical experts, in which cryptologists were no more (or less) important than engineers, mathematicians and mechanics. Thus, between 1939 and 1948, Britain brought codebreaking and codemaking into the industrial age and then the cybernetic era.

5

THE BRITISH ARMY

Signals and security in the desert campaign, 1940–1942

Speed, flexibility, reliability and security are the characteristics required of any signal system. Without these it cannot provide the means whereby immediate and accurate information is supplied to commanders and timely and effective execution of operational and administrative plans can follow. These characteristics are of especial importance under desert conditions where distances are great and dispersion considerable, where there are constant and rapid changes in the situation and where units and formations move frequently from one command to another.[1]

The following examples of the misuse of routine may serve as a guide to [the] proper use [of radio-telephones]:

(a) In June 1942 an Italian Second Lieutenant in a radio intercept company was awarded the German Gold Cross for "Saving the 15th Panzer Division in the Western Desert near Bir Hachem." The 15th Panzer Division was cut off from its supply trains and was almost out of fuel and ammunition. The Italian intercepted a conversation *in the clear* between two British commanders concerning their *intended actions* in disposing of the unfortunate German division. This information enabled the German commander to collect and fuel a few of his tanks and break through the encircling British forces to reach his supply trains, and so to extricate his whole division.

(b) During the British stand on the Alamein line, a British regimental commander whose position was near the south flank sent a desperate call, *in the clear*, saying, in effect: "I am out of fuel, out of ammunition. Will someone please do something." Fortunately, in this case the Germans did not.

(c) Two British brigade commanders were talking on the air. One asked: "Can you do anything about closing the 3000 yard gap between your left and my right flank?"

The second replied, "No, I can't. Can you?"

"No, I can't either."

Twelve hours later the Germans did something about it.

(d) A British Armoured Division on the Tunisian front intercepted a message *in the clear* from a German air support party calling for a dive bomber attack on a British position at a stated time, and stating that the target area would be indicated by ringing it with artillery smoke. The British commander ordered his artillery to register on a nearby German strongpoint. When the Stukas arrived on schedule the British artillery ringed this point with smoke. The subsequent Stuka attack was thorough and effective.[2]

Only a traitor used radio, only a fool did not; this dilemma haunted all commanders of the Second World War. In order to control the operations of millions of men scattered over as many square miles, states had to rely upon the least-trusted medium of communication on earth. Although radio was a uniquely supple and speedy form of signalling, it was also extraordinarily vulnerable to interception. The use of this device increased the ability of a state to coordinate its forces and the chance that an enemy would discover its intentions. Without radio there was no certainty of command. With it there was no guarantee of secrecy. The rise of radio led to a new system of relationships (which might be called "C^3IS") between command, control, communications, signals intelligence and signals security, and to a revolution in the art of war. The connection between information, command and communications lay at the heart of this revolution.[3]

Intelligence shapes a commander's understanding of how best his forces can be used to further his aims, while communication systems carry the messages which lead both to knowledge and to action. If it can maintain adequate communications, or deny the enemy access to accurate intelligence, an army should be more likely to defeat its opponent. Ideally, it should be able to establish technically the maximum standard both of signals and of security at one and the same time. The more dangerous the enemy's source of intelligence, the greater the standard of defence needed against it. All this seems simple; all becomes complex when that threat is the most deadly of them all—signals intelligence. For any improvement in an army's standard of communication will tend to weaken that of its signals security; any tightening of security will tend to strangle signals; any improvement in signals or security may hinder an army's ability to achieve victory. These paradoxes stem from the dialectical nature of C^3IS.

Command is more than generalship. It is a medium and a message, and the link between leader, machine (staff, formations and units) and men. The process of command is shaped by the quality of generals, the training of soldiers, the structure of organization and the flow of communications. One would expect orders and information to move most efficiently through an army with a simple and flexible command structure. One would expect this level of efficiency to fall as that structure becomes more complex and hierarchical, especially as more levels of command are interposed between a field commander and his fighting units. Too many generals spoil the battle. Of course, any headquarters will have a limited span of command: it can control only so many sub-units and assimilate just so much information at any one time. A general needs intermediate levels of command to amplify his power over his fighting units and to filter out the information rising from below. In principle, these intermediate levels should be as few as possible and they should serve primarily as relay stations for the transfer of orders and information. The more intermediate levels of command, the greater the likelihood that the transfer of messages will be slowed and their meaning misunderstood. The more independent and powerful these levels, the more likely they will be to pursue their own aims and confuse the process of command. Nothing would seem less efficient than a C^3 system with many intermediate levels of command, each having a small span of command, all joined by rigid hierarchical bonds. The ideal C^3 system would have the maximum possible span and the fewest possible levels of command.

An army could exert its power to the full through such a fine-tuned system—if every part always functioned with high efficiency and without interruption. Armies, however, must sometimes enter a realm of friction where only the crude survive. Under the stress of war, some or all command links will disappear, the transmission of orders and information will be delayed unexpectedly, action and knowledge will be hampered. To survive these conditions, units must be able to cooperate without coordination from above, and headquarters to act even when enveloped in the fog of war. This is most likely to occur when an army has many intermediate levels of command, each an independent centre of power with a small span of command, all connected by rigid hierarchical bonds which can control large segments of a force even when under the gravest stress known to man. Such robust C^3 systems will be far less efficient than fine-tuned ones; even this diminished quality of command can be maintained only when signals systems operate at their maximum level of performance.

The purpose of military signals is to transfer across a chain of command that volume of information and instructions at that velocity which an army needs to achieve its task. The volume and velocity which can be provided depend upon the efficiency of a signals service. What is needed will vary with the aim and with the army at hand. The more urgent and unpredictable the problem, the greater the call for speed; the larger and structurally more complicated the army, the greater the need for size. Modern military organizations require fast-working and dense signals links with subordinates, superiors and hosts of other units which fight beside them or which meet their logistical needs. These communication structures must be complex; they are correspondingly vulnerable to dislocation.

The efficiency of a communication system may be measured crudely in terms of its volume (the maximum quantity of groups of traffic which can be transmitted between all its stations at any one time) and of its velocity (the mean, the minimum and the maximum times required for any station in the system to receive messages of a given length from any other). A military communication system will be most efficient when all its traffic can be sent at the highest possible rate of speed through an uninterrupted set of links. The friction of war will degrade this level of efficiency. Whether for technical reasons or because of enemy action, individual stations or links in a network may cease to function, without warning and with effect. At worst, this problem can wreck communications during critical periods. While less spectacular, another form of friction is no less deadly.

Security against traffic analysis and cryptanalysis will degrade the functioning of any communication system. The use of the most simple and rapid modes of signalling, such as radio transmission in plain language, will be curtailed; the adoption of time-consuming matters like code and cipher will become essential. One lapse from a complex and continually changing set of procedures, and security will slide toward the pit. Only well-trained and constantly monitored personnel can avoid such slips and only at a price. Every security system offers a compromise between the need for secrecy and the usability of signals. Speed of transmission is crucial in communications; secure systems are slow. In 1944 operators using Morse code by key could transmit about 300 plain language groups of traffic in ten minutes. When they used high grade British systems such as the Typex cipher machine or one-time pad (OTP), the encipherment and the transmission of this traffic required a period six to fourteen times greater. Earlier in the war, British personnel could transmit just three to six cipher groups per minute.[4] Such friction will occur whenever any signals security system is used. The more communication an army needs to function, the greater the effect of this problem. The aggregate effect of these delays in the velocity of traffic and the reduction in its volume may be a signals failure. In any case, when guarded by the full panoply of security precautions, any communication network will function at a small fraction of its full theoretical efficiency. Effective procedures for signals security will cripple again the already diminished level of efficiency of any C^3 system. In no other case does the mere pursuit of defence against a hostile source of intelligence so harm the work of any army; security against the enemy's sound-ranging service will not reduce the scale of one's artillery fire by two-thirds. A signals intelligence service need not read a single message in order to hamstring its enemy.

In using means of communication which an enemy can intercept, the more technically perfect signals become, the less so security becomes, and vice versa. A robust C^3 system will have dense layers of main and fallback communication links between units and headquarters. Effective signals security procedures will be more difficult to enforce upon this increased number of operators; the enemy's codebreakers and traffic analysts will receive more traffic to attack. Conversely, reductions in the number of links will make a communication system more secure but more fragile. Only a signals system which is never used is certain to be secure; any form of signals security is certain to cripple communications. Of course, one can sometimes establish secure means to transmit traffic by plain language; or reduce the volume of communications necessary during operations, by training forces to act automatically without first requesting and receiving orders; or devise techniques to transfer information and orders quickly and flexibly. These means can reduce the scale of the problem; they cannot eliminate it. The imperatives of communication and of security are in conflict; the stakes at risk are the quality of one's command and the secrecy of one's strategy.

There is no simple escape from this dilemma. Signals security is not an absolute virtue; an unbreakable but unworkable cryptographic system is worse than none at all. Communication is the primary purpose of signals, security a secondary consideration. Despite this relative ranking, each of these matters is vital: to ignore signals security is to risk destruction. One cannot escape the need to choose between evils; one can merely select the least of them. "The old struggle between 'security' and 'signals' "[5] must end in a complex compromise. Their requirements must be balanced at the highest possible level of marginal efficiency, where no further gains can be made in either direction save by suffering greater losses in the other. It is difficult enough to create a technically effective system for either C^3 or signals security; one must strive to achieve both results at the same time.

It is never easy to balance these imperatives. During 1940–1942 it was even harder than usual for the British Army to draw the "most effective compromise between theoretical security and operational requirements",[6] because it was poorly prepared for either the use or the security of radio. Britain discovered that virtually no such compromise was possible at all. The combination of small numbers of radio operators, and those inexperienced, of large volumes of traffic, of emergency conditions and of poorly designed cryptographic systems, created this danger: any use of security procedures might cause a breakdown of communication, any use of radio one of security. During these years the British army was notorious for lax signals security, constant signals failures and poor command. From late 1942 until 1945, however, it possessed the most powerful, flexible and secure system of military communication on earth combined with an effective system of command. An examination of how the British army entered into and escaped its predicament will contribute to the study of the desert campaign, of the signals intelligence struggle of the Second World War, and of the relationship between command, control, communications, intelligence and security. A study of signals will illuminate our understanding of command.

The purpose of military communications is to support the operations of armed forces; the shape of signals reflects an army's approach to war. Between 1919 and 1939 the British army suffered from financial stringency, from Whitehall's refusal to let it prepare for major wars, and from its own misunderstanding of the nature of modern ones.[7] Similarly, the Royal Corps of Signals was starved of funds, denied the opportunity to train with higher formations and to prepare for mobile operations. If the army was Britain's Cinderella service, signals was its Cinderella corps.

In 1939 Britain had 1,400 regular signals personnel, augmented by another 38,500 less-well-trained Territorials. This total strength increased fourfold to 154,661 men by 1945, while the signals strength of the Indian army (including seconded British personnel) increased tenfold, from 6,411 to 71,395 men. This expansion was particularly marked with radio personnel—in 1939, each infantry division had an establishment of seventy-five radio sets, but by 1944 this had risen to 100—and with predictable consequences.[8] Genius was not required to handle signals equipment: as the Chief Signals Officer (CSO) of the Eighth Army noted in 1945: "Gurkhas, who are notoriously thick in the head, make good signallers."[9] Proper training, however, was essential: another authority stated in 1943 that "signals personnel are either good or useless. There is no half-way. To be good, they must have long periods of combined training, and they must specialize in the particular job for which they are to be employed".[10] Years of training would be required to make these British personnel "good". Moreover, the British army would have to recentre its entire signals system while within earshot of the sound of the guns.

For the army entered the Second World War with its communication system of the First. This elaborate structure of telegraph and telephone lines had a symbiotic relationship with a stable front. Neither could exist without the other. In 1917–1918, signals sustained the great and complex set-piece attacks by which Commonwealth forces wrecked their German foe. This signals system could do anything but move; during mobile operations it could not carry a large or rapid flow of instructions and information between a commander and the commanded. Radio was a tertiary component within this system. It was used far less than technically possible and was handled with neither security nor effect. Confronted with the choice between the risk of interception and the inconvenience of code, signals personnel tried to avoid the use of radio, but when this proved impossible usually sent their messages in clear.[11] Most of these characteristics resurfaced in British signals during 1939–1941.

Of course, all forms of communication are complementary and no single one can handle all tasks. Even in the desert, landlines were an essential signals service: by 1942 the Signals Officer-in-Chief (SO-in-C), Middle East, noted that "the pendulum has now swung" and the value of these systems was underestimated.[12] They were less vulnerable to interception than radio and hence a more secure medium of transmission. Since landline links could carry plain language traffic they reduced, to a degree out of all proportion to their number, the problems caused by signals security. Where available, cable was more than worth its weight in radio sets. In mobile operations, however, landlines were not enough: radio-telephone (R/T) and wireless-telegraphy (W/T) were necessary to maintain tactical and operational control.

In September 1939, unfortunately, these systems were not available to the British army. Thousands of radio sets were on order, but too few to meet the army's existing needs, let alone additional ones, and those available for traffic between headquarters proved clumsy and fragile in mobile operations. Ninety-five per cent of them were designed for and allocated to armour and artillery units. Corps and army headquarters had, respectively, two or three and six to nine radio sets. One set each for forward, rear and lateral communication, linked divisions to brigades and the latter to infantry battalions or armoured regiments. Battalions had no forward radio links at all, although armoured car squadrons, artillery batteries and most tanks were equipped with a radio set. R/T and W/T did not even provide a full fallback network for the British army. Their tactical use was limited to purely armoured operations or to artillery support. Individual command links did not possess a dedicated communication circuit: a corps might have to command three divisions, or a division three brigades, through one set and frequency. This would be a certain cause of apoplexy for command. The artillery circuits were the only element of redundancy in the system; throughout 1940–1942 these links all too often provided the only means for communication within infantry brigades during emergencies. No allowance was made to carry administrative messages. Radio was treated as an auxiliary service which would handle a small load of traffic. Should this system suddenly become a principal means of communication, it would not carry enough operational traffic to maintain a high standard of control: the standard volume of administrative messages would bury it alive. The throat of command might be cut if accident or enemy action wrecked even one radio set.

Not only would these failings become obvious, but they had been predicted. During the interwar years radical thinkers argued that armies would move more quickly and more flexibly in the future than in the trenches, and hence would require new modes of communication; so did chiefs of the imperial general staff (CIGS). In 1922–1923 the conservative CIGS, Lord Cavan, wanted the army to abandon landlines entirely and trust in wireless.[13] In 1927, after witnessing the first "Experimental Brigade" manoeuvres, the more radical CIGS Lord Milne reminded officers "to what extent communication is going to govern action. It is exactly the same question and an even more difficult one than that which confronts an Admiral when dealing with his destroyers". Armoured formations, Milne noted, though not necessarily infantry divisions, would need new modes of command.

> Command is going to be very difficult. You want special determination and quickness…There is no time for argument in command. In a force of this kind you must have quick decision. It is not for the Staff Officer to give advice. It is for the Staff Officer to learn what

his commander wants and go away and get it done. In a force of this kind more than in any other force we have no time to waste nor tempers to get ruined by staff officers expounding how they think it ought to be done. It is for the commander to command and give his orders and the staff officer to carry out these orders to the best of his ability. That is one of the points in a force like this—orders out as soon as possible.

For another point. It seems to me that, as in the cavalry, the commanding officer must be far forward. I cannot help thinking—I may be wrong—that he has not got much time to spend over too many reports; that he must really be like a cavalry divisional commander in former days, well up to the front; and that as in the case of Nelson's Captains, he must have so instructed his commanding officers beforehand that, even before he can send his messages, the different units will be brought up by them in accordance with his wishes. You have got to act quickly, think quickly, and so train the force that they know instinctively what you want.[14]

Milne outlined the style of operational command which proved necessary in 1940, and defined those parts of the 1918 system which required change. He was as prescient about modes of communication as of command. In 1929, after two further years of experience, he insisted that instead of being "tied up in an network of line communications tending to paralyze rather than invigorate its functions", the army needed "mobility and elasticity in [its] means of communication". Only R/T and W/T offered this possibility. They should, therefore, become the principal means of communication in front of corps headquarters. While this view remained official policy until 1939, as with so many of Milne's proposals, haste was made too slowly.[15]

Signals experts supported Milne's policy, and over the next decade they pursued it, developing many different prototypes and procedures for the use of radio in war, and appreciating the limits to other modes of communication.[16] However, financial restrictions and institutional inertia hampered their drive and the adoption of radio, while Milne's warnings about command were forgotten. The army did not prepare signals or command systems fit for mobile war, because it did not believe the latter would occur. The Cavalry and the Royal Tank Regiment wanted a thick radio net for command in mobile battles, and gunners for fire control in set-piece operations, but most officers held that any new continental war would be akin to the last; hence a variant of their old signals and command system would meet the army's needs. Operations would unfold at a stately pace. Command could be exercised in a sure rather than swift fashion, with plenty of time to receive information, to assess options, to consult staff and superiors, to issue orders and to execute them. Shielded from enemy action by a stable front, a landline network would carry with the requisite rapidity an enormous volume of instructions and information; dispatch riders on motorcycles carrying detailed written orders could provide the flexibility and speed needed in emergencies. In the great war such procedures had allowed hastily improvised headquarters to turn the largest, most complex, most unwieldy, human organizations ever known into the most perfect meat-grinding machines ever seen. Surely this could be done again.

By 1939 the army's use of radio had advanced little since 1918; its procedures for security had regressed. In 1917–1918 its system for signals security matched that of any belligerent.[17] Between 1919 and 1932 the War Office preached the necessity of this matter to its officers. It emphasized the vulnerability of radio traffic in the field, particularly between divisions and brigades. It provided hints on the best means to minimize such risks; it planned to establish signals security sections to do so in war.[18] Yet this material was neither taught nor learned well, and the official approach to signals security became fossilized, with counterproductive results. Officers came to regard signals security almost as impossible in itself and incompatible with the use of radio, and to underestimate the power of traffic analysis and what the enemy could gain from intelligence on one's own order of battle. In 1929, signals personnel argued "that rapid communications are of more importance than radio security; that the two are at present incompatible; that rapid communications are becoming more and more the prerogative of radio and that therefore, radio must be used, and the standard of security demanded must be definitely lowered". While information of "immediate tactical value" must be protected, no other kind need be; indeed, enemy intelligence would be overwhelmed by the volume of material it would intercept, and therefore could gain nothing from it. Similarly, after one movement exercise in 1938, Aldershot Command concluded that enemy traffic analysts could not even detect a few new sets operating "behind a front where there is already a considerable volume of W/T traffic"; not so. Even worse, the army's official instructions emphasized that before battle, W/T and R/T would rarely be used, and only when covered by elaborate security, but that during operations they should be adopted freely, with most messages passing in plain language. These principles led soldiers to underestimate grossly the degree to which radio would be used in war and the scale of the security problems which would ensue. Ironically, during 1940 soldiers and officers in the Norwegian and French campaigns reversed the official view, believing that through direction finding, the enemy would immediately locate and shell every radio station when it began to operate, for which reason they rarely used wireless even when it was available. Due to this confusion, the army would receive the worst of all worlds from wireless in 1939–1941.[19]

Nor did the genius of the army's signals security between 1919 and 1939 lie in an infinite capacity for detail. Although during 1936 British forces in Egypt noted that "great importance has always been attached in strict wireless discipline", the War Office's preparations in these areas were lax. For example, the basic elements of signals security were systems of code names for units and places and call signs for communication stations. Until October 1941, however, each army radio station received an individual call sign. Through patience and direction finding, an enemy could follow the movements of each station and often identify the units to which they were attached. Then, through inference and scrutiny of the patterns and the levels of intercommunication, an enemy could determine Britain's order of battle in any theatre and forecast British intentions with striking accuracy. Although these individual call signs changed every day, British forces did not simultaneously change their patterns of intercommunication. Thus, an enemy could quickly identify some of these new call signs, connect these to their sets or nets (communication stations which serviced given command links) and finally reconstruct the entire system. If British procedures for signals security were too primitive for safety's sake, British personnel were also too untrained to use them. In 1939 GHQ France warned that "unless something [was] done to simplify communications while at the same time ensuring a reasonable degree of security, the whole mechanism of command and administration was in danger of breaking down"—all because the personnel of the BEF could not handle a system of unit and geographical code names![20] In the British army the phrase "signals security" essentially meant "wireless silence"; this offered little security once silence ceased.

Between the wars, superenciphered codebooks were the main high-grade cryptographic system used by the British Army.[21] Such systems, however, were extremely slow (in 1937, for example, two hours were needed to encipher, transmit and decipher a message of 110 groups on the RAF's superenciphered codebooks)[22] and were cryptographically vulnerable when used to transmit large quantities of radio traffic. Nor, contrary to the implication in *British Intelligence in the Second World War*, did the use of Typex cipher machines overcome this problem. Although these devices were issued down to divisional headquarters in the British Expeditionary Force (BEF), they were rarely used during May–June 1940. They were agonizingly rare in the Middle East. During 1940 Typex was barely able to cover the most important categories of intercommand traffic in that theatre, forcing reliance on two unsatisfactory alternatives: OTP, or a high grade codebook known to be compromised. This situation slowly improved in late 1941. Typex carried 75,000 of the 89,000 groups sent by GHQ Middle East during the "peak day" of transmission during Crusader. It was first used for operational traffic in the Middle East (between Tobruk and Cairo) during October 1941. Although Typex machines were issued to corps headquarters during the Crusader offensive of November 1941, however, their value was initially limited. Until special vans were devised to shield these devices "from sand and rain ... Typex machines were more often out of order than in order—now [spring 1942] very much the reverse is the case". Even during the Gazala operation of May–June 1942, Typex carried only rear headquarters, essentially administrative, traffic.[23] Until early 1943 British divisions and corps had no simultaneously secure and flexible high-grade system to carry operational messages, such as Germany had in the Enigma machine.

In any case, formally powerful systems are not the only ingredient of cryptography. As the head of RAF signals security noted in 1944, "the mistakes of cypher operators form almost the principal weakness of cypher systems in general. Left to themselves, it is extraordinary what mistakes even trained operators can make".[24] During the first years of the war, the British Army was desperately short of trained operators. In the Ethiopian campaign of 1941 and the Burma one of 1942, it overcame this problem only by conscripting almost every English woman in Khartoum, Nairobi and Rangoon.[25] Not that these women necessarily were bad choices. One cipher operator at GHQ Middle East remembered how the commander's daughter, Miss Felicity-Ann Wavell,

> an energetic and most efficient worker would ask one of the sergeants to call aloud the deciphered groups whilst she rapidly flicked through the cipher volume for their English equivalents at the same time writing the plain language version on to a signal pad. The rest of us would be sitting working in dead silence apart from the sergeant's voice intoning the four-figure groups. Suddenly Felicity's voice would ring out in a authoritative tone, "Check!", making us jump and look up from our work. The sergeant would rework the offending group until it met with Felicity's approval.

None the less, in January 1941 the radio operators of even so critical a centre of command as GHQ Middle East constantly made errors so elementary as to respond in plain language to messages sent in the signals service code.[26] The army's cipher personnel had to master their trade as they practised it; signals and security alike were crippled in the interim. These problems were even greater at lower levels of cryptography and command.

During the great war the army had found it hard to construct proper low- and medium-grade systems for front-line traffic; by 1918 all these codes and ciphers had proved either clumsy or insecure. The army retained this tradition throughout the interwar years. Though signals personnel recognized the need to develop "improved ciphering arrangements" for traffic in the field, the War Office did not do so. The army's low- and medium-grade systems offered little security and gravely hampered communications. As in 1918, this would tempt operators and officers alike to square the circle by sending all their traffic in clear. In any case, during May–June 1940 many British units had no low- or medium-grade systems at all. Staff officers planning the evacuation of British forces in Narvik over the Norwegian civil telephone system were forced to rely on the use of "parables" for security—so too were staff officers in London and commanders in the BEF using the civil telephone systems of Britain and France to discuss developments on one bad day, as France fell on 22 May.[27] The withdrawal orders for one British infantry battalion in Belgium were "given over the telephone by means of a code which involved discussion on the film *The Invisible Man*". The orders issued to one British armoured regiment attached to the First Armoured Division on the Somme front arrived "on a grubby bit of paper, one paragraph of which read: 'Frequencies and code names as for last brigade exercise in Wimborne.' Luckily somebody had a copy of the code".[28] By 1939 the British army was prepared for neither the safe nor the effective use of radio in the field. As the War Office admitted in 1946,

> From the examination of captured documents and interrogation of German intercept personnel, it has been established that valuable information at all levels was acquired through the insecure use of wireless.
>
> At the beginning of the war very scant attention was given to signal security and it was only by painstaking effort and by perseverance that this aspect of training was given the attention it deserved as a operational necessity.
>
> Signal security reached a high level only during the latter years of the war.

It concluded that throughout the war, signals interception provided 70 per cent of German intelligence on the British Army.[29] During the initial years of this conflict, Britain and its army alike paid dearly for these failures of signals and those lapses in security.

This British system provided an ideal target for *blitzkrieg*, that style of warfare into which the *Wehrmacht* stumbled during 1939–1941. The latter forced its foes to fight for high stakes and at a fast pace. Unexpectedly rapid decisions had to be made by armies with confused command structures over fragile communication networks. Poland, France, Britain, Russia, all learned in succession that ineffective command and communication systems were a combat divider. The Germans struck straight at the heart of these systems; the centre could not hold, neither could the front.

In 1940, for example, information and orders percolated through the many levels of an extraordinarily rigid and convoluted Anglo-French C^3I system, a decadent version of one appropriate to 1918. The actions of formations could not be coordinated until a complete sequence of communications had been completed up from units, through every single intermediate headquarters to the high command, and back down again. If any link broke, every action would be paralyzed. Moreover, during days when critical decisions had to be made, these armies had first to determine who should make them. No action could be taken against the Germans until several higher headquarters with overlapping responsibility had been consulted. This process was often completed only after the possibility of successful action had already been forestalled, or never at all.[30]

This failure stemmed in part from the unusual weakness of the Allies' signals network. In early June 1940 only four international telephone circuits linked London and Paris, producing great congestion for emergency planning.[31] The French higher commands relied for communication upon notoriously poor civil telephone systems; the highest of them possessed fewer telephone sets than did a British battalion. One British officer attached to the French First Army during 1940 later described his experiences with this system in these words:

> You could get through to no one, you could beg, you could beseech, you could implore, you could curse but nothing melted the cast-iron obduracy of the operators. It was if some telephonic sadist was gloating over [one's] agonies ... The French members of the staff were made of sterner stuff and never seemed to tire of shouting into the microphone, "Priorité, Priorité d'opérations, Priorité de première urgence", but I don't think that they achieved much.

Another British witness wrote of General Billotte, commander of the Northern group of armies of 800,000 men: "After the second day of the battle [of France] his sole communication was one civilian telephone. He had no telegraphic communication between his H.Q. and Armies at all. The result was that he completely lost touch with his Armies and was never in the picture at all."[32] Billotte soon died by accident; the French command by its own hand.

The British army, too, inflicted wounds upon itself. When its forces failed to find a stable front, its signals system had to play a role which it had not rehearsed, that of movement. It was simultaneously exposed to enemy action. The ability of this system to carry orders and information declined, crippling command precisely when it most needed power. Although the army sought to solve this problem by increasing its use of radio, this could not carry all the requisite traffic. Neither could undertrained and overstrained operators maintain an adequate level of wireless security. These problems increased the chances that an enemy could damage the British army, which in turn exacerbated the initial difficulties with signals and security, *ad infinitum*. Once within this vicious circle, the British army found it hard to escape.

By 1939 the German army, like its British counterpart, had developed a signals service fit for the war it expected to fight, a different sort of war. Again, communication systems were shaped by styles of command and ideas about operations; not coincidentally, the craftsman of the Panzer Divisions, General Heinz Guderian, was a signals officer by origin.

Although German wireless equipment was technically better and more plentiful than British, these advantages were marginal; the real difference was not material but mental. The *Wehrmacht* expected war to be immediate, mobile and decisive. The communication system which it devised to meet these circumstances proved all too suitable for those of *blitzkrieg*, in particular because Germans were motivated to exploit the flexibility and range of radio. In the British army, wireless serviced Stonehenge—self-contained and isolated pillars of command. It provided a series of separate point-to-point links between headquarters, with few lateral connections between columns of command, content staying within each loop unless one of its members consciously chose to relay messages outside. The Germans, conversely, developed a cybernetic system, with more point-to-point links and stronger lateral connections between nets, where content flowed automatically through the whole system rather than waiting for willed relay at each connection between loops. During 1940–1941, German artillery and armour had few more radio sets than their British equivalents, but infantry units and formations had perhaps half again as many, while generals had distinct frequencies to control different subordinates, all augmented by the *Luftwaffe* communication system for ground support. The German system transformed point-to-point links into signals nets. Dedicated frequencies and sets joined all units or headquarters relevant to any function, whose individual members simultaneously maintained links with the elements of other nets, thus robustly stitching the whole together. Simply by listening to the net, units could tap the flow of information and receive orders, while generals could follow the course of operations, without having to wait for intermediate links to relay messages, or else control nets at far lower levels of command. By 1939 the German army was approaching optimality in C^3I, each level of command capable of independent action and initiative, all joined by powerful, flexible and redundant organizational and communication links.

The *Wehrmacht* was more willing to rely on radio than the British army, had a better idea of its value and limitations, and had drawn a more efficient balance between the needs for signals and for security. Thus, it utilized a system (which the British later called the "link sign" or the "single call" procedure) which assigned call signs not to radio sets but to radio nets: on a given day each member of any net used the same call sign. Only skilled operators could handle this system, but they could cripple the ability of hostile traffic analysts to identify nets and sets, and to observe changes in their composition and interaction. In signals as in all areas, during 1940–1941 German soldiers were better trained than British ones, and commanders more experienced, and they exploited that advantage. Again, in the British army, signalling and ciphering were separate processes, handled by different people, with all the confusion that entails; in the German case these two processes were one whenever the Enigma cipher machine was used. Hence, German formations down to divisional headquarters could transmit large volumes of operational traffic with great speed and security. The Enigma should not be judged a failure just because it was ultimately solved: until summer 1942 it was the most flexible and secure means to transmit operational traffic possessed by any army on earth. With a car, a radio set and an Enigma machine, a German general could roam at will throughout his command and yet be in constant and secret touch with all his superiors and subordinates—if he so wished. Erwin Rommel, of course, held that even by this means no commander could simultaneously appreciate the shape of a mechanized battle and communicate with his rear. He preferred to maintain physical contact with some of his leading troops, at the cost of abandoning signals touch with all of his headquarters for days at a time.[33] This was simply a poor approach to command. As better Panzer leaders showed, German signals let any general lead from the front while keeping in touch with his rear. Without this system, *blitzkrieg* could never have come into being.

Not only had the German army raised the standard level of its security; it had also learned when to reduce that level. In particular, it understood the proper role of plain language, which it used for tactical traffic and operational emergencies, when the need for speed out-weighed the risk of interception, when the enemy could not use the information thus compromised before one had acted upon it. As the Bartholomew Committee, the British army body established to assess the lessons of the battle of France, noted, the Germans "appeared to use wireless to the maximum extent and mostly 'in clear'. We had no difficulty in intercepting information but there was so much that it was rarely possible to extract items in time to take action on them".[34] Conversely, without the lubrication provided by the constant use of plain language, Britain's entire C^3 system would grind to a halt. During 1939–1941 the German army often suffered from breakdowns of communication and of security, yet still it possessed the finest signals service of any army on earth. As the War Office's directorate of radio intelligence noted during 1941, "the elaborate, complex, yet reliable and highly flexible wireless networks which their system allows them to conjure up, as it were, at a moment's notice form one of the major sources of the characteristic speed and coherence of [German] operations".[35] Only if the British army entirely abandoned security could it match the ease of use of German signals; it could match the latter's security only if it did not use radio at all.

In signals as in all areas of the British army, the bill for eighteen years of neglect fell due in May 1940. Throughout 1939–1940, as an ideal, the BEF pursued a style of war which focused on set-piece battles of high intensity, complexity and precision, with tightly controlled firepower. Much can be said for this approach—when it finally worked in 1942–1945, it wrecked Axis armies—but like all systems particularly reliant on form, it could easily become fossilized. It needed well-trained personnel to function at all and radical recalibration to meet the many conditions which had changed since

1918. Such a recalibration would have taken a good army much time to complete. The British army was not good. It had just swelled massively in size, its small cadre of experienced, not always able, regulars swamped by hordes of new recruits whom officers had no idea how to prepare quickly and effectively for operations. Inertia ruled during the phoney war. Officers focused on garrison work, using soldiers for routine duties. In the normal British system, tactical training was a matter not for generals but regiments. Few commanders seriously trained their personnel for operations, the chief exception being Bernard Montgomery and the Third Division.

No section of the BEF faced greater problems than the Royal Corps of Signals. It was desperately short of equipment and personnel, especially with regard to radio. GHQ received its signals staff only by stripping them from the divisions sent as labour to the Somme. Even in May 1940 it could establish its radio service solely by borrowing two wireless sets from its corps, while no sets at all were available to service some links between divisions and corps. These shortages crippled GHQ's ability to meet its functions; those relating to cipher personnel almost negated it. Thus, by 19 May 1940, with the debacle in full swing, the War Office pressed GHQ to send by radio "live cipher messages" regarding operations. This order had to be cancelled after precisely two such messages had been sent "owing to the congestion in Cipher Offices" at GHQ. When, over the next two days, GHQ had to rely on hand-speed wireless for communication with London, "the cipher office got inundated and delays on cipher messages became very serious". Yet some days later, with the operational situation deadly, GHQ was forced to order, "Vital cut down signal traffic within B.E.F. Till cable repaired all telegrams must be wireless".[36] Similarly, within the BEF GHQ used cipher for all communications with subordinate formations, which produced long delays (in one case, thirty-six hours). Not surprisingly, the Bartholomew Committee recommended that the army learn to use radio more often and better and replace "cumbersome" cipher" with simpler codes.[37]

The BEF faced difficulties not simply with communication but also with security, for reasons which would recur continually until 1942. With so few trained personnel and so many signals problems, security was even more a secondary concern than usual. The army also lacked interest and expertise in these issues. The BEF had precisely one full-time signals security section in April 1940, while the army established its first one in the Middle East in autumn 1940.[38] All this reduced the sophistication of the signals security precautions which the army could follow. The BEF was reluctant to adopt so elementary a precaution as to change its radio call signs and frequencies regularly. In December 1939 it discovered that its call sign procedure was less secure than the German "link sign" one. The BEF, however, declined to use the latter;[39] when adopted by the Eighth Army in October 1941, this system inflicted immediate and irreparable blows upon German signals intelligence. Finally, as would continue for two years, until it ceased to be the only accepted practice for signals security, a religious devotion to wireless silence before battles began made it impossible to detect and to correct signals and security problems before they became operational ones.

When the British army entered Belgium, its communication system had to move for the first time since 1918. Not until 17–19 May, however, when the BEF began to retreat under continual pressure, did signals problems emerge. In the midst of chaotic operations, BEF signals had to improvise a service based on all available channels of communication and with unprecedented reliance on radio. GHQ, meanwhile, seemed bent on increasing the BEF's signals problems. General Gort established a small tactical headquarters, isolated from the bureaucracy at main headquarters, with the hope of reaching quick decisions; this sudden action instead decapitated the army and fragmented its command system. For forty-eight hours, the BEF had three different centres of command: Gort's small band, main headquarters, and an intermediate body keeping the other two in contact![40] Meanwhile, a characteristic lack of liaison between signals and operational staffs hampered communication. The head of GHQ signals discovered only "by chance" on 19 May that the BEF planned to launch a corps level assault the next day near Arras. "When G. Staff were remonstrated with for not informing Signals, they pleaded that they thought Signals had no resources so that it was not worth worrying them about it."[41]

Amid this chaos, the Royal Corps of Signals achieved a remarkable feat. Up to the moment that the BEF escaped at Dunkirk, it generally received the volume and velocity of communication between brigades, divisions and corps needed for operational purposes. This reflected the ability of the signals corps and the fact that the BEF was spared the worst of the German onslaught. None the less, these weeks revealed that the army's C^3IS system was unfit for mobile war. Land lines could not meet the speed of operations; dispatch riders on motorcycles had little value. In some cases, only the fortuitous working of wireless and liaison officers could carry the messages needed to save corps from destruction, while elementary confusion over coding systems contributed to the capture of the 51st Highland Division after Dunkirk; the attempt to evacuate it by sea from St. Valerie occurred "just at the moment when a new card for the Inter-Service stencil cipher had been issued. The despatch rider with the new cards for the Division had been unable to get through, and it was some time before it was discovered that the ships and the shore were working on different cards". Ironically, during the battle of France, British cryptography damaged the British army more than German cryptanalysis. Communication vanished when under any serious pressure; a serious German assault would probably have smashed the entire C^3I system of the BEF. Within the formations which suffered the heaviest blows, such as the BEF's rearguard or the divisions on the Somme front, signals within and between brigades constantly broke, often for up to twelve hours at a time, a deadly problem given the army's style of operations and state of danger, and its half-trained officers led to expect command to be stable and hierarchical.[42] Divisions shifted continually from one headquarters to another, which were constantly reorganized. One staff officer, General N.M.S. Irwin, described the difficulties in

> trying to get in touch and give information to your next Higher Commander, with whom we had no wireless contact at all and it simply meant I think that Divisional Commanders were fighting their battles by the light of God and hoping that the M.C.O. (motor contact officer) who had pushed back would in the course of his journey pick up one of the headquarters under whom the division thought it was operating.[43]

Meanwhile, the British system for the security of tactical traffic collapsed. This failing was irrelevant to that campaign, small beer when compared with the successful rupturing of the Allied front. In other circumstances, this problem would have had greater consequences. These experiences showed that the British army needed a far larger and better wireless service; however, it took eighteen months to produce the equipment and personnel needed to meet these needs. They also showed that the army had many lessons to learn regarding command, signals and security. These flaws in its procedures would not be addressed for another year because defeat by the Germans was followed by victory over the Italians. Even more, this process of education would occur in circumstances which magnified all the problems found in Belgium.

During the two-and-a-half years following the evacuation from Dunkirk, the lands around the eastern part of the Mediterranean Sea and in the Middle East became the centre for the operations of the British Army, and the locale of many of its worst disasters in history. These defeats are frequently blamed on the failings of this British general or that, and with truth—they can all be seriously criticized. Yet so can their opponents; and many Britons who failed in the desert fought well elsewhere later in the war. To explain failures by focusing on generals is to personalize a systematic problem. The real problem was not that these generals were worse than their German counterparts, but that their system of command was. In the Middle East, even more than in France, the collision between flimsy communication and command shattered the foundation for operations.

British campaigns in Ethiopia, Crete, Egypt, Greece and Libya were all dogged by shortages of signals equipment and personnel. In August 1940 the army had exactly six (soon raised to fourteen) wireless stations for inter-command communication within the Middle East.[44] In January 1941 General Wavell reported that his operations in the western desert, Greece and Ethiopia were "all in danger of coming to a halt, not from want of fighting troops, but for want of transport, signals, workshops and such ... Commanders in all three theatres are seriously hampered by lack of signals personnel". More irritably, his Signals Officer-in-Chief (SO-in-C) noted, "we have not got signals growing on gooseberry bushes".[45] Two months later, the War Office still could not overcome the deficit in radio sets for tanks. Imperial assistance alone let Britain meet these needs. More Australian, New Zealand and Southern Rhodesian than British radio personnel may well have served in the desert; India and South Africa provided virtually all the signals for the Ethiopian campaign.

Until mid-1941, radio communication between Middle East Command and its subordinate headquarters in operational areas was poor, though this was assisted by cable. In January 1941 Cairo could not establish even one dedicated radio link with Khartoum, a centre for the offensive in Ethiopia. Only help from the RAF maintained such links with Athens. In summer 1941 communication between Cairo and Baghdad was in a "parlous state".[46] Throughout the theatre, critical signals functions could be met only by robbing those marginally less vital. In June 1940, General O'Conner's Desert Force could find its signals only by borrowing those of the New Zealand Division, which held the key base of Mersa Matruh. New Zealand also provided the radio staff for the Long Range Desert Group, a battalion with better wireless facilities than any British infantry division had before 1942. In May 1941 the headquarters on Crete found its signals staff only by stripping them from its units, increasing the communication troubles which soon crippled their operations. Three months later the headquarters at Baghdad reversed the process, surrendering most of its radio personnel to its divisions, despite the "danger of breakdown of Signal Communications at this H.Q.".[47]

Equally critical problems emerged in the system and process of command. The Eighth Army is often thought to have been inferior to the *Afrika Korps* because its leaders led from behind the lines through paper and signals, wedded to hierarchy, opposing innovations like "battle groups"—far from it; in fact, the German machinery of command was more rigid than the British one, and that in turn was one reason for Rommel's success. British practices of command were similar to German ones, but simply less effective, and for many reasons. Given its doctrine and training, the *Wehrmacht* could more easily accommodate the revolution in C^3I than the British army. Exploitation of that edge strengthened German blows against a foe tripped up in a transition from a written to a verbal culture of command. Under the 1918/1939 British model, after much staffwork and consultation, divisions or corps formulated detailed plans and sent them on paper to brigades and battalions, which executed them without exercising initiative. Between the wars Milne challenged this model while Montgomery claimed that a general could not command through signals, even W/T and R/T, let alone through staffwork and paper, but only through personal presence at the front and directive orders, executed by well-trained officers and men, who could use their initiative to achieve the desired end.[48] The experiences of 1940 discredited this 1918/1939 model. Where commanders in Britain wished to reform it, those in the Middle East rejected matters central to that system, like staff and signals, and pursued radical alternatives. This opened a long period of experimentation conducted by half-trained forces, led by officers who misunderstood the need and the means to prepare personnel for war, who romanticized the role of personal contact in command and who underrated the power of signals.

When considering command in mobile warfare, British officers in Egypt focused on the (admittedly essential) superstructure, relations between generals, rather than on the structure—the signals and staff and training which formations needed to work. They mistook the power to contact generals for the ability to command men. They assumed that talk between officers would ensure action by units, because the machine of command would work. Liaison officers and personal contact (rather than radio) replaced dispatch riders as the means by which commanders imagined that they could make fast decisions. Wavell concluded that "in battle the proper way to issue orders is verbally and by means of liaison officer rather than by written order". In hindsight, he thought it "quite fatal, especially in rapidly moving warfare, for a Commander to remain at his Headquarters and to try and control formations through signals". The solution was "personal command, i.e. by the superior Commander constantly visiting his lower formations, discussing the situation with them, and issuing instructions verbally, to be confirmed later by his Headquarters". Alan Cunningham shared these views, defining a small airplane, by which to reach formations on the battlefield, as "by far the best means" for a commander to control.[49] Nor was command from the front the habit of Rommel alone. British divisional generals, in particular "Straffer" Gott and "Jock" Campbell, habitually drove forward to assess the situation, while Wavell, Cunningham and Claude Auchinleck flew in—sometimes flying off one end of an airstrip just as the *Afrika Korps* entered the other! Meanwhile, these generals underestimated the need for basic training. Wavell blamed the failure of the "Battleaxe" offensive of 14–17 June 1941 on "lack of training" in a host of simple areas, for which he offered this penetrating explanation: "I should have known all this, and should have taken steps to prevent a good deal of it. I had serious doubts about the wisdom of committing the [Seventh Armoured] Division to battle so soon after its re-equipment, but had not fully realized how raw it really was."[50] Similarly, before the "Crusader" offensive, Auchinleck knew the Eighth Army was not well trained, just not how badly.

These problems were long standing and well known. In autumn 1940 one Indian Army general noted that senior officers in the desert condemned the Army's training as inadequate, and held that "our Manuals or their interpretation cramp initiative, close the doors on progressive thought and adjustment to the ever and rapidly changing methods of modern war and encourage paper which is now a definite enemy". In February 1942, John Harding, then Director of Military Training in the Middle East and later CIGS, emphasized that training must become far more thorough and less

> dogmatic than in the past. This can be done without cramping tactical initiative by establishing standard methods of battle drill covering the more common sets of circumstances and tasks [with] which units and formations find themselves faced when in battle. Battle drill should cover such matters as standard formations, order of march, system for reconnaissance and preparation for action, establishment of communications and system of control. By preparing drills covering these subjects, time will be saved in instruction and also in battle, uniformity of method will lead to less dislocation when individuals, units and formations move from one command to another, and such drills need not cramp the tactical initiative of Commanders.[51]

Such work behind the scenes over the next six months, reinforced by Montgomery's fanaticism on the topic, finally established a decent basic level of training in the Eighth Army by August–October 1942. Until that time, however, British commanders pursued an ambitious approach to command, finely tuned, close to technical perfection, which only a machine of command in excellent condition, with well-trained forces and effective signals, could have executed. These conditions did not exist—even worse, generals misunderstood the scale of Britain's problems in these areas. Thus, they strove to create a command system remarkably like that of Rommel, with all its weaknesses, but without the strengths in trained staff and soldiers that made up for them. In the end, the British army overcame these problems only after Rommel had trained it through disaster and Montgomery through design, and the latter had imposed a command system at the highest possible level of marginal efficiency it could sustain— one more primitive than those which he or Milne had advocated before 1939. From this basis, however, the British army recalibrated the 1918 system with effect and speed.

Britain had not prepared to fight a great war in the Middle East. In order to do so, it had to jury-rig a large imperial army from several sources— regular forces, a British armoured division and an Indian infantry division; and freshly raised ones, a British armoured division, and a mechanized infantry division from each of India, Australia, New Zealand, South Africa and Britain. These forces had few officers experienced in higher levels of command or staffwork. Their most seasoned generals, Wavell and Thomas Blamey, had been senior staff officers in 1917–1918 but not field commanders. Most unit and staff officers learned to fight as they fought, with unfortunate consequences. In 1917–1918 Commonwealth forces had routinely coordinated powerful and precise blows by corps and, less consistently, by armies, combining the power of twenty to fifty brigades in one operation. During 1940–1942, this improvised army drawn from so many different institutions found it hard to coordinate forces of more than one brigade at a time. Between December 1940 and October 1941, no British operation involved much more than two divisions, which usually fought separately, yet elementary problems of command dogged them all.

Thus, General O'Connor's offensive of December 1940–February 1941 originally aimed to disrupt Italian forces in the western desert, on the Egyptian–Libyan frontier, while Britain concentrated its strength against Ethiopia. Wavell warned O'Connor that if his attack succeeded, three weeks after it began, half his forces, the Fourth Indian Division, would be redeployed to Ethiopia. In fact, Wavell suddenly withdrew that division five days after the unexpectedly successful attack began. O'Connor then had to improvise a new plan of operations and to integrate an inexperienced Australian Division into his forces. He did so with success but no guidance. One month later he noted that he had received no orders since the operation began. This "has suited me admirably"; even so, he was subordinate to two headquarters in Egypt, whose disagreements about his duties were hampering his actions.[52] When, one month later, O'Connor wanted permission to advance on Tripoli so to annihilate Italy in Africa, he had no means to discuss the matter by telephone, radio or telegraph. Instead, he sent his message via an officer in a staff car, who spent two days driving to a senior headquarters, arriving too late to shape the signal decision that the campaign should stop, for the moment.[53] Military communications were even worse in Ethiopia. The campaign in that country occurred so far from Cairo, at a time so many crucial events were occurring elsewhere, that Wavell "made no attempt to control their operations"—perhaps fortunately, since his telegrams sometimes took five days to reach the commander, Alan Cunningham. Every time his headquarters advanced, Cunningham's command and communication system shattered for several days, yet he had to control three divisions which at one point were 740, 570 and 250 miles away from him, in different directions. In effect, he did so by flying in to oversee whichever division happened to be in battle at any time.[54] In Libya and Ethiopia, imperial divisions fighting a series of separate battles, often just one brigade at a time, killed or captured 500,000 Italian soldiers, but this weakness was fatal against Germans. In Battleaxe, for example, an Indian infantry division and a British mechanized infantry brigade, infantry tank brigade and cruiser tank brigade, might have attacked as a corps. Instead, they fought in four packets, and were so wrecked.

These problems grew when Auchinleck replaced Wavell at Middle East Command. Between June and November 1941 the number of brigades in the desert doubled to eighteen and the British attempted to control six divisions in one battle. Their fragile system of battlefield command cracked under this weight. As soon as "Crusader" began, the Eighth Army's plan collapsed, largely because it had assumed that British C^3I would be perfect. GHQ directed its commander, Cunningham, to "deploy his forces on as wide a front as possible in order to deceive the enemy".[55] Formations were widely distributed, yet too weak to win without concentration. Only excellent C^3I could square this circle. Cunningham expected this to occur, because he believed experience derived against the Italians could automatically be applied to the Germans. In Ethiopia, scattered formations had mounted coherent pressure against the Italians while, Cunningham noted, "there can seldom in the history of war have been a campaign in which the Commander was so continuously served with accurate information of the enemy's movements and dispositions. The bulk of this information was received from 'Y' sources".[56] He assumed that the quality of intelligence in Crusader would match that in Ethiopia, and that he could use this knowledge and retain the initiative through a sophisticated approach to command. He failed not because he embodied military reaction but precisely because he was a revolutionary, in pursuit of the technically ideal C^3 system, with the maximum span of command and the fewest possible intermediate links. Cunningham wished to avoid "detailed operational orders. Circumstances change with time. Enemy dispositions in particular are liable to alter and necessitate frequent amendments to orders. Any plan made should, he considered, be elastic".[57] Unfortunately, his plan stretched elasticity to the breaking point. When Crusader began, XXX Corps, controlling the Seventh Armoured Division and the South African Division, was to advance deep into the desert—and wait eighteen hours until the British learned the German reaction. Cunningham doubted that XXX Corps

> could take on the enemy armoured forces on its own and should therefore make for Tobruk. We should not go for Tobruk, unless we knew we could hold it. Our armoured forces must take up a central battle position. If the enemy observed what was happening and decided to make a stand, he must either concentrate his armour to defend Bardia or Tobruk, or divide his forces. If he split his forces, we could split ours. If he made no move, we could hem him in. If he tried to get away, we could not cut him off even by making straight for Tobruk. The approach march was unlikely to pass unobserved by the enemy, and from his reactions we should know what he meant to do. By the first evening his intentions would be known, and the decision could be taken.

Meanwhile, the besieged forces in Tobruk would wait until XXX Corps approached and then break out. XIII Corps would surround and contain Axis forces on the coast with the Fourth Indian Division, while the New Zealand Division thrust inland toward Tobruk. Its flank would be covered by the 22nd Armoured Brigade, ordered to attack inferior Axis armour but to fall back on the Seventh Armoured Division if the *Afrika Korps* appeared, and so provoke a decisive clash between British and Axis forces.

This complex plan assumed that intelligence could track the enemy precisely, commanders instantly receive this information and units immediately act on it. It was a plan designed on a large-scale map and the assumption of perfect C^3I, even though the headquarters of both the Eighth Army and XXX Corps were jury-rigged and untried bodies, while experience might have indicated that atmospherics in the desert would wreck wireless signals when night fell, fourteen hours after the attack began— precisely the time when the British could expect to receive news of the German response to their attack and must begin their counter move. The commander of XXX Corps, Willoughby Norrie, doubting that these conditions could exist, argued that the plan would dissipate strength and cause confusion.[58] He was overruled but right. In the first hours of "Crusader", eighteen imperial brigades fell into five isolated groups, while their C^3I collapsed. As Cunningham's *aide de camp* noted thirty hours into Crusader: "Army Comdr was much concerned throughout this day at lack of information, indecisive nature of operation, apparent slowness of Armd Div in getting on and his own inability to force the pace."[59] This experience convinced Cunningham "that it is quite impossible to exercise any close control over the modern battle by normal wireless and cypher procedures"—precisely the assumptions which had underlain his plan.[60] The failure to determine enemy actions led British commanders into disastrous decisions, to divide XXX Corps into its five component brigades (and thus the Eighth Army into eight unconnected parts!) and then to attack.

Eight days into the battle, Cunningham was replaced by Neil Ritchie, one of Auchinleck's staff officers. Ritchie, who had never commanded more than a battalion, was expected to lead an army while serving more as his chief's microphone than an independent general—Auchinleck took the helm at the crucial period. During Crusader, decisions were improvised between the commanders of corps, divisions and brigades, with frequent interjections from Ritchie and Auchinleck. To their credit, imperial officers kept their nerve and reknitted the structure of their command in confusing circumstance, and to good effect, partly because the catastrophe forced them to return to the orthodox system, and so to tap some of its residual power. After six days of disaster, the Seventh Armoured Division reestablished control over British tanks. Corps coordinated divisions and brigades, which cooperated well, even at the battles around the airstrip of Sidi Rezegh, where scattered forces were thrown into a pell-mell defence against the entire *Afrika Korps*. Infantry fought as divisions. The ability of the Fourth Indian Division and especially the Second New Zealand Division to execute their orders and act as formations was fundamental to British victory. XIII Corps was the first imperial formation to recalibrate its C^3I system in order to surmount the conditions of *blitzkrieg*, because it included two of the Commonwealth's three best divisions and divisional commanders, Frank Messervy and Bernard Freyberg, and aimed to reform the command system of 1918 rather than to abandon it.

With Crusader done, command slipped in quality. Ritchie so interfered with tactical decisions during the last days of Crusader that the able commander of XIII Corps, General Austin-Godwin, resigned. The difficult relationship between Ritchie and "my dear chief" created uncertainty in command. An official historian later noted one "frightening" aspect of the battle of Gazala of May–June 1942: "Ritchie who appeared so confident at the end of May was very soon appealing to the Auk for confirmation of any order he issued. The latter seems to have 'butted in' so much with messages and by personal visits that he was really controlling the operations that were moving too fast for anyone not intimately in touch to understand."[61] Ritchie also lacked the prestige and self-confidence needed to control his more experienced subordinates. The who and how of command became open questions. Virtually all of its aspects were worse in the battle of Gazala, May–June 1942, than in Crusader—command virtually disintegrated above the level of brigade. Infantry, broken into brigade boxes, were never commanded above that level, rendering divisions or corps irrelevant, jettisoning precisely the command links which had worked best during Crusader. Neither Auchinleck, Ritchie nor their corps commanders—all crucial nodes of control during Crusader—coordinated armoured divisions or infantry brigades, leaving them to command themselves. Coordination between any two formations required a complex process of consultation between semi-independent generals, which always took two or three days and led to cancelled operations or failed ones. One junior officer recorded how, during the crisis of the Knightsbridge battle on the evening of 13 June, the commanders of XXX Corps and the Second Armoured Division, Gott and Herbert Lumsden, and other staff officers, spent five hours in intense discussion, unable to reach any decision at all.[62] Armoured divisional and corps generals like Messervy, Lumsden and Gott habitually challenged the plans of their superiors (often for good reason). Gott and Lumsden did so at what the New Zealand Division commander, Freyberg, called "the Old Boy Level", of arguing with Ritchie's orders; Montgomery termed the process "belly aching".[63] All this was swiftly followed by a disintegration of command, when coordination failed and the army collapsed, and then by its decapitation between June to August 1942, as virtually every British and Indian commander of a division or higher formation died or was sacked (not all of them fairly).

The question is why this process occurred. The answer has many parts. One problem was poor relations between the parts of this Commonwealth army, where armoured divisions were British and infantry divisions came from India or the Dominions. The differences between British and Indian army officers have been heralded and overrated. Though some heat was produced by issues such as the appointment of Messervy, an Indian army officer and an infantier, to command the chevaliers of the Seventh Armoured Division (a position for which his qualifications were open to question), and the politics surrounding the sacking of commanders during the summer of 1942, the Indian army was the least controversial component of this Commonwealth force; like the gunners, it had a universal joint, and was able to work with every other branch of this Commonwealth army. Military politics, however, distorted cooperation between its other components. The two (just integrated) components of British armour, the Royal Tank Regiment and the Cavalry, had an uneasy relationship. As one staff officer during Crusader, General Galloway, recollected twenty years later: "In 1938 & 9 the R.T.R. were accusing the Cavalry of only being able to use polo ponies and sticks. The Cavalry referred to the R.T.R. as garage mechanics. Both trained their Commanders with green and yellow flags 2/6 each, representing Army Groups, etc!!!"[64] Despite the rivalry between them, each of these components favoured battle independent from the rest of the army, through imbalanced and self-contained mobile forces, with specialist gunners tacked on to protect the base, fighting single-handed war. This sparked two disastrous problems: a separation of armour from the army, excepting the substantial force of "infantry tanks", and the habitual attacks of British armour alone against German forces which combined tanks, anti-tank weaponry, guns and infantry. Equally serious and even more virulent problems divided British and Dominion officers. By March 1941 Blamey thought

> It is clear that, broadly speaking, the fighting is the province of the Dominion troops, while supply and Line of Communication is the main function of the British ... But experience has taught me to look with misgivings on a situation where British leaders have control of considerable bodies of first class Dominion troops while Dominion commanders are excluded from all responsibility in control, planning and policy.[65]

Winston Churchill, too, credited troubles with Australia to the fact that no British infantry divisions were "in the various actions, thus leading the world and Australia to suppose that we are fighting our battles with Dominion troops only".[66] During Auchinleck's tenure, Commonwealth relations worsened. He treated Dominion generals with less tact than Wavell had shown or Montgomery would show. Experiences in Greece, Crete and Crusader led Antipodean commanders to question British competence. Their own spotty performance, and the Australian government's demand that its forces be evacuated from the besieged port of Tobruk, whatever the complications for Cairo, fuelled English dislike of "Private Armies", which used their Prime Ministers to challenge the decisions of British generals. Auchinleck, infuriated that his Deputy Commander-in-Chief, Blamey, had overturned his own policy regarding Tobruk through such means, considered resignation, and demanded that Blamey not replace him should he himself die.[67] This situation helps to explain why Auchinleck usually kept the Australian and New Zealand divisions, two of the three best formations under his command, from the desert. As he said in 1956, "he would not have been inclined to used [sic] dominion troops because this would have meant more negotiations on an inter-government plane".[68]

Inter-commonwealth disputes stemmed from another problem, one central to the crisis in the desert and to the debate over it. In 1939 the British army had a centralized C^3I system like that of 1918, but in a decadent form—rigid, brittle and weak. It also lacked the large numbers of experienced personnel which this finely tuned machine needed to function effectively. After their experiences of 1940, army authorities in Britain wished to reform but not to destroy the structure of command. The Bartholomew Committee wanted to modify the role of senior formations in command while increasing that of a lower one. Armies, corps and divisions were fundamental to command and *ad-hoc* formations useful only in "exceptional" circumstances. However, when frontages could not be restricted, "it is obvious that the lower the formation which can be organized and equipped to fight by itself, the better". The brigade group should be "the lowest self-contained fighting formation ... within the division. The tactical handling of the division should be based on these self-contained groups, which will be *normal* both for training and fighting".[69]

Whereas the Bartholomew Committee recommended that brigade and battalion commanders receive more initiative and responsibility, in the Middle East many officers wished to go further—to make brigades the basic node of command and *ad hoc* coordination the norm, to treat divisions and corps almost as holding companies. Old desert hands often viewed armoured brigades as the basic level of tank command, and wanted other arms to work as brigade groups or "Jock columns" (combat teams of battalion strength, centring on troops of artillery for anti-tank protection). Just before "Crusader", the Seventh Armoured Division summarized its prior experiences: "In the vastness of the Desert, Div. H.Q. functions more like a Corps H.Q. and Bde. like a Div. H.Q. ... The Bde. is the highest formation which can handle a battle in detail. Bdes. were seldom close together ... Corps exercised little control."[70] Thus, the formation commanding most British armour went into Crusader aiming precisely to repeat the disastrous arrangements of "Battleaxe". Auckinleck, too, favoured radical moves from "rigid organizations which are supposed to be suitable for every part of the world" toward decentralized command and brigade groups. He claimed later:

> there was no scope for the employment of corps (plural) in modern army practice as meaning a formation with a fixed composition.

"Old Blamey" and the Australian Government derived their ideas from the first war and the western front in France. They were quite inapplicable to modern mobile war in the desert, where flexibility in the use of formations in the desert was essential. The use of a "fixed" corps would have been wasteful and impracticable.[71]

Against this, Dominion and Indian officers wished to maintain centralized control and to fight as divisions, opposing what Blamey called "the deadly habit of disintegrating formations, so typical of British methods".[72] This debate was doctrinal and political. The brigade group concept would in effect break Dominion divisions, incorporate their units in the British army and render unemployed any Dominion officer above the rank of Brigadier. Yet if Auchinleck adopted the corps as a basis for organization, the question would be "Why not have a Dominion officer command one, especially a man so well qualified but so badly trusted by British officers as old Blamey?" After all, politics had driven Wavell to appoint Blamey his Deputy Commander-in-Chief. This same problem would have hamstrung Auchinleck's plan of 1942 to turn his divisions, purely infantry or armour, into more balanced formations, with two mechanized infantry brigades and one tank brigade.[73] That idea was good in technical terms, but with problems. These "new model" divisions would have been large (each equalling a German infantry and armoured division, or two-thirds of the *Afrika Korps*, in strength) and correspondingly hard to control even by good officers, let alone the mixed bunch at hand. Nor would this change in organization necessarily have combined arms or concentrated force better; the predilection of armour for independent action and of Auchinleck for brigade groups might well have produced a worse result, with tanks continuing to fight single-handed battles, infantry losing any means to cooperate above the brigade and gunners sacrificing themselves even more to save the wreck in rout. Again, most of Auchinleck's infantry were Dominion or Indian and the armour all British. Would he have let Dominion officers command English armour? Would British armoured commanders have accepted command by Antipodean infantries? Would Dominion officers, their faith in Auchinleck and his armour shrinking, have let British armoured divisional generals control their infantry brigades? Neither could such integration easily have been fostered between the British and Indian armies.

Dominion generals like Blamey and Freyberg, and British ones like Montgomery, argued that the army must fight as an army and ultimately their views became orthodoxy. As William Slim noted as CIGS during 1951,

> The first thing is don't break up your ordinary organization, you can do any operation in war with the organization you have got. Do remember that the division is meant to fight as a division, don't let's have any of those Jock columns. If you can't win your battle with

honest-to-God battalions, brigades and divisions, you won't win it by inventing fancy things.[74]

Such views were correct in principle, but not entirely applicable before April 1942. The original point behind Jock columns, for example, was reasonable enough—when speaking to another officer, their originator, Colonel "Jock" Campbell,

> was very definite that they were an improvised answer to a particular problem—that of keeping touch with the enemy after a long advance, when our own armour was largely immobile by casualties or lack of spares and petrol. Acting behind or in conjunction with an armoured car screen, his columns were in fact battle patrols which—containing 25 pdrs [sic], as well as 2 pdrs [sic]—could fight for information and deliver tip and run raids by fire when necessary.[75]

By using artillery as anti-tank guns, "Jock columns" and brigade groups also let infantry operate with security in the desert. They solved specific problems in 1940, and later. Yet they were bad as a universal panacea, preventing the British army from deploying its trump card of 1918 and 1944, the concentrated use of divisions and guns, and in 1941–1942 desert forces and Auchinleck leaned in that direction.

Against these points, the "ordinary organization" of 1939–1940 was designed for high-intensity warfare on narrow fronts in highly developed country. This system could not easily be made to fit the conditions of the desert, doubly so because its central elements were badly prepared against armour. In 1939 it was expected that imperial infantry formations would cooperate closely with infantry tanks for offence and defence, while a few light anti-tank weapons would check enemy armour; the failure of this approach dislocated Britain's entire way of war. In 1941 German anti-tank guns demolished infantry tanks, British anti-tank weapons were few and poor, while its cruiser tank forces were badly handled and disliked working with infantry. The latter were vulnerable in the desert unless they had effective anti-tank weapons in large numbers. These were not available until mid-1942. Until then, infantry could check German armour only by using artillery as anti-tank guns. However desperate, this approach was possible—indeed, for eighteen months it was Britain's best combination against the *Afrika Korps*. Everywhere, armour failed and victory turned on British use of infantry and guns against tanks. Imperial infantry formations with guns firing over open sights often held off or crippled the entire *Afrika Korps*, which characteristically attacked with fast head-on charges—precisely the primitive tactics for which British armour is so often criticized. At Tobruk in April–May 1941, thrice during "Crusader" and at Bir el-Hakeim during

Gazala, infantry and guns were aggressively if accidentally used in a strategically offensive/tactically defensive way, taking or holding positions the *Afrika Korps* felt impelled to attack. In these cases, German forces whipped British armour but then suffered murderous losses (often between 33 and 50 per cent of their tanks engaged) and some defeats when attacking an infantry division. British armour managed such a feat just once, on the first day of Gazala when the *Afrika Korps* charged Grant tanks. The difference between defeat in Gazala and victory in Crusader was the British failure to take the initiative with infantry. Until mid-1942, the best British bet would have been to avoid battle with its armour until the *Afrika Korps* had been induced to attack imperial infantry divisions with their guns effectively deployed, not infeasible but not easy. In order to do so, however, generals could pursue victory not through a direct exercise of the initiative, but only by using infantry divisions in a strategically offensive and tactically defensive way, aiming to provoke an enemy attack on men-made-bait—a psychological nightmare for commanders, a means to provoke Commonwealth anger, an operation hard to plan for or to control. More generally, the British approach to war could work as it was intended to only when it systematically checked German armoured superiority and mastered the conditions of *blitzkrieg*. This was impossible until infantry divisions received large numbers of good anti-tank weapons, which began to occur between March and July 1942. Had Montgomery, outstanding as a troop trainer and the creator of an effective C^3I system, been sent to master the desert in 1941, he would not have succeeded nearly as well as he did in more enclosed spaces during 1942–1943—if at all. Of course, he might also have adapted to the change in technical circumstances of spring 1942 better than Ritchie and Auchinleck. He could scarcely have done worse.

Advocates of decentralized command were responding to real problems; as Auchinleck said during Crusader,

> we were looking ahead at the organisation of the Inf. Div. He thought it was generally agreed that there was too much infantry in it. The composition of the Armd [sic] Divisions must certainly be changed. In the recent fighting the support group had hardly at all, if ever, cooperated with tanks as the Germans did, and their tactics were beating ours.[76]

They were also pursuing good solutions—directive control and new model divisions combining infantry and armour brigades and with far more anti-tank weapons—in principle. Yet these means were impracticable and thus the decentralization of command from corps toward brigades had deadly consequences. Within the army of 1939, the only formations where arms were combined and which pursued that aim were armies, corps and infantry divisions. British forces in Egypt rejected precisely these formations and focused on organizationally flawed ones. Infantry divisions were sound bodies needing radical reform in anti-tank defence and speed of decision; armoured forces had fundamental flaws. A British Armoured Brigade had as many tanks as a Panzer Division, but only 10 per cent of its strength in other arms. A British Armoured Division had as many tanks as a Panzer Corps, but 66 per cent less infantry and artillery, which were placed in a separate "Support Group" without armour. These different British brigades and arms could cooperate well at the operational level but not easily in one single engagement, and armour (excepting infantry tanks) never worked effectively at the tactical level with infantry divisions. Artillery and infantry could cooperate well at all levels, most effectively within an infantry division, most frequently in the penny packets of "Jock columns". The real problem with "Jock columns" and "brigade boxes" is that they increased the security of small bodies of infantry at the direct cost of reducing the chances that the *Afrika Korps* would attack infantry divisions and so be wrecked (one of the main reasons why Rommel lost Crusader). A British Armoured Brigade or Division functioned poorly against strong opponents which used combined arms from the unit to the formation, like a Panzer Division or Corps and even the Italian Mobile Corps; doubly so because British armoured tactics at all levels were inferior to German ones. Given their small staffs, all British armoured formations were difficult to command, the higher, the harder.

This produced problems of tactics, command and communications. The combination of arms and the coordination of forces, by units or formation, was normal for a Panzer Division—its intended aim. Within a British Armoured Brigade, combined arms was inconceivable. It was possible within an Armoured Division but unnatural, requiring a willed act of command followed by many more of control, that the machine do something alien to it, to link artillery, infantry and armour closely in one engagement. Within the British system, combined arms could best be done by a corps; the prospect was crippled by the lack of trained personnel, and by the failure to recognize the significance of this level of command or of that function. Given this military organization, a decentralized system of command could succeed only if British field and staff officers were better than their enemies, able to substitute superior expertise for inferior organization. They were not and the price was high—the loss of all the potential advantages of the British style of war. The British would have been better off playing to their strengths, whatever their weaknesses. Instead, imperial forces were dispersed. Command and concentration disintegrated. Without centralized control, artillery could never be massed, especially since the machine naturally divided guns to protect brigade groups and Jock columns against tanks. In their natural state, every British formation was weaker than the *Afrika Korps*, which did what Auckinleck thought "impracticable". It fought as a fixed corps of two or three German divisions, often aided by another of two Italian divisions, combining arms against one British brigade (often, moreover, consisting essentially of just one arm) at a time, its guns used in centralized shoots, its material strength multiplied by a simple and robust command system which aimed to concentrate its forces—and doubled again because the enemy chose to divide its own.

The Germans had better communications than the British and strained them less, because they fought with greater concentration and a more rigid organization, and acted automatically without first requesting and waiting for orders. This British system multiplied the confusion of command, by replacing the solid hierarchical relations between corps, divisions and brigades, with a fluctuating series of co-relations between every brigade in the Army. During Crusader, the 10th South African Brigade had "no less than 10 changes of Higher Command", while at various stages XXX Corps commanded four divisions, three independent brigades, several regiments and the Tobruk garrison—virtually the whole of Eighth Army![77] With formations fragmented, organization inchoate, officers inexperienced, the situation uncertain, command was not exercised but negotiated, or negated—all dangerous matters for undertrained and inexperienced soldiers. One brigade commander caught in the rout of January 1942 complained that his commanders routinely failed to inform subordinates of their intentions, used wireless to issue orders which disrupted local operations of which they were ignorant, and wrote: "I must confess that after a few days I seldom received an order without wondering how soon it would be changed." As Lumsden, the commander of the Second Armoured Division, said about convoluted command structures at Gazala, "no man can serve two masters".[78]

Before Crusader, XXX Corps told its subordinates that orders must include.

(i) Information—where to go, how to get there, who to ask for; or if an operation order, news of the enemy.
(ii) Intention–what you are driving at.
(iii) YOU WILL—what is to happen.
(iv) YOU WILL THEN—where to come back to, or rally.

After Gazala, the Eighth Army issued a lengthy critique of British failures. Among the "main lessons" were these:

> Any commander of any rank must have a definite aim which he must maintain on a definite plan based on a logical appreciation ... Commanders of all ranks must cultivate the habit of making quick, logical and complete appreciations. In no other way can sound decisions be reached ... The more mobile the forces employed on each side the more important it is to save time and to develop the highest possible speed in thought, decision and action ... If a commander is

to exercise quick control he must be in a position to dispense with constant discussion with or reference to his subordinates. He must be able to decide what he is going to do and issue orders on the information immediately available.

This would require "forethought", "anticipatory orders", "battle drill", and the avoidance of "lengthy discussions, gossip and unnecessary questions" over R/T.[79] Such orders were elementary—mere refinements of Milne fifteen years before; the fact that they were required, and so often, is indicative. Given all of these problems, in order to command, obey, cooperate or fight effectively, British forces would require an unusually powerful communication system, one far better than that of Germany. The flaws in British command strained communication and signals security, which returned the favour, producing a vicious circle with terrible costs.

None of these dangers were evident in the initial stages of the war. In late 1940 and early 1941, British imperial armies smashed far larger Italian ones in Ethiopia and the western desert. Radio was the primary means of communication for forces advancing over these vast and undeveloped areas. With signals as with all things, these offensives were run upon a shoestring. The demand for wireless equipment and personnel swelled, the supply to units and formations had not. In September 1940 exactly sixteen wireless sets were available in the Sudan for all field operations.[80] The success of these campaigns was astonishing; so too the fact that signals met the army's needs.[81] These achievements increased the army's faith in the value of R/T and W/T. The Seventh Armoured Division, for example, emphasized that these facilities alone allowed rapid intercommunication within mechanized formations, "in the handling of which information is of such importance and speed so often vital".[82] Unfortunately these successes also blinded Britain to the flaws in its system of signals and security.

After their first encounters with Italian forces, senior officers of the Western Desert Force and the Seventh Armoured Division alike complained of flaws in their signals, especially of inadequate wireless and training with it: "Forward troops won't pass back information for which one is thirsting. Often fault of link officers", wrote one commander.[83] During the operations of December 1940 to February 1941, critical problems continued in these areas. The headquarters of infantry battalions and armoured regiments had only one radio set for rear or lateral communication with other units or brigades. Brigade and divisional headquarters had only two or three sets for forward, rear and lateral signals, while administrative links were limited. The Fourth Indian Division had precisely one (and that unreliable) set to handle all its administrative traffic during the Sidi Barrani offensive.[84] The Australian Division suffered from failures of communication and command during its great successes at Bardia and Tobruk. British commanders took their successes to prove that their machinery of command was superb; in fact, they showed that this fragile web of signals could easily be torn asunder. Not only was tactical communication as vulnerable as ever, but the loss of one radio set could suddenly eliminate control over a regiment; the loss of three, command by a division. Throughout these campaigns accident or atmospherics frequently disrupted signals, while whenever the Italians fought with determination, most notably at Keren in Ethiopia, communication within brigades unravelled for several hours. Here, as in Belgium, the army's communication system could scarcely withstand any operational stress at all. During long and intense battles against an aggressive foe Britain would most need communication; precisely these conditions would wreck its signals system. Moreover, given the small carrying capacity of this network and the untrained nature of its personnel, the army's needs for signals security had to be subordinated to those for communication to an extraordinary degree.

A captured report on Italian signals intelligence during the Somali campaign of 1940 led British intelligence to conclude: "ITALIAN Intelligence in E. AFRICA functioned almost exclusively on information obtained through interception of our wireless traffic." In Somaliland, "the enemy was able to follow and appreciate our every move through interception of our wireless traffic", though it did not exploit these opportunities aggressively. The cause was deemed to be a poor system of signals security, poorly enforced.[85] Again, the Ethiopian campaign of 1941 was a case study in signals insecurity and not just on the Italian side. Small numbers of radio operators, many of whom "only received their cipher training as operations proceeded", transmitted almost all British operational traffic, and mostly in low-grade codes. Profiting from the capture of a British signals procedure codebook, an Italian signals intelligence force with eight intercept sets, roughly equalling in size British military "Y" in all of the Middle East, maintained a clear picture of the British signals system (and hence of its order of battle, movements and deployments) despite changes in frequencies and call signs.[86] Whether the Italians broke British operational codes during the campaigns is unclear; it would not have been difficult. Yet even these elementary security precautions crippled communications. One report noted that

> the delay on coding and decoding under the present system reacts against efficiency and even if there is the risk of ciphers being broken, it is surely better to employ some such machines as the "Syko" [an RAF device intended to provide twenty-four hours' security for messages] rather than owing to the present delay, tempt commanders and staffs to send messages in clear, because there is no time to employ cipher.[87]

Temptation was not resisted in the desert. By July 1940 the signals branch of the Seventh Armoured Division condemned any efforts at signals security in battle, even mere changes to code names and radio frequencies, as "not practical in an Armoured Division". Before O'Connor began his attack on Sidi Barrani in December 1940, wireless silence was almost total; during its course, the use of plain language was almost universal. An American observer noted that within the Seventh Armoured Division, radio had carried all communications without even one failure. All traffic had gone *en clair*, covered by the

> Christian names of tank and unit commanders and pre-arranged code names for key places ... A captured document revealed that Italian intercept had listed some forty Christian names, but there was no indication that intelligent use had been made of this information. Even had the enemy been able properly to interpret messages sent in the clear, during the Western Desert action, movement was so rapid that he could have done little to prevent the action ordered by the intercepted messages.

Influenced by the scale of this success and the limits to its radio facilities, the army concluded that signals security and mechanized operations were mutually exclusive. A staff study of the desert operations of December 1940–February 1941 argued that

> Modern mechanized warfare demands quick movement, quick thinking and quick decisions; and the more open and unrestrained the country the greater the demand for all three. There simply is not time to put a decision into writing or the opportunity to put it into effect may be lost; and it is the *effect* of the decision that matters, not the writing of it. Consequently, we have to seek another means of conveying decisions and, fortunately, such means are available in the form of R/T and of fast moving cross country vehicles by means of which commanders, staff officers and liaison officers can move quickly from one headquarters to another ... Situations develop, and change, so rapidly that more and more it is becoming necessary for subordinate commanders to be "in the mind" of their superior so that they will instinctively take the right course of action in accordance with his general intention, acting upon the briefest of instructions and often upon none at all.

In mechanized operations, the use of cipher was counter-productive. Despite the army's emphasis on verbal orders,

> cases did occur of written orders being transmitted in cypher. Not only did this cause delay but it was frequently found that the material transmitted was out of date before decyphering had been

completed ... the conditions of warfare of this sort are such that, in fact, the use of cypher is seldom justified. The question which staff officers and others should ask themselves before making use of a method which has so many drawbacks in fast moving warfare is: "Will the information (or the Order or Instruction) which I want to transmit really be of any use to the enemy by the time he has intercepted it, translated it and taken action on it?" In the majority of cases the answer will probably be "No".[88]

Wavell commended these conclusions. Because of over-confidence in its own abilities and of a misunderstanding of the need for signals security, because of the strained communication situation in the Middle East, by March 1941 the British army had scarcely modified its system for signals and security from that of September 1939. This fragile system, however, had worked only because of the strategic passivity and the tactical ineptitude of the Italian army. It might have been tailor-made to suit Rommel.

The *Afrika Korps* was not composed of supermen, while the reputation of Rommel's generalship outshines its reality. His flaws as a commander were legion. His tendency to lead from the front while breaking contact with the rear sometimes let him react to situations before his enemy knew that they existed. More often it left Rommel leading battalions while colonels commanded his corps. Rommel was ever-ready to take hasty decisions based upon incomplete and misinterpreted fragments of information. This behaviour was particularly shaped by his most formative moment as a soldier. Whenever he scented confusion in the enemy command he no longer saw the desert but Caporetto, where his aggression and initiative as a regimental commander had led to the capture of 11,000 prisoners from a routed Italian army. For Rommel, nothing was easier than to imagine an enemy on the verge of collapse, nothing more natural than to gamble everything he had for the highest of stakes. This daring led him to remarkable successes against inferior enemies; this recklessness led him to ruin against able ones.

Rommel, none the less, was a good tactician, an excellent trainer of troops, an inspiring leader of men, a formidable enemy. He moved rapidly and sought to exploit every opening which fortune offered him. He was also lucky in his army and his enemy. The *Afrika Korps* was tough, aggressive, amply supplied with first-rate officers, better suited to armoured operations in the desert than the British and perfectly formed to exploit the latter's system of signals, security and command. It could force the British to fight long, intense and mobile battles, during which they would increasingly need to communicate and be decreasingly able to do so. German signals were better placed to withstand such strain. Even if they did not, German command was better prepared than that of its enemy for life in the fog of war. The superior German battle drill, training, flexibility of command, initiative and tactics were well suited to conditions of broken-backed warfare. British officers, conversely, would seek authorization before action, they would debate options, they would question commands, and they would do so via R/T and in the clear.

Not only would Germans smash the fragile signals of the British army—they would also feed upon its flimsy security. The German army emphasized the acquisition of signals intelligence at a tactical level; the British army specialized in offering it. Under Rommel's command was the Third Radio Intercept Company, later renamed Strategical Intercept Company 621, led by Captain Alfred Seebohm. This was a large force for this theatre, though it never filled its establishment of ten officers and 322 other ranks. Still, in March 1941 the British army in the Middle East had just eighty "Y" personnel; not until late 1941 would it match the Germans numerically, or in the ability to intercept traffic in the field. Seebohm's company, moreover, had already operated with Rommel in France, and established trust and a working relationship with their chief consumer. While one can scarcely blame the Germans for boasting of their successes in intelligence—they have not been plentiful—this company was no better than its Italian or British counterparts.[89] Initially, however, Seebohm's company had easy hunting. This, in part, was because German success in understanding how radio would be used in war also illuminated preparation for tactical "Y". The company was trained to focus in general precisely on what would prove to be the most vulnerable points in the British system—traffic analysis, the interception of plain language messages, especially on artillery and armour circuits, the breaking of low-grade codes. In the long term, these strengths were balanced by weaknesses; the company's capability to break encoded traffic was limited, and it apparently devoted little attention to that task. Until autumn 1941, however, owing to poor British call sign systems and R/T procedure, this company easily traced British strength, movements, condition and intentions, maintaining detailed card indexes which followed the careers of individual British officers and of units from the moment they first used radio in the theatre. For Rommel this material was equivalent in value to ULTRA. Whatever his other flaws, he thrived on intelligence which was "hard" and "hot"—this was about all the intelligence he was competent to handle. Before the war, he emphasized that an army must be "untiringly active in determining [through physical reconnaissance] precise information regarding the enemy and the terrain", and stressed the need to "report observations rapidly, for delay lessens the value of any information". During the war he stated that "reconnaissance reports must reach the commander in the shortest possible time; he must take his decisions immediately and put them into effect as fast as he can. Speed of reaction decides the battle".[90] Given information which stated unambiguously what an enemy intended or was able to do, and in time to act, Rommel could strike like a snake. Seebohm and the British gave him precisely this.

By the spring of 1941, a lack of trained signals and cipher personnel, of sound procedures for security, and of radio facilities placed the British army in tragic circumstances. It had no effective and secure means of signalling in the field. It could barely meet the minimal operational demands for communication, let alone balance this need against that for security. Given the army's lack of radio circuits and its clumsy low-grade ciphers, it could maintain a high volume and velocity of communication in the field only by plain language over R/T—which would inform Rommel of British intentions as fast as these were formulated. The British would find it extremely difficult to enforce stricter signals security, and even if it did so, that would slow and confuse its reactions. Nothing could be more fatal against Rommel's style of operations; nothing would play further into his style of intelligence than poor signals security. Rommel did not need genius to win in the desert during the first half of 1941. He merely needed the British army as his enemy.

Between April and June 1941, the flaws in British signals and security became as plain as their language. Campaigns in Libya and Greece, in Crete and Libya, were marked by extraordinary failures of communication which sparked failures of command. At the start of the Greek campaign, the units of the Second New Zealand Division were scattered 500 miles apart. During it, so General Maitland "Jumbo" Wilson, the commander of British land forces in that theatre, wrote, "generally speaking it was the exception to be in communication with any H.Q. except by liaison officer, a process which involved at least 24 hour round trips".[91] Cyrenaica Command, the headquarters for British forces in Libya during April, quickly lost its ability to communicate with and to control its subordinates. Its infantry formations had few signallers, the vehicles of its armoured-car regiment could not recharge the batteries of their radio sets when one recharging truck was lost. The main formation defending that region, the Second Armoured Division, frequently could contact neither subordinates nor superiors for twenty-four hours at a time, and failed its vital tasks of passing information, controlling units and obeying orders.[92] Communication on Crete was even worse.[93] Throughout these campaigns, signals failures frequently left units and formations such as the Fourth New Zealand Brigade standing next to annihilation.[94] During "Battleaxe", communication between and within the two divisions involved shattered, though it did, just barely, sustain the key decision to break off the battle. The commander of the Seventh Armoured Division informed his seniors by R/T in plain language that consultation was imperative, an airplane carried Wavell and the commander of the Western Desert Force, General Beirsford-Pierse, forward, and withdrawal orders were sent to the Fourth Indian Division in Hindi over R/T. Beirsford-Pierse held that without a major increase and improvement in radio equipment, "control is bound to be lost at one stage or another" in battle; Wavell agreed that the "issue of tank battle" must turn on "wireless control".[95]

Lack of cipher staff further multiplied the handicaps on command. On 24 May Freyberg's headquarters on Crete had one trained cipher officer; not surprisingly, when this body moved during the crisis of battle, it asked GHQ Middle East to keep "cipher traffic minimum during next 24 hours".[96] Soon afterwards, reported one operator at GHQ, cipher signals from Crete "were badly mutilated and corrupt. Mr. Kirby the WO I shift leader kept repeating: 'Poor chaps, no wonder, what they must be going through.' " In Libya only the occasional presence of landlines saved the cipher staffs of the Second Armoured Division "from complete breakdown". Without landlines, "delays in priority messages of 8 hours or more were not uncommon and the use of clear, with all possible security precautions, was authorised more than once in order to relieve the Cipher Staffs".[97]

The Germans stamped their confusing and fast-moving style of warfare upon these battles. The collapse of communications brought down British command, leaving each individual unit to fight alone, leading the army to defeat in detail. Luck and leadership allowed Commonwealth commanders to survive potentially the most disastrous of these circumstances, the retreat from Greece. Here, imperial forces followed a simple plan and, blessed by geography, were generally able to make their enemy fight according to the British timetable of phased withdrawals. Still, Freyberg offered this bitter post-mortem:

> The charges of bad command and staff work are many ... during the seven weeks we were on Greek soil, once we were deployed no tactical decision on major strategic decision ... was even taken unless it was dictated by the German advances ... everybody bolted on the 25th except the New Zealand Divisional Headquarters ... when our senior commanders left us there was no further control of any description in Greece.

He "could not get any decision" from headquarters: "It is possible that he ['Jumbo' Wilson] drew lines in his Headquarters and gave orders, but we were in such a state of disorder that there was no question of establishing a proper defensive position."[98] Similar problems marked the border between triumph and disaster for Freyberg's command in Crete. When all signals links disintegrated, his headquarters lost its touch with operations and its ability to command. As he noted, "there was no signal service ... military organization had broken down and the power to issue orders or to obey them had gone before the 26th May".[99] Energetic actions were not taken to overcome this wasting malady, while without constant coordination from above, too many British and Dominion units failed to cooperate or to take any positive action at all, save to retreat.

During these campaigns every previous problem in the sphere of security emerged, and some new ones. No means had been arranged to change call signs, code words and radio frequencies in battle. So they were not changed; no regimental commander was "willing to risk failure of communications during operations in order to gain in signal security", by adopting new callsigns which his squadrons might not have received.[100] Brigade and divisional headquarters had neither medium-grade facilities nor special systems for use in dangerous areas where capture was possible. In Greece and Crete they had only one secure system, the army's universal high-grade codebooks, with absurd results. Officers could either use these systems in battle, risking their capture and the compromise of much of their service's traffic throughout the world, or destroy both these books and the possibility of secure communications for any operational traffic.

During the Greek campaign most units "destroyed their books in ample time [but] in certain instances the books were destroyed before they need have been". For several days some units could communicate with GHQ Greece only by plain language or a slow and insecure transposition cipher.[101] Conversely, one RAF officer held his books in hand through all the perils of evacuation, "under the mistaken impression that he was making a praiseworthy effort".[102] Nor was this the only example of amateurish preparations. On 24 April, three days before the covering forces withdrew from Greece, the cipher and signals branches of the battle headquarters ashore were separated, which "meant, of course, that all cipher messages reaching the headquarters remained indecipherable".[103] Even during "Crusader", contrary to orders, one armoured brigade was given a high-grade codebook to cover its operational traffic.[104] On Crete such failures proved costly. At Maleme airstrip the Germans captured much of the high-grade superencipherment system and codebook used by the RAF throughout the world. Meanwhile Freyberg could communicate with his brigades, which had destroyed their high-grade systems, only in plain language. By 28 May he could contact GHQ Middle East solely through one "badly working R.A.F. set and only code SYKO which is easily broken".[105]

These cryptographic failings endangered all British operational traffic carried by radio during the campaigns in Crete, Greece and Libya, and produced a longer-lasting problem: for about a year in 1941–1942, the German army cryptanalytical section IN 7/VI at OKH read what it called the "War Office Cipher—Middle East". This was "War Office Cipher 'W' ", the army's universal high-grade codebook, which carried traffic between Whitehall, commands, armies, corps and, later, divisions. It reconstructed "W" through cryptanalysis and then captured a copy of it in Libya during early 1942. Meanwhile, *Luftwaffe* signals intelligence read an RAF high-grade codebook, presumably aided by the material lost at Maleme. British military authorities quickly appreciated that "W" was compromised but could not do without it; hence, they pursued means to live with insecurity. They no longer used "W" for operational traffic, which was covered by OTP and, increasingly from October 1941, by Typex. They aimed to defend traffic carried over "W" by dividing categories of messages between different superencipherment series, for which the tables were changed regularly. By December 1941, "W" was covered by four "W.O. Tables", used for traffic across the world, General, Special, "M" and "I (E)"—the latter initially intended to defend the transfer of signals intelligence material, though fortunately OTP and Typex covered all messages referring to ULTRA—by distinct "M.E. Local Tables" for the Eighth and Ninth Armies and the forces in East Africa, and probably also by some series for forces in Great Britain. Which of these superencipherment series IN 7/VI broke is unclear, though the title "War Office Cipher—Middle East" suggests it was one or more of the "M.E. Local Tables", those most immediately useful for German intelligence. Whatever the case may be, IN 7/VI had great access to the secondary levels of some significant British military traffic, which provided much general information and frequently revealed the movement or locations of units. During 1941–1942, IN 7/VI arguably had as much success against high-grade British army traffic as Bletchley Park did with that of the German army, though apparently Seebohm and IN 7/VI did not cooperate in an attack on this material, while Rommel received none of it; at best, it simply aided the accuracy of card file indexes in Berlin. IN 7/VI sometimes broke and circulated material within a week of its interception in Greece and Africa, not much slower than the contemporary speed of ULTRA; the elementary nature of the codebook, British failures in the use of the superenciphering system and the German application of automated techniques (Hollerith machines) aided the attack. This experience also assisted German work in 1943 against the "War Office Cipher—Home Forces" (presumably, the same basic book with a different superencipherment series, used to cover similar medium-level matters in Britain). Similarly, *Luftwaffe* signals intelligence provided valuable order of battle intelligence on the RAF in the Middle East while, until mid-1943, the Germans exploited another codebook, the Inter-Departmental Code, which revealed details about British diplomacy in the Near East. Again, Britain understood the vulnerability of the basic book and hoped to cover it through changes in superencipherment systems; again, with mixed success.[106] British signals security hinged not on its skill but rather on the limits to that of its enemy. Nothing better demonstrates the poverty of German cryptanalysis than its failure to exploit its golden opportunities of 1940–1942.

Until these campaigns such failures had slowed signals within divisions, shattered command within brigades, and caused tactical setbacks. Now communications within divisions could vanish for a day, commands lose their ability to control, and campaigns be lost.[107] Of course, German signals were no better in Libya and worse on Crete. The German army faced a harsher environment—its command and communication systems were far more fit to survive. These circumstances broke the British army's system of command and signals security. It needed what one Chief Signals Officer (CSO) called "one hundred per cent efficiency"[108] in communication to function; the German Army did not. British failures in signals security had no less serious results. The Middle East commands concluded that during the Greek campaign, "a failure to appreciate the finer aspects of signals and cipher security ... was responsible for the enemy being aware of the dispositions of our forces and the movements of our aircraft".[109] What was inconvenient in Greece became fatal in Libya. After the debacle of April, the Second Armoured Division concluded that in mobile operations, the enemy would be bound to capture copies of operational codes; hence, most of them "should be done away with". Perhaps because they acted on this belief, forces in the desert did not improve signals security and soon paid for it. Before "Battleaxe", wireless silence masked the advance of the Fourth Indian Division to the front, but failures in signals security by the Seventh Armoured Division and supply units in rear areas gave the *Afrika Korps* an accurate picture of British dispositions, nine hours' warning of its start, and information on British intentions, perceptions and concerns during its course. The German counterstroke was based on an almost letter-perfect knowledge of British dispositions, which revealed a deadly gap between forces; its development was blessed by accurate indications of the confusion at higher levels of command, the heavy losses and the shortages of ammunition and supplies and confidence which haunted the foe.[110] Rommel need not have asked for anything more. British intelligence soon concluded: "The following may sound a startling statement but it is not far removed from the truth to say that, in the recent operations, in CYRENAICA, the enemy command directed his operations largely from information given in clear by our units."[111]

However bitter these failures, they forced the British army to recognize its desperate position regarding signals and security. The poverty of its approach to cryptography was obvious as was the fact that "the British Army is painfully behind the German Army" in signals.[112] As the CSO of the Fourth Indian Division noted after Battleaxe: "In mobile operations of this nature where distances are considerable, the problem of intercommunication will require the most careful thought and on the signal plan may depend success or failure."[113] The British army began this process in June 1941; it had much to think about. It would learn these lessons with remarkable speed but would not fully profit from this technical education because of its failures in greater spheres.

Large amounts of equipment and numbers of trained personnel were needed to overcome these problems in signals and security, things in short supply for the British army in the Middle East. In November 1941 it was apparently 6,000 men short of its needs. By April 1942 its continual requests to redress that problem sparked this rebuke from London: "Your demands for signals drafts greatly exceed our ability to supply." Again, in January 1942 Auchinleck told the War Office that "to equip and train armoured divisions as intended depends very largely on provision of adequate number wireless sets and charging engines. Position regarding these is extremely serious". His complaints were accurate—Auchinleck's command was perhaps 10 per cent (or 350 sets) short of its establishment of the obsolescent

No. 9 tank radio set and had received just seventy of the better No. 19 sets. They were also heeded. The CIGS, Alan Brooke, demanded a change to this "desperate shortage ... the efficiency of Armoured Forces depends entirely on the provision of their wireless equipment".[114] By the late spring of 1942, the army in the Middle East finally had the equipment and personnel needed to meet its needs for radio.

This was not, however, the end of trouble. This very success forced the Army to train raw personnel in large numbers and to establish an entirely new structure for signals, based primarily on radio. This task could not be done to perfection, and the insistence on strict wireless silence before operations masked these failings. The CSO of the Advanced Eighth Army headquarters wrote during the Crusader offensive that many problems were obvious once silence was lifted "but it took, to me, an agonisingly long time before they could be put right". Men and officers had not even tested in exercises the signals system on which they would rely. Many signallers—*enthusiatic amateurs*, mostly borrowed from the South African Division, noted another staff officer—had never handled their equipment in the field before the operations; others could not even find nets or maintain frequencies. Liaison officers were often incompetent. Staff officers were reminded that "brevity is the spice of wit and war" and that they must apply elaborate security procedures to R/T; but they received inadequate opportunity to practice these principles. As Norrie, commander of XXX Corps noted, staff and field officers had little sense of proper R/T procedure, hampering communications and security. They attempted to use R/T even when "it is a waste of time and blocks traffic ... the chief failures in R/T security appeared to occur when a commander was asked a question he did not expect". As the War Office noted later, "short, carefully thought out, reports and orders, passed by means of correct procedure, seldom gave anything away, as the enemy hardly had time to pick them up. It was the long rambling discussions which were most fraught with danger".[115] After Crusader, the Eighth Army noted that "all sides of Signals had to learn a lot and run themselves in during the campaign itself ... this was done quickly but during the first days of the campaign when as in any campaign good communications are of vital significance, Signals was learning its job".[116]

The Eighth Army suffered through this learning period. Before Crusader, 20 per cent of the tanks in one of the army's three cruiser tank brigades had no wireless sets; as Norrie noted, this reduced "flexibility and speed of manoeuvre, as the 'dumb' tanks have frequently to be called in or visited in order to give them information and orders, and they are of little use for recce [*sic*]". This danger threatened to become a general one during Crusader. Radio could not be issued to all replacement tanks—barely to all those of troop commanders. The Seventh Armoured Division met its internal needs for communication only by cannibalizing all signals personnel from units which had been fortuitously (in this sense, if no other) withdrawn for refitting. It warned that unless these problems were overcome in the future, "there will be a grave risk of a complete breakdown in communications". The single most significant wireless link, between the Eighth Army and XXX Corps, essentially broke for the first thirty-six hours of battle, and thereafter key messages were often delayed for twelve to twenty-four hours. Once, wireless communication between the headquarters of the Eighth Army and XIII Corps, forty miles apart, was possible only when relayed from a warship to Whitehall and back "in accordance with normal Fleet practice"![117] When exactly four wireless sets were knocked out on 22 November, command in and control over the Fourth Armoured Brigade, the Eighth Army's only reserve armoured formation, equivalent in numerical strength to a Panzer Division, vanished for a day during the crisis of the battle because no fallback signals system existed. Infantry units and formations had exactly the same unsatisfactory signals establishment as in 1939. Communication to brigades and divisions often hinged on a radio set borrowed from neighbouring armoured or artillery units. Administrative links were strained.

These signals shortages and failures made it difficult for higher commands to grasp the reality of Crusader, to coordinate their actions and to control their units. As would continue until August 1942, the continual and sudden reorganization of commands during battle magnified every problem of signals, forcing formations to enter entirely new systems of intercommunication, often with overlapping frequencies and different equipment, producing "very dangerous results" which crippled the very value of the reorganization. Formations did not draw the optimum balance between "the wish to get forward for operational control and the necessity to avoid outstripping administrative control". (After the Gazala battle, the CSO of XIII Corps argued that an advanced headquarters should be placed within W/T reach of its headquarters and R/T reach of those of its subordinate commands.) The paucity of circuits made communication a bottleneck for command at all levels. Corps were expected to control two divisions (which might be fighting complex battles separated by 100 miles) over exactly the same links. As would continue until the "J" service was formed in summer 1942, the tactical information contained in the signals of British units and lower formations took far too long to pass up the British chain of command, and often never passed down at all. The Second New Zealand Division later reported that "information was always scanty about formations on our flanks except when we were able to make contact with them ourselves". Thanks to Seebohm, Rommel was often better informed of such British communications than his opposite numbers.

These failings produced the confusion which marked all levels of British command during Crusader. As one well-placed liaison officer at Seventh Armoured Division headquarters noted on 22 November, all appeared chaos. Enemy were all over the place and it was impossible, listening in on the Command set to the Brigade Commanders talking to each other in the thick of it, to make head or tail of it ... Willoughby Norrie hit it on the head in giving orders to the South Africans. "Tell them there's the biggest bloody tank battle going on in history and that's all we know."

One South African armoured officer summarized the experience of many Commonwealth units: "We were to get used to the daily 'swans' into nothingness after nothingness, pursuing mirages of enemy conjured up by imagination and fear, mixed-up communications, mistranslated codes and nerve-racked commanders." The disintegration of communication links left armoured brigades scattered throughout the southern part of the battlefield, each to fight alone. Commonwealth infantry divisions in the north learned of even the most critical of events to the south of them only by establishing communications themselves with other formations and by intercepting the traffic of forward British units. The Eighth Army and XXX Corps failed to meet their central tasks of circulating information to or coordinating the activities of their formations. Their own knowledge of events was all too often twenty-four to thirty-six hours out of date. The tempo of delay in communication contributed to a remarkable cycle of exultation and despair on the part of senior British officers.[118]

These problems were serious, yet their scale should not be exaggerated. Even by Crusader the army had more units in the field with more W/T and R/T links than ever before; even during Crusader its communications never collapsed so badly as they had done so universally in the spring of 1941. After the first week, failures of communication produced uncertainty and fear but no longer disaster, though the balance was close—just one fortuitously placed wireless set linked the Second New Zealand Division with XXX Corps as it ran from death on 30 November–2 December. Compared to Battleaxe, Crusader marked major technical advances for British signals. A dedicated "Command R/T" link joined Eighth Army, XXX Corps and the Seventh Armoured Division, though not XIII Corps. Corps commanders and senior armoured officers received armoured command vehicles with radio, letting them move forward while maintaining contact with their rear, and both the Eighth Army and the Seventh Armoured Division established units to tap the traffic of front-line units for the benefit of higher commands. Neither innovation worked perfectly, but they marked substantial improvements. If this system was more fragile than was desirable, it proved less so than the German one.

Even on 22 November, four days after the battle began, Rommel wrote: "Our signals networks could hardly be worse. This is war the way the ancient Teutons used to fight it. I don't even know at this moment whether the Afrika Korps is on the attack or not."[119] A day later, the *Afrika Korps*' headquarters, its signals and its cryptographic equipment were captured, while Rommel's dash to the wire confused his own no less than his enemy's command structure. From that moment, British communications were simultaneously more secure and more effective than those of the Germans. The new headquarters of the *Afrika Korps* had only two radio sets and no usable operational codes. As Auchinleck noted by 30 November: "Enemy has been sending all operations orders in clear for last two days, which is significant of haste and disorganisation."[120] This source revealed crucial information, such as the fact that on 3 December, *Panzer Armee Afrika* had just fifty working tanks, 20 per cent of its strength when the battle began.[121] Meanwhile, British signals carried that volume of traffic at that velocity which a steady command needed in order to salvage a gravely threatened position.

The system tested under such stress in Crusader was modified in detail over the next six months. It was not for want of a radio set that Gazala would be lost—indeed, this was the first battle in which British signals matched those of the *Wehrmacht* at its best. Again, especially during the first week of the struggle, British signals worked more effectively than those of the *Afrika Korps*, handicapped, as ever, by Rommel's own love for fragmenting his command structure. Dedicated R/T and W/T circuits linked all connections of command between formations and from them down to armoured car, tank, artillery and infantry units. Every armoured car and tank, each artillery battery and most infantry companies had a radio set for rear and lateral communications. The system was shielded by dense layers of redundancy. For the first time each infantry division had a forward R/T link with its brigade headquarters while a W/T net supplemented the old R/T one between armoured divisions and their brigades. These and other channels provided flexible signals during operations and robust fallback systems during emergencies. Thus, when on 27–28 May the headquarters signals of the Seventh Armoured Division had to flee from the enemy, were overrun and then forced to flee again for half a day, divisional communications were not seriously disrupted for more than two hours—a far cry from the situation with the Fourth Armoured Brigade eight months before. The same was true when the joint tactical headquarters of the Seventh Armoured Division and the Fifth Indian Division were overrun on 5 June. Although control over sub-units broke down for the best part of a day in these instances, the communication system needed to establish command remained in being, just not the ability to use it.

During Gazala the British had another advantage over Crusader: instead of carrying their signals with them into battle, until the last stages of the operation they fought from a prepared position with an established landline network. This system carried a vast quantity of clear yet secure traffic for higher formations and solved much of the problem surrounding administrative messages. One headquarters officer even claimed that communications in Gazala were "almost faultless, there being few occasions when Army HQ was out of telephonic communication with either Corps". Landlines carried much inter-formation traffic even during mobile operations. Within armoured divisions temporary cables were laid each night between brigade and divisional headquarters, allowing a much freer and more secure discussion of such essential matters as "tank states" (unit strengths) and the question of "tomorrow's plans", so eliminating the greatest single type of material which Seebohm had provided during Crusader. Until the Eighth Army itself was smashed at the Knightsbridge battle on 14 June, communication at and above the brigade level was rarely impaired for more than a few hours at a time. Even during the debacle of the following month, signals never fell near to their nadir of Crusader. After Gazala, commands and CSOs wanted detailed improvements in their communication system, yet they conceded that it had worked through the shock of a devastating defeat.[122]

British signals in the desert are usually mentioned only in the context of failure, of an inability to maintain communication at this, that or the other vital moment. As one account noted regarding Crusader: "There were comparatively few radio sets, and at all levels down from Army H.Q. they could be relied upon to fail, or for traffic to become indecipherable when most needed."[123] One must not, however, confuse the failure of a medium with that of its message, of signals with command. Slow and faulty communications are a part of war, one which armies are designed to overcome. Such situations may result not from technical failures by a signals service but from the nature of a campaign. In the desert small numbers of men fought in confusion over vast areas. There was no stable front—headquarters and signals units rather often experienced the sharp end of war. To an equal extent for British and Germans alike, headquarters were overrun, signals facilities smashed, the flow of information and of orders dammed. British signals matched the quality of their German counterparts in these circumstances; British commanders did not.

Rommel preferred to fight battles of manoeuvre; he made the British do so. He believed that such circumstances would cripple the regular transmission of messages; his tendency to operate out of radio contact with his headquarters made this a self-fulfilling prophecy; but whatever the flaws of his system of command, it was least suited in part to this problem. Moreover, when out of communication with Rommel his subordinates acted with speed and with effect. On 30 November 1941, at Sidi Rezeg, General Cruwell commanded the *Afrika Korps* as he saw fit rather than waiting an hour for an order from Rommel, already received, to be decoded. Subsequently, in violation of Rommel's orders but in accordance with realities, a colonel at rear headquarters ordered the abandonment of the *Afrika Korps*' dash to the wire. The Germans lost battles but no minutes. British commanders were less willing to act until they had received enough information to form a clear picture of events, which with Rommel ran like quicksilver. The British machine needed more orders and more time to work than the German one. It could not win in the desert with the best signals it could receive; the failure was not of communication but command. Moreover, because the Eighth Army needed better signals in order to function than the *Afrika Korps*, it would suffer to a greater extent from the imposition of effective signals security.

The months between Battleaxe and Crusader witnessed the most radical improvement in the signals and cipher security of the British army during the Second World War. The Director of Military Intelligence in the Middle East told senior commanders "we were scandalized about what the Germans knew of our intentions and Order of Battle during the last operations in the Western Desert ... the Italians had been good in the same way, but they had never 'totted us up' in the same way the Germans had".[124] Meanwhile, after assessing the operational disasters of mid-1941, military cryptographic authorities doubted "that leakage of information was due to insecurity of ciphers. It is true that certain ciphers were overloaded but many mistakes seem to have been made in other directions which could easily have provided useful intelligence to the enemy". These conclusions were accurate and these authorities understood the greatest cipher compromise confronting British forces in the Middle East: "It must be assumed that the 'W' Cipher Book is in enemy hands. Security must therefore be maintained by frequent changing of tables." These authorities also realized, "It is obvious that confidence in the security of ciphers in the Middle East [has] been shaken." These problems of confidence, communications and cryptography could be overcome only by tightening then-current modes of security, and abandoning the old tendency to oppose the use of ciphers and to rely on plain language traffic. These authorities recommended that, as in current practice, high-grade systems carry all intercommand traffic about operations, with particular emphasis on OTP for the present but with greater reliance on Typex, and that this approach should reach down to divisional headquarters, which should receive codebooks or Typex. The existing cipher system for communication between divisions and brigades must be replaced, and a new syllabic cipher should be introduced for traffic below the brigade level.[125] In order to explain the need to accept and enforce such time-consuming improvements, staff and middle-level field officers were told of Italian and German successes against British traffic.[126] By October a common inter-service programme for these matters was instituted down to unit level in the Middle East. More signals security officers were provided and their status was enhanced. These personnel received more professional training, including practical courses in cryptanalysis without which they "would be of little use and would not know what faults to look for".[127] The army monitored its signals for signs of weakness and publicized the problems widely among its personnel. The transmissions of

British operators were continually monitored, a necessary precaution given their lack of experience. All this was essential if the army was to improve its signals security. The need for these practices was spurred by the experiences of Crusader, particularly by the capture of fragments of Seebohm's records at Bardia, which showed some of his unit's success and hinted at more.[128]

Progressively after Battleaxe, firm steps were also taken against the perils of traffic analysis, and effective ones. After August 1941, Seebohm's company maintained a tight grip on the imperial order of battle throughout the Middle East, but lost track of key operational developments on Rommel's front, culminating in its entire failure to forecast the Eighth Army's strength and intentions before Crusader. In August 1941, for example, the Seventh Armoured Division withdrew from the front, yet the *Afrika Korps* later noted, "as a result of the enemy's skillful masking of wireless traffic and his retention of the same organization of command, this withdrawal passed unnoticed by us".[129] Although "many heads were shaken" in doubt that operators could use so complex a system, on 16 October 1941 the Eighth Army adopted the link sign procedure for call signs. These heads were shaken in vain, for this was one of the army's greatest achievements in signals security of the entire Second World War. As Seebohm's company noted after Crusader, the institution of this system

> *eliminates practically all the basis of former wireless intelligence work* ... the difficulties of wireless intelligence in the ensuing period caused a decline in results and later further measures were taken to increase the security, notably the reduction of traffic sent in clear ... *The new procedure* made possible no important identifications of the units taking part after the commencement of the battle on the first days of the attack. Mention must also be made of the smart passing of wireless traffic as well as of the excellent wireless discipline within the 7 Armd. Div. This allowed little scope for the Interception Service ... Neither the time of the attack nor the strength of the forces employed at the commencement were known. The reasons for this were the wireless silence, the measures taken to preserve wireless security, and *the new wireless procedure* adopted.[130]

From Crusader onward, all German observers praised the "excellent wireless security" of the Eighth Army before battles began. Not that the link sign procedure was perfect. During Crusader, XIII Corps found it impossible to change call signs for its formations every day, instead doing so every four days, which eroded the security value of the system. By April–May 1942, assisted by operators' errors and the capture of sections of the link sign book, Seebohm's company penetrated part of the system and reconstructed elements of the British order of battle.[131] This success, however, required great effort and produced limited success. At one stroke Seebohm, and through him Rommel, lost the ability to monitor British dispositions or intentions before operations began. Their only source on these matters were the solutions of the encoded radio traffic of the American attaché in Cairo, Colonel Fellers, in whose "little fellers" Rommel placed great faith.[132] These were, however, no replacement for traffic analysis: simply because a great technical achievement is required to produce a source of intelligence does not make it a better one. Rommel began all of his battles between October 1941 and August 1942 with strikingly inaccurate assessments of British strength and intentions—the scale and the timing of the Crusader offensive caught the *Afrika Korps* by surprise, while it underestimated by one-third the number of British tanks on the front before the Gazala operation. The paradoxical nature of intelligence and of its denial are revealed by the comment about this last failure by Rommel's chief of intelligence, F.W. von Mellenthin: "Perhaps, fortunately, we underestimated the British strength, for had we known the full facts even Rommel might have baulked at an attack on such a superior enemy."[133] For the British army, less security in signals might have produced less damage in battle.

In late 1941, the reform of British cryptography achieved two great successes; it heightened all forms of security before battle, and it stopped the rot at the point of gravest danger, German penetration of British inter theatre or strategic traffic. Compared with its triumph in these spheres, the British army proved less able to improve the defence of its traffic once operations began, at all levels between corps headquarters and the front line. In the summer of 1941, it flirted with the idea of using high-grade systems for interformation traffic in the field. Thus, in the Syrian campaign OTP was to be used for "all repeat all" operational messages between divisions, corps and force headquarters, and the practice became standard in the coming months. During Crusader, a senior military cryptographer noted: "Practically all secret operational messages are now sent in 'One Timers'." OTP, however, was far too clumsy, slow and labour-intensive to carry much traffic, and not easily used by small headquarters on the move. In 1942–1943 it would be used only to defend categories of information warranting absolute security, such as tank states and ULTRA. In 1941, the only secure system available to carry operational traffic was able to cover only small amounts of it, and was extremely difficult to use. Although Typex was issued to corps headquarters during Crusader and Gazala, it carried primarily administrative traffic. Not until the Tunisian campaign was this device with its combination of high security and volume available to help British operational traffic.[134] Denied the use of high-grade systems for such messages, the British turned to devise effective low- and medium-grade ones. Unfortunately, it failed to do so. Through this chink in its cryptographic armour Britain suffered wounds from Rommel.

Low- and medium-grade systems are, for any army, the most difficult to create; they must be used by a host of often poorly trained operators or officers and carry an extraordinary volume of traffic which refers to matters of which the enemy knows. It is hard to make such systems usable, harder to make them secure, hardest to achieve both ends at once. The Germans found as many troubles in this sphere as the British. Throughout 1941–1942 the British army experimented with many field ciphers and R/T codes to meet these needs. None proved very suitable—even those of 1945 had flaws. The combination of these weaknesses and the conditions of the desert war proved almost fatal to the Eighth Army.

Before Crusader, according to plan, the army altered its ciphers for use within divisions and introduced a syllabic code within brigades.[135] In technical terms, however, these systems offered little security. Given the absence of the records of Seebohm's codebreaking *Staffel*, any conclusions regarding German exploitation of this opportunity must be provisional. None the less, during Crusader Seebohm's company penetrated many (probably most) of the Eighth Army's field codes. In July 1942 the Germans found "little difficulty" in solving the "Sheetex" R/T code, which was then in common use; during 1943–1945 they often read its successors, the "Codex" and "Slidex" systems. Further, the Eighth Army's field ciphers were cryptographically weak, widely distributed and, like their German counterparts, often captured when headquarters were overrun. One report after Gazala noted that the "very frequent compromisation of ciphers and keys seriously interrupted cipher work"; another, that circumstances "when the Army MEBC [Middle East Brigade Cipher] keys have been compromised [is] a common state of affairs".[136] Altogether, the Germans probably had some access to British R/T codes and field ciphers, and thus to all operational communications from corps headquarters down. They scarcely needed to bother, however; they could have had all this simply by tuning their radio sets to British frequencies.

The real flaw of these middle-grade systems was not insecurity but clumsiness. During Crusader, XIII Corps used cipher and six different codes; its divisions had to use all of these systems alongside other R/T codes with their own units. Every comment on codes or ciphers made after Crusader pleaded that they be simplified. As XXX Corps noted, "there were too many [codes], they were too complicated, and it was difficult to change them when they were compromised". Formations could not cope with this bewildering situation, which threatened dire results. At a desperate moment on 1 December 1941, the Second New Zealand Division could not conduct secret communications with XXX Corps because the latter did not have the appropriate code, and had to plan a dangerous withdrawal in veiled language.[137] During operations the use of cipher caused a "bottleneck" in communications, particularly because trained cipher operators were, as ever, in short supply. By 2 December 1941 the advanced headquarters of the Eighth Army noted, "Cipher office swamped. 3 day delay on D messages. Outstanding cipher messages"—scarcely surprising, since it had only one trained cipher officer. On one occasion it took twelve hours for a "MOST IMMEDIATE" cipher message from the Eighth Army to reach XXX Corps—and then only because it was retransmitted in the clear! After Crusader, the CSO of the Seventh Armoured Division stated "the lack of use of Cipher was amply justified as the consequent speed up in communications was enormous. In the latter stages of the operations, the Division was placed under Command of a Corps which used Cipher very extensively and the consequent delay in traffic was very apparent".[138] Even worse, small errors in the use of code or cipher could have catastrophic operational effects: a counter-attack central to the "cauldron" battle on 5 June 1942 collapsed because the commander of the Second Armoured Brigade misread an encoded order and attacked west instead of east of the Knightsbridge box, precisely into deadly fire he had been intended to avoid.[139]

Throughout Crusader and Gazala the Eighth Army used far more R/T and W/T than ever before. This was handled by imperfectly trained personnel and by senior officers having little experience with the medium, who treated the "blower" as though these were telephones on a party line, transferring to it their old habits of debate over details rather than precision of orders. Precisely the increase in signals multiplied the problems in security. For these officers, even this unprecedented volume and velocity of signals was not enough, and the need for quick communication as overwhelming as Rommel. The combination of poor systems, emergency and untrained personnel led, as ever, to the use of plain language, which was officially approved. Norrie recommended "what I term Chinese" for communication. "Commanders who know each other well can talk a mixture of Urdu and Veiled English, which no enemy can interpret", though he also "thought that too much use was again made of Christian names: This is secure for a short period but not for days on end." Of course, so one German intelligence officer noted, these messages were usually "masterpieces of understatement ... [which] seldom [revealed] the real state of affairs in all its seriousness". Still, aware as it was of British habits of expression, the *Afrika Korps* naturally placed weight on statements like the following from the Fourth Armoured Brigade on 29 November 1941: "I am without ammunition and in urgent need of it." The British tried to minimize these risks through the use of guarded language, substituting officers' nicknames for those of formations, or sending operational orders in veiled allusions. One can, however, call the 22nd Armoured Brigade, one of the best and strongest British tank formations, "Scotty" only so many times before the meaning becomes obvious; then so too becomes the significance of the fact that on 25 November 1941 the commanders of neither XIII nor XXX Corps "know where Scotty is—nobody knows!"[140] There was often poetry in guarded language—"the fox is killed in the open" after Beda

Fomm; "come on the Greys, get out your whips" during the crisis at Alem el Halfa. There was little security.

In the heat of operations even veiled speech evaporated. Thus, on 1 December 1941, while planning the breakout of his surrounded Second New Zealand Division, Freyberg

> called up Headquarters 30 Corps by RT and spoke to General Norrie about his intentions. Sergeant Smith stood by the set while the General spoke and listened in horrified silence while he described his plan in the plainest of plain language, quite unblemished by the merest pretense of RT procedure or security precautions. Smith bounded over to OC A section: "Did you hear what he said? Did you hear?" he yelled and, without waiting for answer, "Tiny [General Freyberg] said that we are going to break out at dusk—four miles east, nine miles south-east over the escarpment and then flat out for the wire! *All in the clear!*" The last words were almost a shriek. Throwing out his arm in the direction of the sinister black shapes squatting on the distant skyline to the north, he turned and peered earnestly into the face of Lieutenant-Colonel Agar, who had come up to see the fun. "And what does he think those bastards out there are going to do about it, sir?" As he sauntered off dejectedly, fragments of his mournful soliloquy floated back to his hearers. "... nine miles to Point 192 ... east to wire ... nine miles to Hell, more like ...".[141]

All this was inevitable in the circumstances; so was the result. Throughout Crusader and Gazala, the more intense and confused the battle, the more routinely did British regimental, brigade, divisional, corps and army commanders communicate in clear. As one cynic wrote, "there were codes to be fumbled with and compromised so that resort had to be made to veiled language ... the more senior the officer on the wireless, the more likely he was to break the code" [sic].[142] Seebohm was a passive partner to these discussions, Rommel a recipient, the Eighth Army a victim. Interception of plain language transmissions was the simplest form of signals intelligence during the Second World War and ULTRA the most sophisticated. Rommel gained as much from the former during operations as any Allied land commander ever did from the latter.

Judging from the *Afrika Korps*' intelligence diary, Seebohm's company was Rommel's best source of intelligence during Crusader—more important than all of the rest together. It maintained as accurate a picture of British strength and dispositions as did the commanders of the Eighth Army. From the second day of Crusader, Seebohm's company reconstructed most of the British order of battle. Between 23 November and 24 December, it provided detailed accounts of the perceptions and intentions of senior British commanders twenty-five times. One example from Seebohm's signals intelligence diary from 27 November, just before the dogfight at Sidi Rezeg, will show the nature of such reports.

Extracts from intercepted wireless communications 27 Nov 41.

From YWP (13 Corps): Ronny (Tobruk?) and Bernhard (2 NZ Div) have *not* joined up. Tell your late Lord Master.

From 13 Corps to Eighth Army: I have some information for you. Bill's (?) and Bernhard's (2 NZ Div) boys are changing over and everything is going well. My Neptune (commander?) is on the way to visit Bernhard, and if possible to look up Ronny (Tobruk?) at the same time.

Eighth Army to 13 Corps: ... Keep an eye out in Frank's (4 Ind Div) and Scraper's (?) direction.

13 Corps to Eighth Army: In your direction and where Willoughby was?

Eighth Army to 13 Corps: No, more towards Frank and Hargess (Hargest?).

13 Corps to Eighth Army: Everything is jacked up with me, and everything concentrated on that corner.

Eighth Army to 13 Corps: Well then, keep particular watch towards Insect (?) and also in Hargess's and our direction.

Eighth Army to 13 Corps: I am sorry that Bernhard's party did not come with Scotty (22 Armd Bde). That causes me some anxiety. It is not impossible. In the meantime you should aim to co-ordinate arrangements with Ronny, so that he may have more freedom.

13 Corps to Eighth Army: The arrangements made with Willeby will be carried out on time, and he will do everything as arranged. It would of course be better if you could get hold of Hargess. As soon as you run into difficulties get in touch with Hargess.

Eighth Army to 13 Corps: Yes, I will keep that in mind. As soon as things become difficult for you, tell me, and I will arrange help immediately with U.G.'s (1 Army Tk Bde) eldest son.

13 Corps to Eighth Army: Yes, I will tell you when we need U.G.[143]

Such information helped the *Afrika Korps* to aim its blows and to assess their effect, but far less so than during Battleaxe. All the problems of communication and command which confused British forces did the same to Seebohm. After months of rigourous wireless silence, 120,000 men and 600 tanks suddenly attacked. Almost immediately, the British plan collapsed on the southern axis but worked like clockwork in the north. Noise from the failure filled the airwaves—success was silent. During the first week of the attack Seebohm provided excellent intelligence on XXX Corps in the desert but little on the formations of XIII Corps in the north. Meanwhile, his company had mixed success against the three forms of British communication security. Apparently, it never broke the Eighth Army's field ciphers, which protected some important traffic (though probably not most of it, because of their clumsiness and the problems of communications). Even so, this was a harbinger of what could happen if only the British army developed usable means of high-grade security for field traffic. Conversely, two days into the offensive Seebohm's company broke the formal code system referring to formations. Thus, he knew the entire British order of battle whenever code was used, which provided key hints about intentions and actions. However, the cryptographic weakness of codes no longer compromised one key issue. Before Crusader, the British abandoned their earlier practices of reporting mechanical casualties "by R/T using code, 'crawler', cruiser, 'creeper', light tank, etc. But we learnt enemy were intercepting this, so latterly crocks were reported in writing through liaison officer, and false crock reports sent out over the air".[144] Hence, the Germans found it far more difficult to determine enemy casualties than before—Seebohm's company appears to have provided nothing on the matter—and grossly distorted them as Crusader wore on, contributing to Rommel's disastrous decisions in the middle part of the battle.

The situation regarding plain and veiled language was the most peculiar. British commanders often used this procedure, which betrayed more information to the enemy than did broken codes, but in the midst of the confusion veiled language did have some security value. Unfortunately, one could not know whether this would be the case when one conducted such a conversation, only afterward—literally, to use veiled language was to gamble. Seebohm's men apparently had no means to translate communications in Urdu and Afrikaans, which they did not even write down, thus losing an easy opportunity to acquire information from two of the five divisions in the battle. When dealing with messages in English, they quickly learned which Christian name referred to which regiment or brigade, and thus always understood significant elements of most intercepted conversations. This success, however, was crippled by major errors about the names and nicknames of imperial divisional and corps commanders. Seebohm's company often misinterpreted names like "Straffer", the nickname of the Commander of the Seventh Armoured Division, who was referred to as "Scraper", and constantly misunderstood references to the names of both British Corps commanders, Norrie and Godwin-Austin. Thus they missed key elements in the conversation. Even fifteen days after the start of Crusader, they interpreted a reference to a proposed action by a corps for one by a brigade! Worst of all was confusion over Commonwealth formations during the crisis of the battle. On 24–25 November, Seebohm's company presumed "Bernhard" to be the commander of the South African Division instead of the most dangerous formation they confronted, the Second New Zealand Division, which they thus did not even know was at the front. Consequently, it missed several chances to appreciate the reality on the northern axis, before Rommel dashed to the wire and threw the battle away.

For such reasons, the Germans missed the point of perhaps half the significant discussions in plain language they intercepted, showing the not inconsiderable security value of plain language, augmented by their simple failure to intercept morse key conversations (including Freyberg's message in "the plainest of plain language"). Again, Germans frequently heard British officers use the phrase "usual source" (jargon for communications intelligence ranging from plain language intercepts to ULTRA) over the radio or read it in captured documents. Seebohm's company knew the meaning of the phrase but, because it covered so many sources while ample proof (intercepted or captured) showed that such material often came from middle-grade Italian traffic (which the *Afrika Korps* constantly condemned as insecure) and German material in plain language or low-grade codes, it concluded that their own high grade systems were secure.[145] Even worse than these limits to intelligence were the problems with its interpretation. Above all, on 30 November, Rommel, who "used to get this hunch that I knew where the enemy would give way",[146] interpreted fragments of intercepted traffic to indicate that the enemy would give way all over. He took wireless intelligence regarding the panic of one South African brigade in the south and silence in the north to mean victory was at hand. In fact, it was the Second New Zealand Division. On the assumption that silence meant security, Rommel turned from annihilation in the desert before him to pursue the mirage of Caporretto on the horizon. Instead of crushing the remnants of XXX Corps, and achieving a guaranteed victory, Rommel chose to drive into Egypt. He hoped to destroy the entire British position. Instead, he wrecked his own. As Rommel drove to the wire the New Zealanders captured his headquarters and unravelled his entire position.

In January 1942, however, Seebohm's company contributed to Rommel's revenge. Units of the main British force on the new front, the Second Armoured Brigade, adopted changes in the code names for units which betrayed the relief of forces at the front, and broadcast their tank states in clear, revealing their weakness. These failures showed that the British had not enforced the improvement of signals security on reinforcements entering the theatre. These revelations sparked Rommel's second offensive into Libya; the debate which senior British officers carried out in plain language over R/T regarding their reactions guided his steps towards victory.[147]

Unfortunately, the records for Seebohm's organization during Gazala have not survived, so any judgment regarding the value of its work is unusually provisional. However, remaining evidence indicates that during the first two weeks of Gazala, Seebohm's company provided far less useful material than it had done during Crusader. Even the problem with the use of plain language, the gravest flaw remaining in British signals security, had declined in scale. Still, this source gave the *Afrika Korps* unnecessary advantages, including perhaps the single most valuable one it ever received from signals intelligence, by showing how best to save one of the two German armoured divisions from deadly peril after the first day of the battle. In any case, by 11 June 1942—the eve of the decisive engagement in Gazala—through the interception of plain language messages, Seebohm's company reconstructed the Eighth Army's strength and dispositions. It also provided a useful if not entirely accurate picture of British intentions, which spurred Rommel on to one of his greatest triumphs. After the Knightsbridge battle, signals security seems to have been increasingly forgotten and senior British commanders driven to use R/T in the most desperate of circumstances. For a week, Seebohm's organization briefly matched its success in Crusader. It revealed the collapse of British command and the tempo of the rout of the Eighth Army, providing background knowledge which no doubt helped Rommel to score his stunning victory at Tobruk. However, this triumph was fleeting: in late June and early July 1942 at Mersa Matruh and El Alamein, the *Afrika Korps* experienced intelligence failures which were remarkable even by its own chequered standard.[148] By July 1942, it provided far less significant material than it had done in November 1941, though this still uncovered British deployments around El Alamein and provided useful hints as to their intentions.[149]

This decline in the success of German signals intelligence against the British army continued throughout the high summer of 1942 and down to the end of the war. Indeed, an authoritative postwar German study concluded, the British army's radio communications became "the most effective and secure of all those with which German communication intelligence had to contend". It is usually argued that the capture of Seebohm's company in July 1942 provided such proof of the flaws in British signals security that the latter immediately and radically tightened its procedure.[150] This is inaccurate. The British army more fundamentally improved its techniques of signals security in autumn 1941 than in autumn 1942, when, in essence, it simply strengthened the details of its system and reinforced its enforcement. Indeed, the reasons for this change do not even stem directly from technical improvements in signals security.

Throughout the British army's success in Crusader, its humiliation during Gazala and its triumph at El Alamein, its system of signals and security did not fundamentally change. By Crusader Britain had evolved a basic approach to such matters which it retained until 1945. The value of this system was initially constrained, however, because signals and security are the servants and not the masters of the field. Until July 1942 Rommel made the British fight the war he wanted, and at his pace. He could create confused conditions of warfare which broke the British command. Given their superior training and tactics, even when out of communication German units fought with effect; even Rommel in the course of his desert excursions had sometimes to appear at a decisive place before the British knew that it existed. British units, meanwhile, came on and went back in the same old way. British commanders, losing faith in their men and themselves, desperately striving to reassert their grip on events, looking for the means to form a picture of the battle, reached for the radio telephone like drowning men. This medium amplified the context of command but at a price: it increased the power of poor no less than of sound decision making. In the case of the British command this medium magnified all their worst characteristics: indecision, lack of discipline, the debating of orders, "belly-aching".

Yet after July 1942 this same system of signals and security met British needs, not because the former changed but because its circumstances did. The British army ceased to make war as the Germans wished. Instead, it made the *Afrika Korps* stand and fight like Englishmen. Fighting in enclosed spaces, possessing effective anti-tanks weapons and experienced personnel in large numbers, the British army finally had the opportunity to make a modified version of its C^3I system of 1939 function well. It was also led by the officer who was best suited to achieve this end. Montgomery mastered the British army which then beat the German one. He forced Rommel to fight surely rather than swiftly, a style of war at which the British matched the Germans and Montgomery surpassed Rommel. Montgomery quite deliberately slowed the pace of battle; he forced Rommel to fight at a speed which suited the less flexible British system of command and its less well-trained forces. It was precisely to deny Rommel the opportunity of ever again stamping his mark upon events, of regaining the initiative, that Montgomery adopted the cautious approach for which he has so often been criticized. The new commander of the Eighth Army, moreover, reached back for old memories. He adopted a modified version of the style of war by which British and Dominion armies had smashed the Germans in the summer and autumn of 1918. They would do so again. British units would come on in a new way while the level of confusion on the field would decline. This eased the psychological strain on British commanders, who needed to use R/T less often and with less desperation, and hence did so with greater security. In the British case, security was sapped by failure in the field and bolstered by success. From this basis the British army would shortly forge the most powerful and flexible C^3IS system of the Second World War.

6

INTELLIGENCE, UNCERTAINTY AND THE ART OF COMMAND IN MILITARY OPERATIONS

This paper will explore the connections between intelligence, the conduct of military operations and the art of command. It will first examine this relation in the period before the industrial revolution and the development of real time communications, particularly as it was reflected in the influential arguments of Carl von Clausewitz. It will also examine how far his ideas on intelligence and uncertainty shaped his theory of military operations. Second, this paper will study the relationship between intelligence, operations and command in the modern period. For this purpose, it will rest on a mature case study—Edward Drea's account of the use and misuse of intelligence in the Pacific War by General Douglas James MacArthur. Finally, this paper will consider the relationship between intelligence, operations and command in the future. It will link together such issues as one general's use of ULTRA and the interrelationship between intelligence, uncertainty and command in one war, and in the theory of war; it will use Clausewitz to illuminate a campaign and vice versa. This paper cannot develop every point which it mentions, but the hope is to show that these points merit further development and to provide a conceptual framework which may assist that process.

Intelligence and military operations

Any discussion of intelligence and war must begin with Clausewitz's arguments about uncertainty and the psychology of command. Such a discussion may also illuminate those ideas, which are fundamental to modern theories of war. The limits to this approach must be emphasized from the start. Both war and *On War* are complex matters. The discussion at hand will focus on only certain variables, excluding issues like technology, doctrine and politics. It will discuss only part of a phenomenon, not the whole.

Clausewitz believed that: "At the moment of battle, information about the strength of the enemy is uncertain, and the estimate of one's own is usually unrealistic."[1] The inability to collect accurate, relevant and complete data about the battlefield, about one's own forces no less than the enemy, was fundamental to Clausewitz's view that war lies within "the realm of uncertainty ... the realm of chance". These views about intelligence were axiomatic but not simplistic. Clausewitz was referring not to man's ability to know the world but to a commander's ability to understand a battle. He was a practical man writing for practical men, through generalizations drawn from his own experience and study. He matured in a military environment where accurate operational intelligence was difficult to acquire, while rumours in battle were rife, where many important factors (perhaps most of them) were known to be unknown, where slow and unreliable communications systems rendered information which was accurate when it was acquired inaccurate when it was received or, indeed, prevented it from ever being transmitted at all. In the short period of time available to act on the battlefield, the command, communication and intelligence services of his era could not provide clear, consistant and accurate information. A general could not know the facts about operations that he needed to know when he needed to know them. He could not know the enemy or the battle, therefore he would have to act without knowledge.

From these specific circumstances Clausewitz derived universal generalizations, which were accurate for his century but not necessarily for ours. He concluded that

> Many intelligence reports in war are contradictory; even more are false and most are uncertain ... most intelligence is false, and the effect of fear is to multiply lies and inaccuracies. As a rule most men would rather believe bad news than good, and rather tend to exaggerate the bad news. The dangers that are reported may soon, like waves, subside; but like waves they keep recurring, without apparent reason.

Under these circumstances, more intelligence reports make "us more, not less uncertain".[2] As will be shown below, that observation remains true even today, though the nature of the uncertainty has changed.

Some of this analysis was commonplace—soldiers had often emphasized the limited value of intelligence. Xenophon, for example, wrote "in time of war enemies often form designs on one another but seldom know the state of things among the party against whom their designs are formed. Therefore there is nothing other that can give counsel in such a case but the gods. They know all things and give signs to whomever they please by sacrifices, omens, voices and dreams".[3] Since his time, bureaucracy has replaced the gods. Clausewitz, moreover, essentially focused on the operational level during war, and on this plane, rather than that of strategy, is where the comments in this paper pertain. Clausewitz assumed that commanders should usually possess accurate intelligence about strategic issues, especially before war broke out. This, incidentally, explains why Clausewitz thought that strategic surprise was a good idea in theory but extremely difficult to execute in practice. "The movement of the enemy's columns into battle can be ascertained only by actual observation … but the direction from which he threatens our country will usually be announced in the press before a single shot is fired." "But uncertainty decreases the greater the distance between strategy and tactics; and it practically disappears in that area of strategy that borders on the political."[4] Similarly, whereas Clausewitz concluded that boldness was fundamental to operations, he specifically denied that it had the same place in strategy.

Clausewitz's views about operational intelligence were not simple, nor were they absolutely accurate, as the experience of at least one of his contemporaries shows. The Duke of Wellington believed and demonstrated that useful tactical and operational intelligence could be collected on the enemy, and devoted much personal attention to the task. A small but notable minority of British and American generals of that era adopted a similar view. Similarly, from an examination of the same base of data as Clausewitz, the Baron de Jomini drew different conclusions about operational intelligence. Over 2,000 years before, the influential Chinese theorist of strategy, Sun Tzu, had also praised—in fact, had exaggerated—the military value of intelligence.[5] Nonetheless, Clausewitz offered a powerful generalization about the effect of operational intelligence before the modern era, and these views were central to his theory. For Clausewitz, the lack of sure, current and effective intelligence causes uncertainty to dominate the field of battle, the psychology of command and the art of war. This is one of the major causes for the "friction" which distorts all attempts to act on intentions in the operational sphere. So deeply do these ideas about ignorance and uncertainty shape his logic and his theory of command and war, that amendments to them automatically force one to reconsider Clausewitz's arguments from the start. In fact, if these variables were to receive new values, then Clausewitz's equations would produce new solutions. This is true of Clausewitz's view that deliberate deception is almost always useless in war while intentional strategic surprise can rarely be achieved;[6] and, by extension, of even more fundamental matters, such as Clausewitz's belief that uncertainty and friction together prevent commanders from achieving precisely intended results precisely as intended; and of emphasis on intuition and determination in thought, on boldness in operations, his theories of understanding, command and action.

According to Clausewitz, few men function well amidst the uncertainty and ignorance, the friction and danger, of the battlefield. That environment can be mastered only by the "military genius", a man with "a very highly developed mental aptitude for a particular occupation", war. This figure combined the faculties which, "taken together, constitute the essence of military genius. We have said in combination, since it is precisely the essence of military genius that it does not consist in a single appropriate gift—courage, for example—while other qualities of mind or temperment are wanting or not suited to war."[7] Gifts of character, thought and action fuse into one to form the military genius. While pedantry—Clausewitz's favourite word of denigration—killed command, other intellectual powers gave it life. War "cannot be waged except by men of outstanding intellect",[8] possessing "a special type of mind ... a strong rather than a brilliant one",[9] with "a sensitive and discriminating judgement ... a skilled intelligence to scent out the truth"[10] and presence of mind, the ability to respond quickly and competently to the unexpected.

When assessing the personal characteristics of commanders, Clausewitz used the language of ideal types and the logic of the golden mean, recognizing that the absence from or the predominance in a personality of virtually any characteristic could be costly and that desirable characteristics were linked on a spectrum to undesirable ones. Thus, carried too far, determination could "degenerate into obstinacy".[11] Moreover, he was never dogmatic—to every "rule" or "principle" he describes, he immediately notes the exception or the limitation. None the less, two faculties in particular were the bedrock of military genius. Strength of character, the "ability to keep one's head at times of exceptional stress and violent emotion" allowed the reason of the commander to dominate his passions without destroying their drive.[12] Equally fundamental was determination—a willingness to "stand like a rock",[13] to act on belief despite uncertainty, to hold to a consistent course of action amidst confusion. Clausewitz commended the consistent pursuit even of an inferior course of action. He understood the old principle: order, counterorder, brings disorder.

> The role of determination is to limit the agonies of doubt and the perils of hesitation when the motives for action are inadequate ... when a man has adequate grounds for action—whether subjective or objective, valid or false—he cannot properly be called "determined". This would amount to putting oneself in his position and weighing the scale with a doubt that he never felt.[14]

Determination "is engendered only by a mental act; the mind tells man that boldness is required, and thus gives direction to his will. This particular cast of mind, which employs the fear of wavering and hesitating to suppress all other fears, is the force that makes strong men determined."[15] Determination (in Clausewitz's sense) alone could prevent action from being paralyzed by uncertainty and the delays and hesitation caused by thought.

The mind of the military genius combined reason and intuition—"an intellect that, even in the darkest hour, retains some glimmerings of the inner light which leads to truth ... the quick recognition of a truth that the mind would ordinarily miss or would perceive only after long study and reflection".[16] It combined thought and temperament into one whole greater than its parts.

> Knowledge must be so absorbed into the mind that it almost ceases to exist in a separate, objective way ... Continual change and the need to respond to it compels the commander to carry the whole intellectual apparatus of his knowledge within him ... By total assimiliation with his mind and life, the commander's knowledge must be transformed into a genuine capacity.[17]

Clausewitz's statement that "all great commanders have acted on instinct"[18] refers to this union of thought and temperament, which might be called informed intuition. This faculty of *coup d'oeil* alone can master uncertainty and ignorance and understand the battlefield.

> Circumstances vary so enormously in war, and are so indefinable, that a vast array of factors has to be appreciated—mostly in the light of probabilities alone. The man responsible for evaluating the whole must bring to his task the quality of intuition that perceives the truth at every point. Otherwise a chaos of opinions and considerations would arise, and fatally entangle judgement. Bonaparte rightly said in this connection that many of the decisions faced by the commander-in-chief resemble mathematical problems worthy of the gifts of a Newton or an Euler.[19]

> In the dreadful presence of suffering and danger, emotion can easily overwhelm intellectual conviction, and in this psychological fog it is so hard to form clear and complete insights that changes of view become more understandable and excusable. Action can never be based on anything firmer than instinct, a sensing of the truth. Nowhere, in consequence, are differences of opinion as acute as in war, and fresh opinions never cease to batter at one's convictions. No degree of calm can provide enough protection: new impressions are too powerful, too vivid, and always assault the emotions as well as the intellect.
>
> Only those general principles and attitudes that result from a clear and deep understanding can provide a comprehensive guide to action. It is to these that opinions on specific problems should be anchored. The difficulty is to hold fast to these results of contemplation in the torrent of events and new opinions. Often there is a gap between principles and actual events that cannot always be bridged by a succession of logical deductions. Then a measure of self-confidence is needed, and a degree of scepticism is also salutary. Frequently nothing short of an imperative principle will suffice, which is not part of the immediate thought-processes, but dominates it: that principle is in all doubtful cases to stick to one's first opinion and to refuse to change unless forced to do so by a clear conviction. A strong faith in the overriding truth of tested

principles is needed; the vividness of transient impressions must not make us forget that such truth as they contain is of a lesser stamp.[20]

Intelligence and risk-taking

This is the background to Clausewitz's art of war, the means by which the intelligent commander without intelligence should function in conditions of uncertainty. Boldness is central to this theory of operations.

> in what field of human activity is boldness more at home than in war? ... [B]oldness in war has its own prerogatives. It must be granted a certain power over and above successful calculations involving space, time, and magnitude of forces, for wherever it is superior, it will take advantage of its opponent's weakness. In other words, it is a genuinely creative force.

To Clausewitz, "a distinguished commander without boldness is unthinkable. No man who is not born bold can play such a role, and therefore we consider this quality the first prerequisite of the great military leader".[21]

Daring was valuable because it made commanders act and because, when they did act on its dictates, it multiplied all the conditions of uncertainty which frightened their opponents. In fact, a bold commander tended to create timid enemies—his own confidence thrust the burden of uncertainty onto the foe. While, in Clausewitz's view, a general might never be able to increase his own certainty, his boldness would heighten the enemy's uncertainty and thus indirectly compensate for his own limited intelligence. These observations remain true for all wars. Two hostile commanders stand at the opposite ends not only of the field of battle but also of a balance of uncertainty and an equilibrium of intelligence. This relationship is relative—by increasing the enemy's uncertainty, you decrease your own—and complex. Even when the quality of intelligence is better than assumed by Clausewitz, pursuit of an unexpected and high-risk strategy can still upset the balance of uncertainty—indeed, the subjective certainty engendered in a commander's mind by better intelligence may actually increase his opponent's chances to achieve success through an unexpected strategy. Daring also maximized one's chances to surprise the enemy in general and even to surprise him in a specific way through deliberate intent. Clausewitz held that this was impossible to do on the strategic or strategic/operational levels, but that it could be achieved at the operational or operational/tactical levels through a combination of boldness, determination, creative imagination and intellect. "Only the commander who imposes his will can take the enemy by surprise; and in order to impose his will he must act correctly."[22] Today, of course, the reverse is true—given such reliable and widespread devices as radar, complete surprise is almost impossible to achieve at the operational level and almost impossible to avoid at the strategic level.[23]

Scarcity multiplied the value of boldness. To Clausewitz, audacity is less dangerous in commanders than caution and less frequently found. "Given the same amount of intelligence [in a commander], timidity will do a thousand times more damage in war than audacity"; "a general cannot be too bold in his plans, provided that he is in full command of his senses, and only sets himself aims that he himself is convinced he can achieve"; "we always have the choice between the most audacious and the most careful solution. Some people think that the art of war always advises the latter. That assumption is false. If the theory does advise anything, it is the nature of war to advise the most decisive, that is, the most audacious"; "boldness grows less common in the higher ranks"; "no case is more common than that of the officer whose energy declines as he rises in rank and fills positions that are beyond his abilities".[24] In Clausewitz's equation, uncertainty and its psychological consequences reduce the frequency of boldness among commanders and increase the value of this scarce commodity on the field of battle. If all commanders were aggressive risk takers, this characteristic would define the military art but it would no longer offer a comparative advantage to any general. When most commanders are cautious, then audacity is at a premium. In a world of risk takers, the deliberately cautious man is king.

Yet boldness in itself is merely a matter of animal spirit and is inferior to temperament guided by reason. Few generals combine these characteristics, but they are the greatest of military geniuses.

> Boldness governed by superior intellect is the mark of the hero. This kind of boldness does not consist in defying the natural order of things and in crudely offending the laws of probability; it is rather a matter of energetically supporting that higher form of analysis by which genius arrives at a decision; rapid, only partly conscious weighing of the possibilities. Boldness can lend wings to intellect and insight; the stronger the wings, then, the greater the heights, the wider the view, and the better the results; though a greater prize, of course, involves greater risks.[25]

In the most desperate of hours, when material strength cannot prevail, the day may yet be saved by a commander who unifies "boldness and cunning"[26] (not intellect but "secret purpose", a combination of intuition and practical knowledge).

Clausewitz also noted a third combination of temperament and reason, one pointing away from the others and also from all of his own generalizations about the psychology of command. Caution was generally produced not by choice but by character, by an instinctive reflex to uncertainty. Worst-case analysis, he argued, was the natural response to the unknown. "Men always tend to pitch their estimate of the enemy's intentions too high than too low, such is human nature."[27] Sometimes, however, caution was the deliberate decision of a superior or cunning intellect. This combination of characteristics was the most rare, the most balanced, the most powerful of them all.

> Whenever boldness confronts timidity, it is likely to be the winner, because timidity in itself implies a loss of equilibrium. Boldness will be at a disadvantage only in an encounter with deliberate caution, which may be considered bold in its own right, and is certainly just as powerful and effective; but such cases are rare. Timidity is the root of prudence in the majority of men.[28]

Certain dimensions to Clausewitz's argument about "boldness" and "caution" merit careful attention. His main tool for analysis and synthesis was the ideal-type method. He distilled complex issues into their basic components and developed his concepts by posing simple and often extreme or contradictory statements against each other. Hence, if one takes any statement out of its context, one will distort his entire argument. The context for his discussion of "boldness" and "caution" is Book Three of *On War*, which defines the general phemonena which shape strategy as a whole. Here Clausewitz uses a conceptual model of the relationship between moral and mental qualities, and explains how all of these matters affect generalship as a whole. Not surprisingly, given this context, he treats commanders as if they possessed one and only one psychological characteristic. They are "all bold" rather than a mixture of characteristics, such as "mostly bold with a shade of caution". He also discusses the military effect of these psychological traits in the abstract, that is, how the characteristics of "boldness" or "caution" are affected by and affect the condition of "uncertainty". His generals are avatars of an ideal type rather than human beings. Clausewitz does not discuss in precise historical terms how the relative "caution" or "boldness" of one commander fighting another works within and affects specific circumstances. Indeed, no doubt he would have regarded this point as pedantic, and viewed these characteristics as being absolute rather than relative—that one is either bold or not, and when comparing two audacious commanders the point is that both are daring, not that one is more daring than the other. Given his concerns and his level of analysis, it was reasonable for Clausewitz to adopt such a means of assessment, but commentators must take care in transferring his generalizations about psychological characteristics to their own assessments of specific commanders. What is true of ideal types need not be true of individuals, especially not when, as will be shown below, "uncertainty", the central component in his theory, is open to revision.

Nor is it ever easy to define psychological characteristics such as "boldness". Are they determined by a general's behaviour—his usual or universal practices when selecting options—or by his essential and innate temperament? In any case, few commanders always behave in what is commonly regarded as an "audacious" or "cautious" manner. In the Second World War, for example, Erwin Rommel was daring in the desert but not at Normandy. Bernard Montgomery usually adopted a deliberately cautious approach, but he veered occasionally toward both daring and timidity. The behaviour of most commanders fluctuates within a given range on the spectrum between these traits. It usually involves some mixture of them.

Above all, confusion arises from terminology. In common usage, "boldness" is defined by such words as "aggression" and "high risk" and is identified with field commanders such as Rommel. This is not Clausewitz's usage—or, more precisely, not his only usage. He defined daring by reference not to a few specific sorts of behaviour but to the ability to act in an unexpected fashion. Under his usage, if everyone follows a mindless cult of the attack, then the risk taker would be reckless while the truly bold commander might be he who turns to a carefully calculated defensive battle. This is especially pertinent because he defined defence rather than any form of attack as being the strongest form of war. Clausewitz, of course, did not regard such circumstances as the general rule. In practice he usually did associate boldness on the battlefield with aggressive and high-risk actions. None the less, paradoxical as it might seem, in the Clausewitzian sense "boldness" could sometimes be defined by such words as "caution" and "calculation", if used in a creative or unexpected way. To Clausewitz, Fabius Maximus or Pericles would be "audacious"—indeed, Montgomery at Alam el-Halfa might have seemed a bolder commander than Rommel, by daring to use the tactics of 1918 against those of 1940, in an unexpected fashion and with unexpected success.

For example, Clausewitz defines deliberate caution as being "bold in its own right", presumably because, in his theory, this stems from the same combination of thought and temperament which produces "boldness governed by superior intellect". In another context, Clausewitz emphasizes that "when a man has adequate grounds for action—whether subjectively or objectively, valid or false—he cannot properly be called 'determined' ".[29] The same logic can be applied to "caution" or "daring"—the more adequate the grounds for action, or the greater the degree of certainty, the less significant the effect of psychological characteristics on decisions. To Clausewitz, daring is essential in circumstances of uncertainty, where it substitutes for lack of strength or intelligence. If, however, one possesses accurate and usable intelligence on the enemy and greater strength, then what seems to be a bold action by common usage would simply be an act of calculation by Clausewitz's terminology—a calculated risk. Under such circumstances calculation can replace boldness. If perfect intelligence could be acquired on the operational plane, daring would be no more relevant to a commander than it is to a chess player choosing whether or not to sacrifice a piece. Little daring is required to bet on a sure thing, little caution to avoid certain destruction. Intelligence can turn caution into daring, and daring into calculation. One must not confuse a calculated action for a bold one, nor aggression for audacity.

Hereafter in the text, to avoid confusion, we will refer to the common usage of the word "boldness" with the phrase "aggressive risk taking", as distinct from "boldness in Clausewitz's sense". At different times, the analysis will focus on two distinct issues—how intelligence affects (a) the range of behaviour of specific commanders on the spectrum between "caution" and "boldness"; and (b) the relative value on the battlefield of these psychological characteristics as ideal types, in the age of accurate and real-time intelligence.

It was on the foundation of uncertainty that Clausewitz formulated all his normative rules for command—especially the "imperative principle" ("in all doubtful cases to stick to one's first opinion and to refuse to change unless forced by a clear conviction") and the value of boldness. It is on this foundation that he defined the psychological characteristics for his ideal general. Only the "harmonious combination of elements", which make up "the essence of military genius"—in particular, daring, determination and informed intuition—can prevent the psychological effect of uncertainty from wrecking the quality of command. "With uncertainty in one scale, courage and self-confidence must be thrown into the other to correct the balance."[30]

During the twentieth century, however, changes in the status of intelligence at times eroded—although not ended—the reign of uncertainty over the field of battle. ULTRA and uncertainty may represent opposite poles regarding a commander's understanding in war. This is not to say that ULTRA represents perfect knowledge, but rather the closest approximation to perfect and usable knowledge that commanders can expect to receive. How has this affected the validity of the Clausewitzian paradigm? How has increased knowledge affected the psychology of command, the art of war, the qualities required for military genius and the value of caution against boldness as a characteristic of commanders? If intelligence provides "adequate grounds" for action, what significance do daring and determination (in Clausewitz's sense) retain? Any answers to these questions must take three general points into account.

First, intelligence does not produce command decisions, commanders do. Their personalities, their attitude toward risk, their military education, are the single most important factor in the use of intelligence and in the practice of operations.

Second, given the paradoxical nature of strategy, the greater the influence of Clausewitz's analysis of the psychology of war and his prescriptions for handling it, the less their accuracy, because by solving a problem he transformed it. Clausewitz defined means to manage uncertainty without reducing its scale, particularly through determination in the mind of the commander and boldness in his deeds. In the century and a quarter following his death his theory had mixed fortunes, but his prescriptions regarding these specific characteristics were influential, largely because they fit with those of other authorities and with the lessons which officers intuitively derived from the Napoleonic and Nelsonic experience.[31] Many armies, preeminently those of Germany, Japan and France before 1914, did follow his prescriptions, in however vulgarized a fashion; simultaneously, the Nelsonic tradition affected the British, German, Japanese and American navies in a similar way.

John Keegan has recently argued that Clausewitz's views are irrelevant to historians because they have never influenced soldiers.[32] One might as well argue that Newton has never influenced a gunner. Nor can Keegan's view survive contact with primary documents. The writings of several American generals of the Second World War, for example, are permeated with both pure and vulgarized forms of Clausewitz. Consider George S. Patton's lecture on "victory" of 1926:

> War is an art and as such is not susceptible of explanation by fixed formulae ... War [is] ... violent simplicity in execution [and] pale and uninspired on paper ... Insist on: Maximum distances; BOLDNESS; Prompt and accurate reports. Speed is more important than the lives of the [men at the] point. THE ENEMY IS AS IGNORANT AS YOU ... You must not be delayed by blufs. Bluf your self ... BE BOLD ... YOU ARE NOT BEATEN UNTIL YOU ADMIT IT, Hence DON'T ... The "Fog of war" works both ways. The Enemy is as much in the dark as you are. BE BOLD!!! [sic].

Similarly, in 1943 Patton wrote: "Never take counsel of your fears. The enemy is more worried than you are. Numerical superiority, while useful, is not vital to successful offensive action. The fact that you are attacking induces the enemy to believe that you are stronger than he is ... IN CASE OF DOUBT, ATTACK." Even Dwight Eisenhower insisted that instructors should

> treat war as the drama that it is rather than constantly reducing it to a science of marching tables and tonnage calculations. I do not decry the necessity for the scientific end of the education, I merely think that too many officers develop their thinking more and more along lines of mathematical calculations rather than realizing that calculations always go wrong.
>
> Many generals constantly think of battle in terms of, first, concentration, supply, maintenance, replacement, and, second, after all the above is arranged, a conservative advance. This type of person is necessary because he prevents one from courting disaster. But occasions arise when one has to remember that under particular conditions, boldness is ten times as important as numbers.[33]

None of this proves a direct connection between Clausewitz's ideas and these commanders' actions, but it does show that they explained their views to each other in Clausewitzian language. Until Keegan can come to terms with the evidence, his assertions are useless.[34]

Generals, of course, were not Clausewitzians in a concious sense. In taking fractions of his argument out of context and placing them in the context of the Napoleonic tradition, soldiers turned his precepts on their head—thus, Clausewitz's insistence on the importance of determination was used to defend obstinacy; his arguments about boldness did influence a mindless cult of the offensive; his idea of the military genius did justify the idea of commander as great man—or dictator. The point is simply the effect of this vulgarized variant of Clausewitz. While boldness (in Clausewitz's sense) remained as rare in the twentieth century as ever, aggressive risk taking did become more common among commanders than usual. In principle, as aggressive and high-risk behaviour on the battlefield becomes more common, it changes the context which defines its own value: the higher the ratio of generals who are aggressive risk takers, the less scarce that characteristic and therefore the smaller the comparative advantage it offers. The same is true of determination (in Clausewitz's sense). Increasingly, aggressive risk takers will fight each other, and both will lose the operational benefits stemming solely from this characteristic of temperament: indeed, the less aggressive of them might have the advantage. The more common aggressive risk taking is, moreover, the more other (and temperamentally cautious) commanders will be forced to find a counter to it, and the more they will succeed in doing so. For commanders on the battlefield, psychological characteristics do not have an absolute value but a relative one, defined against those of their adversaries. Their value will vary entirely with the circumstances. As aggressive risk taking becomes common, other commanders are given an incentive—an imperative—to create such circumstances. Thus, one might conclude, as a direct result of his observation, empirically based and tolerably accurate, aggressive risk taking tended to become less effective than Clausewitz had predicted and caution, though not timidity, more so.

Third, many commentators, merging Clausewitz, the cavalry spirit and the notion of "Great Captains", have treated aspects of war such as boldness of command and skill in manoeuvre as though these were universally the most—perhaps, the only—fundamental factors for victory. The following points apply not to Clausewitz but to views common among modern commentators. This view is most commonly attached to the influential ideas of Basil Liddell Hart, although many other military commentators have expressed such views. George S. Patton also spoke of "the Great Captains" and "the immortal line of mighty warriors".[35] Exponents of such ideas have tended to view war in romantic terms (as a form of art rather than a type of fight) and to adopt such beliefs as the idea that mobile operations must represent a higher form of the operational art than set-piece battles. While Clausewitz himself despised such an approach, it is particularly pronounced among members of the romantic school of military history, with their adulation of the romantic school of military commanders, especially in its German form. They embrace several fallacies. These views fall prey to the idea of the "master cause"—in effect, they treat just a few of the many factors involved in a process as being the only necessary causes and therefore sufficient causes for it. As a result, certain factors in a process are overemphasized while others, perhaps equally important, are forgotten, because they are treated as passive conditions.[36] The views in question, moreover, are ahistorical. The role of each individual aspect of command and military prowess varies with the conditions of time and place. There is no universal value for any one of these characteristics nor any constant basket of weights for the whole—the importance of all of these matters varies from one period to another. *Ipso facto*, this is also true of the characteristics of any single commander. Furthermore, one common means used to derive the nature and determine the value of these characteristics—the comparison of commanders across the ages and the pursuit of the "Great Captain"—is useful as a heuristic device but fatally misleading when applied as a precise and meaningful tool of analysis. "Great Captains" are not people, they are a Platonic ideal—an idea regarding how to gauge the quality of individual commanders. This ideal, in turn, rests on implicit assumptions about the universal value of specific military characteristics—that is, intellectual presuppositions are smuggled into an analysis and then uncovered as empirically demonstrated conclusions. Certain military qualities are fetishized, others are ignored, without any rigorous justification being offered for this selection of values, and then certain commanders are treated as archetypes for these allegedly universal qualities, as if the characteristics of Hannibal would have automatically made him master of the western front. While a historical record demonstrates the usual (although not universal) inferiority of a Blucher to a Bonaparte, how can one meaningfully compare two contemporaries who never fought each other, let alone commanders from different epochs; and from these hypothetical comparisons, how can one derive lessons regarding the universal value of any single characteristic of command or of war?

These issues of theory can be illuminated through a study of the war fought by Douglas James MacArthur and his lieutenants against Japanese enemies, powerful but ignorant, who could not use intelligence to reduce the scale of uncertainty but instead simply sought to manage this effect through a vulgarized version of the Clausewitzian art of war and of selected traditions from their own warfare. These conclusions can be compared to Allied experiences in Europe between 1942 and 1945 against a German enemy with similar characteristics. This intelligence record will provide a mirror for generals—by comparing what a given officer believed was the case with his actions one can reconstruct his calculus of military actions, his nature as a commander—and for generalship.

ULTRA in the Pacific

Seven months in the Pacific produced two of the most celebrated events in the history of intelligence. While ample attention has been paid to the role of codebreaking in the United States' disaster at Pearl Harbor and its triumph at Midway, the studies of "ULTRA" (or "special intelligence", as American officers more commonly called it) in any other part of the Pacific War have been limited in quantity and quality. A bridge has now been thrown across this gap in scholarship. The primary strength of Edward Drea's *MacArthur's Ultra, Codebreaking and the War Against Japan, 1942–1945*[37] is his analysis of how one source of intelligence worked, how it fit in with the rest, how the material which it produced was assessed and used by commanders in a single theatre and how all of this affected the course of one campaign. The evidence on these issues is better than usual in the study of military intelligence and Edward Drea has mined it with energy and craft. Drea, a master of the American records on MacArthur's campaigns, has also utilized the surviving Japanese documents with unprecedented thoroughness. *MacArthur's Ultra* possesses greater analytical sophistication and covers more chronological terrain than the best previous accounts of intelligence during the Pacific War, and good ones, the works of Gordon W. Prange *et al.*[38] It is entirely superior in analysis, synthesis and research to lesser but still useful studies, such as those by John Costello, Edwin Layton, Ronald Spector and Ronald Lewin. Drea's account is sober and multi-causal. It is far from the speculation, sensationalism and exaggeration of the role of intelligence which mark so many studies of that subject such as those by Ladislas Farago and James Rusbridger, and which mar even the works of Lewin and Costello.[39] Drea does not stretch evidence, misquote it, invent it or ignore it, nor does he ever forget that intelligence by itself can never win a war. On the other hand, he demonstrates that ULTRA was the decisive source of intelligence in the southwest Pacific, one which fundamentally shaped the course of the Pacific War.

MacArthur's Ultra is essential on two counts. It is the first serious study of signals intelligence in the southwest Pacific theatre and it is the best single study of that campaign as a whole. While Edward Drea is far from ignorant of the practice of intelligence, he is not a specialist in its study. Thus, he is immune to ills which specialists are heir to, particularly the tendency to exaggerate the significance of intelligence, and his judgments on such issues are of special value. Drea's discussion of the technical aspects of the topic— the communication and cryptographic systems of the Imperial Japanese Army and Navy (IJA and IJN), the techniques by which allied cryptanalysts attacked these codes and the process by which the product was distributed, analyzed and utilized—is useful to the expert while remaining comprehensible to the common reader. His account of codebreaking organizations and the role of data-processing machines as a cryptanalytical tool in the South West Pacific Area Command (SWPAC) will particularly interest students of cryptology. Nor does Drea overrate the role of codebreaking. He places it in the context of all sources of information and he pays unusual attention to often-overlooked elements of signals intelligence, such as traffic analysis. No other book about the Second World War explains with more authority exactly what information was available to any Allied commander and his staff on a daily basis and how this affected their decisions. Few match the rigour by which Drea compares the causal role of ULTRA to that of its fellow factors—operational, logistical, doctrinal, topographical, personal—in the shaping of events. This work ranks alongside those of Ralph Bennett among the best, not to mention, the few, scholarly studies of signals intelligence during the Second World War.[40]

Drea takes as his text the dictum of Bennett and of F.H. Hinsley that there was not one ULTRA but several—that the role and importance of special intelligence varied with time and theatre. Certainly there were fundamental differences between the ULTRAs of the Pacific and Europe, and for technical, tactical, organizational and political reasons. In Europe, ULTRA emanated from a centralized bureau controlled by one country, which coordinated the attack on every code of two others. Codebreaking against Japan was produced by several agencies of three allies (Australia, Great Britain and the United States) working in a decentralized fashion. The USN and the American army ran separate organizations, each divided between autonomous bureaus in Washington and the Pacific, while the cryptanalysts in Delhi had greater independence than any other sub-section of British codebreaking. This frustrated those who at the time held that only a centralized system could foster efficient cryptanalysis, and that frustration has shaped the historiography of the period. It has led, in particular, to the claim that because SWPAC sabotaged centralization, it must have abused ULTRA.[41] This may be true but no one has proved it. Certainly the loose system of the Pacific met the needs of the USN in 1942, while Drea argues that it always worked for SWPAC. However effective in technical terms, this system had obvious political consequences: it left ample room for bureaucratic buccaneering. Nothing could have better suited MacArthur—a commander of messianic self-confidence, a well-honed public relations machine, remarkable political power, a desire for total sway over his own sphere and the determination to control Allied strategy against Japan. He had unique control over codebreaking in his theatre: "Central Bureau", MacArthur's signals intelligence agency, was never subsumed in the integrated Anglo-American cryptanalytical system. This remained his private intelligence bureau. It produced MacArthur's ULTRA for MacArthur's aims—to crush the foe and to influence his friends.

Drea, by implication, leaves his readers with the impression that ULTRA in Europe became technically more successful and militarily more useful in a steady, regular and virtually unbroken fashion as time went by. While this argument is tolerably accurate as a broad generalization about the whole period between 1939 and 1945, it is not true of specific matters during smaller periods of time, such as the campaigns in the Atlantic and in Africa between 1940 and 1943. The history of ULTRA in these two theatres and in the southwest Pacific is very similar, replete with sudden and complete cryptanalytical successes or defeats, reversals of cryptological fortune, situations where a total inability to penetrate one of the enemy's cryptographic systems coincided with total access to others, fluctuations in the military value of a mature source of intelligence. Moreover, in these campaigns technical achievements in cryptanalysis and success on the field of battle were not linked in a simple pattern. Arguably, in the Mediterranean campaign ULTRA could have been most useful when it was technically most primitive rather than most mature, because of the prevailing strategic and operational conditions. When it was most primitive, force to space ratios were low as were both sides strengths; hence, victories with decisive consequences were possible. By the time that it became mature, both sides were locked into a prolonged struggle of attrition.[42] The differences between the history of ULTRA in Europe and the Pacific are not so stark and simple as Drea suggests. They also exist in areas which are not discussed in his formal and explicit analyses. In his formal explanations of the causes for events, Drea appears to explain the differences between the effect of ULTRA in Europe and the Pacific primarily in terms of the technical success of cryptanalytical bureaus and the personal predilections of commanders. He does not always explicitly incorporate two other factors, the limitations to ULTRA as a source of intelligence—what material it could and could not provide—and the issue of how far such material could and could not be used in distinct operational and strategic circumstances. On the other hand, these matters are integrated implicitly into his narrative, and effectively so.

The history of ULTRA in Europe and the Pacific also differed. In Europe the sequence of events regarding Allied success against German cryptographic systems was broadly similar, although the date at which the process began varied significantly with the German service in question. First came a period of limited and often fragmentary access to specific Enigma keys, coupled with major problems in assessing such material. Then followed a cryptanalytical breakthrough, which produced high-level material on a continual and current basis and led, finally, to a long period of mature exploitation, when analysts had determined the main lines of the enemy's organization, could draw powerful conclusions about its operational intentions and precise ones about its capabilities, and were almost always accurate about such fundamental matters as the enemy's order of battle.

Little of this was true of the Pacific, although that theatre was at first glance ideally suited for signals intelligence. Forces were scattered over millions of square miles and often lacked direct links by cable; hence radio dominated communications. Prisoners of war and agents were less effective sources of intelligence than usual while captured documents, photo reconnaissance and signals intelligence were much more important than usual. In the wireless war the Allies had two further advantages: the IJA and IJN lacked sophisticated signals intelligence services and placed rare faith in the formal security of their cryptographic systems. The operational circumstances of the Pacific increased these opportunities (See Maps 6.1 and 6.2). Force-to-space ratios were extraordinarily low. Most elements of both sides were rarely in direct contact with the enemy and the disposition, strength and intentions of such forces were masked and difficult to calculate. Rarely has possession of the initiative carried such consequences. It was unusually difficult to recover one's balance if struck by an unexpected blow—weeks might be required to redeploy naval or air forces from one base to another, months to build the infrastructure needed to maintain large forces in a new

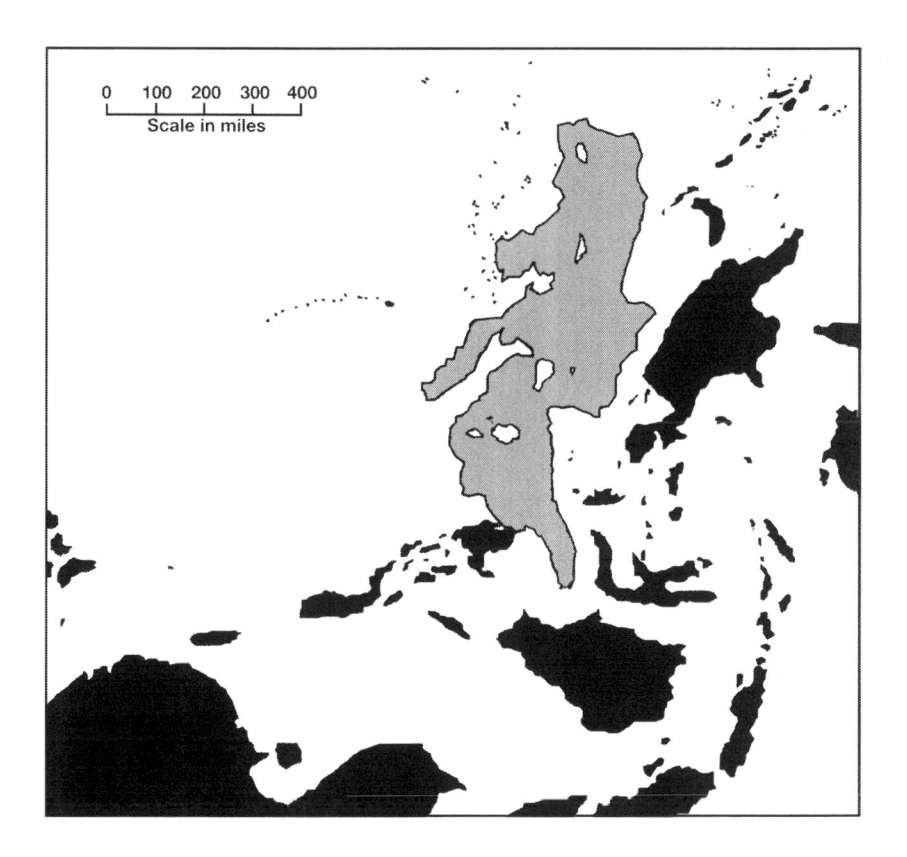

Map 6.1 The Mediterranean and Western Pacific theaters compared

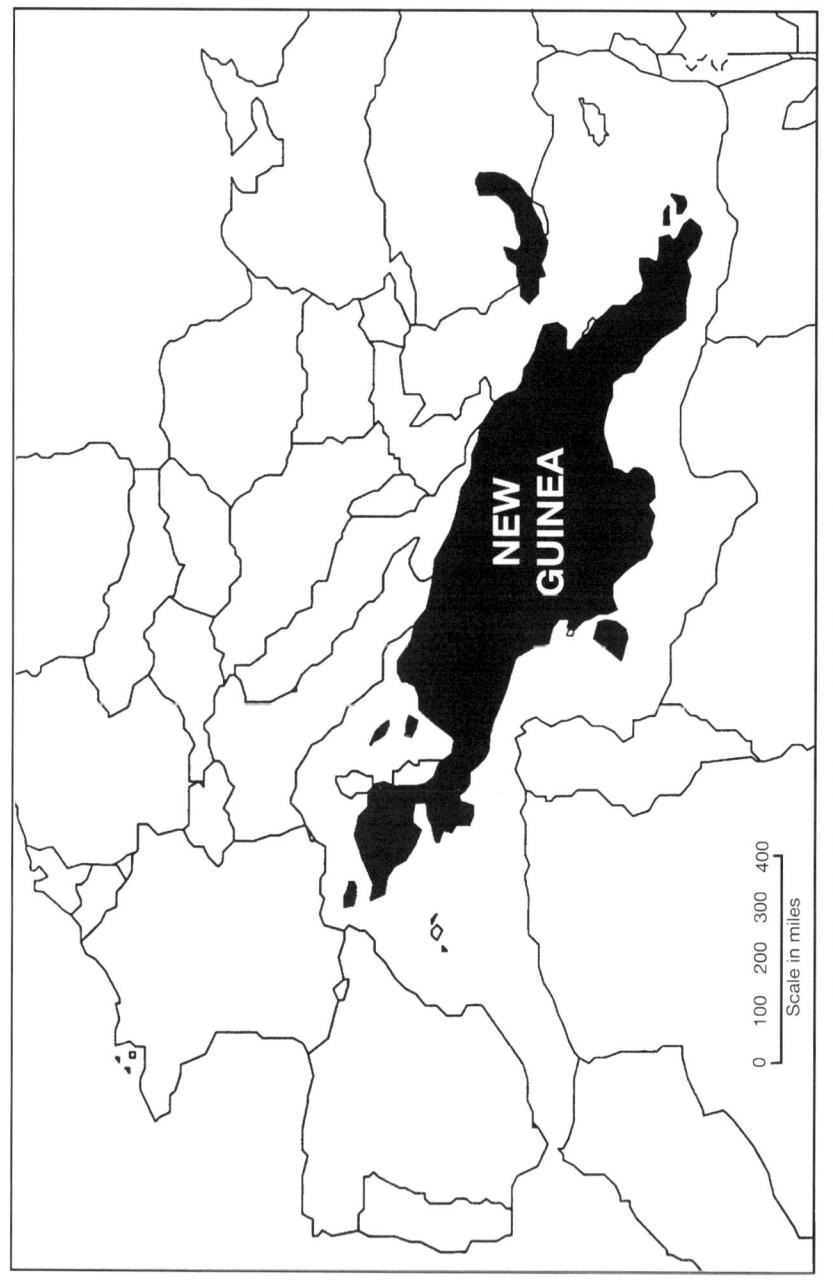

Map 6.2 The New Guinea and Mediterranean theaters compared

rea or to move soldiers by sea or land. The war in New Guinea, in particular, was a sideshow in which neither side could easily replace its losses. The destruction of 20,000 men or 200 airplanes, or the capture of one supply base could transform a campaign in a territory with the geographical space of the Mediterranean theatre. Operations in New Guinea, for example, turned on the annihilation of forward Japanese airbases in August 1943 and on the battles of the Bismarck Sea and Hollandia, in all of which absolute Japanese material losses were quite small. The ability to concentrate one's strength against the enemy's weakness, to catch it by surprise and to profit from a knowledge of its intentions were unusually large; this was doubly true for that most risky and complex of military operations, amphibious assaults. Such circumstances generally provide the greatest opportunities for success through signals intelligence.

Events did not work quite as might have been anticipated, because of the IJA's organization and its cryptographic systems. The IJA and the IJN relied on superenciphered codebooks. While the latter were slower to use than the machine cipher systems of the era, more labour intensive and unable to carry as heavy a load of traffic before becoming cryptologically vulnerable, and the distribution of new books and tables was dogged by difficulties, they were a perfectly good means of defence if used with parsimony and skill. In practice, they were as secure as the technically more sophisticated Enigma and Purple systems; at least changes in superencipherment tables sometimes denied Allied cryptanalysts complete access to Japanese codes. Moreover, these systems often were used with skill, if not always so. From early 1942 the IJN's most important radio signals were more frequently read by the enemy than not, although access might be lost for several weeks at a time when codebooks or superencipherment tables were changed. In December 1941, however, none of the IJA's systems had been penetrated. Thereafter its security procedures were sound. They were always better than the practices of the armies of Germany, Italy and the Soviet Union and, until 1944, at least equal to those of the American or British Commonwealth forces. There was one solitary if crucial exception to that rule, the IJA's "water transport" system, used for Army traffic about troop and logistical shipments by sea. This was created in December 1942 and solved by Allied cryptanalysts four months later.[43]

Thus the Allies had more or less complete mastery over all codes regarding Japanese maritime matters. That was the fundamental priority in this genuinely combined services war, where the struggles on land, sea and air were far less self-contained than in Europe. However, the IJA's cryptographic systems for use within divisions (and sometimes between garrisons and their immediate superiors) were the most secure of any army of the entire Second World War. They were never once solved. Admittedly, the elements within Japanese divisions needed relatively little intercommunication by radio, given their operational circumstances—had they been forced to signal to the degree required under European conditions, either Japanese command within divisions would have been strangled or the security of their codes would have collapsed.[44] The IJA had not found a general solution to the problem of middle-grade cryptographic systems and communications within divisions, merely an effective solution to its own particular difficulties in that sphere. Until January 1944 western cryptanalysts also failed to penetrate the superenciphered codebooks used for communication between Japanese formations. Only when the Japanese 20th Division failed to destroy its codebooks during a withdrawal in New Guinea did the Americans finally break in, assisted by subsequent compromises of a similar nature.[45] As so often, defeat on the field of battle crippled signals and cryptographic security, and compromises of security fathered operational catastrophes, in a vicious circle. None the less, for the first half of the Pacific War, more signals intelligence about Japanese land operations was acquired through cryptanalysis of naval than of army traffic, just as at the same time solutions of *Luftwaffe* traffic were the main source of ULTRA on the German army. Of all the Axis fighting services the IJA, along with the German U-boat command, possessed by far the hardest cryptographic shell. In both cases the nut cracked only because the Allies acquired copies of the system without the enemy knowing the fact. Hence, from the spring of 1942 Allied commanders in the southwest Pacific could profit from traffic analysis against IJN and IJA stations, along with mastery of the IJN's operational traffic, its "water transport" systems and, after April 1943, of the IJA's "water transport" systems. Until January 1944, however, rather late in the day, they had no access to the IJA's operational traffic. After that date, material of this sort flooded in.

Nor was this the only problem at hand. In both world wars, the primary task of signals intelligence was to master the enemy's order of battle, after which its capabilities were much easier to define and its intentions less difficult to determine. This task worked best against an enemy with a predictable chain of command. It was difficult to achieve against the IJA, because the success of signals intelligence varies with the cultural, structural and doctrinal background of the target. The IJA did not organize its forces on the conventional western pattern. To a greater degree than any other army of the Second World War, Japanese commands were established in the form of *ad hoc* task forces, composed of a unique *mélange* of units drawn from many different formations, often designated only by the name of their senior officer; elements of a single division were routinely distributed hundreds of miles from the others. The location of a given German regiment normally indicated the presence of a specific division. The strength of such forces could usually be calculated with a tolerable degree of accuracy, and sometimes with extraordinary precision. This was not true of the IJA nor of many non-western armies during this century, such as the Turks during the First World War and the Iranians during the Gulf War of the 1980s.[46]

Structural links between the IJA's units and formations were loose, by western standards—the identification of a given unit did not necessarily indicate anything about any formation, or vice versa. When reconstructing the IJA's order of battle, the basic building block was the battalion rather than the division; this rendered reconstruction more difficult by an entire order of magnitude. In 1937 the British Military Attaché in Tokyo, F.S.G. Piggott, who had controlled intelligence for the Second British Army during the last phase of the great war, wrote that "it was easier to draw up the German Order of Battle in France in 1918, than the Japanese Order of Battle in China in 1937".[47] This difficulty continued in various forms throughout the Pacific War. Until early 1944, the Allies had a surprisingly limited grasp of the enemy's order of battle both in theatres and garrisons. Then, through the break into IJA operational traffic and the difficult technical task of assessing "address groups" (the elements within any cryptographic system which identify the transmitter and recipient of messages), Central Branch was able to determine the location, boundaries and titles of all IJA headquarters, and therefore the disposition and deployments of all its higher formations. Such material had obvious strategic value. Here, as ever, intelligence was entirely irrelevant to grand strategy, and secondary in the formulation of strategic objectives at the theatre level—such issues are decided by the interests of states and the attitudes of statesmen. The material from ULTRA, however, was sometimes fundamental to the execution of theatre-level strategy. It frequently guided the selection between and the planning for major operations, and it was essential for the success of the most effective operational options available to SWPAC, outflanking or bypassing. At the same time, however, it was too imprecise to meet many critical operational needs, such as to uncover with certainty the strength and composition of specific commands.

When compared to the norm with signals intelligence, ULTRA in the southwest Pacific was unusually effective in tracing enemy intentions but surprisingly unsuccessful in determining their capabilities—usually an easier task. When compared to its peak in Europe, ULTRA in the Pacific never achieved complete mastery over the enemy's order of battle. After accounting for these differences, the two were roughly equal as sources for strategic intelligence and had a roughly equal effect on strategy and the planning of major operations. The situation was more complex at lower levels of war. Compared to western Europe, ULTRA in the southwest Pacific was generally a less thorough and accurate source of operational intelligence, but conditions on the battlefield allowed intelligence more easily to shape dramatic operations. Therefore, in the southwest Pacific ULTRA of technically lesser quality contributed to operational triumphs which matched anything in Europe. In the Pacific, ULTRA's greatest value lay in addressing the issues of how to execute lines of strategy and where (or where not) to begin major operations. Once direct contact had been established with the enemy, however, most information was acquired through tactical means in which the Allies had no particular advantages, and the balance of intelligence between the IJA and the Americans moved toward equilibrium.

These characteristics stemmed not merely from Japanese cryptographic and military–bureaucratic systems, but from the nature of ULTRA and of intelligence assessment at SWPAC. ULTRA was the most sophisticated source of intelligence during the Second World War. It was never a perfect one; it was not always the best. ULTRA took words straight from the enemy's mouth, but those words were not always straightforward. As Ralph Bennett has written: "Ultra always told the truth, but not always the whole truth."[48] ULTRA's output fell between two poles, one best described by words such as "transparent" and "self-evident" and the other by terms like "opaque" and "ambiguous". The meaning of messages of the first type seemed to be intuitively clear when compared to the framework of common sense, as when an enemy commander outlined his imminent intentions, or his quartermaster defined their order of battle, or a convoy signalled its location. In all such cases, the nature of the content was intuitively self-evident. Conversely, the content of traffic of the second type was, in itself, ambiguous—its meaning could be determined only through formal and frequently elaborate analysis. Fragmentary bits of intelligence about the enemy's dispositions and order of battle, for example, often provide value only through the derivation of inferences which can be acquired solely through the application of a reasoned, but seemingly arbitrary and arcane, process. The first sort of material is relatively easy to understand and trust and use; the second is more difficult on all of these counts. MacArthur's headquarters handled material of the first kind very well. This was not true of the second. It could not master the higher level of analysis needed to exploit such material, work which Bletchley Park and Allied commands in Europe did so well. Hence, SWPAC's intelligence assessments were flawed and often dismally bad.

In this sphere MacArthur's headquarters was the least successful and among the least competent senior commands of the western allies. Here the critics of SWPAC's use of ULTRA have much ammunition to find. Drea does not quite recognize the weakness of SWPAC's performance, but close reading of his narrative proves the point. He describes a constant pattern. SWPAC made effective use of unambiguous information, "hot" and "hard", about enemy intentions and capabilities, while its assessments of ambiguous material ranged from mediocre to poor. In particular, SWPAC misconstrued the enemy's strength and dispositions in its planning before battle after battle. While such errors were most routine and extreme during the first year of the war, they occurred even to its end.

This stemmed primarily from the personality of MacArthur himself. He was not the type of officer to encourage the objective analysis of intelligence. He wished to see material which supported the aims he had already defined and proved that they were good. Anything else he would ignore—nothing else could more easily be baked to suit his appetite than ambiguous material. MacArthur defined the nature of his meals through the selection of a cook who would always season his meals according to his master's taste. His intelligence chief, General Charles Willoughby, was almost always and significantly wrong whenever his data was not self-evident and extraordinarily precise in nature. Even then his estimates were usually mediocre, with a few brilliant exceptions, derived from self-evident ULTRA traffic, most notably before the attack on Hollandia in 1944. MacArthur once stated that there had been only three great military intelligence chiefs in history "and mine is not one of them".[49] This was an understatement—under MacArthur, Willoughby is a candidate for one of the three worst intelligence chiefs of the Second World War. It was also self-condemnation. Intelligence can only be as good as its master. Enlightened and open-minded generals will always gain more from it than will those who know what they want to be told and who refuse to hear anything else. Some men use lamposts for illumination, some simply for support; and several subordinate headquarters under MacArthur's command, American or Australian, did assess ULTRA on the IJA better than SWPAC.

MacArthur, Willoughby and other staff officers at SWPAC also failed to understand the Japanese way of war, the strategic calculus which determined the range of options Japanese commanders believed that they had and how they would choose among them. Drea does not systematically assess American preconceptions about Japan and its army and their effect on American military operations, although few historians are better suited to this task and he does not entirely share the influential views of John Dower on that topic.[50] None the less, Drea demonstrates that SWPAC's predictions of Japanese behaviour rested on cultural and military ethnocentrism, ignorance of the enemy's doctrine and the belief that the enemy must act as Americans would in their place. Not surprisingly, down to the end of the war, Japanese decisions continually surprised SWPAC and many of its subordinate commanders—although not all. The Australian General Thomas Blamey and the American General Walter Krueger understood the IJA's style of operations quite well and that knowledge shaped their professional if unpublicized operations against it. ULTRA sometimes preserved MacArthur from the costs of such errors. It was perhaps the only kind of intelligence which could have overcome the combination of ethnocentrism and mediocre assessment at SWPAC and the unusual problems involved in determining the enemy's capabilities. Thus ULTRA may have been even more crucial to MacArthur's success than Drea allows, yet he allows a great deal. His account merits attention and some extension.

In the Pacific War, the period between August 1942 and September 1943 was one of equilibrium and attrition between forces roughly equal in quantity, quality and initiative. The build up of Allied strength in New Guinea and the Solomon Islands turned the forward edge of Japanese conquest into the central battlefield of the Pacific War. The operations in these areas cost Japan more than the United States. Japan was less able to replace losses, because its casualties in aircraft, pilots, transport vessels and soldiers substantially exceeded those of the Allies, while the latter used their forces with greater economy and effect. In this campaign, the sources and targets of military power were armed men and the means to keep them armed. Both sides strove to maintain large forces in some of the least developed places between the poles, where virtually no logistical infrastructure or networks of physical communications existed. In such a war and such an environment, the United States held the strongest cards. Nowhere could it more thoroughly outmatch Japan than in creating an entirely new system of military logistics and in fighting a war of material attrition. Japan, conversely, had made precisely the errors defined by Clausewitz:

> Since the object of the attack is the possession of the enemy's territory, it follows that the advance will continue until the attacker's superiority is exhausted ... What matters therefore is to detect the culminating point of victory with discriminate judgement.
>
> One defence is ... not exactly like another, nor will defence always enjoy the same degree of superiority over attack. In particular this will be the case in a defence that follows directly the exhaustion of an offensive—a defence whose theater of operations is located at the apex of an offensive wedge thrust forward deep into hostile territory ... a defence that is undertaken in the framework of an offensive is weakened in all its key elements.[51]

Japan, instead, expanded until it could go no further. There, at its level of incompetence, it fought with all its power and to the death. The battlefields of New Guinea and the Solomon Islands were simply too large and too far forward to suit its tiny logistical and transport capabilities. Every mile further the battles were from its main centres of power, Tokyo, Manila and Singapore, the greater relatively its logistical problems and the more exposed its lines of communication. Japan was fighting precisely the war which least suited its material resources, a prolonged and costly battle of attrition beyond easy reach of its supply system.

This drove Japan, as a matter of routine, to take great and often costly risks, such as shipping divisions to the most forward ports under its control, and into the maw of enemy air and naval strength, or operating hundreds of aircraft from the same base, all vulnerable to one massive onslaught. Japan's fighting and logistical services entered a vicious circle, which progressively weakened their ability to fight anywhere at all. For as both sides strained their muscles to strangle the other in New Guinea and the Solomon Islands, Allied forces began to slash the exposed limbs of Japanese logistics. The southwest Pacific witnessed a terrible campaign of maritime interdiction, rendered even more deadly and one-sided by Japan's failure to retaliate in kind and its incompetence in convoy escort. These engagements eroded still further the relative ability of Japanese logistics to support a prolonged war of attrition. By early 1944, exactly as the IJA adopted a strategy of human (though not material) attrition, Japan had lost the naval and air strength needed to back it. Japan was on the verge of losing any use from every single soldier and tons of supplies on its forward defensive perimeter from the Marshal Islands to Burma.

These American engagements also directly shaped operations—the battle of the Bismarck Sea drowned not merely a division but any hope for Japanese strategic initiative in New Guinea. Similarly, preemptive airstrikes wrecked Japan's forward airbases on that island, largely because it failed to develop an effective early warning system for air defence or to use properly its few radar sets. This crippled Japan's air performance and increased the scale of its aircraft losses.

Between August 1942 and February 1944 the great American victories in the Pacific lay in the war of attrition. No doubt some such success would have occurred in a world without ULTRA but, as Drea demonstrates, in the world as it was these triumphs did rest on the foundation of signals intelligence. As a result, small American forces were used with optimum effect against their logistical and air targets. A few hundred aircraft and a few dozen submarines on station did not have to hunt tiny and elusive targets in an area of a million square miles. The location, strength and intentions of those targets were known; little American effort was wasted and few opportunities were missed. Intelligence was the father of both the economy and the concentration of force. It came close to ending uncertainty. It allowed precisely intended actions to be executed precisely as intended. It ensured that all available American naval and air power would be used effectively against the enemy. It turned aggressive risk taking into calculated risk. MacArthur's air force commander, General George Kenney, was no better than SWPAC in dealing with ambiguous information. Yet Kenney received vast amounts of "hot" and "hard" material from ULTRA, which he trusted and used in one of the most successful campaigns of interdiction and the acquisition of air supremacy ever waged by any air force. Few commanders have married intelligence to operations so well and with such effect.

Events on the ground in New Guinea during 1942–1943 took a different form. Despite the breathtaking self-sacrifice of Japanese soldiers and their formidable military qualities, the IJA lost more men than the Allies in every major engagement. Nor could it match their material resources. On the tactical and operational levels, however, the IJA's attacks often caught the Allies by surprise and made them fight in areas where their advantages in material could not easily be deployed. When on the defence, the IJA forced the Allies to launch slow and costly battles of attrition. All this offered

Japan the chance for perpetual check in New Guinea. If forced to fight on the IJA's terms, the limited resources of SWPAC could do no more than slowly reconquer a wilderness. This is precisely what happened during the middle game of this campaign. Whether the Allies used their armies clumsily, as under MacArthur in the summer of 1942, or with skill, as under Blamey in the spring and summer of 1943, they were not pursuing a winning strategy. Instead, they played directly into the IJA's policy of delay, human attrition and the grinding of American will. Nor was ULTRA of great value in these operations. In technical terms, it was in a primitive state. ULTRA produced little material directly relevant to land operations and that which did pertain was difficult to interpret. It sometimes illuminated the enemy's strategic redeployments to the theatre but MacArthur's armies (unlike his air forces) were in no position to act on that material. Given the nature of the terrain and the naval and air balance between the adversaries, Allied land forces had a limited range of options, all of which led to a pattern of stereotyped operations along narrow and predictable channels of advance. So long as this continued, SWPAC could never take centre stage in American strategy nor could ULTRA offer more than marginal assistance on the field of battle.

At the turn of 1944 all of these things changed, for a brief but crucial period, as did MacArthur as military commander. His record in the Pacific before April 1944 and after November 1944 was mixed in quality. On the one hand, he evinced aggression, willpower, a gambler's instinct and a flair for amphibious operations. Against that stood his penchants for misreading enemy intentions, for issuing unrealistic orders to his men and for attacking directly where the enemy was strongest; his operations on land, moreover, tended to become bogged down in battles of attrition, a style of operations in which he was not gifted. Conversely, in mid-1944 MacArthur conducted an impressive campaign which turned his command from the periphery to the centre of Allied strategy in the Pacific. Not coincidentally, this occurred precisely when ULTRA finally and suddenly penetrated into the IJA's operational traffic. That was a necessary cause for MacArthur's successes, but it was not a sufficient one. The side with superior intelligence also possessed greater military power and favourable opportunities to fight a war of manoeuvre. The war of attrition had gutted Japanese naval and air resources, the bulwarks needed to brace its defence perimeters against major blows. American military power heavily outweighed that of Japan in quantity and quality, while the breaching of the Bismarck barrier and the cracking of the shield of the Marshal Islands opened a 1000 mile line of sea room for a campaign of manoeuvre toward Japan's inner defence perimeter. On New Guinea the IJA remained formidable, with roughly as many soldiers as SWPAC possessed, but it was strong in only a few locations along a 1,000-mile coastline. Elsewhere it was not merely weak—it almost literally did not exist. Its logistical structure consisted of one major supply centre and a handful of small ones, linked by coastal shipping and portage on human backs through roadless bush. This system could sustain the forward crust of the IJA against the heaviest direct thrust which SWPAC could launch, but just one deep and heavy amphibious blow might shatter it beyond hope of repair. In 1944, unlike 1943, such blows could be launched. Japanese air forces on New Guinea might endanger or annihilate amphibious operations but they were far weaker than Kenney's command and, as ever, they were vulnerable to preemptive airstrikes. Admiral Halsey's Third Fleet in the south/central Pacific generally tied down the IJN. The latter, however, could still despatch naval forces greater than those under MacArthur's command for short periods of time to the waters around the northern half of the New Guinea theatre.

The erosion of Japanese naval and air resources, combined with the rise in his own logistical and amphibious capabilities, gave MacArthur the opportunity to strike long and heavy blows at Japanese positions. The potential range of his amphibious assaults increased from eighty to 800 miles from his main base. In principle, a repetitive pattern of stereotyped operations in predictable sectors of attack could be avoided. But in practice, as Drea demonstrates, without ULTRA MacArthur would not have used these material resources with maximum effect—he might not even have understood the new range of options open to him. Certainly in early 1944, before the intervention of ULTRA, MacArthur still pursued a stereotyped line of operations: to strike directly at Hansa Bay, the enemy's main line of resistance. This would have played straight into Japan's hands. The IJA treated east-central New Guinea as a forward glacis on which to delay the enemy and weaken its strength. Meanwhile it prepared to make northwestern New Guinea a bastion for part of the inner defensive sector, the Phillipines. As Drea emphasizes, a direct attack on the outer crust of Japanese defences at Hansa Bay might well have failed and, had it done so, the southwest Pacific theatre would have been completely marginalized.

Once ULTRA of a self-evident nature uncovered Japanese deployments on New Guinea, in particular, the strength of its forward crust at Hansa Bay and the weakness of its main supply base at Hollandia, MacArthur threw his plans out the window. To precise knowledge and superior force he added aggressive command and the calculated pursuit of great gains at the risk of moderate losses. In March–April 1944 Kenney's forces demolished enemy air strength in central New Guinea, followed immediately by the seaborne seizure of Hollandia. This shattered Japanese defences in the southwest Pacific and broke its forces on New Guinea into two halves. Over the next two months a fast and aggressive amphibious campaign seized northwestern New Guinea before Japanese defences could be solidified while, simultaneously, several IJN counterattacks were parried. During the four months from April to July 1944, MacArthur leapt five times further than he had in the previous twenty-four months, annihilated or isolated five IJA divisions for small American losses and stove in Japan's external defensive perimeter—just as Halsey's forces were doing 1,000 miles to the north. MacArthur also seized bases for the assault on the Phillipines, the projected date for which advanced by five months. Then the attack on the relatively weak garrison of Leyte in the Phillipines during October 1944 caught Japan by surprise. Ultimately, the American hammer smashed three divisions and what remained of Japan's regular naval and air forces on the anvil of Leyte. This gave MacArthur the opportunity to render irrelevant and bypass much of the inner perimeter of Japanese defences, the Phillipines. In any case, he could now directly attack the most vital and vulnerable components of the Japanese Empire—its line of maritime communications from Singapore to Tokyo, and the Japanese home islands.

These operations and MacArthur's entire strategy of bypassing enemy strongpoints and concentrating his power against weakly held but strategically vital areas which could serve as forward logistical and air bases, rested on intelligence, in particular, on ULTRA. In the battle for Leyte, ULTRA also allowed American airforces to smash several units and portions of the Japanese 23rd and 26th Divisions at sea, thus crippling the defence of that island and the quality of several good formations. Yet ULTRA increasingly lost that function and this value once American forces entered the Phillipines. Tough fighting could no longer be avoided, since strong garrisons held each position in the innermost perimeter of Japanese defences. MacArthur refused to bypass most of the Phillipines but insisted on assaulting many of its main islands, because he viewed the conquest of the Phillipines as an aim rather than a means—and an aim defined far less by the dictates of strategy than those of his own personal prestige. The logic of the battlefield and of MacArthur threw American forces directly against centres of Japanese strength, instead of around them. This situation was like that in New Guinea during 1943, with one difference—given a vast increase in their firepower, American forces ground down the IJA more quickly and cheaply than before. By 1945 the Japanese command on Okinawa calculated that every American division possessed five times more firepower than any Japanese one.[52] Even so, MacArthur's operations cost time and American lives, and many of his assaults were unnecessary for the advance upon Japan.

Simultaneously, these battles required the support of precisely that sort of intelligence which SWPAC could least provide. MacArthur's great campaign of March–October 1944 had rested on the basis of self-evident ULTRA. It had required exactly the material which ULTRA was best able to acquire and SWPAC to understand and use, on the enemy's strategic intentions, perceptions, dispositions and redeployments. Intelligence on these strategic issues could differentiate enemy strongpoints from their centres of weakness. If SWPAC could determine where the enemy was weak, it did not need precise intelligence about the composition of garrisons which were known to be strong, so long as it proposed to bypass them. This was fortunate, since even in mid-1944 its assessments of such operational intelligence were mixed in quality. The lacunae in ULTRA and errors in its analysis led to gross miscalculations of the strength of several garrisons which American forces did have to attack, failures in assessing the maritime movement of some Japanese reinforcements, especially its First Division, to Leyte, and a misunderstanding of the enemy's intentions before the divisional strength attack at Aitepe in New Guinea.

Once the strategy of bypassing was abandoned, once American forces were condemned to attack Japanese strength head on, these problems in the acquisition and assessment of intelligence acquired greater importance than ever before. With the near annihilation of the IJN and of Japan's ability to move soldiers and supplies by sea, cryptanalytical access to traffic about maritime matters became irrelevant. Yet that had previously been the main source of signals intelligence and of self-evident ULTRA, the material which SWPAC used most effectively. While the IJA's operational codes yielded far more material than before, this could not be used in a straightforward fashion. In essence, this traffic provided opaque ULTRA, SWPAC's traditional weak point, about the least comprehensible aspects of the IJA, its order of battle and the strength of its formations. Moreover, there must almost always be gaps in the material provided by any single source of intelligence. Continually from November 1944, SWPAC misunderstood these issues, while MacArthur ignored ULTRA whenever it did not say what he wished to hear. Not only this—to a large extent his strategy threw away the potential advantages offered by ULTRA.

When American forces entered the Phillipines ULTRA became less and less useful. Due to a combination of fragmentary intelligence, especially regarding the strength of smaller formations and support troops, and an analysis which rested on wishful thinking, Willoughby underestimated the number of Japanese defenders on Luzon in the Phillipines by 50 per cent, or 130,000 soldiers. SWPAC's planning for the invasion of Luzon rested on this assumption. MacArthur in particular wished to fight a rapid and risky campaign which would have played straight into the hands of a strong, effectively deployed and well-led enemy. Fortunately, working from exactly the same data, Krueger's headquarters assessed Japanese strength accurately and far better than SWPAC did. Krueger, not MacArthur, ran the battle, and he did so through a broad and cautious advance which took Japanese power properly into account. This reduced to a minimum American casualties but also the speed of the campaign. On Luzon as on Okinawa, isolated and outnumbered IJA forces substantially reduced the American strength available to attack the Japanese home islands. By 1944, alone among the Axis armed services, the fighting quality of the IJA had not generally collapsed from its peak of 1942. A strategy of bypassing rendered most of its strengths irrelevant and exploited all of its weaknesses. Once bypassing was abandoned, the abiding power of the IJA could again support Japan's strategy of delay and attrition of American manpower and willpower.

Gaps in ULTRA and mistakes in its interpretation did not hamper the invasion of Luzon, but neither did signals intelligence particularly help it. ULTRA showed Krueger that he must fight a careful and cautious campaign, but this was his predelection in any case, and not an unreasonable one given the known quality and characteristics of the IJA. ULTRA certainly had little effect on his operations once ashore.

In Operation Olympic, the projected invasion of Kyushu, ULTRA was more successful. It was the only source of strategic intelligence available to American planners and in some ways a strikingly effective source. It located thirteen of the fourteen divisions on Kyushu and uncovered the IJA's entire defensive strategy. Conversely, ULTRA did not define the strength of these units. Thus Willoughby underestimated the number of Japanese soldiers on Kyushu by some 40 per cent. MacArthur rejected this calculation as defeatist and held that Japanese forces were even smaller than Willoughby supposed. Fortunately, the plan of campaign which rested on this optimism was not put to the test, largely because of the indirect influence of ULTRA.

ULTRA also shaped the politics of American strategy at the theatre level throughout 1944–1945. It was not the only factor at play, but until ULTRA is accounted for, the decisions to invade the Phillipines and to use the atomic bomb will be misunderstood.[53] During 1942–1943 SWPAC was a command of tertiary importance. The operations of 1944 made the territory under its control a plausible base for the assault on the Japanese home islands, and MacArthur immediately brought the Phillipines to the forefront of American strategy. While Chester Nimitz and "Bull" Halsey, potential rivals for dominance over American strategy in the Pacific, accepted MacArthur's case, the Joint Chiefs of Staff were less accomodating. Here ULTRA became the trump suit for MacArthur. During the debate over the future of American strategy between June and August 1944, assessments of Japanese capabilities and intentions rested primarily on the basis of ULTRA. MacArthur's operations of the period, his drafting and redrafting of plans for the invasion of the Phillipines, were shaped by ULTRA not only in operational terms but also in political ones—by the need to overcome the arguments, often themselves derived from interpretations of ULTRA, put forward by opponents to his strategy. Conversely, ULTRA may have saved Americans and Japanese alike from paying the price on Kyushu for MacArthur's ambition to command the largest amphibious assault the world had ever seen.

ULTRA was fundamental to the American decision to use the atomic bomb: indeed, Edward Drea has demolished the view that intelligence should have led Washington away from any use of that weapon. The best source of strategic intelligence available to American decision makers in the summer of 1945 was not "Magic" but ULTRA. Magic demonstrated—

indirectly—the intentions of the liberal Japanese faction, which had routinely lost power struggles in Tokyo for fifteen years. It revealed that even they pursued peace terms which the United States would not accept. ULTRA revealed—directly—the capabilities of the IJA and the intentions of the faction which dominated Japanese policy. It showed that the IJA intended to make Kyushu a second Okinawa and fight to the death, taking tens of thousands of Americans killed and hundreds of thousands of wounded with them, not to mention millions of Japanese. An assessment of the intelligence record as a whole—as against merely Magic—makes the attitudes of American decision makers toward the atomic bomb more explicable. ULTRA directly pressed the United States toward the use of the atomic bomb and away from a conventional amphibious assault.

In hindsight, though not at the time, the Pacific War was a classic case of military overkill. Japan was so outweighed by western technology and American industry that a single-handed Japanese victory was impossible. Even its survival as an independent state was unlikely. Only if Germany had won the war in Europe and come to rescue its ally (which, in turn, might have been possible only if Japan had joined in an attack on Russia during 1941 instead of starting the Pacific War in the first place) would any kind of Japanese victory be conceivable. So, even though signals intelligence was clearly involved in Japan's defeat, obvious questions remain—how important was ULTRA? Was it necessary to victory? Could the war have been won without it and in what way? While these questions cannot receive a definitive answer, they can be addressed through three arguments.

First, in 1942 ULTRA was a necessary although not a sufficient cause for the elimination of the IJN's superiority at sea in the battle of Midway—luck, Japanese errors, American strength and Chester Nimitz were of equal significance. Then, through shaping the American decision to invade Guadalcanal, traffic analysis helped to lead Japan toward a campaign of material attrition in the south and southwest Pacific.[54] Ultimately these events significantly hastened the withering of Japanese military power.

Second, in 1944 ULTRA was necessary to the strategy of bypassing, which short-circuited Japan's hopes to grind down American will through human attrition. This Japanese strategy was not necessarily foredoomed—even accounting for the desire to avenge Pearl Harbor, the United States would not have paid an unlimited price simply to annihilate Japan. Had conventional forces been the only kind involved, the United States might have been made to accept a more favourable kind of negotiated peace than Japan in effect received. After all, in Korea and Vietnam between 1950 and 1975, states with no more firepower than Japan and a similar style of military operations so damaged American will and killed American soldiers as to make the United States tolerate a military and diplomatic stalemate. The United States suffered heavy losses on New Guinea and Tarawa in 1943, Leyte in 1944, Luzon, Okinawa and Iwo Jima during 1945. This butcher's bill would have been far higher had the United States been unable to leap through Japan's defence perimeters by attacking only a few and weakly held islands. Of course, even then it can never be established whether the United States would have refused to pay this bill for the simple pleasure of making Japan surrender unconditionally.

Third, however, that argument is not merely hypothetical but irrelevant. Even had the American Army been ground to a halt on the field of battle, atomic weapons would probably still have forced Japan to surrender—and Pearl Harbor ensured that these weapons would be used. Thus, signals intelligence clearly was not necessary to American victory in the Pacific War—only if Germany had won the struggle in Europe and the United States been forced into a simultaneous two-ocean war might ULTRA have become the straw which broke the back of Japan. On the other hand, very few single factors are absolutely essential for victory in a prolonged war of attrition, and signals intelligence clearly was a major contributing cause to American victory. It allowed the United States to defeat Japan far more speedily and at a lower cost than otherwise would have been the case. This, of course, was exactly what ULTRA allowed the western Allies to do against Germany in Europe at the same time.[55]

This analysis rests largely on the narrative of Edward Drea. Yet he has also provided several general observations about ULTRA and MacArthur which contribute to an examination of intelligence and military operations. Contrary to Drea's own expectations, ULTRA never shaped MacArthur's strategy; it rarely affected the formulation (as against the execution) even of his major operations. Whatever intelligence indicated, MacArthur's aims never changed—to make his command the centre of the American effort in the Pacific, to retake the Phillipines and to win the war through an invasion of Japan. These objectives, Drea insists, stemmed from vanity no less than rationality, although to some degree they were defensible on strategic grounds. For MacArthur, ULTRA was a tool to achieve his own aims rather than to help him choose between them. He used intelligence when this helped him further his objectives and ignored it when it would not. While this is conventional for many commanders, it is not always so. MacArthur falls among the group of generals in the twentieth century who were least likely to change their aims or means because of intelligence. Finally, Drea offers a brief and tantalizing statement about the effect of intelligence on commanders of specific personality types—"ULTRA appears to have reinforced basic personality traits. It convinced forceful commanders to take risks and push forward, just as it persuaded prudent ones to go even more slowly".[56] From a study of this generalization, combined with the use of the intelligence record as a mirror of generalship, one can link together different issues: several general's use of ULTRA and their style of command; the relationship between ULTRA and uncertainty; and the role of intelligence in war. All of these issues, in turn, illuminate matters which are fundamental to Clausewitz's arguments and to the study of war—the importance of intuition and determination in thought, of boldness in operations, the nature of understanding, command and action in war.

Intelligence and modern war

When his actions are compared to his knowledge, Kenney stands out as a bold, flexible, quick-thinking and far-sighted commander. Relatively superior intelligence of a high absolute order was fundamental to his success, yet he acted on knowledge with skill, resolution and audacity. Here is a commander who embodies what generally would be regarded as a superb union of knowledge, boldness, superior intellect and cunning. Krueger and, to a lesser extent, Blamey, fell into the psychological category which Clausewitz regarded as the norm—cautious commanders who wanted reinforcements against uncertainty. And of course overwhelming superiority is the most effective guarantee against uncertainty—not surprisingly, the first rule in Clausewitz's art of war is to be as strong as possible, especially at the decisive point.[57] Yet one must not separate psychological characteristics from their operational and doctrinal context. Caution, if guided by knowledge or intuition, as against being merely an irrational response to uncertainty, could be a valuable characteristic against an enemy whose offensive operations were stereotypically aggressive and whose defensive positions were well prepared. To adopt an aggressive but unbalanced defence against a Japanese attack was to give the IJA its greatest chance to play its strong cards of speed and manoeuvre and to avoid the allied trump suit of prepared firepower; conversely, caution, allied to knowledge, intuition or cunning, could force the IJA to attack Allied strength head on. Similarly, for an Allied commander to launch aggressive and unprepared assaults against thick Japanese defensive positions would be to throw away his trump suit and to gamble on the weak card of the ability to tolerate losses. Daring in operational manoeuvre through such matters as outflanking or bypassing often, though not always, was an effective way to bypass IJA positions—it certainly led to the greatest of Allied successes against Japan; but when forced to attack prepared Japanese positions, boldness in tactics and in operations was almost by definition recklessness, for precisely the same reasons that it had been on the Western Front during 1915–1917. Set-piece battles were the rational response to this situation. Caution rather than boldness might best allow a commander to exploit the known offensive and defensive characteristics of the IJA.

For Blamey and Krueger caution, combined with skill in set-piece operations, did pay great strategic dividends. Blamey's plan for the drive on Lae and Salamaua in New Guinea between June and September 1943, for example, deliberately eschewed the boldness preferred by MacArthur, and properly so. As Blamey calculated, by instinct rather then knowledge, to advance further than Nassau Bay would be to attack the IJA where it was strongest. By stopping at

Nassau Bay, he could force the IJA to advance and attack him, out of effective range of its own air support and into the maws of his defensive firepower. All this, in turn, would weaken the IJA's rear defences, ease the success of another and deeper amphibious strike and, when that happened, trap more enemy forces than would otherwise be the case.

This plan worked as intended, which is unusual in war. It was similar to a successful approach adopted by the Canadian Corps against the German army in the battle of Hill 70 in 1917 and by the Canadian and Australian Corps at Amiens in 1918—proof that caution, the use of the operational offensive combined with the tactical defensive, and set-piece battles guided by knowledge and intuition, have a proven track record against armies which institutionalize aggressive risk taking alongside defensive systems which rely on tactical or operational counter-attack.[58] This approach to operations made Dominion forces, division for division, the Germans' most effective enemies in both world wars. It could easily be used against any enemy that followed German defensive systems, including the IJA. At Lae/Salamaua, Blamey conciously applied the style of operations which the Dominion armies had used to smash the Germans in 1917–1918 and which they were using to the same purpose in the Middle East and Europe. His understanding stemmed both from an instinctive grasp of how the IJA fought and of how set-piece battles were fought, and from better intelligence than Clausewitz would have expected, though this stood far from the standard of perfection. ULTRA informed the Allies of the overall strength of Japanese forces on New Guinea, but their specific deployment remained very unclear. Hence Blamey's strategy rested one-third on information, one-third on cunning and one-third on a Clausewitzian technique to manage uncertainty. The attack on Nassau Bay acted as a magnet for the IJA, and thus uncovered its deployment in the forward area; this also threw the enemy off balance. Caution "governed by superior intellect" overcame uncertainty and an aggressive enemy.

Krueger lacked Blamey's brilliance. He was a cautious, methodical and deliberate commander, perhaps more so than is justifiable, but his approach, none the less, was effective. He cannot be criticized for adopting a bad means to deal with the IJA, merely for not choosing the best, and even this criticism is of dubious accuracy. During the course of his operations ULTRA had reached a state of technical maturity, while Krueger also established an able intelligence staff. Professional assessments of intelligence shaped his operational aims and means no less than was true of Kenney. The intelligence record explains and to a large extent justifies the controversial decisions to adopt slow and methodical means to clear both Leyte and Luzon which have hampered Krueger's reputation. His caution stemmed from two distinct but related qualities, a personality reflex and a rational response to specific circumstances. Headlong charges against deep and prepared Japanese defences would produce far greater American casualties for no better results in battle than would prepared attacks, and perhaps for no quicker results.

The mirror of ULTRA offers an odd reflection of MacArthur, one which should be considered by students of his operations during the Korean War. He had a closed mind regarding aims. He was remarkably reluctant to change even his means once he had defined them. When on the defensive, in conditions of uncertainty, against an enemy with the initiative and superior force, as between June and August 1942, during the period surrounding the Japanese invasion of Buna and Milne Bay, MacArthur could be a cautious, even a passive, commander. When gripped completely in the toils of uncertainty and facing an enemy with overwhelming power and virtually complete initiative, as on the Phillipines in the hours immediately following the outbreak of the Pacific War, MacArthur could be utterly paralyzed. He was at his worst in adversity, and at his best when he possessed superior force and the initiative. Then, daring and tenacity of purpose were MacArthur's cardinal characteristics—if not always desirable ones, as Blamey appreciated at Salamaua and Krueger on Luzon. As MacArthur wrote in February 1942:

> Counsels of timidity based upon theories of safety first will not win against such an aggressive and audacious adversary as Japan ... The only way to beat him is to fight him incessantly. Combat must not be avoided but must be sought so that the ultimate policy of attrition can at once become effective. No matter what the theoretical odds may be against us, if we fight him we will beat him.[59]

MacArthur fits the crude version of Clausewitz's "military genius", with the emphasis upon the determination, willpower and aggressive risk taking of the commander. In fact, however, with MacArthur as with Douglas Haig, the vulgarized version turned the model on its head. Strength of character, boldness and determination became close-mindedness, obstinacy and lack of originality. The value of MacArthur's psychological characteristics as commander turned on intelligence and military conditions. Given the knowledge and the chance to manoeuvre away from the enemy's strength and toward its weakness, MacArthur's aggressiveness produced impressive actions. Without that knowledge (or the willingness to use it), without that opportunity and will, MacArthur's weaknesses as a commander came to the fore and aggression tended to became liability. Time and time again he took great risks in order to win the biggest stakes, a kind of mentality which must inevitably lead a commander to a crushing defeat. Time and again he preferred to assault the enemy where it was strongest. ULTRA staved off the potential consequences of these weaknesses. The latter achieved their inevitable result along the Yalu River in 1950.

A combination of several things—superior power, room to manoeuvre, good intelligence and luck—were necessary to turn MacArthur's daring to use. Of these four, the first two were necessary in individual terms. The latter two were collectively necessary but on its own each was merely a contributing factor. MacArthur could live without luck so long as he had intelligence. He could often live without knowledge so long as all of these other conditions held true—but intelligence always made his operations easier and it was necessary for his great successes between March and November 1944. MacArthur also acted on secret information with resolution and speed—when he wanted to believe it. Unlike Kenney and Krueger, however, he was not an intelligence-driven commander. In effect, he acted on Clausewitz's "imperative principle"—he changed his first opinion only when forced to do so by clear conviction, and only when irrefutable evidence pointed toward a better means to achieve his prime directive, and never changed his aims. With MacArthur, the better and more trusted the knowledge, the more daring and determined the action; the less certain the situation, the more pedestrian the response. Yet this was just a tendency, a strong but not an invariable pattern. MacArthur finally turned the Bismarck barricade in late 1943 through the invasion of Arawe, which rested on a gamble rather than knowledge, through an instance of aggressive risk taking that Clausewitz himself would most likely have regarded as bold.

The intelligence record determines some of the characteristics of MacArthur and his lieutenants and also indicates their quality. Although Kenney's reputation needed little refurbishing, this record enhances it. The latter rehabilitates Krueger's reputation to a substantial degree, and shows Blamey to have been a shrewd commander, a surprisingly able one who understood both the enemy and the art of war in his theatre. MacArthur does not come out of the study at the level indicated by Drea—as one of the four or five best commanders of the war—but he certainly stands out as a good and gifted one, of mixed qualities and achievements. The intelligence record demolishes the hero-worship and self-mythologization of earlier works along with the uncomplimentary assessments of the recent revisionist literature. It shows him warts and all, as a far from average commander—weak in some ways, strong in others. A reading of Drea also leads to a surprising conclusion: while intelligence staffs notably improved their ability to handle ULTRA, there was no learning curve in its use by MacArthur and his lieutenants. They started as well as they finished, with regard to ULTRA of both categories, fragmentary and finished material. Indeed, MacArthur handled intelligence in Korea exactly as he had done in the Pacific. In particular, during the drive to the Yalu his refusal to consider objectively intelligence which challenged the aims he had laid down, and his use of intelligence in policy debates with his superiors, were identical to his practice of 1945. The record also sustains part of Drea's argument that ULTRA reinforced the "basic personality traits" of specific commanders. It certainly led aggressive risk takers to become even more audacious, but it led cautious ones to become not more prudent but rather more calculated. This observation has significance for the theory of command and decision making in war.

Intelligence, operations and the future of war

Some provisional observations may be drawn about the modern relationship between intelligence and uncertainty, and its effect on the art of war, the psychology of command and the nature of and need for military genius. These conclusions pertain specifically to a situation where superior and knowing forces fight inferior and ignorant enemies, which adopt a vulgarized version of the Clausewitzian formula for managing uncertainty and, more generally, to cases where one side possesses intelligence services which are (a) of an absolutely good quality; and (b) superior to those of the enemy. These conclusions might not pertain to different circumstances. When both sides possess equal and effective intelligence, for example, the result may be the military equivalent of chess. Alternatively, when intelligence of such quality and equality is derived from sources which can easily be destroyed if only they are known to exist—as would have been true of many types of ULTRA—the same situation may lead each side simultaneously to blind the other and plunge the battlefield back into darkness. Similarly, when both sides possess equally poor intelligence, Clausewitz's predictions may pertain. However, when confronting a poor intelligence service, a mediocre one may give its master a remarkable edge. One need not move far from uncertainty before Clausewitz's rules cease to apply with certainty.

In the case at hand, when intelligence helps the stronger side but not the weaker, the latter fights in the fog of war, the former merely in mist. The debilitating effect of confusion and uncertainty is reduced for one but only one army. Only reduced—never eliminated. Intelligence can never achieve complete and absolute perfection; no sane commander will ever expect it to be so. As E.T. Williams, the head of intelligence for the British 21st Army Group, wrote about his experience with ULTRA:

> Perfect Intelligence in war must of necessity be out-of-date and therefore cease to be perfect. We deal with partial and outmoded sources from which we attempt to compose an intelligible appreciation having regard to the rules of evidence and our soldierly training and which we must be prepared constantly to revise as new evidence emerges. We deal not with the true but with the likely. Speed is therefore the essence of the matter.[60]

Any single piece of information can remain accurate for only a certain period of time: completeness in intelligence requires the collation of many such pieces, and during the time required to achieve perfection in that process, some of these pieces cease to be accurate. Given the dialectical and paradoxical nature of strategy and intelligence, moreover, good information well understood about a phenomenon is likely to make commanders take actions which change the phenomenon and thus render imperfect the information, its assessment and the actions which flow from them.

INTELLIGENCE, UNCERTAINTY, COMMAND

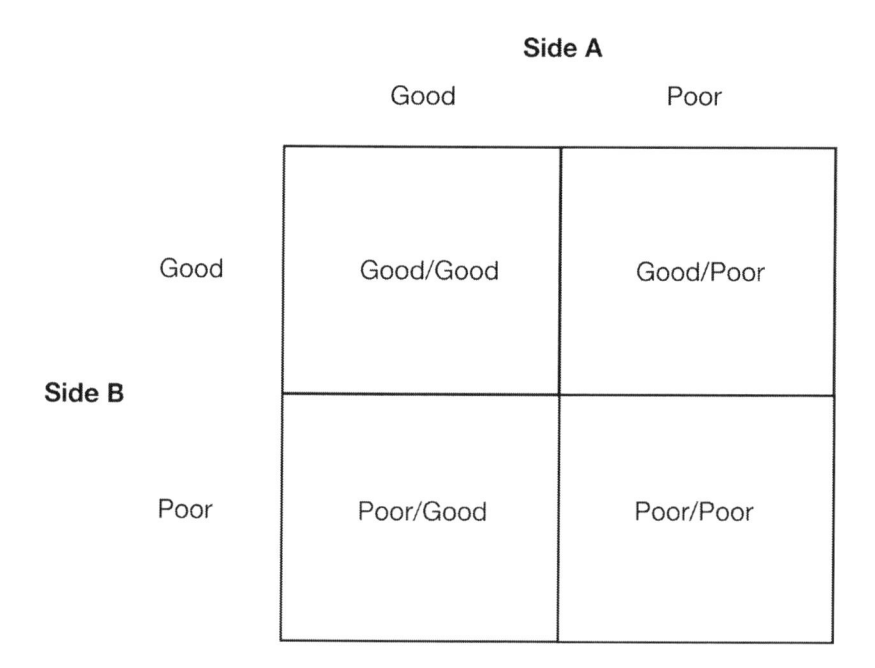

Side A

	Good	Poor
Good	Good/Good	Good/Poor
Poor	Poor/Good	Poor/Poor

(Side B: Good / Poor rows)

Figure 6.1 Possible combinations of high/low quality intelligence between two opponents.

By definition, even with excellent intelligence, the effect of friction and the reciprocal nature of war ensure that uncertainty will still exist, if in a different form and, perhaps, to a lesser degree. Nor are intelligence and uncertainty linked in a simple linear relationship. As one first moves a certain distance away from the pole of ignorance, more intelligence may create more certainty; but as one moves closer still toward the pole of knowledge, the greater the volume of information, again the greater the uncertainty; indeed, a new kind of uncertainty will be produced. Nor can intelligence ever be a universal panacea in war. Its value will always vary with the operational circumstances. Good intelligence well understood may be useless: a good army with bad intelligence may well defeat a bad army with good intelligence.

None the less, such instances as MacArthur's operations of 1944, Kenney's air campaigns and the allied amphibious assaults on Europe, all point to one thing. Against a bold, powerful but ignorant enemy, especially one whose forces are unbalanced or taking substantial risks, a daring and powerful force reinforced by knowledge can strike far more precise blows than Clausewitz would have dreamed possible. The greater degree of precision will render these blows all the more deadly. This may also be true of inferior but informed forces, as shown by Nimitz's decision to gamble on knowledge at Midway. Yet, as Blamey, Krueger and Bernard Montgomery at El Alamein and Medennine demonstrate, the frequency and the success of calculated styles of command have also risen, particularly when attacking a strong and effectively deployed enemy.

Clausewitz's rules of thumb and estimates of probable outcomes do not completely fit modern circumstances, because some of his assumptions do not. Far more frequently than he expected, for example, generals were able to strike precisely intended blows precisely as intended and to surprise their enemies in specific ways through deliberate intent. Moreover, a larger fraction of generals seem to have been able to function effectively under conditions of knowledge than had been the case under circumstances of ignorance. Many of these generals may not have been military geniuses, but perhaps military genius is less fundamental to command in circumstances of knowledge; perhaps in such cases military competence augmented by good intelligence will suffice. While not all men can be good commanders, some previously barred from that status now could achieve success on the battlefield when the heightened power of intelligence reduced the scale of uncertainty and the density of the fog of war. This reduced some—not all—of the friction of war; arguably, so too did other improvements in the workings of military technology and organization, such as communication systems. In particular, during the era of Clausewitz, the commander almost literally did perform the entire function of command: his staff was nothing but a small secretariat. Since then, command has become the joint function of a man and of an institution: the staff has become a bureaucracy and the commander anything from chairman of the board to CEO. Room remains for the freedom of action of the commander and the influence of his personality and the exercise of his genius, especially at a tactical and operational level, but these factors are none the less restrained. The corresponding loss in potential drive and creativity is balanced by the improved general efficiency of the military machine. This has changed the nature of the personality which understands and acts on intelligence—it once was a single mind, now it is one mind harnessed in different ways to an institution. In some cases, the commander becomes an executive implementing a collective decision and his personality becomes less relevant to command; in others, his personality remains the dominant factor at play.

The heightened power of intelligence altered the intellectual faculties which Clausewitz thought necessary for command. He regarded "presence of mind" as valuable, for example, because it alone let one make immediate and competent decisions when some of the fog of war suddenly lifted. But for that group of commanders who knew in advance what lay behind that patch of fog, this faculty became less significant than the ability to act effectively on such knowledge. Informed intuition probably remained essential to military genius, but, perhaps, not to military competence so long as that faculty was augmented by intelligence. Above all, the heightened value of intelligence sapped the value of determination (in Clausewitz's sense) as a factor in military genius. That commander who dogmatically followed Clausewitz's "imperative principle" of sticking tenaciously to first opinion despite contradictory material was a fool. Many more commanders had "adequate grounds" for action than Clausewitz thought possible, and therefore had less need for determination (in his sense). When time was short, of course, presence of mind remained as crucial as ever—when battles became fluid, and very often good intelligence and real-time communication systems failed, then determination (in Clausewitz's sense) remained vital. None the less, qualities fundamental to command in the age of uncertainty often proved counterproductive in the era of ULTRA—of good intelligence and real-time communication. Indeed, military genius itself may actually be counterproductive in an era of excellent and reliable intelligence. Geniuses do not need great knowledge to perform effectively. They often make a fetish of faith in their intuition.[61] Military competents need all the help they can get and often know that fact. They have far more than military geniuses to gain from reducing the environment which makes genius so formidable—uncertainty—and this obviously can be done through a use of intelligence no less than through the concentration of superior power. Greater intelligence, that is, cuts at the roots of the superiority of the military genius—it may altogether eliminate that edge.

Nor is that the end of the story. Intelligence affects another important condition of war. The effect of "fortune"—of unforeseen, unforeseeable and unintended matters—was central to all classical theories of strategy. Thucydides and Machiavelli, Clausewitz and Napoleon, all regarded luck as fundamental to success or failure in war. Many premodern commentators implied that strokes of fortune were caused by the intentional intervention of providence or else somehow were the natural and consistent product of a commander's character. Thus, so goes the story, when considering whether to make a man a general, Naploeon asked one question—"Is he lucky?" Clausewitz, conversely, stripped connotations of intention and of the consequences of character from his idea of "chance". To him, chance meant nothing more or less than random events produced by the interplay between a huge range of unforeseeable and uncontrollable factors.

Precisely these issues have changed in the modern age of better intelligence, real-time communication, and powerful staffs. What once were random actions now often can be predicted and controlled. Armies can foresee far more than before, and execute their intentions far better. Thus, the effect of "fortune" on war has declined; so has its plausibility as an excuse for defeat. Not that luck can ever vanish from war. It will particularly affect the tactical and lower operational levels, often as much as it has ever done. On the plane of higher operations and strategy, however, its significance will decline. Luck will remain a factor in calculated risks, though far less important than in the era of uncertainty. When two armies with informed but opposing intentions clash, moreover, much that they know will change and so will their ability to execute their intentions. Above all, where one side has better intelligence than the enemy, it will rely on knowledge while the fate of its foe will hinge on chance. Intelligence can directly replace luck. "Fortune", so long queen of the battlefield, has been dethroned by a pawn.

The heightened power of intelligence in the Second World War did not change the relationship between generals who evinced Clausewitz's two kinds of unregulated temperament—aggressive risk takers remained superior to timid generals. Intelligence, however, did increase the superiority over these two of every case of temperament guided by reason—it provided a more solid and rational basis for audacity governed by superior intellect or cunning, and deliberate caution. It also increased the frequency of these cases. Krueger, perhaps even Montgomery or Blamey, might have been timid generals in a different era of uncertainty and intelligence, but in the Second World War they were calculated ones. Hence, aggressive risk taking became a conditional virtue. Sometimes it produced all the rewards which were promised by boldness (in Clausewitz's sense). Aggressive risk taking, however, was automatically and without warning converted to recklessness whenever it confronted boldness or deliberate caution guided by intelligence. Clausewitz himself noted: "Even in daring there can be method and caution; but here they are measured by a different standard." They must be measured by a different standard again in conditions of greater certainty. Thus, the exceptions to Clausewitz's generalizations about audacity became increasingly common—so much so as to challenge the rule.

All told, between 1914 and 1945 increased intelligence reduced the value of certain characteristics in the Clausewitzian equation, particularly determination and nerve, and increased that of others, especially calculation and the ability to act on sure knowledge in a precise way.[62] Certain gifts of character declined in value, some others of intellect and technique rose. Clausewitz most prized the gifts which allowed commanders to act without knowledge. All these gifts have different values when one can act on knowledge. His prescriptions were formulated to suit the intelligent commander without intelligence; they had to be revised to suit the intelligent (or the competent) commander with intelligence.

But this situation may have changed again. The world wars of this century were, perhaps, that period when the ability of armies to acquire, assess and act on intelligence was at its peak in history. The relationship between uncertainty and intelligence may have changed as much since 1945 as it did between 1815 and 1914. Since 1945, armies have become increasingly bureaucratized. In business, bureaucratization kills the entrepreneur. In war it kills the general. Clausewitz wrote about the characteristics and role of just one type of general, the field commander in battle. Today the perfect general also requires other kinds of traits—a genius for logistics, intelligence, military diplomacy, the management of a large planning staff and machine.[63] No single commander or military system may be able to develop all of these traits fully and simultaneously—indeed, strength in one may necessarily cause weaknesses in another. Thus the German army may have been so bad at strategy precisely because it was so good at operations, just as the British army lost every battle but the last. Whether those rules which govern field command hold true for battle management is unclear, but one thing is clear: this issue will be fundamentally affected by the nature of intelligence in the age of the bureaucratization of war. Since 1945, armies have massively increased their ability to acquire information, but this has been mostly opaque in nature, requiring complex analysis to be of use. The ability of armies to analyze such material with accuracy and speed has not kept pace with the increase in its volume; meanwhile, staffs have expanded in size and the quantity of their paperwork has been multiplied by their ability to communicate in real time.

In particular, modern command, control, communication and intelligence systems have revolutionized the art of operations and the nature of generalship. One can acquire reliable information on issues which, for Clausewitz, were highly problematical, such as the location and strength of one's own forces. Even mediocre intelligence services can reduce the depth of the fog of war regarding the enemy's location and strength. Good intelligence services can almost entirely eliminate the fog on such issues, and even fathom the enemy's intentions before they are executed. In Clausewitz's theory of operations, intelligence and prolonged calculation handicapped command. In this century they have become a prerequisite for commanders.

Meanwhile, the relation between time and space in operations has changed. In Clausewitz's theory, and in his day, communications were slow, the speed of movement was low and operational theatres were relatively small in size. A battle could be affected by forces within just a day's march of one's forces, or roughly twenty miles. Of course, on the intersection between the operational and strategic levels, when planning major operations or the beginning of a campaign, one had to account for the forces in an entire country. In this century, real-time communication exists between forces scattered over millions of square miles. The increased duration of operations in time and their expansion in space, combined with the greater speed of movement of military forces, have dramatically increased the size of the area from which enemy forces may affect a battle. For Clausewitz, the area of battle and the theatre of operations overlapped and they did so in a relatively small space. The tactical and the operational spheres were almost identical. In this century, increasingly, the tactical, operational and strategic spheres have come to overlap. MacArthur's battles could be immediately affected by forces hundreds of miles away, his operations by enemies based thousands of miles away. For commanders in the 1990s, this situation has become even more notable.

Hence, contemporary commanders may face a situation unprecedented in history. Intelligence and communications have improved, but so have the

Table 6.1 The evolution of the role of intelligence in military operations and war

	1800*	1914–1945	Present and Future
The Commander's Interest in Intelligence	*Ad hoc.* As needed immediately before and during battle. Low trust in the quality, reliability and relevance of intelligence. Most decisions are based on personal and intuitive judgment.	Intelligence is used extensively before and during battle. Trust in its quality, reliability and usefulness is medium to high. Decisions are partly personal but increasingly depend on intelligence much less on intuition. Intelligence can be ignored or overruled by personal decisions but increased reliance on intelligence input.	Major decisions without intelligence are unlikely. Great dependence on intelligence and much less reliance on personal judgment. "Addiction" to intelligence makes independent-creative *ad hoc* decisions less likely. "Collective decisions", team and staff work. Heavy reliance on intelligence.
Organization	No permanent organization. Initiated by local requirements of the commander.	Large permanent intelligence organizations and bureaucracy, primarily military. Relatively small peace-time, greatly expanded in war.	Very large and permanent intelligence organizations and bureaucracies, both military and civilian.
Scope and Range	Mostly short-range "line of vision" direct observation. Primarily tactical/operational.	Short and Longer-range. Entire theatre of war – tactical, operational, and strategic.	Global and theatre on all levels.
Sources and Reliability	Humint – spies, direct observation. Difficult to transmit in real time. Low reliability, hence little trust in its values.	All sources – Humint, Photint, Sigint can readily be transmitted in real time. Reliability and trust varies drastically once battle begins, depending on circumstances.	All sources and all levels – Humint, Photint, Sigint can be transmitted in real time. An increase capacity for the commander to collect his own reliable intelligence in battle.
Problems	Lack of trust, lack of interest. Uncertainty created by dearth of intelligence (uncertainty of type A dominates).	Often poor understanding of what intelligence can and cannot do. Trust is based on past personal experiences. Attitude still shaped by doctrines formulated in premodern time (i.e. 1800s).	Greater dependence on intelligence, though not always better understanding. Over reliance on intelligence while art of command and war are neglected. Uncertainty created by too much intelligence (uncertainty type B dominates).
The Balance of Intelligence	All sides face equal problems.	Some sides are better or much better in intelligence gathering. Advantage can shift permanently or temporarily from one side to another. Intelligence becomes a major weapon or force multiplier/divider.	As in 1914–1945 but the gap between the best and worst is widened. The optimal use of modern precision-guided weapons requires more and better real-time intelligence.
Solutions to Problems and Better Use	Greater reliance on the experience and intuition of the commander, the art of warfare. Transference of uncertainty by initiative, movement and offensive to other side. Maximum concentration, keeping reserves at hand. "Stand like a rock." Intuitive risk-taking.	Better understanding of the value and limits of intelligence; positive experience. Art of War as in 1800 though increased reliance on intelligence. Calculated risk-taking.	Need for better education in intelligence matters. Relearning and formulating the art of war in relation to intelligence. Need to know when to take action and not wait for the last bit of intelligence. More dedicated real time intelligence. Better organization preparation distillation and distribution of intelligence.

* Occasionally, commanders like Wellington and Sherman pay great attention to intelligence. Such marginal improvement can upset the balance of intelligence in one side's favour and have major operational consequences.

speed of battle and the need for quick decisions increased. More information is available more rapidly on more subjects; the one thing which has not changed is the speed required to make human judgments and decisions. Commanders need far more information on a far greater range of matters than in the past. They can also acquire it. Once most pieces of intelligence were false; now, they are true, but trivial in quality and overwhelming in quantity. More can be worse. Certainly, a massive volume of accurate but opaque intelligence will produce information overload and two opposite problems. The first is the Clausewitzian dilemma of ignorant uncertainty, bewilderment and paralysis of the will. The second is self-confident error, the tendency to interpret this otherwise unmanagable mass of material solely through preconception. This problem renders an increased quantity of intelligence counterproductive. Virtually any preconception will plausibly explain some intelligence. Hence, an increased quantity of opaque intelligence will support any and every mistake in assessment—volume reinforces error. The greater the quantity of such material, the greater the amount of intelligence any preconception will seem to explain and therefore, intuitively, the more accurate it will seem to be.

Simultaneously, the nature of "uncertainty" has changed. Once it stemmed from the lack of accurate knowledge; now, it stems both from that situation and from a new one—the lack of usable knowledge. In fact, contemporary commanders confront two distinct varieties of uncertainty, which have different causes and different solutions. One of them is as old as war, the other is the direct product of an attempt to solve the first. "Type A" uncertainty is that one described by Clausewitz, characterized by ignorance and the inability to receive accurate and useful intelligence in time to act on it. "Type B" uncertainty stems from the power of modern C^{3}I systems, which collect anything and everything that can be collected and communicate anything and everything which can be communicated simply because it can be done. In modern war, too much has to be known too quickly and too much can be known too often; and by the time what can be known has been understood, new factors are known which have to be understood before one can act, *ad infinitum*. Type A uncertainty was literal and perceptual—(a) one could not know the facts and (b) one knew that fact. With Type B, the literal problem has declined while the perceptual one has changed—(a) sometimes one can know the facts and (b) one knows that one can do so but (c) one cannot predict how or when one will know the facts one wants to know or determine how to separate them in time from the mass of irrelevant facts that surround them, or to distinguish "signals" from "noise", to use Roberta Wohlstetter's classic terminology.[64] Type B uncertainty produces the "Schwarzkopf syndrome", the desire to wait just one more moment in order to read just one more report, the reluctance to act on imperfect knowledge because it is known to be imperfect and that at any point another report might well produce perfection. Clausewitz offered an elegant and practical solution to "Type A" uncertainty—to ignore intelligence and to act exclusively on informed intuition, because only through this means could generals hope to deal with the world. Neither this solution nor a simplistic application of Clausewitz's "imperative principle" can appeal to commanders confronting the second sort of uncertainty.

All this is affected by yet another problem. Pieces of intelligence are a perishable commodity in war—their value declines over time (see Figure 6.2). Two issues define the "half-life" of military intelligence, or the speed with which it must be used in order to be of use: the level of war (tactical, operational or strategic); and the fluidity of the engagement. Generally speaking, the higher the level, the longer the half-life. There is, however, one fundamental limit to this generalization. The central issues at hand are the degree to which a military situation is constant and a piece of intelligence is unique. The more continual the situation and the more continuous the information, the longer the half-life; the less the continuity, the shorter the period of value. The half-life of the intelligence available to a battalion before the start of a prepared battle may match that of a corps midway through a mobile engagement. The tactical intelligence available to Canadian companies before the assault on Vimy Ridge in 1917 remained useful for weeks. The operational intelligence available to Rommel's headquarters during the "Crusader" operation of 1941 often had a half-life of half a day.

The rate of decline in this "half-life" from higher to lower levels varies directly with the fluidity of the engagement. This rate is most gradual in set-piece battles, fought from fixed positions after days to months of preparation. In such circumstances, much of the deployment of enemy forces will remain stable for long periods and can easily be determined, while one's own chain of command and flow of intelligence will remain strong. Intelligence services will tend to function at their highest level of efficiency, producing and cross-checking useful, reliable and accurate intelligence. Staffs will have ample time to assess this intelligence, which will let the highest and best organized of them guide their subordinates. Often, neither the purport of intelligence nor the military situation will change notably from day to day. A broad framework of things constant and known will surround even those things which change and become unknown. In prepared operations, finally, whether one acts on a piece of intelligence immediately or two weeks later as often as not will be irrelevant. In many cases, actions taken immediately will not be completed for two weeks. Under such circumstances, the half-life of tactical intelligence will be measured in days or weeks, operational intelligence in weeks or months, and strategic intelligence in months.

In mobile war, none of these rules hold true. The deployment of one's forces and those of the enemy will frequently change. So will intelligence about them. The chain of command and the flow of information will often break; intelligence and operational authorities at higher headquarters will not be able to guide their subordinates, who will often have to act with little time

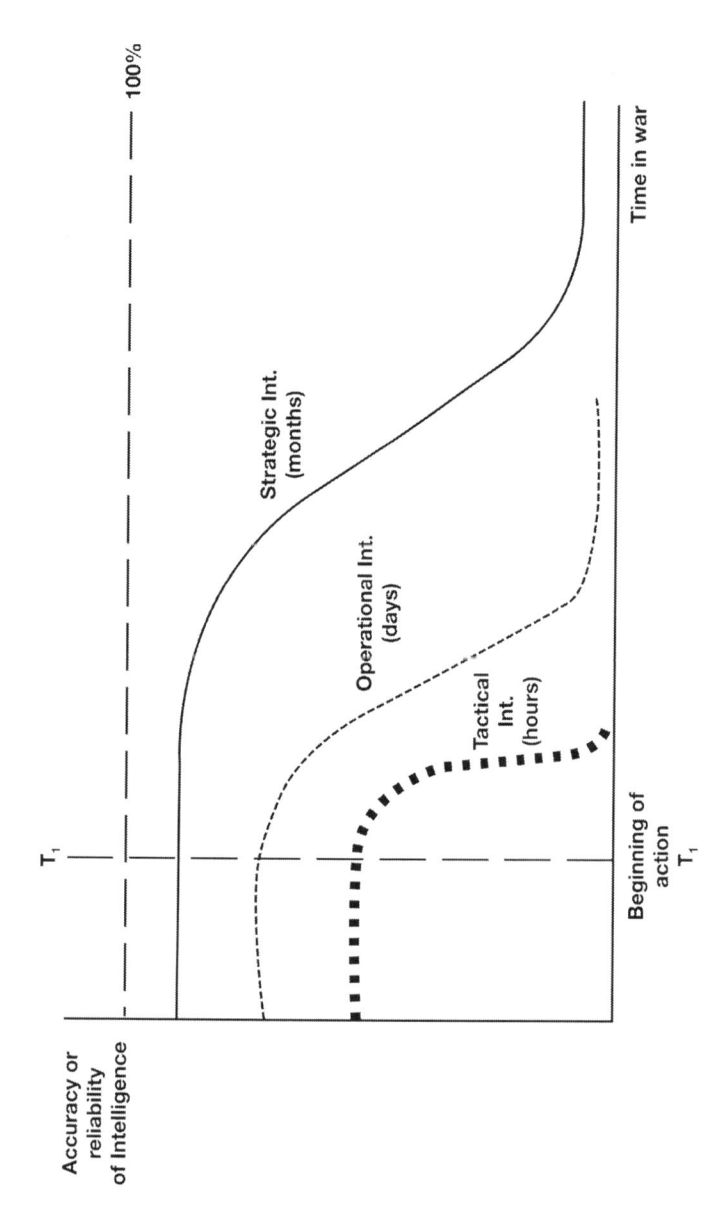

Figure 6.2 Intelligence as a perishable commodity of war

for assessment or preparation. Hence, in mobile war, the lower the level of the engagement, the less the accuracy of the intelligence and the power of assessment, and yet the greater the speed with which intelligence must be used to be of value. Therefore, in mobile war the half-life of intelligence declines sharply—from months at the strategic level to days at the operational level and hours at the tactical level. Intelligence has the shortest "half-life" of all in the middle of a fluid engagement at the tactical sphere. Here, military situations and military intelligence are most fleeting and unique. Under such circumstances, intelligence literally must be used within a few hours or never at all; often one must act immediately in ignorance rather than wait an hour for accurate information to arrive. At the operational level, the "half-life" of intelligence is greater, but nowhere else does assessment confront such technical complexity. Assessing staffs are small while irrevocable decisions often must be made within the space of several hours.

Each of these combinations of level and fluidity of war produces distinct problems regarding the collection, assessment and use of intelligence. Each of these problems has a different ideal solution. The lessons learned from any one need not apply to any other—in fact, they may be precisely the solution not to apply. Thus, elaborate intelligence organizations and careful calculation are essential for prepared operations, but counterproductive for fluid ones; experience of tactical command in a mobile war cannot prepare one for the accuracy and half-life of intelligence available at the strategic level.

These issues are not merely of academic significance. They are fundamental to command decisions and to military education. Mere intellectual knowledge of them will not make good generals, but ignorance will make bad ones. Such knowledge cannot tell generals how they should act. It will show them the environment in which their actions take place: it will illuminate the problem and indicate the solutions. Perhaps commanders can be taught to recognize that the relationship between intelligence, time, uncertainty and decision takes different forms, each with distinct characteristics and problems. Perhaps new rule-of-thumb solutions can be found to these problems, through focusing on the collection of transparent intelligence, or on kinds of opaque intelligence which cannot be explained by every kind of preconception, or by developing more effective means of formal assessment or schooled intuition, or by formulating a version of the art of war resting on the basis of a higher base of knowledge. Perhaps one can define indicators which are most likely to reveal what one needs to know at a time that one can act on it. Perhaps a new version of the "imperative principle" can be formulated to help commanders know when they know enough to act, to know when they should cease to wait for new intelligence reports and to disregard the constant flood of incoming trivia. Perhaps the main requirement of determination will be the ability to know that the time has come to "stand like a rock" and move—despite the sure knowledge that new and relevant information will arrive while one is doing so. When one can know everything, the problem is to know when one knows enough. None the less, the dilemma is clear. Once commanders had to be taught to consider intelligence. Now that they have begun to do so, they must be taught how to overrule it, when and why. Perhaps only a "military genius" will be able to deal with these new circumstances—but, if so, this genius will have different characteristics than those defined by Clausewitz.

Whatever may prove to be the case in this realm, more definite statements may be made about the effect of all these issues on prevailing theories of strategy and generalship. In wars of the future, intelligence just as much as uncertainty will shape what commanders will know and how they should act. War will remain an act of violent, frightening and dangerous competition, characterized by uncertainty of old kinds and new; only remarkable traits of character and mind can come to terms with it. Yet the nature of that uncertainty will not necessarily be the same as in Clausewitz's time. In a world of real-time communications, an abundance of intelligence and, often enough, a reduced number of known unknowns, the nature of the military genius will change. In the age of military machines, the personal traits of the commander will be less fundamental than in Clausewitz's day, although still important. He will have to know how to deal with both types of uncertainty. The nature of his intuition, his ability to understand intelligence and to act will be different.

In particular, the nature of military genius varies with circumstances. No single and universal mixture of characteristics produces this state at all times through the ages; under some circumstances military genius is less necessary for success on the field of battle than in others; under others it may in fact be unnecessary or counterproductive. When intelligence reduces the reign of uncertainty, such personality characteristics as caution, daring and determination are transformed: they enter an alloy with knowledge, which alters many of the characteristics of the original element. Hence, one must take care in comparing the "Great Captains" of this age with those of earlier epochs, because the greater degree of knowledge available to captains has fundamentally changed the characteristics which make them great. Bonaparte's determination literally is Haig's obstinacy. Intelligence allows far more commanders to achieve the status favoured by Clausewitz, where boldness is "governed by superior intellect". It also allows caution to become deliberate—to become calculation.

All this, in turn, affects fundamental aspects of Clausewitz's theory of war. Whereas Jomini compared war to a game of chess, Clausewitz argued that "in the whole range of human activities, war most closely resembles a game of cards".[65] But which game? with what range of chance and what room for skill and what degree of uncertainty? Vingt-et-un? Poker? Whist? Clausewitz also saw war as an act not of reason but of will, where intellect matters less than character. Daring and determination were more valuable to generals than knowledge; greater military consequences were produced by marginal changes in personality than in brain cells.[66] The characteristics required of a commander were those of an expert at poker rather than a master of chess. Yet in the modern era war can also be an act of intelligence. When this is so, character is no longer by necessity the only central issue, and the nature of the metaphorical game itself has changed. The realm of chance is changed and the room for skill increased.

Commanders are no longer playing poker, but games where the realm of uncertainty is reduced, such as happens to different degrees in chess or whist. Nothing can be more fatal than to play chess or whist as though they were poker against an opponent who plays by the rules of the game. In particular, when intelligence lets one side play chess against the enemy's poker, caution ceases necessarily to be the mark of the undistinguished mind or the mere product of psychological weakness—aggressive risk taking may well be so. Caution can cease to be just a personality reflex. It can become a rational response to knowledge. The most careful solution can be better than the most aggressive. A calculated chess player will have an advantage over a aggressive one who plays that game by the rules of poker. One cannot win at poker without bluffing; one cannot bluff at chess.

All this modifies Clausewitz's insights into the art of command. In principle, boldness—both in his sense of the world or in the common palance of aggressive risk taking—can become more common and more successful than he predicted. Yet deliberate caution may also become more common and even more effective than Clausewitz predicted. To err on the side of caution is no longer necessarily to err. Caution as well as boldness can be linked with effect to superior intellect or to cunning. The rise of intelligence and the decline of uncertainty in modern warfare have affected the actions of generals. They must also affect our judgment of generalship.

7
NCW, C⁴ISR, IO AND RMA
Toward a revolution in military intelligence?

No military forces have ever placed such faith in intelligence as American ones do today. Advocates of the "revolution in military affairs" (RMA) assume that information (as technology or superhighway or revolution or age) will transform the knowledge available to armed forces, and thus their nature and that of war. This faith is central to American doctrine and policy. Joint Visions 2010 and 2020, which guide strategic policy, predict forces with "dominant battlespace awareness" (better knowledge than) a "frictional imbalance" with and "decision superiority" over an enemy, and unprecedented flexibility of command: the ability to combine freedom for units with power for the top, and to pursue "parallel, not sequential planning and real-time, not prearranged, decisionmaking".[1] Officials have created new concepts about intelligence and command, aiming to pursue power by fusing, into systems, matters which once were split into "stovepipes", and new forms of information technology. These concepts include net-centric warfare (NCW), the idea that armed forces will adopt flat structures, working in nets on the net, with data-processing systems at home serving as staff for the sharp end through reachback; C⁴ISR (command, control, communications, computers, intelligence, surveillance and reconnaissance; loosely speaking, how armed forces gather, interpret and act on information); the "infosphere", the body of information surrounding any event; and "IO" (information operations), the actions of secret agencies.

Progressives and revolutionaries (conservatives need not apply) debate these issues in detail and in principle. The Marine Corp's draft doctrine on IO denies that technology can solve all problems, and defends "our timeless fighting principles". Army doctrine too gives C⁴ISR a Clausewitzian cast. It can "reduce the friction caused by the fog of war" and help impose one's will on the enemy, but "achieving accurate situational understanding depends at least as much on human judgment as on machine-processed information —particularly when assessing enemy intent and combat power ... Uncertainty and risk are inherent in all military operations".[2] Conversely, the Pentagon's Director of Force Transformation, Admiral Cebrowski, claims that all principles of classical strategy, like "the relatively high value accorded mass", stemmed from "the dearth of timely, accurate, and comprehensive information. In the relative absence of information, mass provided the insurance against what Clausewitz called the fog of war". These problems had ended; classical strategy was dead; a "new theory of war based on information age principles and phenomena" was needed. Revolutionaries assume C⁴ISR will function in a system precisely as a person sees the world, turns data to knowledge and acts on it. They believe armed forces can comprehend an enemy and a battle perfectly, and act without friction. David Alperts, a founder of NCW, holds,

> we will effectively move from a situation in which we are preoccupied with reducing the fog of war to the extent possible and with designing approaches needed to accommodate any residual fog that exists to a situation in which we are preoccupied with optimizing a response to a particular situation ... we will move from a situation in which decision making takes place under "uncertainty" or in the presence of incomplete and erroneously [sic] information, to a situation in which decisions are made with near "perfect" information.[3]

All sides in this debate assume intelligence will have great power. They take its triumphs for its norms. Thus, in 1995, the USAF chief, General Fogleman, discussing ULTRA and FORTITUDE, said: "Throughout history, soldiers, sailors, Marines and airmen have learned one valuable lesson. If you can analyze, act and assess faster than your opponent, you will win!"—unless, of course, it is stronger or smarter or luckier than you.[4] The military exponents of information warfare (IW) assign unprecedented weight to intelligence in war. In 1995 Colonel John Warden, USAF planner and theorist of airpower, held "Information will become a prominent, if not predominant, part of war to the extent that whole wars may well revolve around seizing or manipulating the enemy's datasphere". George Stein wrote: "Information warfare, in its essence, is about *ideas and epistemology*—big words meaning that information warfare is about the way humans think and, more important the way humans make decisions ... It is about influencing human beings and the decisions they make."[5] Faith in intelligence and IO underlie command and control warfare (C²W), the main form of operations the United States plans to fight, a version of *blitzkrieg* which seeks "to deny information to, influence, degrade, or destroy" the enemy's "information dependent process", so to shatter its ability to perceive and command.[6] Revolutionaries advocate a higher mode of war, rapid decisive operations (RDO), which features "High Quality Shared Awareness", "Dynamic Self-Coordination", "Dispersed Forces", "De-massed Forces", "Deep Sensor Reach", "Compressed Operations and Levels of War", "Rapid Speed of Command" and the need to "Alter Initial Conditions at Increased Rates of Change", by exploiting all these principles "to enable the joint force, across the cognitive, information and physical domains of warfare, to swiftly identify, adapt to and change an opponent's operating context to our advantage". RDO will open with the pursuit of a "Superior Information Position (Fight First for Information Superiority)" and become "knowledge-centric":

> The creation and sharing of superior knowledge are critical to RDO ... Decision makers, enabled by study, judgment, and experience, convert information into knowledge and situational understanding, which is the key to *decision superiority* — the ability to make better decisions faster than the adversary ... IO are the information equivalent of maneuver and fires ... In planning for effects-based operations, *knowledge* is paramount.[7]

The premier US military exercise of 2002, "Millenium Challenge 02", tested every transformed force and component of RDO, particularly "information/knowledge superiority" and the establishment of "a knowledge network". The USAF commander noted that the aim was "machine-to-machine talk", so that a commander can "create an air tasking order with one push of a button. I can see the entire battle in a way that if there's something I don't like, I can fix it". The "Unified Quest 03" and "Quantum Leap" wargames of 2003 addressed such issues in more detail, while advocates pushed strategy from the age of Clausewitz to that of the Borg.[8] Cebrowski held that power soon would be defined by " 'information fraction' ... the measure of a system's ability to access and contribute to a larger information network" through NCW and C[4]ISR.

> *This is the age of the small, the fast, and the many.*
> Small: Power and size are uncoupled.
> Fast: A shorter response with a faster rise time more precisely placed in time and space.
> Many: The power of the collective at lower cost over a larger area.
>
> *Rebalance for the information age.*
> "Demassification" through increased information fractions.
> Simplification through adaptive relocation of complexity and the human.
> Networked components vice integrated systems.
>
> *Operations based on assured access, information superiority, control of initial conditions and rates of change.*
> *A priori* access to the domains of conflict.
> Secure a superior information position and convert it to a competitive advantage.
> Leverage the path dependency of conflict.[9]

The revolutionaries conceptualize war as game and strategy as shooting. They assume that to be seen is to be shot, to be shot is to be killed, and to be fast is to win. Warden defines "a very simple rule for how to go about producing the effect: do it very fast ... the essence of success in future war will certainly be to make everything happen you want to happen in a very short period of time—instantly if possible".[10] These tendencies are reinforced by the use of Colonel John Boyd's OODA cycle—observe, orient, decide, act—to describe all conflict on all levels of war, with the aim usually defined as moving through the cycle faster than one's opponent; wiser heads urge that this edge be used to think more rather than simply act faster. That model, derived from Boyd's reflections on his experience as a fighter pilot in the Korean War, is a good means to conceptualize one-on-one combat. It is less useful for war. In a boxing match, speed may equal victory; in strategy, cries of "faster! harder!" produce premature ejaculation. Focus on the OODA cycle, "sensors to shooters", "one shot one kill" weapons and the idea that armed forces can act almost without friction on near perfect knowledge, has led to a fetishization of speed and the tacticization of strategy.

These ideas frame those about intelligence. The assumption is that intelligence will be an engine fit for a finely tuned, high-performance machine—reliable, understood, useful, usable, on call. One can learn exactly what one wants to know when one needs to do so, and verify its accuracy with certainty and speed. The truth and only the truth can be known. It will show what should be done and what will happen if one does this. Action taken on knowledge will have the effect one intends, nothing more or less. Intelligence experts in the military–academic complex have attacked these ideas. Williamson Murray notes that a key to RDO, the idea that "Operational Net Assessment" (ONA) will turn knowledge to power by constantly updating and fusing all data on everything related to a war, ignored every known problem in intelligence. At a strategic level, net assessment rarely did more than bean counting. It usually fell victim to worst- or best-case assessments and mirror-imaging. Achieving ONA would require "a revolution in the culture of intelligence", a "move away from the search for the predictive to an emphasis on a broader, intuitive understanding of potential opponents", from focus on collection and technology toward foreign languages, culture and history. Michael Handel argued that intelligence, once undervalued, had become oversold. "If it sounds too good to be true", he briefed officers, "maybe it is."[11] American doctrine about intelligence and operations, too, treats the relationship between these matters carefully and well.[12]

The Pentagon expects normal intelligence to be as good as it ever has been, more central to planning and operations, and to be transformed along with every other element of power. In January 2003, the Chairman of the Joint Chiefs of Staff, General Myers noted:

> we have always tended to have this situation where intelligence people are in one stove pipe and the operators in another and we are real happy if they talk together. When today's world requires

that they be totally integrated ... you can't have an intel pod, throw it over a transom to an operator and say, here's what we know. This has got to be [a] continuous, 24/7 sort of relationship and synergistic to the point where operations help with intel and vice versa.[13]

Commenting on Operation Iraqi Freedom, Cebrowski noted

the intelligence analysis problem, where we have all of these intelligence sources, and they all produced their products and reports and fed databases, all of which are stove-piped. The analysis functions are similarly stove-piped. Essentially, we have an intelligence community that is organized by wavelength.

But it needn't be that way. It could be more like this, where your intelligence is organized around the demand functions of warning, force protection, and warfighting intelligence, where you have data mediation layers that are able to pull together all source information, plot it geo-spatially, and generate the kinds of displays in which a senior leader's question can in fact be answered at very, very high speed.[14]

He advocated "a new demand centered intelligence system". Since 1970, Cebrowski held, intelligence had become unbalanced as the quantity of information rose exponentially, the power of analysis grew in a linear fashion, while specialists alone collected and processed (and hoarded) material from each source. This caused overload and strangulation in information. Too much data was available, too little of it used and even less coordinated, because it was divided into watertight pots defined not by function but source. Never was all the data on any topic brought together. Agencies collected what they did because that was what they did; the customer was forgotten. So to solve these problems, material from all sources should go to an "Information Dominance Center" (IDC) for analysis characterized by "Continuous merge ... Megadata, All Source, Open Source and Geospatial Data, Dynamic Collection, Visualization". This idea, like that of ONA, assumes analysts constantly can gather, analyze, synthesize, fuse and update intelligence from all sources on all aspects of an enemy in real time and make it useful to decision makers. This rolling product would be returned to agencies and to an office of an Under Secretary of Defense Intelligence, with three analytical–operational functions, "Warning, CI/Force Protection and War-fighting intelligence".[15] At every level of command from Pentagon to platoon, decision makers would receive and discuss all relevant intelligence through "horizontal fusion".[16] At first glance, such a body might solve the problems caused by uncoordinated single-source agencies, but not that of information overload in analysis, unless one assumes that to centralize and automate and computerize information must transform its nature. Precisely that is the assumption. As its name indicates, the IDC is intended to unleash the power of information: to bring intelligence into the information revolution, and vice versa.

Here, as often in the debates over the RMA and intelligence, vague language and jargon obscures a clash between ideas and agencies. Advocates of the RMA view the intelligence services which survived the cold war as legacy forces, industrial-age dinosaurs, muscle-bound and clumsy, too focused on technique, security, secrecy and the source of their collection as opposed to the material it provides; too divided in acquiring their evidence and presenting their analyses; too reluctant to disseminate their data; providing too much useless information; too little able to answer key questions fast and accurately. In the cold war, American intelligence focused on supporting millions of soldiers in a worldwide competition against a peer, with the trump suit being the collection of data on strategic issues through technical means; in the information age, the foci are terrorists or expeditionary forces. To meet these needs, the revolutionaries want intelligence services to become nimble, to simplify their techniques and reduce their emphasis on them, to alter their priorities and their focus on one source; to cease being monopolists of knowledge and oracles of assessment; to distribute their material widely and freely, to fuse it constantly in a rolling fashion, to cooperate in assessment with each other and the military in *ad hoc* teams, and to emphasize broad strategic or political issues less and military operational ones more, to provide less but better information. Advocates of the RMA see the attack on the twin towers as illustrating the flaws in American intelligence, but their criticisms are more fundamental. They want a revolution in military intelligence.

These ideas have political consequences, intended even if unspoken. If an IDC is created, one analytical bureau, a military one, reflecting its aims and means, will handle all information from all sources, and dominate analysis in the intelligence community. If ONA is practiced, power in analysis will move from Washington to theatre commands. All this will revive demarcation disputes between collectors and customers over priorities and between the military and the Central Intelligence Agency (CIA) in analysis. Again, the problems in American intelligence can be solved by many means, not merely those proposed by advocates of the RMA. Intelligence services can adapt to the times; they do so all of the time. Without transforming or detracting from other work, refined "push" and "pull" techniques should let them flexibly and immediately meet many of the needs of each of five divisions in an expedition, a good thing in itself. However, such reforms (even more those in the revolutionary programme) raise the dangers of the militarization and the tacticization of intelligence. Junior commanders always want to control intelligence, more than ever in an era of C^{4}ISR and expeditionary forces; yet such steps threaten to erode the advantages of critical mass or centralization.

Again, the rise of precision weapons and ISR blurs the boundary between target acquisition and intelligence. After Afghanistan, one intelligence officer noted "As weapon sys become more 'intel centric' the importance of ISR increases proportionately ... Think of Intel as a modern gun director", while Myers said bombs "can be used like bullets from a rifle, aimed precisely and individually". After Iraq, Cebrowski held "'the real fight is a close-in sensor fight', with fused intelligence and surveillance products that reduce the number of steps and time between identifying a target and attacking it"; later, he advocated "an Intel/Surveillance based force".[17] The concept of C^{4}ISR has the virtue of placing its components in a process, each affecting and affected by each other, but it has eroded older boundaries of meaning. Somehow, in moving from C^{3}I to C^{4}ISR, "computers" have eaten qualities once assigned to "command" while "intelligence" has diminished, as an idea connoting "to think" slips into one meaning "to sense". The same link between sensors and intelligence also characterized the heart of the older intelligence system, the collection of data on Soviet nuclear forces, but since the point was not immediate action (indeed, precisely the opposite, to avoid it!) there was breathing space for thought. This is less the case when the aim is to immediately kill a soldier.

When considering C^{4}ISR, it is tempting to focus on the aspects most easily changed, machines, to assume improvements to them must raise the performance of the human ones, or the whole, and to believe solutions to one set of problems (target acquisition) will solve another (net assessment). In fact, one can improve every technological aspect of C^{4}ISR without aiding any of the human ones, possibly even harming their performance. The same action can help target acquisition and harm net assessment. These pressures bolster the tendency in American intelligence to focus on technology. Some revolutionaries hold that only non-human means can allow a C^{4}I and NCW system to work. Contributors to the *Air Force 2025* project predicted a C^{4}ISR system with the self-awareness of a man, or a god: "a series of intelligent microprocessor 'brains' ... all-knowing, all-sensing"; "an intelligence architecture with human-like characteristics. It will simultaneously sense and evaluate the earth in much the same way you remain aware of your day-to-day surroundings". One theorist concludes: "Future generations may come to regard tactical warfare as properly the business of machines and not appropriate for people at all."[18] Against this pressure is the cry for "humint", but that takes many forms. Some call for a change in the culture of intelligence; others on the need for human intelligence, while soldiers define "humint" vaguely, taking it to mean everything from cultural awareness or linguistic knowledge, to a focus on humans as sources of information and for subversion, to paying some attention to humans, or to anything but technology. Beneath the debate on intelligence is an inchoate struggle between emphasis on humans or machines.

Many of these ideas about intelligence are naive or misguided. Their advocates cannot achieve exactly what they intend. Still, their actions will have consequences. They may cause a revolution, even if not the one they plan. The RMA is the greatest matter affecting intelligence today, and one of the greatest it has affected.

Ideas on these issues have affected American intelligence services, most notably those most closely linked to the military. Since 1995 they have focused increasingly on serving C^{4}ISR, especially by improving their databases, links with customers and reachback. The Defence Intelligence Agency (DIA) aims to provide "Fused, Tailored Intelligence Essential to Battlefield Dominance" and "Dominant Battlespace Intelligence for the Warfighter". Among the five "Core Competencies" in the National Security Agency's (NSA) "National Cryptologic Strategy for the 21st Century" is

> Goal 2—Military Operations, Ensure Dominant Battlespace Knowledge Through Integration of Cryptology with Joint Operations ...

(2) Integration of cryptology with point operations to ensure dominant battlespace knowledge. NSA seeks to:
 (a) Anticipate warfighter intelligence needs—on time, anywhere, at the lowest possible classification ...
(3) Integration of cryptologic support to enable policy makers to promote stability and thwart aggression. NSA seeks to ...
 (b) Work with policy customers to improve interoperability and ensure that intelligence can be tailored to meet customer needs.
 (c) Expand "pull" dissemination capabilities to enable customers to initiate real time requests to improve crisis support.
 (d) Work with the IC [Intelligence Community] to create interactive databases that will enable searches for information gathered by members of the IC.

In Afghanistan during 2002 (and no doubt, in Iraq in 2003) NSA personnel, "integrated with the combatant commander staffs ... ensured field commanders and others had access to NSA operations and crisis action centers; developed a collection system that supports military forces abroad" and coordinated reachback. On 17 October 2002, the NSA's Director, Michael Hayden, said: "As we speak, NSA has over 700 people—not *producing* SIGINT—but sitting in our customer's spaces *explaining* and *sharing* SIGINT". The National Imagery and Mapping Agency (NIMA), too, deployed "the Target Management System Network", giving its "customers direct access to targeting support and navigation data from the NIMA precise point database".[19] By January 2003, NIMA and NSA exchanged personnel and combined imagery, geospatial and signals intelligence at the point of first production, before it was sent to consumers.[20] After Operation Iraqi Freedom, the director of the CIA praised "the seamlessness, fusion, speed and quality of what is being provided on the battlefield" and held this proved his organization must transform like other intelligence services.[21] These agencies all aim to distribute normal intelligence better than the best performance ever reached before. Though they are reforming rather than transforming, this pressure may reinforce the military's role in intelligence and the latter's tendency to focus on technology, technique and tactics, despite the rhetoric about the need to develop human sources and cultural awareness.

Meanwhile, the intelligence community began to enter the information age. By 2001 the United States government had several web-based but enclosed intelligence intranets, linked to the military's "SIPRnet" (Secret Internet Protocol Router Network), a self-contained internet gated from the conventional one. Intelligence and government agencies were joined to "Intelink Intranet", which had further sub-sections—"Intelink Commonwealth" (between American, Australian, British and Canadian agencies), "Intelink-SCI" for the "top-secret, compartmented intelligence level", "Intelink-S", a "SIPRnet at the secret level" for military commands, and connections between the main intelligence agencies and their consumers, like the CIA's "Intelink PolicyNet" and the DIA's "Joint Intelligence Virtual Architecture", a web-based interactive system which joined 5,300 analysts worldwide for normal work and reachback. These nets were supported by steadily improving collection, search, and analysis functions which, the head of the Joint Military Intelligence College noted, must allow "mining of data not only of what the analyst knows is important but also of—while unthought-of by the analyst—what might be of importance".[22] By 2003, the agencies were beginning to deploy an "Intelligence Community System for Information Sharing" (ICSIS) system, with secure gateways for the transfer of messages between networks of different security classifications.[23] The inability of the CIA, the NSA and the Federal Bureau of Investigation to coordinate their databases before the attack on the twin towers shows the limits to this work, but one should not over-generalize from that failure. Even on 10 September 2001, intelligence databases on traditional military and diplomatic matters were probably linked fairly well. No doubt they have been made to work rather better since.

These steps were in pursuit of greater visions. The "Strategic Investment Plan for Intelligence Community Analysis" noted that by 2007, the agencies aimed to achieve a

> virtual work environment enabled by collaborative and analytic tools, and interoperable databases ... the breaking down of barriers and the sharing of databases of critical and common concern ... a virtual work environment that connects databases across the IC, enabled by collaborative tools, policies, and a security framework to allow analysts to share knowledge and expertise and link them to

collectors, consumers, allies, and outside experts ... Efforts and electronic tracking and production systems to capture and make available intelligence "products" that can be recovered and reused by customers and other analysts (knowledge warehouses).

The aim was to create the "secure and classified sub-set" of the infosphere, "the intelsphere, which is the virtual knowledge repository of authoritative intelligence information, relevant reference material, and resources used to store, maintain, access and protect this information". The DIA had taken the lead "in developing the concepts underpinning knowledge management in order to provide full battlespace visualization to warfighters and military planners", but all military intelligence providers "are automating their request, tasking, and response systems—at both the front and back ends—to serve a scattered and diverse constituency", and creating

> an integrated electronic production environment. The large organizations, for example, are making strides, albeit somewhat uneven, in tracking customer requests and in recording and capturing production flow, an effort that will become increasingly critical if we are to develop common "knowledge warehouses" that are easily accessible to our customers and to each other.

To this system must be allied search techniques which would sidestep information overload, and "reveal connections, facilitate analytic insights and deductions and stream-line search by prioritizing information, automatically populating databases, and integrating data". The ultimate aims were:

- Dynamically integrating national intelligence analysis from multiple sources with the timely reporting of tactical sensors, platforms, and other battlefield information.
- Providing customer, user, and producer interfaces so that organizations at all levels (national–allied/coalition–theater–tactical) have access to digital data that each can retrieve, manipulate.
- Using advanced models, architectures, automated metrics/management tools and authoritative production templates within a collaborative environment to dynamically assign, prioritize, track, and measure the operations/intelligence infosphere content.

By 2010, the intelligence community hopes to have "a dynamic knowledge base ... fully accessible from anywhere at any time by authorized users ... Knowledge base linkage to collectors with information needs/gaps automatically identified".[24] So too, the army's Deputy Chief of Staff for Intelligence held that in the "knowledge-centric" army, analytic operations will be executed collaboratively in a distributive environment with extensive use of virtual-teaming capabilities. Analysts at every level and in multiple locations will come together in virtual analytic teams to satisfy unit of action and employment intelligence requirements. Each analyst will have access to the entire body of knowledge on the subject at hand and will draw on interactive, integrated, interoperable databases to rapidly enable understanding. Communities of analytic interest will create and collapse around individual issues. The commander forward will be supported by the entire power of the formerly echeloned, hierarchical, analytic team.[25]

No doubt, some of this is mere rhetoric, a political response to pressure, while much that matters remains unsaid. Collectors and analysts fear the uncontrolled distribution of their best material, or that transformation might degrade their work. According to an informed commentator, Bruce Berkowitz, in 2001–2002 the CIA's Directorates of Intelligence (DI) and Operations (DO) had incompatible databases. Each DI analyst had one computer linked to their own (poor) database, another to the internet, neither to other official systems. "The CIA view is that there are risks to connecting CIA systems even to classified systems elsewhere." Merely to send intranet e-mail to intelligence officers outside the agency was hard. Few CIA computers were linked to SIPRnet, though models which could receive but not send messages were quickly being introduced. The CIA disliked Intelink because it could not control dissemination of documents sent there. It did "post almost all of its products on CIASource, a website maintained on the Agency's network that is linked to Intelink", to which few outsiders had access (this required approval both of a person and a computer). No one outside the agency had much electronic access to CIA material. In order to study any topic, DI analysts had to search separate databases, on the DI system, Intelink, and the internet, and often they simply ignored the last two. "When it comes to IT, the CIA's approach is not 'risk management' but 'risk exclusion'." All this had cultural causes and consequences. Access by outsiders to CIA data threatened its hierarchical system of assessment and quality control, while "by making technology a bogey-man rather than an ally, the CIA is reinforcing the well-known tendency toward introversion among most DI analysts".[26] This critique was accurate for the time, but changes seem to have occurred since. By 2003, the CIA claimed to be creating secure but flexible inter-agency databases and intranets, including the ICSIS (which had languished since 1998) and a browser-based system allowing document sharing and e-mail.[27]

So too, in 1999, Hayden had two teams investigate the NSA. Both condemned its culture and rejection of the internet. The internal team noted "we focus more on our own 'tradecraft' than on our customers, partners, and stakeholders". It advocated the NSA's "transformation ... from an industrial age monopoly to an information age organization that has entered the competitive market place", embracing "the Internet as a force-multiplier ... a means of creating numerous virtual centers of excellence with colleagues around the world". The external team held that the NSA must be recentred around the internet, and overcome its "culture that discourages sending bad news up the chain of command ... a society where people were afraid to express their own thoughts". "NSA generally talks like engineers. NSA will talk about the technic parameters of constructing a watch, describing gears and springs, when the customer simply wants to understand that we have just developed a better way to tell time. Even more important, NSA needs to learn to communicate what the ability to tell time might mean to a customer."[28]

Advocates of the information revolution view the CIA and NSA as anal and ossified, unable to see the need to provide fast, flexible, fused material. Such criticisms have force. Yet, Hayden noted, the NSA "is a very conservative, risk-averse organization" because these characteristics, and "consistency and thoroughness and care", fit the cold war.[29] They also suit any intelligence agency which dislikes error or insecurity. The rhetoric of transformation obscures the key issue—who gets what from whom? It is easy enough to produce good intelligence or coordinate analysts, or push material effectively in a crisis, or send fused information fast from Washington to a theatre command, or from there to an aircraft or unit commander. These are standard problems with school solutions: reachback, tailoring, fusion, and pull techniques are old hat, they do not require transformation. To give thousands of people access to the databases of secret intelligence services, to use them as they wish, however, is unprecedented, and an aim of the revolution. "Information typically has been retained in agencies' channels until the product becomes intelligence", said John Osterholtz of the DOD's chief information office. "We don't want to hoard data until it is done. We want to provide it as soon as possible."[30] To do so, however, is to give intelligence services cause to fear for their security and tradecraft and the integrity of their data. There are concerns to be balanced. The question is, how?

Since 1995, the intelligence agencies have learned how better to push their product to the military, who have honed their means to pull it. Reachback is a reality, which it will reshape. Already, it has magnified the power of intelligence. Colonels can tap data from the centre to solve problems in the field and guide immediate strikes; junior analysts at home can warn sergeants at the sharp end of danger or promise just ahead. Yet in all fairy tales, curses accompany blessings. Search engines augment analysis. They cannot replace analysts. Intelligence is a human process—it cannot simply be automated. Machines cannot command. C⁴ISR has solved only some problems of command and changed none of its conditions. As ever, the issue is how much information a system contains, how fast and flexibly it circulates, and how well it is used. In communications, intelligence and decision making, more or faster is not necessarily better; the value of multiplication depends on what is being multiplied; changes in quantity cause changes in quality, sometimes for the worse. If intelnets work as advertised, collectors can more easily distribute their product, analysts can find the material they want and correlations be made, expected or unexpected, actions can be aided—and everyone can receive far more data than ever before, perhaps too much. So to justify their existence, intelink agencies will stock "knowledge factories" and an IDC with reports *en masse*, many trivial, some competitive, all well advertised; analysts will be swamped in sites, losing their way down hot-linked detours; analysis will be constipated by the quantity of information, conflicts of interpretation and of interest; need and politics will keep security restrictions in being, often blocking users precisely from the material they need or hiding all the best evidence. This situation calls for education in intelligence and its pathologies, and the creation of a new culture for assessment and use. If this aim is achieved, analysts and engines will just be able to prevent the increased mass of detail from adding more friction to general decision making, while making great gains in two areas: when one knows what one wants to know, the answers will come with unprecedented power and speed; and the chances for discovery by serendipity will rise. If this aim fails, more will mean worse.

Again, by making intelligence more central than ever before, the United States has made C^{4}ISR the centre of gravity for its power and its greatest vulnerability. It has also increased the importance and the difficulty of security. SIPRnet is the richest treasure ever for espionage, and intelink agencies its crown jewels, which will shine the brighter the better intelligence is fused and distributed. In principle, the "intelsphere" is walled from enemies but accessible to friends, who communicate with freedom. If this firewall collapses, that web-based communication will become the equivalent of plain language traffic over wireless. If an enemy penetrates your "intelsphere", it will have more chances than ever before to gather intelligence on you or to pirate your intelligence and use it as its own, and an unprecedented ability to corrupt your data. That danger, whether occurring in secret, in known form or even just as a suspicion, right or wrong, is the Achille's heel of the "intelsphere". If soldiers cannot trust the "intelsphere", how will they act on it? One successful corruption of information, producing one failure in the field, might cripple the machine or the trust on which it relies. A virus may be little more damaging than the fear of one. Thus, as ever, security will trump flexibility. Databases are most easily defended when they are accessible only to regulated computers. SIPRnet, however, is easily accessible—anyone capturing intact any one of thousands of vehicles in Operation Iraqi Freedom in theory could reach any database linked to it. Penetration is common. In 2001, 16,000 attempts were made to enter United States Navy computer networks, "of which 400 gained entry, and 40 traveled the networks". In 2002, twenty-nine attacks on USAF networks "resulted in some compromise of information or denial of service". In 2003, the American Chief of Naval Operations, Admiral Vern Clark, said: "If you are a parent today, raising a youngster, one of the areas you ought to push them toward is network security. This is going to be a job market that is crying out for people for the next 200 years."[31] This danger will limit the significance of intelligence easily reached through SIPRnet, and force intelligence agencies to shelter their best material behind secure gates or else on separate intranets. The "intelsphere" must stand apart from the "infosphere", while still being linked to it through secure and flexible procedures, which allow information to be pushed from the top and pulled from below, and more coordination between databases, and between analysts and users. These links may be more rich, thick, flexible and fast than ever before, or alternately below the standards of 1944 or even 1918, depending on the relationship between the techniques of cyber attack and defence. At worst, C^{4}ISR may follow the classic downward spiral of C^{3}I over radio, where jamming and the need for security sapped most of its flexibility and power.

The mechanization of intelligence and command has also transformed the security dilemma. The new killer applications are spies to steal information and cyberwar to corrupt databases. The key danger from hackers is less an ULTRA than a nuclear strike on data; an agent in place, conversely, could betray one's entire database of intelligence and command. In the cold war, sergeants-turned-spies pillaged storehouses of paper secrets—now, a Walker family could loot "knowledge warehouses", or corrupt them. Cyber defence must be geared to handle every possible enemy everywhere all of the time, though for the United States mercenary hackers may be the greatest problem for decades, until the rise of a peer competitor. Other states will have to reckon with peers, or superiors. American authorities recognize these threats and act against them. Thus, in 2002, "a layered cyber-defense system" protected the Defense Information Infrastructure, combining "local DoD intrusion detection systems" with an NSA-controlled "computer network defense intrusion detection system ... a network of sensors that are strategically placed within the DoD infrastructure, providing analysts the capability to identify anomalous cyber activities traversing the network". The Pentagon hosts annual cyberwar competitions which, in 2003, included "a so-called rogue box in each network that the red team could use to simulate insider attacks".[32] Though no American headquarters may ever feature signs reading "He who uses the computer is a traitor!", this will happen to smaller states. The electron is a weapon. It can be used by you as well as against you.

Compared to C^{4}ISR and NCW, IO is a less novel and less problematical concept. It describes its subject better than any extant term, like "covert action". IO embraces many "disciplines"—deception, operational security, electronic warfare and psychological operations, but also civil and public affairs, that is, public and press relations. Initially, the latter were added to IO to meet the army's distinct problems with peacekeeping, but the relationship grew to include political warfare, both defensive and offensive. During the campaign in Afghanistan, the Pentagon briefed journalists about the techniques of Serb and Iraqi propaganda and press manipulation, or "enemy denial and deception".[33] This concern shaped its media policy during the 2003 war in Iraq, and also led to the short-lived "Office of Strategic Influence" of 2002, a military organization to shape international media coverage. Due to bad publicity, that office closed a day after its existence was announced, and no doubt reopened the next under a new title. That American doctrine about IO fuses in one category matters once treated as "black" (psyops) and "white" (public relations), and regards their combined practice as normal, presents problems for journalists, the public, and the military itself. With the significant exception of computer network attack (CNA), IO does not involve pouring old wine into new bottles, merely placing new labels on old bottles. Functions which intelligence officers might once have conducted in a general staff, perhaps with operations, security and signals personnel in secondary roles, are now treated as a combat arm, controlled by the senior operations officer, with intelligence personnel first among equals of specialist elements. This rise of operations and decline of intelligence is marginal and reasonable; IO are operational matters, but in need of a close relationship with intelligence and other elements. The basic doctrine for IO is sound, and close to the best practices of the best practitioners of two world wars. IO should be controlled by an officer directly responsible to a commander, guided by a small "cell" of specialists, able to provide expertise and liaison, deliberately organized in an *ad hoc* manner, cut to fit the cloth; the various "disciplines" of IO should be "fused"; not merely coordinated, but combined.[34]

Thus, American doctrine on deception regards all aspects of intelligence as force multipliers, to be integrated into every aspect of planning and operations. It defines sound principles — "centralized control"; "security"; "timeliness" in planning and execution; "integration" of deceit with an operation; and, above all, "focus" and "objective", aiming to influence the right decision makers and to affect their actions—to treat the manipulation of intelligence and ideas merely as a means to an end. In order to achieve such ends, practitioners must understand their foe's psychology, "possess fertile imaginations and the ability to be creative"; they must pass a story through many sources which an adversary will find believable, ideally by reinforcing its expectations; and fuse intelligence, psychological warfare and operations security with deception. This doctrine is powerful, but it has weaknesses which stem from the roots of its strength, the influence of the British tradition of deception. The campaigns of 1943–1944 which culminated in "FORTITUDE" stem from so many unique circumstances that they are a poor guide to the average. To treat them as normal is to assume that deception is precise and predictable, that one will have edges equivalent to ULTRA and the "double cross system", while the enemy's intelligence is castrated. These are tall assumptions. Again, "focus" and "objective" are fine principles, but in order to make key decision makers act as one wishes, one must know who they are, what they expect, how to reach them and how to know whether one has succeeded. This is not easy. Deceivers wrestle with uncertainties and pull strings they hope are attached to levers in a complex system they do not understand. Deception rarely has just the effect one wants and nothing else. The unintended cannot be avoided. American doctrine urges that this difficulty and others be resolved through risk assessment, but that is to mistake a condition for a problem. Reason is good, war games are fun; when assessment concludes, risks remain.[35]

IO doctrine has been easier to write than to test. American experience with its components since 1989 have ranged in quality from poor (Somalia) to decent but uninspired (Panama; the 1991 Gulf War; Kosovo). In 1998, one IO colonel with experience in Bosnia and at Fort Leavenworth, Craig Jones, noted "much confusion remains—IO is still many different things to many different people". It lacked measures of effectiveness. "A commander has the right and the responsibility to ask his IO staff officer this simple question: 'How do we know this IO stuff is helping me achieve my overall objectives?'" Between the conception of the idea and 2003, the US military had no experience with IO in war, except in Kosovo, where Serbs matched Americans; its theory was drawn from history, where good examples did abound, some better still than Operation Iraqi Freedom. The theory was good—the problem was *praxis*. In 2000 the IO Franchise, Battle Command Battle Lab, at Training and Doctrine Command, admitted the need for basic studies on IO in war, including "good, reliable means" to assess its impact. "Intelligence doctrine addressing IO remains to be produced, and training remains concentrated on the traditional functions of locating and identifying opposing forces", with "intelligence products ... designed to support force-on-force, kinetic, lethal engagements". Again, in "numerous Army Warfighter Exercises ... attrition-focused command and staff training exercises", time was too short "to employ the less tangible aspects of IO in a manner that would influence the operation", and to understand their value and limits. A division or corps headquarters had just hours "between receipt of mission to course of action selection, allowing as much time as possible for coordination, synchronization, and orders production", and one at theatre level "out to 120 hours and beyond". Deception and psyops, however, might take months to work. "The most important aspect of IO at the tactical and operational levels is execution", yet how far could division or corps staffs "effectively integrate and execute all elements of IO into their decision-making processes, given the time constraints common to tactical operations?" If not, how should IO be organized? Historical experience, incidentally, including that from Iraq in 2003, suggests deception and psyops can work well even within a month from their start, while a theatre-level headquarters should handle these matters for subordinate commands. Again, how should old disciplines like EW be adapted to fit new technology, IO and the information age?[36]

Even experts were unsure how to apply IO. It was practiced only in exercises, peacekeeping, and Kosovo, all experiences with limits. Bosnia illuminated IO's use in peacekeeping but not in war, and perhaps provided some counterproductive lessons: a directing committee of twenty-plus members is possibly too bureaucratic for operations. In 2000, reflecting on experience with IO in divisional work at the Exercise and Training Integration Center, one IO Analyst, Roy Hollis, noted: "All too often, IO is associated with rear area or force protection operations only ... This is only a part of what IO is capable of doing, and we have to unlearn this." Since "many staffers do not fully understand or appreciate the value of IO", without effective "IO staff huddles", "strong leadership" from the IO officer and a supportive Chief of Staff, "the staff will focus on what they already know and give minimal attention to Information Operation requirements". Personnel "lacked actual subject matter expertise in the various disciplines or elements, plus intelligence support, that make up Information Operations", and spent too much time in too many meetings.[37] Amateurishness and bureaucracy are common problems in military intelligence; but for IO, a focus on form may turn revolution into a checklist. Until 2003, these problems characterized American efforts to apply their IO doctrine.

Properly handled, IO are powerful tools, but they do not necessarily work as one hopes, and they can be used by one's adversary. Defence matters as much as attack; it is simply harder. Their power will be multiplied in an unpredictable way by the rise of a new discipline. Unclassified material rarely refers to CNA, but the topic has not been ignored, simply treated with secrecy, just as armies did deception and signals intelligence between 1919 and 1939. One USAF intelligence officer notes "offensive IO weapons ... remain shrouded in limited-access programs"; the Joint Chiefs of Staff's doctrine on IO discusses CNA in a classified annexe; in 2000–2001, the USAF sponsored research into specialist "Cyber-Warfare Forces", "potential targeting issues" and "how to mitigate or minimize collateral damage effects", how CNA would affect "the full-spectrum of Information Attacks" and create new "broadly defined multi-disciplinary activities, such as: cyber-based deception, Electro-Magnetic Interference (EMI), Web Security, Perception Management. How do we integrate/fuse input and provide a COA (Course of Action)?"[38] The Pentagon's Command and Control Research Program describes CNA as "a rapidly evolving field of study with its own concepts and technology".[39] Anyone able to employ a hacker for love or money can hope to gain from CNA, while attack somewhere is easier than defence everywhere. The entry costs are small, the potential payoff large, and the consequences uncertain. Sooner or later some state will let slip the bytes of cyberwar, with uncertain effect. CNA may revolutionize IO by incapacitating computer systems, or replacing true data with false; or it may prove to be Y2K revisited. A first strike may be so advantageous that it creates an imperative to move first, adding a new twist to deterrence. Even when not used, CNA creates, as one veteran noted, "built-in paranoia", the need to fear that hostile states or non-state actors are attacking and to react on that assumption to anything which looks like a threat[40]— doubly so since CNA may be indistinguishable from accident, its authors undetectable, and it may inflict mass destruction (consider the consequences of wrecking the computers controlling air traffic control at Heathrow Airport, or of a nuclear power plant). So too, the nature of power in CNA is unknown: "How do you measure IO power?", asks the USAF's Institute for National Security Studies; "How would one calculate Correlation of Forces à la past Soviet/Russian approaches?"; what are the "units of IW force" or their structure, "e.g. squadrons of IW computers"?[41]

IO is a known commodity; not so, C4ISR and NCW. How will reach-back, intelnets, an IDC or "knowledge warehouses" affect the normal working of intelligence, and its use in crises or operations? Certainly, they will not end uncertainty, but will just create a new kind—what Michael Handel called "Type B uncertainty", the problem of decision making in a context of too much and constantly changing information.[42] Uncertainty is not just about what is seen, but about how we see; not merely what we know, but how we know that we know what we know; because of too few facts, and too many. It is a condition linked to problems. The problems can be eliminated, but attempts to end one often create another. A condition of uncertainty is that one can never solve all of its problems at any one time; merely choose which problems to avoid, or embrace; and the conditions must be endured. One can increase one's certainty, and reduce that of an adversary or gain an advantage over it, and these gains may be great; but none of this is easy to achieve. When facing a serious foe, uncertainty will remain sizable. Even against a weak one, it can never vanish—chess players, knowing their foe's dispositions, remain uncertain about his/her intentions and the clash of their own strategies. C4ISR and "Dominant Battlespace Knowledge" (DBK) will increase uncertainty precisely in the way they reduce it; so too friction. In time of routine, they will provide more data than a general needs. In time of crisis they will produce less intelligence. How far will the ability to collect and process information under routine circumstances affect ideas of what intelligence can do when it matters? Will such a routine not merely hide pathologies and paradoxes and make them even more debilitating when they strike?—which will be when it matters. What will a machine relying on the receipt of facts in hosts do if deprived of them? How will information junkies behave when thrown into cold turkey—just when battle starts?

To date, the answers are unpleasant. The USN's "Global 2000" war games tested the application of NCW. It found both the power of C^3I and its classic problems multiplied; with every member of the net able to post and edit notes, information overload paralyzed command—officers had so much data that they could use little of it, bad coin drove out good. One witness questioned the validity of "visions of a command-and-control structure akin to the civilian internet ... that the natural creativity, spontaneity, and adaptability of war fighters can be unleashed by freedom from constraint analogous to that of the civilian Internet in commercial settings".[43] Experience in the Kosovo campaign led Air Commodore Stuart Peach to sombre conclusions: "the drive to streamline procedures and handle ever more data has had an important side effect; airmen have become driven by process not strategy", "in reality, theory, doctrine and practice collide with process. Airmen claim one thing (centralized command and decentralized execution) and in fact practice another (centralized command and centralized execution)"; "refining the process of airspace control orders, air tasking orders and air task messages became the performance criteria, rather than creative and bold operational ideas or campaign plans".[44] According to a USAF officer, during this campaign the Supreme Allied Commander Europe "had in his office a terminal that allowed him to view what Predator unmanned aerial vehicles in the air were seeing". Once, when Wesley Clark viewed three vehicles he thought tanks, "he picked up a telephone, called the joint forces air component commander, and directed that those tanks be destroyed. With a single call, based on incomplete information, all the levels of war, from strategic to tactical, had been short-circuited".[45] Similarly, during March 2002 in Afghanistan, officers in superior headquarters at home and abroad bombarded commanders with questions and advice based on live pictures transmitted from Predators in flight.[46] A case of friendly fire in that month showed that information overload, friction between layers of command and inexperienced personnel had swamped the USAF's premier operational command, in western Asia. So much information was available that USAF squadrons could not circulate much material in ATOs to their pilots, while staff officers would not change their procedures, ensuring confusion between all layers of command.[47] The system processed and circulated far more information faster than ever before, but in this high-tempo environment, the need to spend just thirty seconds in retrieving data could produce tragedy. It is so fast moving, fragile and complex that system errors are inevitable even without an enemy; the only questions are how often, at what cost, and how much an enemy will multiply them.

A fluid but hardened information and command system will not be easy to achieve. The aims must be to simplify the flood of data and direct it where needed, so avoiding the classical problem with satellite imagery, when one knew what to look for only after the start of the crisis when that knowledge was needed. It will be hard to gain full access to data about known unknowns and impossible to do the same about unknown unknowns. Nor can such systems work unless doctrine and training prepare people to use them. Still, one can reduce these new forms of uncertainty through old-fashioned means. One must start by putting intelligence in its place. It does not make or execute decisions, people do, and more fundamental issues—their education, intuition, doctrine, character, courage, openness of mind, wisdom, attitudes toward risk—determine how they understand and apply it. Knowledge is only as useful as the action it inspires. Decision makers should listen to intelligence, and consider whether their perceptions are accurate, if they are pursuing the best means to achieve their ends or noting all the salient points; yet they must remember that intelligence cannot answer every question. They cannot wait for the last bit of information to be received and for data processing to make their decisions. They must know when to act without intelligence or knowledge—that is why they are leaders. Soldiers need to know well enough to act well enough when they must, and to understand when that moment is; no more, no less. The key questions are: what do you need to know? When and how can you know that you know enough to act, or know that you know all you can use? All shades of opinion recognize that C^{4}ISR and DBK have magnified problems such as information overload, micromanagement and the fruitless search for certainty, for which they share many solutions, such as changing the culture of command. Units must be able to operate in harmony without command, through some new version of "marching to the sound of the guns", or what the revolutionaries term "swarming". Commanders must learn to act when they have a good enough picture of events even when it is imperfect and new information is arriving, and to understand when they have achieved that condition. Sometimes this process is called "to opticize"; Clausewitz termed a similar process the "imperative principle".[48] When combined, these means have power and limits. They can solve many problems of command, perhaps most of them, but not all; and conditions will remain. C^{4}ISR will be a function of a complex system manned by many people. It will suffer from all of the things natural to humans and complex systems, including uncertainty, friction, unachieved intentions, unintended consequences, unexpected failures and unplanned successes.

Operation Iraqi Freedom provides the first test of American ideas about C^{4}ISR and NCW, but not a simple one. The struggle was so unbalanced that one must take care in extrapolating from triumph; judgments from failure are easier to make. How many lessons useful for 1914 could have been drawn from Omdurman? How many of those could a victor have believed? Any lessons drawn from this campaign will be intended to shape policy in 2020, and the nature of (to use the jargon) the "objective" force—yet it was fought by "legacy" forces, using elements of "interim" C⁴ISR. Arguably, the keys to victory were air supremacy, vehicle and body armour, the incompetence and subversion of Iraqi officers and the psychological effect on Iraqi soldiers of the power and invulnerability of Coalition artillery and tanks. A Marine Colonel noted some of his tanks survived seven RPG rounds, and "became the unkillable beast and caused them [Iraqis] nightmares".[49] General Tommy Franks, head of Central Command, wrote that the Coalition solved the problem of irregular forces simply by moving tanks into towns: "the Fedayeen would sacrifice themselves by climbing up on the tanks. They had no tactics to deal with armor."[50] Yet any lessons learned from this campaign will be used to explain why "legacy" forces must be transformed, and heavy tanks are bad. Again, our data on the role of intelligence is limited, though much is available even on the most secret of matters, communications intelligence and deception; times have changed. This paper goes to press in February 2004, before the Pentagon releases any of its "lessons learned" memoranda, though many of those from formations and arms are available to the public. Much good commentary is available, but the database is incomplete, and the assessments of observers vary with their experiences. Signals and headquarters personnel emphasize the power of communications and intelligence. Colonel Dobbins, Base Commander of the 392nd Air Expeditionary Group, thought the GPS satellite constellation gave all participants a "common and accurate picture". The First Marine Division praised GPS, but denied that it shared a "common operating picture" (COP) with outside authorities. The director of C⁴ for the Joint Chiefs of Staff (JCS) said: "We do not believe [the Iraqis] had any situational awareness of what we were doing or where we were ... We could tell you, even in Washington, D.C., down to 10 meters, where our troops were."[51] That may have been true in Washington, but not always in Iraq.

Any "lessons learned" process runs the risk of overgeneralizing from events, doubly so when military politics enters the fray. And this event will be politicized. Already, slogans like "lazerkrieg" have been coined; in a frequently cited and almost officially sanctioned phrase, General Myers, the JCS chairman, described Operation Iraqi Freedom as demonstrating "a new American way of war". The issues merit consideration more than cheerleading. In a study of American operations in Afghanistan during 2001–2002, Stephen Biddle argued that some aspects of war had been transformed, others had not been, and both cases had to be examined in order to learn the right lessons.[52] The same is true for Iraq.

Far more than most campaigns, Operation Iraqi Freedom was intelligence driven. Authorities attempted to apply their doctrine and concepts, to follow all best practices at once and with sophistication, and to harness them to C²W. They did not achieve all their aims, but their actions were able, matching those of the western Allies during 1944 in form, if not necessarily effect. Planning at Central Command, said Franks, assumed "we would not gamble but we would accept prudent risk". It focused on flexibility and surprise, allowing either land or air forces to open the attack, as chance or need required. Intelligence was intended to start the machine, of which IO was a major part. The plan included "five fronts". Conventional forces dominated just one, albeit the central thrust, the assault from Kuwait. They were intended to lead the second front, in Kurdistan, but ultimately deception and Special Forces did so. Special Forces ran the third front, the west, while airpower and subversion did the fourth, working "not only from the outside in, but from the inside out" to prevent the enemy from creating "a fortress in their strategic center of gravity, which was the Baghdad–Tikrit area". The "fifth front was information"—subversion to weaken the regime, electronic warfare to destroy "principal lines of communication for the purpose of giving orders" including pre-war attacks in the "no-fly zones" against fibre-optic links, forcing the Iraqis onto radio and cellphone circuits; "Candidly, we knew we wanted to leave some other communications links up because there is benefit in understanding what orders are being given." This front turned on a "combination of two things. One was as much silence as we could get in terms of public knowledge of the things I previously described, and deception which we wanted to feed into the Iraqi regime to cause them to react in ways that we wanted them to react".[53]

In Operation Iraqi Freedom, the success of C⁴ISR and IO was mixed at strategic–political levels, and overwhelming at operational ones, better at action than calculation, at target acquisition than ONA. Everything based on machines achieved unparalleled power, all things focused on humans were mediocre, with the exception of IO. Authorities got Iraqi politics wrong. They overestimated their ability to subvert Saddam Hussein's regime without having to smash it, the ease of occupation, and the consequences of letting Iraqi soldiers demobilize themselves, rather than be captured. These failures probably stemmed from policy makers rather than specialists, but that is life; C⁴ISR has changed neither net assessment, nor the politicization of intelligence.[54] The failure of subversion weakened the American ability to stop the most dangerous strategy open to Iraq, the creation of a fortress Baghdad; fortunately, Iraqi incompetence and the USAF blocked this threat. Anglo-American assessments of Iraqi weapons of mass destruction (WMDs) were wrong, and their use of intelligence for public relations was incompetent; their dossiers of February 2003 are classic bad examples in that genre. Even more, fears the enemy would use WMDs caused Coalition forces to take counterproductive steps, from forcing soldiers to wear NBC suits to creating fears about a "red line" around Baghdad and the need for a "western" front.[55] This problem stemmed not from the falsification of intelligence, but its limits. As Franks noted, material on the issue came from high-level defectors, low-level agents, and "monumental reams of intercepted information". Yet, "Intelligence information is much more often imprecise than it is precise ... one never knows the validity of the intelligence, much like intelligence preparation of the battlefield, which says this is what we believe, now we must go confirm the existence."[56]

With hostilities commenced the first website war, posing new problems for media influence. Here, American authorities mixed success at home with failure abroad. They did not manage hostile European media nor counter *al-Jazeerah*'s influence on Arab audiences, partly because of IO failures: an American military newspaper conceded that many officials "were hostile to Arab reporters in briefings and in person. And only rarely were high-level U.S. officials offered as interview subjects".[57] Western media gave Saddam Hussein better intelligence than most armies in history have had, while a new problem emerged in the form of websites focused on strategic affairs, which gather and assess information with power, often providing archives and links to other sites. The retired General Lucian Truscott IV noted: "the book says you've got to keep the enemy ignorant of where you are, what you're going to do. And I said to my wife one day, I opened up the *New York Times*, turned it to the back page and said, 'if I was an Iraqi general I could fight the war off of this map'."[58] The problem of operational security for western military forces continues to rise. In a serious war, it might matter.

Conversely, "embed" journalists, attached to units so to counter Saddam, "particularly practiced in the art of disinformation, misinformation, denial, deception, downright liar quite simply" as Deputy Assistant Secretary of State for Defence Whitman said,[59] played to the fad for reality television and provided a ballast of constant good filler for home consumption. The 600 "embeds" attached to American forces and 100 with British ones had mixed success in countering Iraqi disinformation, until Baghdad fell. Yet the military did shape the tone of coverage through "embeds"; the First Marine Division treated them as "an entirely winnable constituency" and told its soldiers "media were not to be 'escorted', they were to be 'adopted' and made members of the Division family". It noted, "sharing austere living conditions, danger and loss, journalistic desires of impartiality gave way to human nature" which "enables our story to be told in a very personal, humanistic way. To the viewers and readers, the 1st Marine Division was not an anonymous killing machine, it was an 18-year-old Marine from Anywhere, USA".[60] As part of the bargain, "embeds" accepted limits on their ability to report sensitive information, meaning they had to understand what that was. Two days before the attack the Third Infantry Division gave its ninety-seven "embeds" a "broad overview of the plan, including tentative timelines, so that the media would understand the context of what they were observing, and avoid filing stories that would tip intentions to the Iraqis. If media were not provided the context, they could report their observations and unknowingly provide the Iraqis sensitive information" or "inadvertently tip adversaries to friendly intentions just by interpreting what they observe". Later on, these "embeds" received "unprecedented access to plans", without compromising them: "We know of no media that violated the trust during the entire operation. After all, they were coming along."[61] This was a reasonable way to balance the needs for operational security and journalistic access (and integrity), but as an inevitable result, without their knowledge (and sometimes without the military's prior intention), "embeds" became a source of military intelligence and a means of deception and media influence. The Third Division noted that "access to leaders and soldiers through embedding provided first-hand accounts and balanced negative press from media not embedded"; in particular, because they had been briefed that the division planned to halt two days in the campaign near An Najaf for between forty-eight and seventy-two hours to refit, embeds "had a more realistic understanding and were optimistic in their accounts", and "balanced the negative press from reporters outside Iraq". Generally, "embeds" followed their professional instincts; their reports were honest, however impressionistic, while casualties were low and action fast. One may wonder how far this experience can be repeated. The greatest attrition suffered by "embeds" came from those who preferred to avoid reality after experiencing training: fifteen of sixty assigned to the First Marine Division bowed out when given the chance, after which another six of twenty-seven assigned to one regimental combat team never showed up.[62] "Embeds" on Omaha Beach in June 1944, conversely, would have transmitted pictures like the first twenty minutes of "Saving Private Ryan". They would not have been taken for entertainment.

American strategic intelligence worked better in purely military spheres, if less on matters of quality than quantity. Its picture of enemy order of battle and characteristics was good. It appreciated fairly well the strength needed to destroy its foe, though it assumed the war would last 125 days, as opposed to twenty-five, and grossly overrated the enemy's quality and rationality. These were major errors yet perhaps unavoidable in the circumstances, and minor in practical import (far less costly than those about WMDs). The Coalition could hardly have attacked with fewer forces than it did, or earlier, or with less damage on either side. Even seasoned analysts had grounds for uncertainty about the capabilities and intentions of enemy forces—would they all be bad, or would some achieve mediocrity? Would they stand in the field, or the cities? As the British Ministry of Defence noted, "very little was known about how [the Iraqis] planned to oppose the Coalition or whether they had the will to fight. Objective analysis had to take into account Iraqi bluster and disinformation ... The lack of clear information meant that the Coalition did not anticipate that Iraqi organized military resistance would collapse so quickly and completely".[63] When the V Corps commander, General Wallace, said the Iraqis were "not the enemy we wargamed", he merely expressed surprise they were foolish enough to fight in the open.[64] He would have been foolish to assume they would—that the foe would be as incompetent as possible and follow the worst strategy available. Clearly, however, there had been no revolution in military intelligence at basic levels, where old problems in assessment recurred, especially for western armies in relation to non-western foes. The First Marine Division noted that American forces grasped enemy capabilities well, but

> we remained largely ignorant of the intentions of enemy commanders ... This shortcoming was especially critical as much of the war plan was either based on or keyed to specific enemy responses. When the enemy "failed" to act in accordance with common military practice, we were caught flat-footed because we failed to accurately anticipate the unconventional response. This was primarily due to a dearth of HUMINT on the enemy leadership. In trying to map out the opposition's reactions we were largely relegated to our OSINT [open source] sources and rank speculation based on our own perceptions of the battlefield to make our assessments ... Our technical dominance has made us overly reliant on technical and quantifiable intelligence collection means. There is institutional failure to account for the most critical dimension of the battlefield, the human one.[65]

American strategic intelligence was mediocre, but better by far than that of the enemy. Iraq was surprised by the time of the attack, its forces caught in normal positions, following disastrous plans involving multiple defence lines and massive redeployments in the open, because it misread its own and the Coalition's capabilities, and perhaps because of deception. According to Franks, throughout 2002, forces for war against Iraq were deployed and strengthened in as "invisible" a fashion as possible, so not to stampede Saddam into undesirable actions and "to achieve surprise in the event we had to go to war". Equipment was moved secretly, in container ships, presumably to avoid detection by satellites or spies. In 2003, the Coalition very much wanted to keep the eleven regular and two Republican Guard divisions in Kurdistan from destroying the northern oilfields, attacking Kurds, or moving south. Thus, the Fourth Division went to ships in the eastern Mediterranean, able to achieve that end whether it could enter Turkey or not.

> You have tactical efficiency if you are able to introduce a division from the north, but you have strategic surprise simply by having the division positioned in the eastern Mediterranean. We believed we could through intelligence means have some influence on the regime through information warfare and deception, and we wanted the regime to believe that force would be introduced in the north, and that the timing of that introduction might be discussed with the Turks. We wanted some uncertainty in the mind of Saddam Hussein about whether the Turks were planning to permit the

landing of the force, so I kept the force waiting long past the point where I knew it would not be introduced in the north.[66]

Though the United States preferred to send the Fourth Division through Turkey, this end was subordinate to freezing Iraqi forces in Kurdistan, and it always pursued a second plan—using deception to pin the Iraqis, with Special Forces and an airborne brigade to create a skeleton front, at the price of slowing the Fourth Division's move to Kuwait by several days. The equation was complex. To Franks, the Fourth Division's role was to pin Iraqis in Kurdistan. If it succeeded, it mattered little whether that formation was ready for other tasks; thus it was not, reducing the divisions in Kuwait on 20 March by 20 per cent, a high cost for deception. However, the Fourth Division and the First Armored Division would be available some weeks into the attack, which Franks thought "took the gamble out of the equation and placed the level at what I call prudent risk". The option of waiting until those forces were in Kuwait would have strengthened the blow but lost surprise; while Franks thought that deploying the Fourth Division in Kuwait from the start, at the risk of letting Iraqi forces move from Kurdistan, would dull the Coalition's edge.

To cover these intentions, says Franks, "we initiated deception operations to pass information to the regime that would cause either uncertainty or chaos".[67] How this was done is not completely certain, given the limits to our data about American intelligence on and means to deceive Iraq, but still much evidence is in the public domain. The campaign involved all the usual sources, diplomatic, intelligence, physical and media. Franks implies that he ran deception virtually by himself, which is unlikely, although no doubt he was central to it—as ever, interest by a commander is essential to make deception work effectively. He warned Saddam, through an Arab leader who was an unofficial link between them, that Jordan and Turkey would aid the United States. He claims to have passed precise disinformation to Baghdad, through an American officer whom Iraqi intelligence believed was one of their agents, but who was actually under United States control.[68] Other diplomatic and intelligence channels may have carried deceptive material, which was also disseminated through the media. The weeks before the attack witnessed classic signs of media-borne deception. Some forces quietly slipped from the record (as the GlobalSecurity website noted) while others were advertised, especially the location of ships containing the Fourth Division. As a Turkish front collapsed, or perhaps merely seemed to do so, press reports from Washington emphasized that this would crack Coalition plans, and indicated the attack would begin only after the Fourth Division reached Kuwait. Meanwhile, Franks passed a different story to Baghdad through his controlled agent, that at the last minute before war, Turkey would let in the Fourth Division, to open a northern front. How far these different stories were coordinated is unclear—Washington may have been as confused as Baghdad on these points. Conversely, this may have been an example of the deception technique called the "double bluff", the passing of conflicting stories, one of which calls the other as a lie. In either case, the Americans pursued surprise through the classic means of encouraging an enemy to focus on the wrong indicators and to assume an attack would occur later than intended, its start signalled by the movements of the Fourth Infantry Division, which would suit their IO doctrine and sense of Iraqi preconceptions.[69] Later, the Defense Secretary, Donald Rumsfeld, agreed that the "inability of forces to enter from the north was disappointing, but keeping 4th ID in the Mediterranean created element of surprise, Iraq did not expect attack to begin until 4th ID arrived in Kuwait". He speculated that Iraq

> very likely expected Gulf War II, a long air war that would give them time to do whatever they thought they wanted to do, leave or take cover and what have you, followed at some distance by a ground war, and probably a massive ground war ... they did not expect a ground war to start without an air war and they did not expect a ground war to start without the 4th Infantry Division while it was still up in the Mediterranean. I also suspect that they didn't expect the first air attack that took place the day before the ground war began.[70]

That attack occurred late on 19 March when, after telling the media the war would not start that day, American authorities struck to kill Saddam when intelligence indicated his apparent location—an improvised and unsuccessful use of deception, which surprised even American staff officers in Qatar. Innocent "embeds" too supported deception. As part of the cover, all embeds were sent to "training exercises" in the days before the operation began, while none went with the Special Forces used to clear the western desert just before the battle; later, others were sent with the 173rd Airborne Brigade as it flew from Italy to Kurdistan, to attract attention there. Between 22 and 30 March, Americans spread disinformation about airborne assaults (rather fewer occurred than were hinted) and their sites; they deliberately overplayed media accounts of their problems in the south so to lure Iraqi forces forward; while small but publicized actions occurred in Kurdistan. In particular, the 173rd Airborne Brigade began its ostentatious activities on 26 March, as Americans approached the Iraqi main line of resistance between Karbala and Kut, but was not fully deployed or conducting operations there until 1 April, almost a week later. Again, a feint covered the thrust through the Karbala gap during 1–3 April.

American deception was sophisticated and followed its doctrine. It aimed to affect enemy actions, not ideas, and did so by aiming for confusion, but for misdirection when enemy preconceptions could be fathomed (thus, the deployment of so many Iraqi forces in Kurdistan signalled an expectation of threat). The evidence does not indicate how far deception shaped Iraqi errors. At the operational level, probably it achieved more through confusion than misdirection, which is the norm. Iraqi commanders seem to have been confused, probably in part because deception did further "uncertainty or chaos", though it may not have mattered much to that effect, given the many factors at hand. Deception did not achieve its full end of pinning Iraqi forces in Kurdistan before or during the war—Saddam needed no encouragement to keep regular divisions there and the two Republican Guard divisions finally did move south, to annihilation by air, though in staying and going they served American plans. Given the fact Coalition forces in Kuwait were small, with big reinforcements on the way, however, deception probably contributed to Iraq, and foreign states to which it listened, being taken by surprise about the timing of the attack. If so, deception shaped the politics of the outbreak of war. Some governments doubted the United States was ready to attack. Saddam routinely walked to the edge of a precipice before signalling a willingness to back down. Meanwhile, American deception indicated that the cliff's edge was some distance away, its location marked by the Fourth Division. If he or they misunderstood when the attack would start, they would not have seen the imperative need to avoid it, and thus not have taken the slim chances to avoid catastrophe. Perhaps deception mattered more through its unintended effects than the intended ones, not for the first time.

Advocates of transformation emphasize what one theorist terms "targeting epistemology".[71] In Iraq, American authorities played such mind games, which Admiral Cebrowski called a "direct movement into the cognitive domain".[72] This American practice in Iraq was among the most sophisticated on record, with some original features. Through television and radio broadcasts and 50 million leaflets, psyops was conducted against Iraqi civilians and soldiers, without apparent impact. It never reached soldiers in some, perhaps most, units, lacking personal radios and surrounded by Ba'athist security. The Coalition failed in a key area of political warfare, to make civilians affect the war. Conversely, it launched a "fused" IO attack on enemy epistemology, aimed to cripple its communications and corrupt its information. Cebrowski claimed that, knowing "a dictator can't trust his information" and Saddam would have to "script the whats and whens" of his war even though "he doesn't know if people will carry them out", the United States aimed to wreck his "feedback loop", his ability to know what was happening on the battlefield.[73] This approach involved the destruction of command and communication targets, and more. The air attacks on Saddam, and the claims they rested on reports from agents in Baghdad, were highly publicized, to shock his subordinates. His trust in his officers, and their mutual confidence, was sapped by announcements that Americans were subverting Iraqi officers, and contacting via e-mail those with access to computers. This combination of psyops, bribery, deception, and a human form of cyberwar, manipulated a Stalinist regime and a paranoid political culture, seemingly with effect. After the war, one Iraqi officer stationed on the southern Iran–Iraq frontier, Colonel Sa'ad, held psyops had little effect on his men whereas e-mails to officers had a "big impact". Even if officers immediately reported all such contacts to a superior, "Imagine him thinking: 'If the Americans are able to get into the mind of a senior commander this way, how can I protect a whole division?'."[74]

At the operational level, the story is mixed. Military planners pursued a COP for commanders and a "Common Relevant Operating Picture" (CROP) for soldiers, to give everyone in any decision-making loop the same, good information, while national intelligence agencies sought to support this expeditionary force. These ambitions seem to have been realized tolerably well at the theatre level, including component commands down to the corps, which historically is fairly common, but not far below. After the war, the NSA boasted that, through laptop computers, staff at Marine regiments, army divisions and USAF theatre command centres "tapped into the most sensitive NSA databases". The experience did not impress one of its consumers.[75] Once it began to advance, the First Marine Division

> received very little actionable intelligence from external intelligence organizations. The Division had to assemble a coherent picture from what it could collect with organic and DS [direct support] assets alone.
>
> The nature of the battlefield, the extreme distances, high operational tempo and lack of a coherent response from a conventional enemy all made it difficult for an external agency to know what was tactically relevant and required by the GCE commander. The byzantine collections process inhibited our ability to get timely responses to combat requirements with the exception of assets organic to or DS to the Division. This made the Division almost exclusively reliant on organic or DS collection assets. The Division found the enemy by running into them, much as forces have done since the beginning of warfare ...
>
> On a fluid high tempo battlefield, a highly centralized collections bureaucracy is too slow and cumbersome to be tactically relevant. The best possible employment option is to push more assets in DS to the lowest tactical level and increase available organic collections ...
>
> OIF presented the intelligence community with unprecedented robust collection architecture to support combat operations. Unfortunately it also presented the community and more specifically the tactical user with the equally unprecedented cumbersome collection bureaucracy.

> The existing hierarchical collections architecture, particularly for imagery requirements, is wildly impractical and does not lend itself to providing timely support to combat operations.

This division faced every standard problem of bottlenecks and overload in information, and the failure of every "push" and "pull" technique touted to manage them. National intelligence sources were "great for developing deep targets, subject to the prioritization of high headquarters [Division and higher]. Navigating the labyrinth of collection tasking processes proved too difficult in most cases to get reporting on Division targets, and certainly for Battalion-level collections". Intelligence sections had better signals, which "inundated" them with irrelevant information. The only exceptions to these flaws were systems organic to the division. JSTARS [the Joint Surveillance Target Attack Radar System] illuminated the location of hostile vehicles. "Because they were close to the point of decision, those JSTARS operators shared the sense of urgency and 'can-do' attitude. They worked aggressively to find ways to answer questions instead of deflect them."[76]

These problems occurred in part because Marine technology and organization for C[4]ISR were less sophisticated than those of the army. The Third Division was led from an "assault command post", which let its commander "freely move on the battlefield with a separate security and communications package", and a Divisional tactical command post (DTAC), "an intelligence node with stable communications and access to corps, theater, and national intelligence products to support the DTAC and forward brigades who were all on the move almost constantly".[77] The Marines' command system was similar, but DTAC had better communications and a divisional intelligence support element (DISE) shaped precisely to receive, collect, collate and assess material from higher levels. DISE did tap the resources of national intelligence services, but could not direct their use. Unlike the Marines, the Third Division did not complain of information overload nor of inability to shoot the rapids of Byzantium nor that higher levels provided only useless material. Still, it too noted that higher authorities would not meet its requests for information on specific topics, and demanded better organic capabilities for imagery and signals intelligence. DISE received live UAV feeds, and had some influence on their missions. Aided by a NIMA team, it accessed NIMA imagery "only hours old" when DTAC was stationary and reestablished these contacts forty-five minutes after ending each of its eight moves in the campaign. The Third Division did not refer to NSA material, meaning little was provided. DTAC used this intelligence to guide orders to its brigades and its organic firepower. The Third Division moved a major step further than the Marines, but it too met unsolvable problems with intelligence. Brigades and battalions made most key decisions. Although DTAC tried to send them information, little arrived, because of problems with communications. As the division later noted about intelligence, "if you aren't talking, you're just camping".

When the division began to move, its main signals system fell apart. The mobile subscriber equipment (MSE) network used FM frequencies to link stationary headquarters about fifteen miles apart. It could not be used by units on the move, usually the case at any time for one or two of the division's three brigades, nor when main divisional signals moved. MSE worked well between adjacent battalions, or when a brigade headquarters stopped and contacted division; otherwise, not. Still, it had to carry most traffic within the division. Fortunately, as MSE failed, Central Command gave the Third Division a jury-rigged alternative, based on a "dumbed-down" version of the next generation, the digitalized Force XXI Battle Command Brigade and Below system, "FBCB^2/BLUEFOR", with geographical tracking and text-messaging systems.[78] Though "BLUEFORCE TRACKER" was intended to let theater staffs locate friendly forces, not carry combat communications, FBCB^2/BLUEFOR had an "awesome ability" to do so, alongside problems of its own. The Third Division had just 150 BLUEFOR sets, far less than did the logistical units for which they were designed, forcing undesirable rationing; and in effect BLUEFOR sent plain language text messages by wireless! "BFT was non-secure and had the potential to be monitored and exploited by a more technologically savvy enemy." MSE and BLUEFOR, backed by commercial cellphones and forty-three military Iridium phones, carried enough traffic during mobile operations to meet the Third Division's central needs, barely. Alas, none of these systems, bar MSE, could carry the digitalized systems "most beneficial" for operations and intelligence (including those needed to transmit any imagery pulled down from above). These systems worked only when MSE did, and when brigade headquarters, often stationary for only four hours, bothered to take the forty-five to sixty minutes needed "to set up and boot" the system. Intelligence and command were transformed above the division, but unchanged and barely adequate within it. The Third Division received little more "actionable" intelligence from above than the Marines, and just as often found the enemy by running into it.

In 2003, divisions, brigades and battalions had no better intelligence in battle than during 1944, though that was useful. Units made good and fast use of prisoners, psyops and Iraqi cellphone traffic.[79] At a higher level, however, intelligence was handled well, as planned and with rare efficiency. It set the machine in motion. On 19 March, American authorities had intelligence on Saddam's location for hours before the ultimatum ended, but did not act until that period ended, when they struck at once. On 20 March, the ground attack opened twenty-four hours earlier than intended, when Iraqi movements toward southern oilfields were detected. Later, intelligence tracked the movement of the Republican Guard, and guided airstrikes on it. Franks noted that commanders had "much more precise technology-based information"; sitting before the main data-processing systems at his headquarters, in front of thin plasma screens, before receiving any reports from below, he detected the "thunder run" (armoured thrusts with close air support) from the Karbala Gap to the Saddam Hussein International Airport via BLUEFOR, GPS and channel-surfing to the reports of a CNN "embed" with the 3/7 Cavalry. "The combination of these technologies was very, very powerful, and at the same time as we had this advantage, we knew for a certain fact the regime was unable to communicate with its subordinate Republican Guard forces to give them instructions to respond, to react." He recalled later: "I've just died and gone to heaven. I've just seen the first bit of network-centric work that has ever been experienced by the highest level of operational command."[80] Frank's Deputy Commander, John Abizaid, held: "Never before have we had such a complete picture of enemy tactical dispositions and intentions. I think largely the speed of the campaign was incredibly enabled by the complete picture we had of the enemy on the battlefield." Intelligence "was the most accurate I've ever seen on the tactical level, probably the best I've ever seen on the operational level and perplexingly incomplete" about WMDs. "Operationally we came up with a remarkably clear picture. We expected to fight the main battle between the line of Karbala, Kut and Baghdad, we expected it to be fought against the four Iraqi Republican Guard divisions and we expected their exact positions on the battlefield." C^{4}ISR and IO worked well and with unprecedented quality, though "we found it difficult at times to assess and measure [IO's] effects during the operation" while "our ability to strike rapidly sometimes exceeded our ability to sense and assess the effects as quickly as we would have liked".[81] The Marines and the British were more critical of the Allies' grasp of enemy intentions and about how the war would be fought.

The Coalition appears to have gained little from agents about strategic matters before the war—the evidence in the public domain indicates that they passed on many false reports, and misled western decision makers, though of course success may be silent—but more on tactical issues during it. According to investigators from the "Joint Readiness Training Center Intelligence Division" (JRTCID), the sixty-nine tactical human intelligence teams (THT) deployed in Iraq were expected to give Central Command 120 reports per day. Instead, they provided thirty, because neither that command nor its units knew what to do with them—THTs often "augmented four-man stacks during building raids (they were usually the number two man, who statistically is the person who gets shot)". The Third Division too thought THTs unable to give "experienced and comprehensive analysis and guidance to operational teams".[82] Even if used inefficiently, THTs provided some useful material to units, and Special Forces. How, how far and how usefully, cryptanalysis or traffic analysis was conducted is unclear, but across the board it appears to have been among the best sources. Frank's comments imply that communications intelligence was at least good at a theatre level, while the Third Division thought "sigint" "performed adequately". Apparently, "elint" and traffic analysis were useful while plain language traffic was often intercepted in real time and used effectively at operational and tactical levels, implying that formation and battalion staffs had interpreters, able quickly to translate colloquial Arabic in the Iraqi dialect to usable English. The Third Division had twenty-four Arabic speakers with its legacy signals intelligence systems, and perhaps as many again with its modern ones.[83] Lack of interpreters, however, was a critical problem for interrogation of prisoners, one cause (along with the inability of the small Allied forces to process prisoners) why Iraqi soldiers were left to melt back into the population, which later created security problems. The American military had just seventy qualified Arabic translators in its ranks, many of whose knowledge of Arabic or Arabs was sketchy. According to the JRTCID, most were competent "basically ... to tell the difference between a burro and a burrito". The US was forced to turn to "contract linguists", "mercenaries" without much physical stamina. "Laugh if you will, but many of the linguists with which I conversed were convenience store workers and cab drivers, most over the age of 40." Nor were they used well. "We can no longer afford to send interpreters in 'support' of units to buy chickens and soft drinks."[84] The Coalition, however, had unprecedented success with innovative technical means of collection, such as imagery; and also UAVs, which the JRTCID tellingly termed "the vacuum through a straw" and the "drug of choice". UAVs may well prove to be crack cocaine for information junkies. For the first time in history, GPS became the leading source of tactical intelligence, and maps wastepaper.[85]

Information surged across the system without swamping it, carried, one journalist wrote, by "an unsung corps of geeks improvising as they went, cobbling together a remarkable system from a hodgepodge of military-built networking technology, off-the-shelf gear, miles of Ethernet cable, and commercial software", and Microsoft Premier on-line help for troubleshooting.[86] Reachback, push and pull techniques and a "Warfighting Web" linked national intelligence agencies to theatre commands, and rear headquarters to ground forces, equipped with 100,000 GPS receivers, one to each vehicle (or to most squads of nine soldiers or five Marines). Commands shared a COP as did the members of any unit, though little passed either way through the interface of divisional and corps headquarters, or national boundaries. Perhaps 3,000 leaders from corps to section shared various intranets (including BLUEFOR) with map overlays. These systems let everyone know where everybody was, and allowed instant contact through text-messaging systems with anyone at adjacent levels of command whose screen name one knew. Although this equipment was installed at the last moment, had design problems, and personnel were poorly trained in its use, BLUEFOR and GPS scored one triumph—they were far better than maps in showing people where they and others were, even allowing precise manoeuvre during blinding sandstorms, reducing uncertainty and the need for signals. BLUEFOR, however, barely boosted operational communications above the best historical norms, and it had a striking flaw—its insecurity; so too commercial cellphones. Iridium phones were also used insecurely, and their transmissions failed "approximately 50% of the time". The Coalition's operational communications worked only because they abandoned signals security—the point is obvious.[87] Conversely, the fact that American forces functioned so well despite their many problems with signals indicates the power of their systems for command and training.

One heralded aspect of C⁴ISR received a test. During 2002 the Deputy Secretary of Defense, Paul Wolfowitz, noted that in the Afghanistan campaign, "young non-commissioned officers routinely integrate multiple intelligence collection platforms by simultaneously coordinating what amounts to several 'chat rooms' ... They display an agility that comes from being completely comfortable with this new way of doing things." Upbringing on the internet made them children of the information age.[88] He did not discuss how well this technique would work in complex operations. This issue arose in 2003. Tactical intranets were based on a chat-room format. Chat rooms on SIPRnet (the classified military intranet) joined Tactical Operations Centers (TOC) at brigades to the world—by sending a question to a TOC, a soldier on the front was one interface from an expert, though the number of chat rooms (fifty for the army and 500 for the navy) and people yearning to join threatened information overload.[89] This danger was avoided. Others were not. Problems with MSE prevented brigades from routinely contacting SIPRnet. One observer noted: "Rumour spreading was rife in particular over the most secure means the SIPRNET. People were using it as a chat room and making unsubstantiated allegations and claims on this means. Commanders lost faith in the SIPR and chose direct voice comms as the best means. It also created confusion and fear amongst Marines that was unnecessary."[90] Like radio, chat rooms solve problems and make them. They are also labour intensive. No unit can use a chat room without having one person monitoring it. The number of chat rooms rises not just because they have value, but because people have time to spare. The more chat rooms you have, the less you need them. It is unclear whether chat rooms gave soldiers useful advice, or how military communications can apply a system commonly used for gossip, in a war against a dangerous foe with the initiative.

The greatest change came in airpower where, heretofore, the need to build and distribute daily air tasking orders (ATOs), often the size of a telephone book, caused bottlenecks and overload in information, and confusion and friction for command. In Iraq, web-based ATOs let commanders change missions at will; carrier-borne aircraft received their target orders just as they got to the edge of Baghdad. Fleeting news or chances which once would have been lost in the shuffle led to precise strikes—in Iraq, as in Afghanistan and Yemen, sometimes the USAF could bomb a ten-by-ten-foot box twenty minutes after its detection by any source. A soldier with a laser range-finder linked to GPS could send the coordinates of a target to a command site hundreds of miles away, which fed those coordinates onto the GPS-enabled bombs of an aircraft in another locale—even changing them in flight. Much of this success stemmed not from transformation but, as one senior officer said, from "having 'lots of airplanes in the air constantly with numerous types of munitions' "—what others called aircraft "racked" and stacked" in a "racetrack" pattern.[91] As with the "cab rank" system of 1944, the flexibility, speed and range of air strike expanded not just because command improved, but because many aircraft were present and opposition was absent. How far this operation reflects transformation in airpower is uncertain. Perhaps it occurred above a margin for the optimum use of airpower, below which performance spirals down. In the Kosovo campaign, after all, against an enemy with good camouflage and air defences and a high degree of political influence, overcentralization and confusion between levels of command crippled the use of a similar system of airpower.

Below the corps level in land warfare, C^4ISR seems to have changed little. Reachback did not work; fusion was cold. In the Third Infantry and First Marine Divisions, the speed of reaction between calls for fire support and the moment batteries received their orders was 180 to 200 seconds—if anything, the system was less speedy and sophisticated than the Allied one at Normandy in 1944, though artillery delivered more accurate and devastating fire. The system for air support was far less good than that of 1944. Marine and army units could not receive tactical air support when they needed it; so too the Third Division at the operational level.[92] C^4ISR increased the power of aircraft in interdiction, but not close support. Much signals kit was clumsy or incompatible, leading to failures in links of the chain which might have mattered against a real foe. Planning cycles to coordinate movement and fire support within Marine and army corps and divisions and with the USAF, were based on forecasts of likely events twenty-four, forty-eight and seventy-two hours ahead. These cycles were so slow compared to action on the field that formations could not harmonize their forces or firepower. This problem was redoubled by slow and clumsy links when formations, theatre commanders and the USAF tried to coordinate overlapping immediate responsibilities.[93] Land forces and the USAF fought separate battles, and argued over the margins of their responsibilities, rather than fusing them. In these key areas, the performance of 2003 fell well below the standard of 1944, let alone of transformation. Below the corps level, the official COP failed; there was no ONA—indeed, there seems to have been little operational intelligence in the classic sense. Though advocates of the RMA claim the operational level of war will vanish, one doubts they had this in mind!

One also may doubt that ground operations were a matter of transformed command and the conscious use of "swarm" tactics. The real picture seems to be one of a big country with few enemy forces, which attackers entered in a dispersed fashion and fell forward, driven by inertia, determined junior leaders and the principle of "point me toward the enemy". This war could be won by divisional or regimental commanders. Precisely they took the key decisions—the "thunder runs" from Karbala to Saddam Hussein International Airport, and from there to Baghdad—without access to intelligence or consultation with superiors. This was for a reason—Franks' "experience in Vietnam was that we did not want the guy we used to call Snowball 6 orbiting overhead and telling our platoons what to do. I made sure I never did that". He avoided overcentralization and micromanagement, at the price of dividing intelligence from operations. Intelligence guided airpower and gave generals a good grip on events, but it did not influence the key actions on the ground. The officers who received this material did not act on it; those who acted did not have that intelligence.[94] Frank's instincts were sound, but this approach would have worked less well against a better enemy. Then, command might have to be more centralized, initiative curtailed, and intelligence would be perhaps more useful. What journalists call swarms look rather like the use of columns in nineteenth-century imperial warfare, less an innovation than a standard procedure. Again, in 2003 signals were not necessarily better than in 1944, nor were all improvements in communications good for command. General Mattis led the First Marine Division as though in the western desert during 1941, through plain language radio transmissions and a vehicle that let him easily and quickly visit his forces in action. And one Marine sergeant noted: "NCOs run the fight no matter how much you get on the radio. Sit back and listen to them. You might just learn something from them."[95]

Operation Iraqi Freedom demonstrates a new standard for conventional war. Cebrowski proclaimed "the discovery of a new 'sweet-spot' in the relationship between land and air warfare and a tighter integration of the two. The things that compel are good sensors networked with good intelligence disseminated through a robust networking system, which then yields speed. Speed turns out to be a very, very important factor".[96] In effect, he claimed the revolutionaries' predictions were coming true. Yet C^4ISR, NCW, C^2W and IO worked as planned, because Coalition forces had the initiative and followed their plan, while the enemy was passive, overwhelmed, unable to strike their forces or C^4ISR, or make them fight hard in towns. Had Iraq jammed GPS or tactical communications, it would have broken the Coalition's enhanced power in intelligence and precision of attack; had it harmed strategic signals or computers, it would have crippled the enemy's command; if it could have profited from signals intelligence, the living would have been easy. American satellite communications came close to the limit even in this simple campaign, especially for forces "on the move", limiting and slowing the transmission of operational traffic at all levels.[97] Nor can this problem be easily solved—the more signals can do, the more is demanded of them. Video-teleconferencing and the transfer of video images are increasingly taken as norms, even though they eat bandwidth for breakfast and crash brigade communications to boot—or reboot.[98]

How far this success can be repeated is unsure—the German army of 1941 or the Red Army of 1945 might have exploited these flaws in C³I; NCW, C⁴ISR and IO worked less well in Kosovo; turkey shoots offer few lessons in tactics. These technical problems in communication and intelligence can probably be overcome, but so too can enemies improve their attack on them. The first step for any rational and capable enemy in a war with the United States might be to jam any communications on the electromagnetic spectrum—this would damage American power far more than their own. C²W worked in Iraq, as sometimes it has in the past; but not always. So one-sided was this war that intelligence served primarily for target acquisition rather than ONA. If ONA was attempted, it failed, which raises questions about the concept of RDO. So too, one may question ideas about ISR and command which assume that in thirty minutes once every two hours, TOCs can receive, update and distribute to division and corps commanders all-source intelligence from all levels in a neat, precise and synchronized fashion.[99] Dust and heat in rooms housing SIPRnet servers and routers endangered C⁴ISR more than did the Iraqis. Sometimes, the tactical intranet broke down, often signals went *en clair* via civilian cellphones.[100] Could this near-NCW system work in complex operations against an able enemy? In Afghanistan and Iraq, precise strikes have often failed, showing that they succeed only when the machine performs without friction. Any friction yields failure; no system can always be perfect. An enemy which fights by its own rules, light infantry willing to die or able silently to steal away, has caught American forces at a disadvantage. One enemy can learn from another's successes and failures, or from American tactics. The latter follow their playbook; they have remarkable faith in doctrine; they do what their doctrine says, and they test the ideas they are discussing. They are more formulaic than they think.

Again, though few forces match the level of American training, still its performance in Iraq leads one to wonder whether these standards can sustain transformation. The JRTCID's verdict on the army's intelligence training is hard. It held that combat officers, especially within units, questioned the competence of their intelligence personnel, and correctly so. Junior officers and enlisted men were unprepared "to take on tactical intelligence roles" at battalion or brigade levels. They "did not understand the targeting process and were unable to produce the products to support" it. They had "very little or no analytical skills" and "weak intelligence briefing skills. If the … senior intelligence analyst was unable to brief, commanders usually forwent the intelligence portion of the brief". Poor "collection management", a "recurring problem" in training, emerged "during real-world operations". At divisions and corps, collection managers often had "no formal training" nor any idea of what questions to ask their intelligence services. They "failed to develop Specific Intelligence Requirements (SIRs), those questions that the tasked assets specifically answer … Most assets had poor SIRs assigned to them, which caused the asset teamleader to guess what was the collection manager's intent".[101] This helps to explain why senior authorities could not meet the needs for specific intelligence of the Marine Division and the Third Division.

C^{4}ISR multiplied some forms of power more than others. The gains were most notable in links between theatre and component commands, in their ability to direct centralized firepower, and to allow aircraft to learn of targets of opportunity and conduct interdiction missions. Airpower was directed with unprecedented speed, power, precision and reach. Yet one should not take the greatest rises in performance for their norm, nor overgeneralize from particulars—by assuming Iraq in 2003 represents the future of war, or that land forces can suddenly behave like they have wings. Since 1933, air forces have been able to apply NCW to some aspects of combat, as have navies since 1955, while armies have not. Technology enables transformation; that in 2003 it multiplied the interdiction power of aircraft far more than it did land tactics is suggestive. Again, American forces had "dominant battlespace awareness" and "decision superiority", but these edges were not revolutionary in nature, merely at the upper edge of historical norms. So too, reachback and flexibility of command and the fusing of intelligence. So far, NCW and C^{4}ISR have not revolutionized communications, intelligence and command; at best, they have more or less reached the standard of 1944. Yet that standard is respectable, and it can probably be improved, in some ways.

Advocates of transformation appreciate the limits to C^{4}ISR and NCW in Iraq. John Osterholtz notes "there were pockets of net-centric operations, but it was not a general operating paradigm". Cebrowski held "what we're seeing is essentially net-centric warfare for the joint task force commander. The next step is network-centric warfare for the warfighter— reflecting increased 'jointness' at the tactical level of war". "People at the bottom, the tactical level, that's the only place where mortal danger lurks, and they are the least well-connected ... We're doing C^{4}I for the admiral and the general. We have a moral obligation to fix this."[102] How far can their hopes be realized? Any answer to this question must start by separating reality from rhetoric. The claims made for the RMA and NCW often are unlikely; but simply because they are wrong does not mean nothing is happening. The foundations of power clearly are changing: they always are. Information (as system, technology and content) is central to those alterations. Armed forces should adapt to changing times, attempts to do so will take them somewhere, if not necessarily where they thought they wanted to go. Adaptation can take armies to useful places, sometimes to the space they wanted to reach, or beyond. Often, however, one cannot get there from here, to the destination one likes. Armed forces do not always succeed in adaptation as planned. Efforts to force the pace of events can misfire. A revolution is not a road one takes to a certain destination. Attempts to ride the road will have unexpected results—your efforts to take the lead may cause a second party to nudge a third into your path and force you to kill a fourth, or fall behind the pack. Human actions may redirect the revolution, turning the road or the terminus. Revolutionaries may destroy the revolution, conservatives realize it.

A key factor in any attempt to learn lessons is the difference between problems and conditions. Problems can be solved, conditions must be endured. National intelligence services can flexibly and immediately meet many of the needs of a few divisions. The Third Division's experience indicates that properly equipped and organized divisional headquarters and national intelligence services can make effective contact in real time, though it will be far easier to improve techniques of pushing intelligence than those of pulling it. The difficulties for communications within and between formations in Operation Iraqi Freedom could probably be overcome for an expeditionary force of similar size, but not for one as large as Allied forces in Germany during 1945. Transformation offers so much because it affects so few forces, while its cost will reduce their size. Conversely, one can never eliminate uncertainty from war. No serious general theory of strategy can assume one will always have perfect knowledge while the enemy will always be blind, or one can always execute one's intentions without any error. Judgments are even harder to make because so many are needed. One can say RMA enthusiasts are wrong, because their system would fail against a serious enemy or a real war; yet if the latter cannot occur in the next twenty years, why does that objection matter? Perhaps as a special case during that period, an "information age" theory of strategy may apply. The point is both the transformation of forces, of their quality, and of their quantity, of one's power relative to one's enemy. When Americans draw lessons from Iraq, they can apply them to one case of conventional conflict, of giant against dwarf. Any other states drawing lessons from this conflict must think of war as a whole.

NCW or C^{4}ISR will not revolutionize (nor even much change) events on the strategic level of war, or the strategic-diplomatic dimensions of peace, which are dominated by human rather than technological matters. Often they will affect such events counter-productively, by increasing confusion in and between levels of command. C^{4}ISR and NCW sometimes will revolutionize tactics and operations where, all too often, friction at the systematic level has reduced the value of intelligence; one actor had information another could have used but did not have in time to act, knowledge available in time could not be used with effect; failures by any one cog prevented the whole machine from working well, or at all. In conventional war, NCW and C^{4}ISR may ensure that every cog of the machine works well at the same time, reducing friction to the lowest level possible. All national intelligence assets will focus on giving every unit every chance to exploit every fleeting opportunity; one's forces will be used to asking for or receiving such information and using it instantly, and well. In 1917, British signals intelligence constantly located U-boats, prompting immediate air or surface strikes, which failed because units were slow and their ordnance weak. By 1943, intelligence on U-boats was little better but Allied forces were far more able to kill. In 1944–1945, Allied air forces, using the cab rank system, could strike any target reported immediately, if not accurately; in the 2003 Iraq war, aircraft launched instant, precise and devastating strikes based on information acquired ten minutes earlier by headquarters 10,000 miles away. C^{4}ISR and NCW will raise the bar on the best use of intelligence, and the frequency of optimum uses, in conventional war; they will multiply any form of firepower relying on rapid, precise and long distance strikes, such as airpower.

Little will change where equals engage, or the weaker side evades one's strength or strikes one's C^{4}ISR, or against guerrillas. If NCW fails in any instance on which it is relied, disaster will be redoubled because of that fact; and fail NCW ultimately must. If successful, it will force one's adversaries to find solutions by evading your strength or by making you play to your weaknesses. It always is convenient when one's enemy chooses to be foolish or weak, or foolish and weak, but sometimes it does not choose to be; and you will be a fool to assume it must be so. A smart but weak foe may refuse any game where you can apply your strengths, and make you play another one, such as terrorism. A tough and able foe might turn the characteristics of your game and machine into a strength of its own, by attacking any precondition for NCW and then by imposing its rules on you. By doing what suits them in the context of our power, they will change their strengths and weaknesses—and yours too. The RMA has done many things, not everything. It has multiplied American strengths but not reduced its weaknesses. It has increased the value of high technology and firepower in conventional war, but for little else; where these things matter, they do more than ever; where they do not, nothing has changed. Iraq shows that the United States will aim to practice intelligence, command and war at a higher level than ever achieved before. When it can play to its strengths, it will succeed.

NOTES

Introduction

1 For works in this vein, cf. John Ferris, *The Evolution of British Strategic Policy, 1919–1926* (Ithaca, NY: Cornell University Press, 1989); "The Theory of a 'French Air Menace', Anglo-French Relations, and the British Home Defense Air Force Programmes of 1921–1925", *Journal of Strategic Studies*, 10(1) (March 1987), pp. 62–83; "Treasury Control, the Ten Year Rule and British Service Policies, 1919–1924", *Historical Journal* (December 1987); "The Symbol and Substance of Seapower: Great Britain, the United States and the One Power Standard, 1919–1921", in B.J.C. McKercher (ed.), *Anglo-American Relations During the 1920s: The Struggle for Supremacy* (Edmonton: University of Alberta Press, 1990); " 'The Greatest World Power on Earth': Britain During the 1920s", *International History Review* (November 1991); "The Air Force Brats View of History: Recent Writings and the Royal Air Force, 1918–1960", *International History Review*, XX (January 1998); "Fighter Defence Before Fighter Command: The Evolution of Strategic Air Defence In Great Britain, 1917–1934", *The Journal of Military History*, 63 (October 1999), pp. 845–884; "Achieving Air Ascendancy: Challenge and Response in British Air Defence, 1915–1940", in Sebastian Cox and Peter Grey (eds), *Air Power History, Turning Points from Kitty Hawk to Kosovo* (London: Frank Cass, 2002), pp. 21–50.
2 For works in this vein, cf. John Ferris, "A British 'Unofficial' Aviation Mission and Japanese Naval Developments, 1919–1929", *Journal of Strategic Studies*, 5(3) (September 1982), pp. 416–439; " 'Worthy of Some Better Enemy?' The British Assessment of the Imperial Japanese Army, 1919–1941, and the Fall of Singapore", *The Canadian Journal of History* (August 1993); "Japan In The Eyes of the British Army and the RAF, 1919–41" and "The Anglo-Japanese War In Asia, 1941–45", in Ian Gow and Yoshi Hirama (eds), *A History of Anglo-Japanese Relations: Military Dimensions* (New York: Palgrave, 2002); "Student and Master: The United Kingdom, Japan, Airpower and the Fall of Singapore", in Brian Farrell and Sandy Hunter (eds), *Singapore, Sixty Years On* (Singapore: Eastern Universities Press, 2002), pp. 94–121; "Armaments and Allies: The British Military Services and the Anglo-Japanese Alliance, 1911–21", in Phillips O'Brien (ed.), *The Anglo-Japanese Alliance* (London: Routledge, 2003).
3 John Ferris, "Far Too Dangerous a Gamble? British Intelligence and Policy During the Chanak Crisis, September–October 1922", in B.J.C. McKercher and Erik Goldstein (ed.), *Power and Stability, British Foreign Policy, 1865–1965* (London: Frank Cass, 2003), pp. 139–184.

4 For my assessment of 2002, cf. John Ferris, "The Road to Bletchley Park: The British Experience with Signals Intelligence, 1890–1945", in Oliver Hoare (ed.), *Intelligence and National Security*, 16(1) (Spring 2002), pp. 53–84. Records have not been released (and may no longer exist) on many key issues, such as the inner structure of SIS and many of its reports; and on political surveillance by MI5 and its imperial counterparts, most notably in India and Egypt, as against its work in security against espionage. For earlier works, not published here, cf. John Ferris, "Whitehall's Black Chamber: British Cryptology and the Government Code and Cypher School, 1919–1929", *Intelligence and National Security*, 2(1) (January 1987), pp. 54–91; "The British Army and Signals Intelligence in the Field During the First World War", *Intelligence and National Security*, 3(4) (October 1988); "From Broadway to Bletchley Park: The Diary of Captain Malcolm Kennedy", *Intelligence and National Security*, 4(3) (July 1989); "Before Room 40: The British Empire and Signals Intelligence, 1989–1914", *The Journal of Strategic Studies*, 12(4) (December 1989); *The British Army and Signals Intelligence During the First World War* (Phoenix Mill: Alan Sutton, 1992); " 'Airbandit': C31 and Strategic Air Defence During the First Battle of Britain, 1915–1918", in Michael Dockrill and David French (eds), *Strategy and Intelligence: British Policy During The First World War* (London: Hambledon, 1996).

1 Lord Salisbury, secret intelligence and British policy toward Russia and Central Asia, 1874–1878

I am grateful to the copyright holders for permission to cite material from the papers of the Third Marquis of Salisbury (Hatfield House), Owen Bourne, Lord Lytton and Lord Northbrook (India Office Library and Records), Lord Beaconsfield (The Bodleian Library) and Lord Minto (the National Library of Scotland). All remaining primary material cited is held by the Public Record Office and appears by permission of the Controller of Her Majesty's Stationery Office.

1 G.J. Alder, *British India's Northern Frontier, 1865–95, A Study in Imperial Policy* (London: Longmans, 1963); David Gillard, *The Struggle for Asia, 1828–1914* (London: Methuen, 1977); R.L. Greaves, *Persia and the Defence of India, 1884–1892* (London: Athlone, 1959); Adrian Preston, "British Military Policy and the Defence of India: A Study of British Military Policy, Plans and Preparations during the Russian Crisis, 1875–1880" (Ph.D. dissertation, University of London, 1966), and "The Eastern Question during the Franco-Prussian War", in Jay Atherton (ed.), *Historical Papers, 1972* (Victoria: Canadian Historical Association, 1972); A.P. Thornton, "The Reopening of the 'Central Asian Question,' 1864–9", *History*, 41 (1956), and "Afghanistan in Anglo-Russian Diplomacy, 1869–73", *Cambridge Historical Journal*, 11 (1954).
2 Seymour to Clarendon, 21 February 1854, *The Oriental Question, 1840–1900, Files from the Royal Archives, Windsor Castle* (Bethesda, MD: University Press of America, n.d.), Reel 5.
3 This argument challenges that of Firuz Kazemzadeh (*Russia and Britain in Persia, 1864–1914, A Study of Imperialism* (New Haven, CT: Yale University Press, 1968), p. 26), but generally concurs with Peter Morris, "The Russians in Central Asia, 1870–1887", *Slavonic and East European Review*, 53 (1975); see also note 18.
4 The best modern discussions of the Central Asian background to these events are Garry Alder, "Big Game Hunting in Central Asia", *Journal of Imperial and*

Commonwealth History, 9(3) (1981); Gillard, *The Struggle for Asia*; Edward Ingram, *The Beginning of the Great Game in Asia, 1828–1834* (Oxford: Clarendon, 1979); M.E. Yapp, *Strategies of British India, Britain, Iran and Afghanistan, 1798–1850* (Oxford: Clarendon, 1980), and "British Perceptions of the Russian Threat to India", *Modern Asian Studies*, 21(4) (1987). These scholars clash violently over most matters of interpretation, offering proof for Salisbury's scepticism about the efficacy of experts. Richard Millman's *Britain and the Eastern Question, 1875–1878* (Oxford: Clarendon, 1979) is the best modern account of British policy toward Turkey, though his unflattering view of Derby has been effectively challenged by John Vincent (ed.), *A Selection from the Diaries of Edward Henry Stanley, 15th Earl of Derby (1826–93), Between September 1869 and March 1878* (hereafter *Derby Diaries*), Camden Fifth Series, Volume 4 (1994), Royal Historical Society (1994).

5 Agatha Ramm (ed.), *The Political Correspondence of Mr. Gladstone and Lord Granville, 1868–1876*, vol. 2, *1871–76* (London: Royal Historical Society, 1952), pp. 353, 433.
6 Alder, *British India's Northern Frontier*, pp. 38–55.
7 The standard accounts are John Lowe Duthie, "Pressure from Within: The 'Forward' Group in the India Office during Gladstone's First Ministry", *Journal of Asian History*, 15(1) (1981), and "Some Further Insights into the Working of Mid-Victorian Imperialism: Lord Salisbury, the 'Forward Group' and Anglo-Afghan Relations: 1874–1878", *Journal of Imperial and Commonwealth History*, 8(3) (1980), to which the analysis contained in this chapter is indebted.
8 FO 519/275, Wellesley to Loftus, 21 February 1872.
9 Napier of Magdala to Duke of Cambridge, 14.7.71, Cambridge microfilms, Reel 27; L/MIL/17/14/80, memorandum by Roberts, "The dangers to which a reverse would expose us", 27.1.91.
10 Millman, *Britain and the Eastern Question*; Duthie, "Pressure from Within" and "Some Further Insights"; and Marvin Swartz, *The Politics of Foreign Policy in the Era of Disraeli and Gladstone* (London: Macmillan, 1985) offer the best modern accounts of these issues.
11 Disraeli to Salisbury, 28 October 1875, Salisbury Papers, Hatfield House, D/20; cf. George Earle Buckle, *The Life of Benjamin Disraeli, Earl of Beaconsfield*, vol. 6, *1876–1881* (London: John Murray, 1920), p. 15.
12 Dep. Hughenden 93/1, memorandum by Salisbury, 30.5.74, Salisbury to Disraeli, 13.10.74.
13 Salisbury to Disraeli, 27 March 1874, Disraeli to Salisbury, 2 June 1874, Salisbury Papers, D/20; Vincent, *Derby Diaries*, entry 6.3.74, p. 168.
14 Gwendolyn Cecil, *Life of Robert, Marquis of Cecil*, vol. 2, *1868–1880* (London: Hodder & Stoughton, 1921), p. 160; John Martineau, *The Life and Correspondence of Sir Bartle Frere*, vol. 1 (London: John Murray, 1895), pp. 491–498, passim; Duthie, "Some Further Insights", pp. 183–195; cf. the older views of B.H. Sumner, *Russia and the Balkans, 1870–1880* (Oxford: Clarendon, 1937), p. 53.
15 Salisbury to Lytton, 22 June 1877, Lytton Papers, India Office Library and Records, E.218/A.
16 Salisbury to Northbrook, 19 February 1875, Northbrook Papers, India Office Library and Records, C.144/12.
17 *Ibid.*, Salisbury to Northbrook, 25 March 1875.
18 Agatha Ramm, *Sir Robert Morier, Envoy and Ambassador in the Age of Imperialism, 1876–1893* (Oxford: Clarendon, 1973), p. 217.
19 Cf. *ibid.*, *passim*, and note 50 below. For background, cf. H. Sutherland Edwards, *Russian Projects against India from the Czar Peter to General Skobeloff*

NOTES

(London: Remington and Co., 1885), which is accurate for the mid-nineteenth century, although not always so for earlier periods; Gillard, *The Struggle for Asia*; John L. Evans (ed.), *Mission of N.P. Ignat'ev to Khiva and Bukhara, 1858* (Newtonville: Shoestring Press, 1984); Kazemzadeh, *Russia and Britain*, pp. 24–44; David MacKenzie, *The Lion of Tashkent, The Career of General M.G. Chernaiev* (Athens, Ga.: University of Georgia Press, 1974), pp. 43–48; Morris, "The Russians in Central Asia"; Alfred J. Rieber (ed.), *The Politics of Autocracy: Letters of Alexander II to Prince A.I. Bariatinskii, 1857–1864* (Paris: Mouton, 1966), pp. 77–78, 107–108.

20 Salisbury to Temple, 20 September 1878, Salisbury Papers, A/21.
21 Lady Salisbury to Lady Ely, 12 January 1877, *Oriental Question*, Reel 27.
22 Minto Papers, MS 12504, Minto Diary, entry 7.6.77, NLS. The son was Salisbury's eldest, James, Viscount Cranborne, then 15 years old.
23 Dep. Hughenden 74/2, Cabinet Paper by Salisbury. n.d., but *c*.7.77 by internal evidence.
24 Salisbury to Derby, 1 August 1874, Salisbury Papers, D/XVI/73.
25 The best account of British intelligence during the later nineteenth century is William Carpenter Beaver II, "The Development of the Intelligence Division and Its Role in Aspects of Imperial Policy Making, 1854–1901" (Ph.D. dissertation, Oxford University, 1976). For other solid studies, cf. Christopher Andrew, *Her Majesty's Secret Service: The Making of the British Intelligence Community* (London: Heinemann, 1985), pp. 21–67; Thomas G. Fergusson, *British Military Intelligence, 1870–1914, The Development of a Modern Intelligence Organisation* (London: UPA, 1984); John Ferris, "Penny Dreadful Literature: Britain, India and Strategic Intelligence on Russia and Central Asia, 1825–1947", paper presented to the Fourth International Conference on Intelligence, Carlisle Barracks, Pennsylvania, May 1989, and "Before 'Room 40': The British Empire and Signals Intelligence 1898–1914", *Journal of Strategic Studies*, 12(4) (1989); Preston, "The Eastern Question", and "British Military Policy", pp. 103–73.
26 T165/49, memorandum, "1922–23, Secret Service".
27 Cranbrook to Lytton, 27 September 1879, Lytton Papers, E.218/6.
28 Sumner, *Russia and the Balkans*, p. 368; Wolff to Salisbury, 30 August 1878, 16 January 1879, Salisbury Papers, A/18. Ferris, "Before 'Room 40' " and David Kahn, *The Codebreakers: The Story of Secret Writing* (New York: Macmillan, 1968), pp. 189–214, provide a background to this matter.
29 Clarendon to Palmerston, 28 February 1856, 7 March 1856, *Oriental Question*, Reel 20; FO 65/574, Napier to Foreign Office, 16 March 1861, passim; Ferris, "Penny Dreadful Literature"; Yapp, *Strategies*, p. 389.
30 Salisbury to Northbrook, 1 January 1875, Northbrook Papers, C.144/12; Salisbury to Currie, 23 August 1875, Salisbury Papers, DX/111/18.
31 Ferris, "Penny Dreadful Literature".
32 Lytton to Burne, 13 April 1877, Owen Burne Papers, India Office Library and Records, D.951.
33 Salisbury to Northbrook, 25 March 1875, Northbrook Papers, C.144/12.
34 *Ibid.*, same to same, 19 February 1875.
35 Salisbury to Temple, 20 September 1878, Salisbury Papers, A/21.
36 Salisbury to Northbrook, 22 May 1874, 19 June 1874, 10 July 1874, 17 July 1874, 12 August 1874, 3 December 1874, Northbrook Papers, C.144/11; Salisbury to Lytton, 19 May 1876, 2 June 1876, Lytton Papers, E.218/3A.
37 Disraeli to Salisbury, 17 October 1874, Salisbury Papers, D/20.
38 G.R.G. Hambly, "Unrest in Northern India During the Viceroyalty of Lord Mayo, 1869–72: The Background to Lord Northbrook's policy of Inactivity", *The Royal Central Asian Journal*, LXVIII (January 1961), pp. 37–55; Bernard

Mallet, *Thomas George, Earl of Northbrook* (London: Longmans, Green, 1908), pp. 99–105 and Edward C. Moulton, *Lord Northbrook's Indian Administration, 1872–1876* (London: Asia Publishing House, 1968), pp. 5–11, 242–245

39 Northbrook to Salisbury, 16 June 1874, Napier of Magdala to Northbrook, 8 March 1874, Northbrook Papers, C.144/11 and C.144/15; India Office to Foreign Office, 11 March 1876, FO 539/14; Alder, *British India's Northern Frontier*, pp. 49–58; John Keay, *The Gilgit Game, The Explorers of the Western Himalayas, 1865–95* (Oxford: Oxford University Press, 1979).

40 Salisbury to Disraeli, 13 October 1874, Salisbury Papers, D/20.

41 Dep. Hughenden 105/1, Lytton to Disraeli, 21.4.76. The best account of the relationship between Lytton, Salisbury and Disraeli is Ira Klein, "Who Made the Second Afghan War?", *The Journal of Asian History*, 8 (1974), pp. 97–121.

42 Dep. Hughenden 74/2, "Memorandum on possible Military Operations beyond our Trans-Indus Frontier" by H.W. Norman, 2.12.76, Government of India to India Office, No. 86 of 1877, 17.5.77, Political, memorandum by Foreign Department, Government of India, 2.7.77, memorandum by Sir Erskine Perry, 8.7.77, "Note on Frontier Government and Policy".

43 Lytton to Davies, 12 May 1876, Lytton to Sandeman, 8 April 1877, Lytton Papers, E.218/73 and E.218/24; Lytton to Burne, 8 April 1877, Burne Papers, D.951.

44 Haines to Cambridge, 23.7.76, Cambridge microfilms, Reel 32: Vincent, *Derby Diaries*, entry 12.10.76, p. 333.

45 Northbrook to Merewether, 22 October 1874, Northbrook to Salisbury, 22 January 1875, Northbrook Papers, C.144/16 and C.144/12.

46 Memoranda by Roberts, 22.3.73, "Proposal for an Intelligence Branch to be attached to Quartermaster Genl.'s Dept." and Captain Collen, 17.6.76, "Memorandum on the formation of an Intelligence Branch, Quartermaster General's Department, India", L/MIL 7/7793; Lady MacGregor (ed.), *The Life and Opinions of Major-General Sir Charles Metcalfe MacGregor*, vol. 2 (Edinburgh and London: W. Blackwood and Sons, 1888), pp. 2–3; Charles Metcalfe MacGregor, *Narrative of a Journey through the Province of Khorassan* (London: Allen, 1879), and *Wanderings in Balochistan* (London: Allen, 1882).

47 India Office to Foreign Office, 24 June 1878, Public Record Office (London), FO 181/567. Also Lytton to Gathorne-Hardy, 18 April 1878; same to same, 8 May 1878; Lytton to Cranbrook, 8 June 1878, 14 July 1878; Lytton to Temple, 18 July 1878; Cafagnari to Lytton, 24 May 1878, passim; same to same, 18 April 1878; these are in Lytton Papers, E.218/25A, E.218/25B, E.218/5, E.218/34, E.218/33.

The events of 1878 provide a good picture of the strengths and weaknesses of the Indian intelligence system. The timings of the Russian actions at issue are: St. Petersburg's decision to mobilize its forces in Turkistan and to send an official mission to Kabul, mid-May 1878; dispatch of the mission from Tashkent, mid-June, and southward movement of about 19,000 Russian troops, 1 July 1878; cancellation of military demonstration, 9 July; mission reaches Kabul, 22 July (after negotiating with representatives of Sher 'Ali *en route* from about 10 July). See Kazemzadeh, *Russia and Britain*, pp. 40–44; Seymour Becker, *Russia's Protectorates in Central Asia: Bukhara and Khiva, 1865–1924* (Cambridge, Mass.: Harvard University Press, 1968), p. 97; I.L. Yavorski (trans. Majors E.R. Elles and W.E. Gowan), *Journal of the Russian Embassy through Afghanistan and the Khanate of Bukhara in 1878–1879* (Calcutta, 1885). Russia did not try to conceal these actions (as opposed to prior preparations for them)—indeed, the mobilization had to attract British attention in order to serve its diplomatic purposes; hence, these events show the most effective way in which the most efficient possible intelligence service run out of India alone during that period could uncover real Russian threats. Indian intelligence sources (primarily, newswriters in Afghanistan and Indian merchants returning from Central Asia) had provided information on Russian military movements for years, frequently inaccurate and alarmist. These sources did not provide any advance warning about the Tsarist intentions of 1878, nor did the Foreign Office pass on its first hint in this direction (cf. note 75). On 24 May 1878, Lytton's intelligence chief in Peshawar, Louis Cavagnari, reported that Russia was placing "all the pressure they can" on Sher 'Ali, including veiled threats to unleash Abdur Rahman, but he doubted that the amir would turn to Russia—that nothing, in effect, was abnormal. Even on 8 June 1878 Lytton regarded reports from Foreign Office sources (probably in Persia) that Russian forces in Turkistan were mobilizing as "all moonshine"; these may in fact have been so, although Russian military preparations were by then under way.

Simultaneously, however, Lytton noted that newswriters in Kabul and Peshawar stated that Russia had informed Sher 'Ali that an official Russian mission would shortly visit Kabul, which had not occurred since 1838. These reports were accurate, and they were provided with remarkable speed. By 19 June "various sources"—Lytton noted that "these reports not yet fully substantiated, and their degree of important [sic] cannot be precisely ascertained"—revealed Russian mobilization and "pressure on Amir to receive important Russian Embassy". Between 29 June and 2 July Cavagnari reported massive Russian troop movements in Turkistan, though Russian strength was exaggerated at 30,000 rather than 19,000 men. Thus, by mid- to late June the government of India was aware that the two main Russian actions might be occurring. Although it was not entirely certain of the facts, the government was in a position to monitor and deal with the problem. Between 14 and 18 July additional garbled reports of Russian military movements and relatively accurate accounts of the details of Russian negotiations with Sher 'Ali led Lytton to intervene in the affair. Thus, Indian intelligence sources could not report on Russian intentions, as opposed to actions; their information on the latter was imprecise and two to three weeks out of date. Information from Kabul was more accurate and more quickly received. Under the circumstances, these sources did provide the advance warning that Lytton demanded. The government of India would have had ample time to respond if Russian military actions had continued, and it did have time to checkmate the negotiations between Russia and Sher 'Ali.

48 Wellesley to Loftus, 28 February 1877, FO 519/276.
49 *Ibid.*; Wellesley to Loftus, 21 February 1872, FO 519/275; same to same, 2 March 1875, passim, FO 519/277; same to same, 17 December 1876, passim, FO 519/280.
50 Since the 1930s, historians dealing with Russian policy in Central Asia and the Balkans during the 1870s have used Wellesley's material as a primary source. This is particularly true of the fine and still standard works of B.H. Sumner, *Russia and the Balkans*, p. 55, and "Lord Augustus Loftus and the Eastern Crisis of 1875–78", *Cambridge Historical Journal*, 4 (1932–1934), pp. 285–286; Wellesley was an essential source for much of Sumner's analysis. Incidentally, Sumner often misunderstands how British decision makers interpreted Wellesley's material. For similar use of Wellesley's reports by other scholars, cf. MacKenzie, *Lion of Tashkent*, p. 110, *passim*. The only exception to this rule is John Vincent (cf. Vincent, *Derby Diaries*, pp. 27–28), whose failure to understand the nature of Wellesley's material wrecks much of his revisionist attempt to defend Derby. Contrary to Vincent, Wellesley is a weighty source as regards

the charges that Derby (or his wife) leaked cabinet secrets to the Russian ambassador, though arguably he may not provide hanging evidence; even more, Disraeli, Victoria and Salisbury would have taken with special seriousness any such evidence emanating from Wellesley. All of this wrecks Vincent's suggestion that one or all of these individuals were involved in a conscious conspiracy to frame Derby through false charges. The scholars who have used Wellesley's material, however, have never explicitly stated what it was and why they have treated it with such unusual regard. This chapter differs from previous works not in having acquired better access to records of Wellesley's work but in asking a different question: how this intelligence affected British decision-making. Given the nature of things, the possibility that Wellesley fell victim to a gigantic Russian gambit of deception cannot be disproved. However, the state of the evidence indicates otherwise. The material pointed in so many directions simultaneously that no deceiver could hope to be certain how it would be understood; moreover, many of the details provided by Wellesley can be confirmed by cross reference to independent sources. If this was deception, it was the most sophisticated programme ever known to have been carried out in peacetime; it involved the transmission of an extraordinary amount of genuine and high-level documents, including evidence that Russian agents were procuring the blueprints of modern British warships. It was as much a failure as a success.

51 Wellesley to Loftus, 20 January 1872, FO 519/275.
52 Same to same, 16 April 1872, FO 519/274.
53 Wellesley to Tenterden, 14 April 1875, FO 519/278.
54 Wellesley to Cambridge, 17.3.75, Cambridge microfilms, Reel 29
55 Granville to Cambridge, 20.6.71, Granville to Cowley, 16.6.72, Cambridge microfilms, Reel 27; Preston, "The Eastern Question".
56 Undated memorandum by Ponsonby (February 1876 by internal evidence) *Oriental Question*, Reel 27; minute by Tenterden, 17 January 1875, FO 65/926; cf. distribution list on Wellesley to Tenterden, 10 August 1875, FO 65/913; Salisbury to Northbrook, 1 January 1875, Northbrook Papers, C.144/12.
57 Wellesley to Loftus, 26 September 1876, FO 519/279.
58 Compare Disraeli's analysis in Buckle, *Disraeli*, p. 246, with memorandum by Wellesley, 10 November 1876, WO 33/29.
59 Wellesley to Cambridge, 22.8.74, 31.3.75, Cambridge microfilms, Reel 30.
60 Vincent, *Derby Diaries*, p. 420
61 Salisbury to Northbrook, 1 January 1875, Northbrook Papers, C.144/12.
62 Wellesley to Cambridge, 10.1.76, Cambridge microfilms, Reel 21: Salisbury to Cambridge, 11.5.78, Cambridge microfilms Reel 34.
63 Dep. Hughenden 71/1, Wellesley to Montague Corry, 24.4.78.
64 FO 519/274, Wellesley to Loftus, 7 January 1873, and FO 539/9. This discussion of Khiva generally concurs with the account based on Russian sources in Becker, *Russia's Protectorates*, pp. 70–72, and Morris, "The Russians in Central Asia", pp. 524–525. As an essay in history, Chernaiev's comments were clearly flawed. Although the Ministry of Foreign Affairs had frequently opposed Russian expansion in Central Asia, Alexander II usually favoured or at least condoned it (Evans (ed.), *Mission of N.P. Ignat'ev*, pp. 5–21, 30–36; MacKenzie, *Lion of Tashkent*, pp. 43–48, *passim*; Rieber, *Politics*, pp. 107–108, *passim*). Even then, however, his frontier officials often set the pace. By the 1870s and 1880s, the split between St. Petersburg and the frontier was increasingly wide. The Ministry of War, however, always favoured expansion in Central Asia and worked covertly with its frontier officers in this direction, while Alexander II authorized Russia's actions in central Asia of 1878, which

was scarcely surprising, given concurrent British actions in Turkey. Thus, though Wellesley's reading of the past history of Russian expansion was inaccurate, it was a useful guide to the present.

65 Granville to Cambridge, 13.4.72, Granville to Cambridge, 20.12.73, Cambridge microfilms, Reels 28 and 29.
66 Granville to Cambridge, 30.12.73, Cambridge microfilms, Reel 29.
67 H.D.G. Matthew, *The Gladstone Diaries, with Cabinet Minutes and Prime Ministerial Correspondence*, vol. 8, *July 1871–December 1874* (Oxford: Clarendon, 1982), pp. 267, 418; Ramm, *Political Correspondence*, pp. 371, 433–34; Lord Edmond Fitzmaurice, *The Life of Granville George Leveson Gower, Second Earl Granville, K.G., 1815–1891*, vol. 2 (London: Longmans, Green, 1906), pp. 411–15; Gladstone to Queen Victoria, 28 November 1873, *Cabinet Reports by Prime Ministers to the Crown, 1868–1916, Reel Two, 1872–75, Cabinet Letters in the Royal Archives* (Microfilm). The best modern accounts of the Anglo-Russian negotiations on these issues are Morris, "The Russians in Central Asia", and Thornton, "Afghanistan".
68 Wellesley to Loftus, 12 October 1874, 10 November 1874, FO 519/277.
69 *Ibid.*, same to same, 25 November 1874, *passim*.
70 *Ibid.*, same to same, 17 March 1875; same to same, 20 January 1876, *passim*, FO 519/279; Wellesley to Tenterden, 21 July 1875, 10 August 1875, FO 65/985.
71 Wellesley to Loftus, 26 March 1875, FO 519/277. For virtually identical strategic arguments by an earlier governor of the Caucasus, see Rieber, *Politics*, 70–73.
72 Wellesley to Loftus, 19 April 1875, FO 519/277; same to same, 7 June 1875, *passim*, FO 519/279.
73 Same to same, 14 April 1876, FO 519/279. In 1881, following the second Anglo-Afghan war, Abdur Rahman did become the amir of Afghanistan and a useful ally to Britain.
74 *Ibid.*, Wellesley to Loftus, 15 April 1876; Salisbury to Lytton, 21 April 1876, Lytton Papers, E.218/3A.
75 Admiral Phipps Hornby Papers, National Maritime Museum, PHI 118 B, Part 3, WH Smith to Phipps Hornby, 25.2.78, 9.2.78, 28.1.78, 9.5.78, 23.2.78, 20.4.78. Matthew Allen, "The British Mediterranean Squadron During the Great Eastern Crisis of 1876–9", *The Mariner's Mirror*, 85(1) (February 1999), pp. 53–67.
76 Salisbury to Loftus, 3 April 1878, Salisbury to Cross, 30 April 1878, Salisbury Papers, A/31 and D/111/17; FO 65/1030, Loftus to Foreign Office, 6 May 1878, *passim*; ADM 1/6455, Foreign Office to Admiralty, 20 May 1878; Dep. Hughenden 93/1, Salisbury to Disraeli, 10.2.78; Sumner, *Russia and the Balkans*, p. 479; Klein, "Second Afghan War", pp. 102–120. There appears to be no evidence that this material was ever sent to the India Office or Lytton. If so, it would have been the material regarding Russian mobilization that Lytton regarded as "all moonshine" (Lytton to Cranbrook, 8 June 1878, Lytton Papers, E218/25B), a phrase he is unlikely to have used in reference to material from Wellesley's source, of which he was aware.
77 N.A. Khalfin, "Indian Missions in Russia in the Late Nineteenth Century and British Historiography of International Relations in Asia", *Modern Asian Studies*, 21 (1987), p. 644.
78 For a discussion of the methodological problems involved in intelligence history, see John Ferris, "The Intelligence Deception Complex: An Anatomy", *Intelligence and National Security*, 4(4) (1989).
79 Salisbury to Loftus, 3 April 1878, 11 December 1878, Salisbury Papers, A/21; Disraeli to Queen Victoria, 30 September 1876, *Oriental Question*, Reel 27.

NOTES

80 Compare Disraeli's analysis in Buckle, *Disraeli*, vol. 6, p. 246, with memorandum by Wellesley, 10 November 1876, WO 33/29.
81 Dep. Hughenden 69/1, Montague Corry to Beaconsfield, Whit Monday, 5.77; Disraeli to Layard, 7.8.77; Dep. Hughenden 71/4, minute by Stanhope, B of T, 5.3.?79, *passim*; Buckle, *Disraeli*, vol. 6, pp. 155, 172.
82 Northbrook to Salisbury, 13 May 1875, *passim*, Northbrook Papers, C.144/12.
83 Haines to Cambridge, 23.7.76, Cambridge microfilms, Reel 32, and same to same, 2.7.77, Reel 33.
84 Vincent, *Derby Diaries*, entries 5.8.75 and 9.7.76, pp. 234, 308.
85 *Ibid.*, entry 12.3.75, p.199.
86 *Ibid.*, entry 20.4.75, p.209.
87 *Ibid.*, entry 17. 12. 74, p. 185; Dep. Hughenden 112/4, Derby to Disraeli, 4.9.75.
88 Gwendolyn Cecil, *The Life of Robert, Marquess of Salisbury*, vol. 3 (London: Hodder & Stoughton, 1931), p. 115.
89 Vincent, *Derby Diaries*, entry 9.6.76, p. 301.
90 *Ibid.*, entry 2.11.76, p. 346.
91 *Ibid.*, entry 7.1.77, p. 365.
92 *Ibid.*, entries 15.7.75 and 11.11.75, pp. 230, 251.
93 *Ibid.*, entry 11.11.75, p. 251.
94 *Ibid.*, entry 9.10.75, p. 245.
95 *Ibid.*, entries 6.4.76 and 22.6.76, pp. 288, 303–304; Dep. Hughenden 112/4, Derby to Ponsonby, 20.6.76.
96 Vincent, *Derby Diaries*, entry 24.12.77, p. 470.
97 Salisbury to Derby, 15 June 1875, Salisbury Papers, D/XVI/73; Salisbury to Northbrook, 11 December 1874, Northbrook Papers, C.144/11; *ibid.*, Salisbury to Northbrook, 16 April 1875, *passim*, C.144/12; Salisbury to Lytton, 21 April 1876, Lytton Papers, E.218/3A; Greaves, *Persia*, pp. 48–49.
98 Salisbury to Northbrook, 19 March 1875, *passim*, Northbrook Papers, C.144/12; Salisbury to Lytton, 19 May 1876, *passim*, Lytton Papers, E.218/3A; George Earle Buckle, *The Life of Benjamin Disraeli, Earl of Beaconsfield*, vol. 5, *1868–1876* (London: John Murray, 1920), p. 434.
99 Salisbury to Lytton, 2 November 1876, Lytton Papers, E.218/3A; *ibid.*, same to same, 16 February 1877, E.218/4A; cf. Gwendolyn Cecil, *The Life of Robert, Marquess of Salisbury*, vol. 2 (London: Hodder & Stoughton, 1921), p. 131. In the context of this letter, the phrase "the Asiatic side" clearly refers to Central Asia and Afghanistan; in other contemporary letters, the phrase means Anatolia or Armenia.
100 Dep. Hughenden 74/2, Cabinet Paper by Salisbury, n.d. but *c*.7–8.77 by internal evidence, "Memorandum on the North West Frontier"; Dep Hughenden 92/4, Salisbury to Disraeli, 18.7.77.
101 Salisbury to Disraeli, 11 June 1877, Salisbury Papers, D/20.
102 *Ibid.*, same to same, 1 June 1877.
103 Cecil, *Life*, vol. 2, pp. 129, 145.
104 *Ibid.*, pp. 124–125; Buckle, *Disraeli*, vol. 6, p. 71. For Ignatiev's report of later and similar views by Salisbury, cf. George Hoover Rupp, *A Wavering Friendship: Russia and Austria, 1876–1878* (Cambridge, Mass.: Harvard University Press, 1941), pp. 345–346. According to Ignatiev's account, under this hypothetical arrangement Britain would control Afghanistan while Persia would be neutralized, with Russia staying on the north bank of the Attrek River. Salisbury would have established everything he wanted in Central Asia and more under this arrangement. Given (1) the support of the influential Ignatiev, and (2) the clear desire of Gorchakov and Alexander II to end

Britain's opposition to Russian policy in Turkey, it seems quite possible that the Russian government would have made some such formal division of Asia into spheres of influence. This may have been the period in which the frequent Victorian policy of neutralization and spheres of influence in Asia between Britain and Russia came closest to fruition.
105 Buckle, *Disraeli*, vol. 6, p. 111; Millman, *Britain and the Eastern Question*, p. 537, n. 48; Sumner, *Russia and the Balkans*, pp. 237–239.
106 Salisbury to Lytton, 15 June 1877, Lytton Papers, E.218/4A.

2 "Indulged in all too little"? Vansittart, intelligence and appeasement

The author is indebted to the copyright holders and to the Masters, Fellows and Scholars of Churchill College, Cambridge; Cambridge University Library; the India Office Library and Records; and the Birmingham University Library, for permission to cite material from the papers of Alexander Cadogan, Malcolm Graham Christie, Thomas Inskip, Eric Phipps and Robert Vansittart; Charles Hardinge; George Curzon; and Neville Chamberlain, respectively. All AIR, CAB, FO, HD, KV, PREM, T and WO files are held at the Public Record Office. All such material falls under Crown copyright and appears by permission of the Controller of Her Majesty's Stationery Office. I am indebted to Keith Neilson for comments on my analysis.

1 "The World Situation and British Rearmament", memorandum by Vansittart, 31.12.36, FO 371/20278.
2 FO 800/309, Halifax to Runciman, 6.9.38.
3 David Dilks (ed.), *The Diaries of Sir Alexander Cadogan, 1938–1945* (New York: Putnam, 1972), p. 29; Donald Cameron Watt, *How War Came, The immediate origins of the Second World War, 1938–1939* (New York: Pantheon, 1989), pp. 613–614, *passim*; Christopher Andrew, *Secret Service, The Making of the British Intelligence Community* (London: Heinemann, 1985), pp. 486, 540–542, *passim*; Wesley K. Wark, *The Ultimate Enemy, British Intelligence and Nazi Germany, 1933–1939* (Ithaca, NY: Cornell University Press, 1985); Norman Rose, *Vansittart, Study of a Diplomat* (London: Heinemann, 1978), pp. 135–147, 205; Donald Graeme Boadle, "Sir Robert Vansittart at the Foreign Office, 1930–1938" (Ph.D. dissertation, Cambridge University, 1979), pp. 162–177.
4 Dilks, *Diaries*, p. 21.
5 The best account of British intelligence during the later nineteenth century is William Carpenter Beaver II, "The Development of the Intelligence Division and its Role in Aspects of Imperial Decision Making, 1854–1901" (Ph.D. dissertation, Oxford University, 1976). Other general surveys include Christopher Andrew, *Secret Service*, pp. 21–67, and Thomas G. Fergusson, *British Military Intelligence, 1870–1914, The Development of a Modern Intelligence Organisation* (Frederick, MD: University Publications of America, 1984). Specialist accounts are contained in Adrian Preston, "British Military Policy and the Defence of India: A Study of British Military Policy, Plans and Preparations during the Russian Crisis, 1875–1880" (Ph.D. dissertation, University of London, 1966) and "The Eastern Question during the Franco-Prussian War", in Jay Atherton (ed.), *Historical Papers, 1972* (Ottawa: Canadian Historical Association, 1972); and John Ferris, "Lord Salisbury, Secret Intelligence and British Policy Towards Russia and Central Asia, 1874–1878", in Keith Neilson and B.J.C. McKercher, *Go Spy the Land, Military Intelligence in History* (Westpoint: Praeger, 1992), pp. 115–152.

6 FO 95/775, Currie to Law, 12.5.90, *passim*; for other instances of how British intelligence was collected during the late nineteenth century, cf. Ferris, "Lord Salisbury", and HD 3/ 77.
7 Beaver, "Development of the Intelligence Division", op.cit.
8 FO 371/673, minute by Hardinge, n.d. but May 1909 by internal evidence, *passim*; Keith Neilson, *Britain and the Last Tsar* (Oxford: Clarendon, 1995), p. 286.
9 For examples, cf. FO 115/977, FO 115/1904 and FO 929/1.
10 For these developments, the best sources are Andrew, *Secret Service*, pp. 297–481, and John Ferris, "Whitehall's Black Chamber: British Crptology and the Government Code and Cypher School, 1919–1929", *Intelligence and National Security*, 2(1) (January 1987).
11 John Ferris, "Before 'Room 40': The British Empire and Signals Intelligence, 1898–1914", *Journal of Strategic Studies*, 12(4) (December 1989), pp. 438–442.
12 Robert Vansittart, *The Mist Procession* (London: Hutchinson, 1958), p. 148.
13 For one example of Vansittarts's comments on an intercepted letter between leading Swedish businessmen, cf. FO 382/911, minute by Vansittart, 26.2.16.
14 For examples of this process, see FO 800/157, Woollcombe to Vansittart, 2.6.21; Vansittart to Curzon, 23.11.22, F. 112/228, Lord Curzon of Kedelston papers, India Office Library and Records; FO 371/8185, Thomson to Vansittart, 20.2.22.
15 Curzon papers, *ibid*.; Ferris, "Whitehall's Black Chamber", pp. 75; Keith Jeffery and Alan Sharp, "Lord Curzon and Secret Intelligence", in Christopher Andrew and Jeremy Noakes (eds), *Intelligence and International Relations, 1900–1945* (Exeter: University of Exeter, 1987); R.H. Ulman, *Anglo-Soviet Relations, 1917–21, Volume III, The Anglo-Soviet Accord* (Princeton: Princeton University Press, 1972); minutes by Vansittart, 1.12 and 4.12 (n.d. in original, but 1922 or 1923 according to internal evidence), Vansittart Papers 11, 1/2, Churchill College, Cambridge.
16 Vansittart, *Mist Procession*, pp. 348–349; John Ferris and Uri Bar-Joseph, "Getting Marlowe to Hold His Tongue: The Conservative Party, the Intelligence Services and the Zinoviev Letter", *Intelligence and National Security*, 8(4) (October 1993), pp. 103–104.
17 T 1/12517/13418, Curzon to Chamberlain, 25.3.19.
18 KV 4/151, "Note by Lord Hardinge", n.d., in minutes of the First Meeting of the Secret Service Committee, 3.2.19.
19 Eden to Neville Chamberlain, 12.12.37, Neville Chamberlain papers, NC 7/11/30/46, Birmingham University Library.
20 Ferris, "Whitehall's Black Chamber", Appendix 2, p. 91.
21 Cumming to Hardinge, 1.7.19, Charles Hardinge papers, Volume 40, Cambridge University Library; Dilks, *Diaries*; FO 371/10841, Sinclair to Tyrrell, 18.7.25, *passim*, E 4206, E 4550; Crowe to Curzon, 28.12.21, Curzon Papers, F. 211/219 B.
22 Vansittart, *Mist Procession*, p. 458.
23 Ian Colvin, *Vansittart in Office* (London: Gollancz, 1965), pp. 171–172.
24 Dilks, *Diaries*, p. 198.
25 FO 370/1497B, Vansittart to Eden, 6.2.43, in "Extracts from Correspondence"; VNST 1, 4/9, Sargent to Vansittart, 30.10.46.
26 Peter Hoffmann, *The History of the German Resistance, 1933–1945*, 3rd edn (Montreal, PQ: McGill-Queen University Press, 1996), pp. 57–59; Klemens von Klemperer, *German Resistance Against Hitler, The Search for Allies Abroad, 1938–1945* (1992), p. 21, 77 n.205, 89–91, 93–96. Despite this flaw, these authors' comments on Vansittart are generally accurate.

NOTES

27 "1934/Secret Service", Blue Notes, T 165/61; Ferris, "Whitehall's Black Chamber", pp. 78–79, Appendix 1.
28 Vansittart, *Mist Procession*, pp. 397–398.
29 Ben Pimlott (ed.), *The Political Diary of Hugh Dalton, 1918–40, 1945–60* (London: Jonathan Cape, 1986), pp. 69–72, 80–81.
30 CAB 53/4, 108th meeting of the Chiefs of Staff Committee, 27.3.33; John Ferris, "From Broadway House to Bletchley Park: The Diary of Captain Malcolm Kennedy, 1934–46", *Intelligence and National Security*, 4(3) (July 1989).
31 Ferris, "Whitehall's Black Chamber", pp. 78–79.
32 *Documents on British Foreign Policy* (hereafter, *DBFP*), Series 2, Volume XIII (London: Her Majesty's Stationery Office, 1973), p. 445.
33 FO 371/20278, "The World Situation and British Rearmament", memorandum by Vansittart, 31.12.36.
34 John Barnes and David Nicholson (eds), *The Empire at Bay, The Leo Amery Diaries, 1929–1945* (London: Hutchinson, 1988), pp. 419, 425.
35 Eden to Neville Chamberlain, 12.12.37, Neville Chamberlain papers, NC 7/11/30/46; *DBFP, Series 2, Volume XIX* (London: Her Majesty's Stationery Office, 1982), pp. 705–706, n.2.
36 VNST 11, 2/19, Vansittart to Warren Fisher, 9.8.38.
37 WO 190/324, MI3 to MOI, 27.4.35; Hankey to Phipps, 11.1.38, Eric Phipps papers, 3/3, Churchill College, Cambridge; Stephen Roskill, *Hankey, Man of Secrets, Volume III, 1931–1963* (London: Collins, 1974), pp. 237–238.
38 CAB 27/627, memorandum by Gladwyn Jebb, 19.1.39.
39 For a discussion of these issues and a bibliography of the literature, cf. John Robert Ferris, *Men, Money and Diplomacy, The Evolution of British Strategic Policy, 1919–26* (Ithaca, NY: Cornell University Press, 1989), pp. 43–49.
40 Vansittart to Curzon, 23.11.22, Curzon papers, F. 112/228; cf. Vansittart to Curzon, 30.3.21, Curzon papers, F. 112/221B.
41 Vansittart to Curzon, 3.9.22, Curzon papers, F. 112/228.
42 FO 371/ 12040, memorandum by Vansittart, 19.10.27.
43 John Connell, *The "Office", A Study of British Foreign Policy and its Makers 1919–1951* (London : Wingate, 1958), p. 102.
44 Gladwyn Jebb, *The Memoirs of Lord Gladwyn* (London: Weidenfeld and Nicolson, 1972), p. 59.
45 Arthur Willert, *Washington and Other Memories* (Boston: Houghton Mifflin, 1972), p. 174.
46 Vansittart, *Mist Procession*, p. 443.
47 Robert Rhodes James, *Eden, A Biography* (London: Weidenfeld and Nicolson, 1986), p. 159; for Eden's mature view, cf. The Earl of Avon, *The Eden Memoirs: Facing the Dictators* (London: Cassell, 1962), p. 242.
48 John Colville, *The Fringes of Power, 10 Downing Street Diaries, 1939–1955* (New York: Norton, 1985), p. 162; NC 18/1, Neville Chamberlain to Ida Chamberlain, 12.12.37.
49 FO 371/20094, minute by Craigie, 5.10.36, *passim*, E 5280.
50 FO 371/20094, minute by Vansittart, E 6768.
51 Aspects of this issue are discussed in Ferris, "From Broadway House to Bletchley Park", pp. 433, 447–449; David Dilks, "Appeasement and 'Intelligence' ", in David Dilks (ed.), *Retreat From Power, Volume One, 1906–1939* (London: Macmillan, 1981), pp. 155–157; Gerhard Weinberg, *The Foreign Policy of Hitler's Germany, Volume 11, Starting World War Two, 1937–1939* (Chicago: University of Chicago Press, 1980), pp. 282–283.
52 FO 371/20278, "The World Situation and British Rearmament", by Vansittart, 31.12.36.

NOTES

53 Compare *ibid.* with FO 371/20286, memorandum by Far Eastern Department, 4.12.36, F 7504.
54 FO 371/20285, mutilated letter to Norton (marked "C/315", dated 29.1.36, from the SIS, according to internal evidence), F 674, shows that even in early 1936 SIS sources in Germany were monitoring signs of Germano-Japanese cooperation.
55 FO 371/20285, minutes by Cadogan, 27.11.36, and Vansittart, 28.11.36, F 7231, F 7223.
56 FO 371/20278, minute by Orde, 26.12.36, F 7781.
57 WO 106/5606, minute by C.R. Major, MI2 (c), 3.12.36; WO 208/859, memorandum by Dennys, MI2, to DMOI, 8.12.36.
58 For Mendl, cf. FO 800/220, and for Rome, cf. FO 395/373, Scott to Koppel, 7.7.22, *passim*; KV 4/151, minutes of the Third Meeting of the Secret Service Committee, 4.3.19.
59 CAB 24/221, CP 125 (31), p. 12; CAB 24/239, CP 52 (32); CAB 24/243, CP 212 (33).
60 Rose, *Vansittart*, pp. 88–119.
61 CAB 24/260, CP 42(36). For similar statements by Vansittart, cf. *DBFP, Series 2, Volume V*, pp. 550–551; *DBFP, Series 2, Volume XV*, p. 731; *DBFP, Series 2, Volume XVI*, p. 154; CAB 24/227, CP 4 (32); CAB 24/248, CP 104 (34); CAB 16/109, third and ninth meetings of the Defence Requirements Sub-Committtee, 4.12.33, 30.1.34.
62 Vansittart Papers, VNST 11, 2/13, "Notes of a Conversation with General Milch, 15.10.37". Though the citation in the text comes from Milch, Vansittart stated that it represented German thinking in general.
63 Dilks, *Diaries*, pp. 47–48.
64 For examples of this phenomenon, compare *Foreign Relations of the United States* (hereafter, *FRUS*), *1937, Volume 1, General* (1954), p. 76; memorandum by Vansittart, 6.7.37, FO 371/20733, C 5933; memorandum by Vansittart, 21.3.38, VNST 1, 1/23.
65 *DBFP, Series 2, Volume XVIII*, No. 8; *Documents Diplomatiques Francais* (hereafter *DDF*), *1932–1939, 2eme. series (1936–1939), Tome XI (3 September–2 Octobre 1938)* (1977), pp. 88–89; Dilks, *Diaries*, pp. 148, 160, 197–198.
66 VNST 11, 1/14, Vansittart to Eden, 3.7.37; CAB 24/221, CP 125 (31); *DBFP Series 2, Volume XIX*, p. 827.
67 VNST 11, 2/15, Vansittart to Eden, n.d.; Peter Wright, *Spycatcher, The Candid Autobiography of a Senior Intelligence Officer* (New York: Viking, 1987), p. 325.
68 AIR 5/489, Air Attaché, Washington, to Air Intelligence, No. 11, 22.9.22, No. 92, 11.1.23, No. 280, 28.5.23, *passim*.
69 AIR 5/489, Air Attaché, Washington to Air Intelligence, No. 11, 22.9.22, No. 92, 11.1.23, No. 280, 28.5.23, *passim*; minutes by Boyle, 1.5.24, and Trenchard, 30.5.24, *passim*; Military Intelligence Division to United States Military Attaché, London, 7.6.23, Bureau of Aeronautics to United States Naval Attaché, London, 23.8.24, United States National Archives, RG 165/9771–249.
70 Biographical details in FO 371/12130, Air Ministry to Foreign Office, 4.4.27.
71 For Christie's views of Germany while Air Attaché, see FO 371/13635, C 9193; for his sources during that period, cf. *ibid.*, C 10133, and Christie Papers, CHRS 1/2, Milch to Christie, 13.1.30, Hugo Junkers to Christie, 14.1.30.
72 AIR 5/343, Steel to Hearson, telegram AM 99, 6.3.22, *passim*, especially Pt. 1 and Pt. IV, Annexes; AIR 5/323, *passim*.
73 CHRS 1/1, Christie to Newall, 17.11.28.
74 FO 371/13635, Christie to Rumbold, 27.12.29, "Junkers Aircraft Company", in Rumbold to Sargent, 27.12.29, and memorandum by Christie, "Aero-political situation in Germany", 29.11.29.

NOTES

75 FO 371/13635, memorandum by Christie, "Aero-political situation in Germany, 29.11.29; CHRS 1/1, Christie to Newall, 17.11.28.
76 CHRS 1/1, Christie to Yencken, 21.9.30, Christie to Jock Balfour, 17.1.31, memorandum, n.d. but summer 1931 (by internal evidence), "The Programme of the National Socialist Party of Germany", *passim*; for material from 1932–1934, cf. CHRS 1/4, 1/6.
77 For discussions of these points, cf. Andrew, *Secret Service*, pp. 540–542; Wark, *Ultimate Enemy*; Rose, *Vansittart*, pp. 135–138; and Bob de Graaff, "The Stranded Baron and the Upstart at the Crossroads: Wolfgang zu Putlitz and Otto John", *Intelligence and National Security*, 6(4) (October 1991), pp. 669–700.
78 AIR 40/2630, B.J. 130, "Dr. Gustav Victor Lachmann", *passim*.
79 I am grateful for this information to David Hayward, a Ph.D. student at Southampton University (e-mail from Hayward to Ferris, 4.3.00).
80 A.P. Young (ed. Sidney Young), *The "X" Documents* (London: Deutsch, 1974), p. 9; Vansittart, *Mist Procession*, pp. 512–513.
81 Von Klemperer, *German Resistance*, pp. 77, n. 201, and 117; CHRS 1/26 B, "Extract from Q's letter dated end of 1938".
82 Von Klemperer, *German Resistance*, p. 104; CHRS 1/26 A, Christie to "Mr. Gilbert" (Vansittart), 15.8.38.
83 CHRS 1/26 B, memorandum by Christie, "October 38".
84 CHRS 1/26 B, memorandum by Christie, 20.12.38, "Notes of a conversation ...".
85 CHRS 1/29 A, Christie to Vansittart, n.d., "Memo dated March 7, 1939"; FO 371/22966, Christie to Vansittart, n.d., *passim*; Hoffmann, *History of the German Resistance*, pp. 32–33, 63; and von Klemperer, *German Resistance*, pp. 28–29.
86 Andrew, *Secret Service*, pp. 580–581; Watt, *How War Came*, pp. 103–104; cf. David Irving, *Churchill's War, The Struggle for Power* (Bullsbrook, WA, Australia: Veritas, 1987), pp. 121–122.
87 For Christie's dealings with Goering and Henlein, cf. CHRS 1/5 and 1/22.
88 Von Klemperer, *German Resistance*, p. 133
89 *DBFP, Series 3, Volume II* (London: Her Majesty's Stationery Office, 1949), p. 686.
90 VNST 1, 1/20, 1, 1/23, memoranda by Vansittart, 6.7.37, 21.3.38; cf. FO 371/20733, memorandum by Vansittart, 6.7.37, C 5933.
91 Young, *"X" Documents*, pp. 150–158, 231–234; FO 371/21659, minute by Vansittart, 7.12.38, *passim*, C 15084.
92 FO 371/21736, memorandum by Vansittart, 9.8.38.
93 F.W. Winterbotham, *The Nazi Connection* (New York: Harper & Row, 1978); similarly, Czech military intelligence provided a copy of the *Langnamverein* memorandum procured by Christie, cf. FO 371/20733, memorandum by Vansittart, 7.7.37, C 5933; FO 371/21736, C 9527.
94 Andrew, *Secret Service*, pp. 531–579; Dilks, *Diaries*, p. 169; *DBFP, Series 2, Volume XIX*, p. 55, 464, 822–824; Winterbotham, *Nazi Connection*, pp. 17–31; Watt, *How War Came*, pp. 100–101; de Graaf, "Stranded Baron", p. 677, *passim*.
95 Hoffmann, *History of the German Resistance*, pp. 60, 63, 66.
96 Interrogation records of Major Richard Ernst Heinrich, No. U.35, "Major Richard Ernst Heinrich", n.d. but *c*. late 1942 by internal evidence; and No. 5107, 26.1.43, "Further Interrogation of Major [name deleted]", KV 2/275; RG 165/179/705, Final Interrogation Report of Eugen Steimle, 12.12.45, 307th Counter-Intelligence Corps Detachment, Headquarters Seventh Army, Appendix No. 5.

NOTES

97 Young, *"X" Documents*, pp. 24, 40–43, 49, 219–228; FO 371/20733, minute by Barker, 4.7.37, *passim*, C 4882.
98 *DDF, Tome 10*, pp. 688–689; Colvin, *Vansittart in Office*, p. 156.
99 Barnes and Nicholson, *Empire at Bay*, pp. 419, 425.
100 *DDF*, pp. 754–5, 769–71.
101 For references to disinformation, cf. *ibid.* and Dilks, *Diaries*, pp. 199, 196; *DBFP Series 2, Volume XIX*, pp. 55; Wesley K. Wark, "Something Very Stern: British Political Intelligence, Moralism and Strategy in 1939", *Intelligence and National Security*, 5(1) (January 1990).
102 Dilks, *Diaries*, pp. 197–198; VNST 1/1/20, memoranda by Vansittart, 6.7.37, marked "Suppressed by Eden"; CHRS 1/24, 1/25.
103 For this issue, cf. Wark, *Ultimate Enemy*, p. 63–98; Andrew, *Secret Service*, pp. 547–551; Boadle, "Sir Robert Vansittart", pp. 162–176.
104 For examples of the use of intelligence in these memoranda, cf. *DBFP, Series 2, Volume V*, p. 549; *DBFP Series 2, Volume VI*, p. 969. For the more conventional uses, cf. CAB 24/260, CP (13) and CP (39) 36; CAB 24/248, CP 104 (34); CAB 16/111, CP 116 (34), and minute by Vansittart, 2.6.34. Christie's reports for the period 1933–1935 may be found in CHRS 1/5, 1/6, 1/7, 1/9, 1/14, 1/15, 1/19.
105 Neville Chamberlain to Ida Chamberlain, 14.1.37, Neville Chamberlain papers, NC/18/1; NC 7/11/29/19, Warren Fisher to Chamberlain, 15.9.36.
106 VNST 11, 2/14, Vansittart to Eden, 3.7.37; VNST 1/1/20, memoranda by Vansittart, 6.7.37, marked "Suppressed by Eden"; the memoranda were entered "for record" in FO 371/20733. Rose, *Vansittart*, pp. 205–206, misunderstands the circumstances surrounding these memoranda.
107 *DBFP Series 2, Volume XVI*, p. 276; *DBFP Series 2, Volume XIX*, p. 53; Rose, *Vansittart*, pp. 192, 205; VNST 1/1/20, memoranda by Vansittart, 6.7.37; VNST 11, 2/15, Vansittart to Eden, n.d.
108 VNST 1, 1/20, memoranda by Vansittart, 6.7.37; VNST 11, 2/13, "Reports on Germany, 1936–November 1937" and "Germany in November 1937", unsigned but both presumably by Christie.
109 FO 371/22419, memorandum by McDermott, 28.7.38; FO 371/21742, minute by Roberts, 4.10.38.
110 The best recent accounts of British policy in 1938–1939 are Williamson Murray, *The Change in the European Balance of Power, The Road to Ruin* (Princeton: Princeton University Press, 1984); R.A.C. Parker, *Chamberlain and Appeasement, British Policy and the Coming of the Second World War* (New York: St. Martin's Press, 1993); and Watt, *How War Came*.
111 Memoranda by Vansittart, 21.3.38, VNST 1, 1/23 and 20.1.38, VNST 11, 2/16.
112 PREM 1/265, Halifax to Chamberlain, 19.3.38.
113 Memoranda by Vansittart, 21.3.38, VNST 1, 1/23 and 20.1.38, VNST 11, 2/16.
114 VNST 11 2/18, two undated minutes by Vansittart, *c*.2–3.38 according to internal evidence; CHRS 1/26A, undated memoranda, presumably by Christie, "A few rough notes of impressions gathered in Germany in December 1937", "March 1938", "Germany's Foreign Policy, March 1938"; CHRS 1/13, Christie to Vansittart, 16.2.38; FO 371/21660, minutes by Sargent and Cadogan, 8.2.38, marginal note by Vansittart; FO 800/309, undated memorandum, but *c*.28.3–1.4.38 according to internal evidence, "Main points from the recent secret reports from Germany".
115 26th meeting of the Cabinet Committee on Foreign Policy (F.P. 36), 18.3.38; FO 800/313, Halifax to Chamberlain; NC/18/1, Neville Chamberlain to Ida Chamberlain, 31.10.37, 26.11.37, 13.3.38, 20.3.28, 22.5.38; for Cadogan's

views, cf. Dilks, *Diaries*, p. 73, *passim*, and Cadogan Papers, ACAD 4/1, Cadogan to Eden, 13.5.36.
116 FO 371/ 21736, C 9527.
117 FO 371/ 21659, memorandum, "What Should We Do?", 18.10.38, C 14471.
118 FO 371/21729, minutes by Vansittart, 22.7.38, 25.7.38, 27.7.38, C 7512, C 7591, C 7634; VNST II, 2/19, minute by Vansittart, 9.8.38.
119 FO 371/21729, Mason-MacFarlane to Henderson, 26.7.38, minutes by Strang, 30.7.38, Mounsey, 2.8.38. Henderson to Strang, 27.7.38, memoranda by Mason-MacFarlane, 25 and 27.7.38, C 7648; FO 371/21663, minutes by Strang and Sargent, 16.7. 38, 23.7.38, C 6825; Dilks, *Diaries*, p. 89.
120 FO 371/21663, minute by Vansittart, 9.8.38, C 6825.
121 Young, *"X" Documents*, pp. 50–59, 75–84; FO 371/21663, minute by Sargant, 7.7.38, C 6577; FO 371/21738, "note of a conversation" with "X" (unsigned, but by Young), C 9591.
122 VNST 11, 2/18, "Dear Friend" letter, dated 12.8.38, *passim*; VNST 11, 2/19, memorandum by Christie, 6.8.38; CHRS 1/26 A, "News from entirely reliable source received 27/7/38", Christie to Vansittart 10.8.38, unsigned memoranda (but by Christie according to internal evidence) dated 14.8.38, 19.8.38, Christie to "Mr. Gilbert", 15.8.38.
123 CHRS 1/26 A, Christie to Vansittart, 10.8.38.
124 *DBFP, Series 3, Volume II*, pp. 683–686.
125 VNST 11,2/19 Vansittart to Warren Fisher, 9.8.38; Pimlott, *Political Diary of Hugh Dalton*, pp. 236–237; FO 371/21663, minute by Vansittart, 9.8.38; FO 371/21736, minutes by Vansittart, 9.8.38, 25.8.38, C 9591 and C 9608. For his views on Czechoslovakia proper, cf. FO 371/21729, minute by Vansittart, 22.7.38, C 7512; FO 371/21735, minute by Vansittart, 30.8.38, C 9377; FO 371/21735, minute by Vansittart, 7.9.38; VNST 1, 2/36, minute by Vansittart, 6.8.38; VNST 11, 2/18, Vansittart to Halifax, 16.8.38; VNST 11, 2/19, minute by Vansittart, 9.8.38; VNST 1, 2/39, minutes by Vansittart, 30.8 and 14.9.38.
126 The most recent analysis of Hitler's position during the Munich crisis is Richard Overy, "Germany and the Munich Crisis: A Mutilated Victory?", *Diplomacy and Statecraft*, 10(2–3) (1999). For assessments of whether the opposition could have launched a coup in September 1938, see Hoffmann, *History of the German Resistance*, pp. 43–44, 75–96, 553, n. 33; von Klemperer, *German Resistance*, pp. 105–107.
127 Dawson to Barrington-Ward, 7.9.38, Geoffrey Dawson Papers, Volume 80.
128 T 273/407, memorandum by Wilson, "Reflections on ...", n.d. but early October 1938 by internal evidence,.
129 CAB 23/94, Cabinet, 30.8.38.
130 T 273/403, memorandum by MI3b, 26.8.38, *passim*.
131 CAB 23/95, CAB 37 (38), Cabinet meeting 12.9.38; FO 371/21729, minute by Sargent, 3.8.38. The best statements of the military balance in August–September 1938, both as it was and as it was perceived by British leaders, are in Murray, *Balance of Power* and "Appeasement and Intelligence", *Intelligence and National Security*, 2(4) (October 1987); and Wark, *Ultimate Enemy*. These sources, and Parker, *Chamberlain*, pp. 150–181, also offer good accounts of British decision making during the crisis, and of how intelligence affected it. The discussion on these points in Andrew, *Secret Service*, pp. 552–561, is inadequate. Peter Jackson, "French Military Intelligence and Czechoslovakia, 1938", *Diplomacy and Statecraft*, 5(1) (March 1994) indicates that whatever was the real balance between Germany and Britain and France, Germany quickly would have overrun Czechoslovakia.
132 PREM 1/265, minute by Wilson, 30.8.38.

133 FO 371/21663, minute by Strang, 16.7.38, *passim*, FC 6825; NC/18/1, Neville Chamberlain to Ida, 11.9.38; NC 7/11/31/123, Halifax to Chamberlain, 21.8.38; FO 371/21659, memorandum by Cadogan, 8.11.38, C 14471; T 273/407, undated notes by Wilson, "Notes for Speech"; Carl von Clausewitz (ed. Michael Howard and Peter Paret), *On War* (Princeton: Princeton University Press, 1976), pp. 85, 180, 191. For discussions of Clausewitz's views on these points, cf. Michael Handel, *Masters of War, Sun Tzu, Clausewitz and Jomini* (1992) and John Ferris and Michael Handel, "Intelligence, Uncertainty and the Art of Command in Military Operations", *Intelligence and National Security*, 10(1) (January 1995).

134 Thomas Inskip, "August 26th–September 19th, 1938, Munich", entry for 30.8.38, Thomas Inskip papers, Churchill College, Cambridge. This typescript was clearly written after the event. Wilson and Chamberlain also read and received several of Vansittart's notes and a "Dear Friend" letter from Christie's sources, dated 19.9.38, PREM 1/249; cf. PREM 1/265, Vansittart to Halifax, 7.9.38; T 273/403, minutes by Wilson, 9.9., on memorandum by Vansittart.

135 *DBFP, Series 3, Volume II*, pp. 40, 58–59, 63, 83–86, 97–98, 116–118, 131–134, 233, 238–239, 299, 257, 280, 283, 649. Many of the original documents cited here are contained in FO 800/309, FO 800/314 and FO 371/21729.

136 For instances of minutes by Vansittart, whether entered for record or read, cf. FO 371/21736, C 9450, C 9504, C 9591, C 9608; CHRS 1/26 A, Christie to Vansittart, 10.8.38; FO 800/314, Halifax to Henderson, 5.8.38.

137 Dilks, *Diaries*, pp. 89, 94, 95.

138 FO 371/21729, two minutes by Sargent, 3.8.38; PREM 1/265, two minutes by Horace Wilson, 5.9.38; FO 371/21735, minute by Roberts, 11.9.38; FO 371/21736, C 9527.

139 Dawson to Barrington-Ward, 7.9.38, Geoffrey Dawson Papers, Volume 80

140 CAB 27/158, memorandum by Wilson, 10/41, "Munich 1938"; cf. T 273/403.

141 Halifax to Chamberlain, 21.8.38, NC 7/11/31/123

142 *DBFP, Series 3, Volume II*, pp. 11, 54, 195; *FRUS, 1938, Volume 1, General*, pp. 560–561, 565–566.

143 FO 371/21735, Halifax to Chamberlain, 5.9.38, C 9378; PREM 1/265, Chamberlain to Halifax, 6.9.38; cf. PREM 1/265, two memoranda by Wilson, 5.9.38.

144 CAB 23/94, Cabinet meeting, 30.8.38.

145 *FRUS, 1938, Volume 1*, pp. 585–586.

146 CAB 23/95, Cabinet meeting 12.9.38.

147 *DDF, 1932–1939, 2e serie (1936–1939), Tome VIII*, (17 January–20 March 1938), Paris, 1973.

148 T 273/403, minutes by HW, 9.9., on memorandum by Vansittart.

149 T 273/403, unsigned, undated memo, but by Wilson, *c.* early 10.38.

150 *Ibid.*; *FRUS, 1938, Volume 1*, p. 560; the British record of these conversations is minuted by Wilson, 30.8.38, PREM 1/265.

151 Dilks, *Diaries*, pp. 89–91; Roskill, *Hankey*, pp. 391–393; Phipps to Hankey, 6.10.38, Phipps papers, 3/3, draft Phipps to Wilson, 13.12.38, 3/5, Phipps to Halifax, 15.12.38, 1/21; FO 371/21742, British embassy, Paris, to Foreign Office, 28.9.38, No. 320, and minute by Roberts, 4.10.38; for Chamberlain's surveillance of the opposition during this period, and its influence on his views in general, cf. Ian Colvin, *The Chamberlain Cabinet* (New York: Taplinger, 1971), p. 264; Irving, *Churchill's War*, pp. 127–128; NC 18/1, Neville Chamberlain to Ida Chamberlain, 9.10.38; Andrew Roberts, *The Holy Fox, A Biography of Lord Halifax* (London: Weidenfeld and Nicolson, 1991).

152 Young, "*X*" *Documents*, pp. 49, 68–73, 85–89.

NOTES

153 FO 371/21736, Halifax to Phipps, 9.8.38, memorandum by Vansittart, 10.9.38, C 9504; FO 371/21736, Halifax to Phipps, 12.9.38, No. 240, C 7561; FO 371/21735, minute by Vansittart, 7.9.38, C 9384; for Halifax's views, cf. CAB 27/623, 26th meeting of the Cabinet Committee on Foreign Policy, 18.3.38, and FO 800/314, minute, 20.8.38 to Oliphant, Sargent and Vansittart; NC 7/11/31/123, Halifax to Chamberlain, 21.8.38. For other instances of Vansittart's tailoring his arguments specifically to affect Halifax's views, cf. FO 800/309, Vansittart to Halifax, 28.5.38).
154 Dilks, *Diaries*, p. 95; cf. CAB 27/646.
155 FO 800/314, minutes by Halifax, 9.8.38, 29.8.38 and Vansittart, 10.8.38; NC 7/31/124, Halifax to Chamberlain, 26.8.38.
156 CAB 23/95, CAB 43 (38), 25.9.38.
157 CAB 46 (38), 27.9.38.
158 Marginal notes, Chamberlain to Halifax, Halifax to Chamberlain, both undated, but 25 September by internal evidence, Earl of Halifax papers, Reel One, copies held in Churchill College.
159 Inskip typescript notes, "August 26th–September 19th 1938, Munich", entry 8.9.38; Amanda Smith (ed.), *Hostage to Fortune, The Letters of Joseph P. Kennedy* (New York: Viking, 2001), p. 271; CAB 27/158, memorandum by Wilson, 10/41, "Munich 1938".
160 Pimlott, *Political Diary of Hugh Dalton*, p. 262.
161 Inskip typescript notes, entry 17.9.38.
162 Dilks, *Diaries*, pp. 163–64.
163 CHRS 1/29A, Christie to Vansittart, 20.1.39.
164 FO 800/309, Halifax to Astor, 23.6.38; CAB 27/263, 26th meeting of the Cabinet Committee on Foreign Policy, 18.3.38. For useful discussions of Halifax's views, cf. Wark, "Something Very Stern"; Bruce Strang, "Two Unequal Tempers: Sir George Ogilvie-Forbes, Sir Nevile Henderson and British Foreign Policy, 1938–39", *Diplomacy and Statecraft*, 5(1) (March 1994); Roberts, *Holy Fox*.
165 Dilks, *Diaries*, pp. 103–104.
166 PREM 1/330, memorandum by Wilson, "Points made by Sir Nevile Henderson", 28.10.38.
167 FO 371/ 21659, C 14471.
168 FO 800/314, minutes by Vansittart19.10.38, and Halifax, 21.10.38.
169 FO 800/311, minute by Halifax, 28.10.38, Halifax to Phipps, 1.11.38.
170 FO 371/22965, memorandum by Jebb, 21.2.39.
171 Dilks, "Appeasement and 'Intelligence' ", pp. 154–158.
172 CHRS 1/26A and 1/26 B, Christie to Vansittart, 19.8.38, memorandum by Christie, "October 1938".
173 Strang, "Unequal Tempers".
174 Dilks, *Diaries*, pp. 128, 130, 153; Young, *"X" Documents*, pp. 119, 134–138, 140–142; for samples of the voluminous material submitted by Vansittart and Christie, cf. FO 371/22966, C 3096, C 3234, C 3235; FO 371/22963, C 1319; FO 371/22965, C 2209; CHRS 1/26 B.
175 Good accounts of the role of intelligence in the change of British policy during the six months following the Munich crisis are Andrew, *Secret Service*, pp. 575–590; Dilks, "Appeasement and 'Intelligence' ", pp. 159–162; Wark, "Something Very Stern" and *Ultimate Enemy*; Watt, *How War Came*, pp. 99–103.
176 Dilks, *Diaries*, pp. 125, 139–144, 153, 155, 169.
177 FO 800/310, meeting with Dominion representatives, 28.1.39, H/IX/14; CAB 27/624, 35th meeting of the Cabinet Committee on Foreign Policy, 23.1.39.

178 FO 371/22963, minute by Roberts, 31.1.39; FO 371/22963, minute by Cadogan, C 1277.
179 CAB 27/624, 35th meeting of the Cabinet Commitee of Foreign Policy, 23.1.39, 36th meeting, 26.1.39; Inskip, typescript, "January 1939 to April 1940", entry for 23.1.39.
180 FO 371/22965, minute by Jebb, 16.2.38; for the reception of Vansittart's material during the early spring of 1939, cf. FO 371/22966, C 3096, C 3097, C 3234, C 3235; FO 371/22965, C 1878, C 1982, C 2072, C 2431.
181 FO 371/22963, memorandum by Vansittart, 18.1.39, C 1319; FO 371/22966, memorandum by Vansittart, 13.3.39, C 3234, cf. 3235; FO 371/22965, memorandum by Vansittart, 20.2.39, C 2209
182 FO 371/22965, Foreign Office to Lindsay, 27.2.39, No. 95.
183 FO 371/23066, minute by Vansittart, 16.5.39; for the standard view in the Foreign Office, cf. FO 371/23560, F 2876.
184 FO 371/22972, C 7253.

3 Image and accident: intelligence and the origins of the Second World War, 1933–1941

This chapter is dedicated to the memory of Michael Handel, who would not have agreed with it all.
1 For examples, Christopher Andrew, *Secret Service, The Making of the British Intelligence Community* (London: Heinemann, 1985); Wesley Wark, *The Ultimate Enemy, British Intelligence and Nazi Germany, 1933–1939* (Ithaca, NY: Cornell University Press, 1985).
2 Donald Cameron Watt, *How War Came, The Immediate Origins of the Second World War, 1938–1939* (New York: Pantheon, 1989); Gerhard Weinberg, *The Foreign Policy of Hitler's Germany*, vol. 11, *Starting World War Two, 1937–1939* (Chicago: University of Chicago Press, 1980); Williamson Murray, *The Change in the European Balance of Power, The Road to Ruin* (Princeton: Princeton University Press, 1984), R.A.C. Parker, *Chamberlain and Appeasement, British Policy and the Coming of the Second World War* (New York: St. Martin's Press, 1993).
3 Sherman Kent, *Strategic Intelligence for American World Policy* (Princeton: Princeton University Press, 1949). Later works in this genre, by a member of Kent's staff and later deputy director for intelligence in his own right, Ray S. Cline, *Secrets, Spies, and Scholars: Blueprint of the Essential CIA* (Washington: Acropolis Books, 1976), and *Strategic Intelligence and National Decisions* (Glencoe, IL: Free Press, 1956) by Roger Hilsman, director of the State Department's Bureau of Intelligence and Research, offer intelligent refinements of Kent's arguments, which address many of the criticisms of the "no-fault" school, as do the best recent studies in this vein, Bruce D. Berkowitz and Allan E. Goodman, *Strategic Intelligence for American National Security* (Princeton: Princeton University Press, 1989), and Michael Herman, *Intelligence Power in Peace and War* (Cambridge: Cambridge University Press, 1996).
4 Robert Jervis, "What's Wrong with the Intelligence Process", *International Journal of Intelligence and Counterintelligence* 1 (Spring 1986), pp. 28–41 and *Perception and Misperception in International Politics* (Princeton: Princeton University Press, 1976); Richard K. Betts, "Analysis, War and Decision: Why Intelligence Failures are Inevitable", in Klaus Knorr (ed.), *Power, Strategy and Security: A World Politics Reader* (Princeton: Princeton University Press,

NOTES

1983), pp. 37–46; Michael I. Handel, *War, Strategy and Intelligence* (London: Frank Cass, 1989); Roberta Wohlstetter, *Pearl Harbor: Warning and Decision* (Stanford: Stanford University Press, 1962); Mark M. Lowenthal, "The Burdensome Concept of Failure", in Alfred C. Maurer, Marion D. Tunstall, and James K. Kegle (eds), *Intelligence: Policy and Process* (Boulder: Westview, 1985), pp. 43–56; Thomas Lowe Hughes, *The Fate of Facts in a World of Men: Foreign Policy and Intelligence-Making* (New York: Foreign Policy Association, 1976).

5 Minute by Eden, 22 September 1937, FO 371/20749.
6 *DDF, 1932–1939, 2e serie (1936–1939), Tome VIII* (17 January–20 March 1938), Paris, 1973, p. 587.
7 Gabriel Gorodetsky, *Grand Delusion, Stalin and the German Invasion of Russia* (Princeton: Princeton University Press, 1999).
8 John Mearsheimer, *The Tragedy of Great Power Politics* (New York: Norton, 2001), p. 11, *passim*.
9 Max Domarus (ed.), *Hitler, Speeches and Proclamations, 1932–1945, The Chronicle of a Dictatorship, Volume Two, The Years 1935 to 1938* (trans. Chris Wilcox and Mary Fran Gilbert) (Wauconda, IL: Bolchazy-Carducci, 1992), pp. 865–869.
10 *DDF, 1932–1939, 2e serie (1936–1939), Tome III* (19 July–19 November 1936), Paris, 1968, pp. 557–559.
11 Neville Chamberlain to Ida Chamberlain, 20.3.38, Neville Chamberlain Papers, NC/18/1, BUL; Malcolm Kennedy Diary, entry 13.9.38, Malcolm Kennedy Papers, Sheffield University Library; Silvio Pons, *Stalin and the Inevitable War, 1936–1941* (London: Frank Cass, 2002), pp. 60–186.
12 *I Documenti Diplomatici Italiani, Ottava Serie: 1935–1939, Volume XII* (23 May–11 August 1939), Rome, 1952, p. 379.
13 Lars T. Lih, Oleg V. Naumov and Oleg V. Khlevniuk, *Stalin's Letters to Molotov, 1925–1936* (New Haven, CT: Yale University Press, 1995), pp. 178, 183, 208, 232.
14 *Ibid.*, pp. 195, 213–214; People's Commissariat of Justice, *The Case of the anti-Soviet Bloc of Rights and Trotskyites* (Moscow: People's Commissariat of Justice, 1938), pp. 767–779; J. Arch Getty and Oleg V. Naumov, *The Road to Terror, Stalin and the Self-Destruction of the Bolsheviks, 1932–1939* (New Haven, CT: Yale University Press, 2001), pp. 148–149, 165, 252, 305, 369, 374, 421–422, 425, 448, 532–533.
15 J.V. Stalin, *Works, Volume 12, April 1929–June 1930* (Moscow: Foreign Language Publishing House, 1955), p. 262 ; *Works, Volume 13, July 1930–January 1934* (Moscow: Foreign Language Publishing House, 1955), pp. 297, 300; *Problems of Leninism* (Peking: Foreign Languages Press, 1976), pp. 875, 881, 884.
16 V.M. Molotov, *Soviet Foreign Policy—The Meaning of the War in Finland* (New York: Workers Library, 1940).
17 *DDF, 1932–1939, 2e serie (1936–1939), Tome VII* (29 September 1937–16 January 1938), Paris, 1972, p. 670; *Tome VIII* (17 January–20 March 1938), Paris, 1973, p. 704; *Tome X* (10 June–2 September 1938), p. 180.
18 J.R. Ferris, " 'Indulged in all Too Little'? Vansittart, Intelligence and Appeasement", *Diplomacy and Statecraft*, 6(1) (March 1995).
19 Helmut Heiber and David Glantz (eds), *Hitler and his Generals, Military Conferences 1942–1945, The First Complete Stenographic Record of the Military Situation Conferences, from Stalingrad to Berlin* (New York: Enigma, 2003), p. 555
20 Holger Herwig, *Politics of Frustration, The United States in German Naval Planning, 1889–1941* (Boston: Little, Brown, 1976), p. 196.

21 Watt, *How War Came*, p. 329.
22 Herwig, *Politics of Frustration*, pp. 197, 212–213; Wilhelm Deist, Manfred Messerschmidt, Hans-Erich Volkmann and Wolfram Wette, *Germany and the Second World War, Volume One, The Build-up of German Aggression* (Oxford: Oxford University Press, 1990), p. 559.
23 The classic in the field of military assessment remains the essays in Ernest May (ed.), *Knowing One's Enemies: Intelligence Assessment before the Two World Wars* (Princeton: Princeton University Press, 1984); a strong collection on the same vein is Williamson Murray and Alan Millett (eds), *Calculations: Net Assessments and the Coming of World War II* (New York: Free Press, 1992). Beyond the essays in these works, among the most useful accounts of military estimates and their impact on policy, for Britain see Keith Neilson, "Pursued by a Bear: British Estimates of Soviet Military Strength and Anglo-Soviet Relations, 1922–1939", *The Canadian Journal of History*, 28(2) (1993), pp. 189–221; Joseph Maiolo, *The Royal Navy and Nazi Germany* (London: Macmillan, 1998); Christopher Bell, "The Royal Navy, War Planning and Intelligence Between the Wars", in Peter Jackson and Jennifer S. Siegel (eds), *Intelligence and Statecraft: The Use of and Limits of Intelligence in International Society, 1870–1970* (Westport: Greenwood, forthcoming); for France, see Martin Alexander, "Did the Deuxieme Bureau Work? The Role of Intelligence in French Defence Policy and Strategy, 1919–1939", *Intelligence and National Security* (1991), pp. 293–333; Antony Adamthwaite, "French Military Intelligence and the Coming of War, 1935–1939", in Christopher Andrew and Jeremy Noakes, *Intelligence and International Relations* (Exeter: University of Exeter Press, 1987), pp. 191–208; for Italy, see Brian Sullivan, "The Impatient Cat: Assessments of Military Power in Fascist Italy 1936–1940", in Murray and Millett, *Calculations*, pp. 97–135; MacGregor Knox, *Mussolini Unleashed, 1939–1941, Politics and Strategy in Fascist Italy's Last War* (Cambridge: Cambridge University Press, 1982); Robert Mallett, *The Italian Navy and Fascist Expansionism, 1935–1940* (London: Frank Cass, 1998). For Germany, see Deist *et al.*, *Germany and the Second World War, Volume One*, pp. 541–567, *passim*.
24 United States Army War College, 1926 course, memorandum 18.1.26, "Intelligence features of specific war plans", AWCCA File 315–3, Center for United States Military History, Carlisle Barracks.
25 SHAT 7N 2484, memorandum, "Le Deuxieme Bureau, Son Role–Son Organisation–Son Fonctionement", 31.1.27, Service Historique de l'Armee de Terre, Chateau de Vincennes.
26 The role of national characteristics is only beginning to be properly appreciated and integrated into studies of military estimates. For France's assessment of those of Germany, see Peter Jackson, *France and the Nazi Menace: Intelligence and Policy Making, 1933–1939* (New York: Oxford University Press); and two works by Andrew Barros, "Le Deuxieme Bureau evalue les forces allemandes: les dangers du sport et de l'education physique, 1919–1928", *Guerres Mondiales et Conflits Contemporains* (forthcoming) and "Finding Weakness in Strength and Strength in Weakness: French Intelligence and the German Air Menace, 1919–1928", in Jackson and Siegel (eds), *Intelligence and Statecraft*. For Britain impressions of Japanese national characteristics see J.R. Ferris, " 'Worthy of Some Better Enemy?' The British Assessment of the Imperial Japanese Army, 1919–1941, and the Fall of Singapore", *The Canadian Journal of History* (August 1993) and "Student and Master: Britain, Japan, Airpower and the Fall of Singapore, 1920–1941", in Brian Farrell (ed.), *Singapore, Sixty Years On* (Singapore: Eastern Universities

NOTES

Press, 2002); Bell, "The Royal Navy, War Planning"; and Antony Best, *Empire Under Siege: British Intelligence and the Japanese Challenge in Asia, 1919–41* (Basingstoke: Palgrave Macmillan, 2002).
27 Watt, *How War Came*.
28 *DDF, 1932–1939, 2e serie (1936–1939), Tome VIII* (17 January–20 March 1938), Paris, 1973, p. 621; *Tome X* (10 June–2 September 1938), pp. 180, 513.
29 Italy, Combat Estimates 30.6.27, 30.6.28, 30.6.29, 30.6.30, 30.6.36, 1.11.39, 18.12.41, G-2, W.D., G.S., *U.S. Military Intelligence Reports, Combat Estimates: Europe, 1920–1943, Reel Two*, UPA.
30 Malcolm Muggeridge (ed.), *Ciano's Diary, 1939–1943* (London: Heinemann, 1947), pp. 9–10, 274.
31 Great Britain, Combat Estimate, 16.12.25, G-2, W.D., G.S, *U.S. Military Intelligence Reports, Combat Estimates: Europe, 1920–1943, Reel One*, UPA.
32 Adolf Hitler, *Mein Kampf* (trans. Ralph Mannheim) (London: Hutchinson, 1971), pp. 144, 658.
33 Baron A. Meyendorff (ed.) *Correspondence Diplomatique de M. de Staal (1884–1900), Volume One* (Paris: Marcel Riviere, 1929), pp. 25–26, *passim*.
34 Norman Rich and Norma Fisher, *Holstein Correspondence* (Cambridge: Cambridge University Press, 1961), p. 551; Norman Rich, *Friedrich von Holstein, Politics and Diplomacy in the Era of Bismark and Wilhelm II* (Cambridge: Cambridge University Press, 1965), p. 438; *Documents on German Foreign Policy* (hereafter *DGFP*), Series D, Volume One, p. 1168.
35 Rich and Fisher, *Holstein Correspondence*, p. 548.
36 MacGregor Knox, *Mussolini Unleashed*, p. 34
37 Muggeridge, *Ciano's Diary*, p. 51.
38 *DGFP, Series D, Volume One*, p. 33; for broader accounts of German perceptions of Britain, see Geoffrey Waddington, "Hassgegner: German Views of Great Britain in the Later 1930s", *History*, 81(261) (1996), pp. 22–39; Deist *et al.*, *Germany and the Second World War, Volume One*, pp. 548–549, 595–604, 627–632, 642–643, 711.
39 *DGFP, Series D, Volume One*, pp. 3–5; Robert Mallett, *The Italian Navy*, p. 150.
40 Memorandum by United States Naval Attaché, Tokyo, 22.6.34, *Confidential US Diplomatic Post Records, Japan, Part 3, Section A*, microfilm Reel 18; Watt, *How War Came*, p. 139; Peter Jackson, *France and the Nazi Menace: Intelligence and Policy Making, 1933–1939* (Oxford: Oxford University Press, 2000), p. 32.
41 Memorandum by Bonner Fellers, 1933, "The Psychology of the Japanese Soldier", Hoover Institution on War, Revolution and Peace, Bonner Feller Papers, Box One, p. 30.
42 J.R. Ferris, " 'Worthy of Some Better Enemy?' The British Assessment of the Imperial Japanese Army, 1919–1941, and the Fall of Singapore", *The Canadian Journal of History* (August 1993).
43 SHAT 7N 3333, "Conference du Colonel Mast a l'Ecole Superieure de Guerre", n.d., 1933.
44 Lecture by Colonel Burdett, 23.11.35, AWCCA, File Number G-2, Number 4, 1936.
45 SHAT 7N 3333-1, "L'Infanterie Japonaise", n.d., probably 1931; SHAT 7N 3334-1, "Les Forces Militaires en Presence en Extreme-Orient", "Conference fait a l'Ecole Superieure de Guerre", 21.4.37.
46 J.R. Ferris, "Student and Master: Britain, Japan, Airpower and the Fall of Singapore"; FO 371/31858, memorandum by Air Attaché, Bangkok, 26.9.41, No. 1; RG 165/2085-947, memorandum by Colonel McCabe for the Chief of Staff, "The Capabilities of Japan in Military Aviation", 23.6.39; AIR 40/2215, Documents Section, Captured Personnel and Material Branch, 26.5.45, transla-

tion of "Japan: Air Armament Industry and Equipment", prepared for the Reich Minister for Air/Air High Command, General Aircraft Head GL/A-Armament", 1.1.42.
47 Bell, "The Royal Navy, War Planning".
48 J.R. Ferris, "Student and Master".
49 For Britain, see Wark, *The Ultimate Enemy*; for France, Jackson, *France and the Nazi Menace*. For German and Italian military services, see Knox, *Mussolini Unleashed*, pp. 32–33; Mallett, *The Italian Navy*, pp. 180–81 Deist *et al.*, *Germany and the Second World War, Volume One*, p. 501.
50 Roger Reese, *Stalin's Reluctant Soldiers, A Social History of the Red Army, 1925–1941* (Lawrence: University of Kansas Press, 1996), p. 163; Geoffrey P. Megargee, *Inside Hitler's High Command* (Lawrence: University of Kansas Press, 2000), pp. 102–116.
51 Andreas Hillgruber, "Das Russland—Bild der fuhrenden deutschen Militars vor Beginn des Angriffs auf die Sowjetunion", in Alexander Fischer, Gunter Moltmann and Klaus Schwabe (eds), *Russland–Deutschland–Amerika. Russia–Germany–America. Festschrift fur Fritz T. Epstein zum 80* (Wiesbaden: Franz Steiner, 1978), pp. 296–310.
52 Despite the plethora of bad books, there are broad and serious studies of the intelligence services of the major powers during the interwar years: David Kahn, *Hitler's Spies, German Military Intelligence in World War II* (New York: Collier, 1978), on Germany; for France, Douglas Porch, *The French Secret Services: Their History from the Dreyfus Affair to the Gulf War* (Oxford: Oxford University Press, 1995); for Britain, Christopher Andrew, *Secret Service*, and the material in Nigel West, *MI6, British Secret Service Operations, 1900–1945* (London: Weidenfeld and Nicolson, 1982) must be read, with some caution; for the USSR, Christopher Andrew and Oleg Gordievsky, *KGB: The Inside Story of its Foreign Operations from Lenin to Gorchakov* (London: Hodder & Stoughton, 1990) and Christopher Andrew and Vasili Mitrokhin, *The Mitrokhin Archive, The KGB in Europe and the West* (London: Allen Lane, 1999); for Czechoslovakia, General Frantisek Moravec, *Master of Spies* (London: Bodley Head, 1975); for Poland, Garlinski and Richard Woytak, *On the Border of War and Peace: Polish Intelligence and Diplomacy in 1937–1939 and the Origins of the Ultra Secret* (New York: *Eastern European Quarterly*, 1979); for Japan, John Chapman, "Britain, Japan and the 'Higher Realms of Intelligence', 1918–1945", in Ian Gow, Yoichi Hirama and John Chapman (eds), *The History of Anglo-Japanese Relations, 1600–2000, Volume III, The Military Dimension* (London: Palgrave, 2003) (also more broadly for the intelligence relations between Germany, Italy and Japan). Louis Allen, *Burma, The Longest War* (New York: St. Martin's Press) offers useful accounts of Japanese espionage and preparations for subversion in Asia during 1940–1941.
53 Alexander Dallin, *German Rule in Russia* (London: Macmillan, 1957), pp. 114–116.
54 Andrew and Mitrokhin, *The Mitrokhin Archive*, pp. 55–110.
55 Watt, *How War Came*, pp. 231, 248–249, 368, 376, 378, offers the clearest assessment of how intelligence probably affected Soviet policy during 1939, though the account is necessarily speculative, and much material was subsequently released on Soviet diplomacy and intelligence during that year.
56 Ferris, "Whitehall's Black Chamber", p. 243; David Irving (ed.) (with introduction by D.C. Watt), *Breach of Security, The German Secret Intelligence File on Events leading to the Second World War* (London: William Kimber, 1968), p. 21, *passim*; Kahn, *Hitler's Spies*, pp. 178–181; Australia Archives Cambera, A 6825/5, memorandum by E. Petrov, "Report on the Organisation of Soviet

NOTES

Cipher Services (with particular reference to the Soviet State Secret Service Department (Spets Otdel)", 10.8.56; RG 457/751, "Assignment of SIS Personnel, August–September 1938" (I am indebted for this information and reference to Dr. David Alvarez); RG 457/764, "First Detailed Interrogation of Bigi, Augusto", CSDIC/CMF/Y, 20.9.44.

57 This figure is calculated by adding together the different *Forshungsamt* reports in Irving, *Breach*, and FO 371/21742, C 11002/1941/18 (in the former case, identified by a six-figure number). RG 457/171, G-12 to D.N.C. Security Coordinating Committee, 10.7.45, includes useful comments on German diplomatic codebreaking, though it is hard to differentiate prewar from wartime success.

58 Stephen Budiansky, *Battle of Wits: The Complete Story of Codebreaking in World War II* (Toronto: Free Press, 2000) has some material on the later 1930s. The best material on French cryptanalysis in the 1930s is Christopher Andrew, "Dechiffrement et diplomatie: Le Cabinet noir du Quai d'Orsay sous la Troisieme Republique", *Relations Internationales* (1976), pp. 37–64; Peter Jackson, *France and the Nazi Menace* (Oxford: Oxford University Press) and "Intelligence and the End of Appeasement", in Robert Boyce (ed.), *French Foreign and Defence Policy, 1918–1940: The Decline and Fall of a Great Power* (London: Routlege, 1998); on British cryptanalysis, Ferris, "Whitehall's Black Chamber" and "The Road to Bletchley Park: The British Experience with Signals Intelligence, 1892–1945", *Intelligence and National Security*, 16(1) (2002), and A.G. Denniston, "The Government Code & Cypher School Between the Wars", *Intelligence and National Security* 1(1) (1986), pp. 48–0; on Italian and American, David Alvarez, "Left in the Dust: Italian Signals Intelligence, 1915–1943", *International Journal of Intelligence and Counterintelligence*, 14 (Fall 2001) and *Secret Messages: Codebreaking and American Diplomacy 1930–1945* (Lawrence: University Press of Kansas, 2000); on German, Irving (ed.) *Breach* and Kahn, *Hitler's Spies*; on Polish, John Schindler, "Polish Signals Intelligence Between the Two World Wars", paper presented by John Schindler to the Cryptological History Symposium, 29–31 October 2003; on Swedish, C.G. McKay and Bengt Beckman, *Swedish Signals Intelligence, 1900–1945* (London: Frank Cass, 2003). Evidence on the Soviet side is fragmentary, though useful material is included in Andrew and Mitrokhin, *The Mitrokhin Archive*. Andrew, on p. 69, indicates that the USSR solved some traffic from every great power and many smaller ones, but the nature and significance of this success is uncertain. He holds: "No Western SIGINT agency during the 1930s seems to have collected so much political and diplomatic intelligence." This claim is dubious. Given the limited Soviet ability to intercept traffic, agents probably gave it more telegrams than codebreaking did. The GC&CS, with roughly similar success against systems and more access to traffic, probably solved as many or more significant telegrams than Soviet codebreakers, while Italy perhaps matched the USSR with regard to the combination of codebreaking and black-bag jobs.

59 L/WS/1/72, Dennys to Henderson, 13.4.1939, Dennys to Stuart, 22.6.1939; WO 33/1500, War Office, 1.1.38, "Order of Battle of the Military Forces of the U.S.S.R."; WO 33/1655 A, MI2b, 15.2.40, "Order of Battle of the Military Forces of the U.S.S.R".

60 Irving, *Breach*, pp. 55–120.

61 Watt, *How War Came*; Andrew and Mitrokhin, *The Mitrokhin Archive*, pp. 83, 107–108, 119; Getty and Naumov, *Road to Terror*, pp. 422, 538–539, 561–562.

62 Watt, *How War Came*.

63 *DDF, 1932–1939, 2e serie (1936–1939), Tome VII* (29 September 1937–16 January 1938), Paris, 1972, pp. 632–633.

64 *DDF, 1932–1939, 2e serie (1936–1939), Tome III* (19 July–19 November 1936), Paris, 1968, pp. 202–206, 250–255; *Tome XIII* (1 December 1938–31 January 1939), Paris, 1979, p. 471; *Tome IX* (21 March–9 June 1938), p. 1049.
65 For the Germans, see Barton Whaley, *Covert German Rearmament, 1919–1939: Deception and Misperception* (Frederick, MD: University Publications of America, 1984), for the Italians, cf. William C. Mills, "The Chamberlain–Grandi Conversations of July–August 1937 and the Appeasement of Italy", *International History Review*, 19(3) (1997), pp. 594–619. OSS archives contain copies of two case files from the *Regia Aeronatica*'s security service about material fed through controlled French agents, RG 226/89/50 and RG 226/89/57.
66 Mills, *ibid*.
67 Jackson, "Intelligence and the End of Appeasement".
68 Some useful specialist accounts of how intelligence affected the outbreak of the European war in 1939 include David Dilks, "Flashes of Intelligence: The Foreign Office, the SIS and Security Before the Second World War", in Christopher Andrew and David Dilks, *The Missing Dimension, Governments and Intelligence Communities in the Twentieth Century* (London: Macmillan, 1984); Ferris, " 'Indulged in All Too Little'?"; David Dilks, "Appeasement and 'Intelligence' ", in David Dilks (ed.), *Retreat From Power, Volume One, 1906–1939* (London: Macmillan, 1981), pp. 155–157; Richard Overy, "Strategic Intelligence and the Outbreak of the Second World War", *War in History* 5(4) (1998), pp. 451–480; Irving, *Breach*, pp. 47–120. The two best accounts of the diplomacy of the period, Weignberg, *Starting World War Two*, and Watt, *How War Came*, also pay attention to the issue.
69 Knox, *Mussolini Unleashed*, p. 15.
70 A collection, not necessarily complete, of *Forshungsamt* intercepts of Czech telephone traffic during the Munich crisis are in FO 371/21742, C 11002/1941/18.
71 Irving, *Breach*, pp. 55–120.
72 Aspects of this issue are discussed in Ferris, " 'Indulged in all Too Little'?"; Dilks, "Appeasement and 'Intelligence' ", pp. 155–157; Gerhard Weinberg, *Starting World War Two*, pp. 282–283; Antony Best, *Britain, Japan and Pearl Harbor: Avoiding War in East Asia, 1936–1941* (London: Routledge, 1995); and John Chapman's many works on the intelligence relations between the Axis states, e.g. J.W.C. Chapman, "Signals Intelligence Cooperation Among the Secret Intelligence Services of the Axis States, 1940–41", *Japan Forum* (1991), pp. 231–256.
73 Dilks, "Appeasement and 'Intelligence' ", pp. 154–158.

4 The British "Enigma"

1 The India Office Records and Library, at the British Library, hold the L/R/5, L/WS and M/3 series; The National Archives, Washington (NAW), hold the RG 38, RG 165 and RG 457 series, and The National Archives of Australia, Canberra Reading Room (NAA), hold the CP 4 and A 451 series. All remaining source references come from the Public Record Office, Kew, and appear by permission of the Controller of Her Majesty's Stationery Office.
2 Peter Calvocoressi, *Top Secret Ultra* (London: Cassell, 1980), pp. 21–31; Josef Garlinski, *Intercept* (London: J.M. Dent and Sons, 1979), pp. 7–10; F.H. Hinsley, with E.E. Thomas, C.F.G. Ransom and R.C. Knight, *British Intelligence in the Second World War, Its Influence on Strategy and Operation*, vol. 2 (London: HMSO, 1981), pp. 631–641. The best general account of

NOTES

machine cryptography is Cipher A. Devours and Louis Kruh, *Machine Cryptography and Modern Cryptanalysis* (Dedham, MA: Artech House, 1985). Their account of Typex is not entirely accurate, unavoidably so, given the limits to the material available to them.

3 ADM 137/1896, memorandum by Fremantle, 22.5.17.
4 ADM 1/8435, report of the committee on mechanical cryptography, June 1914.
5 CAB 1/33, memorandum by Beatty, n.d., "Manoeuvres 1913, Miscellaneous Remarks".
6 ADM 1/8044, Patent Office to Admiralty, 15.5.08, *passim*; ADM 1/8385, memorandum "Cypher type writers", n.d. and no author cited, but by Marrack and *c.* June 1913 according to internal evidence.
7 WO 32/9 153, 10th meeting of the Wireless Telegraphy Committee, 16.3.13; ADM 1/8385, minute by Churchill, 6.5.13, memorandum by Marrack, 6.6.13; ADM 1/8435, report of the committee on mechanical cryptography, June 1914; WO 32/4731, minute by Davies, 30.10.13; CO 323/640, memorandum by Allen, 24.7.14; FO 371/2513, Browne to Montgomery, 1.9.15; George Cockerill, *What Fools We Were* (London: Hutchinson, 1944), p. 23.
8 ADM 1/8435, report of the committee on mechanical cryptography, June 1914; CO 323/640, minute by Robinson, 19.8.14.
9 John Ferris, "Whitehall's Black Chamber: British Cryptology and the Government Code and Cypher School, 1919–1929", *Intelligence and National Security*, 2(1) (1987).
10 CAB 16/89, 1st meeting of the Wireless Messages Committee, 14.2.28; CAB 35/45, ICC paper No. 916.
11 CAB 35/1, 24th ICC meeting, 2.3.22; CAB 35/8, ICC paper No. 633.
12 CAB 35/1, 32nd and 34th ICC meetings, 6.7.23 and 30.10.23; CAB 35/19, ICC paper No. 729.
13 L/R/5/278, Indian War Department History, *General Staff and Analogous Matters*, 1939–1944, p. 39, n.d. and no author cited.
14 Devours and Kruh, *Machine Cryptography*, offers the best general account. Lt. Col. Marcel Givierge, "La Cryptographie et Les Machines a Cryptographier", *La Science et La Vie* (March 1923), pp. 223–31; RG 38/P-10-c/19483 A, Military Attaché, London, No. 30825, 2.7.31, to MID, WO 165/4131-B-2; memorandum by Lt. Wegner, 20.6.32 (4–28). RG 38/P-10-c/19483 A and RG 457/608 include a host of USN reports on cipher machines and manufacturers' brochures.
15 WO 279/54, report on general staff exercise, *c.* November 1922; ADM 116/2101, minute by Fitzmaurice, 20.7.23; CAB 35/1, 34th ICC meeting, 30.10.23; CAB 35/19, ICC paper No. 729; Hinsley *et al.*, *British Intelligence in the Second World War*, pp. 631–641; Garlinski, *Intercept*, pp. 7–10; *The Origin and Development of the Army Security Agency*, 1917–1947, p. 17, no author cited. (Laguna Hills: Aegean Park Press, 1978).
16 Deavours and Kruh, *Machine Cryptography*, p. 7; HW 3/14, memorandum by Peel, "Cipher machine invented by Lieut. Colonel A. Peel, C.M.G., and Mr. G. Critchley".
17 Ferris, "Whitehall's Black Chamber"; CAB 4/13, CID paper No. 636-B; CAB 4/14, CID paper No. 674-B.
18 NAA, CP4/2/1/114, "Cyphers and Codes in the custody of the Cables section of the Prime Minister's Department", 7.1.37.
19 CAB 16/89, 1st meeting of the Wireless Messages Committee, 14.2.28. That Whitehall was attracted to rotor systems and never considered the adoption of two commonly used for government traffic, the Hagelin or Kryha devices, is puzzling; perhaps the GC&CS or the War Office's experts studied them and discerned the weaknesses which would become apparent between 1939 and 1945.

NOTES

20 HW 3/14, memorandum by Peel, "Cipher machine invented by Lieut. Colonel A. Peel, C.M.G., and Mr. G. Critchley".
21 FO 371 Index, 1929, entry "Cyphers"; Hinsley et al., *British Intelligence in the Second World War*, pp. 631–641; WO 32/3057, memorandum by S.D.6., 2.10.29; CAB 35/17, 80th ICC meeting, 30.6.32.
22 RG 38/P-10-b/20363, memorandum by Wenger, 3.6.32, "Auto Cypher Machine", *passim*; RG 38/P-10-c/19483 A, memorandum by Lt. Wegner, 20.6.32 (4–28).
23 *Ibid*; CAB 35/30, ICC paper No. 1428; RG 457/608, Wenger to Chief of Naval Operations (Director of Naval Communications), 6.2.32, JNW:R, memorandum by Naval Attaché, London, 15.1.36, Serial No. 55, UK patents, 4.4.28, 320, 315 and 25.3.36, 70, 905, No. 10129/28, US patent, 4.5.37, 2, 079, 130.
24 RG 38/P-10-b/20363, memorandum by Wenger, 3.6.32, "Auto Cypher Machine", *passim*; AVIA 8/356, memorandum A. 359, "Recommendation for an award to Wing Commander Lywood, O.B.E., in Conjunction with the Type 'X' Cypher Machine".
25 FO 850/134, minute by Travis, 12.6.44.
26 HW 3/14, memorandum by Clarke and Lambert, "Marconi Machine", n.d.
27 CAB 35/45, report of SCC, 8.3.33. One service representative on the SCC, Wing Commander Warrington-Morris, had a long-standing faith in the value of such "scrambling" devices for radio traffic (CAB 35/16, 64th and 65th ICC meetings, 12.12.29 and 18.12.29).
28 AIR 20/1531, Security of R.A.F. signal communications, n.d. and no author cited, but *c*. December 1944 according to internal evidence
29 CAB 4/23, CID paper No. 1157-B.
30 AVIA 8/356, Memorandum A. 359.
31 R.V. Jones, *Most Secret War, British Scientific Intelligence, 1939–1945* (London: Hamish Hamilton, 1978), p. 103, *passim*.
32 AIR 14/3562, No. 26 Group, 12.45, "The Signals War, A Brief History of No. 26 Group".
33 Except where otherwise noted, the material in this and the following six paragraphs is derived from material in AVIA 8/356. Between 1920 and 1932, Britain spent L10,000 on cipher machines, including L1,500 for the O'Brien models. The initial development of Typex Mark I cost L1,260 and the entire project £12,469. This compares favourably with the development of Sigaba, which took three and a half years and US$120,000 (RG 457/591, "Extract from memo of 19 February 1941"). By September 1941 the 3,232 Mark IIs on order were expected to cost L300,000, which would be more than offset by savings on cipher personnel. Lywood and Smith received £500 and £250 respectively for their work on Typex—an award of 75 per cent of Lywood's salary and 100 per cent of Smith's; notably, O'Brien received £30,000 for use of the far less sophisticated "Syko" system. However, these men received other rewards. All officers involved moved a step up in grade and received honours, while two other ranks were made officers. Lywood reached the top of his professional ladder, becoming the Air Ministry's Director of Signals, controller of British strategic communications during the Second World War. After stagnating for fourteen years in the same post, Smith became a warrant officer, and by 1946 apparently reached the rank of Wing Commander—a remarkable rise.
34 AIR 5/424, memorandum by Simpson, 28.7.26, *passim*.
35 NAW, RG 165/2280 A 77, memorandum by Major Evans, Office of the Military Attaché, London, No. 30262, 26.3.31.
36 In January 1936, O'Brien told the United States Naval Attaché in London that BTM was the present manufacturer for his new system, provided photographs of a well-finished machine, and held it was being considered by the British

government. The Naval Attaché doubted the last point, probably rightly so by this time. In 1934–1935 O'Brien was still trying to sell a machine to the government, which BTM probably supported as Creed did Lywood. (RG 457/608, memorandum by Naval Attaché, London, 15.1.36, Serial No. 55, UK patents, 4.4.28, 320, 315 and 25.3.36, 70, 905, No. 10129/28, US patent, 4.5.37, 2, 079, 130). For BTM, see "A Short History of the British Tabulatory Machine Co Ltd", n.d. and no author cited, James W. Birkenstock Collection, CBI 132, Box 1, folder 3, Charles Babbage Institute, University of Minnnesota.
37 Hinsley *et al.*, *British Intelligence in the Second World War*, pp. 631–641.
38 AIR 2/2720 S.43275, Lywood to unknown recipient, 25.6.34; AVIA 8/355, memorandum by Director of Signals, 11.11.37. Ralph Erskine, "The Development of Typex", *The Enigma Bulletin*, 2 (May 1997), pp. 69–81, offers an excellent assessment of the development and role of Typex, especially of its security.
39 I am indebted for this information to Ralph Erskine.
40 AVIA 22/1483, War Office to Ministry of Supply, 18.9.44, suggests the War Office wanted an on-line cipher teleprinter and did not have such a system.
41 Hugh Denham, "Bedford–Bletchley–Kilindini–Colombo", in F.H. Hinsley and Alan Stripp, *Codebreakers, The Inside Story of Bletchley Park* (Oxford: Oxford University Press, 1993), p. 269.
42 Devours and Kruh, *Machine Cryptography*, pp. 73–80; Colin Burke, *Information and Secrecy, Vannevar Bush, Ultra and the Other Memex* (Metuchen, NJ: Scarecrow Press, 1994)
43 "Extract from memorandum of 19 February 1941"; RG 457/591, memorandum by Friedman, "Verbal Statement of CSP 888", 28.2.40.
44 RG 457/188, GC&CS, Naval Section, Cryptographic Memorandum No. 40
45 AIR 20/1531, Security of R.A.F. signal communications; CAB 35/34, ICC paper No. 1692; Hinsley *et al.*, *British Intelligence in the Second World War*, pp. 631–641.
46 AVIA 8/356, Minute by Nutting, 25.9.39.
47 AIR 29/141, Air Ministry Communication Centre War Diary, entry 12.39.
48 AVIA 8/356 contains records for orders and production of Typex machines; there are slight discrepancies between these figures, and somewhat greater ones compared to the records for Admiralty procurement in ADM 1/11770. See Ralph Erskine, "The Development of Typex", pp. 72–73, for production between 1942 and 1945.
49 In 1944 the head of RAF signals security believed Germany had broken some RAF Typex traffic during the Tunisian campaign (AIR 20/1531, Security of R.A.F. signal communications). Postwar investigations concluded that Germany never broke any Typex traffic. Hinsley *et al.*, *British Intelligence in the Second World War*, pp. 631–641.
50 L/WS/1/72, Henderson to Dennys, 9.2.39, *passim*; M/3/8692/39, War Office to Burma Office, 28.9.39; WO 244/99, Morgan to C.S.O., Line of Communications, B.E.F. France, 23.5.40; AIR 23/1338, Air Ministry to H.Q., R.A.F., Middle East, 31.1.41; AIR 23/1293, memorandum by chief signals officer H.Q., R.A.F., Middle East, 27.10.41; CAB 120/321, minute by Dowding, 7.1.42; AIR 23/5692, RAF H.Q. Iraq to Air Ministry, 10.4.42; AIR 20/1531, "Security of R.A.F. Signal Communications".
51 INF 1/380, Cadogan to Radcliffe, 3.2.42.
52 FO 371/32275, Postal and Telegraph Censorship Department, memorandum "Cable Congestion", 17.3.42.
53 INF 1/380, Cadogan to Radcliffe, 3.2.42; FO 850/56A, minute by Codrington, 2.4.43, memorandum by Foreign Office, 6.5.43; FO 850/172, minute by Dunlop, 1.6.45.

NOTES

54 AIR 23/6180, memorandum by Michell, 1.10.41, "Signals Lessons Learned During the Campaign in Libya".
55 AIR 20/1531, "Security of R.A.F. Signal Communications".
56 WO 165/81, Directorate of Signals War Diary, entry 16.7.42.
57 The best account of the Admiralty's policy toward and procurement of Typex machines is in ADM 1/11770, "Ships and Authorities Who Will Hold R.A.F. Type X Mark II Cypher (Coding) Machine", *passim*; other material is in AVIA 8/356. These figures do not always jibe, though the variations are usually only about 10 per cent apart. In case of differences, I have used the figures in ADM 1/11770. Ralph Erskine, "The Admiralty and Cipher Machines During the Second World War: Not So Stupid After All", *The Journal of Intelligence History*, 2(2) (2002), pp. 49–68, destroys previous views regarding the RN's experience with Typex.
58 CAB 120/321, Air Ministry Conference, 20.1.42, *passim*.
59 AIR 23/129X, "Report on Visit to the United Kingdom by Chief Signals Officer, R.A.F., M.E., Chief Signals Officer, Air Formation Signals, and Chief Radio Officer, R.A.F., M.E.", 27.10.41.
60 HW 14/14, "Major Vemba's Report on Tour", n.d. but *c.* mid-December 1941 by internal evidence (misdated in file); AIR 23/5959, HQ RAF M.E., 18.11.41, "Outline Signal Plan for Middle East section of U.K.–Egypt–Russia Air Route".
61 AIR 23/6905, memorandum by S/L Badcock, 22.8.42, "211 Group R.A.F.".
62 FO 370/688/12, Foreign Office Circular No. 128, 11.8.42.
63 CAB 21/2517, "Report on Visit to Certain British and Dominion's Missions and Offices in the United States and Canada by the Cypher Advisor to the Security panel, May–June 1943"; AIR 14/3562, "The Signals War".
64 WO 165/76, Directorate of Signals War Diary, entry 21.10.43.
65 WO 193/211, COS (42) 107; WO 203/5157, Air Ministry to British Commands, 12.7.44.
66 FO 850/172, 108th CSC, 4.7.45, Y 7455.
67 WO 204/4744, Eisenhower to Surles, 11.12.42; WO 204/1557, AFCB Gibraltar to London, 8.11.42, 12.11.42; WO 204/3917, AAG to AOC Eastern Air Command, 23.1.43, AFHQ to US 11 Corps, 13.1.43.
68 WO 204/6378, report by CSO, First Army, "Signals Campaign in North Africa", n.d.; AIR 23/5731, Signals Plans Force 141 (Air) memo, 18.6.43, HQ North African Air Forces to formations, 6.7.43; AIR 23/6636, MAC, Air Command Desert, "Fighter Control, Communications and R.D.F. in the First Fourteen Days of the Sicilian Invasion (Provisional Report)"; WO 204/7870, 15 Army Group, "Note on Signal Communications in Operation 'HUSKY' "; for the comparative transmission of groups, see War Office, *Study on Signal Communications during the Second World War* (1950), WO 222/25, pp. 412–13.
69 HW 14/5, Denniston to "The Director", 6.6.40.
70 John Ferris, "The Road to Bletchley Park: The British Experience with Signals Intelligence, 1890–1945", in Oliver Hoare (ed.), *Intelligence and National Security*, 16(1) (Spring 2002), pp. 53–84.
71 HW 14/2, MI1 to GC&CS, 1.11.39, GC&CS to MI1, 4.11.39.
72 HW 14/3, "Minutes of meeting held on 26th February, 1940, to discuss the introduction of the R.A.F. Type 'X' Cypher Machine in the three Services".
73 HW 14/5, unsigned letter, C/4579, 19.6.40; HW 14/6, Denniston to DDMI (O), 8.7.40.
74 CAB 120/321, Air Ministry Conference, 20.1.42, *passim*; AIR 20/1531 "Security of R.A.F. Signal Communications"; Ralph Erskine, "The Development of Typex", pp. 76–78.

NOTES

75 AIR 23/995, Appendix A to Middle East Standing Orders (Signals), Part 1. B. "War, Signals Security War Organisation", 16.5.42; AIR 23/5023, memoranda by RAF Headquarters, 10.10.42, Signal Instruction No. 42, and 11.11.43, No. 23; WO 203/5157, SACSEA to War Office/Admiralty/Air Ministry, 24.2.44, SEAC to CSO I.A.T., 28.4.45; HQ SEAAC Signals Staff Instruction No. 69, 28.1.44.
76 RG 457/764, "First Detailed Interrogation of Bigi, Augusto", CSDIC/CMF/Y, 20.9.44.
77 RG 547/604, memorandum by COMNAVFORGER, 21.8.51, "Historical, Naval Radio Intelligence ('B-Dienst')", by Captain Bonatz. For a detailed account of attitudes toward Typex by members of OKW/Chi and OKH In/7, see TICOM/1–66, "Paper by Dr. Otto BUGGISCH of OKH/In.7/VI and OKW/Chi on Typex", 12.8.45; and TICOM/1–161, "Further Statements on Typex by Huettenhain, Fricke & Mettig", 31.10.45; R 457/743, 14/TS/50, "Radio Intercept and Cryptanalysis", 18.9.50; RG 457/171, G-12 to D.N.C. Security Coordinating Committee, 10.7.45.
78 RG 457/604, US 8th Fleet (Naval Intelligence Unit), 28.3.45, No. 162308, to CNO (DNI); RG 457/764, "First Detailed Interrogation of Krause, Werner", CSDIC/CMF/Y 3, 31.7.44
79 RG 547/604, memorandum by COMNAVFORGER, 21.8.51, "Historical, Naval Radio Intelligence ('B-Dienst')", by Captain Bonatz; R 457/743, 14/TS/50, "Radio Intercept and Cryptanalysis", 18.9.50.
80 RG 457/145, Major Gamba, "An Account of the Recovery of the Keys of the French–British Interallied Cipher", n.d.; RG 457/145, Admiral Maugeri, "Italian Communications Intelligence Organization", n.d., c.1944; RG 457/770, "Subject: Italian Escapee from Athens" and "Interview with Colonel Giorgio Negroni on 27 September 1943"; RG 457/764, "First Detailed Interrogation of Bigi, Augusto", CSDIC/CMF/Y, 20.9.44.
81 RG 457/764, "First Detailed Interrogation of Bigi, Augusto", CSDIC/CMF/Y, 20.9.44; RG 457/769, "Reports on Interrogations of Werner K.H. Graupe and Herbert S.B. Schwartze", S.I.S. H.Q. Etousa, 9.12.44.
82 RG 457/770, memorandum by Lt. Colonel Schukraft, AFHQ, "German Signal Intelligence Activities", 22.3.44; TICOM/1–161, *op.cit.* The best English-language accounts of German and Italian signals intelligence are David Alvarez, "Left in the Dust: Italian Signals Intelligence, 1915–1943", *International Journal of Intelligence and Counterintelligence*, 14 (Fall 2001), and David Kahn, *Hitler's Spies*.
83 CAB 21/2517, memorandum by Lt. Commander Bull, Secretary, Cypher Security Committee, n.d. but c.12.43, "Special Cypher Precautions *vis-à-vis* the United States".
84 CAB 21/2519, JIC 48 (25) Final (Revise), 22.4.48, "Instructions for Handling Certain Information".
85 FO 850/132, 72nd and 73rd meetings of Cypher Security Committee, 29.12.43, 19.1.44, Y 335/G, Y 421 G; FO 850/134, 83rd meeting of CSC, 14.6.44, Y 3433/G; TICOM/1–66 and 1–161, *op.cit.*; cf. note 47.
86 David Alvarez, *Secret Messages*.
87 CAB 21/2519, Personal Minute by Churchill, 27.1.44, Bridges to Stewart Menzies, 28.1.44, Stewart Menzies to Bridges, 31.1.44, Bridges to Churchill, n.d. but January 1944 and 31.1.44; HW 9/27, Minutes of Second Meeting of Cypher Policy Board, 12.6.44, Minutes of Second Meeting of Cypher Policy Board, 5.10.44.
88 W.G. Welchman, *The Hut Six Story, Breaking the Enigma Codes* (New York: McGraw-Hill, 1982), p. 171.

NOTES

89 David Stafford, *Camp X, Canada's School for Secret Agents, 1941–45* (Toronto: University of Toronto Press, 1986), pp. 154–165.
90 Nigel West (ed.), *British Security Coordination, The Secret History of British Intelligence in the Americas, 1940–1945* (New York: Fromm International, 1999), pp. 447–454. Notably, in a secret patent of 1933, presumably unknown to Bayly, Friedman outlined a different procedure for suppressing stunt characters (US Patent 6.130,946, United States Patent Office, www.uspto.gov).
91 Welchman, *Hut Six*, p. 173; and Stafford, *Camp X*, pp. 161–2, offer variant accounts.
92 Andrew Hodges, *Alan Turing, The Enigma, A Biography* (London: Burnett, 1983), pp. 243–253, 399, 402; Welchman, *Hut Six*, p. 176; for the USN's relationship with data-processing firms and its application to cryptology, cf. Burke, *Information and Security*.
93 Welchman, *Hut Six*, pp. 171–174.
94 West, *British Security Coordination*, pp. 450–451, 457. PRO files between 1943 and 1947 refer to this machine as "Telekrypton". In fact it was "Rockex I"; referring to that machine, which had been on order for two months, i.e. after Bayly developed the prototype, in April 1943, the Joint Staff Mission to Washington stated, "the telekrypton apparatus will be operated on the 'one time' principle and will therefore have the same security as a one time pad, i.e. 100 percent security"; CAB 122/561, Joint Staff Mission to War Cabinet, 24.4.23. For purposes of simplification, I will term this system "Rockex I", though the documents do not.
95 Hodges, *Turing*, pp. 246–248, 269; CAB 122/561, "H.R. Procedure", for Telekrypton; for the programme as a whole, see J.V. Boone and R.R. Peterson, "SIGSALY Secure Digital Voice Communications in World War II, The Start of the Digital Revolution" (www.nsa.gov/wwii/papers/start_of_digital_revolution.htm).
96 CAB 122/561, "Project X-61753, Report by Dr. Turing", n.d., and Joint Staff Mission to War Cabinet, 24.4.23.
97 CAB 122/561, JSM to COS, 17.9.43, and JSM to War Cabinet, 15.12.44.
98 WO 202/917, "Historical Record of the British Army Staff Washington, Part II, Operations, Plans and Intelligence", n.d., c.1946:
99 Welchman, *Hut Six*, pp. 171–174; Hodges, *Turing*, pp. 270–284.
100 FO 850/132, memorandum by Bull, 14.12.43, 72nd meeting of the Cipher Security Committee (CSC), 29.12.43; FO 850/134, minute by weeder, 16.4.73, 88th CSC meeting, 6.9.44; HW 9/27, minutes of Second Meeting of Cypher Policy Board, 5.10.44; PREM 4/34/8A, memorandum by Bridges, 8.12.44.
101 FO 850/134, minute by Communication Department, 3.8.44.
102 HW 9/27, minutes of Second Meeting of Cypher Policy Board, 5.10.44, minutes of Fourth Meeting of Cypher Policy Board, 21.2.45, minutes of Second Meeting of Cypher Policy Board, 19.9.46, Appendix C CPB (46) 2, 25.8.46; AVIA 22/1483, Cypher Policy Board to Ministry of Supply, 30.7.45.
103 FO 850/236, memorandum by Gambier-Perry, 1.10.47.
104 WO 288/122, Annex "D" to Allied Land Force Signal Instruction No. 4, Annex "C" to Combined Signal Instruction No. 2; HW 9/27, memorandum by Cypher Policy Board, 11.11.49, CPB (49) 13; "KL-7 (ADONIS)" (webhome.idirect.com/-jproc/crypto/kl7); NAA, A 451/1/50/5584, memorandum from Jones to Ainsworth, 8.9.53; "INFOSEC History", New Zealand Government Communications Security Bureau (www.gcsb.govt.nz/infist.htm).
105 HW 14/3, "Minutes of meeting", 26.2.40; AVIA 8/356, memorandum "A.352"; AVIA 22/1483, Morrell to DDSRD (1), 22.12.44; Erskine, "The Development of Typex", pp. 72–73.

NOTES

106 RG 457/203, Bayne to Corry, P/1390, 9.5.55.
107 CAB 122/579, Coleridge to Jacob, 21.2.45.
108 AVIA 22/1483, D.D. Sigs (E) to D.D.S.R.D. (1), 5.12.44, *passim*; one of the new machines considered for government use had the euphonious name "Fruitex"; Hodges, *Turing*, pp. 245–247, 266–268, *passim*.
109 HW 9/27, minutes of Second Meeting of Cypher Policy Board, 5.10.44, minutes of Second Meeting of Cypher Policy Board, 19.9.45, *passim*; AVIA 22/1483, first and second meetings of the "War Office Sub-Committee" of "The Cypher Machine Development Committee", 8.12.44 and 8.1.45. I am indebted for information on the RM (26) programme to Peter Freeman.
110 HW 9/27, minutes of the Third Meeting of the Cypher Policy Board, 5.11.46, *passim*.
111 FO 371/22503, Knox to Sargent, 21.20.38, minute by O'Malley, 10.11. 38, *passim*, W 15391.
112 FO 850/291, memorandum by Grey, 3.12.53 and minute by Speaght, 4.12.53.

5 The British army: signals and security in the desert campaign, 1940–1942

I am indebted to Michael Handel, Elizabeth Herbert, Richard Popplewell, Tim Travers and to the participants at the Third United States Army War College Conference on Intelligence and Military Operations in May 1988 for comments upon an earlier draft of this paper. I am grateful to Jill and Michael Handel for hospitality and to Yael, Benjamin and Ethan for entertainment. Material from the papers of Basil Liddell Hart, R.L. Thompson and General O'Connor (Basil Liddell Hart Centre for Military Archives), General Cunningham (National Army Museum), Generals Corbett and Galloway (Churchill College, Cambridge), General Auchinleck (John Ryland Library), A.F. Johnson (Imperial War Museum) and Lord Trenchard (Royal Air Force Museum, Hendon) is cited with permission of the copyright holders. The L/WS series is held at the India Office Records and Library, at the British Library, and materials from the RG 165 series at the National Archives, Washington, DC. All other primary sources cited in this paper are held at the Public Record Office, Kew, and appear by the permission of the Controller of Her Majesty's Stationery Office.

1 WO 169/1016, memorandum by Middle East GHQ, 13 March 1942.
2 AIR 23/5526, training memorandum by Allied Force Headquarters, 17 March 1943.
3 The following comments have been influenced by Shelford Bidwell and Dominick Graham, *Fire Power, British Army Weapons and Theories of War, 1904–1945* (London and Boston: Allen & Unwin, 1982), pp. 248–250; Martin van Crevald, *Command in War* (Cambridge, Mass.: Harvard University Press, 1985), pp. 1–16; and Gordon Welchman, *The Hut Six Story, Breaking The Enigma Codes* (New York: McGraw-Hill, 1982).
4 WO 204/8792, Colonel Bailey to "G", 7 April 1944; WO 203/5157, memorandum by S.O. in C., South East Asia command, 25 March 1945; War Office, *Study on Signal Communications during the Second World War* (1950), WO 222/25, pp. 412–13.
5 WO 169/1016, memorandum by CSO, 13th Corps, n.d. but early 1942 according to internal evidence.
6 AIR 23/6180, memorandum by RAF headquarters, Middle East, 1 October 1941.

NOTES

7 For accounts of this issue see Brian Bond, *British Military Policy between the Two World Wars* (Oxford: Oxford University Press, 1980); and John Ferris, *The Evolution of British Strategic Policy, 1919–1926* (Ithaca, NY: Cornell University Press, 1989). The best account of the British army in the Second World War is David French, *Raising Churchill's Army, The British Army and the War Against Germany, 1919–1945* (London: Oxford University Press, 2000).
8 WO 244/98, memorandum by Signals Staff, Army Headquarters, Delhi, n.d. but late 1943–early 1944 according to internal evidence, *passim*; War Office, *Study*, pp. 6, 13, 17, 90. Cf. R.F.H. Nalder, *The Royal Corps of Signals, A History of its Antecedents and Developments (circa 1800–1955)* (London: Royal Signals Institute, 1958), pp. 223–264.
9 WO 170/4205, memorandum by CSO, Eighth Army, 21 February 1945.
10 WO 204/6595, memorandum by Beddell Smith, 19 February 1943.
11 R.E. Priestly, *The Signal Service in the European War of 1914 to 1918 (France)* (Chatham: Institute of Royal Engineers, 1921); John Ferris, "The British Army and Signals Intelligence in the Field During the First World War", *Intelligence and National Security*, 3(4) (October 1988).
12 WO 201/126, SO in C, Middle East to Director of Military Training, 20 April 1942.
13 WO 279/54, report on army staff exercise, 10–11.22, n.d.; WO 279/55, report on army staff exercise, 4.23, n.d.
14 "Address to the officers of the Mechanized Force by the C.I.G.S. at Tidworth, 8th September, 1927", Trenchard Papers, C.11/19/2, Royal Air Force Museum, Hendon.
15 WO 32/3057, memorandum by Milne, 14 November 1929, *passim*.
16 Cf. WO 287/24, pamphlets, "Summary of Engineer and Signal Information" for 1928–1938.
17 Ferris, "The British Army".
18 WO 33/1073, "Secret Supplement to Signal Training", 1925; "Secret Supplement to the Manual of Military Intelligence in the Field", 1923 and 1931 (copies in Whitehall Library, Old War Office); WO 33/249, "Memorandum on the Security of Wireless Signals in the Field", 11 May 1931.
19 RG 165/2280–9–1121 2 and 4, "Signals Training Volume 1, 1933, Organisation and Intercommunication in the Field", National Archives, Washington; WO 287/24, "Summary of Engineer and Signal Information" for 1929, p. 24; L/WS/1/245, Aldershot Command, "Report on the Road Movement Exercise Carried out by 2nd Division, 28–30 April, 1938", in CIGS to CGS India, Liaison Letter, 31.10.3; WO 33/1662, A 5156, "Notes on the Tactical and Administration Lessons of the Campaign in Norway".
20 WO 191/60, memorandum by Fifth Division, 12 June 1936; WO 197/11, memorandum "Points which have arisen", n.d. but October 1939 by internal evidence, no author cited. A slightly different problem arose for Commonwealth forces in Egypt during autumn 1940, when

> Security became a fetish and censorship was rigid. Code-names were allotted to units and to those holding the principal appointments in them. Telephone conversations thereafter were marked by hilarity or exasperation, according to the mood of the caller and the urgency of his call. To stand by and hear the Adjutant, irascible and red-faced, say "Pansy to Lulu speaking", was too much for the orderly-room staff, and though the business was serious it took some time to train all ranks in correct telephone security procedure.
> (D.W. Sinclair, *19 Battalion and Armoured Regiment, Official History of New Zealand in the Second World War, 1939–45* (Wellington, New Zealand: War History Branch, Department of Internal Affairs, 1954), p. 13)

NOTES

21 John Ferris, "The British 'Enigma': Britain, Signals Security and Cipher Machines, 1906–1946", *Defense Analysis*, 3(2) (May 1987).
22 AVIA 8/356, memorandum A.359, no author cited and n.d., but *c*. autumn 1938 according to internal evidence.
23 F.H. Hinsley *et al.*, *British Intelligence in the Second World War, Its Influence on Strategy and Operations*, vol. 2 (London: HMSO, 1981), pp. 640–641; Ferris, "The British 'Enigma'"; WO 169/1016, memorandum by CSO Eighth Army, 23 October 1941, *passim*; HW 14/14, "Major Vemba's Report on Tour", n.d. but *c*. mid-December 1941 by internal evidence (misdated in file).
24 AIR 20/1531, "Security of R.A.F. Signal Communications", no author cited and n.d., but *c*. December 1944 according to internal evidence.
25 John Ferris, "Whitehall's Black Chamber: British Cryptology and the Government Code and Cypher School, 1919–1929", *Intelligence and National Security*, 2(1) (January 1987); Nalder, *Royal Corps of Signals*, pp. 303–304, 33; Compton Mackenzie, *Eastern Epic, Volume One, September 1939–March 1943, Defence* (London: Chatto and Windus, 1951), p. 518; A.F. Johnson Papers (typescript memoirs, n.d.), *Having Volunteered*, p. 285, Imperial War Museum 80/42/1.
26 WO 201/95, RAF headquarters Greece to SO in C, Middle East, 18 January 1941.
27 CAB 65/13, Appendix Two, W.M. (40), 134th Conclusion, Minute 1, Confidential Annex, 22.5.40.
28 WO 32/3057, Senior Signals Officers Conference, 12 June 1930; Joan Bright (ed.), *The Ninth Queen's Royal Lancers, 1936–1945, The Story of an Armoured Regiment in Battle* (Aldershot: Gale and Polden, 1951), p. 4; David Scott Daniell, *History of the East Surrey Regiment, Volume IV, 1920–1952* (London: Ernest Benn, 1957), p. 80; "Hist (C)1", memorandum by Auchinleck, 19 June 1940, *Great Britain, Cabinet Office, Cabinet History Series, Principal War Telegrams and Memoranda, 1940–1943, Miscellaneous* (Nendeln: KTO, 1976), p. 51; WO 33/1662, "Notes on the Tactical and Administrative Lessons of the Campaign in Norway", n.d., A 5156.
29 WO 165/76, War Office Signals Liaison Letter, November 1946; WO 279/247, "Signal Training (All Arms), Pamphlet No. 12, Communication Security".
30 Michael Glover, *The Fight for the Channel Ports, Calais to Brest 1940: A Study in Confusion* (London: Leo Cooper in association with Seeker & Warburg, 1985), pp. 31–33, *passim*; Brian Bond, *France and Belgium 1939–1940* (London: Davis-Poynter, 1975), pp. 34–35, 81, 96, 103–104; Walter Lord, *The Miracle of Dunkirk* (London: Allen Lane, 1982), p. 15; Gregory Blaxland, *Destination Dunkirk, The Story of Gort's Army* (London: Collins, 1973); Bernard Montgomery, *Memoirs* (London: William Kimber, 1958), pp. 55–58, *passim*.
31 CAB 21/2516, E.E. Bridges to Hollis, 7.6.40 and Bridges to Douglas, 3.6.40.
32 WO 178/8, memorandum by Knox, 17 May 1942; Miles Reid, *Last on the List* (London: Cooper, 1974), pp. 26–27.
33 B.H. Liddell Hart (ed.), *The Rommel Papers* (London: Collins, 1953), pp. 13, 122, 167, *passim*; Bidwell and Graham, *Fire Power*, pp. 219–220.
34 CAB 106/220, Report of the Bartholomew Committee, n.d.
35 WO 208/5032, memorandum by MI8 (a), 18.7.41, "A Note on German Wireless Communications During the Battle of Crete", *passim*.
36 WO 197/11, memorandum "Discussions in London", n.d., no author cited; WO 197/92, "Historical Record of SO in C [*sic*] B.E.F. during the Battle of France", n.d.; WO 165/76, Directorate of Signals War Diary, entry 19 May 1940; WO 208/2036 A, Advanced GHQ to War Office, 23.5.40.
37 CAB 106/220, "Notes of a Conference", 12.6.40, *passim*.

NOTES

38 WO 167/19, BEF, Special Wireless Section C War Diary, entry October 1939; WO 167/7, General Staff Intelligence Weekly Progress Reports, 21 and 28 April 1940; WO 169/420, No. 3 Headquarters Signals Company War Diary, entry 8 November 1940; cf. WO 208/5021.
39 WO 167/17, memorandum by GSO3 Wireless, 29 December 1939.
40 CAB 106/220, "Notes of a Conference", 12.6.40.
41 WO 197/92, *op.cit*.; J.R. Colville, *Man of Valour, the Life of Field-Marshal the Viscount Gort* (London: Collins, 1973), p. 190.
42 For material on problems regarding communication within British units and formations during the French campaign, see A.C. Bell, *History of the Manchester Regiment, First and Second Battalions, 1922–1948* (Altrincham: J. Sherratt, 1954), pp. 342–364; W.R. Beddington, *A History of the Queen's Bays (The 2nd Dragoon Guards) 1929–1945* (Winchester: Warren, 1954), pp. 13–14, 19–22; Blaxland, *Destination Dunkirk*, p. 87, *passim*; Guy Courage, *The History of 15/19 Royal Hussars, 1939–1945* (Aldershot: Gale and Polden, 1949), pp. 26–34; D. Dawnay *et al.*, *The 10th Royal Hussars in the Second World War, 1939–1945* (Aldershot: Gale and Polden, 1948), pp. 13–16; Roger Evans (ed.), *The Story of the 5th Royal Inniskilling Dragoon Guards* (Aldershot: Gale and Polden, 1951), pp. 263–274; Glover, *The Fight for the Channel Ports*, pp. 55–61, *passim*; Basil Karslake, *1940, The Last Act; The Story of the British Forces in France After Dunkirk* (London: Leo Cooper, 1979), pp. 68–69, *passim*; Lord, *Miracle*, p. 65; David Rissik, *The D.L.I. at War, the Story of the Durham Light Infantry, 1939–1945* (London: Durham [UK[Light Infantry, 1954), pp. 40–42; Hugh Williamson, *The Fourth Division, 1939 to 1945* (London: N. Neame, 1951), pp. 18, 22; for the 51st Division, cf. War Office, *Study*, WO 222/25, p. 63.
43 CAB 106/220, "Notes of a Conference", 12.6.40.
44 WO 169/420, SO in C, Middle East to GHQ Middle East, 1 August 1940.
45 "Hist (B) 1 Final", C. in C., Middle East to War Office, 27 January 1941, *Great Britain, Cabinet Office, Cabinet History Series Principal War Telegrams and Memoranda, 1940–1943, Middle East I* (Nendeln: KTO, 1976), p. 39; WO 201/61, SO in C, Middle East to CSO, Crete, 14 May 1941; 3 DRL 6043/1/10 a (I), Blamey Papers, "Extracts from Col [*sic*] Porter's report to CGS GHQ MEF [*sic*]", 9.1.42, Australian War Memorial.
46 WO 201/76, C.S.O. RAF Headquarters, Middle East to Air Officer Commanding in Chief, 4 November 1940, *passim*; WO 169/1092, memorandum by CSO, Iraq, October 1941; WO 169/2677, CSO Sudan Force War Diary, entry 26 January 1941.
47 WO 169/1092, G.O.C. Iraq to Army Headquarters, Delhi, 13 August 1941; D.M. Davin, *Crete, Official History of New Zealand in the Second World War, 1939–45* (Wellington, NZ: War History Branch, Department of Internal Affairs, 1954), p. 47; War Office, *Study*, p. 384, WO 222/25; O'Connor to Freyberg, 20.6.40, O'Connor Papers, 4/1, Basil Liddell Hart Centre for Military Archives, King's College, London.
48 Bernard Montgomery, "The Problem of the Encounter Battle as Affected by Modern British War Establishments", *The Royal Engineers Journal* (September 1937); "The Major Tactics of the Encounter Battle", *Army Quarterly*, August 1938.
49 WO 216/60, minute by Wavell, 9.1.41; Wavell to Liddell Hart, 12.8.43, LH 1/733, Basil Liddell Hart papers, BLHCMA; undated and unsigned memorandum by Cunningham, but *c*. January–February 1942, in "RHH" to Cunningham, Alan Cunningham Papers, National Army Museum, 8303-104/18.
50 CAB 106/1218, Wavell to Dill, 19.6.41.

NOTES

51 CORB 4/1, Memorandum by Corbett, *c.*10.40, "Report on Visit to Egypt and the Western Desert ... September 1940"; CORB 4/10, Memorandum by Harding, "Appreciation of the Training Situation in the Middle East", 28.2.42, Churchill College, Cambridge.
52 CAB 106/685, O'Connor to Galloway, 19.1.41.
53 Dorman Smith to Thompson, 18.9.61, RL Thompson Papers, Thompson 2/2, BLHCMA.
54 Draft memorandum by Wavell, 21.5.42, "Dispatch on East African Operations", Force Nairobi to Mideast, 25.3.41, Cunningham to Wavell, 7.2.41, 17.2.41, Cunningham Papers 8303–104/7; memorandum by Cunningham, 6.6.41, "East Africa Force, Report on Operations from 1st November, 1940, to 5th April, 1941", 8303–104–12–1; memorandum by Cunningham, n.d., "Notes on Operations in East Africa from 11th February, 1941, to 3rd July, 1941", 8303–1–4/14; Cunningham to Giffard, 19.3.41, 8303–104–6.
55 WO 201/358, "Eighth Army, Report on Operations"; GHQ, Middle East, to Eighth Army, 2.9.41, "Crusader, Note by C-in-C, M.E.F.", 30.10.41, Cunningham papers, 8303/104–18.
56 Memoranda by Cunningham, 6.6.41, "East Africa Force, Report on Operations from 1st November, 1940, to 5th April, 1941", "Notes on Operations in East Africa, 11th February, 1941, to 3rd July, 1941", Cunningham papers, 8303–104–12–1 and 8303–104/14.
57 WO 201/358, "Eighth Army, Report on Operations".
58 WO 201/513, Norrie to Cunningham, 1.11.41; Corps Commanders Conference No. 3, 29.10.41, and No. 4, 14.11.41, Cunningham Papers, 8303–104/1 and 8303–104/18.
59 WO 169/996, Eighth Army War Diary, Supplementary Sheets, entry 0945, 19.11.41.
60 Undated and unsigned memorandum by Cunningham, but *c.* January–February 1942, in "RHH" to Cunningham, Cunningham Papers, 8303–104/18.
61 CAB 106/647, Latham to Kippenberger, 21.7.48.
62 Neil Orpen, *War in the Desert, South African Forces World War Two, Volume Three* (Cape Town: Purnell, 1971), p. 268.
63 CAB 106/721, Freyberg to Kippenberger, 26.9.50, *passim*.
64 GLWY 1/6, memorandum by Galloway, n.d., "Comments on your Draft which you sent to me dated 12th Jan., '68", General Galloway Papers, Churchill College, Cambridge.
65 3 DRL 6643/1/2A (vii), Blamey Papers, Blamey to Menzies, 5.3.41, AWM.
66 CAB 65/22, Churchill to Eden, 14.3.41, W.M. (41), 29th Conclusions, Minute 2, Confidential Annex, 17.3.41; CAB 65/23, Churchill to Fadden, 29.9.41, Churchill to Casey, 29.9.41, W.M. (41), 98th Conclusions, Minute 3, Confidential Annex, 29.9.41.
67 CAB 65/23, Casey to Churchill, 17.3.41, No. 2907, W.M. (41), 29th Conclusions, Minute 2, Confidential Annex, 17.3.41; Auchinleck Papers, No. 613, Auchinleck to Brooke, 4.1.42, John Ryland Library, Manchester; CAB 106/737, Wilson to Latham, 13.11.50.
68 AWM 67/3/12, Gavin Long Papers, D.W.B. Maughan, "Note on interview with Sir Claude Auchinleck at Australian Club on 23/6/56", Australian War Memorial, Canberra.
69 CAB 106/220, *op.cit.*
70 AWM 54/44/4/1, "Tactical Questions and Answers by 7th Armoured Division", n.d. but shortly before 18 November 1941 by internal evidence.
71 Memorandum by Maughan, *op.cit.*, AWM 67/3/12; for similar contemporary statements of such views, cf. Auchinleck to Alan Brooke, 12.1.42 and 6.3.42,

NOTES

and Auchinleck to Grigg, 2.3.42, Auchinleck Papers, Nos. 629, 740 and 732; for a later one, cf. LH 1/30/63, Auchinleck to Liddell Hart, 24.10.58, Liddell Hart Papers.
72 3 DRL 6643/115a, Blamey to Sturdee, 1.8.41; cf. CAB 106/776, memorandum by Fourth Indian Division, 27.3.42, "Training—Infantry Tactics".
73 Auchinleck Papers, Nos. 629, 745, Auchinleck to Brooke, 10.2.42, 6.3.42.
74 AWM 51/162, Address by Slim, 1951.
75 CAB 106/618, Memorandum "Training—Infantry Tactics", Lt. Col. D.A. Buteman, Adv 4 Ind Div, 27.3.42.
76 WO 169/922, Minutes of Staff Conference, 12.12.41.
77 CAB 106/150, "Conclusions and Suggestions", 10th South African Brigade; WO 201/518, XXX Corps to Eighth Army, 15.12.41.
78 WO 106/2235, "Statement by Maj.Gen. Herbert Lumsden"; cf. CAB 106/671.
79 WO 201/479, XXX Corps, Training Instruction No. 3, 27.10.41.
80 WO 169/2677, CSO Sudan War Diary; 1 September 1940.
81 WO 201/294, report by Cunningham on Abyssinian operations, November 1940–April 1941, n.d.; J.F. MacDonald; *The War History of Southern Rhodesia, Volume One* (Salisbury: S.R.G. Stationery Office, 1947), pp. 63, 81; Neil Orpen, *The East African and Abyssinian Campaigns* (Cape Town: Purnell, 1968), p. 66, *passim*; P.C. Bharucha, *The North African Campaign, 1940–1943, Official History of the Indian Armed Forces in the Second World War* (Calcutta: Combined Inter-Services Historical Section, 1956), p. 95, *passim*; Anthony Brett James, *Ball of Fire, The Fifth Indian Division in the Second World War* (Aldershot: Gale and Polden, 1951), pp. 36–121; G.M.O. Davy, *The Seventh and Three Enemies* (Cambridge: published for the Regiment by Heffer, 1952), p. 37; William Moore, *The Durham Light Infantry* (London: [Cooper, 1975), p. 45; Dudley Clarke, *The Eleventh at War* (London: M. Joseph, 1952), p. 137, *passim*. Bisheshwar Prasad, *The East African Campaign, 1940–41, Official History of the Indian Armed Forces in the Second World War* (Agra: Combined Inter-Services Historical Section, 1963), pp. 54–56, *passim*.
82 WO 201/352, "Operations of the Seventh Armoured Division in December 1940".
83 CORB 4/1, memorandum by Corbett, c.10.40, "Report on Visit to Egypt and the Western Desert ... September 1940", Churchill College, Cambridge
84 WO 201/353, memorandum by Fourth Indian Division on the operations of November–December 1940, n.d.; AWM 123/878, Australian Army headquarters, Intelligence Report No. 156, 19.12.41; AWM 671–31/348 Pt. 2, undated memorandum by Brigadier Savige in "Notes on Volume V", AWM 67/3/348 Pt. 1 and undated memorandum by Savige, "The Battle of Bardia".
85 WO 169/1107, Appendix "A" to HQ Western Desert Force Intelligence Summary No. 201, 18.9.41.
86 WO 169/3196, memorandum by Callan, 5.12.41; WO 201/294, *op.cit.*; RG 1651 2280-A-112 (19), "Communications System for an Armoured Division", by unnamed United States Army observer in Egypt, 11.4.41, National Archives, Washington; F.H. Hinsley et al., *British Intelligence in the Second World War, Its Influence on Strategy and Operations*, vol. 1 (London: HMSO, 1979), pp. 380–381.
87 WO 201/352, "Lessons affecting Particular Arms and Services from Operations in Eritrea"; Prasad, *The East African Campaign*, p. 79.
88 WO 201/352, "Report on Lessons of the Operations in the Western Desert, December 1940", by Major General Michael Gambier-Perry, copy No. 25; WO 216/60, memorandum by Wavell, 9.1.41; CORB 4/1, memorandum by Corbett, c.10.40, "Report on Visit to Egypt and the Western Desert ... September 1940", Appendix C, Churchill College, Cambridge.

NOTES

89 Hans-Otto Behrendt, *Rommel's Intelligence in the Desert Campaign, 1941–1943* (London: Kimber, 1985), *passim*; and also Albert Praun, *German Radio Intelligence* (paper prepared for Historical Division, Headquarters European Command, United States Army, n.d. but post-1945), pp. 51–56, 117–120, offer useful accounts of the work of Seebohm's company. Neither source is sufficiently critical regarding these issues. Behrendt (pp. 156–158), for example, entirely omits the crucial fact that the *Afrika Korps* badly misunderstood British dispositions before the battle of Gazala. English translations of important primary documentation from No. 3 Company may be found in WO 201/2150 and AWM 54/492/4/75. Some useful material on Seebohm is included in Janusz Peikalkiewicz, *Rommel and the Secret War in North Africa, 1941–1943* (West Chester: Schiffer Publications, 1992), pp. 63, 68, 73, 143–161.

90 Liddell Hart, *Rommel Papers*, p. 200; Erwin Rommel, *Attacks* (Vienna, VA: Athena Press, 1979), pp. 7, 263; Behrendt, *Rommel's Intelligence*, p. 80, recognizes that it "was [Rommel's] intuition, his instinct about his opponents' likely behaviour that was the decisive factor", but fails to address critically the question of the quality of Rommel's use of intelligence. J.A.I. Agar-Hamilton and L.C.F Turner, *Crisis in the Desert, May–July 1942, Union War Histories* (New York: Oxford University Press, 1952), p. 17; David Hunt, *A Don at War* (London: Kimber, 1966), pp. 72–73, 113; and David Irving, *The Trail of the Fox* (New York: Dutton, 1977), pp. 122–126, show clearly how poor that quality could be.

91 WO 201/53, memorandum by General Wilson, n.d. but 1941; 3 DRL 6643/1/2a (111), Blamey Papers, Signals, 6th Australian Division, "Report on Signal Operations in Greece", 26.5.41; AWM 54/423/6 (92), Appendix B, "Report on Operations of 6th Australian Division in Greece" in Thomas Blamey, "Report on Operations Anzac Corps During the Campaign in Greece", 21.7.41.

92 WO 169/1016, memorandum by CSO, Second Armoured Division, 2 November 1941; Nalder, *Royal Corps of Signals*, p. 299; CAB 106/767, memorandum by Neane, "Operations in Cyrenaica" n.d. but *c.* late spring 1941.

93 WO 201/99, memorandum by Inter-Services Committee on the Crete campaign, June 1941.

94 C.A. Borman, *Divisional Signals, Official History of New Zealand in the Second World War, 1939–45* (Wellington, NZ: War History Branch, Department of Internal Affairs, 1954), pp. 118–119; Howard Kippenberger, *Infantry Brigadier* (London: Oxford University Press, 1949), pp. 40–41.

95 AWM 54/44/4/1, "Tactical Questions and Answers for the 7th Armoured Division", n.d.; WO 216/9, Middle East to War Office, 31.5.41, O/69213; WO 201/357, WDF No. 3382/G (O), 5.8.41, "Battle of Capuzzo, 14–17 Jun [sic]", *passim*.

96 WO 201/101, Crete headquarters to GHQ, Middle East, 24 May 1941, Creteforce Signal Instruction No. 4, 12 May 1941; WO 201/53, *op.cit.*; A.F. Johnson, undated typescript, "Having Volunteered", p. 279, A.F. Johnson papers, Imperial War Museum, 80/42/1.

97 WO 169/1016, *op.cit.*

98 AWM 67/5/17, Freyberg to Editor-in-Chief, New Zealand War Histories, 16.1.51.

99 AWM 67/3/137, Freyberg to Rich, 17.10.49.

100 *Ibid.*

101 WO 201/54, memorandum C.C. (42) 26, 12 March 1942.

102 AIR 23/6180, *op.cit.*

103 Borman, *Divisional Signals*, p. 116.

104 WO 201/369, Appendix B to Signal Officer-in-Chief's memorandum, January 1942.

NOTES

105 WO 201/99, *op.cit.*; WO 201/101, Crete headquarters to GHQ Middle East, 25 April 1941, 28 May 1941.
106 WO 208/3248, CSDIC/CMF/Y 31, Second Detailed Interrogation Report on Two German Prisoners, n.d. but *c.* May–June 1945 by internal evidence; WO 193/211, War Office to Commands, "Major Vemba's Report on Tour", n.d. but *c.* mid-December 1941 by internal evidence (misdated in file); HW 14/14, M.I.1.B. X. 594, 20.8.41; HW 14/18, "Notes on Cipher Security—Middle East"; WO 201/2057, GHQ, MEF, Staff Conference, 1.6.41; HW 14/7, Denniston to Director, 1.10.40.
107 David Belcham, *All in the Day's March* (London: Collins, 1978), pp. 75–9; Bharucha, *North African Campaign*, pp. 176, 179; Borman, *Divisional Signals*, pp. 98–165; Davin, *Crete*, pp. 411–412, *passim*; Kippenberger, *Infantry Brigadier*, p. 41, *passim*; Gavin Long, *Greece, Crete and Syria, Australia in the War of 1939–1945* (Canberra: Australia War Memorial, 1986), p. 37, *passim*; G.H. Mills and R.F. Nixon, *The Annals of the King's Royal Rifle Corps, Volume VI, 1921–1943* (London: J. Murray, 1971), pp. 151–153; Peter Singleton Gates, *General Lord Freyberg, VC* (London: M. Jospeh, 1963), p. 159, *passim*; Tony Sampson, *Operation Mercury, The Battle of Crete, 1941* (Hong Kong: Hodder and Stoughton, 1981), pp. 241–242, *passim*.
108 WO 169/1016, memorandum by CSO, Fourth Indian Division, 30 October 1941.
109 WO 201/54, *op.cit.*
110 Behrendt, *Rommel's Intelligence*, pp. 99–100; WO 201/2150, "Appendix 5, Extracts from Composite Monthly Reports"; WO 208/5040, "Translation of a Captured ITALIAN Document, Italian GHQ North Africa, General Staff Intelligence", 6.7.41; Liddell Hart, *Rommel Papers*, p. 145; F.W. von Mellenthin, *Panzer Battles* (New York: Ballantine, 1955), p. 94; R.H.W.S. Hastings, *The Rifle Brigade in the Second World War, 1939–1945* (Aldershot: Gale and Polden, 1950), p. 73; CAB 106/757, Major General O'Moore Creagh, "The 7th Armoured Division", 2.11.43; WO 201/357, "Notes on Action 7 Armed Div [*sic*] 14–17 June 1941", *passim*; CAB 106/619, for the value of signals intelligence in supporting the German raid on the Halfaya Pass of 26/27 May 1941, cf. WO 201/2769, "Battle Report on the Scorpion Operations", 30.5.41, Von Herff Column, *passim*.
111 3 DRL 6643/1/2b (ii) Pt 1 "I (B) in the Field", Appendix "B" to G.S.I. M.E.F. Army Intelligence Summary No. 449, 12.8.41.
112 WO 201/99, *op.cit.*
113 WO 169/1016, *op.cit.*
114 WO 216/69, C in C Middle East to War Office, 7.1.42, SD/46547, minute by Alan Brooke, 10.1.42, *passim*; "Hist (B) 9 Final", War Office to C in C, Middle East, 18 April 1942, *Great Britain, Cabinet Office, Middle East I*; Bharucha, *North African Campaign*, p. 206; John Connell, *Auchinleck, A Critical Biography* (London: Cassell, 1959), p. 310.
115 WO 277/25.
116 WO 169/1015, CSO Advanced Eighth Army headquarters to SO in C, Middle East 22 November 1941, memorandum by CSO, Eighth Army, 3 March 1942, *passim*; WO 201/361, Appendix "D", HQ 7 Armoured Division Office instruction No. 1, 6.11.41; WO 201/479, "Lessons of the Operations in Cyrenaica—No. 3"; WO 201/518, XXX Corps to Eighth Army, 15.12.41; WO 201/369, "Some Signals Lessons of the Libyan Campaign, November 1941 to February 1942"; memorandum by Galloway, undated but *c.*1968 by internal evidence, "Comments on your Draft which you sent to me dated 12th Jan., "68", Galloway Papers, GLWY 1/6, Churchill College, Cambridge.

NOTES

117 O 201/631, "Conversation between Brigadier Whiteley–Brigadier Galloway, 1030 hrs 19 Nov 41 [*sic*]", "Telephone Conversation Lt. Col. Packard Lt-Col [*sic*] Jennings, 0950 hrs 6 Dec 41 [*sic*]"; WO 169/997, Galloway to Cunningham, 2235 hours, 19.11.41; WO 201/369, Appendix B to memorandum by SO in C, "Signal Lessons", 1.42.

118 *Ibid.*; WO 201/538, memorandum by GHQ, Middle East, 25 March 1942; J.A.I. Agar-Hamilton and L.C.F. Turner, *The Sidi Rezeg Battles 1941, Union War Histories* (London: Oxford University Press, 1957), pp. 220–221, *passim*; Belcham, *All in the Day's March*, pp. 99–102; Bharucha, *North African Campaign*, p. 225, *passim*; Borman, *Divisional Signals*, pp. 180–210; Clarke, *The Eleventh at War*, p. 207; Connell, *Auchinleck*, pp. 348–398; Robert Crisp, *Brazen Chariots, An Account of Tank Warfare in the Western Desert, November–December 1941* (London: Muller, 1959), p. 32; Davy, *The Seventh and Three Enemies*, p. 134, *passim*; David Erskine (ed.), *The Scots Guards, 1919–1955* (London: W. Clowes, 1956), p. 87; Geoffrey Evans, *The Desert and the Jungle* (London: William Kimber, 1959), pp. 91–93; Kippenberger, *Infantry Brigadier*, pp. 132–135; Ronald Lewin, *Rommel as Military Commander* (London: Batsford, 1968), p. 65, *passim*; Barton Maughan, *Tobruk and El Alamein, Australia in the War of 1939–1945* (Canberra: Australian War Memorial, 1966), pp. 456–461, *passim*; G.L. Vernay, *The Desert Rats, The Story of the Seventh Armoured Division, 1938 to 1945* (London: Greenhill, 1954), p. 76; A.D. Woozley (ed.), *History of the King's Dragoon Guards, 1938–1945* (Glasgow: Caxton Works, 1946), pp. 130, 142; CAB 106/582, 7th Armoured Division, An Account of the Operations in Libya; WO 201/518, memorandum by XXX Corps to Eighth Army, 15.12.41; WO 201/479, "Lessons from Operations—Cyrenaica No. 8", 27.12.41, "Lessons from Operations—Cyrenaica No. 12", 26.1.42; WO 201/522, XIII Corps, "Notes on Lessons from Recent Operations"; WO 201/631, "Conversation Between Brigadier Whiteley–Brigadier Galloway 1030hour 19 Nov 41 [*sic*]"; PREM 3/291/5, Fuller to Minister of State, 22.11.41.

119 Irving, *Trail of the Fox*, p. 129.

120 Connell, *Auchinleck*, p. 385; WO 201/374, Auchinleck to Churchill, 30.11.41; CAB 106/715, *op.cit.*

121 WO 201/357, WDF No. 3382/G (O), 5.8.41, "Battle of Capuzzo, 14–17 Jun [*sic*]", *passim*.

122 WO 169/1016, memorandum by H.N. Crawford, *passim*; WO 201/538, memorandum, "Notes on the Employment of L.O.s", 12 August 1942; cf. Reports and minutes of investigation into these operations in WO 106/2234 and WO 106/2235; Agar-Hamilton and Turner, *Crisis in the Desert*, p. 66, *passim*; Brett James, *Ball of Fire*, pp. 195–199, 220; Neil Orpen, *War in the Desert*, pp. 229, 250; I.S.O. Playfair *et al.*, *The Mediterranean and Middle East, Volume III (September 1941 to September 1942), British Fortunes reach their Lowest Ebb, History of the Second World War, United Kingdom Military Series* (London, 1960), pp. 270–273; Vernay, *Desert Rats*, pp. 106–7.

123 Mills and Nixon, *Annals*, p. 182.

124 3 DRL 6643/1/10A (7), "Conference of Commanders", 26.9.41, Blamey Papers, AWM.

125 HW 14/18, M.I.1.B. X. 594, 20.8.41, "Notes on Cipher Security—Middle East".

126 WO 169/1107, Appendix "A" to HQ Western Desert Force Intelligence Summary No. 201, 18.9.41.

127 WO 169/1092, memorandum by Venham, 10 December 1941; AIR 23/722 contains the standing orders for cipher and signals security for the RAF in the

Middle East during 1941–42; AWM 123/877, Australian Army Headquarters Summary No. 145, 3.10.41.
128 WO 208/5040, "Analysis of Captured Documents Showing Results and Efficiency of German Wireless Intelligence (May–Nov [sic] 1941", GSI/21/IS/28, n.d. but c. January–April 1942 by internal evidence.
129 3 DRL 6643/9211, "Captured Report of the Reconnaissance in Force Carried Out By 21 Armoured Divisions on 14 September 1941", Blamey Papers, AWM; WO 208/5040, "Analysis of Captured Documents Showing Results and Efficiency of German Wireless Intelligence (May–Nov [sic] 1941", GSI/21/IS/28, n.d. but c. January–April 1942 by internal evidence.
130 WO 169/1016, memorandum by CSO, First Armoured Division, 13 July 1942; WO 204/3896, Allied Forces Headquarters to formations, 2 February 1943.
131 Von Mellenthin, *Panzer Battles*, p. 94; Behrendt, *Rommel's Intelligence*, p. 180, *passim*; AWM 54/519/7/26, memo by J.D. Rogers and S.H. Porter, "Lessons of the Second Libyan Campaign", 26.12.41.
132 Irving, *Trail of the Fox*, p. 152.
133 Von Mellenthin, *Panzer Battles*, p. 94.
134 WO 201/73, GHQ Middle East to Palestine Command, 5 June 1941; WO 169/1016, memorandum by CSO, Eighth Army, *passim*; AIR 23/6008, memorandum by Leonard Williams, 25 November 1942; HW 14/14, "Major Vemba's Report on Tour", n.d. but c. mid-December 1941 by internal evidence (misdated in file).
135 *Ibid.*
136 WO 169/1016, memorandum by CSO, 10th Indian Division, 9 July 1942, *passim*; WO 201/538, memorandum by GHQ Middle East, 5 December 1941.
137 WO 201/519, memorandum by XXX Corps, 29.12.41.
138 WO 169/1015, Advanced Eighth Army Headquarters Signals War Diary, entry 2 December 1941; WO 169/1016, memorandum by CSO, Seventh Armoured Division; AWM 54/519/7/26, memo by Rogers and Porter, *op.cit.*; WO 106/2235, "Written Statement by Major General F.W. Messervey", *passim*; WO 201/538, "Lessons from Operations—Cyrenaica No. 1", 5.12.41; CAB 106/671, memo by C.M. Valienten, "The First Support Group, November 1940–February 1942", 18.3.49; WO 201/518, XXX Corps to Eighth Army, 15.12.41.
139 WO 106/2234, "Report of a Court of Enquiry Assembled by Order of the C-in-C", n.d.; WO 106/2235, "Statement by Maj Gen H. Lumsden", n.d.
140 Behrendt, *Rommel's Intelligence*, pp. 105, 109, 115; WO 201/518, XXX Corps to Eighth Army, 15.12.41.
141 Borman, *Divisional Signals*, p. 202.
142 Hastings, *Rifle Brigade*, p. 4.
143 AWM 54/492/4/75, "Appx A to Pz Gp Afrika HQ Intelligence Diary, 18 Nov @ 31 Dec 41 [sic]"; WO 201/2150, memorandum by Toyes, "German Wireless Intercept Organisation", 30.7.42.
144 AWM 54/44/4/1, "Tactical Questions and Answers", *op.cit.*
145 WO 201/2150, Appendix 7 to memorandum by Toyes, 30.7.42.
146 Behrendt, *Rommel's Intelligence*, p. 80.
147 *Ibid.*, pp. 100–120; CAB 106/671.
148 Irving, *Trail of the Fox*, p. 154; Playfair et al., *Mediterranean and Middle East, Volume III*, pp. 139–140; Hunt, *A Don at War*, p. 95; Lewin, *Rommel*, p. 105; von Mellenthin, *Panzer Battles*, p. 97; Liddell Hart, *Rommel Papers*, pp. 156, 169, 240; Behrendt, *Rommel's Intelligence*, pp. 105–127, *passim*.
149 WO 201/2150, memorandum by Toyes, 30.7.42.

150 Behrendt, *Rommel's Intelligence*, pp. 168–169; Praun, *German Radio Intelligence, op.cit.*; Ronald Lewin, *The Life and Death of the Afrika Korps, A Biography* (New York: Quadrangle, 1977), pp. 35–36; Irving, *Trail of the Fox*, p. 195.

6 Intelligence, uncertainty and the art of command in military operations

We are grateful to Sebastian Cox, Edward Drea, Christina Goulter, Andrew Lambert and Milan Vego for comments on earlier drafts of this paper.

1 Carl von Clausewitz (ed. Michael Howard and Peter Paret), *On War* (Princeton: Princeton University Press, 1976), p. 233.
2 *Ibid.* p. 117. For a discussion of many issues related to this topic, see Michael Handel, "Intelligence and Military Operations", in Michael I. Handel, *Intelligence and Military Operations* (London: Frank Cass, 1990) and *Masters of War, Sun Tzu, Clausewitz and Jomini* (London: Frank Cass, 1992).
3 W. Kendrick Pritchett, *The Greek State at War, Part III: Religion* (Berkeley: University of California Press, 1982), p. 149.
4 Clausewitz, *On War*, pp. 198–201, 210; and Handel, *Intelligence and Military Operations*, pp. 8–11, 13–21 and *Masters of War*, pp. 107–132.
5 For Jomini, see Handel, *Masters of War*, pp. 107–132. For recent accounts of Wellington and operational intelligence, cf. Jac Weller, "Wellington's Asset: A Remarkably Successful System of Intelligence", *Military Review*, 42 (June 1962); Julia V. Page, *Intelligence Officer in the Peninsula: Letters and Diaries of Major the Hon. Edward Charles Cocks, 1786–1812* (Tunsbridge Wells: Spellmount, 1986), introduction by David Chandler. All modern accounts of Wellington's military organization also refer to his intelligence system: cf. Michael Glover, *Wellington's Army in the Peninsula, 1808–1814* (Vancouver: David and Charles, 1977); H.C.B. Rogers, *Wellington's Army* (London: Ian Allan, 1979); and Lawrence James, *The Iron Duke, A Military Biography of Wellington* (London: Weidenfeld and Nicolson, 1992). Stephen Mark Harris's MA dissertation at the Department of History, the University of Calgary, 1993, "British Military Intelligence in the Crimean War, 1854–1856", demonstrates that at their best, operational intelligence systems in the mid-nineteenth century could provide material which rivals the quality and accuracy of their successors of the twentieth century.
6 Handel, *Masters of War*, pp. 102–107.
7 Clausewitz, *On War*, p. 100.
8 *Ibid.*, p. 110.
9 *Ibid.*, p. 103.
10 *Ibid.*, p. 101.
11 *Ibid.*, p. 108.
12 *Ibid.*, pp. 105–106.
13 *Ibid.*, p. 117.
14 *Ibid.*, pp. 102–103.
15 *Ibid.*
16 *Ibid.*, p. 102.
17 *Ibid.*, pp. 146–147.
18 *Ibid.*, p. 71.
19 *Ibid.*, p.112.
20 *Ibid.*, p. 108.
21 *Ibid.*, pp. 190, 192.

NOTES

22 *Ibid.*, p. 200.
23 For arguments on these lines, cf. "Intelligence and the Problem of Strategic Surprise", in Michael Handel, *War, Strategy and Intelligence* (London: Frank Cass: 1989), pp. 229–281 and the same author's *Perception, Deception and Surprise: The Case of The Yom Kippur War* (Jerusalem: Hebrew University of Jerusalem, 1976); Richard K. Betts, "Analysis, War and Decision: Why Intelligence Failures are Inevitable", *World Politics*, 31 (October 1978), pp. 61–89 and the same author's *Surprise Attack: Lessons for Defence Planning* (Washington, DC: The Brookings Institution, 1982).
24 Clausewitz, *On War*, p. 110, 190–191; Azar Gat, *The Origins of Military Thought, From the Enlightenment to Von Clausewitz* (Oxford: Oxford University Press, 1989), pp. 202, 205.
25 Clausewitz, *On War*, p. 192.
26 *Ibid.*, pp. 202–203.
27 *Ibid.*, p, 85.
28 *Ibid.*, p. 180. See also Handel, *Masters of War*, pp. 151–154.
29 *Ibid.*, pp. 103, 190.
30 *Ibid.*, p. 86.
31 Michael Howard, "The Influence of Clausewitz", in Clausewitz, *On War*, pp. 29–39. For contemporary views about determination, character and daring similar to those of Clausewitz, cf. Marshall Marmont, *The Spirit of Military Institutions* (trans. Frank Schaller) (Philadelphia: J.B. Lippincott and Co., 1974 [1862]), pp. 222–237. Clausewitz's great nineteenth-century competitor as a theorist of strategy, the Baron de Jomini, placed far less emphasis on the topic but his few references to the issue coincide with the views of Clausewitz (The Baron de Jomini, *The Art of War* (trans. G.H. Mendell and W.P. Craighill) (Philadelphia: J.B. Lippincott and Co., 1962), p. 50). The Clausewitzian and Napoleonic tradition about the psychology of command also pervades the views of one of the most representative commentators on strategy before the First World War, Commandant J. Colin, *The Transformations of War* (trans. L.H.R. Pope-Hennessey) (London: Hugh Rees, 1912), pp. 183, 351–353.
32 John Keegan, "Peace By Other Means: War, Popular Opinion and Politically Incorrect Clausewitz", *Times Literary Supplement* (11 December 1992), pp. 3–4.
33 Martin Blumenson, *The Patton Papers, 1885–1940* (Boston: Houghton Mifflin, 1972), pp. 753, 794–797 and *The Patton Papers, 1940–1945* (Boston: Houghton Mifflin, 1974), p. 263; Alfred D. Chandler, Stephen E. Ambrose, Joseph P. Hobbs, Edwin Alan Thompson and Elizabeth F. Smith (eds), *The Papers of Dwight David Eisenhower, The War Years: III* (Baltimore: Johns Hopkins University Press, 1970), pp. 1439, 1754. See also Christopher Brassford, *Clausewitz in English: The Reception of Clausewitz in Britain and America, 1815–1945* (New York: Oxford University Press, 1994), especially pp. 152–187.
34 John Keegan, *A History of Warfare* (New York: Alfred A. Knopf, 1993), simultaneously views Clausewitz as having had no influence while somehow still producing every evil in modern war. Unfortunately, he fails to understand the text he attacks. He describes a Clausewitz who never lived and ignores the one who did. Keegan's understanding of Clausewitz is reminiscent of the Ayatollah Khomeini's views of the United States.
35 Brian Bond, *Liddell Hart, A Study of His Military Thought* (London: Cassell, 1977), pp. 20, 45; John Mearsheimer, *Liddell Hart and the Weight of History* (Ithaca, NY: Cornell University Press, 1988), pp. 48–50; Blumenson, *The Patton Papers, 1885–1940*, pp. 794–797.

NOTES

36 For a discussion of this issue, cf. John Ferris, "The Intelligence–Deception Complex: An Anatomy", *Intelligence and National Security*, 4(4) (1989).
37 Edward Drea, *MacArthur's Ultra, Codebreaking and the War Against Japan, 1942–1945* (Kansas: University Press of Kansas, 1992).
38 Gordon W. Prange, with Donald M. Goldstein and Katherine V. Dillon, *At Dawn We Slept* (New York: McGraw-Hill, 1981), *Miracle at Midway* (New York: McGraw-Hill, 1982) and *Pearl Harbor, The Verdict of History* (New York: McGraw-Hill, 1986).
39 Ronald Lewin, *The American Magic: Codes, Ciphers and the Defeat of Japan* (New York: Farrar Straus Giroux, 1982); Henry C. Clausen with Bruce Lee, *Pearl Harbor, Final Judgement* (New York: Crown, 1992); John Costello, *The Pacific War* (New York: Rawson and Wade, 1981); Edwin T. Layton, with Roger Pineau and John Costello, *"And I Was There": Pearl Harbor and Midway—Breaking the Secrets* (New York: William Morrow, 1985); Ladislas Farago, *The Broken Seal: "Operation Magic" and the Secret Road to Pearl Harbor* (New York: Random House, 1967); James Rusbridger and Eric Nave, *Betrayal at Pearl Harbor: How Churchill Lured Roosevelt into War* (New York: Summit, 1991).
40 Ralph Bennett, *Ultra in the West* (London: Hutchinson, 1979) and *Ultra and Mediterranean Strategy* (New York: William Morrow, 1989).
41 Drea, *MacArthur's Ultra*, pp. 28–29.
42 Cf. note 39 and John Ferris, "Ralph Bennett and the Study of Ultra: A Review Article", *Intelligence and National Security*, 6(2) (1991).
43 Drea, *MacArthur's Ultra*, pp. 74–75.
44 For a general discussion of Allied points, cf. John Ferris, "The British Army, Signals and Security in the Desert Campaign, 1940–42", in Michael Handel (ed.), *Intelligence and Military Operations* (London: Frank Cass, 1990), pp. 255–291.
45 Drea, *MacArthur's Ultra*, pp. 62, 92.
46 John Ferris (ed.), *The British Army and Signals Intelligence During the First World War* (London: Army Records Society, 1992), chapter 8, *passim*; Anthony H. Cordesman and Abraham R. Wagner, *The Lessons of Modern War, Volume II: The Iran–Iraq War* (Boulder: Westview, 1990), pp. 412–423, *passim*.
47 Public Record Office, London, WO 208/1214, memorandum by Piggott, No. 32, 30.11.37. This citation appears by permission of the Controller of Her Majesty's Stationery Office.
48 Ralph Bennett, "Intelligence and Strategy in World War II", in K.G. Robertson (ed.), *British and American Approaches to Intelligence* (London: Macmillan, 1987), p. 147. For a general discussion of these issues, see Michael Handel "The Politics of Intelligence", in Handel, *War, Strategy and Intelligence*; Thomas L. Hughes, *The Fate of Facts in the World of Men* (New York: Foreign Policy Association, December 1976); and Yehoshast Harkabi, "The Intelligence Policy Maker Tangle", *Jerusalem Quarterly*, 30 (Winter 1984), pp. 125–131.
49 Drea, *MacArthur's Ultra*, p. 187.
50 John Dower, *War Without Mercy, Race and Power in the Pacific War* (New York: Pantheon, 1986). For a discussion of the attitudes of the British and American armies on such matters before the outbreak of the Pacific War, cf. John Ferris, "Racism, Ethnocentracism and Strategy: British and American Perceptions of the Imperial Japanese Army, 1919–41", a paper presented to the First International Conference on Strategy, the United States Army War College, Carlisle Barracks, February 1990, and "Worthy of Some Better Enemy? The British Estimate of the Imperial Japanese Army, 1919–41, and the Fall of Singapore", *The Canadian Journal of History*, 27(2) (August 1993).
51 Clausewitz, *On War*, pp. 528, 571–572; cf. Section 6, chapters 5 and 22.

52 Thomas M. Huber, "Japan's Battle of Okinawa, April–June 1945" (Leavenworth Papers, Number 18) (Combat Studies Institute, United States Army Command and General Staff College, 1990), p. 11.
53 Drea, *MacArthur's Ultra*, pp. 202–225.
54 Lewin, *American Magic*, pp. 159–169.
55 F.H. Hinsley, "British Intelligence in the Second World War", in Christopher Andrew and Jeremy Noakes (eds), *Intelligence and International Relations* (Exeter: Exeter University Press, 1987), pp. 217–218, and *The Intelligence Revolution: A Historical Perspective* (Colorado Springs: United States Air Force Academy, The Harmon Memorial Lecture in Military History, No. 31, 1988), pp. 9–10.
56 Drea, *MacArthur's Ultra*, p. 231.
57 Clausewitz, *On War*, pp. 194–195, 204.
58 The best account of the Canadian Corps style of operations, and in particular the means by which it understood and exploited the characteristics of the German defensive system and its reliance on counter-attacks in 1917–1918 is Ian Brown, "Currie and the Canadian Corps 1917–1918" (MA dissertation, University of Calgary, 1991), pp. 34–37, 74–82, *passim*. For other discussions relevant to the topic, cf. G.W.L. Nicholson, *Canadian Expeditionary Force, 1914—1919* (Ottawa: Queen's Printer, 1961), pp. 284–286; Tim Travers, *How the War Was Won, Command and Technology in the British Army on the Western Front, 1917–1918* (London: Routledge, 1992), pp. 110–174; C.E.W. Bean, *The Official History of Australia in the War of 1914–1918, Volume V, The Australian Imperial Force in France During the Allied Offensive, 1918* (Sydney: Angus and Robinson, 1942), pp. 242–626.
59 Larry I. Bland and Sharon Ritenour Stevens (eds), *The Papers of George Catlett Marshall, Volume 3, "The Right Man for the Job"*, 7 December 1941–31 May 1943, pp. 101–102.
60 WO 208/3575, memorandum by E.T. Williams, "The Use of Ultra by the Army", n.d. but *c.*1945.
61 Handel, *Masters of War*, pp. 148–149.
62 For evidence supporting the view that the beginning of the modern age of intelligence was 1914 rather than 1939, see Patrick Beesley, *Room 40, British Naval Intelligence, 1914–1918* (London: Harcourt Brace Jovanovich, 1982); Ferris, *The British Army, op.cit.*; John Ferris, "The British Army and Signals intelligence in the Field During the First World War", *Intelligence and National Security*, 3(4) (October 1988); David Kahn, *The Codebreakers: The Story of Secret Writing* (New York, Macmillan, 1967).
63 Michael Handel, "Clausewitz in the Age of Technology", in Michael Handel (ed.), *Clausewitz and Modern Strategy* (London: Frank Cass, 1986), pp. 73–75.
64 Roberta Wohlstetter, *Pearl Harbor: Warning and Decision* (Stanford: Stanford University Press, 1962), pp. 336–338.
65 Clausewitz, *On War*, p. 86.
66 Gat, *Military Thought*, pp. 181–84.

7 NCW, C4ISR, IO and RMA: toward a revolution in military intelligence?

1 "Joint Vision 2010" and "Joint Vision 2020" (www.dtic.mil/doctrine); for a bibliography, cf. John Ferris, "The Biggest Force Multiplier? Knowledge, Information and Warfare in the 21st Century", in Alistair Dally and Rosalind

NOTES

Bourke (eds), *Conflict, The State and Aerospace Power* (Canberra: Aerospace Centre, 2003), pp. 149–165.

2 Marine Corps Combat Development Command, Draft "Information Operations", 25.9.01, USMC, Doctrine Division Home Page; FM 100–6, 27.8.96, "Information Operations" (www.adtdl.army.milcgi-bin/adtl.dll); FM 3–0, *Operations*, 14.6.01, 5.75, 6.38, 11–47.

3 Admiral Cebrowski, "The Small, the Fast, and the Many", *NetDefense*, 15.1.04, p. 10; David Alperts, "The Future of Command and Control with DBK", in Stuart E. Johnson (ed.), *Dominant Battlespace Knowledge* (Washington, DC: NDU Press, October 1995). For a different reading of the relationship between intelligence and strategy, cf. J.R. Ferris and Michael Handel, "Clausewitz, Intelligence, Uncertainty and the Art of Command in Modern War", *Intelligence and National Security*, 10(1) (January 1995), pp. 1–58.

4 General Ronald Fogleman, speeches, 25.4.1995, "Information Operations: The Fifth Dimension of Warfare", *Defense Issues*, 10(47) (www.defenselink.mil/speeches/1995) and "Fundamentals of Information Warfare—An Airman's View", 16.5.1995 (www.af.mil/news/speech/current).

5 George Stein, "Information Warfare", *Airpower Journal* (Spring 1995); Colonel John A. Warden III, "Air Theory for the Twenty-first Century", *Aerospace Power Chronicles, "Battlefield of the Future: 21st Century Warfare Issues"* (1995).

6 Joint Chiefs of Staff, Joint Pub. 3–13.1, *Joint Doctrine for Command and Control Warfare (C2W)*, 7.2.96.

7 Department of Defense, *Transformation Planning Guidance*, April 2003, APP 4, "Joint Concept Guidance (www.oft.osd.mil); U.S. Joint Forces Command, *A Concept for Rapid Decisive Operations, RDO Whitepaper*, J9 Joint Futures Lab, 2.3, 4.1, 4.3.1.3.

8 USJFCOM, Millenium Challenge 02 (www.jfcom.mil/about/experiments/mc02); 9.8.02, "Air Force portion of experiment ends with positive result" (www.jfcom.mil/newslink/story/archive/2002/no080902); "Unified Quest 03" (www.jfcom.mil/about/experiments/uq03).

9 Admiral Cebrowski, "The Small, the Fast, and the Many", p. 10.

10 Warden, "Air Theory for the Twenty-first Century".

11 Williamson Murray, "Transformation: Volume II", in Williamson Murray (ed.), *Transformation Concepts for National Security in the 21st Century* (Strategic Studies Institute, US Army War College, September 2002), pp. 10–17; an untitled briefing paper by Michael Handel, copy in my possession, c.2000. These papers offer fundamental critiques of assumptions about intelligence in the RMA; cf, Ferris, "The Biggest Force Multiplier?"

12 cf. notes 2, 6 and 34.

13 Defense Writer's Group, 22.1.03, interview with General Richard Myers (www.oft.osd.military/library.cfm?libcol=).

14 "Speech to the Heritage Foundation", 13.5.03, by Arthur Cebrowski, *Transformation Trends*, 27.5.03 (www.oft.osd.mil).

15 Arthur Cebrowski, 17.6.03, "The Path Not Taken…yet" (www.oft.osd.mil).

16 Rudi Williams, " 'Horizontal Fusion' Makes Troops Less Vulnerable, More Lethal", *American Forces Information Service*, 26.9.03.

17 Briefing Paper by Joe Mazzafro, "Operation Enduring Freedom, Intelligence Lessons Learned, An Unofficial Quick Look", JWAD Mini-Symposium, 7.5.02 (www.maxwell.af.mil/au/awc/awcgate/awc-lesn); Jim Garamone, "Myers says Joint Capabilities, Transformation Key to 21st Century War", American Forces Information Service, 5.2.02 (www.defenselink.mil/news/Feb2002/n020520002_200202054); Dawn. S. Onley and Susan M. Menke, "DOD seeks to exploit intelligence", *Government Computer News*, 23.6.03.

NOTES

18 "Preface", "2025 In-Time Information Integrations System (I3S)", "The Man in the Chair: Cornerstone of Global Battlespace Dominance", "Wisdom Warfare for 2025", *Air Force 2025* (1996) (www.au.af.mil/au); Thomas K. Adams, "Future Warfare and the Decline of Human Decisionmaking", *Parameters* (Winter 2001–2002).
19 "Vector 21, Defense Intelligence Agency Strategic Plan, 1999–2000" (www.loyola.edu/dept/politics/milintel); NCS-21 (National Cryptological Strategy for the 21st Century) (www.nsa.goc/programs/ncs21/index); Director of Central Intelligence (DCI), "The 2002 Annual Report of the United States Intelligence Community, 1.03" (www.cia.gov/cia/publications/Ann_Rpt_2002/index); "Statement for the Record by Lieutenant General Michael V. Hayden, USAF, Director, National Security Agency/Chief, Central Security Service, Before the Joint Inquiry of the Senate Select Conmmittee on Intelligence and the House Permanent Select Committee on Intelligence, 17 October 2002" (www.nsa.gov/releases/speeches).
20 Dan Caterinicchia, "NIMA, NSA increasing colloboration", *Federal Computer Weekly*, 30.1.03.
21 Dawn S. Onley, "Success in Iraq due to better info sharing, Tenet says", *Government Computer News*, 11.6.03.
22 "Vector 21", *op.cit.*; Frederick Thomas Martin, *Top Secret Intranet: How U.S. Intelligence Built Intelink, The World's Largest, Most Secure Network* (New York: Prentice Hall, 1998); speech by A. Denis Clift, President, Joint Military Intelligence College, at Yale University, 27.4.02, "From Semaphore to Predator, Intelligence in the Internet Era" (www.DIA.MIL/Public/Testimonies/statement06); "Joint Intelligence Virtual Architecture JIVA" (www.fas.org/irp/program/core/jiva).
23 Dawn S. Onley, "Intelligence analysts strive to share data", *Government Computer News*, 5.28.03.
24 ADCI/AP 2000–01, "Strategic Investment Plan for Intelligence Community Analysis" (www.cia.gov/cia/publications/pub).
25 Lt. Gen. Robert W. Noonan, Jr. and Lt. Col. Brad T. Andrew, retired, "Army Intelligence Provides the Knowledge Edge", *Army Magazine* (April 2002).
26 Bruce Berkowitz, "The DI and 'IT', Failing to Keep Up With the Information Revolution", *Studies in Intelligence*, 47(1), 5.03 (www.cia.gov/csi/studies/vol47/no1/article07).
27 Wilson P. Dizzard III, "White Houses promotes data sharing" and Dawn S. Onley, "Intelligence analysts strive to share data", *Government Computer News*, 28.6.02 and 5.28.03.
28 External Team Report, A Management Review for the Director, NSA, 11.10.99; New Enterprise Team (NETeam) Recommendations, The Director's Work Plan for Change, 1.10.99 (www.nsa.gov/releases/reports.html).
29 Richard Lardner, "Leadership streamlined, chief of staff created, NSA Chief Pushes Ahead with Overhaul of Agency's Culture, Operations", *Inside Defence Special Report*, 16.10.00.
30 Frank Tiboni, "Quantum Leap tests network warfare", *Federal Computer Weekly*, 27.8.03.
31 Charles L. Munns, "Another View: Navy's network services buy pays off", *Government Computer News*, 3.7.03; David A. Fulghum and Douglas Barrie, "Cracks in the Net, Foes of the West Look for chinks in its technological armor", *Aviation News & Space Technology*, 30.6.03; "Statement by John Gilligan, Chief Information Officer, United States Air Force, Before the SubCommittee on Terrorism, Unconventional Threats and Capabilities House Armed Service Committee", 3.4.03 (www.house.gov/hasc/openingstatementsandpressreleases/10thcongress/02–04–03gil).

NOTES

32 DCI, "2002 Annual Report", *op.cit.*; William Jackson, "Cyberdrill carries over to real war", *Government Computer News*, 19.5.03.
33 "Background Briefing on Enemy Denial and Deception", 24.10.01 (www.defenselink.mil/news/Oct2001/t10242001_t1024dd.ht).
34 Joint Chiefs of Staff, Joint Pub. 3–58, *Joint Doctrine for Military Deception*, 31.5.96 (under revision as of time of writing, June 2003); Joint Pub. 3–54, *Joint Doctrine for Operations Security*, 24.2.97; Joint Pub. 3–13, *Joint Doctrine for Information Operations*, JCS, 9.10.98; Joint Pub. 2–01.3, *Joint Tactics, Techniques, and Procedures for Joint Intelligence Preparation of the Battlespace*, 24.5.00.
35 John Ferris, "The Roots of FORTITUDE: The Evolution of British Deception in the Second World War", in T.G. Mahnken (ed.), *The Paradox of Intelligence: Essays in Honour of Michael Handel* (London: Frank Cass, 2003).
36 Center for Army Lessons Learned (CALL), 2 October 2000, Information Operations Franchise, Research Project Proposal #s 4, 5.9, 10 and 12 (www.call.army.mil/io/research).
37 CALL, "The Information Operations Process"; "Tactics, Techniques and Procedures for Information Operations (IO). Information Operations, Observations, TTP, and Lessons Learned" (www.call.army.mil/io/ll).
38 Research Topics proposed by INNS, 25.7.00, "Information Operations (IO) 5.16", Computer Network Warfare, "Information Operations (IO) 5.23, and 5.29"; and Air Force Material Command, 8.28.01, "Effects Based Information Operations" (www.research.maxwell.af.mil/js_Database); Colonel Carla D. Bass, "Building Castles on Sand, Underestimating the Tide of Information Operations, *Aerospace Power Journal* (Summer 1999).
39 "CCRP Initiatives", Office of the Assistant Secretary of Defense Command, Control, Communications and Intelligence, 9.26.2001 (www.dodccrp.org).
40 Dan Caternicchia, "DOD Forms Cyberattack Task Force", *Federal Compuer Weekly*, 10.2.03.
41 Research Topics proposed by INNS 25.7.00, IO 5.48, and IO 5.24, *op.cit.*
42 J.R. Ferris and Michael Handel, "Clausewitz, Intelligence, Uncertainty and the Art of Command in Modern War", *Intelligence and National Security*, 10(1) (January 1995), pp. 1–58.
43 Kenneth Watman, "Global 2000", *Naval War College Review* (Spring 2000). For a more optimistic reading of this exercise, and others, cf. *Network Centric Warfare, Department of Defence Report to Congress*, 27.7.01, pp. E-24 (www.c3i.osd.mil/NCW).
44 Air Commodore Stuart Peach, "The Airmen's Dilemma: To Command or Control", in Peter Gray (ed.), *Air Power 21, Challenges for the New Century* (London: Ministry of Defence, 2001), pp. 123–124, 141. An American Army observer, Timothy L. Thomas, offered similar views: "Kosovo and the Current Myth of Information Superiority", *Parameters* (Spring 2000).
45 Major William A. Woodcock, "The Joint Forces Air Conmmand Problem, Is Network-centric Warfare the Answer?", *Naval War College Review* (Winter 2003), p. 46; the words are Woodcock's, but his source is Michael Short, the Joint Air Force commander in Kosovo.
46 Anthony H. Cordesman, *The Lessons of Afghanistan, Warfighting, Intelligence, Force Transformation, Counterproliferation, and Arms Control* (Washington, DC: Center for Strategic and International Studies, 12 August 2002), pp. 63–64.
47 Verbatim Testimony of Colonel David. C. Nichols and Colonel Laurence A. Stutzreim, Tarnack Farms Enquiry, 1.03: (www.barksdale.af.mil/tarnackfarms/rosenow).
48 *Ibid.*

NOTES

49 "Marine Corps Colonel and First Sergeant, Task Force Tarawa, April 2003" (www.urbanoperations.com/ifaar2.ht).
50 Joseph L. Galloway, "General Tommy Franks discusses conducting the war in Iraq", 19.6.03, Knight Ridder Washington Bureau: (www.realcities.com/mld/krwashington/6124738.h).
51 "What Went Right?", *Janes' Defence Weekly*, 30.4.03; "Operation Iraqi Freedom, 1st Marine Division, Lessons Learned, 28 May 2003", accessible from the website of the Urban Operations Journal, section "Operation Iraq Freedom, AARs, Observations, Analyses and Comments"; for comments by rear area personnel, see Dan Caterinicchia, "Command keeps troops connected", *Federal Computer Weekly*, 1.4.03; Dawn S. Olney, "Network-centric operations score big in Iraq, DOD's Frankel says", *Government Computer News*, 26.5.03.
52 Stephen Biddle, "Afghanistan and the Future of Warfare: Implications for Army and Defence Policy" (Strategic Studies Institute, US Army War College, November 2002); cf. Antony Cordesman, *The Lessons of Afghanistan*, pp. 39–71.
53 Galloway, "General Tommy Franks", *op.cit.*
54 Anthony H. Cordesman, *Intelligence and Iraqi Weapons of Mass Destruction: The Lessons from the Iraq War* (Washington, DC: Center for Strategic and International Studies, 1 July 2003).
55 *Ibid.*
56 Galloway, "General Tommy Franks", *op.cit.*
57 Lisa Burgess, "Iraq War: Swift, Lethal Battle Shot Down Many Cold War Theories", *European and Pacific Stars & Stripes*, "Freedom in Iraq" special section, 27.5.03.
58 Online Newshour, Lessons of War, 1 May 2003: (www.pbs.org/newsho..ddle_east/jan-june03/lessons_05–01/ht).
59 Transcript, "BBC Interview, Deputy Assistant Secretary Whitman on Media Operations During Operation Iraq Freedom": (www.urbanoperations.com/whitman.ht).
60 "Operation Iraqi Freedom, 1st Marine Division, Lessons Learned, 28 May 2003", *op.cit.*
61 "Third Infantry Division (Mechanized) After Action Report, Operation Iraqi Freedom", pp. 41–44 (globalsecurity.org).
62 Ross W. Simpson, "Operation Iraqi Freedom, Going to War", *Leatherneck* (July 2003).
63 *Operations in Iraq, 2003: First Reflections* (London: Ministry of Defence, July, 2003), p. 15 (www.mod.uk).
64 Kamal Ahmed, "Blair 'expected war to last four months' ", *The Observer*, 6.7.03; "Fifth Corps Commander, Live Briefing from Baghdad, 7 May 2003" (www.urbanoperations.com/ifaar4.ht).
65 "Operation Iraqi Freedom, 1st Marine Division, Lessons Learned, 28 May 2003", *op.cit.*
66 Galloway, "General Tommy Franks", *op.cit.*
67 *Ibid.*
68 *Ibid.*
69 Cf. notes 35 and 36.
70 "Summary of Lessons Learned, Prepared Testimony by Secdef Donald H. Rumsfeld, General Tommy R. Franks, Senate Armed Services Committee, July 9, 2003" (www.oft.osd.mil); Anthony Cordesman, *The "Instant Lessons" of the Iraq War, Main Report, Seventh Working Draft* (Washington, DC: Center for Strategic and International Studies, 28 April 2003), p. 186.
71 Colonel Richard Szafranski, "Information Warfare", *Airpower Journal* (Spring 1995).

NOTES

72 Cebrowski, "Speech to the Heritage Foundation", *op.cit.*
73 David A Fulghum, "The Pentagon's force-transformation director takes an early swipe at what worked and what didn't in Iraq", *Aviation Week and Space Technology*, 28.4.03, p. 34.
74 Scott Peterson and Peter Ford, "From Iraqi officers, three tales of shock and defeat", *Christian Science Monitor*, 18.4.03; Douglas Jehl with Dexter Filkins, "After the War: Covert Operations; U.S. Moved to Undermine Iraqi Military Before War", *New York Times*, 10.8.03.
75 Frank Tiboni, "NSA to speed intelligence delivery", *Federal Computer Weekly*, 2.9.03.
76 "Operation Iraqi Freedom, 1st Marine Division, Lessons Learned, 28 May 2003", *op.cit.*
77 Except where otherwise noted, the source for the following two paragraphs is "Third Infantry Division (Mechanized) After Action Report, Operation Iraqi Freedom", pp. 2–5, 51–55, 71–74, 96, 101–03, 183–196 (globalsecurity.org).
78 For a description, see LTC John Charlton, "Digital Battle Command: Baptism by Fire", CALL, *News From the Front, Sep-Oct 03* (www.army.mil/products/NFTF/sopoct03/FBCB2/fbcb).
79 "Marine Corps Colonel and First Sergeant, Task Force Tarawa, April 2003", *op.cit.*
80 Galloway, "General Tommy Franks", *op.cit*; Matthew French, "Franks: Net-centric Tech is 'Heaven' ", *Federal Computer Weekly*, 22.1.04.
81 Jim Garamone, "Abizaid: U.S. Displaying 'Offensive Spirit' in Iraq", AFIS, 25.6.03, (www.defenselink.mil/news/Jun2003/nO6252003_200306251); United States Senate Armed Services Committee, 25.6.03, "LTG Abizaid Senate Confirmation Hearing, Questions and Answers (24 June 2003)", (www.senate.gov/^armed_services/testimony/cfm?wit_id=2312&id=8).
82 CALL Newsletter No. 03–27, 10.03, "Operation Outreach" (call.army.mil); "Third Infantry Division (Mechanized) After Action Report, Operation Iraqi Freedom", p. 15.
83 *Ibid.*
84 Joseph Farah and Jon Dougherty, "Iraq theater's Tower of Babel", Paul Sperry, "U.S. miscalculations left troops vulnerable", *WorldNetDaily*, 18.9.02, 10.7.03; Center for Army Lessons Learned, Newsletter No. 03–27, 10.03, "Operation Outreach" (call.army.mil).
85 *Ibid.*
86 Joshua Davis, "If We Run Out of Batteries, This War is Screwed", *Wired*, 21.5.03.
87 LTC John Charlton, "Digital Battle Command: Baptism by Fire", Center for Army Lessons Learned, *News From the Front, Sep–Oct 03* (www.army.mil/products/NFTF/sopoct03/FBCB2/fbcb); "Third Infantry Division (Mechanized) After Action Report, Operation Iraqi Freedom", pp. 192–193.
88 "Prepared Statement for the Senate Armed Services Committee Hearing", Office of Force Transformation, 9.4.02: (www.oft.osd.mil/library/speeches/speeches.cf).
89 Davis, "If We Run Out of Batteries"; for the navy's 500 chat rooms, cf. Dan Caterinicchia, "Defence IT leaders outline challenges", *Federal Computer Weekly*, 8.5.03.
90 "Notes Based on a Briefing by an Observer of 1st Marine Division OIF Operations", accessible from accessible from the website of the Urban Operations Journal, section "Operation Iraq Freedom, AARs, Observations, Analyses and Comments".

NOTES

91 "What Went Right?", *Janes' Defence Weekly*, 30.4.03.
92 "1st Marine Division, Lessons Learned, 28 May 2003", *op.cit*; "With the 'Marne 500' in Iraq, U.S. Army Officer, 3rd Infantry Division, March 2003" (www.urbanoperations.com/ifaar7); "Third Infantry Division (Mechanized) After Action Report, Operation Iraqi Freedom", pp. 32–33, 103, 106, 140–141.
93 "Third Infantry Division (Mechanized) After Action Report, Operation Iraqi Freedom", pp. 32–33, 101–104; Center for Army Lessons Learned, Newsletter No. 03–27, 10.03, "Operation Outreach" (call.army.mil).
94 Galloway, "General Tommy Franks".
95 "Operation Iraqi Freedom, Quick-Look Tactical Observations, Marine Corps Ist Sergeant, 24 Marine Expeditionary Unit, 'The Warlords', May 2003" (www.urbanoperations.com/ifaar5); "1st Marine Division, Lessons Learned", "Notes Based on a Briefing by an Observer of 1st Marine Division", *op.cit*.
96 "What Went Right?", *Janes' Defence Weekly*, 30.4.03.
97 LTG Abizaid hearing, *op.cit*.
98 Major Ted Nagel, "Command and Control (C2) in TOC Operations", Center for Army Lessons Learned, *News From the Front, Mar–Apr 03* (www.call.army.mil/products/NFTF/marapr03/C2/c2).
99 *Ibid*.
100 Davis, "If We Run Out of Batteries".
101 Center for Army Lessons Learned, Newsletter No. 03–27, 10.03, "Operation Outreach" (call.army.mil).
102 Dan Caternicchia, "Network-centric warfare: Not there yet", *Federal Computer Weekly*, 9.6.03; Dawn Onley and Susan Menke, "DOD seeks to exploit intelligence", *Government Computer News*, 23.6.03.

BIBLIOGRAPHY

Documentary collections

Barnes, John and David Nicholson (eds), *The Leo Amery Diaries, Volume One: 1896–1929* (London: Hutchinson, 1980).
—— *The Empire at Bay, The Leo Amery Diaries, 1929–1945* (London: Hutchinson, 1988).
Colville, John, *The Fringes of Power, 10 Downing Street Diaries, 1939–1955* (New York: Norton, 1985).
Davis, Julia and Dolores A. Fleming (eds), *The Ambassadorial Diary of John W. Davis, The Court of St. James, 1918–1921* (Morgantown, VA: West Virginia University Press, 1993).
Dilks, David (ed.), *The Diaries of Sir Alexander Cadogan, 1938–1945* (New York: Putnam, 1972).
Cabinet Reports by Prime Ministers to the Crown, 1868–1916, Reel Two, 1872–75 (Microfilm) (Brighton, England: Harvester Press, 1974).
The Case of the anti-Soviet Bloc of Rights and Trotskyites (Moscow: People's Commissariat of Justice, 1938; New York: Howard Fertig, 1988).
Confidential U.S. State Department Central Files: Great Britain, Internal Affairs, 1930–1939 (Microfilm) (Frederick, MD: University Publications of America, 1985).
Confidential US Diplomatic Post Records, Japan (Microfilm) (Frederick, MD: University Publications of America, 1983–1984).
Documents Diplomatiques Francais, 1932–1939, 2e serie (1936–1939) (Paris: Impr. Nationale, 1963).
Documents on British Foreign Policy (DBFP) Second Series (London: Her Majesty's Stationery Office, 1946).
Documents on German Foreign Policy (DGFP), Series D (Washington, DC: US Printing Office, 1949).
Domarus, Max (ed.), *Hitler, Speeches and Proclamations, 1932–1945, The Chronicle of a Dictatorship, Volume Two, The Years 1935 to 1938* (trans. Chris Wilcox and Mary Fran Gilbert) (Wauconda, IL: Bolchazy-Carducci, 1992), pp. 865–869.
Ferris, John (ed.), "From Broadway House to Bletchley Park: The Diary of Captain Malcolm Kennedy, 1934–46", *Intelligence and National Security*, 4(3) (July 1989).
Ferris, John (ed.) *The British Army and Signals Intelligence During the First World War* (Phoenix Mill: Alan Sutton, 1992).
Foreign Relations of the United States (FRUS), The Paris Peace Conference, 1919, Volume XI (Washington, DC: US Government Printing Office, 1943).

Getty, J. Arch and Oleg V. Naumov (ed.), *The Road to Terror, Stalin and the Self-Destruction of the Bolsheviks, 1932–1939* (New Haven, CT: Yale University Press, 2001).
Heiber, Helmut and David Glantz (eds), *Hitler and his Generals, Military Conferences 1942–1945, The First Complete Stenographic Record of the Military Situation Conferences, from Stalingrad to Berlin* (New York: Enigma, 2003).
I Documenti Diplomatici Italiani, Ottava Serie: 1935–1939 (Rome: Libreria dello Stato, 1952).
Matthew, H.D.G. (ed.), *The Gladstone Diaries, with Cabinet Minutes and Prime Ministerial Correspondence, vol. 8, July 1871–December 1874* (Oxford: Clarendon, 1982), pp. 267, 418.
Middlemas, Keith (ed.), *Thomas Jones, Whitehall Diary, Volume II, 1926–1930* (London and New York: Oxford University Press, 1969).
Muggeridge, Malcolm (ed.), *Ciano's Diary, 1939–1943* (London and Toronto: Heinemann, 1947).
The Oriental Question, 1840–1900, Files from the Royal Archives, Windsor Castle (Bethesda, MD: University Press of America, 1985).
Pimlott, Ben (ed.), *The Political Diary of Hugh Dalton, 1918–40, 1945–60* (London: Jonathan Cape, 1986).
Ramm, Agatha (ed.), *The Political Correspondence of Mr. Gladstone and Lord Granville, 1868–1876, vol. 2, 1871–76* (London: Royal Historical Society, 1952).
Ramsden, John (ed.), *Real Old Tory Politics, The Political Diaries of Robert Sanders, Lord Bayford (1910–1935)* (London: The Historians' Press, 1981), p. 221.
Rich, Norman and Norma Fisher (ed.), *Holstein Correspondence* (Cambridge: Cambridge University Press, 1961).
Rieber, Alfred J. (ed.), *The Politics of Autocracy: Letters of Alexander II to Prince A.I. Bariatinskii, 1857–1864* (Paris: Mouton, 1966), pp. 77–78, 107–108.
Smith, Amanda (ed.), *Hostage to Fortune, The Letters of Joseph P. Kennedy* (New York: Viking, 2001).
Stalin, J.V., *Works, Volume 12, April 1929–June 1930* (Moscow and London: Foreign Language Publishing House, 1955).
—— *Works, Volume 13, July 1930–January 1934* (Moscow and London: Foreign Language Publishing House, 1955).
U.S. Military Intelligence Reports, Combat Estimates: Europe, 1920–1943, Reel Two (Frederick, MD: University Publications of America, 1985).
Vincent, John (ed.), *A Selection from the Diaries of Edward Henry Stanley, 15th Earl of Derby (1826–93) Between September 1869 and March 1878*, Camden Fifth Series, Volume 4 (London: Royal Historical Society, 1994).
Williamson, Philip (ed.), *The Modernisation of Conservative Politics, The Diaries and Letters of William Bridgeman, 1904–1935* (London: Historians' Press, 1988).
Young, A.P. (ed. Sidney Young), *The 'X' Documents* (London: Deustch, 1974).

Monographs

Adamthwaite, Antony, "French Military Intelligence and the Coming of War, 1935–1939", in Christopher Andrew and Jeremy Noakes, *Intelligence and International Relations* (Exeter: University of Exeter, 1987), pp. 191–208.
Agar-Hamilton, J.A.I. and L.C.F Turner, *Crisis in the Desert, May–July 1942, Union War Histories* (New York: Oxford University Press, 1952).

BIBLIOGRAPHY

—— *The Sidi Rezeg Battles 1941, Union War Histories* (London: Oxford University Press, 1957).

Alder, G.J., *British India's Northern Frontier, 1865–95. A Study in Imperial Policy* (Plymouth: Royal Commonwealth Society, Imperial Studies, No. 25, 1963).

Alvarez, David, *Secret Messages: Codebreaking and American Diplomacy 1930–1945* (Lawrence: University Press of Kansas, 2000).

Andrew, Christopher, *Secret Service, The Making of the British Intelligence Community* (London, Heinemann, 1985), pp. 21–67.

Archer, Christon, John Ferris, Holger Herwig and Tim Travers, *A World History of Warfare* (Lincoln: University of Nebraska Press, 2002).

Avon, The Earl of, *The Eden Memoirs: Facing the Dictators* (London: Cassell, 1962).

Behrendt, Hans-Otto, *Rommel's Intelligence in the Desert Campaign, 1941–1943* (London: Kimber, 1985).

Bell, Christopher M., *The Royal Navy, Seapower and Strategy Between the Wars* (Stanford: Stanford University Press, 2000).

Best, Antony, *Empire Under Siege: British Intelligence and the Japanese Challenge in Asia, 1919–41* (Basingstoke: Palgrave Macmillan, 2002).

Bidwell, Shelford and Dominick Graham, *Fire Power, British Army Weapons and Theories of War, 1904–1945* (London and Boston: Allen & Unwin, 1982), pp. 248–250.

Borman, C.A., *Divisional Signals, Official History of New Zealand in the Second World War, 1939–45* (Wellington, NZ: War History Branch, Department of Internal Affairs, 1954), pp. 118–119.

Buckle, George Earle, *The Life of Benjamin Disraeli, Earl of Beaconsfield, vol. 5, 1868–1876* (London: John Murray, 1910–1920).

—— *The Life of Benjamin Disraeli, Earl of Beaconsfield, vol. 6, 1876–1881* (London: John Murray, 1910–1920).

Burke, Colin, *Information and Secrecy, Vannevar Bush, Ultra and the Other Memex* (Metuchen, NJ: Scarecrow Press, 1994).

Calvocoressi, Peter, *Top Secret Ultra* (London: Cassell, 1980).

Cecil, Gwendolyn, *Life of Robert, Marquis of Cecil, vol. 2, 1868–1880* (London: Hodder & Stoughton, 1921).

Crevald, Martin van, Command in War (Cambridge, MA: Harvard University Press, 1985).

Deist, Wilhelm, Manfred Messerschmidt, Hans-Erich Volkmann and Wolfram Wette, *Germany and the Second World War, Volume One, The Build-up of German Aggression* (Oxford: Clarendon Press, 1990).

Devours, Cipher A. and Louis Kruh, *Machine Cryptography and Modern Cryptanalysis* (Dedham, MA: Artech House, 1985).

Dilks, David, "Flashes of Intelligence: The Foreign Office, the SIS and Security Before the Second World War", in Christopher Andrew and David Dilks, *The Missing Dimension, Governments and Intelligence Communities in the Twentieth Century* (London: Macmillan, 1984).

—— "Appeasement and 'Intelligence'", in David Dilks (ed.), *Retreat From Power, Volume One, 1906–1939* (London: Macmillan, 1981).

Fergusson, Thomas G., *British Military Intelligence. 1870–1914. The Development of a Modern Intelligence Organization* (Frederick, MD: University Publications of America, 1984).

Ferris, John Robert, *The Evolution of British Strategic Policy, 1919–1926* (Ithaca, NY: Cornell University Press, 1989).

BIBLIOGRAPHY

—— "The Symbol and Substance of Seapower: Britain, the United States and the One-Power Standard, 1919–1921", in B.J.C. McKercher (ed.), *Anglo-American Relations in the 1920s, The Struggle for Supremacy* (Edmonton: University of Alberta Press, 1990).

—— "Student and Master: Britain, Japan, Airpower and the Fall of Singapore", in Brian Farrell (ed.), *Singapore, Sixty Years On* (Singapore: Eastern Universities Press, 2002).

—— "The Biggest Force Multiplier? Knowledge, Information and Warfare in the 21st Century", in Alistair Dally and Rosalind Bourke (eds), *Conflict, The State and Aerospace Power* (Fairbairn, ACT: Aerospace Press, 2003).

French, David, *Raising Churchill's Army: The British Army and the War Against Germany, 1919–1945* (Oxford: Oxford University Press, 2000).

Fuller, William, *Strategy and Power in Russia, 1600–1914* (New York: Free Press, 1992), pp. 328–452.

Garlinski, Josef, *Intercept* (New York: Scribner,1979).

Gillard, David, *The Struggle for Asia, 1828–1914* (London: Methuen, 1977).

Gooch, John, *The Plans of War, The General Staff and British Military Strategy, c.1900–1916* (New York: Wiley, 1974).

Gorodetsky, Gabriel, *Grand Delusion, Stalin and the German Invasion of Russia* (New Haven, CT: Yale University Press, 1999).

Handel, Michael I., *War, Strategy and Intelligence* (London: Frank Cass, 1989).

—— *Masters of War* (London and Portland, OR: Frank Cass, 2001).

Harris, Steven, *British Military Intelligence in the Crimean War, 1854–1856* (London, England and Portland, OR: Frank Cass, 1999)

Herman, Michael, *Intelligence Power in Peace and War* (Cambridge: Cambridge University Press, 1996).

Hillgruber, Andreas "Das Russland-Bild der fuhrenden deutschen Militars vor Beginn des Angriffs auf die Sowjetunion", in Alexander Fischer, Gunter Moltmann and Klaus Schwabe (eds), *Russland–Deutschland–Amerika. Russia–Germany–America. Festschrift fur Fritz T. Epstein zum 80* (Wiesbaden: Franz Steiner, 1978), pp. 296–310.

Hinsley, F.H. and Alan Stripp, *Codebreakers, The Inside Story of Bletchley Park* (Oxford: Oxford University Press, 1993).

Hinsley, F.H. with E.E. Thomas, C.F.G. Ransom and R.C. Knight, *British Intelligence in the Second World War. Its Influence on Strategy and Operations, Volume One* (London: Her Majesty's Stationery Office, 1979).

—— *British Intelligence in the Second World War. Its Influence on Strategy and Operation, Volume Two* (London: Her Majesty's Stationery Office, 1981).

Hitler, Adolf, *Mein Kampf* (trans. Ralph Mannheim) (London: Hutchinson, 1974).

Hoffmann, Peter, *The History of the German Resistance, 1933–1945*, 3rd edn (Montreal, PQ: McGill-Queen University Press, 1996), pp. 57–59.

Hopkirk, Peter, *The Great Game, On Secret Service in High Asia* (London: John Murray, 1990).

Ignat'ev, N.P. (ed. John L. Evans), *Mission of N.P. Ignat'ev to Khiva and Bukhara, 1858* (Newtonville, MA: Oriental Research Partners, 1984).

Ingram, Edward, *The Beginning of the Great Game in Asia, 1828–1834* (Oxford: Clarendon Press, 1979).

—— *Committment to Empire: Prophecies of the Great Game in Asia, 1797–1800* (Oxford: Clarendon Press, 1981).

—— *In Defence of British India, Great Britain in the Middle East, 1795–1842* (London: Frank Cass, 1984).

Jackson, Peter, *France and the Nazi Menace* (Oxford and New York: Oxford University Press, 2000).

—— "Intelligence and the End of Appeasement", in Robert Boyce (ed.), *French Foreign and Defence Policy, 1918–1940: The Decline and Fall of a Great Power* (London and New York: Routledge, 1998).

Jeffery, Keith and Alan Sharp, "Lord Curzon and Secret Intelligence", in Christopher Andrew and Jeremy Noakes (eds), *Intelligence and International Relations, 1900–1945* (Exeter: University of Exeter, 1987).

Jervis, Robert, *Perception and Misperception in International Politics* (Princeton: Princeton University Press, 1976).

Kahn, David, *The Codebreakers: The Story of Secret Writing* (New York: Macmillan, 1968).

—— *Hitler's Spies* (New York: Collier, 1978).

Kazemzadeh, Firuz, *Russia and Britain in Persia, 1864–1914, A Study in Imperialism* (New Haven, CT: Yale University Press, 1968).

Kippenberger, Howard, *Infantry Brigadier* (London: Oxford University Press, 1949).

Klemperer, Klemens von, *German Resistance Against Hitler, The Search for Allies Abroad, 1938–1945* (Oxford: Clarendon Press, 1992).

Knox, MacGregor, *Mussolini Unleashed, 1939–1941, Politics and Strategy in Fascist Italy's Last War* (Cambridge: Cambridge University Press, 1982).

Liddell Hart, B.H. (ed.), *The Rommel Papers* (London: Collins, 1953).

Long, Gavin, *Greece, Crete and Syria, Australia in the War of 1939–1945* (Canberra: Australia War Memorial, 1986).

MacGregor, Lady (ed.), *The Life and Opinions of Major-General Sir Charles Metcalfe MacGregor, Volume Two* (Edinburgh and London: W. Blackwood and Sons, 1888).

MacKenzie, David, *The Lion of Tashkent, The Career of General M.G. Chernaiev* (Athens, GA: University of Georgia Press, 1974).

McKercher, B.J.C., *The Second Baldwin Government and the United States, 1924–1929, Attitudes and Diplomacy* (Cambridge: Cambridge University Press, 1984).

May, Ernest. (ed.), *Knowing One's Enemies: Intelligence Assessment before the Two World Wars* (Princeton, NJ: Princeton University Press, 1984).

Mearsheimer, John *The Tragedy of Great Power Politics* (New York: Norton, 2001), p. 11, passim.

Mellenthin, F.W. von, *Panzer Battles* (New York: Ballantine, 1956).

Millman, Richard, *Britain and the Eastern Question, 1875–1878* (Oxford: Clarendon, 1979).

Murray, Williamson, *The Change in the European Balance of Power, The Path to Ruin* (Princeton, NJ: Princeton University Press, 1984).

Murray, Williamson and Alan Millett (eds), *Calculations: Net Assessments and the Coming of World War II* (New York: Free Press, 1992).

Nalder, R.F.H., *The Royal Corps of Signals, A History of its Antecedents and Developments (circa 1800–1955)* (London: Royal Signals Institute, 1958).

Neilson, Keith, *Britain and the Last Tsar* (Oxford: Clarendon Press, 1995).

Parker, R.A.C., *Chamberlain and Appeasement, British Policy and the Coming of the Second World War* (New York: St. Martin's Press, 1993).
Popplewell, Richard James, "British Intelligence and Indian Subversion, The Surveillance of Indian Revolutionaries in India and Abroad, 1904–1920", Ph.D. dissertation, Corpus Christi College, Cambridge, 1996.
Pons, Silvio, *Stalin and the Inevitable War, 1936–1941* (Portland, OR: Frank Cass, 2002).
Rhodes James, Robert, *Eden, A Biography* (London: Weidenfeld and Nicolson, 1986).
Rose, Norman, *Vansittart, Study of a Diplomat* (London: Heinemann, 1978).
Roskill, Stephen, *Hankey, Man of Secrets, Volume III, 1931–1963* (London: Collins, 1974).
Stephenson, Sir William Samuel, *British Security Coordination, The Secret History of British Intelligence in the Americas, 1940–1945* (New York: Fromm International, 1999).
Sumner, B.H., *Russia and the Balkans, 1870–1880* (Oxford: Clarendon Press, 1937).
Swartz, Marvin, *The Politics of Foreign Policy in the Era of Disraeli and Gladstone* (London: Macmillan, 1985).
Ulman, R.H., *Anglo-Soviet Relations, 1917–21, Volume III, The Anglo-Soviet Accord* (Princeton: Princeton University Press, 1972).
Vansittart, Robert, *The Mist Procession* (London: Hutchinson, 1958).
Waller, Derek, *The Pundits, British Exploration of Tibet and Central Asia* (Lexington, KY: University Press of Kentucky, 1990).
Wark, Wesley K., *The Ultimate Enemy, British Intelligence and Nazi Germany, 1933–1939* (Ithaca, NY: Cornell University Press, 1985).
Watt, Donald Cameron, *How War Came, The Immediate Origins of the Second World War, 1938–1939* (New York: Pantheon, 1989).
Weinberg, Gerhard, *The Foreign Policy of Hitler's Germany, Volume II, Starting World War Two, 1937–1939* (Chicago: University of Chicago Press, 1980).
Welchman, W.G., *The Hut Six Story, Breaking the Enigma Codes* (New York: McGraw-Hill, 1982).
Whaley, Barton, *Covert German Rearmament, 1919–1939: Deception and Misperception* (Frederick, MD: University Publications of America, 1984).
Winterbotham, F.W., *The Nazi Connection* (New York: Harper & Row, 1978).
Wohlstetter, Roberta, *Pearl Harbor: Warning and Decision* (Stanford, CA: Stanford University Press, 1962).
Yapp, M.E., *Strategies of British India, Britain, Iran and Afghanistan, 1798–1850* (Oxford: Clarendon Press, 1980).

Articles

Alder, Garry, "Big Game Hunting in Central Asia", *Journal of Imperial and Commonwealth History*, 9(3) (1981).
Alexander, Martin, "Did the Deuxieme Bureau Work? The Role of Intelligence in French Defence Policy and Strategy, 1919–1939", *Intelligence and National Security* (London: Frank Cass, 1991).
Allen, Matthew "The British Mediterranean Squadron During the Great Eastern Crisis of 1876–9", *The Mariner's Mirror*, 85(1) (February 1999).
Alvarez, David, "Left in the Dust: Italian Signals Intelligence, 1915–1943", *International Journal of Intelligence and Counterintelligence*, 14 (Fall 2001).

Barros, Andrew, "Le Deuxieme Bureau evalue les forces allemandes: les dangers du sport et de l'education physique, 1919–1928", *Guerres Mondiales et Conflits Contemporains* (Paris: Presses universitaires de France, forthcoming).
de Graaff, Bob, "The Stranded Baron and the Upstart at the Crossroads: Wolfgang zu Putlitz and Otto John", *Intelligence and National Security* 6(4) (October 1991).
Dithie, John Lowe, "Pressure from Within: The 'Forward' Group in the India Office during Gladstone's First Ministry", *Journal of Asian History*, 15(1) (1981).
Duthie, John Lowe, "Some Further Insights into the Working of Mid-Victorian Imperialism: Lord Salisbury, the 'Forward Group' and Anglo-Afghan Relations: 1874–1878", *Journal of Imperial and Commonwealth History*, 8(3) (1980).
Erskine, Ralph, "The Development of Typex", *The Enigma Bulletin*, 2 (May 1997).
—— "The Admiralty and Cipher Machines During the Second World War: Not So Stupid After All", *The Journal of Intelligence History*, 2(2).
Ferris, John, "Before 'Room 40': The British Empire and Signals Intelligence 1898–1914", *Journal of Strategic Studies*, 12(4) (1989).
—— "The British Army and Signals Intelligence in the Field During the First World War", *Intelligence and National Security*, 3(4) (October 1988).
—— "The Greatest World Power on Earth: Great Britain in the 1920s", *International History Review*, 14(4) (November 1991).
—— "The Intelligence–Deception Complex: An Anatomy", *Intelligence and National Security*, 4(4) (1989).
—— "The Road to Bletchley Park: The British Experience with Signals Intelligence, 1890–1945", *Intelligence and National Security*, 16(1) (Spring 2002).
—— "Whitehall's Black Chamber: British Cryptology and the Government Code and Cypher School, 1919–1929", *Intelligence and National Security*, 2(1) (January 1987).
—— "'Worthy of Some Better Enemy?' The British Assessment of the Imperial Japanese Army, 1919–1941, and the Fall of Singapore", *Canadian Journal of History* (August 1993).
Ferris, John and Uri Bar Joseph, "Getting Marlowe to Hold His Tongue: The Conservative Party, the Intelligence Services and the Zinoviev Letter", *Intelligence and National Security*, 8(4) (October 1993).
Fisher, John, "The Interdepartmental Committee on Eastern Unrest and British Responses to Bolshevik and Other Intrigues Against the Empire during the 1920s", *Journal of Asian History* (2000).
French, David, "Spy Fever in Britain 1900–1015", *Historical Journal*, 21 (1978).
Hiley, Nicholas P., "The Failure of British Espionage Against Germany, 1907–1914", *Historical Journal*, 26 (1983).
Jackson, Peter, "French Military Intelligence and Czechoslovakia, 1938", *Diplomacy and Statecraft*, 5(1) (March 1994).
McKercher, Brian, "'Our Most Dangerous Enemy': Great Britain Pre-Eminent in the 1930s", *International History Review*, 14(4) (November 1991).
Martel, Gordon, "The Meaning of Power: Rethinking the Decline and Fall of Great Britain", *International History Review*, 14(4) (November 1991).
Mills, W.C., "The Chamberlain–Grandi Conversations of July–August 1937 and the Appeasement of Italy", *International History Review*, 19(3) (1997), pp. 594–619.
Morris, L.P., "British Secret Service Activity in Khorassan, 1887–1908", *Historical Journal*, 27 (1984).

Neilson, Keith, " 'Greatly Exaggerated': The Myth of the Decline of Great Britain Before 1914", *International History Review*, 14(4) (November 1991).

—— " 'Pursued by a Bear': British Estimates of Soviet Military Strength and Anglo-Soviet Relations, 1922 1939", *Canadian Journal of History* (1993).

Overy, Richard, "Germany and the Munich Crisis: A Mutilated Victory?", *Diplomacy and Statecraft*, 10(2–3) (1999).

Preston, Adrian, "The Eastern Question during the Franco-Prussian War", in Jay Atherton (ed.), *Historical Papers, 1972* (Ottawa: Canadian Historical Association, 1972).

Strang, Bruce, "Two Unequal Tempers: Sir George Ogilvie-Forbes, Sir Nevile Henderson and British Foreign Policy, 1938–39", *Diplomacy and Statecraft*, 5(1) (March 1994).

Waddington, Geoffrey, "Hassgegner: German Views of Great Britain in the Later 1930s", *History*, 81(261) (1996).

Yapp, M.E., "British Perceptions of the Russian Threat to India", *Modern Asian Studies*, 21(4) (1987).

Dissertations

Beaver, William Carpenter II, "The Development of the Intelligence Division and Its Role in Aspects of Imperial Policy Making, 1854–1901", Ph.D. dissertation, Oxford University, 1976.

Boadle, Donald Graeme, *Sir Robert Vansittart at the Foreign Office, 1930–1933*, Ph.D. dissertation, Cambridge University, 1979.

Preston, Adrian, "British Military Policy and the Defence of India: A Study of British Military Policy, Plans and Preparations during the Russian Crisis, 1875–1880", Ph.D. dissertation, University of London, 1966.

INDEX

Abizaid, General John, 319
Accounting and Tabulation, Co. 143,
Admiralty, 24, 46, 51, 140–41, 154, 161, 173
Afghanistan, 9–13, 16–22, 26, 30–33, 36, 38–39, 41–43, 332–3, 336
Afrika Korps, 199–200, 204, 208–11, 216–18, 222, 225–7, 229–30, 232–4, 236–8
Agar, Lieutenant Colonel, 233
Air Forces: Germany, 61, 72–73, 123–4, 149, 165, 168, 182, 194, 221, 258; Japan, 122–23, 263–5; Royal Air Force, 62, 72–3, 148–51, 155–7, 159–64, 191, 199; United States, 263–5, 271–4, 289–90, 301, 304–6, 208–9, 316, 321–2
Air Ministry, 72–73, 152, 156–8, 164, 173, 176
Air Tasking Orders, 306, 321–2
Akkhal, The: 15, 26, 29, 39, 43
Alexander II, Tsar, 9, 23, 25–34, 37–39, 41–42, 334, 336
Ali, Sher, 12, 17–22, 30–31, 36, 38, 333
Alperts, David, 289
Amery, Leo, 71
Andrew, Christoper, 45
Appeasement, 45–46, 50, 59, 72–3, 77–94, 106, 120
Aras, Tewfik Rustu, 55
Army, Australia, 201–02
Army, Britain, 35–6, 123, 139–41, 154–61, 164–5, 181–238. 275, 280
Anti-Tank weapons, 207, 209–10; Armour, 187–8, 201–11, 218,220, 222–26, 229–30, 232–6; Artillery, 187, 206, 208–9; British Expeditionary Force, 190, 192, 195–8; Cavalry, 188, 206; Columns, Jock, 207,209, 211; Eighth, 162, 186, 196, 199–201, 204, 212, 223–8; Infantry, 187, 201–11; Signals, 186, 196–200, 213–4, 217–9, 222–4; Tactics, 206–12; Western Desert Force, 213, 218, ; Training, 185–91, 195–8, 207, 214, 217, 231
Army, Canada, 274, 283
Army, Commonwealth, 186, 201–2, 205–09, 257
Army, Dominion, 206–08, 219, 274
Army, France, 192–3, 249
Army, Germany, 165–8, 181–2, 186, 192–5, 198, 202–04, 208–19, 226, 249, 257–8, 280, 324; Afrika Korps, 199–200, 204, 208–11, 216–18, 222, 225–7, 229–30, 232–4, 236–8; Tactics, 209–12
Army, Imperial Japan, 121–23, 155, 249, 252, 257–69, 271–2
Army, India, 139, 186, 200–06, 218, 222
Army, Iraq, 308–09, 311, 318–20
Army, Iran, 258
Army, Italy, 181, 198, 202, 211–16, 236–7, 257
Army, New Zealand, 199, 201, 203–04, 207, 218–9, 224–5, 231, 233, 235–6
Army Russia/Soviet, 257
Army, South Africa, 201, 203, 212, 225, 235–6
Army, United States, 123, 142, 154,
Army, Turkey, 258
Auchinleck, General, 200, 202, 204–08, 210–11, 222, 226
Austin-Godwin, General, 205, 235
Australia, 164, 176, 199, 206,
Austria, 16, 58, 127
Auto Cyphers, Ltd., 145

Baldwin, Stanley, 47–48, 61,
Ball, Joseph, 48, 52

387

INDEX

Battle, of: Alam el Halfa, 233, 247; Alamein, 181, 237, 277; Amiens, 272; Arawe, 274; Atlantic, 166, 168, 254
Bardia, 213
Beda Fomm, 232–3
Bismark Sea, 263
BATTLEAXE, 200, 202, 207, 218, 228–9, 234; Bir el Hacheim, 181, 209–10; Caporetto, 216, 236; Cauldron, 232; Crete, 159, 198–9, 206, 218–20; CRUSADER, 190, 202–07, 209–12, 220, 223–6, 228–37, 283 ; GAZALA, 191, 205, 205, 227, 209–10, 212, 226–7,232, 236–7; Guadalcanal, 269; Hill 70, 272; Hollandia, 261, 265; Keren, 214; Marshal Islands, 263–4; Medenine, 277 ; Mersa Matruh, 237; Midway, 252, 269, 276; Pearl Harbor, 252, 269–70; Salamaua/Lae, 271–3; Sidi Barrani, 213, 215; Sidi Rezegh,204 ; Tobruk, 168–9, 203, 206–7, 209, 213, 237; Vimy Ridge, 283
Bayly, Benjamin de Forest, 171–4, 177
Beatty, Admiral David, 139
Beck, General Ludwig, 66, 69, 70–1, 74–5, 81
Beirsford Pierse, General, 218
Bell Labs, 172
Bennett, Ralph, 253, 260
Berlin, Isaiah, 158
Berkowitz, Bruce, 298
Betts, Dick, 101
Biddle, Stephen, 308
Biddulph, Captain, 19
Billotte, General, 193
Bismark, Otto von: 11, 41, 107
Blamey, General Thomas, 201, 206–08, 261, 264, 271–2, 274, 276, 279
Bland, Neville, 48
Boadle, Donald Graeme, 45
Board, Cypher Policy, 174–7
Board, W/T, 141, 143
Bokhara, 10, 30, 36, 41
Bohm-Tettlebach, Lieutenant– Colonel, 70
Bosch, Robert, 65–6, 68, 79
Boyd, Colonel John, 291
Bridges, E.E., 169–70
British Security Coordination, 171–4
Britain, Foreign Policy: 8–44, 45–98, 113–4
British Tabulating Machines, 151, 176, 355

Brooke, General Alan, 223
Bukarin, Nicolai, 112
Burton, Richard Francis, 19

Cabinet, The: 11, 23–24, 26, 30, 45, 73, 78, 84, 87–92, 158, 162
Cadogan, Alexander, 46, 49–50, 52–53, 59, 61, 69–70, 78, 85–86, 88, 90–97
Cairncross, John, 126
Cambridge, Duke of, 22, 24–25, 33, 36
Campbell, Colonel "Jock", 200, 209
Campaign: Arakan, 164; Barbarossa, 110; Burma, 191, 263; Desert, 181–2, 198, 202–38, 254; Ethiopia, 191, 198, 202–03, 214; France, 163, 189–93, 195–8; Greece, 198, 206, 218–22; Japan, 268–9; Kosovo, 304, 306, 322, 324; Malaya, 157; Mediterranean, 159–61, 166–68, 254–5; Murmansk, 166; Norway, 166, 189, 191; Phillipines, 274–9, 266–8, 272–3; Somalia, 214; South West Pacific, 252–67, 271–4; Syria, 230; TORCH, 162; Tunisia, 162, 169, 182, 230
Canada, 164, 171–2
Canaris, Admiral, 70–71
Canning, Stratford, 14
Castlereagh, Lord, 119
Cavagnari, Louis, 333
Cavan, Lord, 187
Cebrowski, Admiral Arthur, 288–90, 294, 315, 323, 325
Chamberlain, Joseph, 78
Chamberlain, Neville, 52–53, 55, 61, 68–9, 73, 77–79, 105–6, 110, 114, 124, 133
Characteristics, national, ideas of: 54, 106, 111, 115–24
Chernaiev, Mikhail,13, 26, 334
Chief of Imperial General Staff, 187, 201
Chiefs of Staff, Britain, 51, 73, 77, 89, 162, 164, 174
Chiefs of Staff, Combined, 173
Chiefs of Staff, Joint, 268, 291, 304, 308
China, 30, 122, 125, 259
Christie, Malcolm Graham, 61–76, 79–80, 86, 89, 93–95
Church, G.R.M., 140
Churchill, Winston, 55, 72–3, 82, 90, 105–6, 114, 135, 140, 158, 169–70, 206
Ciano, Count, 115–8, 129

INDEX

Clark, Admiral Vern, 301
Clark, General Wesley, 306
Clarke, W.F., 146–7
Clausewitz, Carl, 85, 239–52, 262, 271–2, 275–87, 284–91, 307
Cockerill, George, 140
Colonial Office, 140–41
COLOSSUS, 172, 177–8,
Colvin, Ian, 50, 71
Command, 181–88, 238–52, 258, 270–87, 289–91, 294, 301–2, 305–7, 315, 318–27: British Army, 187–8, 192–3, 195–205, 207–13, 216–19, 225–7, 232–8; French Army, 192–3; German Army, 193–5, 208–12, 216, 219, 225–7; United States, 288–91, 316–24
Command and Control Warfare (C2W), 289, 308, 323–4
Command, Control, and Communications, C3, 183–5, 192–3, 195
Command, Control, Communications and Intelligence (C3I), 192–4, 197–9, 202–05, 207, 210, 238, 280, 282, 294, 306
Command, Control, Communications, Intelligence and security (C3IS), 182–5, 197, 238
Command, Control, Communications, Computers and Intelligence (C4I), 294, 308, 323
Command, Control, Communications, Computers, Intelligence, Intelligence, Surveillance and Reconnaissance (C4ISR), 288–90, 293–5, 299–301, 305, 307, 309, 317, 321–27
Committee, Bartholomew, 195, 207
Committee, Cipher Machine, 145, 147, 149, 151
Committee, Cypher Security, 169
Committee, Imperial Communications, 141
Committee, Imperial Economic, 147
Committee, Joint Intelligence, 169
Committee, Strategic Cables, 147–8
Committee, Wireless Messages, 143
Common Operating Picture, 308, 316, 320–22
Communications, 138–80, 181–240, 277–8, 286, 300; Britain, 138,141–3,147–59, 161–2, 171–5, 178–9, 355; British Army, 185–9, 193,

196–200, 202, 204, 212, 217–19, 221–7; Cell phones, 309, 318, 321, 324; Dispatch riders, 189, 197, 200; Fibre–optics, 309; German Army, 193–5, 212, 216–18, 221, 225–7 HYDRA, 171–2: Key Conversations, 173, 178, 236; Liaison Officers, 200, 215, 223; Plain language, 169, 181–2, 184–6, 189, 195, 215–8, 220, 226, 231–5, 300, 318–21, 323–4; Radio, 138–43, 147–8, 150, 155–9, 161–2, 171–4, 177, 179, 185–9, 194–6, 198–200, 202, 204, 218–19, 225–8, 309, 321; Radio-Telephone, 147–8, 150, 187, 189, 199, 213, 215–8, 223, 225–6, 231, 233, 235, 238; Satellite, 323
SIGSALY, 173; SIPRnet, 296, 298, 301, 321, 329, ; Telegraph, 138–9, 141, 143, 156–8, 161, 171–2, 186–8, 197, 202, 226–7; Telephone, 166, 173, 186–8, 193, 197, 202, 226–7; Teleprinters, 149–54, 151–4, 162, 171–6, 178–9; United States, 316–24; Veiled Language, 191, 215, 231–6; X-System, 172
Computer Network Attack, 300–02, 304–5, 316–7
Conference, Lausanne, 47
Conference, London Naval, 51
Conference, Montreaux, 55
Connell, John, 54
Conwell-Evans, Philip, 68, 78, 89
Cooper, Duff, 92
Costello, John, 252
Coulson, Lieutenant, 150
Cranbrook, Lord, 15
Creed and Co, Messrs., 151,154, 157, 175–6, 355
Crisis, Abysinnian, 133
Crisis, Chanak, 1922, 54
Crisis, Great Eastern, 8, 25–26, 31, 34–36, 40–43Crisis, Munich, 76–94, 116, 124, 133–5, 156, 178
Crisis, Trieste, 178–9
Crisis, Rhineland, 71
Critchley, Mr., 144, 150
Crowe, Eyre, 49
Cruwell, General, 227
Cumming, Mansfield, 49
Cunningham, General Alan, 200–04
Currie, Philip, 46
Curzon, Lord, 47–49

389

INDEX

Cyphers: Call signs, 190, 194, 196, 217, 219–20, 229–30; Code names, 190; Codes low-grade, 157, 167–8, 191, 218, 222, 228, 230 31; Codes, medium grade, 191, 196, 220, 230–2, 234–5, 231, 258; Communications effect on, XXX, 184–5, 196, 215–16, 232; Inter-Allied, 167; Inter-Departmental, 160, 221; Inter-Service Stencil, 197 ; One Time Pads, 139, 155, 159–62, 171, 174–5, 184, 190, 220–1, 228, 230; Operators, 185–6, 190–1, 194, 196; Playfair, 139; Substitution, 139; Superenciphered codebooks, 139, 141–2, 147–8, 154–6, 159–61, 167, 177, 190, 220–21, 257–8; Syko, 157, 165–6, 167–8, 214, 22o,355; transposition 139, 220; War Office Cypher 'W', 160, 167, 220–1, 228

Cypher machines, 138–80, 354–5, 358; Britain 139–80; C–36, 165; Combined Cipher Machine, 156, 164; Cryptotyper, 140, 143–4; Enigma, 138, 142–45, 149–56, 161–65, 191, 194–5, 254, 257; Germany, 142–4, 154–5, 160–1; Hagelin 143–4, 154–5; Hebern, 142–44, 150l KL-7, 176; KW-26, 176; Kryha 142; Lorenz, 153; M-209, 165, 167; O'Brien/O'Brien-Gardner, 143, 145–7, 149,151, 354–5; On-line cypher teleprinters, 145, 150–54, 171–80; One-time tape mixers, 172; PURPLE, 257; RM-26, 177; Rockex, 173-8, 358; Secratype; 175; Sigaba 145, 153–6, 162, 164,169, 176, 354; Telekrypton, 171–3, 358,l Typex, 144–45, 149–65, 169–70, XX, 175–7, 184, 190–91, 220–21, 228, 230; United States, 142, 144–6, 154–5

Cypher Machine Development Committee, 177–8

Cypher Machine Development Unit, 177–8

Czechoslovakia, 66, 69, 71–2, 76–90, 97, 111, 120, 126, 129, 134

Dahlerus, Birgir, 71
Daily Herald, The, 91
Daily Mail, The, 90
Daladier, Edward, 105, 121,133
Dalton, Hugh, 51, 82, 90, 92–3

Data Processing, 151, 253, 288. 297–8, 300, 318–9
Davies, Francis, 140
Dawson, Geoffrey, 83, 87
Deception, 71–72, 93, 132, 135, 241, 301–4, 308–9, 311–5, 334
Defence, Ministry of, 311, 319
Defence Teleprinter Network, 149, 151,
Defense, Department of, 288, 291, 299, 301–02, 304
Denham, Hugh, 154
Derby, Lady, 11, 23, 334
Derby, Lord, 11, 23, 25, 28–9, 33–34, 36–38, 41–42, 333–4
Dilks, David, 45
Disraeli, Benjamin, 8, 11–12, 18–19, 24–26, 28, 31, 33–36, 38, 40, 43, 334
Dobbins, Colonel, 308
Dominions, 143, 156–7, 178,
Dominions Office, 143, 156–7
Doudeville, General, 28,
Dower, John, 261
Drea, Ed, 239, 252–4, 260–1, 263, 265, 268, 270, 274

Eastern question, 8–9, 11–14, 18
Eden, Anthony, 49, 52, 55, 59, 61, 73–4, 76, 90, 98
Egypt, 158–60, 168, 189
Eisenhower, General, Dwight, 162, 249–50
Elliott Bros., Messrs., 145
Elphinstone, Keith, 145
Embeds, 310–11, 314

Fellers, Captain Bonner, 121
Fogleman, General Ben, 289
Foreign Office, 24, 46–98, 105, 134, 140–41, 156, 170, 174, 176–7: American Department, 53, 61; Communications Department, 126, 158, 175, 177–79 ; News Department, 54, 58, 90; Southern Department, 55; Far Eastern Department, 56–7; Central Department, 58, 62–3, 74, 76, 79, 86
Foreign Policy, Cabinet Committee on, 70, 77, 96–97
FORTITUDE, 289, 302
France, 14, 48, 49, 54, 58, 63, 71–2, 85, 88–91, 94–5, 105–6, 113–4, 116–7, 119, 122, 124–37, 142, 144, 154, 165, 192

INDEX

Francois-Poncet, Andre, 131–2
Franks, General Tommy, 308–9, 312–15, 318–19
Frere, Bartle, 10, 12
Freyberg, General Bernard, 205, 208, 218–20, 233–5
Friedman, William F., 150, 153–54
Fritsch, General Werner von, 67, 74–5
Fund, Secret Service: 15, 19, 24, 50–51, 175

Galloway, General, 206
Gambier-Perry, Richard, 171, 177
George, David Lloyd, 54
General Post Office, 174, 178,
Geographical Positioning System, 308, 319–23
Germany, 49–52, 56–98, 103, 105–6, 109–13, 115–6, 119–38, 141–4, 153–5, 160–69, 269
Germany, resistance, 50, 64–72
Giers, M. de, 119
Gladstone, William, 10, 26–27, 41
GlobalSecurity, 313
Goebbels, Dr, 56
Goering, Herman, 56–7, 67–8, 70, 71, 77, 79, 105, 114, 127, 134, 168
Gorchakov, Prince, 13–14, 33, 336
Goerdeler, Carl, 64–5, 67–9, 71, 74, 79–80, 90–1
Gordon, General, 18
Gort, General, 197
Gott, General, 200, 205, 234–5
Grandi, Count, 119, 132–3
Granville, Lord, 10, 26–27
Great Captains, 250–1, 286
Gregory, Maundy, 48
Grey, Hugh, 178–9
Grey, Lord Edward, 91
GUARD, 169–70
Guderian, General Hans, 193

Haig, Douglas, 115, 273, 286
Haines, General, 36
Halifax, Lord, 45, 53, 61, 69, 70, 77–98, 106, 114
Hall, Admiral Reginald ('Blinker'), 50
Halsey, Admiral, 265–6, 268
Handel, Michael, 101, 291, 305
Handley Page, Messrs., 64
Hankey, Maurice, 51, 53, 73, 90
Hannibal, 251
Harding, John, 201

Hardy, Gathorne, 24–25
Hart, Basil, 250
Hardinge, Charles, 46, 48–49
Hayden, Michael, 295, 298–9
Henderson, Arthur, 51
Henderson, Nevile, 53–54, 74, 84–86, 89, 91, 95
Henlein, Konrad, 54, 67, 71–2, 78,
Hess, Rudolf, 115
Hideki, General Tojo, 106
Hinsley, F.H., 253
Hitler, Adolf, 54, 58–61, 66–8, 71, 72, 75, 77–98, 102, 105–7, 110, 111, 113–16, 118–21, 123–4, 131–35,
Hoare, Samuel, 97
Hohenlohe, Prince, 70–71, 78,
Hole, Sidney, 143
Hollis, Roy, 304
Hollerith machines, 151, 160, 165, 167–8, 221
Huettenhain, Dr. Erich, 165,
HUSKY, 162,
Hussein, Saddam, 309–10, 312–14, 318–19

Ideology, 53–54, 56, 102–03, 105–15, 135–7; liberalism, 100, 105, 107–111, 113–5, 119; marxism-leninism, 105, 107–13, 115; fascism, 105, 110; militarism, 105, 111, 113; national-socialism, 105, 107, 111; Social Darwinism, 54, 111, 113, 115, 120; conservatism, 110; nationalism, 110
Ignatiev, Nicolai, 9, 14, 28, 42, 336
India, 9–13, 16–17, 20, 22, 24–25, 29–30, 33, 35–39, 47, 105, 156,159, 164, 199, 332–5
Influence: 34–44, 77–98, 111
Information: 99, 102–4, 239–42, 280, 282–3, 288–90, 305–06, 309, 320, 325
Information Age, 289–90, 293, 299, 321, 326
Information Dominance Center, 292–3, 300, 304–5
Information Operations: 288, 290, 301–05, 309–16, 319, 323
Information overload, 178–9, 183–4, 282, 292, 305–7, 321–2
Information Warfare, 289, 305, 312
Inskip, Thomas, 92, 97
Intelligence, Analysis: 25, 33–45, 47–48, 50, 55–58, 62–64, 72–75, 92–93, 105–6, 131–37, 258–61; balance of,

391

INDEX

244, 259–60, 281; Diplomatic, 15–44, 46–98, 123–37; Document Stealing, 15–16, 22–33, 99, 125, 127–28, 134–35; estimates: 24–7, 35–41,53–4, 58–60,62–4,68–9, 71–98, 115–25l Ethnocentrism, 13–14, 115, 117, 121–3; failures: 114–15, 120, 124, 130–37, 183–4; human: 16, 20–33, 46, 99, 125–6, 128–29, 294, 296, 309, 312, 317–20; images: 114–25, 135–7; imagery, 307, 317–8, 320; learning from: 8, 12, 37–44, 88–98, 104, 117, 122–4, 135–7, 270, 274, 294; Logic, best-case, 84–85, 102, 104, 291; Logic, worst case, 43, 84–85, 102, 104, 132, 245–6, 291; Mirror-Imaging, 102, 124, 291; nature of: 34, 48–49, 99–105, 130–31, 135–7, 260–61, 270; Operational, 165–8, 202–4,214–5, 217, 222, 228–37,239–87, 307–27; Operational Net Assessment, 291–3, 310, 322, 324; politicisation of, 51–53, 55–58, 72–98, 253, 265–9, 293–4, 309–10; perceptions: 106, 135–7, 307, 312; preconceptions, 104–05, 270–71, 282, 285

Intelligence, Agencies: Abwehr, The, 64, 66, 67, 70, 125; B-Dienst, 160, 165–7; Central Bureau, 253–4, 259; Central Intelligence Agency, 293, 295–6, 298–9; Defense Intelligence Agency, 295–7; FBI, 172; Forshungsamt, 125–27, 134; Government Code & Cypher School, 46–52, 55–7, 61, 98, 125–28, 133–5, 141–43, 145–8, 151–2,155, 159, 161,163–7, 169–170, 174–5, 177, 221, 351; Intelligence Branch, War Office, 46, 48; MI 5, 64, 70, 85, 94, 329; National Imagery and Mapping Agency, 295, 317; National Security Agency, 295–6, 298–9, 301, 316–7; OKH/IN7, 168; OKW/Chi, 165; Pers Z, 125–27; Room 40, 141, 166; Secret Intelligence Service (SIS), 46, 48–50, 52–53, 57, 69–70, 73, 76–78, 85, 94, 125, 133, 171, 173, 329; Signals Intelligence Service (Italian), 167; Signals Intelligence Service (United States), 125–6

Intelligence, national: Australia, signals intelligence, 253–4; Britain: on Russia and Central Asia, 8–44; on Nazi Germany, 51–98; interwar, 48–52, 55–58, 61–62, 69, 76–9, 105, 110–11,123–8, 130–38; Christie-Vansittart network/"private detective agency", 52–53, 58, 61–72; military intelligence, interwar, 53,57, 84, 128; World War Two, 203, 214, 217, 228, 253–4; Victorian, 15–44, 46, 332–3; Czechoslovakia: 126, 129; France, 115, 122–4, 126–29; Germany: 47, 123–29, 132–36; signals intelligence, 125–9, 134, 160–61, 165–9, 173, 181, 192, 197, 212, 217, 220–21, 228–37; India, British: 16–17, 19–22, 332–3; Italy: 124, 126–7, 133–35, 351; signals intelligence, 165–7, 181, 214–5, 217, 228–9; Japan: 125–26; Poland: 126–27, 129; Russia/USSR, 16, 23, 47, 112–3, 115, 124–29, 351; codebreaking, 16, 23, 125–8 ; Sweden, 127; United States, 115–16, 118, 122–25, 127–29, 326–27; codebreaking, 169–70, 172, 252–71, 295–6, 309, 319; contemporary doctrine, 289–327

Intelligence, Signals: codebreaking, 16, 23, 45–46, 49, 55–57, 61, 95–96, 98,125, 131–35, 138–80, 184–6, 252–71, 319–20, 351; cryptography, 128–9, 138–80; direction-finding, 189–90, 217; electronic warfare, 302, 304, 309; traffic analysis 61, 184, 190, 217, 229–30, 253, 258, 269, 319; telephone intercepts, 76, 90, 125–27, 134–5, 166

Intelligence, Surveillance and Reconnaissance: 294, 324

International Business Machines, 151, 172, 175–6

Irwin, General N.M.S., 198

Italy, 49, 55–8, 68, 72, 73, 92, 95, 103, 106, 111, 115–6, 120, 124–36, 154, 156–7, 165–7

Japan, 49, 56–7, 68, 95, 98, 105–6, 111–3, 115, 120–31, 133–5, 142, 154, 157, 167, 254–74

Jebb, Gladwyn, 54

Jervis, Robert, 101

Joint Staff Mission to Washington, 170, 173–4, 358

Jomini, Baron de, 241, 286

Jones, R.V., 149

392

INDEX

Junkers, Hugo, 62

Kashgar, 29, 41
Kaufmann, General von: 13, 17, 21, 26, 28–30, 33, 36, 38
Keegan, John, 249–50
Kennedy, Joseph, 84, 87, 88, 90, 92,
Kenney, General George, 263, 265, 271, 274
Kent, Sherman, 101
Khalfin, N.A., 33
Khiva, 9, 26–27, 334,
Kieper, Dr, Otto, 67
King, John, 126
Kipling, Rudyard, 16
Kleist-Schmenzin, Major von, 68, 70, 71, 80–81
Knox, Dilwyn, 146
Kokand, 10
Kordt, Erich, 65–6
Kordt, Theodor, 65–6, 68, 70, 86
Krueger, General Walter, 261, 267–8, 271–4, 276, 279

Lachmann, Gustav, 64
Lambert, L.H., 146–7
Lawrence, John, 10
Layton, Edwin, 252
Leaks, 52, 73, 90–91
Leger, Alexis, 90
Leeper, Rex, 88, 90
Lenin, Vladimir, 130
Letter, Zinoviev, 48
Lewin, Ronald, 252
Loftus, Augustus, 31–32
Lumsden, General Herbert, 205
Lytton, Lord, 16, 20–21, 31–33, 35–36, 39–40, 44, 333, 335
Lywood, O.G.: 149–53, 354–5

MacArthur, General Douglas, 121, 239, 252–3, 260–1, 263–8, 271, 273–6, 280
MacDonald, Ramsay, 47, 51
MacGregor, Charles Metcalfe, 21
Macchiavelli, 278
Marines, United States: 288–9, 308, 310–11, 316–19, 322–3
Mason-MacFarlane, Neil, 70, 79 , 85
MacLean, Donald, 126
Masyrk, Jan, 83
Mattis, General, 323
Maximus, Fabius, 247
Mayo, Lord, 10

Mearsheimer, John, 106–7
Mellinthin, F.W. von, 230
Mendl, Charles, 58
Merv, 9, 12, 15, 19, 22, 26, 30, 36, 41–42
Messervy, General Frank, 205–06, 234–51
Michael, Grand Duke, 13, 29–30, 36, 39
Milch, Edward, 62
Miliutin, Dmitri: 13, 23, 28, 31, 36
Milne, Lord, 187–8, 199, 201, 213
Minto, Lord, 14
Molotov, Vyascheslav, 113
Montgomery, General Bernard, 199, 201, 205–06, 208, 210, 238, 247, 276, 279
Mounsey, George, 79
Muller, Joseph, 66
Murray, Williamson, 291
Mussolini, Benito, 82, 103, 105–6, 117, 119–21, 124, 128, 130–33
Myers, General Richard, 291–2, 294, 308

Napier, Captain, 19, 29
Napoleon, 243, 249–51, 278, 286
Navy:German, 141–2, 153, 155, 164–7, 249, 258, 326; Imperial Japanese, 121–2, 249, 258, 326; Italian, 155; Royal, 32, 123, 139–141, 143, 146, 155, 157, 160–61, 163, 166–7, 224, 229; United States, 123–4, 142, 154, 172, 176, 249, 253, 265, 301, 306
Nelson, Horatio, 249
Netcentric Warfare, 288–90, 294–301, 306–7, 319, 323–7
Newton, Isaac, 243, 249
New Zealand, 176, 199
News Chronicle, The, 71, 91
Nimitz, Admiral Chester, 268–9, 276
NONSUCH, 169–70
Norrie, General Willoughby, 204, 223, 225, 232–5
North Atlantic Treaty Organization, 176
Northbrook, Lord, 10, 13, 17–21, 33, 36, 43
Nostitz, Gottfried von, 67
Nutting, Charles, 156

O'Brien, Mr, 145–147, 150
O'Conner, General, 199, 202
Oldham, Ernest, 126
Oster, Hans, 66–7, 70,
Osterholtz, John, 299, 325
Ougree Steel Trading Co., 145–6

393

INDEX

Pact, Anti-Comintern, 56–7, 95, 134–5,
Pact, Hoare-Laval, 73
Palford, Giffard, 18–19
Palmerston, Lord, 119
Patton, General George, 249–50
Peach, Air Commodore Stuart, 306
Pechel, Rudolf, 65
Peel, Lieutenant Colonel, 143–5, 150
Pericles, 247
Phipps, Eric, 90
Piggott, Colonel F.S.G., 259
Poland, 58, 62, 68, 79, 98, 112–3, 125–30, 192
Press relations, 302, 309–11
Propaganda, 119
Pulitz, Wolgang zu, 65–6, 70
Punch tape, 171–2, 174–6
Psychological warfare, 302–03, 315–6, 318

Racism, 11, 13–14, 18, 54, 63–4, 113–17, 120–23
Rahman, Abdur, 30, 38, 333
Rapid Decisive Operations, 289–91, 324
Rawlinson, Henry, 10, 12
Realism, 11, 53–54, 58–59, 105–14
Revolution in Military Affairs, 200, 203, 288, 293, 295, 322
Ribbontrop, Joachim, 56, 61, 66–8, 72, 74, 84, 95, 105, 111, 115, 127, 134
Ritchie, General Neil, 204–05
Ritter, Hans, 65–7
Roberts, Lord, 11
Rommel, General Erwin, 195, 201, 216–8, 221–2, 224–8, 230, 233, 236–8, 247, 283
Roosevelt, Franklin, 105–6, 135, Rose, Norman, 45
Rosenberg, Alfred, 69
Ross, Mr., 150
Rothermere, Lord, 48
Rowlett, Frank, 155
Rumsfeld, Donald, 314
Russia, 8–44, 46, 49, 55–6, 62, 68, 72, 90, 105–6, 110–11, 112, 115–6, 122, 124–36, 148, 154, 168, 192, 269, 294, 324, 332–4, 337

Salisbury, Lady, 13–14
Salisbury, Lord, 8, 11–20, 22, 24–25, 28, 33, 37–44, 46, 334, 336
Schacht, Hjalmer, 67
Schellenberg, Walter, 71

Schwartzkopf syndrome, 282
Security, 123, 128–29, 299–301, 310–13, 361
Security, Signals, 138–80, 181–6, 214–28, 257–8, 299–301, 317, 321, 361; Radio silence, 155, 190, 197, 215, 212
Seebohm, Captain Alfred, 217, 221, 224, 227, 229–31, 233, 235–7
Selzam, Edward von, 65
Sherman, General William, 281
Shuvalov, Count Petyr, 23, 29
Signals, diplomatic: 111, 120, 134–6, 315
Sinclair, Admiral Hugh, 48–50, 76, 78–9, 95
Skobolev, General : 13
Slim, General William, 209
Smith, E.W., 150, 178, 354–5
Smith, Sergeant, 233
South Africa, 157, 199
Southern Rhodesia, 199
South West Pacific Area Command, 260–1, 263–8
Special Forces, 309, 313–4, 319
Spector, Ronald, 252
Stalin, Joseph, 105–6, 112–3, 120, 124, 129
Stewart-Menzies, General, 170, 175,
Strang, William, 79, 85
Strasser, Otto, 64, 66
Strategy: 239–51, 288–95; Bluff, 11, 43, 76, 83–85, 96, 111, 121, 125, 128, 134, 249, 287; British, 8–13, 15, 19, 22, 25, 35, 38–44, 54–60, 81–84, 129–31; Deterrence, 11, 36, 40, 59, 81–85, 111, 120–21, 124, 128–29, 133–6, 305; Fog of war, 243, 249, 277, 288–9; Friction of war, 183–5, 241, 276–7, 288–9, 291, 300, 305–06, 324, 326; Imperative Principle, 243. 248, 274, 278, 283, 304; and Intelligence, 99–100, 135–8, 275–89,288–95, 323–7; Intuition, informed, of commanders: 242–3, 271–2, 277–8, 281, 283–6; Rules: 106–08, 111, 135–7, 286–7; Russian/Soviet, 12–13, 28–31, 112–13
Streseman, Gustav, 130
Subversion, 31, 35, 40–41, 47, 77, 111,
Sudetenland, The: 58, 71, 77–78, 81–4, 86, 88, 91, 93
Sumner, B.H., 31, 333
Supply, Ministry of, 157, 174, 178,

394

INDEX

Surprise, Strategic: 240–41, 244–5, 277, 312–3
Sweden, 127, 142
Systems, International, 106–11, 130–7

Times, The, 83
Thucydides, 278
Travis, Edward, 146–7, 169–70, 172, 177
Treasury, 51, 145–6
Trenchard, Hugh, 62
Truscott, General Lucien IV, 310
Turing, Alan, 172–3, 177
Turkomans, Tekke, 9, 15, 19–20, 28, 39–42
Turkey, 8, 9, 13–14, 16–17, 31, 35–38, 40, 46, 53, 129–30, 334, 337
Turkistan, 10, 19, 21–23, 28, 31, 38–39, 332–3
Tyrrell, William, 49, 58
Tzu, Sun, 241

Ukraine, 58, 95, 125
ULTRA, 138, 171, 173, 217, 221, 230, 233, 236, 239, 248, 252–4, 259–61, 263–70, 271–5, 278, 289, 303
Uncertainty, 42–3, 82–3, 95–8, 107–9, 130–8, 239–42, 244–8, 263, 270–3, 275–89, 305, 307, 312, 315, 326
United States, The: 49, 61–2, 105–6, 109, 114–6, 118, 122–31, 133, 135–6, 144–6, 151, 155, 157–8, 162, 164, 166, 169–75, 262
Ustinov, Klop, 65–6, 70

Vansittart, Guy, 64
Vansittart, Robert, 45–98, 114
Victoria, Queen, 24, 35, 334
Vincent, John, 333–4,
Vyshinsky, Andrei, 112

Wallace, General, 311
Warden, Colonel John, 289, 291
W.Watson and Sons, Co., 145–6
War:Anglo–Afghan, First, 10; Anglo–Afghan, Second, 1878–79, 33;
Gulf War, 292, 294–6, 300, 302–4, 307–27; Iran–Iraq, 258; Korea, 269, 273–4; Russo–Turkish, 18, 23; Spanish Civil 135; United States–Afghanistan, 294–5, 302, 306, 308, 312, 321–27; Vietnam, 269; First World, 141, 186, 258–9, 272, 326; Second World, 155–75, 239, 252–81, 308, 311, 326
War Office, 23–24, 140–44, 146, 156, 163, 192, 195–6, 199, 222–3
Wark, Wesley, 45
Warren Fisher, Nicholas, 51, 53, 73, 81, 83
Watt, D.C., 45
Wavell, Felicity-Ann, Miss, 191
Wavell, General, 198, 200–02, 206, 216, 218
Weapons of Mass Destruction, 309, 311, 319
Welchman, W.G., 171–2, 174, 177
Wellesley, Captain Frederick, 22–43, 333–5
Wellington, Duke of, 241, 281
Wenger, Lieutenant, 145–6
Western Union, 171, 176
Whitney, Christine, 310
Wilhelm II, Kaiser, 68, 107, 119
Willart, Arthur: 54
Willhelmstrasse, The: 64, 66–7, 70
Williams, E.T., 275
Willoughby, General Charles, 261, 267–8
Wilson, Horace, 83, 85–7, 89–92, 94, 97
Wilson, General Maitland, 218–9
Wilson, Rivers, 18
Wright, Peter, 61,
Wohlstetter, Roberta, 101
Wolfowitz, Paul, 321

Xenophon, 240

Yard, Scotland, 47
Yarkand, 9, 18–19, 22, 29–30, 39, 43
Yezhov, Nikolai, 112, 129
Young, A.P., 68, 71, 79–80, 90–91

eBooks – at www.eBookstore.tandf.co.uk

A library at your fingertips!

eBooks are electronic versions of printed books. You can store them on your PC/laptop or browse them online.

They have advantages for anyone needing rapid access to a wide variety of published, copyright information.

eBooks can help your research by enabling you to bookmark chapters, annotate text and use instant searches to find specific words or phrases. Several eBook files would fit on even a small laptop or PDA.

NEW: Save money by eSubscribing: cheap, online access to any eBook for as long as you need it.

Annual subscription packages

We now offer special low-cost bulk subscriptions to packages of eBooks in certain subject areas. These are available to libraries or to individuals.

For more information please contact webmaster.ebooks@tandf.co.uk

We're continually developing the eBook concept, so keep up to date by visiting the website.

www.eBookstore.tandf.co.uk

An environmentally friendly book printed and bound in England by www.printondemand-worldwide.com

PEFC Certified
This product is from sustainably managed forests and controlled sources
PEFC/16-33-415
www.pefc.org

MIX
Paper from responsible sources
FSC® C004959
www.fsc.org

This book is made entirely of sustainable materials; FSC paper for the cover and PEFC paper for the text pages.

#0222 - 210114 - C0 - 234/156/22 - PB